AVID

READER

PRESS

ON AIR

The Triumph and Tumult of NPR

STEVE ONEY

AVID READER PRESS

New York   Amsterdam/Antwerp   London   Toronto   Sydney   New Delhi

AVID READER PRESS
An Imprint of Simon & Schuster, LLC
1230 Avenue of the Americas
New York, NY 10020

First Avid Reader Press hardcover edition March 2025

AVID READER PRESS and colophon are trademarks of Simon & Schuster, LLC

For information about special discounts for bulk purchases,
please contact Simon & Schuster Special Sales
at 1-866-506-1949 or business@simonandschuster.com.

The Simon & Schuster Speakers Bureau can bring authors to your live event.
For more information or to book an event, contact the Simon & Schuster Speakers Bureau
at 1-866-248-3049 or visit our website at www.simonspeakers.com.

Interior design by Ruth Lee-Mui

Manufactured in the United States of America

1   3   5   7   9   10   8   6   4   2

Library of Congress Cataloging-in-Publication Data

Names: Oney, Steve, 1954– author. | National Public Radio (U.S.) History.
Title: On air : the triumph and tumult of NPR / Steve Oney.
Description: First Avid Reader Press hardcover edition | New York :
Avid Reader Press, 2025. | Includes bibliographical references and index.
Identifiers: LCCN 2024050597 (print) | LCCN 2024050598 (ebook) | ISBN 9781451656091
(hardcover) | ISBN 9781451656107 (paperback) | ISBN 9781451656114 (ebook)
Subjects: LCSH: Public radio—United States—History.
Classification: LCC HE8697.95.U6 O54 2025 (print) | LCC HE8697.95.U6 (ebook) | DDC
384.54/0973—dc23/eng/20241104
LC record available at https://lccn.loc.gov/2024050597
LC ebook record available at https://lccn.loc.gov/2024050598

ISBN 978-1-4516-5609-1
ISBN 978-1-4516-5611-4 (ebook)

To the memory of my mother,

Eleanor Jane Malone Oney,

who taught me to love the news

CONTENTS

PROLOGUE: DO OR DIE

On the evening of July 27, 1983, a Jeep Cherokee stopped outside the Washington, DC, offices of the Corporation for Public Broadcasting (CPB), the agency that regulates National Public Radio (NPR) and the Public Broadcasting Service (PBS). Upstairs, the CPB board was holding an emergency meeting to determine the fate of NPR, which after thirteen years of existence had entered a financial tailspin. With $20,000 in the bank and $9.1 million in debt, the network was near collapse. It might not last through the next day.

The men in the Jeep—Congressman Tim Wirth, a Democrat from Colorado and chairman of the House Telecommunications Subcommittee, and David Aylward, his chief legislative counsel—hoped to charm their way into the meeting. "I took over a couple cases of beer," Wirth said later. The two believed that a few drinks might lighten the mood during what they knew would be a contentious session, allowing them to influence the outcome in National Public Radio's favor.

Sharon Rockefeller, chairman of the Corporation for Public Broadcasting, believed that any such involvement would be inappropriate. "Sharon met us on the sidewalk and implored us not to come up," recalled Aylward.

"We don't have much to do tonight," replied Wirth. "So, we're just gonna sit out here and drink."

The congressman and his aide returned to the Jeep. As eight o'clock became ten, then eleven, they got smashed. "Drinking beer and smoking Merit cigarettes on Sixteenth Street," Aylward said later. "We were both crazy." Crazy, however, had little to do with it. Wirth was in possession of a Motorola DynaTAC, the first commercially available cell phone. About the size of a brick and priced at $3,995, the device enabled the men to do something that even a year prior would have been impossible—dial into a closed-door meeting from their car. Every hour or so, Wirth called upstairs.

The attendees at the session sat around a table in the CPB's sixth-floor conference room. At one end was Rockefeller, various agency vice presidents, and their general counsel. At the other, NPR chairman Don Mullally, his team, and their lawyers. The back-and-forth was as ugly as Wirth had feared. "It was like a union negotiation," one of the NPR executives said later. "They'd walk out. Then we'd walk out." The only respites came when a phone atop a credenza on a far wall lit up. Rockefeller would take the call. It would be Wirth telling her, "You've got to settle this."

That a five-term congressman—a future United States senator—was jawboning a federal agency on behalf of near-insolvent National Public Radio was the result of a desperate, ethically dubious undertaking by three of the network's most influential reporters. Known at NPR's M Street Washington headquarters as "the troika," Linda Wertheimer, Cokie Roberts, and Nina Totenberg had for weeks been trying to persuade the officials they covered as journalists to intercede with the Corporation for Public Broadcasting on the network's behalf. "Cokie and Linda each called two or three times," Aylward said later. "I remember standing in my kitchen near Chevy Chase Circle talking to them about what was going on." (Totenberg, NPR's legal affairs correspondent, worked indirectly. "I never talked to anybody on the Hill," she recalled. "Anything I did I got somebody else to do.") According to Aylward, the women believed "that the CPB held all the cards" and that the contingent from NPR conducting the negotiations was "overmatched." The troika feared that in exchange for bailing out the network, the Corporation for Public Broadcasting would restrict its journalistic independence, which would be intolerable. It would be the end of NPR. "Lots of people had roles.

Lots of people did things," Wertheimer said later. "I sensed the urgency," recalled Wirth.

Since its broadcast debut in 1971, National Public Radio had become a major part of the American media landscape. Its two premier programs—*All Things Considered* and *Morning Edition*—aired on more than two hundred stations nationwide and reached millions of listeners daily. Susan Stamberg and Bob Edwards, the shows' hosts, were well known across the country, possessing a celebrity on par with their network television counterparts. The same could be said for many NPR reporters—not just Wertheimer, Roberts, and Totenberg, but Scott Simon in Chicago and Robert Siegel in London— and a roster of eccentric commentators, among them Kim Williams, Vertamae Grosvenor, and Andrei Codrescu. What set public radio apart was its approach to journalism. Unlike most commercial outlets, it presented the events of the day with depth and flair, taking the time to provide context. The storytelling was innovative, sometimes inspired. Not that NPR was flawless. Occasionally, its efforts were so earnest that they provoked parody or so liberal that they drew conservative ire. Regardless, in its decade-plus on the air, the network had established a sound that imaginatively conveyed the times and suggested that radio—the aging and often-overlooked progenitor of electronic mass communications—might eventually lead a journalistic revolution. With its emphasis on well-produced, character-driven dispatches that brought issues to life and highlighted the human voice, NPR was at the forefront of new ideas about broadcasting. Compared with TV news, which with few exceptions was in a glossy rut, the network was adventurous. First, however, it had to survive.

National Public Radio's financial woes had been nearly two years in the making, but they'd become known only in the spring of 1983. Frank Mankiewicz, former press secretary to the late Robert F. Kennedy and from 1977 to 1983 president of NPR, had taken the network to great heights, then driven it into the ground. In an attempt to position NPR at the forefront of the dawning digital age, he made multiple risky investments. His efforts to develop online delivery systems that could tap new sources of income were ahead of their times and, on some level, warranted. Republican president Ronald Reagan was demanding devasting budget cuts for public radio. But Mankiewicz's actions were scattershot, their execution bungled. Auditors had only started to examine NPR's books, and they'd already found that since the first months of 1983, the network had stiffed its landlord, its utilities providers, and the bulk of its freelance contributors. Worse, during the same period NPR had not deducted federal payroll taxes from the salaries of its hundreds of employees, putting it in arears to the IRS. The situation was so bad that even some of the network's biggest supporters were ready to give up. Jack Mitchell, the original newscaster on *All Things Considered* and part of a group of radio veterans who came to Washington to institute austerity measures at NPR, recalled thinking, "It deserves to die."

The Corporation for Public Broadcasting was National Public Radio's court of last resort. Although Ronald Bornstein, Frank Mankiewicz's replacement, had already secured a $1 million bank loan for the network, it barely covered operating expenses. The only remaining option was a government bailout, but the relationship between NPR and the Corporation for Public Broadcasting was strained. Mankiewicz and Sharon Rockefeller had long been at odds. Each was the scion of a powerful family—the screenwriter father of the deposed network president had written *Citizen Kane*; the father of the CPB's boss was Illinois senator Charles Percy, and her husband, one of America's richest men, was governor of West Virginia. But pedigree was all the two had in common. Mankiewicz regarded Rockefeller as an uptight snob. She "didn't care about radio," he said later, adding that she was overly enamored of more glamorous public television. Rockefeller regarded Mankiewicz as a Hollywood blowhard. When she backed increasing the broadcast time of a favorite PBS news show, *The MacNeil/Lehrer Report*, from a half hour to an hour, the NPR chief, in a comment mocking what he regarded as the show's self-importance, cracked, "I thought it already was an hour." Mankiewicz enjoyed taunting Rockefeller. Likewise, Rockefeller wasn't shy about putting her nemesis in his place. Under Mankiewicz, she told the press when news of NPR's financial troubles broke, "there was gross mismanagement and lack of management direction. There were unrealistic expectations of the amount of revenues and few financial controls."

The Corporation for Public Broadcasting board made plain that it would not provide National Public Radio the funding it needed without securing radical concessions. First, the network would have to cut its $26 million annual budget by $10 million—the approximate amount of its debt. Second,

NPR's clients—its member stations—would be required to cosign any note, making themselves financially liable if the network defaulted. Third, NPR would have to alter its business model. Since the network's founding in 1970, the Corporation for Public Broadcasting had given it yearly grants that funded the programming it produced in Washington and transmitted to stations nationwide. Now the agency wanted to give the money directly to the stations, allowing them to buy shows not only from NPR but also from public radio outlets in cities such as Boston (WGBH) and Saint Paul (Minnesota Public Radio). Overnight, the stations would be in competition with the network. Finally, NPR would be forced to cede ownership of its instrument of distribution—space on the Westar IV satellite that beamed its programs around the country. The board "wanted control of the satellite, so NPR couldn't mismanage" it, too, said Linda Dorian, a lawyer for the agency. It was drastic, but Mankiewicz's profligacy demanded no less a price.

National Public Radio was not without leverage. As Bornstein later put it, "NPR was the gold standard," and as the night of July 27 became the morning of July 28, he informed the Corporation for Public Broadcasting board that if the network went out of business, he would work to assure that Rockefeller's agency was blamed for killing it. When *All Things Considered* and *Morning Edition* fell silent, when the voices of Stamberg and Edwards disappeared from the airwaves, the world would learn that the CPB was the reason. Bornstein was adamant. He would paint the agency's board members and chairman as heartless bureaucrats who in acceding to a Republican president's budget cuts had destroyed a source of journalistic excellence. To back up what amounted to an ultimatum, NPR chairman Don Mullally was packing the corporate version of a terrorist bomb. "We hired a law firm to draw up bankruptcy documents," he recalled, adding, "We told CPB that if we did not get the loan, we were going to liquidate the company—pull the plug."

The leaders of National Public Radio and the CPB board members were playing a high-stakes game of chicken, and Tim Wirth, at the urging of those NPR reporters who feared their guys lacked what it took to see the game to a successful end, was part of it. Initially, he'd used his calls to Rockefeller to remind her that Congress was watching. "Our intent was to be a hovering presence," Aylward said later. "NPR was in the room with the authorities, but we were the big brother waiting out on the street. The whole idea was to convey the message, 'You can beat him up, but don't beat him up too bad.'"

After midnight, Wirth changed tactics. As Tom Rogers, his chief legal counsel, recalled, the congressman began using his Motorola DynaTAC to give Rockefeller a polite version of what she was hearing from Bornstein and Mullally. If the agency failed to come to NPR's rescue, it "would not only affect public radio but the CPB." The chairman of a key House subcommittee intended to help network executives pin the onus on the Corporation for Public Broadcasting and its politically and socially prominent chairman.

At one thirty, Wirth and Aylward were still sitting in front of the Corporation for Public Broadcasting building. They had no idea how the negotiations upstairs would turn out, but they weren't going anywhere. "NPR had become a force—a shining example of what media could be," said Aylward. Which was why the two kept pounding back bottles of beer while keeping the bulky DynaTAC charged.

ONE

THE PHILOSOPHER KING

Hulking and unkempt, typically clad in denim and hobnail boots, Jeff Kamen was referred to around the offices of National Public Radio as El Lobo. He came from the world of big-market rock 'n' roll news. During the late 1960s at Chicago's WCFL, a fifty-thousand-watter that blasted music across the Midwest, he'd race to crime scenes and press conferences in an Olds Cutlass, the doors bearing the station's call letters in green, purple, red, and gold. His idea was to be in the middle of the action, and his aim was to produce pieces that emerged from WCFL's playlist. To him, stories weren't all that different from Buffalo Springfield or Rolling Stones songs. Everything he did was antic and driven by a beat. While he numbered both cops and Black Panthers among his friends, Kamen would take on anyone. "He would talk back to Mayor Richard J. Daley," said Jeff Rosenberg, a fellow member of NPR's original staff who as a Northwestern student had been a fan. "Most of us thought he would be found dead in an alley." Instead, WCFL fired the reporter.

Kamen did not leave quietly, telling the *Chicago American* that the station's manager accused him of putting too many "niggers and Puerto Ricans" on the air. Liberal Illinois congressman Abner Mikva quoted Kamen to this effect in the *Congressional Record*, declaring, "Last week a bright young radio newscaster lost his job in Chicago—not because he was faithless to the traditions of integrity, rather because he took them seriously." On the morning of May 3, 1971, Kamen, the most improbable participant in an improbable new enterprise in American broadcasting, stood at an intersection near Washington, DC's Tidal Basin, ready to go to work. Weeks earlier, NPR executives had picked this Monday to introduce their first program, *All Things Considered*. "I felt sorry for the poor bastards," Kamen said later. "They put a pin in a calendar, not having any idea." But there was no turning back. The ad in the *New York Times* was unambiguous: "The radio revolution starts at 5: NPR."

What the men and women behind the fledgling network could not have foreseen was that a group called the Mayday Tribe would choose May 3 to stage a protest intended to shut down the US government. It hoped to bring an end to the Vietnam War. Twenty thousand demonstrators took to Washington's streets. Most were peaceful, a few carried Vietcong flags, and a fringe wielded stones, bottles, and bricks. They were met by not only 5,100 DC police officers and 1,400 National Guardsmen but also some 8,000 army regulars who'd come in by transport plane and truck from as far away as Fort Bragg, North Carolina. The show of force was at the direction of the president. No one, Richard Nixon vowed, would disrupt business in the nation's capital.

By nine a.m. Washington resembled a battlefield. The protesters intended to control the bridges and roads over which federal employees traveled to reach their offices. The police and the military—cops in white helmets with visors down, National Guardsmen carrying rifles with fixed bayonets, army troops swooping in by helicopter—sought to keep the bridges and roads open. They did so by moving on foot or by motorcycle through the demonstrators, spraying tear gas, and making mass arrests. Soon seven thousand people were in custody. Overwhelmed lawmen transformed practice fields near Robert F. Kennedy Stadium into gigantic outdoor holding pens. Acrid haze hung over the city.

The National Public Radio reporters who joined Kamen in covering the demonstration were almost as unlikely as he was. Jim Russell, a rotund twenty-five-year-old who'd done a tour in Vietnam for United Press International (UPI), took up a position at a traffic circle opposite the Lincoln

Memorial. Stephen Banker, an older freelancer (Harvard, 1955) who contributed frequently to the Canadian Broadcasting Corporation, was at the Pentagon. Mike Waters, a veteran of both commercial and college radio known for his melodious voice, staked out the mall. The sole advice that Bill Siemering, NPR's programming director, gave his charges was "that they filter what they saw through who they were." In truth, nothing could have prepared them. Almost immediately, Kamen was detained by the police, but he wasn't held long. As he would tell it, Frank Sullivan, an official from the Chicago Police Department bearing credentials from Nixon, quickly interceded on his behalf. At some point, Waters gave his press pass to two demonstrators to help them avoid arrest. Meanwhile, a cop gassed Russell. Protesters urged him to urinate into a handkerchief, then hold it over his nose. The ammonia, they said, would neutralize the poison.

It was chaos, but no matter how unguided and overmatched, the NPR reporters kept their lightweight Sony TC-100 cassette tape recorders rolling. They interviewed protestors, police, and office workers. They described the mayhem unfurling around them. Most telling, they employed their equipment to collect huge gouts of ambient sound, the discordant melodies of Washington's largest demonstration against the Vietnam War.

National Public Radio was initially headquartered at the Cafritz Building, a modernist structure from the late 1940s at 1625 Eye Street, two blocks from the White House. Although this home was temporary, the network had invested in a sleek Master Control room, superb Scully reel-to-reel recording machines, and high-end Neumann microphones. Presiding over everything was NPR president Don Quayle, a shrewd but good-hearted Utah Mormon with roots in both midwestern college radio and public broadcasting (WGBH in Boston). The engineering staff, a buttoned-down bunch, reported to the authoritarian operations chief, George Geesey, a veteran of WAMU in Washington. The programming staff included a few experienced journalists, but it consisted mostly of scruffy young men in jeans and attractive young women in miniskirts.

Bill Siemering looked as if he were a sociology professor at a suburban junior college. Tall and stoop-shouldered with pale blue eyes, a shock of thinning blond hair, and a reddish beard, he owned a tie but rarely wore it. In his view, a gold corduroy sports jacket, white shirt, and khakis were dressy enough, even in the nation's capital. Yet, as unimpressive as the thirty-seven-year-old programming director appeared, he was a charismatic figure known for fervid pronouncements. "Let's hold hands and have a race" was a favorite. Intoxicated NPR staffers heard in it what they wanted to believe—that the communal and the competitive could coexist.

Siemering envisioned something audacious for the premiere of *All Things Considered*. He would lead the show with a twenty-one-minute documentary on the day's events in Washington pieced together from the audio his people collected in the field. At ABC or NBC, such a production would take a week. He was going to turn it around in a few hours. We can do this, Siemering insisted when Kamen, Waters, Russell, and Banker returned to the newsroom about noon and began dubbing from cassettes onto tape reels. It was insanity but also inspired. Primary sources, multiple perspectives, a narrative not just enhanced by but at times solely advanced by sound. Waters, in addition to his vocal skills, was an accomplished editor. As he and a jack-of-all-radio-trades named Rich Firestone, a longtime Siemering associate who'd just arrived in town, cut and spliced the material, a band of researchers, producers, reporters, and wannabe reporters—among them Rosenberg, Linda Wertheimer, Susan Stamberg, Carolyn Jensen, Barbara Newman, Gwen Hudley, and Kati Marton—prepared feature stories that would fill out the broadcast. Meantime, Jack Mitchell, a PhD who had strayed into broadcasting, polished the news summary he would deliver at some point in the program.

In the midst of all this activity sat *All Things Considered*'s first host, Robert Conley. Forty-two and graying, Conley was a former foreign correspondent for NBC and the *New York Times*, but like many newsmen of his generation, he seemed as sheepish about his credentials as he was proud. He loved to talk about world leaders he'd met in Cairo and other exotic spots. Nonetheless, he disparaged straight journalism. His generation of reporters was cautious and out of it. What mattered in the new world was to be loose and in the moment. That meant dispensing with notes and scripts. Conley took his place in NPR's glassed-in studio for the debut of its flagship show with only a few basic facts in his head about the day's events. He would wing it.

At five p.m. sharp, Conley intoned, "From National Public Radio in Washington, I'm Robert Conley with *All Things Considered*." The program's first theme song—a piping melody composed by Don Voegeli and played on a Moog synthesizer—wafted from radios in ninety cities that boasted NPR stations. The demonstration documentary was not ready. Conley extemporized. He had a professional style, and he was sufficiently informed to be able to report the real news from the protest: Despite the madness, government functions had not come to a halt. Yet, as the minutes passed, he ran out of material and began to pad. (Robert F. Kennedy Stadium, he told listeners, was "named for Senator Robert F. Kennedy.") The best you could say, recalled Jack Mitchell, was that Conley "was not horrible." Finally, at four minutes and fifty-two seconds into the broadcast—an eternity in live radio—the documentary was finished, and the host announced, "Rather than pull in reports, we thought we might take you to the event."

Like an overture, the insistent voice of folk singer and antiwar sympathizer Phil Ochs, performing "Power and the Glory," led listeners in: "Come on and take a walk with me through this green and glowing land. / Walk through the meadows and the mountains and the sand / . . . / Her power shall rest on the strength of her freedom." Then demonstrators shouted, "Come on, people! Stop the war now!" Army helicopters thundered. Police motorcycles roared. Ambulance sirens screamed. A voice-over proclaimed, "Thousands of young people came to Washington. . . . It was their freedom ride, their Selma march." Whereupon the outlaw journalist spoke. "A line of young people has just come across the highway," said Jeff Kamen. "Traffic is stopped. Here come the police. One demonstrator knocked down by a motor-scooter policeman . . . Anger now . . . anger of the young people."

After soliciting onlookers' descriptions of what happened, El Lobo approached an officer and asked, "Sergeant, excuse me. Jeff Kamen, National Public Radio. Is that a technique where the men actually try to drive their bikes right into the demonstrators?" At most other news outlets, the question would have been deleted as editorializing. But for all his moxie, Kamen kept a civil tone and elicited a revealing reply. "No, it's no technique," said the sergeant. "We're trying to go down the road, and the people get in front. What are you going to do? You don't stop on a dime."

From Kamen, the story jumped to Banker at the Pentagon; then back to Kamen, by this point at the Department of Agriculture; then to Russell at the Lincoln Memorial, who reported that he'd been tear-gassed; back again to Kamen, now on Independence Avenue, where an interviewee vowed, "We're gonna shut the fucking city"; and finally to George Washington University Hospital, where a priest speaking to Kamen ticked off the injuries of arriving patients.

Act one of the documentary expressed the demonstrators' point of view. Act two belonged to an unidentified police officer, who asserted that the protesters were using tear gas, too. "The Weathermen organization," he said, is "here to do as much bodily damage as they possibly can." Act three featured businesspeople who criticized both the demonstrators and the police. Act four offered a snippet from a news conference by organizers of the Mayday Tribe, among them Rennie Davis, a convicted member of the Chicago Seven. The protest leaders conceded that despite the havoc they'd wreaked, they had failed. "It is true," said one, "we didn't paralyze the city." The production ran to twenty-five minutes (four minutes longer than scheduled), and while there was a token effort at evenhandedness, there was no doubt where *All Things Considered* stood. The telling line: "Today in the nation's capital, it is a crime to be young and have long hair."

The new network billed itself as *National* Public Radio, but thirty minutes into its inaugural broadcast, its programming sounded as if it were produced by an insurgent subset of the populace. As its coverage proceeded, the disposition of *All Things Considered* stayed to the left, and it added some loopy countercultural elements. Following a roundtable discussion about the demonstration featuring several reporters, Siemering cued a Canadian Broadcasting story about World War I poetry. The actors giving the readings all but stated that Flanders Fields were a stand-in for Vietnam. Conley then introduced a piece from the Midwest: "In this age of unshorn locks, with shagginess transformed into a lifestyle, people don't get their hair cut as often." A correspondent from the Ames, Iowa, station reported that a local barber shop was making up for lost revenue by shaving women's legs so they could wear hot pants. Jack Mitchell's news insert didn't air until six p.m., meaning that the day's Supreme Court decisions, front-page stuff in the traditional press, became an afterthought. But that's what Siemering wanted. NPR was freeform. As the debut of *All Things Considered* drew to a close, the programming director offered a Gwen Hudley story about a heroin-addicted nurse. Midway through, he went to a bluesy Roy Buchanan guitar riff that underscored the account's tragedy. The show reached an appropriately weird end with an interview by Fred Calland, NPR's classical music producer, of 1960s avatar Allen Ginsberg and his father about their opposing views of the times. Among the subjects was LSD.

"Drugs are a source of peace and enlightenment," Allen Ginsberg said.

"Drugs embezzle the development of the youth," countered Louis Ginsberg, a high school teacher and, like his son, a poet.

"Allen, I'll give you the last response," said Calland.

"Ohm. Body. Speech. Mind. Diamond. Teacher. Flower Power. Ohm. Flower power."

So concluded the first edition of *All Things Considered*. The broadcast, however, wasn't over. Although Siemering had prepared a log, the time necessary to complete the protest documentary played hell with his calculations. To make everything fit, he threw out a planned story on the 1971 Pulitzer Prizes, which had been awarded that day. But now the show was too short. Again, the programming director needed Conley to ad-lib. The host missed the instruction. "He was off in dreamland," Mitchell said later. Six and one-half minutes short of a scheduled ninety minutes, the program just stopped, and up came NPR's jaunty theme song. Like a computerized nightmare, the Moog-generated tune—charming for a few seconds, torture in constant rotation—played over and over and over until six thirty p.m., when the stations in NPR's small network at last returned to their regular schedules.

At 1625 Eye, as the staff referred to NPR's first digs, the reactions varied from relief ("We'd at least gotten through it," said Mitchell), to chagrin ("I winced when I heard Kamen ask if the motorcycle stuff was a technique," said Russell), to pride ("It was a happy day," said Siemering. "We had that occasion to show what radio can do. That was a textbook illustration of what we were talking about."). Never before had anything like this coursed over the nation's airwaves. The program was a contraption hammered together from disparate ingredients, a vibration from a realm where youthful conviction commingled with Merry Prankster lunacy, land-grant-university idealism, and a native instinct for storytelling. The protest documentary, its biases aside, would stand as a time-capsule account of a historic day. (That same night, Walter Cronkite gave the story only a few minutes on the CBS *Evening News*.) Somehow a new network had emerged. It was up there—and it was out there.

• • •

Bill Siemering's contributions to establishing NPR's sensibilities were critical, but what he did not do was even more critical. In early 1971, several months before *All Things Considered* premiered, the network's president, Don Quayle, learned that Edward P. Morgan, one of the best-known names in American broadcasting, was available to host the program. During the 1950s and 1960s, Morgan had been the face of ABC television news. In 1960, he was a panelist at the second presidential debate between Richard Nixon and John F. Kennedy. In 1963, in tandem with Howard K. Smith, he anchored coverage of Kennedy's assassination. More recently he had hosted what champions of quality television regarded as one of the medium's greatest achievements, *Public Broadcast Laboratory (PBL)*, a two-hour Sunday-evening experiment in high-mindedness conceived by former CBS News president Fred Friendly and produced by his protégé Av Westin. From 1967 to 1969, the show—airing on National Educational Television, a precursor to PBS—brought antiestablishment politics, racially charged drama (the Negro Ensemble Company's *Day of Absence*, in which Black actors in whiteface sent up small-town southern prejudice), and Ivy League professors into American living rooms. Even some liberal critics were put off by *PBL*'s pretentions, but most loved it. Now Morgan wanted to join NPR, and the Ford Foundation was dangling an alluring incentive: $300,000 to cover his salary for the first several years.

Around 1625 Eye, news that the great man might be signing on was met with hurrahs—by everyone except Siemering. The programming chief didn't want any part of Morgan. If NPR hired him it would lose the chance to establish its own identity. It would not be National Public Radio but Edward P. Morgan Radio, with all the eastern condescension that suggested. Quayle, while hating to lose the $300 grand, backed up his programming boss. NPR said no. It would instead go with Robert Conley, a friend of the network's news director, Cleve Mathews, also a recruit from the *New York Times*.

With that one stroke, Siemering separated NPR from commercial broadcasters. In the weeks before the debut, the programming director expanded on the thinking behind the choice, enthusing to fellow executives about the opportunity the new network had to dispense with the "plastic, faceless men" who delivered the news on traditional American outlets. Nor would it be stiff, like the BBC. NPR would "share the human experience with emotional openness." It would not "rip and read" headlines. It would "bring the people to the people." If this sounded less like a news operation than a vehicle for achieving a more perfect society, that's because in a way it was. "Siemering had this vision of radio as an instrument of education in the finest sense," said Jim Russell. "He saw radio as a totally different animal."

Quayle and the others wanted specifics. NPR didn't have much money—$3.3 million that first year—and the executives demanded to know where the money would go. How, for instance, would the network's initial program—a newsmagazine slated for afternoon drive time—work? The best Siemering could do was say that Conley would front the show, but that he would not be a host in the traditional sense, because he would not read the news. He would instead present produced segments, many originating from stations outside Washington. Sometimes he would interact with reporters, other times with sources. The opinions of nonexperts would be as valued, maybe more valued, than those of political and business insiders, and the arts would receive as much attention as public affairs. As for the shape of the show, Siemering couldn't be sure about that, either. "One of the most critical aspects of putting such a program together," he said, "is the ordering of items, the internal rhythm of the program and the weight of each item, which is not possible to transmit in printed form."

It was a little vague, but there was an underlying theory. "I tried to offer a skeletal outline, a framework for them to fill in," said Siemering. "You know, as you walk down streets in Washington—I was thinking of N between 17th and Connecticut—there's a variety of architectural styles. And I said, 'Each producer contributes their architectural style, but it needs to blend in with the street. It needs to conform to principles of architecture. It can't just be a shack next to a slick townhouse, but it's a producer's program, and you bring your uniqueness, your style.'" In other words, he would establish the range, but the producers and reporters would fashion the stories. What Siemering sought for NPR was distinctive contributors, and while he might have struggled to spell it out, he made it plain in his personnel decisions. "Bill didn't hire people on the basis of competence," said Jack Mitchell. "He wanted to do something new and original. Anyone who had experience had the wrong kind of experience." He was not looking for people with impressive résumés.

He was looking for people who possessed the sort of intangible qualities that would make the network stand out.

Linda Wertheimer was among the first to undergo Siemering's vetting process. Twenty-eight years old with a torrent of brown hair and powerful connections (an aide to Senator Jacob Javits had suggested she apply to NPR), Wertheimer had every reason to believe when she arrived at 1625 Eye that she would leave with a job. A Wellesley graduate, she had spent a year in London working for the World Service of the BBC. From "the Beeb," she'd gone to WCBS Newsradio 88 in New York, an all-news CBS affiliate that featured Charles Osgood, Pat Summerall, and a young Ed Bradley. About midway through her interview with the NPR programming director, however, she sensed that he was not impressed by her stellar bona fides.

"What did your father do?" Siemering asked.

Wertheimer responded that he ran Morrison's Grocery Store in Carlsbad, New Mexico, and that as a girl she had taken orders by phone, standing on a crate by the butcher's case "being a well-spoken child who wrote well."

"Do you mean a neighborhood grocery store?"

"About three times the size of this office," she replied, looking around the programming director's cramped quarters. Suddenly, she wasn't just a Wellesley graduate but someone who understood what it was like to work in a small, family business.

Siemering offered Wertheimer a position. "He decided that I wasn't so uppity after all," she said afterward, "although I was right on the raggedy edge."

If job applicants were "thoughtful and bright," Siemering grabbed them whether they had broadcasting skills or not. Carolyn Jensen, who came from *Der Spiegel*, knew nothing about radio, but she was studious. He brought her aboard to set up NPR's library. Kati Marton, although still in graduate school, had been raised in Hungary, the daughter of a legendary Associated Press reporter, Endre Marton. Gwen Hudley and Rich Adams were neophytes, but both were Black, and the programming chief wanted a network that not only sounded like America but also looked like it. As for those with experience, they, like Wertheimer, needed a counterbalancing attribute that indicated depth—or quirkiness. In his early twenties, Jeff Kamen had been an announcer at Korvette's department store in New York: "Ladies lingerie, upstairs." Susan Stamberg, an ex-producer at WAMU in DC, had financed her education at Barnard as a typist for Jacques Chambrun, a controversial literary agent who represented Grace Metalious (author of *Peyton Place*). She spent the mid-1960s in India with her husband, a program officer with the State Department's International Development Agency. At thirty-two, Stamberg was the oldest successful job applicant. Filling out the group was a handful of people—Mike Waters and Rich Firestone among them—with whom Siemering had worked in the past.

"It was an odd assortment of folks," said Russell, who at least had wire service experience. "He hired me as a safety in case these crazies went off the deep end."

At the same time Siemering sought variety among his reporters, he fought for the equipment they would need to do a specific type of work. He wanted his people to be able to cover events on the fly, to capture raw sound—whether ugly or beautiful, gunshots from a riot or footfalls from a hike on the Appalachian Trail. He thus requested lightweight Sony cassette recorders. As the debut of NPR's first show grew closer, this choice brought him into conflict with George Geesey. The network's operations chief was a formidable character with a creative bent. Indeed, just a month before NPR was to go on the air, he walked into a programming meeting where staffers had penciled prospective names for their still-untitled effort on legal sheets taped to a wall. Each suggestion was worse than the last. Reaching into his wallet, Geesey removed a card on which he had jotted down inspirations and said, "It sounds like this program will include everything. How about *All Things Considered*?" Siemering couldn't thank him enough. One of the great names in broadcasting was born.

That aside, Geesey had his own ideas about audio, believing that journalists on assignment should use reel-to-reel recorders. No one disputed his view that when it came to high fidelity, the Nagra, the state of the art in reel-to-reel machines, was superior to the compact Sony. But Nagras presented a practical problem. They weighed twenty-five pounds. Covering a chaotic event or a breaking story with one was like trying to play football while carrying a big, old hard-shelled suitcase. The ensuing debate became absurd. NPR would transmit its shows over twelve thousand miles of AT&T long lines looping around America in what was known as a "round robin."

While audio would leave the Washington studio at a fulsome 15 kilohertz, it would drop to 6 kilohertz as soon as it hit the wires and degrade to a tinny 3.5 kilohertz by the time it reached distant stations. In much of America, NPR would sound as scratchy as an overseas phone call—which meant that in terms of quality, the kind of recorders reporters used was irrelevant. It would be bad regardless.

The compromise was to go with Sony TC-100s—but to customize them. Cassette machines record at a plodding 1⅞ inches per second. By altering them to record at 3¾ inches per second (the more rapidly tape moves across a recording head, the higher the fidelity), NPR could enhance the sound. Siemering would get the compact recorders that enabled his reporters to venture about more easily, and Geesey would get the quality he wanted. Only after making the changes did the two realize that the tape the Sonys produced would be unplayable on the machines used by everyone else in broadcasting. Whether a bold move or a futile gesture, the decision underscored an emerging truth: NPR would chart its own course.

At planning sessions Siemering had begun hosting each day at 1625 Eye, his people started to sense what they'd signed up for. Sprawled across the floor (few dared sit on NPR's flimsy, cast-off furniture for fear it might collapse), the staff listened as their programming chief played a selection of radio pieces. One of the tapes came from Susan Stamberg. It was a segment of a WAMU series titled *A Federal Case*. She had produced it, and she was proud of it. It had a serious topic and a voice-of-God male narrator, and it could have aired on CBS or NBC. As the piece concluded, Siemering hit the stop button and uttered what for an unfailingly good-natured man was a pointed rebuke: "This is exactly what we don't want to sound like."

Really? Really! thought Stamberg, who was both hurt and intrigued. "It had never occurred to me not to sound like that on the radio."

Siemering demanded that his troops employ a conversational tone, and he insisted that they conduct interviews politely. He wanted reporters to behave in an uncharacteristic manner. He wanted them to be nice. "Granted, there are different situations where you need to nail someone if they're lying," the programming chief said later. "But you get a lot more by being open rather than attacking, because if you start attacking you get their defenses up."

Siemering, Stamberg realized, was less a programming director than a, well, philosopher king—in his hires, his choices of equipment, his maxims. That's what she dubbed him. Around the news department, others also began using the term, realizing that they were working for someone staking out new ground. True, a few of the higher-ups—among them Quayle and Geesey—rolled their eyes. Philosopher king? "We'd hired all these people who knew about content but not about broadcasting," said Quayle, "and what they needed was direction." While Siemering was expounding, Quayle feared that such critical matters as story inventory and planning were being ignored. *All Things Considered* would be a monster, and it would demand close supervision, not oracular utterances.

Siemering was not deterred. On the eve of NPR's premiere, he told the staff: "We have a blank canvas. There'll be a lot of paint put on this canvas over the years. But the very first brush strokes are critical in terms of the color and style that we establish."

The twin transmitting towers of WHA, the University of Wisconsin educational radio station, stood outside the capital city of Madison near a failed housing development named Lake Forest, better known as Lost City. Eveline and William Siemering Sr. and their family lived in Lost City in a frame home two hundred yards from the towers. Cornfields and forests stretched to the horizon. It was the tag end of the Depression, and half the lots were empty. There were few children to play with, and the neighborhood could seem desolate. Occasionally, though, the transmitter operator threw open the door to a tiny redbrick building at the towers' base and switched on a radio monitor, making WHA's shows—*Chapter a Day, The Farm Program*—audible to William Siemering Jr. For a shy and gawky boy, the youngest in a family of four, it was transporting.

As a first grader at Silver Springs School, whose eight grades occupied two rooms (classes were separated by roll-up dividers), Bill, as everyone called him, began to understand what WHA meant to his community. "The teacher would turn on the radio, and we'd have *The Wisconsin School of the Air*. I learned nature, social studies, music, art, science—all from the radio." Equipped with guidebooks, instructors led students through readings, experiments, and drawing projects featured in the broadcasts. "From first grade on, I regarded radio as this wonderful source of imagination. It was something so different in the classroom. Each program was twenty minutes long—morning and afternoon, five days a week."

History, drama, and the human voice—the boy loved them all, which was no wonder. His parents had met in theater school in Minneapolis during the late teens. Both aspiring actors, they went on the road with a Chautauqua circuit—"typical of America at its best," said Teddy Roosevelt—performing sketches and Dickensian set pieces in band shells on town squares. They played small, dusty places that craved culture and political discourse. After a couple of years, William Sr. opened a movie theater in rural Wisconsin, and booked films with an eye not to the box office but to edification. The business failed. He took a job with the Veterans Administration in Madison and settled into family life. But the excitement of those early days remained, and the couple's two sons and two daughters grew up hearing about them.

Bill was hardly a rugged young man, but he absorbed the rhythms and virtues of his rural world. He worked summers for a local fellow who did custom combining and hay-baling. The pair would go from farm to farm. Bill labored late into the twilight, never slacking off until the dew formed on the ground. "It was hard work but it was good work. There was a satisfying ache. I learned about stewardship."

By the time Bill started at Madison's West High School, the Siemerings had moved into the city. It was less lonely there. Even so, he was plagued by moments of alienation. His mother was a Christian Scientist, and she raised him in her faith, teaching him that if he was sick something was amiss in his soul—he was out of alignment with God. Practitioners bearing copies of Mary Baker Eddy's *Science and Health with Key to the Scriptures* would pray for him. Bill felt different from his classmates, more inward-looking. A speech teacher, Ruth McCarty, encouraged him to get involved in student productions. Soon he was building sets and, from time to time, acting. Before graduating in 1952 and heading to the University of Wisconsin, he told Mrs. McCarty he wanted to design sets for television. She urged him to talk with her husband, the director of WHA. Harold B. McCarty told the incoming freshman that he couldn't offer him a job in TV, but he had one in radio.

WHA was located in Radio Hall, a low, limestone structure with an interior wall adorned by a mural depicting the founders of 9XM, a University of Wisconsin experimental station that in 1917 transmitted America's first radio news and music broadcasts. The figures in the mural include a physicist wearing a duster and holding vacuum tubes, reporters sitting at a table covered with paper, and a man at a microphone. For a student enthralled with broadcasting, Radio Hall was Mecca, and Siemering threw himself into the activities there, working twenty to thirty hours during school weeks and full time in the summers. He lugged gigantic Magnecorders—you needed both hands to carry one—into classrooms, where he taped segments for the *Wisconsin School of the Air*. He auditioned to be an announcer and was soon reading the news. He also embraced the underlying notion—particularly strong on heartland campuses, where the Progressive Era had never completely ended—that college stations exist to spread wisdom beyond school boundaries. WHA was a far-reaching source of enlightenment. To Siemering's agriculturally attuned mind, the station functioned like a seed broadcaster, although the seeds were intellectual. This was his first serious idea about radio.

After graduating in 1956 with a degree in geography and a minor in speech, Siemering, who had enrolled in the ROTC, was called to active duty with the army. He became a "broadcast specialist" and hoped to work in Armed Forces Radio. He instead ended up at the United States Disciplinary Barracks in Leavenworth, Kansas, a maximum-security lockup. There he supervised prisoner education and produced a closed-circuit program of inmate news for an audience that included barely literate murderers. On weekends, he manned the mixing board at nearby KCLO, which played country music and billed itself "The Heart of the Nation Station."

Out of the army in 1958, Siemering taught speech at a high school in Eagle River, Wisconsin—a resort town on the Michigan border. He married Carol Kane, an organist at a Christian Science church. Spurred by the launch of Sputnik the year before, he applied for a National Defense Education Act scholarship to pursue a master's degree in counseling at the University of Wisconsin. The thinking behind the scholarship was that recipients would later encourage students to study space-age subjects. Siemering was ambivalent; his heart wasn't in math and science. Still, this was a heady time to be in Madison. Carl Rogers, the central figure in humanistic psychology, was on the faculty. In 1961 Rogers published his seminal work, *On Becoming a Person*. Siemering did not take a class from Rogers, but he saw him around campus and was smitten by the book. Rogers's premise—captured in the phrase "unconditional positive regard"—was that therapists could effect change by fully accepting patients, notwithstanding their ugly past acts or utterances. Some said the permissive 1960s started here. To Siemering, the concept was immediately relevant, and it led to his second big idea about radio. If broadcasters practiced unconditional positive regard and spoke *directly* to listeners instead of *down* to them, they could establish a new level of intimacy in the medium.

Siemering took a job at his alma mater, Madison's West High. During the summer of 1962, he got a call from a former member of the Wisconsin faculty who had become dean of students at the University of Buffalo and needed a manager at WBFO, the college station. That fall, Siemering, his wife, and their two daughters drove their green Nash Rambler east. The dean challenged him to make WBFO as relevant to Buffalo as WHA was to Madison. It would not be easy. The station operated like a club. It did not broadcast year-round. The programming consisted largely of jazz and folk LPs students brought in from their home collections and plopped on the turntable. Whoever felt like reading the news did so.

Buffalo, industrial and dirty, had a large Black population. Its heart was "the Fruit Belt," a neighborhood so called for a profusion of streets with names like Mulberry and Grape. Siemering was intrigued by the area, and he had such a sincere way about him that when he visited, residents invited him to sit on their porches and talk. From what he learned and recorded during these conversations, he produced a three-part series for WBFO titled *To Be Negro*. This was the first of several specials he put together on ethnicity in western New York (*The Nation within a Nation* focused on the Tuscarora tribe of the Iroquois), and it signaled a shift in content at the station that was both dizzying and in keeping with the times. In 1969, following tense negotiations with community leaders ("I remember one woman saying, 'I don't feel comfortable talking with whitey'"), Siemering opened a fully equipped WBFO satellite studio in a Fruit Belt storefront. It aired twenty-seven hours of programming each week. Black music. ("We were the first station to broadcast Roberta Flack locally.") Black art. ("We sponsored a festival.") Black public affairs. ("The Chicago activist Saul Alinsky had a project in Buffalo called BUILD" to promote racial equality. "The TV stations barely mentioned it. I thought, maybe we need to devote more than three minutes a night to this.") Local painters installed a mural in the lobby depicting the history of Black communications, starting with African drums. "It wasn't quite what they have at WHA, but it was the same idea."

Siemering's transformation of WBFO, while political—"I wanted to use radio to give voice to people who didn't have one"—was as much about aesthetics. The station was headquartered at the university student union in a small suite that included offices, a room with a teletype machine, and a studio whose glass windows were papered over to separate it from an adjoining studio occupied by the school's resident genius, Lukas Foss, an experimental composer who had conducted the premiere of Leonard Bernstein's *Symphonic Dances*. Foss had founded the Creative Associates, a group of avant-garde performers. In May 1967, Buffalonians tuned to WBFO received a shock. *City-Links*, a twenty-eight-hour sound sculpture featuring live audio from several urban locations and conceived by the Creative Associates, was on the air. The broadcast cut back and forth among feeds, immersing the audience in the clangs of machinery at a Bethlehem Steel factory and the sibilance of street traffic. "It's said there's music all around if you'll just listen," said Siemering.

Programming at WBFO jelled for Siemering in early 1970. By this point, the station had acquired a degree of professionalism. Not only did it employ some talented undergraduates, among them Ira Flatow, a reporter, and Jonathan "Smokey" Baer, an editor, but it had also hired Mike Waters, a former newscaster at a local country-and-western outlet. As a result, WBFO was ready when in March a violent, anti–Vietnam War rally hit the university. The protest targeted the student union, and the police tear-gassed it. But WBFO stayed on the air. "We broadcast a kind of play-by-play of this event," said Siemering. "I interviewed the leader of the movement and asked him, 'You went to a parochial school. How did you find yourself here?' I interviewed the acting university president. 'Where were you when you decided to let the police tear-gas this building? Was your decision influenced by your desire to become president?' On the air, I said, 'There isn't a right or wrong in this. People are acting on their perceptions of reality. That's what we're talking about. If you haven't heard your views expressed, come on down and we'll put you on the air.' We were a force of reason."

The impact of WBFO's exhaustive coverage was far reaching. Much of Buffalo listened. For Siemering, the broadcast was galvanizing. He combined what he'd learned from covering the riot with what he had discovered at the Fruit Belt satellite studio and what he had realized when he put the work of the Creative Associates on the air. It gave him one more big idea about radio: the best and most vivid material originates not from the top but from somewhere else, often the bottom. Opinions expressed by demonstrators were as valid as those of administrators. Instead of being dispensed from on high, news should bubble up. The commercial networks had it wrong. They were missing the story.

Out of Siemering's musings emerged a daily WBFO show called *This Is Radio*. On it he would play raw tape from Buffalo City Council meetings, then bring on his reporters to assess the contents. He would follow that with a side of *Tommy*, the Who's new rock opera. Then he would air a chat with a writer or professor. The program was a product of its era, sometimes unfocused, other times on point. "*This Is Radio* was Bill's experiment in breaking the format," said Flatow. "In other words, 'Let's not define what a show is in a box. Let's not say it's a talk show. Let's not say it's a magazine show. Each day, let's just let the show find a life of its own.' What was going on that day was the way we would program that day."

This Is Radio was Siemering's landmark creation at WBFO. He was so thrilled with it that he'd occasionally burst out, "*This Is Radio*—damn it!"

Bill Siemering's timing was impeccable. As it happened, a number of radio executives were meeting at various locations in 1970 to draw up plans for what would become National Public Radio. Educational broadcasters, represented by WHA's manager, Karl Schmidt, the chairman of the just-formed NPR planning board, were dominant. Also important were representatives from powerful independents such as WGBH in Boston, which functioned in their cities like civic institutions akin to symphony orchestras and museums. Then there was Pacifica, a Berkeley-based, quasi-Marxist outfit with outlets not just in the Bay Area but also in Los Angeles and New York. Finally, there was the gentle dissident from Buffalo. All told, it was an incongruous bunch united by a common cause—bringing to life a new radio enterprise, funded by the government and dedicated to elevating the electronic news media. Adding urgency to the moment: everyone involved knew that NPR had almost been stillborn.

On a Saturday three years earlier, Jerrold Sandler, a Washington, DC, educational radio lobbyist and former production manager at WUOM, the University of Michigan radio station, got bad news. It was about what was at first called the Public Television and *Radio* Bill, the last piece of President Lyndon B. Johnson's Great Society program. The bill had grown out of a Carnegie Commission study proposing "the utilization of a great technology for great purposes." Audiences would receive "wonder and variety . . . excellence within diversity . . . awareness of the many roads along which the products of man's mind and man's hands can be encountered." The legislation's key advocates, most of them in TV, had never wanted radio to be part of it. They saw the medium as obsolete, and they'd deleted the words *and radio* that would enable something like NPR. The legislation, now called the Public *Television* Bill, was headed to Congress that Monday. When Sandler learned that the initial language had vanished, he phoned Dean Coston, an old Michigan friend who'd become an undersecretary at the Department of Health, Education, and Welfare—the agency that sponsored the bill. Coston and a sympathetic White House adviser sat down with a typewriter and scotch tape and reinserted the two critical words. They copied the doctored pages, then reassembled the bill. The result was a mess. Typefaces did not match, and tape marks showed, but in all the appropriate places the legislation again read "and radio." The administration submitted this version.

Television supporters were furious. But following a campaign on Capitol Hill by Sandler and Ed Burrows, a former WUOM station manager, the opposition capitulated. Not only that, the legislation itself received a new title. That fall, Congress passed the Public *Broadcasting* Act, creating the Corporation for Public Broadcasting, an entity that encompassed both skies-the-limit television and down-at-the-heels radio.

Future PBS executives condescended to radio. Radio powerhouses such as WGBH and WHA were exceptions. Most outlets were awful. To determine how awful, the CPB's Al Hulsen—the founding director for radio—engaged WGBH president Hartford Gunn, who in turn hired Sam C. O. Holt, an urbane Alabamian who'd done time at both the Boston station and in network television. From an office in Harvard Square, Holt surveyed the nation's educational radio broadcasters. He was dismayed. Of the 425 stations he examined, half were "10-watters," meaning their signals didn't reach beyond their campuses. Many were adjuncts of school audio-visual departments. Few possessed adequate control rooms, equipment, or staffs. Programming was spotty, often consisting of just college lectures. "It was pitiful," Holt recalled.

Gunn and Holt agreed on part of the solution. Public radio needed professionalizing. Federal grants soon enabled a number of stations to purchase such basic equipment as typewriters. Less obvious, public radio also needed a uniform sound. TV viewers watch programs. Radio audiences listen to stations. Gunn imagined a network that broadcast "tightly formatted, in-depth national and international news and public affairs, with the emphasis on analysis, commentary, criticism and good talk." Holt concurred, but he differed on a critical point. Where Gunn wanted big-city independent stations like his WGBH in Boston to create the programming, Holt realized that key midwestern outlets would chafe at this arrangement. He asserted that production should be centralized in Washington. The Corporation for Public Broadcasting saw things Holt's way, setting public radio on a path distinct from that of public TV. Unlike PBS, which would air programs produced by stations all over the country, NPR would broadcast *and* produce its own shows.

The heartland stations subscribed to a populist ethos, while those in cities like Boston wanted something more sophisticated. In this context, Bill Siemering, whose well-known work at WBFO made him a champion of open-mindedness as well as highbrow programming, held the middle ground. During the meetings to create National Public Radio, its board selected him to write a mission statement. He finished it in the spring of 1970, and by that summer, when network leaders gathered in Chicago to approve the hiring of Don Quayle as president, everyone in public radio was talking about it. The WBFO manager read the document aloud to the room.

"National Public Radio," Siemering began in his quietly forceful way, "will serve the individual. It will promote personal growth. It will regard the individual differences among men with respect and joy rather than derision and hate. It will celebrate the human experience as infinitely varied rather than vacuous and banal. It will encourage a sense of active constructive participation rather than apathetic helplessness."

Siemering was not just pitching an idea—he was issuing a call.

In its cultural mode, National Public Radio will preserve and transmit the past, will encourage and broadcast the work of contemporary artists and provide listeners with an aural experience which enriches and gives meaning to the human spirit.

In its journalistic mode, National Public Radio will actively explore, investigate and interpret issues of national and international import. The programs will enable the individual to better understand himself, his government, his institutions and his natural and social environment so he can intelligently participate in effecting the process of change . . .

National Public Radio will not regard its audience as a market or in terms of its disposable income, but as curious, complex individuals who are looking for some understanding, meaning, and joy.

On he went, concluding: "National Public Radio should not only improve the quality of public radio but should lead in revitalizing the medium of radio so that it may become a first-class citizen in the media community."

When Siemering sat down, Schmidt turned to Quayle and asked, "Do you think that if you come onto NPR as president that you can implement that?"

"Well, if the author comes along with me as director of programming," replied Quayle, "we probably could."

No one at the meeting, least of all Quayle, anticipated this turn.

"I did it on the spot," he said later.

Ten days after *All Things Considered* debuted, station managers from the nearly one hundred members in the National Public Radio network—a hodgepodge of outlets as various as the nation itself—gathered at the Twin Bridges Marriott in Virginia just across the Potomac River from Washington. They had come to discuss what NPR had wrought—and the consensus, articulated by WHA's Karl Schmidt, was not kind: "Our child has been born, and it is ugly."

Like its premiere, succeeding broadcasts of *ATC* (as the staff had begun to call it) were erratic. They had good moments. Jim Russell contributed a sharp, three-part series pegged to the first anniversary of Ohio's fatal Kent State shootings. The stories stressed the need for upgraded training of the National Guard, which had killed four students and wounded nine. Jeff Kamen, covering yet another DC antiwar demonstration, this one featuring Hosea Williams from the Southern Christian Leadership Conference, explored the links between the civil rights movement and peace activists. He also captured Williams on tape leading a moving rendition of "Down by the Riverside." Mike Waters, in a montage about a summer sunset in the capital, produced four minutes of incantation of a sort rarely aired since radio's golden age in the 1940s. The piece, said Susan Stamberg, was "fabulous."

There were happy accidents as well. Early one evening, Kati Marton burst into 1625 Eye fresh from hearing Germaine Greer speak at the National Press Club. *All Things Considered* was already in progress as she stood in a hall filling in Susan Stamberg and Linda Wertheimer about the event. During a break, Robert Conley, who had witnessed the conversation through the studio window, emerged. "He just grabbed me by the wrist," said Marton, "pulled me in after him, and said, 'Kati, keep talking.' I did. We were live. He wanted that burst, the reality of a young girl's entrancement with this iconic feminist."

Such successes were exceptions. Most of *ATC*'s fare consisted of droning audio from obscure congressional hearings (a school lunch advocate citing alleged deficiencies in the program), bits and bobs from the BBC, conversations with *Christian Science Monitor* reporters about stories they were covering (the network had a deal with the newspaper), and hokey features from member stations. In truth, the show was lucky to get even these on the air, for the day's material was typically unready at deadline. "At the start of a ninety-minute broadcast," said Jeff Rosenberg, "there was supposed to be a stack of tapes" containing all the completed stories. "To stand there at five p.m. and there's only one tape—that's frightening." The result was that from the outset, *ATC* relied on music as padding. Usually the selections were brief, but sometimes they went on and on. (Siemering played Crosby, Stills, Nash & Young's "Ohio" in its entirety between pieces about memorial observances at Kent State.) Staffers termed the musical interludes "panic buttons," because at times of panic—and at first there were many—musical filler was all that stood between the network and dead air.

No wonder the assembled station managers were perturbed. "We were castigated," Jack Mitchell said. "What a horrible mess *ATC* was. It was unprofessional." Not only this, "the southern stations were after us about language and race." Don Quayle did what he could to allay the concerns, declaring, "I think we have a good program," but "none of us are satisfied with it. We are attempting to do something different." Most accepted his assurances of better days ahead, particularly if NPR could fix what they told each other was the central problem.

That problem was Robert Conley. He never should have been chosen to host *All Things Considered*. He was prone to flubs, plagued by a flawed sense of timing, fond of clichés (he trotted out "the shifting sands of policy" whenever discussing the Middle East), and often made bizarre, impromptu comments. While segueing from a straight news report about polluted oceans to a piece that satirized automobile owners for poisoning the air with carbon monoxide, he said this:

Mercury, most of us know, is that silvery substance in thermometers. Ninety-five percent of all samples of swordfish are contaminated by it. It is in the waters. On land, we might think in terms of the highways. Originally, people used to call them turnpikes, because there was a hinged bar blocking the way. That hinged bar is an invention we owe to the British, who legally established turnpikes in 1346. Once, to get through that pike, you had to pay a toll. Thereby was born legally one of the first toll roads. From turnpikes, we call them expressways. Then, with the glut of cars, we began to wonder whether or not these expressways, as some people say, may indeed be the longest parking lots in the world. The growth of automobiles, almost the overpopulation of automobiles, has become a subject for a singular radio drama produced by the National Center for Audio Experimentation.

There were other head-turners as well, the wildest of which heard Conley offer up the recipe for Alice B. Toklas's hash brownies following a story about marijuana use. "The guy on paper really looked good," said Jim Russell, "but he was a space cadet." From his colleagues' perspective, Conley's worst sin was his refusal to type his monologues in script form that would have given the *ATC* staff the ability to time and make room for them in the program. "His idea was that he would just talk it through," said Linda Wertheimer, who became the show's first full-time director. "He wouldn't write it down." Every afternoon at five, Conley jetted into the broadcasting stratosphere without informing producers of his intended remarks. All they knew was that at six thirty he would—maybe—end the show.

Conley was not without strengths. Because of his years at the *New York Times*, he offered the new network much-needed credibility. He gave NPR "get" access. More people knew him than knew the network. Reporters would call sources and ask for an interview, and the response would be, "Oh, you mean the place Conley's gone?" There was also his voice, "wonderful and glib," in Mitchell's words. But the man's mind was a different matter. "I'd hear comments about him being an alcoholic," said Todd Easton, who joined *ATC* as an editor soon after it started. "His grasp of reality wasn't always precise," added Mitchell.

Had Conley been humble about his failings, he might have been regarded by his young NPR associates as a difficult eccentric, but despite his desire to repent from straight journalism, he never let them forget that he was more qualified than they. "The kids who cut tape," he called them. "He was pompous," said Kati Marton. "I think he felt above it all," said Jeff Rosenberg. Indeed, as stories aired during a broadcast, Conley would throw his feet up on the desk as if he owned the place. Not surprisingly, there wasn't much sympathy when just over a month into the show the inevitable happened.

"Conley leaned back in his chair and fell flat," said Wertheimer. "I'm screaming into the talk back [the interoffice hookup through which a director communicates to on-air talent], 'Get to the microphone. Get to the microphone.'" Only after Conley—on his knees, clutching the edge of his desk—began to speak, assuring that *ATC* stayed on the air, did Wertheimer ask, "Are you all right, Robert? Did you hurt yourself?"

Susan Stamberg, despite her junior position at NPR, had been around public radio long enough (she started at WAMU in the early 1960s and returned there following her time in India) to have strong opinions. She chose this juncture to go to Cleve Mathews, who functioned as Siemering's number two. Not only did *All Things Considered* need an overhaul in "shape, form, style and personality," she told the news director, but Conley had to go. She got no disagreement. Quayle concurred, and ordered his programming director to do the dirty work, presenting him with his first test as a manager. "Bill didn't like confrontation," said Rosenberg. Indeed, Siemering had structured the news department along nonhierarchal lines, so much so that there was confusion about who did what. Conley "could be brilliant," the programming director said later, "but then he'd plummet. He'd lose his way." On a June Sunday Siemering dismissed the first host of *ATC*. Conley would assume the nebulous role of "producer/on-air voice/director."

The next afternoon at five, *All Things Considered*'s theme song gave way to the program's new cohosts: Jim Russell and Mike Waters. The plan was to split the show into two segments. The first—and at sixty minutes, the longest—would be devoted to news and presided over by Russell. The second, softer half hour would belong to Waters.

Russell was one of those newsmen whose gifts emerge from his contradictions. Son of a CIA agent, he was a conservative, but he was not judgmental about the rebellious NPR atmosphere. He saw himself as radio documentary maker and was open to a variety of ideas. As an undergraduate at American University, he'd worked for Stamberg at WAMU and applied to be a *Playboy* bunny for a feature about sex discrimination. He was, however, a serious journalist who during his time in Southeast Asia for UPI got into Cambodia. "He had reporting chops," said Stamberg. "He had the entire package," said Todd Easton. "He sounded great on the air. His writing was phenomenal."

Waters was impressive in a different way. Short and lively with a wispy beard and bright eyes, he was a devout Roman Catholic. "Lace curtain Irish," Wertheimer called him. "He had this impish quality," said Siemering. "He was a good storyteller. He had great ears. He'd say, 'I want you to hear this' about something he'd just recorded." Along with his ravishing voice and knack for editing, this love of storytelling made him perfect for back-of-the-book pieces.

The pairing looked good, but put together as fast as it was ("I got a call from Siemering on Sunday," said Russell, "and he said, 'Hey, Jim, you're gonna host the show tomorrow'"), it was troubled from the start.

Russell's experience may have created the impression that he possessed the entire package, but there was a missing piece: maturity. *ATC* had put a twenty-five-year-old at the helm of a complex production, and like a lot of twenty-five-year-olds in radio, he liked to play around in the booth before airtime. With his microphone switched off, he'd boom, "This is *The Big Old Fat Old Jimbo Show.*" Everyone was amused, but many worried that someday that microphone would be live.

"We sent out two versions of *ATC*," said Russell, "one at five p.m. eastern and one at eight p.m. for the West Coast. When you finished the five p.m. show at six thirty you corrected any errors. I was running to the airport to catch a plane, and I wanted to fix something I got wrong in the intro during the first broadcast. I read the correction quickly, made a mistake, and did it over. When I was leaving the studio, I said, 'You got that?'" His colleagues did not get it. At five o'clock Pacific, *ATC* listeners in California just tuning in heard Russell snort: "Oh, shit. Take two."

While Russell's on-air cursing infuriated NPR affiliates ("I had messages from stations saying that I find another line of work," he said; "an apology wasn't good enough"), Waters's problem generated concern inside 1625 Eye. His vocal gifts and lapidary delivery sprang from a tortured sensibility. "He was under a lot of self-imposed pressure," said Mitchell. Where most hosts require only a couple of takes to nail a bit of narration, he sometimes needed fifteen. "That's a bridge over troubled waters," cracked a staffer as he watched an engineer construct a transition—known in radio as a bridge—between sections of a story that had gotten the best of Waters. Each day before airtime, the man Stamberg described as "having a cathedral in his head" rushed to a toilet and vomited.

Whatever the travails under Conley, a man-child and an agonizing perfectionist now fronted *ATC*. The show sometimes felt as if it might come apart. Furthermore, deadlines were still being missed, and contents remained uneven. There was a growing sense, especially among NPR's executives and on the technical side, that Conley had not been the problem. It was the programming director himself who was starting to strike them as a shabbily clad incompetent.

That Bill Siemering typically eschewed a necktie bugged George Geesey. Not only did the head of the operations department wear a tie, so did everyone on his staff. "George insisted on it," said Dick Cassidy, the chief engineer. In Geesey's domain at 1625 Eye, the dress code was respected and the protocols adhered to. His people were serious broadcasters, not a pack of mangy and defiant wildebeests like those Siemering had assembled, men and women who, in the words of one engineer, gave *NPR* an upsettingly apt second meaning: "Non-Professional Radio." Early in the summer of 1971, to impose building-wide order, Geesey introduced a new rule governing the use of some vital equipment that had already been a source of disagreement—the tape recorders. From here on out, when reporters wanted replacement batteries for their machines—a basic supply they'd grown accustomed to scooping up as needed—they had to fill out a form in triplicate. Nobody was happy about this, but Geesey might just as well have dangled a red flag in front of the newsroom's most confrontational figure.

Even in the NPR news department, Jeff Kamen was a divisive character. At his best, he was as good as the network got in its first months. "Not until I heard Kamen's work did I know what Siemering was going for," said Mitchell. Call it audio verité. "In TV," said Kamen, "there's an old saying that if your pictures are too weak, try getting closer. Covering radio news with a microphone is the same thing. If you want the richness of a story, you have to be in the middle of it." A two-part *ATC* piece Kamen did in the summer of 1971 comparing the lost-cause campaign of antiwar congressman Pete Mc-Closkey against that of Richard Nixon for the next year's Republican presidential nomination was a gem of the form. The reporter recorded the quiet, polite sounds of McCloskey's headquarters; then, for the next segment, the brisk, brusque sounds of Nixon's headquarters. In the finished stories, the audience can *hear* the differences between the organizations and candidates. The audio—not the narration—tells the tale.

That was Kamen. But there was also El Lobo; and, as Stamberg put it, "you just couldn't manage him." Whether tromping through the office muttering imprecations or racing around Washington in his unforgettable car—a black 1963 Lincoln Continental—he was out of the wrong movie. "He was not fitting in," said Rosenberg. "People would make jokes about him," said Easton. "He wasn't in the public broadcasting mold." Years later Kamen simply said, "I'm impulsive, self-absorbed." All of which explains why when he grabbed some batteries from the engineering department after the new rule went into effect and one of Geesey's men said, "Hey, Kamen, we don't do that anymore," he exploded.

Cursing and foaming, Kamen stormed into Cleve Mathews's office and told him what had happened. The new regulation was a violation of a core principle—the talent did not submit to the suits. It was, he added, also a betrayal of promises the news director and Siemering had made the day he was hired. "Reassure me," Kamen recalled telling them, "that you won't become a government-style bureaucracy, because that will drive me nuts, and I won't be able to do my work."

"It's just batteries, Jeff," said Mathews. "It's just batteries."

"I quit," said Kamen. For him, it was more than just batteries. He saw in this grain of sand a coming NPR of red tape and inhibitions. El Lobo, whose rock 'n' roll yelps had announced *ATC*'s birth, was gone.

Kamen's departure did not end the tension between Siemering and Geesey. As NPR stumbled into the fall of 1971, executives from all over the network were starting to criticize the programming director. Don Quayle found Siemering's pet phrase "Let's hold hands and have a race" increasingly galling. "It never occurred to him to say, 'I'm in charge and you do what I tell you.' *No, let's all hold hands.*" Several of Quayle's top assistants— principally Chuck Herbits, the legal counsel, and James Barrett, the publicity director—made fun of the programming chief. Herbits, an athletic, good-looking wiseacre, was vicious. He divided the world into "stubby fingers"—pragmatists like himself who did tough jobs—and "limp wrists" like Siemering who couldn't make decisions. "To Quayle's buddies Bill was a joke. They were funny, cruel smartasses," said Mitchell, and they had Quayle's ear. If the programming director had been producing consistent improvements at *ATC*, their criticism would not have mattered, but the show continued to be all over the map. On the upside, Barbara Newman, NPR's first investigative reporter, was breaking stories about cost overruns in the Defense Department's Minuteman missile program. Also, editing and production values were marginally better. Nevertheless, unsuitable "panic buttons"—the phrase, shortened to "buttons," would hereafter be used at NPR to indicate all interstitial music—predominated. Nobody was exercising editorial judgment. Station managers complained that the network was airing stuff that exposed them to ridicule in their communities.

The basic fact remained: Don Quayle had hand-picked Siemering. The NPR president, hoping both to stabilize the network and enable the philosopher king to do what he did best, brought in a fixer.

Joe Gwathmey, a lanky Texan who'd managed KUT in Austin, was only thirty when he joined NPR in October 1971. His job was assistant programming director, but his mandate was to negotiate peace between Siemering and his antagonists. From the start, he realized it would be hard. "What I found was a lot of tension between Bill and the technical staff and pretty much the whole organization," he said. "The tension stemmed from the mismatch between Bill's visionary view of how things ought to be and the very structured, inflexible expectations" of everyone else.

In Gwathmey's view Siemering was "sloppy." Worse, he did not accept criticism well. "It's fair to say that Bill had a high opinion of himself," said Gwathmey. "He wasn't a timid man by any means." Meanwhile Geesey was overbearing and minced no words when telling Siemering to shape up. "George might have genuinely disliked Bill. His view of the world was radically different. He was organized and demanding. In my role as mediator I had more run-ins with George than with anybody."

Still, Gwathmey was hopeful. "I wasn't intimidated. I thought things could be salvaged. I was excited. This was a brand-new organization trying to do something that hadn't been done. I was on board about offering listeners a resource to help understand what was going on in the world, because I thought our society was undergoing a revolution. I thought radio could bridge this gap, because you don't have visual cues to reinforce your prejudices. On the radio you don't know if someone has on a tie-dye T-shirt or a Brooks Brothers suit."

Accommodation, however, could go only so far. On the last Tuesday of October, just four weeks after Gwathmey arrived, an incident that exposed how mismanaged the organization was occurred in front of not just the network staff but also much of official Washington. That evening, Siemering's enemies phoned Quayle: "Turn on your TV and watch the news."

Doug Terry was, at twenty-four, one of those young journalists who want it all—not just to bear witness to history but to be a part of it. He had been in and around radio news since his teens, most recently at stations in Texas. At the same time, he'd participated in the Mayday Tribe protests, where he'd been arrested. That's what brought him to NPR: he heard about the new network and applied. During his first months, he covered the Apollo 17 launch and impressed people with his enthusiasm ("He was passionate," said

Stamberg) and craft ("He had a nice way of putting a piece on the air," said Wertheimer). Following Kamen's departure, Terry took over war coverage. It was no secret where he stood. In early October, reacting to a less-bloody-than-usual weekly Pentagon casualty report, he broadcast a mocking commentary on *ATC*:

> And now they tell us only eight have died this week—eight only! Only sixteen parents to grieve, only eight wives—and how many never-to-be friends—to cry. . . . We are trapped in the Vietnam War. What will it take for some bureaucrat or would-be leader to find a means to get us out? We wait. We wait for the end of our nightmare. Somewhere in the endless corridors of official Washington there must be a computer that keeps track of statistics on the Vietnam War. Someday, somehow, when the numerical truth adds up to the simple reality of human suffering, the computer will print out: ENOUGH. But when?

On October 26 Terry turned his press pass into NPR. Believing that he was free to exercise his constitutional rights, he went down to join the demonstration.

Rennie Davis, along with his Chicago Seven codefendant David Dellinger, was back in Washington. The plan was more limited in scope this time. With only several hundred marchers, the organizers did not have the numbers to shut the city. But that's not to say that their hopes were modest. We have come, Davis told followers, to evict Richard Nixon from office. At the height of evening rush hour, he led a throng of 450 toward the executive mansion. They chanted: "One, two, three, four, we don't want your fucking war." Terry was with them as they sat down in the middle of Pennsylvania Avenue.

Outside the White House, matters grew tense. Two hundred police officers, operating as in the spring on foot and on motorcycles, pushed into the protestors. "All around me people are screaming," Terry recalled. "Women are screaming particularly, and the motorbikes are going '*Rurrvum*.'" At this moment, a big, forceful cop moved into Terry's line of vision. The guy seemed to be in charge. "I was schooled," said Terry, "that you talk back to police. You don't say 'Yes, sir, no, sir.' If they're doing something wrong, you tell them." Terry jumped up and grabbed this commanding figure, raking the front of his dress jacket. Something ripped.

Jerry V. Wilson, chief of the Washington, DC, Metropolitan Police and one of the best-known faces in American law enforcement (he had been on the cover of *Time* the previous summer), glowered at Terry. The NPR reporter had torn off his identification tag. A camera crew from WTOP, the capital's CBS station, captured it all, and the story led its late broadcast. There was also a front-page picture in the *Washington Star* of Terry seated in the street and an account of what happened: "Another demonstrator arrested was one who scuffled with Police Chief Jerry V. Wilson."

The next day at 1625 Eye, the incident was a sensation. One of the producers got hold of the TV footage, and staffers screened it repeatedly. It was a party to celebrate a disaster. NPR executives were mortified but relieved that neither WTOP nor the *Star* identified their man by name or connected him to the network. They convinced themselves that because he'd relinquished his credentials, he'd been free to participate in the rally. The police booked Terry on felony destruction of federal property, although prosecutors reduced the charge to a misdemeanor and, after he pled out, expunged it from his record. Soon, he was back on the air, unrepentant. "I was opposed to the war. I saw this industrial, technology-rich nation attacking a small, backward people."

In November, Cleve Mathews—frustrated by the Terry debacle (many outfits would have fired the reporter) and the general drift—resigned as news director. A week later, Quayle enticed him back. As far as Quayle was now concerned, the weak link was Siemering. Sensing that his position was threatened, the programming chief installed Jack Mitchell (who not only held a PhD but had interned for a year at the BBC) as producer of *All Things Considered*, surrendering a role that to this juncture he'd performed. He would focus on larger issues. Quayle was not appeased. In March 1972, he put Siemering on notice. Either NPR improved, or he was gone.

In this moment of flailing uncertainty Jack Mitchell picked Susan Stamberg to join Mike Waters as cohost of *All Things Considered*, making her the first woman to front a national American news show. Not that the press marked the occasion. NPR's profile was practically nonexistent. (Early in its life *ATC*'s audience was so miniscule that Arbitron, the ratings service, did not keep track.) Still, it was a breakthrough for both the network and the nation's media, and it had not been easy to achieve. NPR's new board chairman, Dick Estell, manager of the Michigan State station in East Lansing, didn't like Stamberg's speaking style and hadn't wanted her. "She's too New York," he told Mitchell, meaning that she was too Jewish. Karl Schmidt, manager of WHA in Madison, NPR's biggest station, and the former board chairman, also hadn't wanted her, but for a different reason: he didn't believe a female could handle the job. Although the network had influential outlets on both coasts, it remained, said Mitchell, "conservative, male, midwestern."

More centered than the others at *ATC*—she was married and had a child—Stamberg was responsible to a fault. "I wasn't nearly as radical as the young ones," she said. She also possessed what for a host is a defining skill— the ability to listen attentively to anyone from the most scintillating conversationalist to the most veteran bore. She had picked this skill up in India. "She was the perfect diplomat's wife," said Mitchell. "She found something interesting in everyone she met. It was a wonderful gift, and it was genuine." At the same time Stamberg possessed another strength: she was a ham. "She had enthusiasm, energy, and presence," said Siemering. Also, she could write, and as much as newspapers or magazines, radio is a writer's medium.

Although Stamberg had not been hired as an on-air performer, she'd been appearing on *All Things Considered* almost since the start, and nearly everything she did stood out, because she interjected herself into her pieces. In a June 1971 interview with Dick Gregory about an anti–Vietnam War hunger strike he'd staged, she caught the comedian's self-righteousness by describing how he took it upon himself to read her fortune at the end of their encounter, "working the numbers, listening to what his head was telling him" until "his messages stopped, and I was dismissed." In a conversation a month later with Buck Lanham, a close friend of Ernest Hemingway, she used her superior knowledge of the late novelist to draw her guest out.

Stamberg and Waters developed a strong rapport. "What came across was like the old Arthur Godfrey show," recalled Jim Anderson, a young engineer at NPR's Pittsburgh station who would soon join the network. "The two had voices made for radio—Susan a beautiful contralto and this deep, throaty chuckle that Waters called 'a two-bit whore laugh.' And Waters had this bass that could lull you into anything." From the start, it was clear that *All Things Considered* was Stamberg's program, and it was also clear that there was no place for the sort of discursive rambling that had initially marred it. Nearly any time she or Waters made what seemed like an off-the-cuff remark, it had been scripted in advance. The best radio might feel immediate, but that immediacy was achieved by calculation. "I learned the art of ad-libbing with her," said Ira Flatow, "and I learned our best ad-libs had to be written first."

Mitchell was behind it all. While Siemering's notions may have worked on *This Is Radio* back at WBFO, *ATC* was a ninety-minute national news show, and it demanded a strict format. "The program needs to be more structured," the new producer announced in a memo. "Listeners should be able to count on hearing the same general type of material at the same time each day."

The Stamberg-Waters-hosted *ATC* was not an immediate success, but the show improved quickly enough that when on May 15, 1972, Arthur Bremer gunned down George Wallace, the Alabama governor and presidential aspirant, at a Maryland shopping mall, Mitchell could respond quickly and confidently. "We had a staff full of egos and people who resented each other," he said, "but we threw out the previously planned show, and everyone came together, and everyone had ideas. In a couple hours we covered a lot of angles. We seemed like a team for the first time." This program was tighter and better informed than listeners had heard previously, and as luck had it, NPR station managers were again in DC for their annual convention. The banquet was that night. The reporters and editors were met by applause when they walked into the Washington Hilton. "It was," said Mitchell, "a big change from the previous year."

Still, except for Stamberg, *ATC* lacked star power. To remedy this, Mitchell hired several commentators. Barbara Mikulski, a member of the Baltimore City Council, did a number of superb pieces about her town's tough neighborhoods. Goodman Ace—along with wife, Jane, half of the Easy Aces (a 1930s radio comedy team) and in the 1950s a writer for NBC's *The Big Show*—found a new life on NPR. Mitchell also resurrected another forgotten voice, the Texas humorist John Henry Faulk, blacklisted decades earlier after running afoul of Wisconsin senator Joseph McCarthy.

It was a start, but *All Things Considered* did not yet have the reach of a genuine national news show. The contributions from the member stations were largely pathetic. (The stories were so bad that Flatow, in an attempt to illustrate what NPR did not want, dubbed copies of one of the worst—a piece by an Arizona station about the rebuilding of the London Bridge at a new location on the Colorado River—and circulated it through the system. He hoped to improve future submissions. Instead, he ignited a near rebellion, having held a local effort to ridicule.) There was a potentially simple solution.

"I thought the telephone" was the answer, said Mitchell. The instrument would allow NPR to contact people all over the country and put them on the air. George Geesey, however, was opposed. "They did not build the studio to do things on the phone. Everything was in stereo." Mitchell traveled to Toronto, where the Canadian Broadcasting Corporation relied on the phone to cover the Canadian vastness. Back in DC, he convinced the engineering department that "telephone callbacks" would work. "Susan took charge. She had regular people she checked in on: Charlie White in Kansas, a woman from Wisconsin. One thing I remember: there was a strike at the Lordstown Chevrolet plant in Ohio. It got nasty. We called the lunchroom and talked to whoever answered." This sort of work, while in contrast to the highly pro-duced audio NPR intended to rely on, enabled the network to create the illusion of far-reaching coverage.

Stamberg excelled at long-distance confabs. "On the phone, I'm not distracted by the ugly tie, or the nervous tic, or the exquisite manicure. By phone, it's strictly voice-to-voice, and I can concentrate totally on what's being said. I also like the crackle of the phone line and the kind of electric punch it gives the conversations. Then, too, the telephone receiver is a mi-crophone everyone knows how to use. People are relaxed and comfortable speaking on the phone and that quality comes across. A recording studio, with all its equipment and electronic gear, is a pretty intimidating place. People freeze up in a studio. Call 'em on the telephone, though, and they'll curl right up for a chat."

It was intimacy and breadth. By the fall of 1972, *All Things Considered* was starting to jell, yet it retained its identity as an alternative to the network news. Stamberg brought this home that Thanksgiving by debuting Grandma Stamberg's cranberry relish recipe, lavishing as much attention on this fam-ily-centered chestnut as CBS would devote to a groundbreaking report from Vietnam. An institution was coming to life, and it hadn't been as hard as Mitchell had feared. "What surprised me, what surprised Siemering" was that "it didn't take much to fix *ATC*."

As far as management was concerned, Siemering was no longer essential to *All Things Considered*, and he was OK with that. "The Quayle people were happy with what I was doing, and so was Siemering," said Mitchell. "He could go out and be the philosopher king."

Freed from day-to-day responsibilities, Siemering, who'd always had a bit of the Age of Aquarius in him, began to dress differently. Early on, he looked like an academic, "but as he went along," said Mitchell, "he became more psychedelic," wearing purple and pink shirts. He was "kind of a flower child," recalled Marton. The shift in wardrobe accompanied a change in life—Siemering left his wife. "Carol was not engaged at all in my work, which was all right," he said. She moved back to Wisconsin, taking their daughters with her.

To be the programming director of NPR in 1972 and to be single was not the worst thing. "Siemering had an aura," said Todd Easton. "He lived as a free man," said Mitchell. "I think there were women," said Russell. For several months, Siemering had been hanging out with Keith Talbot, a long-haired radio madman. A graduate of Franconia College, an experimental school in New Hampshire, Talbot had grown up in a broadcasting family (his father founded Fremantle International, which syndicated TV shows, among them *The Dating Game* and *Romper Room*). Although Talbot was nearly fifteen years younger than the NPR boss, they shared interests in psychology (they met at a symposium of the Washington Psychoanalytic Institute) and sound production. Talbot was the editor of *Soundlink*, a quarterly audio magazine, which he produced on three Sony reel-to-reel recorders in the attic of his frame duplex near American University. Painted white, filled with collages depicting the moon, and dominated by a "Model of Ideas"—a strip depicting consciousness and unconsciousness in three dimensions—the "Dream Attic," as Talbot dubbed his studio, represented either the vanguard of audio news production or the lunatic fringe. The young radio savant distributed his magazine on Norelco cassettes to a select group of fellow freaks.

In September 1972, just as NPR was starting to become more conventional, Talbot sold an idea for an unconventional series to *All Things Considered*. Although "Sound Portraits" was his concept, it was infused with Siemering's spirit. "I drove all over the country with a Sony 800-B reel-to-reel, and each week I turned in an essay that conveyed the sounds of peoples' lives," Talbot recalled. "I did one on Johnny Wright, the police chief in Timmonsville, South Carolina. Another one was on a soldier just home from Vietnam, George Longo. He talked about coming back from Saigon, talked about what it felt like. He was beautiful, amazing. There was nothing else like this on the air. I would spend two days editing an hour-long tape: seventy-five cuts to get to five minutes. I did it all at home on my tape recorders. NPR gave me fifty dollars, sometimes one hundred a week."

While Siemering had enough self-awareness to realize that his protégé's segments might not be what *ATC* was now all about, he seemed largely blind to the fact that many at NPR viewed his support of "Sound Portraits" as confirmation that he was out of touch. As Talbot, who admired the programming chief, observed, "I don't think Bill had the imagination to put himself in other people's shoes." The visionary lacked political instincts, and even when he tried to deal with bureaucratic tasks, he seemed either obtuse (asked to write a job title for Mike Waters on a form, Siemering jotted: "Mike Waters") or inept. If two employees with a disagreement came to him and said, "We have a problem," he'd nod like a therapist and dispassionately respond, "You're right. You have a problem."

By this point, said Mitchell, the term *philosopher king* was mostly used derisively at NPR. Siemering and the organization were moving in different directions, and no one was more aware of it than Jim Russell, who after leaving his cohosting position had returned to being a reporter. He was close to Siemering and to George Geesey. In fact, he and Geesey lived in the same Maryland suburb, and the two often drove home together. One night, Geesey invited Russell in for a drink. Cocktail in hand, the operations chief led his guest to his basement, which contained the most elaborate HO model railroad layout Russell had ever seen. Diesel engines pulled rolling stock on tracks lined with countless industrial buildings, all handmade by the proprietor. Each train had a task. "It was perfect," said Russell. "A light bulb went off: George and Bill were on different tracks." As the reporter understood, for Geesey—and for the other executives—the trains had to run on time.

On Sunday morning, December 10, Bill Siemering awakened in his tiny apartment at the Grayln Hotel to a phone call from Don Quayle. A turn-of-the-century complex on N Street with bare light bulbs and leaky faucets, the

Grayln was grim. Most tenants were, like Siemering, separated or divorced men. Quayle wanted his programming chief to come to 2025 M Street, the future home of NPR. Under construction since just before the network went on the air, it was nearly finished.

An hour or so later, Siemering arrived. Work on the new headquarters had progressed sufficiently for executives like Quayle to move in, although the reporters and *ATC* staffers were still at 1625 Eye and would remain there until the studios in the long-awaited facility were ready. The network would start broadcasting at 2025 M in 1973. The person who created it all would not be part of it.

"I think it's time for you to leave," Quayle said.

"I thought I'd addressed all your concerns."

"It's too late," asserted the NPR president.

There was no reply to that, and Siemering emerged into the frigid, winter day disoriented, disbelieving. Again and again, he told himself that this had not happened. The next morning, he still denied it. He got up, dressed, and walked to 1625 Eye, entering the newsroom as if everything was OK. It was unnerving for the staff to see their deposed boss, and it got worse. Maybe, Siemering proposed, this might still be remedied. He called Quayle: Could he return to NPR in the position of tape editor? He had created *All Things Considered*. Now he was begging to start over at the bottom. Quayle said no. Siemering stumbled back onto the street. His head throbbed. His face and body felt aflame.

At NPR, no one knew what to say. "He comes in as this great designer and conceiver of the system, then is run out of town by the very system he conceived of," said his WBFO protégé Smokey Baer, who joined NPR in the immediate wake of Siemering's leave-taking. Ira Flatow, another of the Buffalo boys, said, "I was shocked. He was my mentor. How could people not see the value I saw in him?" Stamberg, although a bit more realistic, was also upset. "I couldn't believe it. I knew things kept being dropped. I knew that there were often unpaid bills on his desk. But it was awful." As for Quayle, the consensus was that he'd regretted hiring Siemering all along. He'd acted on impulse, made a mistake, and had to rectify it. "I'd known for six months that he had to go," the network president said later. "I didn't want to. I thought his vision was good for us. I wanted to retain the vision and the philosophy.

I brought in Joe Gwathmey to get him to manage and do the administrative kind of leadership that a staff requires. But Bill wouldn't do it. He didn't want to do it. He didn't like to do it."

A few people reached out. Jack Mitchell threw Siemering a small party. Susan Stamberg invited him to dinner. But with his marriage over and children gone, the deposed philosopher king was alone. He had thoughts about the future. Landscape architecture seemed appealing. For now, he craved mindlessness—and needed money. "I went down to the *Washington Post.* They hired people to stuff the sections together when the paper came off the press. You did it by hand." Which was why the Christmas holidays found Siemering collating preprinted inserts into the great daily. Sometimes he viewed it all humorously. "At least I could say I worked for the *Washington Post.*" But there weren't many such moments. He was a failure, and the future of NPR was unclear. In such a state of mind, the new job was a blessing. All Siemering had to do was keep pace with the newspapers ratcheting off the machinery. It was a captivating and rhythmic sound, one he might once have put on the radio.

TWO

ENCOUNTER SESSION

aucus Room 318 of Washington's Russell Senate Office Building—also known as the Old Senate Office Building, or the SOB—overflowed with reporters, photographers, and the merely curious. All eyes were on Sam Ervin, the jowly North Carolina senator who chaired the Select Committee on Presidential Campaign Activities. "An expectant standing-room-only crowd," Josh Darsa told National Public Radio listeners on this morning in the spring of 1973, was "witnessing day one of the Watergate investigation." Alone among America's radio broadcasters, NPR had chosen to cover the hearings gavel to gavel. Live. The probe into the 1972 break-in at the Democratic National Committee headquarters, with its ominous overtones of culpability and cover-up by President Richard Nixon, played to the network's greatest strength—the ability to air an event in real time at length and find theater in the clash of ideas. The proceedings took place just up the street from NPR's offices; they would start at the same hour each morning; and the network had the right man for the job.

Josh Darsa was a veteran journalist who at first glance seemed out of place at scruffy, antiauthoritarian National Public Radio. Given to Jermyn Street suits, cotton dress shirts, and silk neckties, the forty-year-old reporter wore his wavy, dark hair smoothed down and parted on the side, and when not talking into a mic was puffing a pipe. He had come to the network midway through Bill Siemering's tenure from CBS Television News, where he'd been based in Chicago, Europe, and Los Angeles. Although he'd never been a regular on the *Evening News* with Walter Cronkite, he'd had his moments—JFK's "Ich bin ein Berliner" trip to Germany, anti–Vietnam War protests in Berkeley. In November 1963, he'd won brief fame when Alexander Kendrick, the network's London bureau chief, intoned the following nine words on the *Morning News* with Mike Wallace: "Reporter Josh Darsa talked to the Beatles in their dressing room." This was the first American TV interview with John Lennon, Paul McCartney, George Harrison, and Ringo Starr.

The exchange lasted only a minute and twenty-seven seconds, a sound bite in Kendrick's sweeping piece about Beatlemania. For all his panache and background (Columbia grad, army vet), Darsa was mannered on camera. He came across as not so much himself as someone playing himself. On the radio he was more at ease, and NPR brought him on board to produce "Live Events," the typically staid stuff of official Washington that provided filler during the midday hours between morning classical music broadcasts and the five p.m. start of *All Things Considered.* The no-fault insurance hearings of the Senate Commerce Committee, the Congressional Conference on Constitutional Powers—Darsa's job was to bring the drab and the droning to life. Now one of these forums had become the main event. Accompanied by Gary Henderson, an engineer who arrived at the capitol each day by taxi in order to tote a big Nagra tape machine (George Geesey's high-end favorite) capable of recording pool feed, commentary, and interviews, Darsa became a fixture at the Watergate hearings. While PBS also offered continuous coverage of the sessions, its correspondents—Jim Lehrer and Robert MacNeil—weighed in from WETA's studios in Arlington, Virginia. From the first to the last, NPR's correspondent was the sole on-air reporter in the hall with the senators—Ervin, Howard Baker, Herman Talmadge, and the rest—and a who's who of witnesses from the White House.

Darsa's delivery bore traces of the stuffiness that had plagued him at CBS. His style, recalled *All Things Considered* producer Jack Mitchell, "was dramatic and pretentious. Something is important because 'I Josh Darsa am here.'" The reporter, in a line that became the signature of his work during the proceedings, introduced every session by proclaiming: "Live . . . from the nation's capital . . . this . . . is NPR's continuing coverage of . . . the Watergate hearings." He drew out each phrase (and it was always "the nation's capital," never "Washington") with a gravitas that bordered on camp. As his colleague Jim Russell subsequently observed, "He was like a cross between Edward R. Murrow and Rod Serling."

Nonetheless, Darsa was a conscientious professional, probably the most thoughtful and certainly the most experienced broadcaster at National Public Radio. His work on Watergate was thorough and on point. During recesses, he interviewed committee members and staffers and, when no one was available, vamped authoritatively. Not only that, but when the hearings adjourned each afternoon, he rushed back to M Street and produced ten-minute recaps on deadline for *All Things Considered*. The pieces, edited by Todd Easton and Ira Flatow, were mini-documentaries of an ongoing national tragedy. One evening that spring, after playing a sharp exchange between Talmadge and White House Counsel John Dean, Darsa predicted where the crisis was headed:

> If it wasn't vivid before, today's session of the Watergate hearings conclusively illustrated the one fact in this investigation upon which hinges the future course of this committee, this administration, and history.
>
> That fact is that . . . if John Dean can be corroborated by other figures involved in Watergate, if his testimony before this committee can be cemented, if what he is saying is the truth then the ramifications are enormous.

The work took a toll on Darsa—five hours of live, daily broadcasts followed by intense sessions at the studio constructing nightly stories followed by a couple more hours of reading to be ready for another round. "I remember very, very long days and nights with all the Watergate coverage," recalled Easton. "Josh looked so tired and bedraggled. He would have the sleeves of his shirt rolled up above the elbows, and he would walk around or sit at his desk looking like he was in great pain. It always appeared he was talking to himself. His lips and head would actually move slightly as if he was having a conversation. I wondered if he was working out scripts in his head and talking them through. He was intense with an incredible work ethic."

Darsa was the first to reach 2025 M Street each day and the last to leave.

"He slept at the office," Susan Stamberg said later. "He pitched his tent there. His dry cleaning was there. He had no place else to go. He was sort of home-less." Family? A mystery. Girlfriend? No one knew. Once NPR turned off the lights, Darsa curled up on the floor among stacks of old newspapers and fell asleep beneath walls hung with his prized possessions—dramatic color photographs he'd snapped in foreign lands while on assignment for CBS.

NPR's live coverage of the Select Committee on Presidential Campaign Activities rolled on and on: five hours and three minutes, May 17; five hours and twenty-eight minutes, May 22; six hours and thirty-six minutes, June 25; five hours and five minutes, July 12. At first slowly, then in increasing number, listeners began to take note. "Only on public radio, FM's rational, healthy side, was there evidence of a brain and heart out there in radioland," reported the media critic for the *Richmond Times-Dispatch*. "The great drumbeat of Watergate unified stations in Winston-Salem and Knoxville as the public radio network carried the minute details of America's agony." The radio-TV critic at the *Cincinnati Enquirer* was more effusive:

> The National Public Radio Network has provided the only "live" and complete radio coverage of the Senate Committee hearings. On WGUC here . . . that coverage has made a difference whose impact cannot be measured by ratings . . . Public radio has emerged as a recognized and functioning member of the broadcasting family.

NPR had indeed emerged, but some two years into its existence, it remained a secondary news source. The year 1973 could hardly have been more eventful. The United States Supreme Court issued its *Roe v. Wade* decision legalizing abortion. Former president Lyndon B. Johnson died at his Texas ranch. An Israeli fighter jet accidently shot down a Libyan Arab Airlines 727, killing 108 people. But if an event did not happen in Washington, the network sent no one to cover it. NPR instead relied on the wire services or, as in the case of LBJ's death, taped conversations with reporters from established journalistic outlets.

Then there were the internal travails at *All Things Considered*, which the ministrations of Jack Mitchell notwithstanding, continued to be an improvisation that aired each day as much by dumb luck as design. "Since many of the pieces were not ready on time, the program that went out was not necessarily the program that was planned," recalled Rich Firestone, who'd recently taken over as director, freeing Linda Wertheimer to pursue the job she really wanted—reporting from Capitol Hill. "Whoever was in charge had to figure out what was available, what was a good order to put it in, and let the hosts know with enough time that they didn't panic when they had to do a different intro."

Despite the lack of traditional news and the frequent lapses, *All Things Considered* continued to offer something ABC, CBS, and NBC rarely did—rebelliousness, empathy, and the occasional charmed moment. Barbara Newman kept staking out her turf as NPR's muckraker. "She was our investigative reporter," recalled George Bauer, a new NPR hire. Added Todd Easton, "She fancied herself a rock turner." Short and lithe with spiky hair, a grating voice, and a penchant for hiked-up skirts and revealing blouses, the Brooklyn-bred Newman believed journalism should afflict the comfortable and was not hung up by the concerns about objectivity that constrained reporters at the major networks. "What's advocacy and what's not?" she asked. "It's very easy to present both sides and let it go at that. Maybe you become biased because you did all the research and you could come to no other conclusion." If Blue Cross insurance was setting unfair rates and it could be proven, if Wall Street interests were exposing coal miners to danger and they could be nailed, Newman saw no reason to back off. She was the sort of journalist who while working on a story could with no irony proclaim, "I smelled a rat."

Jim Russell was also intent on causing a stir, but where Newman was driven by prosecutorial zeal, Russell, a disciple of Siemering, was pushing the boundaries of radio storytelling. In the summer of 1973, when NPR news director Cleve Mathews sent him to cover a briefing by several noted economists on the impact of poverty in America, the well-upholstered reporter blew off the assignment. "I thought that was the single most boring subject," he said later in explaining why he instead headed to a grocery store in a lower-class Washington neighborhood. There, his Sony TC-100 in hand, he buttonholed an elderly female shopper who agreed to let him accompany her and tape her thoughts as she pushed her cart through the aisles. Each time she selected an item, Russell asked her to tell him how she would use it at home:

"I'm buying a can of peas, and that will be three meals."

"No, no," replied Russell. "You mean that will go with three meals."

"Maybe that will go *with* three of your meals," she corrected him, "but that will be three *of* my meals."

Russell knew he was getting remarkable material, and he kept his recorder rolling, grabbing the evocative sounds—squeaky wheels on linoleum, a cash register ringing, paper bags snapping—with which he could illustrate the stark truth of the woman's words. The resulting piece was the aural equivalent of an ashcan school painting. Listeners heard the impact of poverty. No sooner had it aired than Mathews accosted the reporter.

"God damn it, that's the last time I'll assign you to cover a story."

"Just let me ask you one question," Russell replied. "Do you think it was better than what we'd have gotten if I'd gone to the briefing?"

"That's not the point."

"Oh, yes, that's the point."

If the hard news *All Things Considered* aired frequently echoed the values of the underground press, the program's softer, cultural reports bore a passing resemblance to such period touchstones as the *Whole Earth Catalog*. The wisdom of plain folk was prized, the crassness of the marketplace chided. In a periodic series produced by local stations and called "The Village Well," men and women from across the country reflected on their daily lives. There was also a regular feature titled the "Commercials for Nicer Living Contest" that played off NPR's ad-free status by giving listeners the chance to submit ideas for life-affirming commercials, then hear professionally recorded realizations of the ideas on the radio.

"We'll create an ad for something you love, so tell us what it is," Stamberg would urge the audience.

One was for homemade pies ("Cherry pie, apple pie, pie baked from pumpkin. When you bake pie from scratch you really got something"), and a doozy celebrated a habit most people abandon in childhood. "Life got you down?" a studio announcer asked. "Come along and enjoy the mellow, back-to-nature bliss you knew as a child. Give it a chance. Know your thumb. Share it with a friend." After that last one, Mike Waters could only say, "A commercial for thumb sucking. Well, why not?"

Fred Calland, NPR's arts producer, added erudition to nearly every show.

Tall, with a large, jack-o'-lantern face and pencil-thin mustache, he worked out of a tiny office stacked floor-to-ceiling with 78 rpm recordings of Enrico Caruso and other artists of an earlier era. He contributed to a growing roster of NPR music programs—*Concert of the Week*, *Jazz Alive*, and *International Concert Hall*—while functioning as a deadline poet for *All Things Considered*. He could turn around a lovely piece in mere minutes—those old recordings weren't just for show—and he was at ease with the high and the low. His specialty was birthday stories. For Mozart's 219th, he intoned, "After two hundred years, the enigma of Mozart is unresolved. Even his name is a paradox: Wolfgang Amadeus—stride of the wolf, beloved by God." When Elvis Presley hit forty, he waxed elegiac. "The young, sexy, smoldering-voiced kid made it big. He gathered adoring fans by the millions. Time passes, and that generation is now in its forties. So is Elvis. A whole generation would rather not think about it."

All Things Considered was open to whimsy, and sometimes that whimsy was born of the show's failings. Near the end of an episode early in 1973, Stamberg and Waters faced what seemed like an insurmountable dilemma. Firestone, who sat in a glassed-in booth adjacent to the studio, waved his hands at the cohosts while mouthing the word "Fill!" After the tape then airing concluded, the cupboard was bare. Waters, while anxious when putting together a piece demanding forethought, had a gift for the spontaneous. He smiled reassuringly and off-mic asked an engineer to cue up Irving Berlin's "Cheek to Cheek" on the control-room turntable. When Waters and Stamberg were again live, he swiveled in his chair to face her.

"Would you like to dance?"

"Sure," Stamberg replied with a puzzled look but followed his lead as the music played.

"Come here often?" Waters asked.

"No," she replied. Then, picking up on his intent, she squealed, "Ooh," as if Waters had just stepped on her toes.

"Aw, I'm sorry," he offered.

Although Stamberg and Waters were in a utilitarian space filled with audio equipment, in their minds they were a couple of lonely people on a dance floor. "It was like we'd just met," she remembered, "but we were sitting there with our headsets on. We were pretending. It worked because we had no time to think, no copy to read. That's how we took out the program." It was a flawlessly realized ad-lib. Everyone who heard it was entranced. Everyone involved knew that dead air had barely been averted.

In the spring of 1973, in recognition as much for what it was attempting as what it had achieved, *All Things Considered* received broadcasting's highest honor—the Peabody Award for "distinguished and meritorious public service." The prize honored the show for its body of work, but in an irony not lost on the denizens of M Street, it was given for an October 1972 episode produced when Bill Siemering was still programming director. The lineup for the winning broadcast, fronted solo by Waters (Stamberg had the night off), offered a snapshot of NPR at its early best. Bauer was up first with the news summary (the World Series between the Cincinnati Reds and the Oakland A's was starting; GM employees were striking in Doraville, Georgia). Robert Conley, who continued to serve in the awkward role of "producer/ on-air voice/director," contributed an intro to a BBC dispatch on a North Vietnamese demand that South Vietnam's premier resign as a condition for a peace accord. Siemering's protégé Keith Talbot provided a "Sound Portrait" about the start of deer-hunting season in Virginia and a hunter's quest for a mythic buck named Blackie ("We haven't ever got a shot at him so far"). The heart of the program, however, was devoted to an interview with the pediatrician and author Dr. Benjamin Spock. In answer to a question about his influence on the baby boom generation, Spock declared:

> The young people, at least many of them, are willing to give a part of their life to improving society. And they've got a lot of courage. I think the most characteristic thing about them is they can't be intimidated. This is because their parents didn't intimidate them all the way through childhood the way I was intimidated as a child. I was scared of my parents and my teachers. The reason young people today can't be intimidated is their parents trusted them when they were children.

Although NPR's Rich Adams registered some skepticism ("There are many who say this society has grown up to lack any interest in taking responsibility"), Spock basically delivered an uninterrupted monologue that amounted to a salute to the *All Things Considered* demographic, a portrait of the tiny but devoted group who listened. The program was synching up to its audience.

That National Public Radio had made it this far, this fast, was largely the work of Don Quayle. Many at M Street still resented the network president for firing Siemering, but there was wide accord that without Quayle NPR would have foundered. "He kept this screwy organization together on the force of his very appealing personality," Jack Mitchell said later. "He knew how to schmooze, how to make us feel important," added Ira Flatow. At forty-two, Quayle was old enough to be the father of many of his charges, and he looked out for them. They could count on him for help if their cars broke down or if a spouse fell ill. He signed up the entire staff for a TIAA-CREF retirement policy, assuring all who remained with the network a degree of financial security for life. At the same time, Quayle was young enough to identify with his twentyish reporters, and he accepted their vices, because he was no stranger to life's appetites. Although he was part of a small group of NPR executives known as "the Mormon industrial complex," he didn't act it. "Quayle was not a good Mormon," Mitchell recalled. "He drank coffee. He drank liquor. Politically, he was a Massachusetts Democrat."

Quayle was ambitious not just for National Public Radio but for himself. Midway into the summer of 1973 while flying from Washington to San Diego for the dedication of a studio for member station KPBS, he was summoned from his seat in coach to the first-class cabin by Henry Loomis, the new director of the Corporation for Public Broadcasting. Loomis asked Quayle to resign from NPR and work for him. Several days later, Loomis engineered a call to Quayle from someone the NPR executive admired. Jim Killian, the president of MIT, urged him to take the position. Convinced that the move offered a clear path to bigger opportunities—chiefly, the top job at PBS—Quayle made what he later termed "the worst professional decision" of his life. He resigned from National Public Radio. "Quayle went off to CPB, and it broke our hearts," recalled NPR producer Jeff Rosenberg. With Quayle's departure, the network—in the space of little more than six months—had lost both the philosopher king who conceived its mission and the winning leader capable of realizing it.

• • •

Lee C. Frischknecht was Don Quayle's handpicked successor. A product of Utah State University, he'd worked his way up at educational TV stations around the country (among them WNET in New York), joining NPR at its launch as director of network affairs. But where Quayle was a bad Mormon, Frischknecht was a good one. "Unfailingly polite and humble," the *Deseret News* described him. Just five feet, six inches in height with a bushy mustache and heavy, dark-rimmed glasses, he was industrious and self-contained, more comfortable with flowcharts than with people. "He was not by any stretch of the imagination charismatic," recalled assistant programming director Joe Gwathmey. "His tendencies were conservative. He did not inspire people on staff or at the stations." More than that, Frischknecht harbored an instinctive dislike of journalism. The news business, as he saw it, was not just distasteful but politically risky. Well-reported stories had a way of upsetting powerful people, and Frischknecht did not want to upset powerful people. His vision of public radio was that it should uphold the status quo while disseminating reassuring information that would promote humanity. He wanted NPR to be warm and glowing and useful.

Considering the political climate at the time, Frischknecht's approach was not unreasonable. In January 1973, Patrick Buchanan, Richard Nixon's speechwriter and point man in his public defense against the growing Watergate scandal, appeared on the *Dick Cavett Show* to denounce NPR's sleeker and more prominent sibling—PBS. It's "them versus us," Buchanan told the talk-show host in a statement that reiterated the promise of John Rose, a White House aide, "to get the left-wing commentators who are cutting us up off public television at once—indeed, yesterday." To accomplish this goal, Nixon was filling vacancies on the board of the Corporation for Public Broadcasting with Republican partisans who floated the possibility of taking control of PBS programming and canceling such pesky shows as *Washington Week in Review* and *Bill Moyers Journal.* "The long-predicted emasculation of public television has begun," reported the *Los Angeles Times.*

The threat to PBS was real, but no one at the Nixon White House ever mentioned NPR. Josh Darsa's reports from the Watergate hearings notwithstanding, the radio network just wasn't on the administration's radar. Its audience was too small, its impact too slight. At a meeting with the NPR staff shortly after his arrival, Frischknecht mentioned the threats against the net-work's TV counterpart, then with an air of relief added, "I'm so glad we're not part of that problem. We're lucky we're not as well-known as public television."

To producers and reporters who'd labored for two years to gain recogni-tion for National Public Radio, Frischknecht's comment—no matter that it held a grain of truth—was an insult. "I looked at all my colleagues," recalled Jim Russell, "and said, 'It's the first time I've thought of a news organization aspiring to invisibility.'"

Still, there was no avoiding the headline-grabbing Watergate crisis. For major pieces about it, NPR turned to a new reporter, thirty-three-year-old Robert Zelnick, a University of Virginia School of Law graduate who'd worked at the *Anchorage Daily News* and the *Christian Science Monitor*. Relying on his legal training, he dug into constitutional issues ("It is possible," he re-ported in mid-1973, that the "scandal will ultimately touch President Nixon in so direct and personal a way that his resignation or impeachment will become inevitable") while bringing zeal to the act of covering a big story. "I remember him dancing down the hall and singing a little song when one of the important Watergate events occurred," recalled Smokey Baer. To provide perspective, *All Things Considered* hired the most senior cub commentator in the business: eighty-five-year-old Emanuel Celler, the former US con-gressman from Brooklyn. During his half century in office, Celler had seen a lot of political malfeasance, but nothing, he declared, compared with this:

I wonder how many of our citizens were as frightened as I was by the ways of the Watergate revelations. But for the courage of a federal judge and the per-sistence of some of the press, a perversion of our whole political process would have become a standard. . . .

Not even a Reichstag fire can compare, or even compete. The lies, the per-juries, the destruction and attempted destruction of character, the moneys washed, the conspiracy of silence, reads like a handbook, "How to Secretly Capture a Country," or better yet, "Dictators without Labels."

After the highlights of Darsa's live reports from the Ervin commit-tee—and compared with the revelations then appearing in the *Washington*

Post—NPR was simply covering the bases. But the desire to do more never diminished, which was why on the morning of April 30, 1974, the network's only star was standing in line outside the Government Printing Office. The White House Tape transcripts—1,300 pages of secret recordings of Nixon and his men—had just been made public.

"I went down there myself without a producer or anyone," Susan Stamberg recalled. The plan was for staffers from every level of the organization to read the entire document aloud over the air during a two-day marathon, the plum roles awarded by lottery. "I was assigned to be someone I'd never heard of," Stamberg said later with a whiff of still-simmering disappointment. "Donald Segretti. It was a minimal part. I wanted a larger part."

On Saturday, May 4, Mike Waters, kicked off the broadcast by laying down the ground rules:

> You're listening to National Public Radio's reading of the edited transcripts of White House conversations relating to Watergate. We are reading the complete texts. . . . Our readers are being careful to read dispassionately, avoiding dramatic interpretation. We recognize the way sentences are spoken often affects what they mean. But since we have no way of knowing how the words in this transcript were spoken, our readers are being deliberately nondramatic.

NPR opened with a conversation between John Dean and President Nixon from April 16, 1973, during which Nixon suggested that Dean resign for the good of the administration. But the lawyer, fearing that he'd become the lone scapegoat, proposed linking his departure to that of H. R. Haldeman and John Ehrlichman. Dean handed his boss a draft of a statement designed to show that the White House was painstakingly investigating the Watergate break-in. Joe Gwathmey, NPR's assistant programming director, played Dean; a minor network functionary, Nixon. Both men sat at mics at an M Street conference table as colleagues milled around outside awaiting their turns.

> NIXON: Hi, John.
> DEAN: Mr. President.
> NIXON: Well, have you had a busy day?

DEAN: Yeah. I have been . . . I spent most of the day trying to put together a
statement . . .

Recalled Robert Malesky, a new NPR producer, "It was not great radio."
It was, however, "a public service." NPR beat the *New York Times* in making
the full transcripts available (the typesetting task overwhelmed the paper).
Also, it was on NPR's broadcasts that the repetition of the two simple words
"expletive deleted" helped alert Americans to the obscenity commonplace in
the administration. In the end, the content mattered less than the context.
"You had a sense of eavesdropping," engineer Jim Anderson said later. "It fit
the aesthetics of the sixties." Added Stamberg: "There was something about
us all reading, a collective force in the voices."

The House impeachment hearings soon followed, and NPR carried them
live—this time Todd Easton was on the Hill, while Darsa provided commentary from M Street. The end was now inevitable, and the network was
ready when Nixon resigned on August 8. NPR began its coverage with what
amounted to national town meeting. Using the network's jerry-rigged telephone distribution system, Waters called stations around the country, then,
All Things Considered carried conversations between affiliate hosts and
their listeners. Richard Malawista of WBFO interviewed callers from Buffalo. Doug Brown of WOI interviewed callers from Ames, Iowa. Something
about this patchwork resonated. "I felt as if we had reached out across the
country and held hands," recalled Wertheimer. All of it was a prelude to a
tour de force. During the eighteen months since the scandal started, Darsa
had been saving snippets of his nightly reports and organizing them into
coherent sections. He was not quite done, so when his twenty-nine-minute
summary hit the air, he read an intro to the first act, then sat by as Easton
continued work on the rest in an adjacent editing booth. "I'd rush into the
studio from the booth with the tape in four-minute segments," Easton recalled, "and the engineer wouldn't have time to rack it onto the take-up reel.
He just placed it on a tape head, and it spooled onto the floor." Darsa had
been getting ready for this since those first hearings with Sam Ervin, and he
succeeded. "Our broadcast the day Nixon resigned," Wertheimer later noted,
"stayed with me for years." Malesky agreed. "That was great radio."

•   •   •

Greatness was not sustainable. National Public Radio lacked the financial resources and, with the ascent of Lee Frischknecht, the support to do more than get by. On most days, even getting by was not a given. With everyone underpaid and overworked, anyone could falter. One night a couple of months before Nixon's resignation, Darsa and Easton were alone in the newsroom preparing for the next installment in their impeachment coverage when the telephone rang.

"Josh was in his zone editing," Easton said later, "so I picked up. An authoritative voice on the other end of the line said he was with the Los Angeles County Sherriff's Department and that there was a firefight going on in the streets of LA—and Patty Hearst had been killed."

For all the interest in Watergate, there could have been no bigger news. During the year since the Symbionese Liberation Army had kidnapped the publishing heiress, her whereabouts and fate had become a national obsession. Now her life seemed to have ended in a conflagration sparked by a shootout between the Los Angeles police and her abductors.

"What happened next," Easton recalled, is "a blur. I thought it was pretty strange that the wire machines weren't spitting out the story, but I told Josh that Patty Hearst was dead and we had to commandeer the airwaves. I didn't double-check any sources. Josh didn't either. I thought we had a scoop." At any other news network, established protocols or good judgment would have kicked in. At NPR, there were no boundaries and little inclination to second-guess an impulse, so the network's most experienced reporter picked up a microphone and was live and nationwide.

"There has been a report," Darsa said in a dispatch that aired as a special bulletin on the East Coast and as an insert into the western edition of *All Things Considered*, "that Patty Hearst has been in a firefight and is dead." He then gave a summary of the story leading up to the shootout before concluding in his orotund way: "And so the saga of Patty Hearst ends."

The next morning, as America awakened to word that Patty Hearst was very much alive—she hadn't been present at the Los Angeles firefight that had taken the lives of several of her captors—NPR news director Cleve Mathews lit into Darsa and Easton. But that's as bad as it got. "No heads rolled," remembered Smokey Baer. The network did not acknowledge the error—to its listeners or to most of the staff. "We just skated past it," added Baer.

Throughout the initial months of Frischknecht's tenure, NPR continued to fall short of achieving consistent professionalism. Darsa was particularly plagued. On December 19, the journalist stumbled into M Street wearing a rubbery "Tricky Dick" Nixon mask of the sort then much in vogue. His sole assignment—to make a ninety-second introduction to the network's live coverage of Nelson Rockefeller taking the oath of office as Gerald Ford's vice president. But it seemed beyond him. "Josh had been drinking and wouldn't take off his mask," recalled Jim Anderson, who was engineering the broadcast. Darsa's speech was muffled, making it impossible to get a recording level. Anderson panicked, opening the wrong mic. The result: Darsa got on the air two seconds late. As soon as Anderson switched to the right mic Darsa gave him reason to wish he hadn't. In a smirking reference to Rockefeller's sixteen-year pursuit of the top job, the reporter remarked: "It's what he wanted—but not quite." The line would have worked on late-night TV, but not at NPR. Again, the network made no effort to clean up after the incident.

NPR's small staff, while continuing to believe in the institution and in its ability to approach broadcasting in smart and novel ways, began to come to its senses about the overall quality of the programming. "The editorial process hadn't developed," recalled Malesky. "There was overindulgence and crap journalism." Exacerbating the problem: the audience for *All Things Considered* remained miniscule, which meant that on those occasions when the network did air something worth bragging about, few people heard. Not only did the anonymity sting, but it made it difficult for the reporters to do their work. "I recall making calls to a senator's press person and saying, 'I need to talk to the senator.'" Jim Russell said later. "They would say, 'What is NPR?' And I would end up saying, 'It's like *Sesame Street*. Can I get the interview?'"

A seminal part of the NPR zeitgeist, a paradoxical blend of elitism and defeatism, was thus born. To work at the network was to buy into the idea that you were both better and worse than your competitors. Many employees were simultaneously holier than thou and pusillanimous. Like a troubled kid, the place had a chip on its shoulder, yet it would fold at an unkind glance. This duality would imprint itself into the organizational DNA, and those who couldn't handle the contradiction usually ended up leaving.

By the end of 1974, a number of NPR managers had resigned. Al Hulsen, the former Corporation for Public Broadcasting executive instrumental in the network's founding, had been recruited by Frischknecht to run the programming department, but he quit after a year, saying he was "fed up" with the place. (Hulsen's one accomplishment: he fired Robert Conley, bringing an end to the career of the first *ATC* host.) Most painful, Cleve Mathews, the only journalist in NPR management, departed for a teaching position at Wichita State University, a move that said much about the network—a faculty post in a flyover state was more appealing than that of NPR news director.

Lee Frischknecht's solution was to implement more bureaucracy. He split NPR into two divisions. Corporate Affairs would include the president's office. Programming would include all on-air activities. Programming itself was also carved up. The National News and Information Bureau would handle current events, while cultural coverage would be organized into something called Modular Arts. Jack Mitchell would become the president's assistant and preside over all. Jim Russell was named producer of *All Things Considered*. After years of what amounted to communal living at the network, Frischknecht believed it was time for top-down organization. That he was further isolating himself from NPR's embattled staffers, not to mention fracturing relationships among reporters accustomed to working in concert on all types of stories, seemed of little concern to him. "Lee was interested in the chain of command," recalled Ernest Sanchez, at the time NPR's in-house counsel.

The new big dog in news was Robert Zelnick. Dark-haired and intense, he was a genuinely solid journalist. "He was the only one I would say was really competent," recalled Jack Mitchell. He also exuded the self-confidence of a former US Marine who'd done his duty when, by his lights, others of his generation had shirked. His opening move was to hire some like-minded hard-asses. The first one he brought through the door set the tone.

The college dropout daughter of a virtuoso violinist, Nina Totenberg had met Zelnick during a break in the trial of Watergate defendants Bob Haldeman, John Mitchell, and John Ehrlichman. At thirty-one, she was both promising and a bit of risk. In her brief career, she'd done splendid work for the short-lived but influential *New Times* magazine (a portrait of Washington's ten "dumbest" congressmen) and the *National Observer*, where she'd been a staff writer. However, she'd been fired from the *Observer* for plagiarizing from a *Washington Post* story about House leader Tip O'Neill. By her own admission, Totenberg was guilty, but she maintained there were extenuating circumstances. "The head of the *Observer* was hitting on me," she later said. "And I don't mean suggestive comments. I mean grabbing me. And I kept saying no." The harassment, she felt, prompted the editor to overreact when she transgressed. According to Zelnick, Totenberg fessed up to everything during her job interview. "I asked for a full account, and she told me of the alleged plagiarism. I thought on a scale of badness it wasn't too high and shouldn't disable her career and would, in fact, make her more careful. So I hired her."

Petite, blunt, and self-involved, Totenberg made a quick and not entirely positive first impression at M Street. One evening just after she arrived, another new reporter, David Molpus, asked her for some outtakes of a long story she'd done for *All Things Considered*. He wanted to use them on *A Closer Look*, a new weekday morning news summary. Typically, NPR reporters saved their outtakes on a reel, but Totenberg had not done so, tossing hers onto the floor. That's what she gave to her colleague. "It was a rat's nest," recalled Jim Anderson. Later, Totenberg said it was just a rookie mistake. She'd spent her entire career in print and was still learning. Others didn't buy it. "She was officious and kinda above the rest of us," said Anderson. Todd Easton concurred. "Nina was full of herself. It was: 'Gotta do it my way.'"

Richard Holwill was next through the door, and he possessed just the credentials Zelnick wanted: Louisiana native, graduate of LSU, and Marine Corps veteran with a zeal for hard news acquired at a small public radio station in Missouri. Straightforward and enlightened on race, he was the sort of southerner whom northerners often misread. Because Holwill had embraced civil rights and opposed the war in Vietnam, he struck his new associates as a progressive. But he was a conservative, and within a few days he realized that his coworkers were "real liberals and crazy." Any resulting tension was fine with Zelnick, who wanted to rattle some cages. "He was our White House correspondent, and a good one." More important: "He was loyal to me."

Zelnick and his troops set a brisk and purposeful tone that for all of

Frischknecht's aversion to journalism sent an encouraging signal to those within National Public Radio who hoped to elevate the quality of its reporting. Barbara Newman plunged into the sort of work the network previously didn't do. Accompanied by a congressional investigator named Peter Stockton, she flew to Oklahoma in December 1974 to probe the November death of Karen Silkwood. A twenty-eight-year-old worker at a Kerr-McGee plutonium factory in the little town of Crescent, Silkwood had died in a single-car accident en route to meet a *New York Times* reporter and a union official to discuss alleged safety violations at the plant. For a week Newman and Stockton, whose assistance was covered by a grant from the Fund for Investigative Journalism, interviewed local law enforcement figures and Silkwood's coworkers and friends. Kerr-McGee was a major employer in the area, and the two met resistance, but Newman was a force. "She was like a dog with a towel," recalled Stamberg. "She wouldn't let go." By the end of the month, she had something, and on December 28 she went on *All Things Considered* to report that the Crescent facility could not account for "44 to 66 pounds of plutonium." Only 4.4 pounds were needed to construct a nuclear bomb. "She went out and came back with the story," Jim Russell said later. It was NPR's first major scoop.

The next day NPR found itself in the unheard-of position of seeing its work cited atop the front pages of America's newspapers. Laudatory editorials followed. There was, to be sure, dissent from Kerr-McGee, which in a *Wall Street Journal* article challenged Newman's findings, arguing that the amount of missing plutonium was overstated. There were also doubts within the network itself—not about the reporter's accuracy but about her methods. "She tried too hard," Rich Firestone recalled. Of course, most investigative reporters try too hard, but Newman tried even harder. "Barbara ransacked Silkwood's apartment," Stamberg said later. "She was going through her drawers and found a vibrator at her bedside. I was shocked."

In *Plutonium: A Question of Life and Death*, a one-hour NPR special that summarized her findings, Newman asserted: "Karen Silkwood was right about health and safety hazards at Kerr-McGee. She was right about quality control falsifications. And the dramatic circumstances surrounding her death have served to focus attention on the apparent inadequacies of the plutonium industry and its regulators." While Newman's story didn't answer the big question—was Silkwood killed to stop her from talking—it was investigative journalism at its best. "Barbara rubbed a lot of people the wrong way," remembered Howard Kohn, a reporter for *Rolling Stone* who covered the Silkwood case (he and Newman cowrote one story for the magazine). "But she was dynamic. The lights were on."

Judy Miller, a twenty-seven-year-old reporter who began freelancing for National Public Radio in 1973 while also working as Washington bureau chief of *The Progressive*, a left-leaning monthly, was likewise emboldened by the new boss. "When Zelnick took over they were really interested in breaking news," particularly about the Middle East, she said later. Since her college days at Princeton, when she'd interviewed Egypt's Hosni Mubarak, she'd been obsessed by the region. On a trip to Jordan she'd befriended King Hussein. "He thought I was very funny and wacky," she recalled. "He used to say, 'Call me Sayidi,' which in Arabic means sir" and is pronounced *Seedy*. "I said, 'I can't.' So we settled on 'King.' I was pretty exuberant."

Others at NPR would have put it differently. Beautiful and flirtatious, Miller had a way with powerful men, particularly if they could help her on a story. "There were some important people she was cultivating as sources, if you will," recalled Richard Holwill, who sat next to her at M Street. "It was evident that her conversations, while never untoward, were more intimate than you would normally have with a source." Zelnick did not care. When the phone at Miller's desk rang and she piped up, "Hi, King," he knew that *All Things Considered* would soon be airing an interview with the Jordanian monarch that no one else could get.

National Public Radio was also broadening its cultural coverage. On a Sunday night in September 1974, the sound of a whispery breeze wafted from radios tuned to the network. "Lend me your ears," the show's host said. "We shall all profit therefrom, for the voices we shall pour therein shall be those of exciting people, creative people—*Voices in the Wind*." So began NPR's attempt to do for the arts what *All Things Considered* did for news. In the words of the program's producer, Robert Montiegel, *Voices in the Wind* would be "a report on the creative experience in a contemporary world."

The show's host, Oscar Brand, was part beatnik, part folk singer, part provocateur, and a longtime TV and media personality. Open faced and youthful at fifty-four, he betrayed his age only by wearing sweaters and skinny ties more suggestive of the Brothers Four than Bob Dylan. The Canadian-born Brand came to prominence in the late 1930s as part of New York's protest music scene, singing with Pete Seeger, Lead Belly, and Burl Ives at pro-labor rallies. After serving in the army during World War II, he premiered *Folksong Festival*, a weekly extravaganza for WNYC in New York that was entering its twenty-ninth year on the air. Although the program was in many ways a conventional celebration of America's musical roots, it courted controversy, building evenings around, say, revolutionary anthems favored by Fidel Castro. Brand's career had come close to faltering when his name appeared, along with those of 150 other entertainers and writers, in *Red Channels*, a book that listed purported Communist sympathizers in show business. Yet he did not suffer during the blacklist era. He was too buoyant a figure. Preternaturally busy, he lived by the motto: "If you flower, you get picked frequently." When NPR approached him about fronting its inaugural arts effort, he replied, "I'll try anything once."

The chance to work with Montiegel was a major part of the allure for Brand. In the world of public radio, the thirty-five-year-old producer was regarded as a wizard. Steeped in both James Joyce and pop culture, he'd come to NPR two years before from WGBH in Boston, and since his arrival he'd been the creative force behind some of the network's most ambitious live music broadcasts, among them concerts by the jazz artists Carmen McRae and Herbie Hancock and the folk autoharpist Bryan Bowers. Not only was Montiegel a virtuoso in the booth but he was also great behind a mic. "He was one of those people who could read the phone book, and you'd be riveted," recalled Robert Malesky, who would serve as his assistant. Montiegel was also gay. Neither closeted nor out, he appeared not to give a damn about sexual identity. He was defined by what he put on the air.

From the start, *Voices in the Wind* offered a hospitable venue for cultural figures famous and not. "*Voices* wasn't designed to challenge art or artists," Malesky later reflected. "We put on writers, musicians, actors, and directors we thought were good and ignored the rest." Among the show's guests during its first weeks were the bandleader Stan Kenton, the pianist George Shearing, the actor Richard Burton, the conductor Neville Marriner, the poet Nikki Giovanni, the director Paul Mazursky, the singer Merle

Haggard, and assorted weavers, interpretive dancers, and regional theater impresarios. Brand, who took the train down from New York to record each episode, conducted most of the interviews, but Fred Calland also chipped in. Between conversations, Brand cued up vintage recordings of Serge Koussevitzky, Woody Guthrie, and Aaron Copland or, if the spirit moved him, belted out such musical fare as songs from Shakespeare's *Twelfth Night.*

Voices in the Wind was celebratory and unusual, yet in a public radio kind of way it could be biting. In October 1974, when Washington's Hirshhorn Museum opened to negative reviews from the nation's leading architectural critics (Ada Louise Huxtable of the *New York Times* dismissed the building as a "maimed monument" that created a "maimed mall" and then, for good measure, added that a "major part of the collection it has been built for is maimed"), Montiegel grabbed his tape recorder. In the lobby of the scorned structure, he interviewed tourists who told him they loved the place. He put them on the air to rebut the wisdom from on high.

Also cheeky was Brand's November 1974 interview with Gore Vidal about his then-new novel, *Myron*, a follow-up to his controversial *Myra Breckinridge.* The host didn't need to encourage his famously impolitic guest to break broadcasting taboos. "We must tell our eager listeners," Vidal began, "that in *Myron* I substituted the words for the sexual parts of the anatomy and also various sexual activities for which we have usually brutal Anglo-Saxon words that cause great distress and bring many a blush to the cheek of a maiden of either sex." More precisely, Vidal explained that in the novel he had transformed the surnames of the United States Supreme Court justices who voted for tougher pornography laws in the 1973 *Miller v. California* decision into obscenities. In *Myron*, Blackmun is ass, White is cunt, and Burger is fuck. To Burger a White is a different thing than to Burger a Blackmun. NPR was making a point. "The show," noted Jay Kernis, a member of the network promotion staff who would later supplant Montiegel as the producer of *Voices in the Wind*, "said that cultural coverage was as important as news coverage."

For all of that, *All Things Considered* remained National Public Radio's one true success (Of the network's by this point 170 outlets, "probably only 100 carried *Voices in the Wind*," Kernis conceded), and the program had just made a change that promised to bring it into even sharper focus. Increasingly unable to handle the pressure of a highly formatted production, Mike Waters had been demoted. "He fell apart every other day," Todd Easton said later. "One night," added another colleague, "he was asleep in the M Street library. The room smelled like wine." As it happened, a successor had been sitting in the studio a few minutes each night with Stamberg and Waters for nearly a year.

Bob Edwards arrived at NPR in February 1974 in the position of news editor. His responsibility was to read headlines during *All Things Considered*. The twenty-seven-year-old broadcaster was a native of Louisville, Kentucky. The son of a city government employee and the grandson on both sides of Louisville and Nashville railroad workers, he grew up in a middle-class neighborhood. After putting himself through a local college, he landed a job as a deejay in New Albany, Indiana. While serving in the army, he anchored and produced radio and TV programs for the American Forces Korea Network in Seoul. Out of the service, he attended graduate school at American University, then landed a position at WTOP-AM, Washington's all-news CBS affiliate.

Edwards was lean and tall with a mop of blond hair and a dry sense of humor—so dry that some people missed it. He wrote tight copy, worshipped Edward R. Murrow, and regarded himself as a consummate pro. What distinguished him, however, was his voice. There was never another voice at NPR quite so perfect and captivating. Part of it sprang from Edwards's roots in the border south, a section of the country that has produced so many popular musicians and broadcasters because it bequeaths them with the perfect hybrid accent. In their mouths you hear the soft vowels of Dixie, the flattened syllables of the Midwest, and, if they're from a river town like Louisville, the vernacular ease that Mark Twain popularized on the printed page. It might be called the native tongue. This alone would have been enough to distinguish Edwards, but he had one other great vocal attribute: he was a baritone. In an on-air world dominated by tenors, a baritone is a trombone in a roomful of kazoos.

With the pairing of Edwards and Susan Stamberg, *All Things Considered* became urbane yet down home, cosmopolitan yet folksy. The two were not only from different parts of the country but they were also different sorts.

Neither tried to hide it, and the contrast came into relief every evening just as airtime approached.

A few minutes before five each afternoon, Stamberg—who always wore a tasteful dress when on the radio and, if she was chilly, a sweater, which she kept hanging at the ready near her microphone—disappeared into the women's room to fix her hair and put on lipstick. "The lipstick is a kind of preparation, recognition that I'm company," she later noted. As she stared into the mirror, she made a mental checklist of what she hoped to accomplish during the broadcast. This process, she added, indicated respect for the audience. "Soon I will be greeting listeners and asking for ninety minutes of their attention. I want to make sure their time is well spent."

Edwards, meanwhile, was already in the *All Things Considered* studio in jeans and a flannel shirt, leaning back in his chair and blithely removing a five-dollar bill from his wallet. "I'll buy if you'll fly," he would crack to the nearest production assistant, who would grab the money and rush to nearby Colonial Liquor for Schlitz tall boys, returning to M Street just as the *ATC* theme music—recently reworked and now called the dinks in reference to its bright tones; this would remain the program's signature tune—played. At the sound of the last dink, Edwards popped the top and took a long pull, a toast, he felt, to the regular folks who constituted his tribe. Alone among the nation's network news hosts, Edwards drank on the air, and he had it down to a science, tossing an empty can into a wastebasket at six thirty sharp. "A tall boy," he said later, "is the perfect ninety-minute beer."

Stamberg and Edwards were the lady and the tramp of public radio, and they got along on air and off. "I really learned from her," Edwards recalled. "He was tall and very easy on the eyes," Stamberg added with a hint of devilry. The hosts even shared the same vice. They each smoked nonstop during the show, Stamberg tugging on Marlboros, Edwards on Benson & Hedges 100s. ("We had a Black engineer named Jim Napper," Edwards remembered, "and he said, 'Bob, you're the only white man I know who smokes a menthol cigarette.'") The two were so hooked that engineers regularly had to remove the foam baffles that encased their mics and rinse them out. The water ran brown.

All Things Considered as fronted by Stamberg and Edwards was simultaneously tighter than it had been during the Waters era and, thanks to

Edwards, a bit more working class. Because of Stamberg's willingness to talk to anyone and everyone by phone, the show could reach almost any newsmaker. In the spring of 1975 following the fall of Saigon, she spoke to Peter Arnett, an AP correspondent who'd stayed in the city after the last American soldier left. He provided a coda for the war and the era that birthed NPR: "All the years, it seemed to me, just an incredible waste." Edwards, meanwhile, produced features on a part of the nation the network had previously ignored: his Kentucky homeland. *ATC* was sounding more and more like America.

Lee Frischknecht's restructuring of NPR, whatever the programming improvements, was doomed to fail, for it addressed only the surface of the organization, not the core, and the core was a bubbling caldron. The eruptions started in the newsroom with the March 18, 1975, appearance by the director of the Central Intelligence Agency. William Colby had come to ask network executives not to broadcast a story. The day before, Barbara Newman had learned that several of the country's best news operations, among them the *New York Times* and *Time*, were sitting on an explosive piece about the efforts of the United States to raise a Soviet submarine that had sunk in the Pacific Ocean in 1968 off Hawaii. In a partial account, the *Los Angeles Times* had reported an intriguing detail: the government was relying on Howard Hughes for help. The billionaire had dispatched a ship named the *Glomar Explorer* to the wreck. The ship was equipped with a powerful grappling device that would enable it to lift the sub from the bottom. The California newspaper's account was incomplete. Its rivals had backed off. Newman wanted to go on the air with a story that provided the facts and exposed what she saw as an effort by the government to intimidate the media.

The arrival of Colby at M Street was sufficiently momentous for Frischknecht to emerge from his corporate aerie to hear what the CIA director had to say. "At the meeting Colby explained the situation and asked for our cooperation," Jack Mitchell wrote in a March 19 staff memo. "We made no promises one way or another."

During the roughly six hours between Colby's visit and the five p.m. broadcast time of *All Things Considered*, Newman, Mitchell, Frischknecht, and Zelnick debated what to do. "We had the information that had already been published by the *Los Angeles Times*. We had some new details," Mitchell wrote. "About 4:00 we learned that the story was probably going to break that evening or in the morning papers."

From what Mitchell had heard, the news would most likely run first in Jack Anderson's widely read syndicated column, although Frischknecht, whose distaste for journalism had never been more palpable, dismissed that possibility.

"Anderson is a Mormon and won't use it," he declared.

Even if Frischknecht was wrong and Anderson went with the story, NPR could still beat everyone else. "The question then became," Mitchell added, "did we want to rush ahead with what we had that night? Did it matter that we be first? We could go with a fragmentary story or somebody else would. . . . It seemed to all of us involved in the discussion that we would not gain enough merely being first to warrant throwing together a piece in the half hour or so before airtime."

Although Newman and Zelnick disagreed with Mitchell's assessment, the decision had been made. *All Things Considered* capitulated to Colby's request and dropped the story. That night, Jack Anderson put it on the wire, and, as Mitchell conceded in his memo, "the floodgates opened." NPR had not just lost a scoop to Anderson but to the journalistic world.

Mitchell took responsibility for the decision. "This earned Jack the enmity of the newsroom," Russell recalled. Barbara Newman was incensed. The anger of Zelnick's hard chargers only increased as Washington scuttlebutt focused on how easily NPR had been played. "Richard Cohen of the *Washington Post* wrote a column about the whole thing," Mitchell recalled. "His cutting line: 'Even NPR knew about it, so it couldn't have been much of a secret.' It was an insult, but it was apt. We were not much of a news organization, and I think Frischknecht was quite happy with this."

Frischknecht was not alone at NPR in believing that Mitchell had made the right choice by spiking the piece. Whatever the story's merits, it ran counter to what many viewed as the network's mission. Bill Siemering's conception of an information and news program was broader than hard news. Jim Russell, while bemoaning the specific decision, looked askance at Zelnick's attempt to make hard news a priority. "He wanted NPR to become the finest—but I would say the finest conventional organization, you know

ABC, CBS," Russell said. News and culture had lived in relative harmony during the network's early years, but by cleaving them into separate fiefs, Frischknecht had exacerbated an inherent tension. On one side were those who wanted to beat the competition. On the other were those who thought the Johnny Deadline stuff was unwarranted and came at the expense of humanistic coverage.

No sooner had the *Glomar Explorer* crisis ended than National Public Radio experienced its first racial tensions. Equal opportunity, at least as NPR's founders defined it, was baked into the organization's identity. The initial staff had, of course, included two Black reporters—Gwen Hudley and Rich Adams. "NPR made a bigger effort to stop discrimination than any other news organization," Jack Mitchell said later. But by the mid-1970s, some felt that the network had wavered in its commitment. In hopes of addressing the perceived problem, NPR invited Pluria Mitchell, director of the National Association of Black Journalists, to address the staff. According to Mitchell, the session was a disaster. "They sat on one side of the table, we sat on the other, and they just yelled at us."

Among NPR's Black journalists at the time was Bill Green. Cleve Mathews had hired him out of historically Black Howard University. Green mostly did feature stories (among them a piece on the history of Kwanzaa), but his new boss, Bob Zelnick, wanted to push him to do "harder" fare. "When I took over as leader of the news division," Zelnick later said, "we had an incident with Bill Green." According to Zelnick, Green altered the facts of a story. He "covered a press conference by the Congressional Black Caucus during which the group protested a grant for Vietnamese immigrants." The group said the grant "should have gone to poor blacks," Zelnick recalled, adding, "Bill's lead sentence was: 'The Congressional Black Caucus held a press conference to express their sympathy for Vietnamese refugees.'" Green wrote the opposite of what occurred, and he admitted he had done so "to protect the congressmen's reputation."

Zelnick was outraged. He found Green's actions journalistically reprehensible. "Zelnick wanted to fire Green," Mitchell said later, "but I said, 'We're not going to be in a situation without a male, black reporter. Find another one and we can talk.'"

Mitchell's refusal to dismiss Green led to an extended period during which

the reporter and Zelnick were at loggerheads. As their relationship deteriorated, the news director said, it poisoned his dealings with another young
Black NPR reporter—Marti Griffin, a recent graduate of Ohio's Miami University. "She needed a lot of coaching," Zelnick recalled. "I worked with her
until I had the confidence to send her to cover the White House for a week
when the beat reporter was off. Bill Green came up to her and said, 'Don't do
it. He's setting you up to fail.'"

At a cocktail party a few weeks later, Zelnick met Charlie Cobb, a thirty-
two-year-old ex–field secretary for the Student Nonviolent Coordinating
Committee. He was at the time working as a reporter for WHUR, the public
radio station at Howard. When Cobb agreed to accept a position at NPR
covering foreign affairs with a focus on Africa, Mitchell told Zelnick, "You
can now let Green go." At which point Green and Griffin filed a racial discrimination lawsuit against the network. Green claimed he'd been unjustly
terminated, Griffin that she'd been denied a promotion. The case, Jim Russell said later, "was without merit. Both were inept reporters and did inept
work." Be that as it may, there was support for the two within NPR, and it
sprang from the view that while Zelnick may have been right on the professional merits, he and those who thought like him were wrong about the big
picture. NPR's reporting, many at the network believed, should focus less on
news and more on community building. As Mitchell later wrote, those holding this view thought programming should highlight "identity politics that
championed women, gays, and racial . . . minorities." NPR was caught up not
just in a lawsuit but in a battle facing other newsrooms in the 1970s.

David Cashdan, the lawyer who represented Green, Griffin, and ultimately Ernie Moye, a Black job applicant who charged that NPR had denied
him employment because of his race, believed he had a strong case, both on
its merits and because he'd hit the network in a vulnerable place. "NPR was
embarrassed," Cashdan recalled. "They didn't like the suggestion that public broadcasting, which most people would have suspected of being liberal,
would have to defend itself on race."

NPR fought back. In-house counsel Ernest Sanchez brought in the firm
Miller, Cassidy, Larroca & Lewin (Cassidy was Richard Nixon's personal lawyer), which assigned the case to a bright new associate, Jamie Gorelick, who
would go on to become the United States deputy attorney general. Under

her guidance, Zelnick said in a deposition that race had no bearing on his decision to terminate Green or frustrate Griffin's ascent. "Zelnick claimed any decisions he made were about merit, not race," Cashdan said later. As for Moye, NPR maintained that the network was so understaffed (the personnel department consisted of only two people) that it had lost his application. "Jim Russell put the material on a credenza behind his desk," Sanchez said later. "It wasn't bad intention. It was inefficiency. His office was like the Bermuda Triangle."

During pretrial proceedings, Cashdan received a call from NPR's counsel. "The lawyers told me things about Marti that were a major concern about whether it made sense for her to continue with the litigation. She had some issues. There was an incident." Jack Mitchell was more specific. "Marti tried to commit suicide."

The upshot, Cashdan later said, was to "resolve the case. It was in the interest of both parties." The out-of-court agreement, supervised by Judge Cornelius Waddy of the DC division of the United States District Court, required NPR, in Mitchell's words, to make a small "financial settlement." In those days, Cashdan subsequently explained, "civil rights lawyers were more focused on remedy than on money." In this instance, the remedy was a consent decree. "NPR agreed that it would do better," recalled Sanchez. Under the agreement, the exact nature of doing better was left vague, meaning that until the network satisfied some ill-defined requirements, it would operate under a cloud, one that would create a suspicion among outsiders that NPR had a problem hiring Black reporters and leave insiders feeling that their grievances had not been addressed.

Had NPR been a professionally solid organization, it would have quickly implemented concrete solutions, but, recalled Sanchez, "it was a struggle to follow through." There were too many other problems. As it happened, NPR was facing increasingly vocal salary demands from employees of all colors. In terms of compensation, the place lagged far behind its commercial competitors. Bob Edwards earned $17,000 a year, Nina Totenberg $15,000. Smokey Baer, who many nights single-handedly got *All Things Considered* on the air, $6,900. Don Quayle was so charming, he'd been able to make everyone forget how inequitable it all was. But Frischknecht possessed few interpersonal skills, and, having shunned regular contact with reporters, no understanding of their concerns. When Linda Wertheimer complained to him that she and other news staffers earned the same as his secretary, he replied, "At NPR, everyone is a star."

Ultimately, the expected outcome occurred: the NPR programming staff voted to unionize and wrote Frischknecht seeking formal recognition. Not only did the NPR president not grant the request but he hired a union-busting law firm to advise him how to fight the effort. He was "adamant," recalled Jack Mitchell. The response from network staffers—chiefly Linda Wertheimer, Nina Totenberg, Richard Holwill, and Bob Edwards—was defiant. Totenberg took the lead by placing a copy of the book *Organizing and the Law* atop her desk. She also started bringing in leaders of various labor unions to meet with employees at the M Street conference room, a glassed-in fishbowl visible to NPR executives. As 1975 progressed, emissaries from the Newspaper Guild, the American Federation of Television and Radio Artists (AFTRA), and the United Auto Workers marched in and out. Then Totenberg increased the pressure. "I invited the Teamsters, and they looked like Teamsters," she recalled. "They were big: square heads, square bodies. They had no idea why I invited them to come, but they were willing to give it a try. The brass kept walking by—looking, watching."

NPR's bosses were put off by the theatrics. "Nina was loud," said Gwathmey. "She was a pain in the neck, and her assessments were unfair. There were unrealistic expectations. This was a tiny organization. We couldn't afford what they wanted." As a result, Frischknecht hardened his position. He was never going to recognize a union vote.

By the end of the Gerald Ford years, NPR was in duress. "People were asking, 'Who is in charge of the place?'" Russell said later. "Was it the reporters? That's what they believed, what they wanted. It was a journalistic enterprise. Nothing else mattered." To them, Zelnick was the authority. In the cultural department, only Montiegel's voice counted. "Then there was the rest of the company," Russell added, by that meaning Frischknecht. "They had the illusion they were running things." For NPR executives, just getting through the day was a triumph. "I was trying to keep the lid on sufficiently to meet programming obligations," Gwathmey maintained. "That was my main focus."

Everywhere Lee Frischknecht turned, he spotted trouble. The Corporation for Public Broadcasting typically allotted 17 percent of its annual budget to radio and the remaining 83 percent to television. But in 1975, PBS had demanded a bigger share and a reduction in NPR's take. The parties reached a compromise, but it favored TV: although PBS would still receive 83 percent, NPR was guaranteed only 10 percent—the remaining 7 percent was up for grabs. A group of influential NPR station managers—chiefly Bill Kling of Minnesota Public Radio and Ronald Bornstein of WHA in Madison, Wisconsin—blamed Frischknecht for this reversal. They also blamed him for the union movement and for the strife between the network's news and cultural divisions. And they had begun to chafe at M Street's role as the network's central production house. (The network's sole bureaus were in San Francisco, manned by Leo Lee, the ex–city editor of the *San Francisco Examiner*; and New York, where Bill Toohey, a veteran local reporter, relied on a police scanner to cover spot news). Feeling shut out, station managers wanted changes that would enable local outlets to play a bigger role. Because of a quirk in the structure of the public radio system, they believed there was an opening to do something—and in the process get rid of Frischknecht.

Shortly after NPR began broadcasting, its executives had decided they did not want to lobby Congress. There were too many opportunities for conflicts of interest. The Association of Public Radio Stations was founded to handle the task. The station managers who opposed Frischknecht controlled the Association of Public Radio Stations—a three-man operation that worked out of a tiny DC office—and they launched what NPR's leaders regarded as a conspiracy to oust its president and take control of the network. The "minnow," as Mitchell would later put it, hoped "to swallow the whale." Hammered from within and threatened from without, Frischknecht was at a loss. He was looking for someone to tell him what to do.

Deborah Campbell had been at National Public Radio from the start (Don Quayle had brought her to Washington from WGBH to be his secretary) and was beloved by almost everyone. Nurturing and warm, she was a free soul, intrigued by alternative ways of life and the occult. She'd read the horoscopes of most employees. "NPR had been born under a lucky star," she said, "but it was subject to being misunderstood." (As for Lee Frischknecht, he possessed a "water sign," meaning he doused creativity). Campbell had enrolled at a satellite branch of Antioch College in Baltimore for advanced studies in psychology and sociology. There, she'd taken classes from a professor who directed the school's Center for Social Research and Action. She'd never met anyone like him. He was brilliant, mesmerizing. In late 1975, she confided in him about the problems at NPR. Communications troubles, she called them. Would he meet with the network president? He said yes, and Campbell set it up. Several weeks later, the professor and his graduate assistant had an office at M Street. Officially, they'd been hired as consultants to do an "institutional assessment." In truth they were there to save Lee Frischknecht's job—and start a revolution.

Al Engelman was every inch Herr Doctor—"big body, big personality," recalled Jack Mitchell. Even sitting, as he often did that winter at the head of the NPR conference table surrounded by reporters and producers, he commanded attention. He was six feet tall, and while he'd just turned forty, he didn't look it. He had the barrel chest and thick mustache of a Cossack, and sometimes away from the office staffers spotted him walking his Russian wolfhound. But Al Engelman was no rough beast. He'd graduated from Brandeis and studied with the great Swiss psychologist Jean Piaget, who'd charted the four stages of cognitive development. Engelman dressed like an academic—corduroy jackets with elbow patches, repp ties. A contradictory mix of aggression and erudition, he was hard to figure out until, during lectures, he took off his jacket and rolled up his sleeves. Then you saw the tattoo: Russian displaced-persons camp. As a boy in the 1940s, Engelman had picked cotton in Uzbekistan. The work was brutal, and it made him strong, but there were untold emotional scars, and his degrees and many faculty positions—Boston University, avant-garde Franconia College—had not healed them. He was terrified of confinement and the police state, and he reflexively sided with the downtrodden.

Engelman and Steve Symonds (the graduate assistant) didn't need long to diagnose what they believed was wrong with NPR. The staffers had fallen into ruts. Their daily routines and work relationships needed disrupting. "They were concerned with doing the programs," Engelman recalled. "I was concerned with something else." He argued that the staff's obsession with the shows was its principal problem. "There were enclaves, different interest groups, and people struggling for resources all the time. People were running their own little shops, separate from everybody else. There was the news service. There were the production people. There were people writing stories. The engineering people were concerned with the quality."

To each small group that met with him, Engelman asked: How does your job "relate to the long-range plan? How does it relate to the founding NPR goals?"

With that, Engelman would intone his mantra. "When goals don't define roles, roles will define goals."

The analyst wanted NPR staffers to recommit themselves to the network's mission—the goal. By returning to the faith as laid down by Siemering, workers would stop bickering, elevate their horizons, and, not incidentally, save Frischknecht's job by both undermining the narrow-minded zeal of journalists like Zelnick and stealing a march on the public radio outsiders who wanted change. They would also remake NPR to suit Engelman. It would become an ecumenical refuge where ethnic programming was on equal footing with news, contributions from stations far from Washington supplanted DC-centric shows, and *All Things Considered* periodically stuck it to the man.

Jim Russell agreed that he and his colleagues were overwhelmed by daily responsibilities and had lost sight of the aspirations that brought them to NPR. At the same time, he felt the organization was stretched too thin to undergo such a radical process. "Engelman was trying to take apart a bicycle while we were riding it," he said later. "He had no idea what we actually did for a living and didn't care." Jack Mitchell was less charitable. "Engelman's philosophy was that we were going to have to kill a few people to create a workers' paradise."

The meetings, which Symonds taped and transcribed, devolved into frenzies of name-calling, sobbing, and near fisticuffs. "They'd go on for hours," recalled Jeff Rosenberg. "People would yell and point fingers. The loudest were Bob Zelnick, Jim Russell, and Jack Mitchell. It was personal vituperation." Zelnick, Russell, and Mitchell had reason to raise their voices: they were fighting for competing visions of NPR's future. As for the others, they just seemed unnerved by the process, which was chaotic and threatening. "It was about making trouble," Rosenberg added. "Stand up and indict someone. It wasn't self-criticism. It was: Me! Me! Me! Me! Nothing got solved."

The Antioch version of Werner Erhard's EST had come to M Street. All winter, NPR held encounter sessions. "There was an incredible amount of psychobabble," recalled Jim Anderson. When Engelman wanted to chide a reporter for obsessing over a breaking story without regard to the higher calling, he'd say "You've *perimeterized* your workplace." When he wanted to dissuade a producer from sweating over a deadline as opposed to considering the underlying rationale for journalism, he'd say, "You've been *role-ified*."

Engelman denied that he introduced the topic of sex into the NPR analysis, but those who attended the gatherings say he did. "I was in a meeting in which Engelman said institutional analysis includes who's sleeping with whom," Mitchell recalled. Such inquiries were certainly in character. At Franconia, Engelman had once told a student, "Masturbation is good because it allows you to assert yourself." (After the student alerted her parents to this remark, she transferred to another college.) At M Street, rumors and innuendo ran rampant. "Engelman and Symonds were sleeping with people on the staff," Rosenberg later swore (both men dismissed the claim). The speculation also went the other way, as the consultants from Antioch pondered the sexual predilections of their interviewees. Nina Totenberg, Symonds said, "was a cold fish," while Barbara Newman was "a sex-starved JAP on the prowl." Fred Calland, the cultural guru, "was Captain Kangaroo—asexual."

The NPR staff could take only so much of this. "There was a fury that someone would have unleashed this big, clumsy force," Linda Wertheimer said later. "In an organization that always had all it could do just to get its work done, it seemed like the most monumental waste."

Engelman and Symonds kept pushing. They were doing what Frischknecht had hired them to do, and they believed that the process, while messy, was productive. "My job was to do an assessment of National Public Radio," Engelman recalled. "What was going on? Why was there so much conflict internally?" It was, he said, "an intervention." Symonds took it a step further, saying that they were there to do more than take notes. "There was a lot of pent-up hostility in the company. It had gotten to the point where there were armed camps. The idea was to assist Frischknecht in developing methods for changing the situation—not just assessing it. It involved mixing it up a little bit to find out what was really going on. What was underneath their statements of protestation, their feelings of alienation?" The two weren't backing down. They believed that the nastier the meetings became, the closer they were getting to the truth. "I don't recall Engelman saying, 'Enough of that,'" recalled Rosenberg. The two were cocky. "We saw ourselves," said Symonds, "as Butch Cassidy and the Sundance Kid."

The fissures Lee Frischknecht had hoped to close and heal instead cracked wide open. The NPR reporting staff went after the interlopers from Antioch and anyone at the network who supported them. A few weeks into the assessment, Engelman was in Frischknecht's office when the phone rang. An administrator at the University of Massachusetts, Engelman's ex-employer, was calling to say that a team of reporters was trying to dig into his past.

"Where are they from?" Engelman asked.

"NPR," replied the administrator.

"How do you know?" asked Engelman.

"They're on the other line right now."

Engelman jumped up and ran down to the NPR newsroom, where he discovered Nina Totenberg, Susan Stamberg, Linda Wertheimer, and Bob Zelnick hunched over a telephone.

"This is inappropriate," he roared. "It's a violation of my rights."

"We're reporters," the four replied almost in unison.

"I'm not the story," he countered.

To them, he was the story, for the chaos he and Symonds had introduced into NPR made it harder for them to cover the news—any news. They intended to find out who he was. "People not familiar with news organizations," recalled Wertheimer, "don't understand one of the key things about news organizations—reporters report. It's impossible to keep things secret in a news organization."

By early spring, Engelman and Symonds had finished a draft of their report, and on April 14, Frischknecht summoned Mitchell and Stamberg to give them a heads-up regarding its contents. It was worse than they expected, striking a blow at NPR's journalistic identity while instituting a regimen designed to uplift various racial and ethnic groups. First, Engelman and Symonds recommended that the network disband its news bureau and replace it with "The Department of Program Content Resources." They also advocated the creation of a new enterprise called "Special Audiences," which would produce stories tailored to the interests of specific races, genders, and religious groups. The consultants believed that multicultural coverage was in keeping with the Siemering idea, but they pushed far beyond that. The inventor of *All Things Considered* believed in hiring reporters who looked and sounded like America—not in shaping stories to fit preconceived notions about inclusiveness. Finally, in a move designed to give NPR increased radical standing, Engelman and Symonds suggested that Frischknecht dismiss Zelnick and replace him with the in-house firebrand Barbara Newman.

Mitchell and Stamberg were stunned. The next morning, they huddled with Zelnick. The three agreed that the proposal seemed to indicate, in Mitchell's words, "a lack of familiarity" with working realities and made "little sense." Hoping that they could convince Frischknecht to reconsider, they decided not to inform fellow staffers and instead write the NPR president a private note. With Mitchell typing, they began diplomatically. "Our first thought is to acknowledge and support your general objectives. Susan and Jack—and yes, Bob, too—are very aware of the imbalance that is now reflected in our program." They then unloaded on their boss, asserting that the destruction of the news bureau would damage *All Things Considered* and that there was no need for a Special Audiences department because NPR already did "an outstanding job" covering the interests of minorities. They also decried the idea of putting Newman in charge. "No one," they wrote, "who has ever worked with her would consider her for a management position." Their verdict: "We cannot say too strongly that your proposed solution is nothing short of suicidal." In a handwritten postscript, Stamberg added, "Because of the predictable withdrawal of key personnel from the *All Things Considered* staff if these changes are made, the staff will fall like a house of cards. The staff will be unable to function under the proposed changes. There will be no point in staying around to pick up the pieces that have been so assiduously put into place at such intellectual and psychological cost over these years. SS"

Stamberg had toiled for half a decade to professionalize NPR. *All Things Considered* was unconventional, but it aspired to journalistic excellence. Under Zelnick the show's reporting had improved and its focus had sharpened, and Stamberg enjoyed fronting the increasingly newsworthy product. The more she thought about what was about to happen, the angrier she became. So angry that she said to hell with keeping the changes proposed by Engelman and Symonds under wraps. She began telling coworkers what was in store. By dark everyone at M Street knew.

That evening, the staff gathered in Jim Russell's office to draft a mass resignation letter. The signatories included Stamberg, Edwards, Wertheimer, Totenberg, David Molpus, Ira Flatow, Richard Holwill, and Russell. Although Mitchell did not sign, he gave his blessing—a violation of his status as member of NPR management. About midway through the meeting, Jay Kernis, curious to see what was going on, stuck his head in. As a nonreporter, he was seen as a member of the enemy camp, and almost at once the group ordered him out. When Kernis didn't move fast enough, Holwill, as one witness described it, "began to physically eject him, pulling him by the neck." Holwill later said he was just playing around with one of the "artsy-fartsy" types, but that's not how Kernis saw it, and this was not Holwill's only run-in that night. After the session ended, he shoved Newman, the main beneficiary of the Antioch consultants' proposal. Holwill said it was an accident, but Newman felt otherwise.

The next morning, to avert an insurrection, Frischknecht pounded out an all-staff memo accusing unnamed employees of "breaking" his confidence and organizing an "ill-informed" meeting. "I caution you not to take action until you have all the facts," he urged. The NPR president was trying to appear in control, but in truth he was in shock. He spent most of the day doodling on a yellow legal pad, punctuating his thoughts with arrows and exclamation points. "We must stop the brutalizing," he wrote. "People cannot and should not stand it. I cannot stand much more." Further down, he wrote bluntly: "This shit must stop." Then, remembering what was at stake—NPR's ability to broadcast—he prayed.

On Monday, April 20, National Public Radio released the final, forty-five-page version of the reorganization plan. Although it appeared over Frischknecht's signature, it had been written by Engelman. Just as the NPR president had told Mitchell and Stamberg, he was shutting the news bureau, inaugurating the Special Audiences department, and would begin seeking programming from member stations. In a summary paragraph, the document stated:

News will include the vast and vitally important area of human behavior and existence. And in this category will be the way various minorities view issues, the way they view existence, the kind of struggles they must overcome to accomplish that one great overriding human goal, namely, survival.

The new master plan was rife with reeducation projects ("Socializing the basic philosophy into managers and supervisors" would be a priority, as would "putting a process into place to ensure compliance"). It also relegated personal ambition to the sidelines ("Widespread acceptance of our goals will be the glue. Goals must preempt individual pettiness"). There were also bromides from therapists (Erich Fromm) and the expected elevation of Barbara Newman.

Frischknecht had emasculated Zelnick and NPR's reporters. In a written response, the deposed news director called the plan "a regurgitation of raw data collected by the consultant" and a "simplistic assault on the bureau. Nothing in the methodology reflects either a basic competence on the consultant's part to judge program content or a rational technique for accurately sampling and presenting the views of others." As for the language, he declared:

> The memorandum takes refuge in what seems to be an alien jargon and proceeds from there to recommend structural changes with no apparent understanding of how these will solve problems that have not been adequately defined. None of the very practical problems confronting NPR programming can be solved by a hollow repetition of goals and missions or a mea culpa recitation of ideological dogma to the apparatchiks [Engelman and Symonds]. To those of us whose commitment to this organization's goals and missions is reflected in the time, effort, and pride we assign to our work, Engelman's failures are both offensive and inexcusable.

National Public Radio was on the verge of war between management and staff. This was a hell of a story—just not for NPR. As every journalist knows, the best place to plant a news item is not on the front pages but in a gossip column, which Totenberg did, forwarding a Xerox of Zelnick's thoughts to a writer from The Ear at the *Washington Star*.

"Mouthing Off," declared the headline atop the item in the next day's *Star* that hinted at the shift from hard news to soft at NPR, scuffles in the M Street halls, demotions, and a renewed interest in the stalled union movement. "Ear just hates it when people are mad," the piece archly concluded. Brief and tantalizing, the story was bait for more coverage, and the *Washington Post* and the *Christian Science Monitor* followed with longer articles, but it was the *New York Times* that hit hardest. Beneath the headline "National Public Radio Network Downplays News," the paper's Edward Cowan reported that Frischknecht's decision to remove Zelnick and disband his department had "led to an ebbing of morale in the public radio news staff." In his defense, the network president was quoted saying he was giving member stations what they wanted: "More jazz and more programs for women, minorities, and the elderly in the hope that such a shift will make public radio a genuine alternative." Maybe so, but the piece raised the notion that the specter of labor activity also had something to do with it. The news operation was the source of the union stirrings, and by targeting it, NPR's boss was making a preemptive strike.

Hoping to prevent mass defections, Frischknecht held a daylong retreat for the NPR staff at George Washington University's Marvin Center, with the network springing for breakfast, lunch, and beer and wine at cocktail hour. Although the NPR president was heartened by the kind words of a few employees (many in the cultural department supported his plan), the day belonged to Zelnick, who announced he'd written a five-thousand-word manifesto "to alert those concerned to the many aspects of the . . . reorganization I regard as damaging if not disastrous to NPR."

The hostilities at National Public Radio had reached an even more vitriolic level. In a crack designed to highlight Frischknecht's well-known fear of making journalistic waves, Zelnick wrote, "Perhaps the survival of NPR depends on mediocrity and a 'low profile.' Perhaps it is getting too good and too accepted by the public. Perhaps the public radio system really does not want to be much more than it has been." Then he took another shot at Engelman and Symonds, asserting that their tape-recorded staff sessions were "a poor substitute for adequate analytical methodology." Revealing his contempt for the NPR president, he demanded that the network pay to photocopy and distribute his diatribe.

Frischknecht had heard enough from Zelnick. "Distribution of it to the NPR staff and board of directors and CPB board of directors," he replied, "would constitute an act of such grave and prejudicial nature that the public credibility of NPR would be endangered. Your request is denied." Still, the NPR president seemed paralyzed by the chaos. In meetings with other network executives, he agonized over whether to fire Zelnick or offer him a reporting job contingent on his "discontinuing his public opposition." He also was at a loss over what to do about Totenberg. Should he reprimand her for leaking Zelnick's broadside to the *Washington Star*, or would he risk charges of union-busting? Richard Holwill likewise presented a problem, as did Jack Mitchell.

The negative reaction to NPR's planned change of direction continued to mount. Harrison Salisbury, a Pulitzer Prize–winning former *New York Times* reporter and the new press critic for the CBS *Morning News*, eviscerated the network, informing his viewers in a late-May broadcast:

> For reasons that have not been made very clear, the news and information section of National Public Radio is being turned into a department of "Program Content Resources"—whatever that means. One thing this policy has been designed to do, however, is reduce coverage of news events by National Public Radio and increase its attention to such areas as jazz, the Women's Liberation Movement, problems of minorities and the elderly. No doubt all these are worthy of attention, but it seems a shame that public radio should curtail an excellent existing news service in order to introduce experiments.

NPR was also hit by criticism from the sort of academics who might have been expected to endorse Engelman's attempt to practice social engineering via the radio. In an exasperated note to Frischknecht, a professor at the historically Black Spelman College wrote, "I was very distressed to learn recently that there is a possibility of change of emphasis in the program *All Things Considered*. I would consider this a great mistake indeed, as we here in Atlanta do not have available on either television or other radio stations (or the local newspapers for that matter) anything as informative and professional."

By mid-May, Frischknecht was spending most of his time conducting damage control. In letters to concerned NPR listeners, he defended the network's planned shift and attacked the institution he believed had misinterpreted his intentions—the press. He was obsessed with refuting the *New York Times'* account, informing a professor at Bowdoin College that the paper's article "represented a distortion of the facts and the intentions of myself, the NPR Board and our membership."

As the back-and-forth played out, Susan Stamberg, the personification of NPR, felt her anger turn into something darker. "She was devastated," remembered Jack Mitchell. To the *All Things Considered* host, the sessions with Engelman and Symonds had been intellectually dishonest, a form of corporate bait and switch. "We thought they were trying to brainwash us in some way to back off of the real grievances we had at the time like salary and hours," she said later. The stress was unending. "We'd go to these meetings. Zelnick would rev us up against management. I was trying to be the reasonable one—to calm the waters." Ultimately, she came apart. "I had panic attacks. I had heart flutters. I remember getting so agitated." To recover her composure, Stamberg dove to the bottom of a valium bottle. "Terrible. I was just popping these pills and smoking Marlboros in an effort to be calm. It was so upsetting." As Mitchell later put it, "She had a psychological breakdown."

With Stamberg reeling and NPR experiencing its first bout of bad publicity, Frischknecht implemented the changes proposed by Engelman and Symonds—the news bureau was kaput, the Special Audiences project was up and running. The network president meted out penalties to some—Holwill was suspended for three days without pay—but not all. Totenberg was in the clear; so, too, Mitchell. Meantime, NPR offered Zelnick a reporting position at a fraction of his regular pay. He quit, but not before tossing off another indignant memo: "I am neither in the habit of eating my own flesh or making charitable contributions to my employer." The only recommendation Frischknecht didn't follow involved Newman. The opposition to her was just too strong. In her place, he appointed Jim Russell to the position of content director, elevating a champion of the old NPR.

The whole experiment had been a catastrophe. "Our job," recalled Symonds, "was to get people to stop organizing around power poles and organize around Lee. But as it turned out, Lee didn't have it. He couldn't step up. He couldn't articulate a strategy. It was like asking a cat to be a dog. It wasn't gonna happen." Because of Frischknecht's weakness, the powers behind the Association of Public Radio Stations—Kling and Bornstein—aided by Tom Warnock, the director of radio at the Corporation for Public Broadcasting, succeeded in merging their small organization with NPR. Although the new outfit was still called National Public Radio, there were different ambitions. The first move: Frischknecht was out. Presley Holmes, a network VP, took charge on an interim basis.

Jack Mitchell, fed up with everything, also left, taking a position at WHA in Madison. Josh Darsa joined Jim Russell in management, and they hired several reporters who, unlike the hard-news types favored by Zelnick, were interested in telling narrative-driven stories illustrated by sound.

The influx began with Robert Krulwich. A twenty-nine-year-old Columbia Law School graduate, he started in radio at Pacifica and had more recently been working as the Washington bureau chief of *Rolling Stone*. Krulwich had one responsibility there: getting the magazine's star reporter, Hunter S. Thompson, to meet his deadlines. "My job was to get Hunter to file something so we could justify putting him on our cover, which meant we'd get a four-color ad for the back," Krulwich said later. "Hunter was living in Key West with a soon-to-be-famous friend [Jimmy Buffett] with a parrot. Because of the success of *Fear and Loathing on the Campaign Trail '72*, he was getting invitations to go to Colgate and Oberlin and places like that and get onstage in his half-drunken state and everybody would love that. He had no reason to write anything for us."

At Pacifica, Krulwich had shared office space with *The Progressive*, where he'd become friends with Judy Miller. When he told her of his trouble wresting copy from Thompson, she replied, "Well, Zelnick's just been offed. I'm going to see if I can help," which she did, putting in a word for him at NPR. Krulwich's first task at the network was to edit feature stories for *All Things Considered*. "Russell made up some title—humanities editor or something. I got to do the lighter stuff."

Russell and Darsa also brought on an old friend of Krulwich's, although at first not all shared their enthusiasm. "I don't think so. That nasal voice is not pleasant to hear," said Susan Stamberg upon listening to a sample tape.

Robert Siegel nonetheless got the job. A self-described "New York depressive" and a Columbia graduate, the twenty-nine-year-old Siegel had become intrigued by broadcasting while working at the college station during student protests against the Vietnam War in 1968. "I was at the microphone when we covered the Columbia strikes and had felt, wow, this thing, this alternative to real work, is actually real work and it's actually fairly useful." He started his career at WRVR in New York, a jazz station owned by the Riverside Church. At NPR, he began as the news reader on *All Things Considered*, but soon Russell made him Krulwich's counterpart. He edited the hard news. The two worked at facing desks in an M Street hallway.

Just before leaving *Rolling Stone*, Krulwich had teamed up with the reporter Timothy Crouse to get to the bottom of a rumor. A barber in Seattle, Washington, claimed to be in possession of the mummified body of John Wilkes Booth. According to a long-standing urban myth, the assassin of Abraham Lincoln had escaped when Union troops wrongly identified a Confederate officer during their manhunt and shot him. In the 1930s, carnivals displayed what was said to be Booth's actual corpse. "Tim found this plausible," recalled Krulwich, "so we had to find someone who could lead us in our ability to do a forensic analysis of the skeleton." He called the Abraham Lincoln Book Shop, run by Ralph Newman in Chicago. Krulwich told Newman that this was his last assignment for *Rolling Stone*. "I'm going to this thing called National Public Radio." To which Newman replied: "I have a stepson who's really good at radio. I'm going to get you a cassette of his work."

The stepson was twenty-four-year-old Scott Simon, who was working in public TV in Chicago. "I took the cassette," Krulwich recalled, "and put it in the machine, and it was incredible right off the bat. It was as good as anything I'd ever heard. So I get it to Jim Russell and say, 'We should hire this guy like yesterday.'"

In a matter of weeks, three of the most promising reporters in public radio history had arrived at NPR, and to some extent they stanched the bleeding. Simon, true to expectations, contributed first-rate pieces, particularly his coverage of the December 1976 death of Chicago mayor Richard Daley and, several weeks later, his coverage of a dramatic, fatal crash on the city's El system. His stories, even short ones, were classically constructed. Siegel also attracted good notices, although not because of his style. Short, bearded, balding, and overweight ("He looked like he'd swallowed a raccoon," recalled a coworker), he put news into an academic frame, and he had the knowledge to do so. "He's the college professor," Stamberg said later.

Krulwich summed up his view of broadcasting with one simple phrase: "Let's play on the radio." Early on, however, he didn't know when to stop playing. During the 1976 presidential campaign, NPR took Krulwich off the desk and put him on the trail. On October 11, he accompanied a group of Jimmy Carter supporters to the State Fair of Texas in Austin. Surrounded by people in cowboy boots and ten-gallon hats, he couldn't help himself. "I inadvertently adopted a Texas accent in the middle of my coverage. As I was interviewing I became incredibly more Texan." Back at M Street, Darsa admonished him. "You can't do that. You can't become a Texan when you go to Texas."

During the first days of the Carter administration, Zbigniew Brzezinski, the new national security adviser, dropped by M Street to talk with NPR about his plans. No one was available to interview him. Krulwich, over his protestations that he didn't follow foreign affairs, was drafted. He walked into the studio and began.

"Where are you from?

"Lutsk," Brzezinski said, referring to his hometown in Poland.

"Lutcchskk," Krulwich repeated, stretching the word into a consonant-crammed, multisyllabic car wreck. That's all it took. Krulwich was Polish.

"So, youch halfs all dese peeples."

If Brzezinski was upset, he didn't show it. "It didn't register on him," Krulwich recalled. "Or maybe he was just a diplomat." As the interview continued, the reporter drifted deeper into a cacophony of eastern European gibberish.

After a minute or so, Krulwich noticed that "people wearing ties" were gathering behind the glass wall of the studio. A woman in the group removed a lipstick tube from her purse and on a napkin wrote, "Stop it."

Only then did Krulwich realize the gravity of his actions. "This is not in any way good," he remembered thinking. "I'm mimicking the president's top adviser."

Krulwich walked away from the interview in a daze. "You seem to be

insane," someone snapped. NPR suspended him for two weeks ("Today," he
said later, "I would be fired"). Despite the lapse, however, there was a consensus within the network that it was all unintentional. "His gift for voices was
unconscious," recalled Totenberg, "even unbidden." Soon enough, Krulwich
and Stamberg began presenting business briefs on *All Things Considered* in
the style of Vaudeville sketches. "Susan and I would put on imaginary straw
hats," he recalled. "I'd get my cane, and we both did accents." Subsequently,
Krulwich would undertake major stories as if they were operas, with libret-
tos and choruses.

NPR had regained something of its old, weird self. The Engelman-
Symonds intervention had done damage, but most of their proposals were
scrapped. (Not that Engelman was forgotten: Wags occasionally took to the
in-house PA system to intone: "Paging Al Engelman." The announcement
could still prompt worried looks.) There was a resurgent energy, so much
so that when ABC advertised Barbara Walters's appointment as cohost of
its evening television news with a campaign proclaiming her America's first
woman anchor, NPR took out a full-page ad in the October 4, 1976 *New York
Times*:

We love you too Barbara

BUT

You're not the first woman to co-host a national news program

Susan Stamberg has been co-anchoring a national news show since 1972 . . .

And Susan does it without pictures.

Still, in all, National Public Radio had done no more than right the ship.
Thanks to the merger of the Association of Public Radio Stations with NPR,
however, there was a new board, and its members possessed tremendous ambitions. With a Democratic administration in Washington, it seemed time to
act. Six years into NPR's history, the moment had come to look for a president outside the world of public radio. The board's chairman, Edward Elson,
whose Georgia-based firm owned some two hundred airport newsstands,
headed the search committee. Elson happened to live near Bert Lance, the

incoming director of the Office of Management and Budget, in Atlanta. In the early spring of 1977, Lance slipped his neighbor the names of a few Democratic Party big shots angling for jobs in Jimmy Carter's White House. One name resonated. At an NPR board meeting, Elson told the group that he'd convinced this dream candidate to drop by. He was in the lobby. It was presented as a take-it-or-leave-it proposition. Either the board jumped at the opportunity, or it would lose the potential savior of NPR, a figure so winning that the network could ride his prestige and clout to the highest realms of power and influence. After the stagnant years under Frischknecht and the disarray wreaked by Engelman and Symonds, the board was in no mood for skepticism. Following a brief interview, they made the man an offer.

THREE

CITIZEN MANKIEWICZ

Frank Mankiewicz was not a big man—only five feet, nine inches in height and, at fifty-three, thickening around the middle. Nor were his features remarkable. Jowly with the nose of a boxer who'd taken too many shots to the face, he could have passed as the manager of a minor-league baseball team. Not that anyone who knew him would have made such a mistake. Mankiewicz was so well connected and evoked so many associations that when he strode into the National Public Radio conference room at 2025 M Street on August 1, 1977, his first day as network president, the assembled staff gazed upon him as if he were a dazzling and omnipotent giant.

The indelible event had occurred nine years earlier at Good Samaritan Hospital in Los Angeles. There, a haggard Mankiewicz stepped before a clutch of microphones and said: "I have a short announcement to read. Senator Robert Francis Kennedy died at 1:44 a.m. today, June 6, 1968." As the slain leader's press secretary, Mankiewicz delivered the news. Soon enough, as director of George McGovern's 1972 Democratic presidential campaign, Mankiewicz became the news, in no small part because *Rolling Stone*'s Hunter S. Thompson told much of the story over his shoulder. "McGovern's alter ego," Thompson dubbed him in *Fear and Loathing on the Campaign Trail '72*. All this would have been sufficient to wow the validation-starved souls at NPR, but the new network president was, of course, more than just a political insider.

Not only was Frank the son of *Citizen Kane*'s screenwriter Herman J. Mankiewicz, he was the nephew of the director Joseph L. Mankiewicz (*All about Eve*), and he grew up in show business's most rarified precincts. Groucho Marx and F. Scott Fitzgerald were regulars at Sunday brunches. Orson Welles rehearsed his Mercury Theatre dramas at the kitchen table. During World War II, Frank joined the army, fighting in the Battle of the Bulge. After returning to California. he enrolled at UCLA, where his freshman year saw him reading *Ulysses* aloud in its entirety under the tutelage of the critic Eric Bentley. Journalism school at Columbia, a law degree from Berkeley, a couple of years practicing in LA, and, the big leap, a stint as director of the Peace Corps in Latin America—that someone of this stature would take charge of the network was head spinning. To be sure, there were skeptics. Don Quayle, NPR's founding president, worried that the new network chief, who after all had presided over McGovern's lopsided defeat, was irresponsible: "His reputation preceded him. He was a profligate." In her 1975 autobiography, the actress Shirley MacLaine wrote, "Mankiewicz could be abrasive and insensitive." A longtime acquaintance of the family, she noted that one of Frank's cousins told her, "He will probably self-destruct. Just when things get going, he'll shit on it." But these were minority opinions.

Addressing the National Public Radio staff, Mankiewicz lived up to the high expectations. Congenitally incapable of dullness and blessed with a gravelly voice that could be reassuring and ironic, he told his new charges that he was fortunate to be at NPR and believed in what they were doing. He said what "we'd wanted to hear from Lee but never had," recalled Linda Wertheimer. He said, "'You guys are the best. If more people heard you, they would love it.'" Mankiewicz then took questions. Everyone wanted to know not just what he was going to do but when. To which he responded with vagaries until someone pressed him, whereupon he cracked, "We'll take care of this within a couple of weeks—or before Shavuot." For a second, the place grew quiet. Finally, several Jews on the staff began to chortle, explaining to the rest what this meant. Shavuot was the day Jehovah gave the Torah to the Israelites. Mankiewicz was at once testing the waters to see who would appreciate his Mel Brooks–infused humor and proclaiming a new era. The

Torah was coming. "After he got the laugh," said Jay Kernis, "he looked at a couple of us. He didn't exactly wink, but it was a nod. At that moment he realized: 'I can work this room.'"

There were many rooms at National Public Radio, but from the beginning, Mankiewicz made it plain that he was interested in just one. He did so by moving his office from the third-floor executive suite that Lee Frischknecht had occupied alongside various network vice presidents to a corner on the second floor, where his window overlooked a trash-filled alley. "It was a shithole," said Jim Russell, but it opened into the newsroom, where the reporters, editors, and producers worked, and it was a short dash down the stairs to the quarters of *All Things Considered*, which occupied street-front real estate. No sooner had the new president set up his desk—atop which he plopped the biggest rolodex anyone at NPR had ever seen—than he started roaming around the building. Outfitted in a navy blazer and khakis from DC's old-school Lewis & Thomas Saltz, tie tethered with a PT-109 clip, cigar clenched between his teeth, and a Washington powerbroker often in tow, Mankiewicz was everywhere: the *ATC* studios, the editing booths, Master Control. For a staff that had rarely seen the previous boss, this change was dizzying and, as the early weeks progressed, disconcerting. After he waltzed by Ira Flatow's work space for the umpteenth time, the correspondent, who'd begun covering science full-time, mustered the courage to say something.

"Frank, I'm really feeling paranoid. You stop at my desk, look at me, and walk away. Am I doing something wrong?"

"Oh, no, just the opposite," Mankiewicz responded.

"What do you mean?"

"I know science reporters have the messiest desks of anyone in the business because they have all these journals and papers they're reading, and I just want to point out that I have the best science reporter in the business because he has the messiest desk around."

That was Mankiewicz—a compliment wrapped inside of a joke and all of it delivered with bravura. The guy was exciting to be around. More significant from the news department's point of view, he wasted no time addressing the most pressing concern.

"Morale was terrible," Mankiewicz recalled, "so really the first thing I did was sit down with the union." The results of the meetings at the Embassy

Row Hotel thrilled NPR's news staff. "Mankiewicz came in, and I think it was within forty-eight hours that he'd settled on a contract," said Nina Totenberg, who along with Linda Wertheimer and Bob Edwards, had ultimately helped AFTRA organize the network. "I nearly doubled my salary overnight. I'd been making $15,000—suddenly it was $25,000." It was the same across the board. Diane Dimond, a twenty-four-year-old newscaster who'd just joined the network, saw her pay jump from $15,000 to $30,000. All told, the deal cost NPR $474,000, increasing its payroll 70 percent over a three-year period. Where the money would come from was uncertain, and Mankiewicz's willingness to settle without a fight sent tremors through other parts of the organization. "Frank agreed to everything they asked for," recalled Joe Gwathmey, the assistant programming director, who'd been involved in the negotiations. "I thought he gave them stuff we couldn't afford. Afterward, I got up as quietly as I could and walked back to M Street. My feeling was this was not going to have a good ending. I didn't think the institution could afford what the union won."

Mankiewicz entertained great plans for NPR news, although his public utterances did not offer a precise picture of what those plans were. "There's a certain attitude that we might want to work on around here," he told a trade reporter early on. "We're going to make NPR less of a wine and cheese party and more of a bowling league." Expanding on this view, the new president added that NPR was afflicted by "a little bit of what I suppose in New York would be called Upper West-Sidedness . . . a certain sneering at popular culture, or at least a certain condescension." Mankiewicz came across like a populist, but in truth he was not. "I don't know of any decision that Frank ever made that was consistent with" encouraging a "more blue-collar appeal," said Robert Siegel. The fact of the matter was Mankiewicz did not think NPR was too elite. He thought it was too effete. Where his predecessors revered the university savants and multicultural ideologues who wanted to make America better, he revered the athletes, movie stars, politicians, and industrialists who made America what it was. While he had a soft spot for truck drivers and beer drinkers, racial minorities and afflicted souls, it was in the same way the Kennedys did. When asked during his job interview what he would do at NPR, he'd replied: "Whatever is necessary so that people like *me* would have heard of it." He wanted to play big casino, and to him the biggest casino was the nation's capital. "Frank's interest," according to Siegel, "was very much Washington politics and getting NPR to be in the center ring of coverage of Washington politics."

The byzantine NPR structure Mankiewicz inherited would not be easy to move in a new direction. Josh Darsa now ran the shows. Jim Russell, as head of Program Content, generated what aired on the shows. The broadcasts and the contents originated from different departments staffed by people at cross-purposes. Hoping to rationalize the process, Mankiewicz, in his first major personnel move, hired Sam C. O. Holt as vice president of programming. Since overseeing the 1969 study that had led to the professionalizing of the university stations that largely formed NPR, Holt had worked at the Corporation for Public Broadcasting and as programming director at PBS. Darsa and Russell would both report to him. But despite this addition, NPR's new chief did not envision a streamlined chain of command as the solution. "Mankiewicz was not a corporate leader," said Russell. "He had no inclination in that area. There was no organization he had any faith in."

Mankiewicz believed in informal alliances, and he preferred to cement them outside the office. His chosen gathering place was the Bagel Den, a deli across the street from NPR. There, as he was getting acclimated, he glad-handed and kibitzed like the pol that he was. His goal was to build blocs of support, the most influential of which would be composed of the network's female reporters. "Mankiewicz wanted those women around him all the time," producer Jeff Rosenberg remembered. "He charmed them. He didn't like male figures." For the women, the attraction was reciprocal, and the upside was obvious: "That's how they cultivated power."

Susan Stamberg was not just the most important woman at National Public Radio; she was the most important person. "Frank made you feel great," she said later. "He was—manly. The women loved being around him. He was our delight." Stamberg was not the primary object of Mankiewicz's attention. She was already established. To transform NPR, the new president needed women on the rise, women who in elevating themselves would elevate him. Those he homed in on, recalled Russell, "wanted to be big shots in Washington media, to achieve stature in that community."

Like Mankiewicz, Nina Totenberg was a renegade from an artistic family. The new president appreciated both her profane wit ("Do you want brains or balls?" she snorted when informed that funds were available to hire a reporter half-time) and her increasing reputation as a demon investigator.

In the spring of 1977, as Mankiewicz was preparing to join NPR, Totenberg had achieved something unprecedented. Bob Haldeman, John Ehrlichman, and John Mitchell had asked the US Supreme Court to hear an appeal of their Watergate-related convictions. For weeks, the nation had been anticipating the decision. "Nina figured out that Chief Justice Warren Burger had failed to get the justices to grant cert," recalled Siegel, "but for some reason he was sitting on it." The court had voted not to take up the case but had yet to make it public. "We put out a news release the story was gonna air," said Siegel, "then at five o'clock Nina went on *All Things Considered.*" For the first time in American journalism, a reporter had broken a Supreme Court decision before that decision was announced.

The next morning, the *New York Times* confirmed NPR's story, crediting the network on its front page. That was a high compliment, but it was what Totenberg perceived as a low blow that attested to the measure of her achievement. "The *New York Post* suggested I'd gotten the story from a justice by sleeping with him," she said. The justice in question: Potter Stewart. "The *Post* called me up, and I wasn't experienced" in this, "so I said, 'Yeah, right, Potsy gave it to me.' And they quoted me as if it were straight. They made me sound like an ass. It was extremely unpleasant. It was pure sexism." For NPR, you couldn't buy such publicity. William Safire, a close friend of Mankiewicz, termed Totenberg's piece stunning a few days later in his *New York Times* column.

If Totenberg was the journalistic dive-bomber Mankiewicz envisioned bringing attention to NPR by flying down the smokestacks of Washington's most influential institutions, Linda Wertheimer was the plugged-in and gracious student of those same institutions who he hoped would win them over by explicating their inner workings for the network's listeners. As the new president plotted his opening moves, he conceived a bold project for Wertheimer.

No radio or television entity had ever broadcast live from the floor of the United States Congress. The rhetoric and debates, filibusters and grandstanding—none of it had ever gone out to the public as it was occurring. Hoping to make a splash, Mankiewicz approached Senate Majority Leader

Robert Byrd seeking permission not just to air coverage from the upper chamber but to inaugurate it during what was likely to be the most contentious moment in the first half of the Jimmy Carter administration—the hearings to ratify the controversial Panama Canal treaty, which proposed that the United States cede control of the vital waterway to Panama. Byrd, a fiddle-playing West Virginian, was a fan of public radio, especially of a weekend bluegrass show on DC station WAMU hosted by NPR engineer Gary Henderson (the architect of Darsa's Watergate coverage). He gave the idea his blessing.

That, Mankiewicz thought, was the hard part, but when he summoned NPR engineers and producers to the network conference room to share the good news, he learned that the true obstacles were internal.

"We can't do it," someone declared. "We don't have one hundred microphones."

Under Frischknecht, this might have ended matters. But Mankiewicz was undeterred.

"Tell you what, gentlemen, ladies," he said. "I'm gonna leave this room for half an hour. And when I come back, I would like you to have solved this problem. Or have your resignations in front of me."

Just as it had been years since anyone in a position of authority had complimented the NPR staff, it had been years since anyone had challenged them. Upon his return, Mankiewicz got what he wanted. The network would use lapel microphones on the Senate floor, run the feed through a Shure mixer on the chamber's gallery level, and send it back to M Street to put up on the phone lines. Russell, who attended the meeting, was impressed. "Mankiewicz had the big picture in mind. His job was to erase NPR's invisibility."

Beginning on February 7, 1978, National Public Radio carried the treaty ratification debate live, gavel to gavel, for thirty-seven days. Wertheimer, who sat with engineer Gary Henderson, kept her commentary sparse, functioning almost as an announcer at a baseball game. She set the scene, introduced the players, then got out of the way. The exchanges on the floor amounted to the crack of the bat and the roar of the crowd. It was not scintillating radio. "If NPR ever had any listeners," a senate staffer told *Broadcasting* magazine, "they're going to lose them." Back at M Street, where Frank

Fitzmaurice produced and Robert Siegel provided color commentary (the highlight was an interview with David McCullough, the author of *The Path Between the Seas: The Creation of the Panama Canal*), there was also some head wagging. "It went on and on," recalled Gwathmey. There was resistance from the stations as well. Fewer than half of the network member stations carried the coverage. Most relied on recaps that Wertheimer and Fitzmaurice spliced together at the end of every session to air at night following *All Things Considered*.

Still, the broadcasts were a success, as was a Mankiewicz-ordered series of stories from Panama by Scott Simon, whom NPR dispatched as the vote to turn over the passageway neared. Senators from both sides of the aisle praised the network for its evenhandedness. NPR had let America hear what lawmaking sounded like. Noah Adams, who had recently joined *ATC* as a production assistant, later termed the event a "turning point." The direction was toward a newsier network.

The event also marked the coalescing of a power center at National Public Radio in which Mankiewicz, Totenberg, and Wertheimer formed the nucleus, with Siegel, Krulwich, and, to a lesser degree, Russell orbiting around it. Soon afterward, Totenberg and Wertheimer solicited an addition. Cokie Roberts, the daughter of Louisiana congresswoman Lindy Boggs and the late House Majority Leader Hale Boggs, had hosted *Meeting of the Minds*, a weekly public affairs program on Washington's WRC television. She had recently returned to the capital from Europe, where her husband, Steve Roberts, had covered Greece for the *New York Times* and she'd worked as a stringer for CBS News. She was looking for a job. "Steve came to NPR, and I opened the glass door and let him in and he handed me her résumé," Totenberg recalled. "And Linda said, 'I know her from Wellesley.'" Russell, who would technically be Roberts's boss, was unimpressed, feeling that Roberts lacked on-air presence, but Totenberg and Wertheimer prevailed on their patron. "I sneaked her in," Mankiewicz boasted. The newcomer brought the inner circle to critical mass. As for the department heads, programming directors, and producers who nominally ran NPR, they were on the outside looking in. Siegel, who relished being among the chosen, nonetheless recognized the clubby inequity. "A whole chain of command was routinely being bypassed in terms of the management of the organization," he later said. "All those lunches we had with Nina, Cokie, and Linda were cutting out people who in theory were vice president and executive vice president."

National Public Radio was becoming, informally at least, an institutional matriarchy. Save for Mankiewicz, it was a realm in which men, if not subservient, were no longer in absolute control. "The news division was basically dominated by four very powerful women," a male executive who joined NPR during this period later noted. "Susan Stamberg, Linda Wertheimer, Nina Totenberg, and Cokie Roberts really ran things. Other people kind of surrounded their star, so to speak. They were close, jealous of their airtime." To American feminists, NPR was a beacon. Yet any fantasy that the network was a utopia where women nurtured women was just that—a fantasy. The attraction for Totenberg and the others was less sisterhood than influence, and they were as willing to use that influence against women as against men.

Around the corner from Mankiewicz's office was the office of the only NPR reporter with a door that closed. It belonged to Barbara Newman, the investigative journalist and early member of Siemering's staff. For years, she had been the principal source of groundbreaking stories at the network, and regardless of her involvement in the Engelman-Symonds imbroglio, she had never stopped doing good work. Newman's private quarters might have been seen as a reward for seniority and achievement. It was, however, the opposite—a cage meant to separate her from fellow correspondents. "She was so disliked by the staff that she was put there," said Russell. "It was kind of an Edgar Allan Poe approach to walling her in."

The hostility toward Newman was across the board. "She was a nut bag," said Todd Easton, who'd been promoted to a producer's job at *All Things Considered*. "She was egoistic," added another *ATC* producer. "She came into my office one day and proposed a story on a day in the life of Barbara Newman." But Newman's fiercest nemeses were Totenberg, Wertheimer, and Roberts. Not only did Totenberg and Wertheimer blame her for throwing in with Engelman and Symonds but they all objected to her persona. She showed too much bosom and leg, rejecting the Laura Ashley aesthetic that with the arrival of the conservatively attired Roberts was becoming de rigueur. "She was brassy and Brooklyn," Frank Fitzmaurice would later say. "They were more cultured." Nina, Linda, and Cokie "got together on something and it was their dislike of Barbara Newman," said Russell. "They had

Mankiewicz's attention." They tried to get him to fire her. Russell interceded. While he, too, was put off by Newman's behavior, he respected her journalistic skills.

"This is a lady who has broken several major stories," Russell told Mankiewicz, "and they want to get rid of her because they don't like her. I don't believe you can fire someone for offending a lot of people but being otherwise good and productive."

"You can if the entire staff is against her," Mankiewicz responded.

Newman fought back. "She was always asking, 'Got any dirt on Wertheimer?'" recalled Rosenberg "'Got any dirt on Totenberg?'" It was too little, too late. Mankiewicz "made Newman uncomfortable," Russell would say later. Added Siegel: "We gave her a negative evaluation." Eventually, she left.

To Russell, Newman's departure was dismaying on several levels. He believed that the objections to her by Totenberg, Wertheimer, and Roberts were rooted in self-interest. Newman's brashness was an obstacle to their careers, which they regarded as synonymous with an increasingly conventional, DC-centric NPR. More troubling, Russell realized that Mankiewicz, who shared their aspirations, had no hesitation about bowing to their demands. "He clearly undermined his management by dealing directly with the women," Russell later said. "I quickly decided there was nothing I could do about it, and it would be silly for me to waste my time worrying. I said, 'I can't stop him from talking directly to them. I think it's improper. But there's no such thing as channels when it comes to them.'"

For all of Frank Mankiewicz's coalition building, he could not change NPR unless he changed its programming, which for the majority of listeners consisted solely of *All Things Considered* and, starting in fall of 1977, its offspring *Weekend All Things Considered* (*WATC*). Under twenty-eight-year-old David Creagh, who'd taken over as executive producer of *ATC* after Russell's promotion in 1976, the daily weekday show was inconsistent. Although Creagh, the son of a Washington-based AP correspondent, grew up in a news-steeped household, he was, a coworker would later say, "out of his depth." He'd started at the network as a sound tech, and he was more enamored of high-end audio than current events. During the new NPR president's first week on the job, he chastised Creagh for cuing Jimi Hendrix's version of

"The Star-Spangled Banner" following a report on government malfeasance. "It was a legitimate piece," recalled Mankiewicz, "but the music was mocking. I told David that I thought it was in bad taste."

The occasional scoop notwithstanding, *All Things Considered* was more of a features-magazine program than a news show. By the end of the daily, ten a.m. editorial meeting in Creagh's cramped office, the so-called Road Map—a big whiteboard on which producers jotted down the lineup for the five p.m. broadcast—was complete. The program was locked in before the day and the news it would bring began. Moreover, in keeping with the egalitarian ethos in the NPR DNA, anyone on the *ATC* staff from the top executive to the lowest flunky could commandeer a spot on the schedule for an idea, meaning that space for journalism was often ceded to an assistant's whim.

Then there was the editing, or lack of it. Although Siegel and Krulwich marked up each piece originating from Russell's Program Content division, the material generated by the *All Things Considered* staff itself—interview introductions, interstitial copy, questions for chats with reporters in the field—went straight from a production assistant's typewriter to the hosts. Most of the show hit the air raw. Not only did this mean that *ATC* was flabby ("There was an awful lot of self-indulgence," recalled Sam Holt) and lousy with small errors but that inconsistencies in pronunciations and facts would crop up in the course of a broadcast, with the bottom of the program often contradicting the top.

Even so, the show that Stamberg and Bob Edwards fronted featured a remarkable amount of ambitious work. In fact, the *All Things Considered* of Mankiewicz's first months frequently boasted the sort of lengthy, freewheeling, sound-saturated radio storytelling that Siemering had championed. On an April evening in 1978, against an aural backdrop of boots crunching snow, tree limbs groaning from seasonal melt, and sap dripping into a cup, producer Art Silverman took listeners through the agonies ("The tree's willing, but it can't do it," a New England farmer grimaced) and ecstasies ("It's like you breathe the coming of spring," enthused another farmer) of an annual maple syrup harvest. A couple of weeks later, Hartman Turnbow, a seventy-three-year-old Black Mississippian who'd led the campaign for voting rights in the tiny town of Tchula, gave David Molpus some Delta wisdom regarding what life for Black men and women had once been. "You heard that story about 'A heart's a heart and a figure's a figure—everything for the white man and none for the nigger.' That was about the law. There was no law, not for no Negro." As Joe Gwathmey later observed, "I think the high-water mark for creative presentation of information was in 1978."

At the center of this daily symphony sat Stamberg. While she worked in an aural medium, her skills as an interviewer were almost visual. In the same way that an exacting photographer crops his pictures in the camera viewfinder before he shoots, she framed her conversations in the orbit of the microphone before she spoke. Since one of Stamberg's chief interests was the changing role of women, her work—varied though it was—comprised an unfolding oral history of the gender battles of the late 1970s. One day the author Shere Hite, just back from an Asian book tour to promote *The Hite Report*, told her, "In Japanese, there is no written character for a female orgasm. There is only ejaculation, which means, of course, male orgasm." Soon thereafter, the novelist Lois Gould, addressing why the sexes were socialized differently, opined, "In childhood boys are trained to play on teams. If your team requires eleven kids to play football, they are not going to be best friends. Boys know they have a choice. Either they can play with their best friend, or they can play football. Women—little girls—are never given that choice. They play by themselves or with one best friend. They are gymnasts, solitary skaters, rope jumpers." Such insights didn't just materialize. It was as if Stamberg preordained them, and she could do it with nearly anyone on nearly any topic.

In mid-1978, the Broadway belter Ethel Merman, who'd made her debut in George and Ira Gershwin's *Girl Crazy* in 1930, sat down across from Stamberg in M Street's Studio 2. A lover of musicals, Stamberg knew that Merman, despite her accomplishments, was plagued by the career-long criticism that she took an assembly-line approach to performances, cranking them out almost by rote. Stamberg also knew that Merman hated reporters bringing up the topic, which was why midway through the conversation she did:

"Was it Buddy De Sylva who said about you, 'Watching Merman is . . . '"

"'Like watching a motion picture. She never varies.'"

"And you said that was the greatest compliment you ever got."

"One of them."

"He meant that night after night . . . "

"Consistently."

"It was always the same."

"Never varied, never let down."

"Yes, but what I don't understand is how . . . then why not go to a movie of you? I mean, if you're going to do it the same night after night, then . . . "

"*Because*," Merman finally and inimitably snapped, "*people enjoy live theater! I know people who have come to see Gypsy dozens of times. They just love live theater.*"

"We're almost finished," Stamberg told her aggravated guest. This was the key line of the encounter—not because it signaled the end but because it offered contrast, highlighting Merman's defensiveness. Where many broadcasters would have cut the line before the conversation aired, Stamberg left it in, which was why she was a master.

Nonetheless, *All Things Considered* remained, as one executive recalled, "a blinkered, parochial, self-satisfied little program." In the fall of 1978, hoping to capitalize on its strengths—principally, Stamberg—while fixing the broken parts, Mankiewicz, Holt, and Gwathmey gave their blessing to a huge change. On a Friday night at the end of the broadcast, Josh Darsa appeared in *ATC*'s street-front bailiwick and relieved David Creagh of his duties, reassigning him to a different department. Russell, Siegel, and Krulwich supported the move, but equally involved were two relative newcomers: Rick Lewis and Neal Conan. Lewis, a chain-smoking, twenty-eight-year-old midwesterner, had served two years in the Peace Corps in Central America before getting into radio at NPR's Ames, Iowa, station. He moved to Washington in 1976, becoming a newscaster, then rising to an associate producer's job on *ATC*. Conan, although only twenty-seven, had already been in radio for a decade. The son of a New York physician, he'd started at the Pacifica station WBAI after graduating from high school. He'd intended to stay just a year, but the business grabbed him ("Life is what you heard," he later said), and he never left. Soon, he was freelancing for *All Things Considered*. When the show expanded to weekends, he, too, took a position in Washington.

No sooner had Creagh departed than Lewis and Conan joined Darsa at the producer's old desk. When Conan stood to leave, Darsa announced, "No, you stay. You're part of this." With that he named Lewis the executive producer of *All Things Considered* and Conan its first dedicated editor. "Rick was in charge of grand strategy," Conan recalled, "I was in charge of tactics. I essentially was the line producer."

The new bosses of *All Things Considered* spent their initial six months in attack mode. "We blew up the show," recalled Conan. Henceforth, the Road Map would not be laid out until two p.m. Late-breaking pieces could now find their way into the lineup. As for the pieces themselves, they would have to be shorter. Lewis and Conan fired all but one of *ATC*'s commentators, a group that Conan characterized as "tired, dull hole-fillers." The sole commentator to survive was the idiosyncratic Kim Williams of Missoula, Montana, who mused about collecting and eating wild foods and spoke in a shrill, bumpy voice that reminded Stamberg of a cross between Edith Bunker and a twelve-year-old. That Williams lived to comment another day was proof that the program wasn't turning its back on its roots, but it was turning.

The most critical transformation Lewis and Conan made went to the program's heart. No longer would there be any pretense that the hosts of *All Things Considered* were created equal. "We decided to make it 'the Susan Stamberg Show,'" Conan said. "She provided more material of high quality than anyone else. She would rise to any challenge. I'd say, 'I need this done,' and she did it. She would complain afterward, but she was brilliant." Equally important, she was becoming something of a celebrity—*The New Yorker* featured her in a cartoon in 1978. If Bob Edwards didn't like it (and he was starting not to), that was his problem. "Susan was the star and he wasn't," Lewis recalled. "She was a brilliant interviewer, and he wasn't." Not long after the change, a listener wrote Stamberg, "I love your work and that of your competent, deep-voiced colleague." Those in charge would have put it that way, too.

At Mankiewicz's insistence, *All Things Considered* was moving still further away from where it had begun as an alternative to the network TV news. "Frank used to say that in a strict sense that if you're alternative it means you're defined by someone else," Jim Russell said later. "Every time the other guy copies you, you must change or you're no longer alternative. His version of alternative was 'better.' He'd say, 'Better is alternative. We can do a better job of news coverage. We don't have to . . . '" For a second, Russell's voice trailed off. "Frank never said it, but others completed the sentence for him:

'We don't have to dabble in light, feature-y, back-of-the-book kind of things. We can be the main act.' Frank's view of NPR and mine were different: explicitly different, not subtle."

As 1978 wound down, Russell recalled, he and Mankiewicz debated these differences.

"Frank, I don't think you understand *All Things Considered*," said Russell. "It's like a finished chef d'oeuvre, a measure of this, a measure of that—a finished piece."

"You're having metaphysical objections," Mankiewicz rejoined, before articulating his own definition: "*All Things Considered* is a river of news, all the time, at a very high level."

"Here's the problem with that," Russell countered. "Rivers never know where they're going. They just go. They meander."

Mankiewicz, of course, got the last word. "I wanted to make this a major news organization," he said later. That was the end of Russell. Having lost the battle over the influence of Totenberg, Wertheimer, and Roberts and now a much bigger battle over the nature of NPR itself, he resigned, taking a job in public television with Minnesota's Bill Kling. He was not the only casualty. Josh Darsa was also done. "He was marginalized," said Lewis. "Frank," recalled Conan, "wanted somebody shinier."

Early on the afternoon of New Year's Day 1979—an hour when journalists are typically hungover and still in bed—Barbara Cohen, the managing editor of the *Washington Star*, picked up the telephone at her home on Woodley Road in DC's leafy Kalorama neighborhood.

"I see the *Star* didn't publish today," Frank Mankiewicz began, opening the conversation on what for Cohen was a painful note. The night before, as a party at her house roared on without her, she'd remained at the afternoon newspaper's offices, maintaining a sober vigil. Time Inc., the paper's owner, was trying to complete a deal with its back-shop unions. At the last minute, negotiations hit a snag. There would be no *Star* on January 1, 1979.

What Cohen regarded as awful news, Mankiewicz saw as an opportunity.

"Do you think it's now time to come down and visit the NPR office?"

At thirty-three, Barbara Cohen was not the sort of journalist who would have ordinarily taken a professional interest in NPR. Vivacious and well educated (Swarthmore and Columbia), she was already a force among the reporters and columnists who made up DC's media elite. She and her husband, the *Washington Post* writer Richard Cohen, socialized with Carl Bernstein, half of the *Post* team that had brought down Richard Nixon, and his wife, the journalist and screenwriter Nora Ephron. (It was Ephron who introduced Mankiewicz to Barbara Cohen.) For Mankiewicz even to think about luring her to his network was almost delusional. "I was one of the few women who'd ever been managing editor of a major metropolitan newspaper," she recalled thinking. "Why would I give that up?" But NPR's president had been pursuing her, and he held a couple of strong cards—the *Star*'s labor issues being just one of them.

By the winter of 1979, plans to create a new show that might do for American mornings what *All Things Considered* did for its afternoons were starting to take shape at NPR. "Sam Holt was always saying we should have" such a program, Mankiewicz said years later, "but it was my idea." Although the network president does deserve credit, it was Lawrence Lichty, a numbers-crunching PhD from the University of Wisconsin, who came up with the concept. Working with several audience researchers at the Corporation for Public Broadcasting and a graduate assistant named David Giovannoni, Lichty had studied Arbitron ratings in six markets, among them Washington, DC, and Boston. Their report, blandly titled "The Audience of Format of Some Public Radio Stations," delivered incontrovertible findings. "It was clear," Lichty recalled, "that the audience for public radio was between six and nine in the morning, and it was also clear that NPR was never going to have any impact unless it had a morning show." In the spring of 1978, after finishing his project, Lichty got on an elevator at Vilas Hall on the Madison campus, where he ran into Ronald Bornstein. An influential NPR board member, Bornstein could not have reacted more enthusiastically to Lichty's findings: "Go to Washington and meet Sam Holt." Holt was convinced, and soon his boss was, too.

Mankiewicz was so bowled over by Lichty's numbers that he set to work trying to find the money to fund the show that he now believed could transform NPR into a nationwide force. Help was close at hand.

By job description and political affiliation, Henry Loomis, the president of the Corporation for Public Broadcasting, was not the sort of man who should have been simpatico with Frank Mankiewicz. Not only was Loomis a bureaucrat but he was a Republican, and not only was he a Republican but he was a Nixon appointee. The truth, though, was that Loomis and Mankiewicz had much in common. They were both insiders who regarded themselves as outsiders. Loomis had grown up the son of the eccentric Wall Street millionaire Alfred Loomis, who forsook the stock exchange in the late 1930s to found a scientific lab in Tuxedo Park, New York. The elder Loomis was something of a tinkerer (at night he would attach electrodes to his sleeping boy's head and whisper to him through a microphone to test the powers of persuasion on the unconscious mind), but he nurtured a serious goal. Believing that the United States would soon be drawn into the conflicts boiling up in Europe and Asia, he'd bankrolled research into the technology that he believed could assure victory: radar. His advisers included Enrico Fermi, Niels Bohr, and Albert Einstein. The younger Loomis matured into a similar sort of maverick. As a naval officer during World War II, he used a chance encounter with Secretary of War Henry Stimson to beg that the city of Kyoto, whose artworks he'd studied at Harvard, be spared from the atomic bomb. After returning to college following VJ Day, he earned a degree in physics and ran a defense firm before being named director of the Voice of America in 1958. He remained there until 1965, when rather than capitulate to an order from President Lyndon Johnson that the network stop carrying reports of US Air Force activity over Laos, he resigned. Mankiewicz was impressed. When Loomis told him that the CPB would end fiscal 1978 with a big cash surplus and asked what he would use it for, the NPR president had his opening.

"Start a morning radio show," Mankiewicz replied.

"Wonderful. What would you do the second year?"

"Blackmail you."

"What do you mean?"

"Do you want me to go to your board and say you're the man who killed morning radio?"

It was, Mankiewicz recalled, "a jocular conversation"—a couple of like-minded souls bantering about how to invest a small fortune. The NPR boss would now spend months lobbying Congress for the increased funding, some of which was contained in new public broadcasting legislation offered by Jimmy Carter. Ultimately, NPR would see its share of the CPB budget grow. There would be more than enough to launch a morning show, which was why Mankiewicz hired the idea's progenitor. Lichty started work at the network in September 1978.

This, then, was the ace Mankiewicz played in his courtship of Barbara Cohen: a once-in-a-lifetime opportunity to create a national morning radio program. The research showed there was a market, and the money was there. For the managing editor of a newspaper hemorrhaging cash and facing extinction, it seemed like a godsend. Cohen recalled, "I'd been at the *Star* eleven years. It was always scrimping. You were running a shrinking operation. At NPR, we were going to be building something new. That was appealing." In March 1979, Cohen took control of NPR News.

Mankiewicz was determined to make Cohen's transition smooth. To placate 2025 M Street's true powers, he organized several of what he termed "sorority rushes" with Stamberg, Wertheimer, Totenberg, and Cokie Roberts. To allay worries that Cohen lacked radio experience, he appointed Rick Lewis, the executive producer of *ATC*, as her second-in-command. The network boss took these steps because as he was wooing Cohen, he'd watched the man who'd created the opening for her take a beating. Mankiewicz and Holt had picked a committee of fifteen producers and editors—among them Lewis, Frank Fitzmaurice (supervisor of the coverage of the Panama Canal hearings), Robert Krulwich, Alex Chadwick (host of *A Closer Look*, the daily a.m. news summary), and Jay Kernis—to help Lawrence Lichty give shape to the idea for a show that at this juncture was little more than gaseous matter. The reception was brutal.

"We voted not to let Lichty into the room," Lewis recalled. Where the numbers guru saw himself as the messiah, the staff saw him as a philistine who would bring the dark powers of demographics and Mammon into a realm where commercial considerations were disparaged. Lichty, however, was not easily deterred. He ignored the vote by his colleagues and barged into that first meeting, demanding that Lewis and the rest listen to what he had to tell them. According to Fitzmaurice, he said, "This is an opening for you. You're going to have to trust us." To affirm that Lichty had his support,

Mankiewicz gave him an office next to his, overlooking the second-floor newsroom.

Despite Mankiewicz's efforts, Cohen encountered similar resistance. As she would later put it: "All of a sudden, I realized, 'Uh, oh.'" With her arrival, a major new program was a real prospect, and the opposition became substantial and organized.

The consensus at NPR was that a serious morning show would pose a threat to the network's one success—*All Things Considered.* "Susan Stamberg thought the program" would take "resources from *All Things Considered*," recalled Kernis. "She had NPR unofficially wired so that either no or very few reporters would ever work for the new show." Lichty's recollections were less measured. "The person who was most hostile was Stamberg. She did not want to have a morning program. She would have nothing to do with the program. She shut us out." As for Stamberg, all she could say was she did what she had to do. "I stood my ground."

Even if Stamberg hadn't made her feelings known, it's doubtful that NPR reporters would have embraced the idea of a morning program. "They thought they would have to work twice as hard," recalled Mankiewicz. Added Cohen: They were "not anxious to do a piece for *All Things Considered*, then turn around and stay late to cut a piece for the morning." The reactions, she said, ranged from foot-dragging to hostility. Steve Reiner, a new *ATC* producer who'd come to the network from WGBH in Boston, bringing both strong journalistic skills and radical leanings (a University of Wisconsin grad, he had been in Madison during the school's anti–Vietnam War protests), was astonished by the reporters' vehemence. "I remember Nina Totenberg pointing her finger in my face and screaming, "'I'm never going to do a story' for that show. 'Fucking ever.'"

Soon enough Cohen herself became the object of the resentment. Although she struck Mankiewicz as bright and shiny, she was regarded by many inside NPR as manipulative ("She was ruthless and strategic," Stamberg recalled) and not overly imaginative. Robert Krulwich, the embodiment of the network's creative wing, later described his conversations with the news director regarding a pivotal decision facing those creating the a.m. show—the selection of a host. Krulwich's choice: Harry Shearer. At the time, Shearer was fronting an LA improvisational company called the Credibility

Gap that drew its material from daily headlines. "My notion about the morning show was that we should take it sideways," Krulwich recalled. "Did we really need another *All Things Considered?*" Shearer flew to DC for an audition ("I met with everybody in the building," the comedian remembered. "They were young people with only some adult supervision. They thought they were going to change the world"), but he accepted an offer from a program better suited to his sensibilities: NBC's *Saturday Night Live.* Krulwich blamed Cohen for losing him: "I was championing difference. She was championing more."

A daily morning news show was in truth not the right venue for a sketch comedian. An a.m. audience is not looking for social satire on the previous day's events. It isn't even looking for *All Things Considered.* "I called a lot of psychologists to find out what should be on a morning show," Mankiewicz said later. "One told me the dominant emotion when you wake up is relief. You're alive. Life is beginning to set into an ordinary pattern. Another day is starting. By late afternoon, people are willing to think about anything, but as the day starts you want routine. You want the stock report at a certain time, the sports at a certain time." NPR's affiliates agreed. A morning program should be less a show than a format, a well-choreographed production featuring short pieces and precisely timed spots where stations could cut away to insert traffic and weather reports.

Cohen was not quite the tin-eared newspaper woman her worst critics at NPR thought she was. She hired Chris Koch to replace Rick Lewis as executive producer of *All Things Considered.* The forty-four-year-old Koch, a former producer for ABC TV's *Close-Up* and a former host of the weekly PBS talk show *FYI,* was out of Bill Siemering's playbook. He had started as a reporter at Pacifica, then spent the mid-1970s driving a taxi in New York, learning to cruise gay bars on Christopher Street for post-midnight fares and that the safest place to walk in the city at three a.m., the hour he dropped his cab off at a 135th Street garage and returned downtown, was the middle of Broadway. There was less chance of being mugged if you avoided the sidewalks. Koch told Cohen he'd take the job if she'd let him "move *All Things Considered* away from its very heavy New York–Washington axis. I wanted to get away from that liberal-centrist position and have opinions from both ends of the spectrum."

Still, conceiving a complicated morning program and then getting it on the air would be a challenge for Cohen. "How do you create a show if you know nothing of radio and the staff is resentful?" Steve Reiner recalled asking as he watched the news director struggle. "The attitude was: 'We've got *All Things Considered* and we're doing great. Who needs a new show?'"

Cohen—backed by Mankiewicz, Lewis, and especially Holt—made the decision many other media executives would have. "She outsourced" the job, said Reiner.

In early October 1979, Ted Landphair, the newly appointed executive producer of the NPR program that would be called *Morning Edition* (when the words *morning* and *edition* popped up separately on a list of potential names, Nina Totenberg, her skepticism about the undertaking notwithstanding, suggested combining them), stood before a cadre of employees on the second floor of 2025 M Street. Although only thirty-six, Landphair, the longtime news director of Washington's WMAL, was a respected radio veteran—a big guy with an academic manner. At his side was Marc Kuhn, the wiry, thirty-four-year-old former programming director at WMAL who would serve as the new show's line producer. This was the duo's first meeting with the staff who would get *Morning Edition* on the air, and to illustrate the hierarchy they expected everyone to respect, they'd brought a flip chart.

"Here's my title," Landphair began as he turned to a page onto which he'd scrawled just one word in giant letters: BOSS.

"And here is Marc Kuhn's title," Landphair added after waiting a beat, then turning to the next page: BOSS WHEN I'M NOT AROUND.

To a group of NPR veterans cherry-picked from programs like *Voices in the Wind*—canceled to make way for this big push—and adherents to the rebellious sensibilities that for all of Mankiewicz's ambitions still defined the network, Landphair's gimmicky attempt to instill order seemed at best ill advised, at worst insulting. "Public radio was never good with authority," recalled Jay Kernis, who had been selected to supervise arts coverage on *Morning Edition* and was the highest-ranking homegrown producer in the room. "Landphair thought the staff lacked discipline," he added, noting that in the wake of that inaugural meeting, the executive producer, with Barbara Cohen's blessing, did something "un–public radio like." He imposed a dress code. For men, this meant slacks with creases (no Levis) and shirts with collars; for women, skirts (no pants) and blouses. "Welcome to the adult world," Landphair and Kuhn appeared to be saying, and the thing of it was, the new show's ragtag army initially went along. "The motivation for hiring them was to break the mold," said Kernis. "They were running WMAL, and WMAL had half the audience in DC. An audience of that size was unheard of."

For official Washington during the 1970s—for decades—WMAL was radio. DC did not listen to rock. It did not listen to country. It did not listen to classical. It listened to AM 630, which carried news, sports—the Redskins, the University of Maryland Terrapins—and *Harden and Weaver*, WMAL's monster morning hit (one of every four listeners in the city tuned in). This was the show that NPR had hired Landphair and Kuhn, if not to clone, then to reconstitute in a form palatable to public broadcast audiences.

Harden and Weaver offered a genteel version of what in other, less staid American media markets was known as "morning zoo." Between serious news segments, Jackson Weaver did schtick and impersonations of fictional Washington characters, among them a bureaucrat, a senator, a socialite "informed on nothing" but with "opinions on everything," and an army colonel, who each day cued up the show's enduring staple: A John Philip Sousa march. Frank Harden, the straight man, gave time checks and local traffic reports. "It was a lot about nothing," Kuhn recalled, "but boy everybody loved it."

Hoping to create a higher-brow version of the WMAL superstars, Landphair hired two relative unknowns to host *Morning Edition*. Mary Tillotson was a thirty-three-year-old Alabamian who'd cut her teeth at Atlanta radio powerhouse WSB. Poised and steely minded, she was "thrilled" to get a job at NPR, which she'd long admired. Pete Williams was the product of public radio's Casper, Wyoming, station. Although he was twenty-seven and came across like a studious teenager, he had a Stanford degree and a strong work ethic.

With the talent in place, Landphair and Kuhn started producing *Morning Edition* pilots. As the debut was set for November 5, there was immediate pressure. "We didn't have time to talk," said Kuhn. "We just hustled." From the outset, however, the divisions that emerged in that first staff meeting made progress difficult. To the newcomers, the NPR veterans seemed clannish and at times rude. "Outsiders were not welcome," recalled Tillotson. "The atmosphere was chilly. Linda Wertheimer, Nina Totenberg, and Cokie Roberts were not warm. It was strange. I'd been hired by an outfit that ostracized me." Kuhn put it more bluntly. "They made us feel like we were not their intellectual equals. We were going to have to prove that we were not jackasses." Conversely, the M Street hands felt that Landphair and Kuhn projected a collective arrogance. "To me they just wanted to take what they knew about commercial radio and jam it into public radio," said Kernis. "To them, what we were doing was not *real* radio. They were going to come in and do *real* radio."

That the task of getting *Morning Edition* on its feet would end up pitting Landphair and Kuhn against Kernis was predictable. Not only was Kernis the top representative of the old NPR guard and not only had he been involved in the show's planning (he'd sat in at a New York studio as composer B. J. Leiderman recorded the score) but he had blueprinted it. Whenever he wasn't producing arts pieces for later use, he was hovering over sheets of blank paper drawing clocks into which he penciled pie-shaped wedges that represented the slots where local stations would cut away for inserts. While the new arrivals were in charge of the content, Kernis was in charge of the operating system. There was a personality clash. "Kernis was a snooty young man," recalled Kuhn. "He was a pain in the ass." Kernis, of course, saw it different. "I'd suggest story ideas—profiles of artists and writers, or pieces about the arts, and Kuhn would respond, 'That's stupid.' They basically said, 'Shut up, we know what we're doing.'"

Disaster struck in late October when NPR transmitted Landphair and Kuhn's pilots via closed circuit internally and over phone lines to the stations. "It sounded more like WMAL than NPR," recalled Frank Fitzmaurice. "It sounded more like a commercial, two-person talk show, because that's what Ted and Marc knew how to do." Added Bob Edwards, "It was a bomb. Susan Stamberg and I listened in our office. I recall laughing. The word many used to describe [it] was 'commercial,' but I felt calling it commercial was an insult to commercial broadcasting. The word I used was chatty. One heard chatty hosts yammering on and on about trivia." The reaction from local stations was worse. "They hated it," Mankiewicz said later, "hated it."

The ax fell first on the hosts. "They had Landphair call us at night,"

Tillotson recalled. "We'd been going in before dawn, but he told us, 'Please go over there now and clean out your desks. I don't want the people still working at *Morning Edition* to get upset.' So we dragged our weary asses in."

The next day, Landphair appeared in Mankiewicz's office to make the case that he and Kuhn should stay. Shortly after he departed, the phone rang at Kernis's desk.

"Do you think" Landphair "can pull it off?" asked Mankiewicz.

"This guy has a family," Kernis responded.

"Don't think about that. Can he get this show on the air?"

"No, he can't."

Landphair and Kuhn were gone, and Kernis had a taste of what power feels like, not that it seemed to be worth much right then. NPR did not have a show. Those still involved with *Morning Edition* did have an idea about where they might find a new host.

Just after Landphair and Kuhn departed, Barbara Cohen, Jay Kernis, Rick Lewis, and Chris Koch appeared in the doorway of the M Street office shared by Susan Stamberg and Bob Edwards. "Bob, can we see you for a minute?" one asked. At that second, Edwards was editing a thirty-minute piece scheduled to air on *All Things Considered* commemorating the fiftieth anniversary of the 1929 stock market crash. He could conceive of no reason why anyone would interrupt him. Considering all that was happening, he was, in fact, apprehensive. "He thought he was gonna get fired," Stamberg recalled, "but they asked him to host *Morning Edition* for thirty days."

Cohen and the others had picked the right moment. Two years into their partnership on *All Things Considered*, Edwards and Stamberg were grating on each other. Although they worked well together on the air, especially when they shared the narration of humorous pieces, almost all the plum assignments went to Stamberg (a few weeks earlier she had been chosen to do a historic, live call-in show from the White House with Jimmy Carter), and Edwards resented it. "He never felt he was getting the attention I was getting," she remembered. "He took everything as a sign. I never heard the end of it about how my desk was bigger and how it was closer to the window. If I'd had more pencils in a jar, it would have upset him." The animosity had long been spilling into the open. At a July editorial meeting, as the staff was reading newspaper articles about Hurricane Bob—the first tropical storm

named for a man, which after a lot of hype fizzled—Edwards announced to
all assembled, "If it had been Hurricane Susan, it would have taken out the
whole country." The remark, Chris Koch said later, was "pointed," and it captured how the hosts now regarded each other. "He was treated as a second
banana to Susan," Cohen recalled. "I thought maybe he would welcome the
chance to be the star."

Edwards did welcome it, although in a grudging fashion. "My story deadline loomed," he remembered, "and I needed to get these people out of my
office so I could finish my script. 'Thirty days? OK.' I figured if I helped them
out of a jam, they'd owe me one."

The gathering two evenings later at Barbara Cohen's house began on an apprehensive note. Each of the nearly twenty NPR staffers summoned knew
that the most ambitious project conceived by the network since *All Things
Considered* was about to implode, and none knew it better than the executives most responsible—Mankiewicz, Cohen, and Holt. "Barbara and Sam
were tense," recalled Frank Fitzmaurice. "It looked like they hadn't slept in a
couple of weeks." William Drummond, a young editor who'd just been lured
to NPR from the *Los Angeles Times*, later said, "It was an emergency." Yet
as those present dug into the pizzas atop their host's dining table, the mood
lightened. "We tried to hash" things out, remembered Jackie Judd, a three-
year NPR veteran picked to voice the news insert at the top of the program.
(Carl Kasell, a forty-five-year-old pro who'd studied drama at his North Carolina high school with Andy Griffith, a then-unknown teacher, would handle the insert at the bottom.) The question of "how do we fill up the show"
dominated the conversation, Judd added. "By the end," said Fitzmaurice,
there was a rough plan: "We've all done radio. We've worked to one degree
or another on *All Things Considered*. Let's go try to duplicate that." Several
people in the room later described the scene as similar to the famous one in
the 1939 MGM musical *Babes in Arms* in which Mickey Rooney, hoping to
impress his Vaudevillian parents, enthuses to Judy Garland and a bunch of
kids: "Let's put on a show." The only element missing was a Mickey Rooney
for *Morning Edition*, but as the night ended, the network president made
his choice from this now-revived group.

"You designed the format," Mankiewicz told Jay Kernis. "Get the show on the air." Kernis would never forget the expression that flashed across his boss's face at that instant. It said, "Don't let me down. Don't embarrass me."

With Kernis and Edwards on board, the staff of *Morning Edition* had one week to prepare for the premiere. The atmosphere, recalled Judd, was "frantic." Plans conceived by Landphair and Kuhn were trashed, stories prepared, and everything rehearsed. Making the task harder was the unwillingness of NPR reporters to contribute. "It wasn't all hands on deck," remembered Judd, "it was some hands on deck." Those in the middle of it—Fitzmaurice, who'd been tapped to be the executive producer; Drummond, who would be the editor; Barbara Hoctor, a new hire at *Weekend All Things Considered* who'd been drafted to cohost; Robert Malesky, who'd replaced Kernis as arts producer; and Lichty, who despite being the numbers man had proved himself to love radio and been adopted by the staff—remained at their desks until past midnight, when they staggered home or passed out on the floor. "We'd watch the rats in the alley," Lichty recalled. "Biggest rats you've ever seen." That would be the last thing he saw before falling asleep on the carpet in Holt's office.

Because Kernis had put all those arts pieces in the can during the summer-long run-up to the launch, he had a stockpile of evergreen stories, and he would build most half hours of *Morning Edition* around one. To compensate for the lack of participation by the so-called bureau, he and Fitzmaurice recruited several smart commentators. Peter Osnos of the *Washington Post* would discuss foreign affairs. John Ciardi of the *Saturday Review* would address culture. Then there was Edwards, who, whatever tensions he'd experienced with Stamberg, was solid. "Bob was not only a great voice but a great writer," remembered Kernis. "Writing and accuracy were important to him." Finally, the producer's biggest asset was himself.

Tanned and fit with layered dark hair that fell into his blue eyes when he was excited, the twenty-seven-year-old Kernis was the antithesis of the pasty, nicotine-stained wretches who produced most of what aired on NPR. By network standards well dressed—Britches of Georgetown shirts, chunky sweater vests in cooler weather, and always immaculate Levis—he was more Jovan Musk than Grateful Dead. "He was striking looking," recalled Cohen.

Added Drummond: "He looked like a matinee idol." He also behaved like one, breaking into show tunes to illustrate the emotions he wanted a reporter to hit in a story or, if disappointed by a colleague's efforts, dissolving into tears. Although Kernis had a girlfriend, around 2025 M Street everyone speculated about his sexual orientation. "You know there are people who act gay but aren't—Jay was one of those," Margot Adler, a reporter who joined NPR in 1979, said later. In Drummond's view, there was simply something "diva-ish about Jay."

A diva was just what NPR needed to bring *Morning Edition* to life. "Part of the reason NPR works so well, why the programming works so well," Kernis liked to say, "is that it's great theater. It's compelling. It's entertaining. It hooks you in. It tells you a remarkable story through great characters. It develops the characters. The individual piece and the individual hour have a sense of texture, a sense of pacing, and many different colors." Where others around the network idolized David Brinkley or Walter Cronkite, Kernis— who as a boy growing up in New Jersey was besotted by Broadway—idolized Stephen Sondheim. Such preferences gave pause to some at NPR. "People had their doubts about putting a guy like this in charge of journalism," recalled Rick Lewis. But for a production as complicated as *Morning Edition*—the cutaways to local stations would require the radio equivalent of stagecraft—an aesthete was preferable to a news junkie, and with the reporting staff all but boycotting the program, the arc of the broadcast would be critical. "Jay was a good choice," Judd said later. "He understood the sensibility of NPR and knew how to be fanciful."

By Sunday, November 4—the eve of *Morning Edition*'s premiere—the staff was feeling confident. The combination of Kernis's dramatic flair and Edward's mellifluous voice and no-nonsense prose seemed right. Success, Edwards recalled, "was not impossible, provided there were no last-minute surprises." But the news being the news, arguably the biggest surprise of the last quarter of the twentieth century occurred just a few hours before the show's debut, when militant Iranian students overran the US embassy in Tehran, taking more than sixty Americans hostage. November 5 dawned with television audiences glued to their sets, awaiting updates. But for anyone listening to NPR's new morning show, there would not be a single story on the crisis. Instead they heard Bob Edwards declare that November 5 was

Guy Fawkes Day and the start of laughably obscure Split Pea Soup week. The only real mention of the situation in the Middle East came during the news briefs by Judd and Kasell. "The NPR reporters had said essentially that they wouldn't report for us," Kernis later said, and most—but not all— didn't. Linda Wertheimer took part in a conversation with Barbara Hoctor about the upcoming national elections. Robert Siegel, who in a Mankiewicz- orchestrated coup had just been dispatched to London to open the network's first foreign bureau, weighed in on British-led talks about Rhodesia that would result in the creation of a new nation: Zimbabwe. Then there was an interview with the actor Martin Sheen about one of the year's defining films, *Apocalypse Now*. Still, the show had missed the only event the world wanted to hear about. Afterward, remembered Lichty, "We all went to this breakfast place. Jay, Bob Edwards, Rick Lewis, and we said, 'This is so terrible. We're gonna get fired.'"

At that exact same hour in Chicago, Frank Mankiewicz, who'd spent the weekend in the Midwest, got into a taxi for the ride to O'Hare to catch a flight back to Washington. The radio happened to be on, tuned to the local public broadcasting outlet, WBEZ.

"What are you listening to?" Mankiewicz inquired.

"That's a morning news program on NPR," the cabbie replied.

As Mankiewicz recalled the moment thirty years later, he smiled. "It was the first day, and already we were becoming a routine." The network's new show may have ignored the biggest story of the decade, but it had estab- lished a beachhead in the American morning. Not only that, it was a solid two hours of radio, well produced and confidently presented. As soon as the NPR president reached 2025 M Street, he dashed off a congratulatory note to Kernis.

During the course of the next months, the future of NPR—and of public radio itself—would reveal itself over the airwaves as an assault upon the old and a flourishing of the new. The process would further enhance Frank Mankiewicz's reputation at the network's Washington offices. It would also offer the first hints that the public radio system was not of one mind about the NPR president. It all began with a banishing of the birds from Boston.

Listeners to WGBH, public radio for New England, had for years awakened to a trill of birdsong, then a voice at once authoritative and soothing and in its plumier ranges unintentionally ludicrous. The voice belonged to Robert J. Lurtsema, host of the quixotic *Morning Pro Musica*. At the top of the show, in a segment introduced by words that had become familiar across Massachusetts—"Edited and read by your *Morning Pro Musica* host, Robert J. Lurtsema"—the host delivered a subjective summary of the news, deleting items he deemed distasteful and lingering on those that intrigued him (in 1976 he devoted fifteen minutes to the obituary of Mao Zedong). He punctuated stories with pregnant pauses in the manner of a Harvard professor contemplating profundities. He then played music—medieval at seven, baroque at eight, and classical at nine. He usually presented symphonies in their entirety and often as part of an ongoing program built around composers' anniversaries, seasonal changes, or historical events. But his signature was that opening avian fanfare, referred to by listeners as the "dawn chorus." Lurtsema was not just legendary in his home town (he was born in Cambridge), but an archetypal cultural potentate. Every major market boasted a Robert J., as he was known, and the station managers in many of them viewed NPR's effort to disseminate *Morning Edition* as part of an unholy plan to homogenize a heterogeneous system. "There was a lot of opposition," Frank Fitzmaurice said later. "The stations had to bump something to put us on."

Before *Morning Edition* premiered, reported the *Boston Globe*, Mankiewicz had leaned on WGBH to cancel *Morning Pro Musica*. What the NPR president got, over Lurtsema's protests, was the station's agreement to delay *Morning Pro Musica*'s start ten minutes each day to carry Jackie Judd's news insert at seven and again at eight and nine. For many in Boston, even this small concession was a betrayal. First, Robert J. no longer performed the headlines. Worse, the birds were kaput.

Letters and calls of protest poured into WGBH, with Lurtsema egging people on. Having Judd read the news on *Morning Pro Musica*, the host declared, had "the same impact on the audience that my playing a rock 'n' roll record by Creedence Clearwater Revival would have." The *Globe*'s columnist David B. Wilson wrote that Judd's voice brought to mind "the Junior League nasalities of a young woman with an accent straight out of Grosse Pointe Farms." Warned Wilson: "What Mankiewicz is exporting to Boston is more squalor, however pretentiously disguised. If he can get away with it in Boston, he can get away with it anywhere."

After several weeks of such testiness—and a threat by Lurtsema to quit—WGBH caved. The birds returned at seven a.m. followed by Robert J., in a station spokesman's effusion, "ad-libbing the important non-sensational stories." Judd would continue to deliver the sensational stories at eight and nine. Ultimately, as the complaints intensified (95 percent of the mail supported Lurtsema), the station decided to end all association with *Morning Edition*.

At 2025 M Street disappointment gave way to defiance. "We said, 'Screw WGBH,'" recalled Lichty. With that NPR secured a home for *Morning Edition* at the ninety-eight-pound weakling of New England public broadcasting: WBUR at Boston University, initiating a pattern. When KUSC, the dominant public station in Los Angeles, rejected *Morning Edition*, the network took the show to KCRW, a struggling outfit at Santa Monica College. When WETA, in Washington, DC, said no, NPR sold it to WAMU. Robert Siegel, although now in Europe, kept track of it all. "Every radio station identifies with what it does in the morning," he said later. "The classical stations say, 'If you take music away in the morning, we lose our identity.'" The interests of NPR and those of many stations differed.

On June 20, 1980, NPR started transmitting its programming via Westar I, a 1,200-pound satellite in geostationary orbit 22,236 miles above the equator. No other radio news organization—not CBS, NBC, or ABC, all of which still transmitted their signals over long-distance phone lines—possessed such a capability. Robert J.'s birds may have resumed their morning song in Boston, but Mankiewicz's network was flying above them. "NPR was the first national service to utilize satellite technology," recalled Pete Lowenstein, the network's longtime vice president of distribution.

The most immediate impact of NPR's leap into the skies was the improvement of its sound. During the decade since the network debuted, audiences at distant points on its round-robin system had grown accustomed to broadcasts that sometimes dropped to 2.5 weak, scratchy kilohertz in quality. Now, NPR was coming in at a stereophonic 15 kilohertz. "Someone wanted to know who that man was who said he was Susan Stamberg," remembered

Sam Holt of a listener who had for the first time noticed the tincture of bass in the *ATC* host's distinctive New York honk. The satellite also gave the network the ability to conduct crisp, live interviews with newsmakers in distant locales. After Bob Edwards, sitting at his desk in DC, told his audience that Senator Alan Cranston, the subject of an early such conversation, was in California, people phoned to complain. They thought the host was lying, Mankiewicz said later. "The quality was so terrific they thought Cranston had to be with Bob in Washington."

NPR's full-bodied audio arrived at the moment American car manufacturers, responding to the influx of FM-radio-equipped foreign imports that followed the 1973 Arab oil embargo, started including FM radios as a standard feature. All over the country, people driving to and from work could tune into NPR and experience its stories as great sound. Fabulous though it was, Mankiewicz was alarmed that this audience might indeed think NPR was cheating. At a meeting with network engineers, he made an unusual request. "I asked them to put some static into the satellite stuff, just a little, so that people wouldn't think there was anything magic going on.

"In army boot camp," Mankiewicz began by way of explaining, "I was doing KP duty one morning. The mess sergeant was cooking powdered eggs for one hundred and fifty-five guys, and he gave me a crazy order:

> "Go down to the special services offices and get all their used Ping-Pong balls. If they've got cracks or holes in them, they throw them away. Bring me as many of those Ping-Pong balls as you can get."
>
> I thought the sergeant was sending me on a snipe hunt, but I did what he told me and came back with seven or eight damaged Ping-Pong balls.
>
> "All right," the sergeant said, "I want you to take a mallet and break them up into little tiny pieces."
>
> "What are you going to do with them?"
>
> "Put them in the powdered eggs."
>
> "Why?"
>
> "The pieces of cracked ping pong balls will convince the soldiers they are eating real scrambled eggs with real pieces of shell—not something from a box."

"That is putting static into the satellite broadcast," the NPR chief told the engineers.

For Mankiewicz, there was nothing more fun than having a satellite as a toy. But Westar I also provided another possibility—an opening for those in public radio who hoped to keep the NPR boss from further centralizing production in Washington.

As originally conceived by the Corporation for Public Broadcasting, the satellite system was meant to function as Mankiewicz wanted. It would be the broadcasting equivalent of a one-way street, albeit one with sixteen lanes (the excess channels were for unknown projects in some unknown future). "NPR's view was there would be" a single "uplink," recalled longtime *All Things Considered* producer Rick Lewis. Programming would originate from the nation's capital pretty much as it always had, and the member stations would carry it. However, a powerful figure in the Midwest saw things differently. At an industry conference shortly after Mankiewicz arrived, Minnesota Public Radio's Bill Kling gave a presentation. "He had a graphic that showed lines going up from cities all over the country to the satellite," said Lewis. "There were fifteen of them going up from Minneapolis. It was tongue in cheek," but his meaning was plain: he intended to use the satellite to turn Minnesota into a competing source of programming.

By this juncture the plans that would put NPR on Westar I were complete. For Kling, there was only one move. At a Corporation for Public Broadcasting meeting chaired by William D. Houser, a former vice admiral of the navy who after retirement brought his expertise in satellites to the CPB, the Minnesotan and a cadre of like-minded station managers issued an ultimatum:

"We need 12 uplinks. We don't need a multi-million-dollar one-way telephone service. We need a satellite system that frees producers around the country to provide programming to public radio stations."

Houser was furious that the group would make a last-minute demand. "He was more used to a well-disciplined military," Kling recalled. "He told us, 'If you don't agree to the earlier plan, there will be no radio system, and you'll be left with your thumbs up your asses.'" The admiral then stormed out.

"When a cooler Houser returned," Kling added, "he'd changed his mind." It so happened that the round-robin system NPR had originally used to distribute shows had featured a cumbersome and rarely used switching device that allowed stations in the outback to upload material. There was a precedent. Houser "looked at us and said we had 24 hours to tell him where the 12 uplinks were to go, as the bid docs had to be completed to get the system underway."

Kling and his fellow conspirators fired off teletype messages requesting applications from stations nationwide. "Very few responded," he recalled, "because they didn't really understand it." But a dozen public radio bosses— among them those in Los Angeles, New York, San Francisco, Boston, Des Moines, and seven other locales—did understand. "Once we had 12 cities," said Kling, "we confirmed with Houser, and that's how the system was built." For the handful who appreciated the long-term ramifications, this was a great day.

Although Mankiewicz knew that the satellite system now featured the equivalent of a dozen freeway onramps, he gave the matter little thought. He didn't believe that NPR's affiliates could produce programming of merit. When he'd arrived at the network, Linda Wertheimer had put him wise to the atmosphere in station land. "Let me tell you what you just got into. You've become chairman of a huge sociology department at a second-rate state college where everyone is up for tenure." In the years since, his dealings with the locals had only confirmed this observation. Almost as infamous for his disdain as he was famous for his charm, Mankiewicz hadn't been shy about voicing his low regard for people who in his view were little more than franchisees. He liked to say, "When you've met one public radio station manager—you've met one public radio station manager," recalled Robert Siegel. Dale Ouzts, a Georgia good old boy who as the network's vice president for representation worked to keep the outlets happy, added, "Frank was always saying, 'The stations are dumber than hell.' I'd reply, 'But they own NPR.' I had to kick his butt so often my leg got sore." Yet even if the NPR president had respected his colleagues across the country, he would not have seen their newfound distribution abilities as a threat. He believed the quality of the material coming out of DC was improving so fast that the stations had no incentive to produce their own programs. From *Morning Edition* at dawn to *All Things Considered* at sunset, the network dominated public radio's broadcast day. "With the satellite," Wertheimer said later, "Frank saw that NPR could be big. We could have a big-time audience." That audience was changing. It no longer wanted to hear Robert J. cuing up Telemann. It wanted to hear Bob Edwards talking about efforts to free the hostages in Tehran.

By the fall of 1980, National Public Radio was a twenty-four-hour operation. Where once 2025 M Street essentially emptied out at six thirty p.m. after *All Things Considered* went off the air, it was now up all night. Bob Edwards arrived at two thirty a.m., Jay Kernis shortly thereafter—and they were late to the party. Bill Drummond got in at midnight, partly to edit copy but mostly to wrangle sources in the Middle East to discuss the Iranian crisis on *Morning Edition*. During the broadcasts, which started at six a.m., Drummond napped in an office, emerging around eight when the *ATC* staff began straggling in, whereupon he, Kernis, Robert Malesky, and a couple of others disappeared into meetings to hash out the next day's show. Not until eleven thirty did Drummond leave the building, but he would be so wired that rather than go home he regularly walked the few blocks to a YMCA on New Hampshire Avenue and swam one hundred laps in the pool. "That was the only way I could wind down," he later remarked.

To help feed NPR's increasingly voracious appetite for stories, Barbara Cohen hired, as she put it, "a six-foot shit-kicker." Bearded and imposing, invariably sporting Levis, a leather vest, cowboy boots, and a pair of antiquated round eyeglasses, John McChesney was a rare breed—the intellectual hippie badass. Born in Missouri, he was partly raised in his mother's native Maine. His paternal uncle Robert, an abstract expressionist painter and back-to-the land lefty who lived in a northern California enclave of Communist chicken farmers, was a major influence. Following four years in the air force, McChesney earned an undergraduate degree at Southern Methodist University and a master's in American literature at Stanford. From there it was an easy jump to a teaching job at Antioch College in Yellow Springs, Ohio, where he fell in with the crowd at WYSO, the local public radio station. This was the life he had been seeking, and soon enough he was producing documentaries. When his girlfriend (Jo Anne Wallace, the WYSO manager) got a job at WGBH in Boston, he followed her, cranking out pieces for the competition, WBUR. Cohen found him there, bringing him to Washington in December 1979.

McChesney's assignment was to create a national desk that would cover all of America. "I wanted us to have roots in the boondocks of the country," he said later. "I wanted us to cover the lives of ordinary people. We weren't doing that." But as his odd title—*acquisitions* editor—suggested, he faced difficult issues peculiar to NPR. The reporters in the M Street bureau were more interested in governmental news than events occurring in the heartland, and the network's member stations were incapable of providing solid work on a consistent basis. So McChesney would have to take what he could from the DC reporters and member stations while building a system of bureaus from which the main office would *acquire* most of its stories—and he would have to do it on the cheap. His budget was miniscule.

The problem was not insurmountable, especially if an editor was willing to exploit young and impressionable journalists, and McChensey, for all his radical credibility, had no qualms. ("I came out of the community radio movement where people didn't make shit," he recalled.) With Cohen's approval, he engaged five contract employees working for next to nothing. In Salt Lake City, there was Howard Berkes, a kid from back east who as a volunteer at KLCC in Eugene, Oregon, had done network-quality pieces for *All Things Considered* on the May 1980 eruption of Mount Saint Helens. To help Scott Simon in Chicago, there was Jacki Lyden, a twenty-four-year-old who'd been turning out superior stuff for WKQX, the local NBC affiliate. To replace Leo Lee in San Francisco there was Laurie Garrett, a young Cal Berkeley graduate with a deep knowledge of science. What these and the others (America Rodriguez in Los Angeles, Ellin O'Leary in Berkeley) had in common was an ambition to become serious broadcasters that superseded a desire or need to make a decent living. McChesney offered them roughly $9,000 a year with no health insurance, no overtime, and an unrelenting production quota. Compared with the $22,500 starting salaries AFTRA had negotiated for reporters back at M Street, it was appalling.

For NPR, the Acquisitions Unit produced an immediate journalistic windfall. In its first year, the operation would bring in 1,400 stories for *All Things Considered* and *Morning Edition*—more than triple the number contributed in 1979 by member stations alone. As for the reporters who did the bulk of work, they got to cover the sort of news that the commercial networks assigned to established stars. Berkes produced pieces on the

Sagebrush Rebellion that would lead former California governor Ronald Reagan to the White House and the Mormon Church's opposition to the Equal Rights Amendment. Lyden explored the travails facing the steel industry, spending weeks in Ohio to do a profile of the Youngstown Sheet and Tube Company, and she turned out a two-part documentary for *All Things Considered* about life inside a federal maximum-security prison in Marion, Illinois. On the few occasions that one of McChesney's underpaid reporters protested, their boss scoffed. According to Berkes, he would say, "Hey, you're working for a national news organization, and you're young and you're green. So don't complain."

Practically overnight, McChesney made NPR a power in national news. "He could find good reporters and get them to the right places," Neal Conan said later. "He understood logistics and how to get people to file." The miracle was that he did it all through sheer force of personality. "He was bluff," explained Conan, "and he was always right." Steve Reiner put it more vividly: "John wore his balls hanging down to the floor."

The volume of material flowing into M Street was enormous, and to get it into broadcast shape Mankiewicz freed up sufficient funding to start hiring editors and production assistants. This incoming class consisted primarily of people approaching thirty who'd spent their postcollege years toiling in obscure media outposts. From North Dakota came twenty-eight-year-old John Ydstie, the son of a Lutheran minister who'd first won attention in public radio circles with a project called "Our Home Town" undertaken for KCCM in Moorhead, Minnesota, at the direction of Bill Siemering, who following his comeuppance at NPR and a few months of confusion had landed there. From KERA in Dallas, where he'd been filing stories for the network about Texas, came Steve Proffitt. A droll Louisianan, Proffitt would work for McChesney before switching to *Morning Edition*, where he would produce feature pieces and Bob Edwards's interviews. Others—John Hockenberry, a determined, wheelchair-bound newscaster from Oregon's KLCC; Frank Browning, a freelance magazine journalist from Kentucky by way of San Francisco; Celeste Wesson, a producer from South Carolina by way of WBAI in New York—soon followed.

For the old-timers at National Public Radio—themselves mostly in their late twenties—the reinforcements had started to arrive. Deborah Amos, a diminutive, twenty-eight-year-old who directed *Weekend All Things Considered*, was overjoyed. A refugee from local TV in Tampa and Orlando, where she'd suffered the indignities of cameramen who got a kick out of mooning women reporters while they were on the air, she was searching for colleagues who shared her commitment to ambitious radio storytelling. Bill Buzenberg, a Kansan who'd joined the network in 1978 after a stint in the Peace Corps and a couple of years as a reporter for the Colorado Springs *Gazette*, was also ecstatic. A straight-news reporter, he, too, harbored high ambitions and knew he could not achieve them until NPR reached critical mass.

Young, brainy, upper middle class, politically liberal, artistically adventurous, and typically white, the NPR archetype was taking shape. Recalled Steve Proffitt, "You walked through this lobby into this place where smart, funky, long-haired people were making radio. It felt like becoming part of an exclusive group."

To join Mankiewicz's NPR was like joining a religious order. "We were on some sort of crusade," Amos recalled. "We were in this new project." It demanded a mendicant's devotion. "We just worked," Bill Drummond said later. Nearly all who signed on during this period saw themselves as radio missionaries and 2025 M Street, its drably modern sterility notwithstanding, as a temple. The studios where the hosts fronted the shows were cigarette-smoke-suffused pulpits. The second-floor news bureau, with its IBM Selectric typewriters and three-ply carbon typing paper, constituted a college of reportorial cardinals. In an adjacent area walled off from the others by filing cabinets was the inner sanctum shared by Linda Wertheimer, Nina Totenberg, and Cokie Roberts. The women not only enjoyed pride of place but they also boasted a sofa, a grungy gold barge where they received visitors and from which they berated meddlesome editors. They relished being known as "the troika," although after some testy dealings with them during the first months of *Morning Edition*, Drummond, improving on a phrase from Henry Miller's *Tropic of Capricorn*, came up with a more pointed moniker: "the Fallopian Jungle." The coinage was meant to be derogatory, but the trio, far from being offended, viewed it as further testimony to their power.

The stories that appeared on *All Things Considered* and *Morning Edition* were assembled in the edit booths—five off the lobby and two more upstairs. In these cramped cells outfitted with phones, tape reels, and Scully reel-to-reel machines set atop tables, the monks of NPR—engineers, producers, and sound editors—toiled for hours on end, playing and rewinding sections of quarter-inch Ampex tape (the network went through ten pancakes of the stuff daily) on which reporters recorded their actualities (ax) and narrations (trax). When the whizzes got a sequence just as they wanted, they marked the spot with a grease pencil and ran the tape onto a block, where they made diagonal cuts with a razor blade to excise superfluous material. They then reattached the loose ends with splicing tape, pressing them together with their thumbnails. Potentially usable outtakes—called breaths, because they featured exhales or other brief bits of audio that might be needed to flesh out a story—were affixed to the walls, but they often fell to the floor, which meant that on deadline someone was typically on their hands and knees going through discards searching for the element that could make a piece perfect. The process of getting a finished story onto a reel was agonizing ("Notch me, sync me, roll me off," ran the lyrics Proffitt wrote to memorialize it), accomplished only with concentration and—those razor blades—an occasional bloody finger. Even when the job was done it wasn't finished.

Due to the way 2025 M Street was laid out, the edit booths were some distance from the studios. To get a story to its destination an editor or producer had to grab the relevant tape reel and clutching it like a football bolt down halls and around corners. (Smokey Baer, who claimed just partly in jest that he could "edit faster than anybody who could edit better and better than anybody who could edit faster," was by all accounts the greatest of these broken-field runners.) "There wasn't a day when I was doing *All Things Considered* that somebody wasn't racing tape reels to the studio as people slammed doors and tried to get out of the way," Reiner said later.

Immersive! Suffocating! Nurturing! Working at NPR in the early 1980s was an all-encompassing experience. "It was hard to have a conversation with someone who wasn't a part of it," recalled Drummond, "because they could have no idea what it was like or what happened to you. The intensity of the production process didn't translate." Added Proffitt: "It was insular. Essentially your whole life was at M Street," which explains why when Nippers—as staffers had begun to call themselves—actually had a night off, they preferred their own company to that of outsiders. They ate dinner together, vacationed together, and many of them lived together, two or three per house, mostly in the raffishly hip Adams Morgan neighborhood, although Reiner and two more recent arrivals—Jim Angle, who'd come from the Longhorn Radio Network in Austin, Texas, to be national editor of *All Things Considered*, and Bill Abbott, a University of New Mexico grad who'd taken a job as a producer on *Weekend All Things Considered*—rented an old mansion in Arlington, Virginia. The parties at these addresses ranged from current-events talkfests—the hostage crisis sustained many a drunken conversation—to dance marathons, mostly to Motown and Bruce Springsteen. The Nippers ignored the wave of punk rock crashing onto America's shores. They were attracted to the things they knew and, naturally, to each other.

"We were all in bed with each other," Deborah Amos recalled. "Everybody," Bill Drummond added, "was fucking everybody else." The proximity of so many young, single journalists, most of them new to Washington and everyone caught up in Mankiewicz's adventure, turned 2025 M Street into a hothouse. For some, it was an awakening; for others it was a continuation of college. "If you were working together all hours," Proffitt later said, "then went home to a communal house with the same men and women, you slept with them."

The edit booths—the claustrophobic sarcophagi where by day NPR staffers made radio magic—became by night where those same staffers trysted. The booths were windowless and the doors locked. "It was the only place in the building where you could be completely private," recalled Robert Malesky.

What amorous reporters and producers gained in convenience and seclusion they lost in comfort, not to mention ambience. Making it in an NPR edit booth required flexibility and, if a couple was lucky, a woman wearing a skirt. The rooms were just too small for two people to remove their pants simultaneously without stepping on feet or ripping fabric. But if the woman was suitably dressed, all she had to do was drop her panties, scoot her bottom onto the edge of the table that held the Scully, and everything else followed—sort of. The more passionate the encounter, the greater became the danger. There was a high chance that to keep from falling one party or the other would accidentally hit the Scully's "on" switch, engaging its roller pins, after which sprockets began whirring and tape reels flying as if in mechanical counterpoint to the intimate encounter: notch me, sync me, roll me off, indeed. Some silenced the machine—others, glad for the cover the sound provided, laughed and kept going.

If a couple wanted more spacious accommodations, they typically repaired to Studio B, a little-used recording facility in the M Street basement. It was roomy and carpeted but worrisomely out in the open. Getting there required walking through the lobby, and soon enough fellow staffers would be saying, "Those two are doing the Studio B."

Some of these liaisons produced significant relationships. Deborah Amos paired off with Noah Adams, who had begun hosting *Weekend All Things Considered*; Bill Abbott started going with a producer named Katie Davis. To sanction those couples who took the next step and exchanged vows, Susan Stamberg created a registry of NPR brides and grooms. In due course, the network's long-wed standard-bearer would enter many names in her book, but in the short term, she was not especially busy. As Proffitt recalled, "Boy A and Girl A would be together for a while, and Boy B would be with Girl B. Then Boy A would take up with Girl B. It was kind of like swapping."

The frenetic nature of life at National Public Radio could explain only part of what was occurring. Under Mankiewicz the network itself had become sexy. Where a few years before *All Things Considered* had to go begging to secure guests, it now had plenty of takers, as did *Morning Edition*. NPR was emerging as a font of power in a city where power and desire are interchangeable. Not only did this give the network's young staffers a heightened sense of their allure, but it made them something of a commodity. "To be on NPR at this point in my career became very cool," recalled David Ensor, who'd been covering the state department for the network since 1975. "NPR got onto the radar screen of the twentysomething women in DC, and that was a good thing for me. All of a sudden it was hot and cold running girls."

Communique was Barbara Cohen's bid to make NPR a factor in international news. A weekly, single-subject foreign-affairs program, it featured a revolving group of hosts, among them Simon Winchester, Washington correspondent for London's *Daily Mail*; Morton Kondracke, a senior editor at the *New Republic*; and Sanford Ungar, an editor of *Foreign Policy*. Each figured in Washington's media hierarchy, but none enjoyed as much cachet

as the program's consultant. The daughter of former British prime minister James Callaghan and the wife of the former British ambassador to the
United States, Margaret Jay circulated in a world of diplomats and celebrities. Blond and tall, she was also literate and smart, and Cohen hired her to
help *Communique*'s producer, Jeff Rosenberg, give the show a plugged-in
quality. There was, however, a problem. Jay didn't understand sound production, so Rosenberg assigned Geri Pizzi, an NPR editor, to implement
Jay's vision. The two women spent hours each day in one of the M Street
edit booths, Jay listening to tape and Pizzi cutting, splicing, and answering
the telephone, which rang constantly, the male voice on the other end of the
line always asking for Jay and Pizzi always saying as she passed the handset:
"It's Carl."

Carl was the *Washington Post* reporter Carl Bernstein, husband of Nora
Ephron, friend of Cohen, buddy of Mankiewicz. Unbeknownst to almost
everyone in Washington but Pizzi—who continued to edit tape as the conversations grew intimate—Bernstein was conducting an affair with Jay. The
most famous journalist in America was making nonstop booty calls at NPR.

The Ear at the *Washington Star* broke the story in early 1980. A frenzy
ensued. In a reference to the boldfaced alliance that was the Bernstein-
Ephron marriage, *People* magazine crowed: "What the media had brought
together, the media last week was rapidly putting asunder." The whole thing
was sad. When Ephron discovered that Bernstein was cheating on her, she
was seven months pregnant with her second child. ("He had the affair in
the last stages," an unnamed friend told *People*. "She figured if that is what
he is like now, what will he be like later?") Jewish and raven haired, Ephron
was the cultural and physical antitheses of the Anglican, straw-maned Jay.
But in *Heartburn*, her roman à clef about it all, Ephron took her revenge,
describing the character based on Jay as "a fairly tall person with a neck as
long as an arm and a nose as long as a thumb, and you should see her legs,
never mind her feet, which are sort of splayed." Many at M Street regarded
the episode as titillating.

Along with the sex at National Public Radio came the drugs. "Damn near
everybody in the organization was doing coke," recalled John McChesney.
All Things Considered producer Chris Koch was more emphatic: "There was

an epidemic." Astonishingly, many users were out in the open, placing their orders over 2025 M Street's intercom. Producers in an edit booth craving a hit or hosts in a studio seeking the same would punch 77 on the phone, accessing the building-wide public-address system. They would then speak into the mouthpiece: "Leo del Aguila, call 6492. Leo del Aguila, call 6492."

A Peruvian-born engineer, Leo del Aguila was twenty-five, and at first glance appeared to be a member of an endangered species. Long haired and bearded, he favored blue jeans and orange-and-red tie-dyed T-shirts purchased at Up against the Wall, a Georgetown head shop that doubled as a clothier. His wardrobe was about as wild as NPR got during the twilight of the Carter administration. Yet Leo (short for Leonidas) was not just the network's last hippie. A member of a well-connected Lima family, he was a person of depth and sophistication, fluent in Spanish, Portuguese, and, although he still spoke with a heavy accent, English. He had moved to the United States just ten years earlier, when he and his parents received political asylum following Peru's 1968 coup. After graduating from high school, he spent two years in the US Army. Still, del Aguila was probably best taken at face value.

In the mid-1970s, Georgetown University, where del Aguila enrolled following his discharge, was home to the most politically anarchic and culturally transgressive student radio station in America—WGTB. The Georgetown outlet had supported the Vietcong during the Vietnam War; urged Patricia Hearst, after she joined her captors in the Symbionese Liberation Army, to help overthrow the police state; and, most heretical for a Jesuit school, advocated abortion rights. The station featured a playlist that ran from Captain Beefheart and Frank Zappa to Miles Davis.

WGTB endured several FCC investigations into allegations of broadcasting obscenity and in 1975 drew public condemnation from former vice president Spiro Agnew, who told the *New York Times Magazine*: "The voice of . . . Communism is pervasive in academia. WGTB in Washington broadcasts what seems to be propaganda for the third world."

All of which made the Georgetown station, in the minds of its listeners, a treasure. With an audience of around 100,000, WGTB employed a stable of outsize personalities—many of whom adopted on-air monikers and most of whom could claim an element of fame. In news, there was John Walsh, better known as "Abalone," who while capable of inspired work (his stories on the Wounded Knee standoff were excellent), was also capable of reporting that the US Air Force had launched a bombing attack on Libya—a gross fabrication that he justified by asserting that the American government *wanted* to bomb Libya. In music, there was Leo del Aguila, better known as Professor Marijuana, or, en Español, Profesor Mota.

Del Aguila, who held down the morning DJ slot, was the voice of radio free cannabis in the DC area. "He was so charismatic," recalled Skip Pizzi, the WGTB programming director at the time and one of the many station veterans who would later land at NPR, "that we soon had him emceeing the live concerts WGTB sponsored." It was at these events—some on the Copley Lawn, a leafy expanse at the center of the Georgetown campus, others at Lisner Auditorium at nearby George Washington University—that del Aguila became an underground hero.

Just minutes before shows began, del Aguila would strut onstage with the spaced-out insouciance of Cheech and Chong but in a getup all his own. Atop his head he wore a mortar board—a nod to the academic element of his on-air persona—while in his hands he clutched the business end of a car-battery jumper cable into which he'd inserted a rolled-up wand of newsprint. The world's largest roach clip and biggest reefer. The professor, Profesor Mota, was in the classroom. While bantering with the crowd, del Aguila would light the joint and in a cry that even years later could conjure his presence to those who had been there exclaim, "I've got a party in my pants!" Then he would introduce the night's headliner.

By 1980, the party Profesor Mota was throwing at NPR headquarters had expanded from a small affair ("At first," he recalled, "someone might say, 'I hear you've got something tasty, can you get me some?'") into a full-blown bash. Del Aguila was moving several ounces of cocaine and a significant amount of marijuana through the building each month. With the coke going for $100 a gram and the grass for $60 an ounce, it was easily a $100,000-a-year business. Del Aguila charged only a $10 markup on each sale "In those days I don't think you thought of making money. It was, 'Let's all have fun.'"

Del Aguila's supplier, a painter in rural Virginia, was a steady guy with a seemingly limitless access to "great quality coke and good pot." When a new shipment arrived, Leo would drive out in his 1979 Honda Prelude. Back in the city, he would use a pharmaceutical scale to measure packages by weight (he never cut the goods with borax or any other medium; he purveyed only quality) and transfer them to a leather shoulder pouch he carried with him everywhere and in which he also kept his wallet, an address book, and assorted drug paraphernalia. Then it was off to M Street. Del Aguila was one of the top engineers at NPR. He had started in 1978 on *All Things Considered* with Susan Stamberg and Bob Edwards and branched out to supervising classical concerts from Heinz Hall in Pittsburgh and the Kennedy Center in DC. When his name was called over the M Street public-address system, he would disappear into a studio or maybe an office and consummate a deal. Many staffers relied on him. "That's where I would go," said Bob Edwards.

That cocaine was del Aguila's best-selling product was no surprise. Although a few NPR reporters were in the habit of repairing to the M Street roof to smoke a joint at the end of the day, grass was ultimately too debilitating. Toot, however, could take you wherever you wanted to go. There was nothing like snorting lines while wrestling with a complex story that required dozens of precise cuts and aural nuances. It was like ingesting a focusing device that enhanced one's powers of calibration. Besides, the tools of radio production—hard, flat surfaces and razor blades—just so happened to be the tools of blow. Much of the consumption at M Street occurred inside those notorious edit booths, and the sanctioned method was to cut the coke into lines on the table that held the Scully, although some preferred to unscrew a tape reel (they came apart into two pieces), lay one platter flat, and cut on the pristine aluminum surface near the hub. "People actually got quite skillful putting a small amount of coke there," del Aguila said later. There was no need to confine one's consumption to the office, and many of NPR's users didn't. "There was coke at every party," added del Aguila, remarking of one zestful coworker: "He was a maniac. He loved cognac, and he loved doing a few lines. You know, we all did."

The list of users was long. Of the four hundred staffers at NPR, Deborah Amos estimated that 25 percent indulged. Del Aguila put it at 30 percent. Regardless, someone in every department was getting loaded. At *Morning Edition*, there were Edwards, the arts producer Robert Malesky, and the editor Steve Proffitt. At *All Things Considered* there was Chris Koch. Noah Adams, host of *Weekend All Things Considered*? Yes. Scott Simon, Chicago reporter? Yes. John McChesney, acquisitions editor? Yes. The question was not so much who was using as who was not. As del Aguila later noted: "Of the group that was my peers, my age," more were than weren't.

The party in NPR's pants seemed like it might go on forever, but almost out of nowhere worrisome portents began to appear, the first of which was a parade of strangers into M Street. "Word had gotten out on the street that toot was available at NPR," recalled del Aguila. "People from outside the building started coming in and making inquiries. I thought to myself, 'This is dangerous.'" Even more ominous for the network's main dealer (business was so good that there were also a couple of smaller operators), someone ransacked his apartment. "I had nothing there, God bless," del Aguila said. "But the trauma of having someone break into your place on a drug quest" was upsetting.

The realization started to arise among some at NPR that cocaine, while not technically addictive, could get its hooks into you. "Many of the people we worked with developed a dependency," remembered del Aguila. "We saw some people get fucked up," said McChesney. "They got paranoid. A production assistant on *Morning Edition* got messed up." Where network staffers once couldn't wait to get their hands on more blow, they were now reassessing. "People started saying, 'This is not worth it,'" added McChesney. "'The short rush is not worth it.'"

Yet as a combination work stimulant and powdered late-night fun gun, cocaine presented a powerful temptation. In mid-1980, when the *All Things Considered* staff decamped to Texas for a week of remote broadcasts from Austin member station KUT, blow awaited them, not to mention lots of booze. ("Chris Koch and I went in a rental car to pick up Susan [Stamberg] at her hotel, and she opened the glove compartment and there was a quart of Wild Turkey," said McChesney. "She just shut it back up and said, 'Boys.'") The trip was a success, so much so that Frank Mankiewicz flew in for a celebratory dinner. That's when things started to unravel.

"We were all sitting around a long conference table drinking wine," recalled Koch, "when one of the producers came in and sat down—and he had a lot of powder in his mustache. Somebody leaned over and said, 'Bob [his name wasn't Bob], you've got some powdered sugar in your nose.' Well, Mankiewicz picked this up, obviously saw this, because it was just totally obvious at the table. And Mankiewicz didn't say a word. Not a word was said."

A snort here or there didn't bother the NPR president. What he wanted to know was whether someone was dealing coke at M Street. Mankiewicz, according to Frank Fitzmaurice, had heard rumors "that Leo was selling drugs out of the building, and he began agitating to find out if that was true. He agitated anyone he talked to." Soon enough, he found out. "Mankiewicz knew," recalled del Aguila.

The story grows opaque here. According to one camp, Mankiewicz had received information that a law enforcement agency was planning to raid 2025 M Street. "It was the FBI or the DC police," recalled McChesney. According to another camp, however, Mankiewicz concocted the prospect of a raid out of thin air. "Mankiewicz started a rumor" that the DEA was opening an investigation, said Koch. "Instead of calling people in or having a meeting or getting drug research," he sent "word out that the DEA was gonna bust a bunch of NPR employees." Lending weight to Koch's version was that by nature Mankiewicz disliked playing according to the rules and by political training understood that the best way to handle a dilemma he didn't want to see reported in the *Washington Post* was to traffic in illusions. That way there were no fingerprints. In other words, he was exactly the sort who would have fabricated a bogeyman in the hopes that it would put the fear of God in his staff. Whichever version is accurate, it reached its intended target. There was, said del Aguila, "the possibility of a crackdown. Once that got out it was trouble to me. There was bad karma. I stopped."

With the primary source of supply dried up, drug use at NPR was over. "It ended, and it ended abruptly," recalled McChesney. Everybody just went back to work. No one lost his job, and no one was arrested. Most remarkably, not a hint of the network-wide binge made the newspapers, and only a few beyond M Street suspected that anything untoward had occurred. The lone casualty was a diminishing interest in the calls piped over the public-address system. A message for Linda Wertheimer or Cokie Roberts to meet a producer in a studio or edit booth just didn't generate the same thrill as a message for Profesor Mota.

Three forces saved National Public Radio from the scandal that would have ensued had the rampant cocaine abuse continued. One was the deftness

of Frank Mankiewicz. Another was that despite the extent of the problem, it
was transitory. "It was a fad," Bob Edwards later observed. Just as the arrest
of Doug Terry at the antiwar protest outside the White House had been emblematic of the early 1970s, and the dissension sparked by the psychobabble
of Engelman and Symonds had been characteristic of the decade's middle
years, the drugs were emblematic of the early 1980s. This was an emerging
truth about NPR: not only did its contents mirror the times, so, too, did
its internal dynamics. When the times changed, the behavior changed with
them. "We moved on," Edwards added. There was also, however, something
else. Although nearly ten years had passed since Bill Siemering left the network, the sense of purpose he'd bestowed remained the biggest part of the
culture. "Drugs were not the central pastime there," noted John McChesney.
"They offered a form of relief" from the pressure, and that's all.

At *Morning Edition*, everything was still an uphill fight. "Cokie, Linda, and
Nina were really committed emotionally to *All Things Considered*," recalled
Bill Drummond. "They thought *Morning Edition* was some kind of succu-
bus. They not only ignored us—they went out of their way to dis us." As a
consequence, Jay Kernis—who had started keeping normal business hours
in hopes of bringing a little stability to his show—became the beggar of M
Street. So desperate was he for usable material that most evenings after *ATC*
went off the air he would sidle up to Chris Koch or Steve Reiner.

"What pieces didn't you use tonight that you're not going to use tomorrow?" he would ask.

"Listen to this," Reiner would respond, then hand the *Morning Edition*
producer a tape containing a story that hadn't quite made the grade or an
interview that while having aired in part still had some fresh material.

Kernis would take *ATC*'s castoffs and retreat to an edit booth, where he'd
spend the next several hours, razor blade in hand, cutting and splicing until
he'd refashioned the discarded stories into usable ones. His vow was not to
leave work until he could assure himself that when combined with the pieces
his staff had received from McChesney's Acquisitions Unit these last-second
additions would compose a nearly finished program

Each episode of *Morning Edition* was a triumph of Kernis's will, yet in
the midst of this unending struggle, something unexpected occurred. The

producer and Bob Edwards formed a bond. "Bob had walls up all the time," Frank Fitzmaurice recalled, "but Jay broke through those walls just by being persistent. Bob was good at pushing people away. He would actually turn his back on you when you spoke to him, but Jay wouldn't take that and got Bob to do what he wanted him to do." What the producer wanted Edwards to do was dispense with the hard-bitten news guy routine that was his preferred demeanor and become a multifaceted network host, one who would make use of that incredible voice to bring emotion—joy, sadness, whatever—to the task of narrating the day's events. In his laconic way, Edwards was intrigued and when his cohost Barbara Hoctor departed the program for personal reasons, he decided in consultation with Kernis to fly solo, making what had at first been a temporary gig permanent. Bob became "a very good instrument for Jay," Susan Stamberg later said.

With Kernis as Professor Henry Higgins to Edwards's Eliza Doolittle, a radio star was born. "Jay helped Bob loosen up and show his human side," remembered Barbara Cohen. "He got stuff out of Bob and put him into situations Bob might not have naturally gravitated to. It all happened in Bob's office between eight and twelve each day, after *Morning Edition* went off the air. There was no big show-and-tell. Jay just worked to bring out in Bob what Jay saw was there."

Kernis also refused to let the troika intimidate him. He kept soliciting the women, in Fitzmaurice's words, "negotiating stuff with them that they would not otherwise have agreed to. Nobody else would have gotten them to do it, but Jay was able to sweet talk them and get them to produce stuff for the show." The women did not act out of charity. Rather, the awareness had dawned around NPR that listeners were increasingly tuning into *Morning Edition*. At first, the evidence was anecdotal, much of it supplied by Robert Krulwich, who had moved to New York to cover the financial markets and kept telling colleagues that his pieces for the a.m. show elicited more comments than ones for *All Things Considered*. Soon, the Arbitron ratings started to back up this view. By November 1980, a year after *Morning Edition*'s debut, stations that carried it had doubled their overall listenership. The program, which in its first week was picked up by only half the member outlets, was now airing on 90 percent of them.

All Things Considered meanwhile affected a magisterial disdain for its younger sibling, but it, too, was undergoing a transformation. Now out front with Susan Stamberg was Sanford Ungar. He'd won the cohosting job vacated by Edwards on the strength of his work at *Communique* and his résumé. Before editing *Foreign Policy*, he had been a contributing editor at *The Atlantic* and a reporter at the *Washington Post*. Then there were his books—a major history of the FBI and, with Allan Priaulx, an account of the 1968 student rebellion in France: *The Almost Revolution.*

Barbara Cohen elevated Ungar to the top of *All Things Considered* for the same reason she had launched *Communique*—to boost NPR's coverage of international affairs. The move sparked grumblings at the network, where weekend *ATC* host Noah Adams had been the favorite for the position. "I think hiring me was an outrageous thing to do," Ungar recalled. "I wasn't of NPR. I was at NPR." Stamberg made a stab at welcoming her new partner ("He was bright, just incredibly bright," she later said), but she did not like him. "She thought he was stiff and didn't know radio," Cohen remembered. Moreover, Ungar—whose broad experience gave him a very un-Nipper-like edge—refused to bow to the network's leading lady. "I think she wanted to treat me like her puppy dog. Edwards had allowed her to do that, but I didn't."

Yet cohosts don't have to get along to work well together, and Stamberg and Ungar were a solid team. "I think at our best we were damn good," he recalled. Not only this, the foreign policy stories that Cohen had hoped for began to materialize, as Ungar pushed *ATC* toward more news from Europe, Asia, and Africa. He masterminded a half-hour feature on Liberia—a breakthrough for NPR at the time.

The biggest changes at *All Things Considered* originated from its producer. Because the network was so focused on the launch of *Morning Edition*, Chris Koch wielded more influence than had many of his predecessors. "We were actually very isolated as a unit," he said later. "We just did our own thing. I had a huge amount of power."

Koch used that power to make good on his vow to take *ATC* in unpredictable directions. Aided by a number of new editors and assistant producers—most, like him, refugees from the Pacifica network—he sought out stories that questioned authority. "Chris was an interesting combination," Ungar remembered. "He was partly this radical guy, yet he had some conservative instincts, some surprising instincts. He didn't buy the Democratic cant about a lot of things. He asked questions." That was refreshing at NPR, where people viewed the liberal agenda "as the revealed word—what you were supposed to think." Koch was a small-*d* democrat. "He always wanted to keep the small man's perspective," recalled Bill Abbott. "He said at one meeting, 'We hear about the stock market and how to invest, but I want to hear how someone without any money invests.'" The ultimate expression of Koch's sensibilities was his most controversial hire. A poet, author (*A Coat for the Tsar*), and writing teacher (novelist Richard Price was his best-known pupil), Richard Elman was a provocateur. He and Koch had been friends since 1962, when both worked at WBAI (they produced what for the time was a groundbreaking interview with a former FBI agent who asserted that the agency routinely invaded Americans' privacy). Elman turned his weekly commentary on *ATC* into a soapbox from which he castigated everything and everyone held sacred by the Right and the Left.

Just as *Morning Edition*'s audience was growing, so was *All Things Considered*'s. The show was pulling in a substantial listenership: 1.6 million a week. National Public Radio, however, offered more than just the two big productions. It now broadcast between fifty-five and sixty hours of programming weekly. Mankiewicz inaugurated a series of original radio dramas called *NPR Playhouse* that commissioned works from the likes of David Mamet and Arthur Kopit and transformed F. Scott Fitzgerald short stories into one-acts. He signed a deal for a production that had the potential to put NPR in a larger spotlight: A multipart adaptation of *Star Wars* featuring film cast members Mark Hamill and Anthony Daniels and originating from the University of Southern California–based KUSC. (George Lucas, a USC grad, sold the rights for one dollar because he was a fan of public radio.) Nearly four years into the job, the network chief felt at home. "I liked going to work every day," he later said. "There was steady progress." This was where NPR stood on November 4, 1980—Election Day.

During remarks at the National Press Club on March 26, 1981, two months after Ronald Reagan's inauguration as the fortieth president of the United States, Frank Mankiewicz startled a crowd of reporters with an unexpected announcement. If the "Program for Economic Recovery," the most radical

package of proposed budget changes since the Franklin D. Roosevelt administration, was adopted by Congress, NPR would cease operation in
October. *All Things Considered, Morning Edition*, and the rest would be
wiped out.

The network boss's assertion was a bluff. "When an agency is threatened
with a budget cut it will immediately announce curtailment of whatever service the public values most," observed Morton Kondracke, whose gig as a
contributor to *Communique* did not keep him from raising an eyebrow in
the *New Republic*. Yet Mankiewicz, for all his guile, was grappling with a
genuine challenge.

Reagan had identified eighty-three targets across multiple federal agencies—the FAA, the FCC, the EPA, and nearly all the others except those that
provided "essential safety nets"—for some $41.3 billion in reductions that he
maintained would lift the economy out of its Carter-era malaise. In the case
of the Corporation for Public Broadcasting, the proposed cuts were devastating. Declared the headline in *Broadcasting* magazine: "Reagan Transition's Verdict on CPB: Termination with Extreme Prejudice." Conservatives,
who generally despised public radio, applauded. "NPR is egregious because
it is so pretentious and ideological," Emmett Tyrrell had noted a few months
earlier in the *American Spectator*.

A six-member presidential panel recommended that Reagan kill the
Corporation for Public Broadcasting by canceling its $162 million annual
appropriation. The group asserted that the government had no business financing PBS and NPR. The networks should solicit support from their audiences and businesses.

To achieve Reagan's cuts, Congress would need to rescind funding that
had already been approved. Thanks to a system adopted during the Ford administration to insulate PBS and NPR from political meddling, the Corporation for Public Broadcasting received its allocations two years in advance,
meaning that the budget for 1982 had already been approved. The process
for clawing the money back would open what even the conservative *Chicago
Tribune* regarded as a "can of worms." Nonetheless, Reagan's advisers were
committed to abolishing the CPB, and if they succeeded, National Public
Radio would suffer the most damage—far more than PBS, which operated
largely at a local level and was somewhat immune from decisions made in

Washington. The feature that gave DC-centered NPR a solid foundation also made it vulnerable.

Although David Stockman, director of Reagan's Office of Management and Budget, eventually backed off the plan to defund the CPB entirely, his compromise proposal of a 25 percent cut still struck Mankiewicz as catastrophic. For the first time since arriving at M Street, the NPR chief began speaking of the network as a business, wondering if there were unexplored entrepreneurial possibilities for generating revenue. Mostly, however, he kept talking about what he talked about from the start—NPR's reporting. "People don't realize how narrow the ambition of commercial radio is," he told the *New York Times* for a story about the emerging crisis. "There isn't an analytical news show like *All Things Considered* anywhere else on radio." Mankiewicz's instinct was to fight the reductions by stressing what was at stake journalistically.

On the evening of April 23, 1981, as the Reverend Jim Jones could be heard raving, "How do you feel about it? You may die tonight," *Father Cares*, the most ambitious program of NPR's first decade, began pulsing outward from Westar I to radios all across America. The broadcast was more than just a documentary account of the 1978 mass murder-suicide by the messianic preacher and 909 of his followers at Jonestown, the failed utopia they had built in the jungle of Guyana. It featured recordings of Jones's descent into insanity and his congregation's zombielike capitulations to his increasingly deranged rants. Pieced together from nine hundred hours of tapes the preacher had made on a cassette machine secreted beneath a wooden throne from which he nightly regaled his flock, the program concluded with a fatal attack on a delegation of visiting Californians (among them Congressman Leo Ryan) and the ingestion by Jones's followers of cyanide-laced fruit punch shortly thereafter. A meditation on free will and an examination of the link between faith and fanaticism, the documentary resides in the realm of the senses. It is the sound of nearly one thousand lost souls preparing to lay down their lives for a madman who spoke to them, said one, "like no other man spoke before."

The events that led to *Father Cares* began three years earlier, when James Reston Jr., a creative writing teacher at the University of North Carolina and the son of Scotty Reston, the powerful Washington bureau chief of the *New York Times*, became obsessed with the tragedy at Jonestown. A week after the news broke, he was on a plane to South America and soon after at the crime scene. While the corpses had been removed, the site remained one of intense horror. The vision Reston could not get out of his mind was of the children's toys and clothing scattered in the brush surrounding Jonestown. Back in Chapel Hill, he needed therapy to deal with the resulting panic attacks, but he was certain that he'd found the story of a lifetime. He had learned of the tapes. On the strength of their existence he received an advance for a nonfiction book. There was, however, a problem. The FBI had taken charge of the recordings and ordered them classified. Reston filed a Freedom of Information Act request, which languished for fourteen months. The government's contention that the tapes involved national security made no sense to the writer. One night at his father's home, he laid out the story to Lloyd Cutler, general counsel to Jimmy Carter. Cutler responded that as a favor to Scotty he'd get the younger Reston five minutes with Attorney General Benjamin Civiletti. He declassified the material.

Reston spent the first weeks of 1980 working at the FBI's headquarters on Pennsylvania Avenue, where he began transcribing Jones's fulminations. A Communist as well as a man of God, the preacher declared that he was the subject of both political and religious persecution, and over time he persuaded his mesmerized parishioners that they were, too. Except for a few federal agents, Reston was the only person who had heard this. In the midst of his labors on his book, he experienced an epiphany. It happened as he was playing a recording of Jones verbally torturing one of his followers. Reston could not get the exchange onto paper. "Jones was brutally crushing this character," he recalled, "and I thought, 'I can't capture the feeling of the moment.'" He'd felt the same way about the photographs he'd seen of Jonestown. "Pictures constricted the event." Then the thought came to him: "This was an auditory experience. In life certain things happen that are perfect for one medium, and this was perfect for radio. It was listening that made the imagination run wild." Reston reached out to an old friend—Frank Mankiewicz. Reston had ghostwritten *Perfectly Clear: Nixon from Whittier to Watergate*, a 1973 book that appeared under Mankiewicz's byline.

"I walked over to NPR, went into Frank's office, and told him what I had,"

Reston said later. "Frank knew instantaneously that this was solid gold, and he gave me to Deborah Amos."

Three years into her job at *Weekend All Things Considered,* Amos was becoming one of NPR's most creative producers. Her show, in contrast to its at times overly serious daily namesake or the highly formatted *Morning Edition,* aired some of the most imaginative stories on the network. ("The executives left them alone on Saturdays," recalled Steve Proffitt.) NPR already boasted a history of ambitious documentaries. Back in 1973, Jim Russell had contributed *Phone Phreaks*—a one-hour investigation into the use of "blue boxes" to replicate dial tones that could provide free long-distance calling—and *Flight 401: The Night Fail-Safe Failed,* a reconstruction of a horrific 1972 Eastern Airlines crash into the Florida Everglades. Josh Darsa had directed *The Man with the White Cane,* a taut drama that told the story of Herman Porter, a seventy-five-year-old who fell off a subway platform in Chicago into the path of an onrushing train and survived. As with his news stories, Darsa's piece was theatrical: crowd noise, brakes screeching, and, most hauntingly, the tapping of a cane. Porter's dilemma was unique— he was blind. For *A Question of Place,* Robert Montiegel focused on writers (James Joyce, Robert Frost) and thinkers (Sigmund Freud). With *Father Cares,* Amos hoped to go further.

Amos was enthralled by the German radio documentarian Peter Leonhard Braun and his influential 1973 work *Bells in Europe.* From tapes of church bells recorded in the years before World War II and battlefield audio of exploding bombs cast from some of the same, melted-down bells, he'd brought to life the tragedy of peace devolving into global conflict. In 1979, Amos and Noah Adams traveled to Berlin's Sender Freies Studios to study with Brown. "They gave us recorders and we went out and recorded stuff," she recalled. "Then we came back and sat in booths and matched the ambience, learning how to integrate the tracks. It was serious radio production, and this was the only place that taught it." After returning to the states, Amos, Adams, and engineer Jim Anderson—styling themselves as AAA Productions—began making documentaries about American topics for NPR. In the spring of 1979 they produced a segment on the southern gothic novelist Harry Crews that caught his fierce sensibility and inimitable south-Georgia drawl. A few months later they produced an hour on the Firecracker 400 stock car race, for which Anderson positioned his equipment above the perilous first turn and at the risk of his eardrums captured the roar of hard-charging Dodges and Fords. Yet accomplished as these productions were, they were limited in that they lacked a key element: a narrative. That's what Amos was seeking.

Reston arranged for Amos's initial listening session to occur in his father's office in the Washington bureau of the *New York Times*. There he played her ten hours of recordings—"Jonestown's greatest hits," as he put it. As the two hovered over a tape machine, *Times* staffers gathered behind the door. "The sounds were bleeding out," Reston said afterward. "Everyone wanted to know what was going on."

Amos spent much of the summer of 1980 immersed in the nine hundred hours of tapes. Soon she could identify many of the voices by name. The dead were speaking to her. "My job was to structure the material, and I laid it out like an episode of *ATC*. I had an opening, a tease. I did a ninety-minute clock. I thought that was a good pacing mechanism." The results were encouraging, but as the documentary began to take form, Amos felt that the contents were so overwhelming that if presented in a predictable fashion they might seem unreal. "We decided to break with radio tradition," she recalled. In a conceit dreamed up by Reston, they invented an observer who along the lines of the stage manager in *Our Town* would tell the story. He would be an ex-member of People's Temple who'd extricated himself at the last second. Throughout, he would refer to Jones as Dad or Father. "There was a lot of guff about that," Reston later said. "Journalists are supposed to be objective voices from on high. But we didn't want a disembodied narrator." The assignment fell to Noah Adams, who had to take his voice down a notch to get the tone right. "The character is flat," he recalled. "There's no inflection whatsoever."

All involved in *Father Cares* were walking a fine line. Amos faced the task of organizing and condensing, Reston that of making sure the script didn't go over the top, Adams that of maintaining his laconic pose, and a phalanx of technicians and editors the responsibility of recording the narration and scoring and mastering the final product. Making matters doubly difficult, everyone continued to perform their day jobs at the network, meaning that most of the labor on the program was done after hours. Furthermore, no one received extra pay. The show cost a mere $15,000, the bulk going to Reston.

By early April, Amos was done, and Mankiewicz, believing that she'd delivered a near masterpiece, drafted PBS's Bill Moyers to host a nationwide call-in show after the program. As the date neared, People's Temple sympathizers issued death threats. KQED, NPR's San Francisco station, posted guards outside its studio. On the twenty-third, Mankiewicz booked a private room at Nora, a highly regarded Washington restaurant. Everyone was on edge. "A guy walked in," Adams recalled, "and said, 'I'm looking for the people who are working on the Jonestown program.' He had on a long coat. He could have had a sawed-off shotgun under it. He opened his coat. He didn't have a shotgun. He was just looking for his old college friend Bill Moyers."

Father Cares hit the airwaves at 9:00 p.m. By 10:20, Congressman Ryan was dead, the fruit drink ready. The available tapes did not contain the actual death throes, but even if they had, Amos said later, she would not have used them. This was not a snuff film. What she included was brutal enough. The final words belonged to Adams:

Dad climbed up into his chair. "I have tried to give you a good life." His voice was strong . . . perhaps the last power he could bring to himself as a savior. . . . Things had happened. The fascists would soon come in. . . . They better not find anyone alive. The line formed. The children were first, the seniors next. "Be kind to the seniors," Dad said. A few resisted. They were held down, the poison injected. Father had said it would not hurt. The screaming was not dignified, not Communistic. One man ran into the jungle and waited there perhaps two hours, listening to the wail of pain, slow to end, and then it was quiet. . . . Father's nurse found him on his pedestal, surrounded by his followers. . . . He had a fistful of barbiturates, but he would not or could not take the poison. And there, in the faint light, Father saw the woman, and he begged her to shoot him. She arranged his hands across his chest in a pious pose. She shot him in the left temple then she flung the weapon away in disgust.

The program was so unnerving that before NPR switched live to the Moyers call-in show, it broadcast the gentle sound of surf breaking on a beach, three minutes of soothing white noise.

The response to *Father Cares* was ecstatic. It won the duPont-Columbia

Award for best radio production of the year and the Prix Italia, the industry's highest international honor. There were naysayers. The BBC filed a protest with the Prix Italia judges contending that because Adams's narrator was a creative device, the program was more docudrama than documentary. Within NPR there were those who felt that the show was mannered and insensitive to the victims, portraying them as cattle as opposed to individuals. In the end, however, the supporters drowned out the critics, and the biggest rave appeared where Mankiewicz wanted, and it made the points he hoped someone would. Anthony Lewis wrote in the *New York Times*:

> *Father Cares* cannot conceivably have been done by any American broadcasting organization except National Public Radio. And it appears at a moment when the Reagan administration is trying to slash public broadcasting funds and, especially, kill all national programming—which would mean the end of NPR.
>
> It is impossible to believe that anyone who hears this program would want to eliminate public radio. The question is not one of ideology; it is one of civilization. . . . The public affairs programs of NPR provide information that Americans can get no other way—and they certainly cannot be done locally. The whole National Public Radio Budget is $21 million. This program cost . . . a derisory amount by commercial standards. Without it we could not understand what this century has seen more than once: Authentic evil.

The flaw in Frank Mankiewicz's notion that NPR's journalism provided its own best argument for continued public support didn't take long to reveal itself. Even as the accolades for *Father Cares* poured in, the network chief was dealing with the fallout from forty-five seconds of audio that *All Things Considered* had broadcast several weeks earlier.

The attempted assassination of Ronald Reagan outside the Washington Hilton on March 30 occurred only a couple of hours before the five p.m. airtime of *All Things Considered,* forcing Chris Koch to remake the show on the fly. He devoted the first half to a recapitulation of the afternoon's events— the shooting of the president and press secretary James Brady and the arrest of the suspect, John Hinckley Jr. He then went to reactions from people nationwide. "We interviewed Maureen Reagan," the producer recalled. "We interviewed Tip O'Neill." This was journalism by the book, but Koch was not a by-the-book producer. The next day he acquired a snippet of recorded conversation that had aired on a call-in show on Washington's Pacifica Station, WPFW. "I just had this habit," Gary Covino, an *All Things Considered* assistant producer, said later, "of recording the Pacifica National News." The tape featured an unidentified Black woman advancing an incendiary sentiment. No other network touched it, but Koch regarded it as newsworthy. Midway into that evening's edition of *ATC*, guest hosts Robert Krulwich and Noah Adams—Stamberg and Ungar were off—cut to the exchange:

"Hi, thanks for calling. You're on the air."

"I feel that the person that shot Reagan should have killed him," the woman began.

"Why do you feel he ought to have been killed?"

"Well," she explained, "I feel that Reagan is an unthoughtful person. I feel that he don't think, he don't care, you know, I just hate to hear the other policemens and other peoples being slaughtered and killed, but this man . . . can create a lot of hardship for a lot of people, especially Black people, and I'm sorry this man [Hinckley] is being incarcerated for something he tried to do. I wish he had succeeded."

Within minutes after NPR broadcast this charged dialogue, its offices filled with Secret Service agents searching for the tape. "They saw it as a threat against the president," Koch said later. The *All Things Considered* boss told the lawmen the recording had been erased, thereby shielding Covino. The Secret Service response would later be dismissed as excessive, but not so other reactions. The network's member stations, in Koch's words, "went bonkers." Barbara Cohen asked the *ATC* producer to hold a conference call with station managers from across the country to explain why he aired the material. "I got on and said, 'Listen, we don't make the news. We report it. There was a lot of Black anger expressed at Reagan when he was shot.' I won that one. Frank backed me." Listeners who complained to their congressmen were harder to placate. "The taped comment was sympathetic to the assassin," wrote one. "Such extremist positions should not be supported by taxpayers." Conservative columnists were incensed. "The folks at National Public Radio obviously travel in different circles than most of us," declared Reed Irvine of Accuracy in Media. "They obviously don't hold Ronald Reagan in high esteem." Mankiewicz spent days drafting conciliatory replies, noting that *All Things Considered* also broadcast interviews deploring the assassination attempt and stressing that "NPR is a private, nonprofit corporation" and that "neither I nor any other representative of National Public Radio support (or for that matter oppose) the points of view expressed on our news programs."

The controversy, occurring against the backdrop of the Reagan administration's efforts to defund the Corporation for Public Broadcasting, emphasized a worrisome truth that Mankiewicz had long known. Journalism is a volatile commodity. If one piece doesn't draw fire, another will. In May 1978, Jody Powell, Jimmy Carter's press secretary, attacked NPR for airing a Cokie Roberts story reporting that while discussing the sale of American warplanes to Egypt and Saudi Arabia, Hamilton Jordan, the president's chief of staff, allegedly vowed to "break the back of the Israeli lobby." Declaring the piece was untrue, Powell demanded a retraction; Mankiewicz, convinced that the piece was accurate, refused.

In late April 1981, Mankiewicz hit on an idea: Instead of imploring Congress to keep providing funding for NPR in the face of the Reagan budget cuts, he would wean the organization from federal support. The network chief, expanding on his thoughts of a few months earlier about entrepreneurial activities, envisioned a freestanding communications entity. There was a huge problem. Although NPR had implemented an underwriting operation (the biggest contributors were philanthropists Ted and Jennifer Stanley, whose names were intoned hourly on the network), it had limited success. Nonetheless, Mankiewicz had made up his mind. Having transformed NPR into a power in news, he would make it self-sufficient. For much of the rest of the year, a team of executives working for an in-house entity dubbed Project ASCOT (Audio Services through Cable and Other Technologies) explored the revenue possibilities of cable radio. The gist of the concept was that NPR, taking its cue from TV, could sell premium news and music programming by subscription. This venture, however, failed to come together. Mankiewicz decided to think bigger. In November, spurred by an increasing urgency for action (Congress's final vote on CPB funding left the network facing a $7.2 million shortfall for 1983), he said that NPR was prepared to pursue "every profession except the oldest one." The line was classic Mankiewicz—sassy and vague. But it conveyed his aspirations.

Beneath banners declaring "Public Radio Means Business" and amid shouts of "Off the Fix by '86!" NPR unveiled Project Independence at the April 1982 Public Radio Conference in the ballroom of Washington's Grand Hyatt Hotel. Frank Mankiewicz told the gathering of station managers, board members, and executives that the nonprofit network, rather than hunker down "like a jackrabbit in a hailstorm," would enter the for-profit arena. "You better watch out, we're serious," he declared before introducing Tom Warnock, who following the Frischnkecht debacle had become an NPR vice president and was the architect of the network's new financial strategy. A public radio insider who in his quiet, studious manner was the perfect foil to his grandiloquent boss, Warnock conceded that it was "schizophrenic" to embark on a bold program during funding cuts, but he assured the room that the network was not putting itself in danger.

Project Independence embraced a number of enterprises. The most audacious was NPR Ventures, which itself comprised multiple elements, each designed to take advantage of the network's greatest technical asset. Westar IV, which had replaced Westar I and now transmitted *All Things Considered* and NPR's other shows, was an unexploited resource. As had been the case two years earlier when the network went on satellite, it still broadcast over just a few of its allotted channels, keeping the remaining ones free for future use. The future had arrived. Corporations hoping to disseminate stock reports, sports scores, inventory and sales figures, and news items coveted access to this excess capacity. Westar IV had the potential to be the money-minting master blaster of the information age.

As opposed to already-existing outfits such as CompuServe and the Source (CompuServe offered an electronic edition of the *New York Times*, the Source UPI stories and restaurant guides), NPR Ventures would not have to rely on sluggish AT&T landlines to send information. Once a customer beamed data to Westar IV, the satellite would relay it to member stations that would distribute it to specific locations and individuals by radio.

FM signals feature built-in subcarriers. Usually reserved for services such as reading for the blind, they could also lend themselves to wide, general use. The only device a business or home consumer would need was a modem to unscramble the signal so it appeared as text on a computer terminal, voice and music over a speaker or, via a printer, hard copy. NPR was offering both dissemination and delivery.

The gaudiest of the Ventures was called INC and was backed by Jack Taub. An emerging player in high tech (he'd parlayed a stamp catalog publisher into ownership of the Source, selling it to *Reader's Digest* for $4 million), he persuaded NPR to let him broker most of the unused space on Westar IV to retail chains that wanted to send overnight price changes to stores. The way the deal was set up, the network owned 20 percent of the business and would receive payments over a twenty-five-year period totaling $87.5 million. In return, NPR gave Taub a majority position and a $500,000 fee. Both sides were thrilled. At a press conference, Taub asserted, INC "will be a total communications company that may well trigger an information explosion." Mankiewicz added that by the mid-1980s the network would be earning $5 million annually. Lending credence to the boasts was the presence of the two men who would get things going. Kemmons Wilson, the founder of Holiday Inn, would handle franchising. He envisioned what he called "data hotels" in cities with NPR stations. They would serve as outlets where customers could buy the necessary hardware. A bigger name would create the software—Steve Wozniak. Following a 1981 airplane crash that left him badly shaken, the Apple computer cofounder had split with his partner Steve Jobs and was dabbling in everything from promoting rock concerts (the US Festival) to taking college classes. Wozniak was excited to be joining forces with NPR, and was entranced by the thought of distributing data over its satellite. "It's such a simple and efficient system and so obvious that you wonder why it hasn't been done before," he told a reporter.

NPR Ventures also boasted partnerships with Dataspeed, a Silicon Valley firm pioneering efforts to transmit information to handheld devices, and Codart, another Bay Area concern, this one offering audiences the ability to automatically record broadcasts onto cassettes for later listening. "NPR Goes on Line," boomed the cover of *InfoWorld* magazine. The less cutting-edge facets of NPR Ventures were also critical to the network's survival. A foray into satellite radio, called NPR Plus, would provide classical music twenty-four hours a day, seven days a week, six evenings a week of jazz shows, and hourly news updates on both. This immense undertaking would triple the amount of programming produced by the network. Member stations seeking to broaden their audiences would pay the bill. The projected return the first year: $1 million.

Finally, there was the most vital component, NPR Fund Raising. Earlier in the spring, the network's board had voted to hire a vice president of development whose job, in the short term, would be to supervise applications for foundation grants, one for a projected $4.5 million and another for $5 million spread out over three years. In the long term this executive would strengthen the network's underwriting operation, transforming *All Things Considered*, *Morning Edition*, and features like *Star Wars* into profit centers.

Project Independence was staggeringly ambitious. Not only did it need to get NPR over the $7.2 million hump in 1983 but it was laying the foundation for the empire Mankiewicz contemplated. "Frank stated to me that he didn't want to preside over a period of retrenchment," Warnock recalled. "He wanted to overcome this. He wanted to take a shot at replacing the money from CPB while figuring out a way to continue growing. It was absolutely a good idea." The NPR board approved the plan, as did the consulting firm McKinsey & Company in a network-commissioned report distributed during the Grand Hyatt conference. As Robert Siegel later put it, "McKinsey koshered the nuts."

Frank Mankiewicz was back on the hustings. "The campaign is coming along pretty well. Why not? We've got a good candidate," he told *People* magazine in a story headlined "A Rebel with Causes Rides to the Rescue of America's Endangered Public Radio." Mankiewicz devoted some energy to seeking support on Capitol Hill (toward that end, he hired the PR firm that had once employed Reagan's deputy chief of staff, Michael Deaver), but he channeled most of his time into winning over the men and women without whom he could not undertake his dream. "The bottom line was to convince the stations that this was worth pursuing," Warnock recalled. "We were faced with this loss of income from the Corporation for Public Broadcasting. There were a bunch of people in the field who thought we should just knuckle under."

For the remainder of 1982, Mankiewicz, usually accompanied by Warnock,

Sam Holt, and David Brugger (a CPB official who supervised the disburse-
ment of funds to NPR), would jet off to regional gatherings of public radio
executives to sell them on Project Independence. The sessions put the network
chief in the awkward position of having to curry favor with people he privately
mocked and, on occasion, had offended. (Before speaking to such a group a
few years earlier, he'd peeked from behind the stage curtain, assessed the audience, and cracked to his host, "It looks like a Diane Arbus photograph out
there," after which the host, ignorant of Arbus's grotesque oeuvre, repeated the
comment in her introduction, forcing Mankiewicz to use all of his considerable charisma to smooth things over.) Yet he was now on his best behavior.

Mankiewicz's pitch to the member stations was a combination of money
and magic. The money, while it might not have sounded like a lot in the
commercial world, struck the struggling yeomen of public radio as potential manna from heaven. From NPR Ventures alone, the network chief told
every gathering, small-market stations would earn $6,000 to $15,000 a
year, while major market outlets would pull in $30,000 to $75,000. As for
what was to be had from the other branches of Project Independence, the
figures were speculative but the possibilities were dizzying. "They were very
high," recalled Brugger, "like twenty-two million dollars the first year," which
would cover both the $7.2 million shortfall and reimburse the stations for
the costs of features like NPR Plus. "There would be so much left over that
NPR would be able to return money to the stations."

The magic was the main attraction. Black and sleek and about the size
of a paperback novel, the prototype QuoTrek that Dataspeed had provided
for the presentations was a showstopper. Outfitted with a liquid crystal
screen, the device, Mankiewicz informed audiences, would enable users to
download market data, weather reports, ball scores, and news bulletins from
Westar IV. Not only that, but it came equipped with a "smart" modem that
would allow them to send messages over the phone to other subscribers. The
NPR chief claimed to hold in his hands the instrument that would transform
the communications world. The gizmo "was very pretty and very sophisticated," recalled Warnock. "It had alerts that would pop up if a stock you were
following went higher or lower." According to Dataspeed, it would cost just
$400 and go on the market in 1983.

Everyone to whom Mankiewicz spoke was astonished. He was promising not only to get NPR off the government dole but also to usher in the future of all media. "The device," Brugger said later, "was a little bigger than an iPhone, and it was a talisman."

Frank Mankiewicz's vision inspired its share of skepticism. "It didn't sound believable to me," recalled Brugger. "My feeling was: This is not the business they're in. They're suddenly talking about tens of millions of dollars in profit from leasing satellite space. I thought that if this was really feasible, private business with a lot of capital would have already done it. There were a lot of private satellites up there, a lot of companies that if the technology existed would have jumped on board, and that's the point: there was no way of evaluating any of it, because no one knew if the technology was there. It wasn't marketed. It was brand new." (In agate type at the end of its report, McKinsey & Company expressed a few of these same doubts.) It wasn't just CPB executives who shook their heads. "When I heard about it," Robert Siegel observed later, "it didn't make sense to me." The "ambitions were way out of whack with what NPR was. We had no deep administrative support, no commercial expertise. There I was in London and NPR couldn't even get my paycheck to me. Envelopes were always addressed surface mail. This was just not a big-league business."

Most who voiced concerns came around to a positive view. You wanted to believe Mankiewicz, recalled Brugger. "You're trying to trust the leadership, because they seemed good at producing news programs." Siegel felt the same way. "Frank was known around the building and the system as a rainmaker. If Frank set out to accomplish something, he could make it happen. When he sent me to London, we didn't have funding for the operation. But after I got there, Frank approached the German Marshall Fund and said they should underwrite our position to improve foreign coverage, and in a few months, we got the grant." As for those who couldn't quite quell their worries about Project Independence, Mankiewicz shushed them with a bright but blunt admonishment: "Mama don't allow no pessimism around here."

On a February Saturday just ten months after assuring the public radio world that Project Independence posed no financial risks, Tom Warnock phoned Frank Mankiewicz at home to tell him that NPR was facing a multimillion-dollar shortfall. Recalled a former network executive, "On Monday, Tom stared down at his notes and told us the budget was to be cut by $750,000. Tuesday, it was $1 million, Wednesday $1.5 million, Thursday, $2.5 million." On March 4, 1983, Mankiewicz summoned his staff to the M Street conference room to announce that the deficit stood at $3.4 million and he was slashing $2.8 million from the budget and firing forty-seven employees. It was "such a quick devolution," said Joe Gwathmey, assistant programming director. "Frank and Tom had been nothing but optimistic about our prospects and our future. The satellite system was going to be a gold mine. Then, suddenly, we have a disaster on our hands."

Disturbing signs had been appearing all along, although they were hard to spot. Mankiewicz, for all of his vigor and skill, had never paid attention to NPR's books, and at the moment he was unveiling the grandest business undertaking in network history, he was running the operation with a heedlessness that bordered on negligence. Where others in his position would have scrutinized details, sought alliances with foes, questioned assumptions, and, if confronted by warnings, cut back, Mankiewicz dismissed doubts and baited enemies while speeding ahead. After everything he'd accomplished, his behavior was so precipitous that it begged for interpretation. Those concerns of six years earlier about carelessness, arrogance, disregard for organizational structure, and a predilection to self-sabotage seemed prescient.

The initial hint of a catastrophe had surfaced in a November 1982 memo from NPR chief financial officer Arthur Roberts to Warnock advising that the network was facing "a stringent cash flow problem." Roberts maintained that the matter was temporary, but he had no way of knowing. In June, NPR had shut down its computer accounting system while installing a new one. The changeover, which was beset by delays, would not be completed until the spring of 1983. As a consequence, for the critical eight months that coincided with the start of Project Independence, executives did not receive precise information on how much money was coming in or going out. Making matters worse, Roberts, who'd come to the network from the District of Columbia Public Schools, was an alcoholic. "People found him in bars a number of times during the day," recalled an associate. (In late 1982 the CFO checked into a treatment center.) As for Warnock, he was so obsessed with NPR Ventures that he didn't stay on top of the network's finances. Yet even if the necessary information had been forthcoming, the network's corporate chain of command (known internally as "Art-to-Tom-to-Frank") had been set up to shield Mankiewicz from messy particulars. "I didn't have to look at the printouts," the NPR chief said later. Many business leaders delegate such responsibilities, but Mankiewicz did more than just keep a distance. He considered the job beneath him. In a story he often told to illustrate his view that the bottom line was a concern for lesser beings, he recalled that when he asked Jimmy Carter back in 1976 to enumerate his hopes for his presidency, the poor man, rather than articulating a dream, stated that he wanted to leave "the agencies of the government running more efficiently." Mankiewicz then shook his head. Indeed, even as the network's plight worsened, he told a reporter, "I don't want my epitaph to read: 'He balanced the budget.'"

The result was that by late 1982 NPR's leaders had abdicated their corporate responsibilities. "Nobody knew where we were on budgets," recalled Gwathmey. "The financial reports were delayed and inaccurate. It was beyond incidental mistakes. There were monumental mistakes." In a move Roberts said he cleared with his superiors before the year ended but that Mankiewicz claimed he did not learn of until months later, NPR stopped sending federal and state agencies the taxes withheld from employees' payroll checks, instead using the money to cover operating expenses. The upshot: by the time the news broke that the network was in dire straits, it owed the Internal Revenue Service and its state equivalents $651,000, an amount that grew to $850,000. By early 1983, this threat from within was ripping a hole in NPR. At the same time, threats from without were also taking shape.

Shortly after the Public Radio Conference at Washington's Grand Hyatt where NPR introduced Project Independence, Frank Mankiewicz received a big envelope at M Street from Minnesota Public Radio's Bill Kling. It contained a couple of cassette tapes of a spritely but shambolic variety show out of Saint Paul hosted by Garrison Keillor, a local radio personality who also contributed stories to *The New Yorker*. In his cover note, the Minnesotan asked the NPR chief to listen to the programs.

A Prairie Home Companion had its premiere on Minnesota Public Radio in 1974. The debut drew a live audience of twelve. Over time, however, the show had attracted a listenership in the Twin Cities and other regional markets. Its fictional setting of Lake Wobegon, where, in the words of the program's opening, "the women are strong, all the men are good looking, and all the children are above average," struck a chord. Kling, spurred by his aspirations to produce national programming, believed this was his chance. At a Corporation for Public Broadcasting meeting in Phoenix later in the spring of 1982, he made his case to Mankiewicz in person.

"This is a show we think has potential," Kling said. "The next time you've got money for new programming, will you consider it?

"No," the NPR chief replied.

Kling was stunned. As he subsequently put it, "Frank's answer was not, 'I don't have the money, but I'll take it under consideration when I do.' His answer was, 'No.'"

Mankiewicz's stated rationale for rejecting *A Prairie Home Companion* was direct. "I didn't like" the program, he said later. "I don't like it now. It mocks the values of middle-class America." His sense was that the show was built on a condescending premise: "We're permitting you suburban people who would never go to Nashville to hear the Grand Ole Opry to scoff at it along with us." To him, "it was the first yuppie program—before there were yuppies." The ads for faux companies like Powdermilk Biscuits and the Ketchup Advisory Council and the college-boy country musicians who'd never hopped a freight train much less spent time in Folsom Prison constituted a form of Kabuki. The NPR chief was the sort of old-fashioned liberal who hated anything inauthentic, and he thought *Prairie Home*—which Keillor created after writing a *New Yorker* article about the real-life Opry's final performance at the historic Ryman Auditorium—embodied inauthentic.

There was another important reason why Mankiewicz declined Keillor's program. He considered it a rival. "Any money I give to you will come out of NPR," he eventually told Kling. Although some maintained that the savvy Minnesota broadcaster had put too high a price on *Prairie Home* ("He wanted half of the moon and a third of Mars," said network vice president Dale Ouzts), Kling countered that his offer was fair. As he saw it, Mankiewicz was not saying no to an expensive show that he didn't care for but to "all outside production." The network president didn't want to provide local stations entrée to the distribution system.

The night NPR passed on *Prairie Home Companion* Kling summoned a handful of station managers attending the Phoenix meeting. "We sat on chairs on the hotel patio. I said, 'We made a mistake when we designed NPR. We didn't give them any incentive to buy programs they didn't create. We've got to create a mirror organization.'"

Out of that impromptu session was born the American Public Radio Association (APRA), which would distribute *Prairie Home Companion* and other programs to stations nationwide via the satellite uplinks that Kling had the foresight to set up years earlier. Mankiewicz, just as NPR was trying to achieve independence, had inspired a restive bunch of locals to launch a public radio competitor.

Mankiewicz's instinctive response was to demonize Kling and disparage American Public Radio. "If Garrison Keillor gets laryngitis," he cracked, "Kling's off the air." Later, the network chief remarked, "Kling was obviously a foe of NPR." This view was adopted at M Street. "They made Kling into a monster," remembered John Hockenberry. "People at NPR thought Kling was an egotist trying to build his reputation at the expense of NPR," added Sanford Ungar. In the larger realm of public radio, however, many sided with Kling, especially after Mankiewicz attempted to scuttle APRA by challenging its legitimacy in a letter penned jointly with NPR chairman Maurice Mitchell. (Negative reaction to the letter prompted Mitchell to resign, robbing the NPR chief of an important boardroom ally.) Mankiewicz, they believed, had unnecessarily transformed a business difference into something personal. Veteran *All Things Considered* producer Rick Lewis, who left NPR to work for Kling, subsequently noted, "I don't think Bill felt the same way about Frank that Frank did about him. Bill's attitude was, 'I'm not fighting anybody. I'm doing what I have to do.' The problem with Frank was he came from politics, where you have to have winners and losers." The NPR chief, at a time when he needed to maintain the support of station managers who backed Kling, further antagonized them.

As vital as the relationship with NPR stations was to Frank Mankiewicz, his relationship with the Corporation for Public Broadcasting was more so. Yet here, too, there was trouble. Henry Loomis, the network chief's friend, had given way in 1981 to a Jimmy Carter appointee: Sharon Rockefeller. From the start, Mankiewicz hadn't gotten along with her. First, he thought she was

more interested in PBS than NPR. More critical, the two differed about how
to respond to the Reagan budget cuts. Where Mankiewicz wanted NPR to go
out on its own, Rockefeller wanted him to join her in petitioning Congress
to increase funding. "We had arguments," Mankiewicz said later. "I told her
I wouldn't participate in a campaign to get more money for public broadcasting." His reasoning was pure partisan Democrat. "Reagan was cutting
money for food stamps and every program for the disadvantaged." In such
an environment, it was wrong to seek more federal dollars for TV and radio.
"We had this argument in several places—her office, my office. I may have
been so unwise as to go public—not in the press, but I made no attempt to
conceal my view."

Had Project Independence brought in even a fraction of the revenue
Frank Mankiewicz had anticipated, NPR's problems might have remained
manageable. But nearly every element of the enterprise was sputtering. NPR
Ventures, which had hired a staff of sixteen, was late getting out the gate.
The network hadn't obtained the Federal Communications Commission authorization that would have permitted its partners to transmit information
over its stations' FM subcarriers. Activists were worried that such business
use would interfere with the subcarriers' more socially minded purpose: the
distribution of reading services for the blind. The issue was resolved in the
network's favor, after which NPR Ventures confronted a more serious obstacle. Even with the software for INC from Steve Wozniak and the prototype device from Dataspeed, the technology was still in its infancy. "It works
today, but look at the companies that make it work," Brugger said much later.
"The problem was that it would have taken years to develop the potential,"
Warnock subsequently admitted. The network needed quick results. It ultimately sank $865,000 into NPR Ventures with no chance of seeing a return.

NPR Plus was also in trouble. The network had estimated that its satellite music service, which went online in early 1983 as scheduled, needed to
attract between 150 and 200 member stations, but fewer than 100 paid the
$5,000 fee. With start-up costs of $860,000, most going to fund thirty-one
additional daily newscasts, the network again lost money.

As for NPR Fund Raising, its projections were little more than mirages,
in part because the network did not hire a vice president of development
until September 1982, when application deadlines for the two massive

grants crucial to its survival were imminent. In the end, NPR, although it had based its 1983 budget on receiving both, received neither. Moreover, due to the early 1980s recession, estimated increases in underwriting never materialized. "We thought *Star Wars* would be underwritten," recalled Holt, "but [an expected] $220,000 never came through." This was a true missed opportunity. Expertly made (director John Madden later directed the Oscar-winning film *Shakespeare in Love*), the series drew 700,000 new listeners to NPR. The network didn't see a cent.

The bottleneck in the NPR business office was such that Frank Mankiewicz could not have at first realized how badly Project Independence was doing, but by the start of 1983, Tom Warnock knew enough to phone Brugger at the CPB.

"David, we need your help," he said. "You've got to see if CPB can do anything. We're already $1.8 million in debt. It looks like we're going deeper. Frank won't listen."

Warnock later asserted that he made several early efforts to get through to Mankiewicz. "He so clearly didn't want to hear it." Or perhaps more accurately, he wasn't willing to hear it from a mere NPR vice president. Robert Siegel later contended that the warnings were ignored because the network president had, in effect, neutered his business staff by so frequently turning to newsroom associates like Linda Wertheimer, Nina Totenberg, and Cokie Roberts for advice. "These vice presidents became yes-men. I'm not sure they were taken that seriously."

In the weeks prior to the reckoning, things proceeded as usual at NPR, and under Mankiewicz that meant continued spending. The network chief welcomed 1983 by giving pay raises to his senior employees. The total: $480,000. Mankiewicz was accustomed to distributing largesse, and NPR staffers were getting accustomed to receiving it. "We had been in a period we used to call Camelot," recalled Warnock. "The company was growing, the programs were going well, and money wasn't a problem." Indeed, an astonishing 110 of NPR's 400 employees now possessed corporate American Express cards. To the old-timers who remembered the lean years under Siemering, it felt odd. "Coming up in public radio, which was always so penny-pinching, I wondered how we could afford this," Susan Stamberg said later. "There was a lot of lavish living," and much of it was unencumbered by receipts. "I didn't have to itemize expenses to get reimbursed," recalled Siegel. "I charged American Express and never saw the bill. NPR just paid it. I could have been hiring dancing girls. It was a good deal, but it was crazy." Ultimately, NPR would be saddled with $800,000 in what auditors termed "poorly monitored" AmEx charges.

Programming meanwhile kept expanding, with NPR introducing several ambitious new shows. On January 2, the network premiered *NPR Dateline*, a single-topic half hour hosted by Sanford Ungar. Airing at four thirty p.m. weekdays, it was designed to provide a lead-in to *All Things Considered* and give Ungar a forum to dig into big subjects. Most of the stories were off the top of the news, and many reflected Ungar's interest in foreign policy—but not all. One of the best took Ungar to Chicago for a raucous conversation with Studs Terkel and Mike Royko about that city's politics. Meantime, Robert Siegel, Deborah Amos, and Neal Conan were working on a series about the threat of nuclear war, which had them flying all over the globe. Then there was *The Sunday Show*, a weekly, five-hour arts-and-culture cornucopia that had debuted a few months earlier and was initially produced and hosted by Dave Ossman, a founder of the Firesign Theatre, the surreal 1960s comedy troupe. Ossman somewhat toned things down for NPR, focusing on American crafts, dance, and poetry—not that he entirely abandoned his rebel ways. "It's in my nature to push against people's conservatism," he said upon taking the gig, and that nature proved too much for the network. After five months Ossman was fired Still, *The Sunday Show* won a Peabody, and Mankiewicz upped its 1982 budget of $750,000 to $1.9 million for 1983.

Among the forty-seven NPR employees Frank Mankiewicz fired in March were the last hired—including the entire seventeen-member staff of *The Sunday Show*, which was canceled—and one of the first: Fred Calland, the Renaissance man who had worked at the network since the inaugural episode of *All Things Considered* (Stamberg interceded on that one, saving Calland's job). Still, those who remained assured themselves that the worst was over. Sanford Ungar recalled: "I remember people saying, 'No one's going to abolish public radio. We're a national treasure. We're like the National Gallery.'" By Ungar's lights, many NPR reporters and producers lived in "an unreal world" and could not grasp that the institution had hit an iceberg.

As soon as the news broke of NPR's difficulties, founding network president Don Quayle called Mankiewicz from his office at Washington's WETA, where he'd recently become a vice president. He was stunned by the reaction. "I wanted to see if I could help get things straightened out," he said later, "but Frank was obstinate. He said, 'Don't interfere with what we're trying to do here.'" David Brugger got the same story. "The problems were bad," but Mankiewicz still had faith in his plan. "They felt they were right in the first place and that the visions of money from NPR Ventures were going to come true. They didn't want to explain anything. They didn't want to show us the books. We had no need to question them. There was no need to talk." At that moment, NPR was preparing a glossy brochure praising Project Independence for distribution at the annual Public Radio Conference later in the spring.

Mankiewicz vacillated between defiance and distraction. One minute, he dismissed the severity of the issue. "It could have been solved fairly easily," he recalled thinking. "I mean, we were talking about three or four million dollars. That was it!" The next, he drifted. "I'm not sure I wanted to stay there much longer anyway. I'd accomplished what I wanted." Neal Conan, who had moved to NPR's New York bureau, sensed that his boss was "bored." More pointedly, he said, Mankiewicz was looking for a bigger job. "He was maneuvering to become commissioner of Major League Baseball." Former *All Things Considered* producer Jack Mitchell, back at WHA in Madison, Wisconsin, had heard from the Milwaukee Brewers' owner, Bud Selig, that Mankiewicz, in anticipation of the retirement of then-MLB commissioner Bowie Kuhn, was angling for the position. A lifelong Saint Louis Cardinals fan, Mankiewicz believed that the joys of the ballpark would be a tonic after the small-potatoes infighting of public radio. But in the end, it was a pipe dream. He was "never seriously considered," a Selig spokesman said afterward. Much as the NPR chief might have liked to escape his predicament, he would have to gut it out.

Several weeks after learning of the $3.4 million shortfall, Mankiewicz received another call from Warnock—the deficit was nearly twice that amount. The NPR chief's reaction was to demote his vice president. Frank "took me out of the loop," recalled Warnock. Many felt the move was overdue. "Warnock wasn't giving the information fast enough and accurately enough,"

Frank Fitzmaurice, *Morning Edition*'s executive producer, said later. Others, however, viewed Warnock, in Ungar's words, as "the fall guy." Regardless, the champion of Project Independence was done. Warnock, noted one colleague, didn't seem like he was "able to fight"—and fight was what Mankiewicz now intended to do. He tapped Billy Oxley, a well-liked figure from the network's satellite operation, as the new finance executive. According to Barbara Cohen, "Billy said we can make it."

The 1983 Public Radio Conference convened in Minneapolis on April 18 at the Hyatt Regency Hotel, but unlike the session in Washington the year prior, no one was boasting that NPR would be off the fix by '86. While Frank Mankiewicz had not released the terrible new figures, "there had been rumors of some kind of financial setback," recalled Bill Kling, who was hosting the event, which the M Street delegation found unbearable.

Mankiewicz, rather than dominate the conference as he had twelve months earlier, ceded the floor to Oxley, who sat beside him at a table of NPR executives facing the packed Hyatt ballroom. After a few minutes, Kling sensed that "the sacrificial lamb," as he called the newly elevated executive, was not "giving us the full picture." The Minnesotan wanted to know the precise amount of the debt. "I asked questions that caused Billy to give bigger and bigger numbers." Still, Kling wasn't satisfied, and he stood to pose another query.

Mankiewicz was done keeping quiet. "Darth Vader approaches the mic," he grumbled from his seat, eliciting a gasp from the audience.

Although most at NPR believed that Kling was the equivalent of the Star Wars villain, many public radio station executives saw it otherwise, and the network president's crack earned him some boos, which gave his adversary the opening he wanted.

"Who has the bottom-line number for the deficit?" Kling demanded.

"$5.8 million," answered Oxley.

NPR was on the verge of bankruptcy. Myron Jones, a former Ford Foundation official who'd replaced Maurice Mitchell as the network's board chairman, observed that the problems were so bad that *All Things Considered* and *Morning Edition* might not survive. After conferring with the board, he made an emergency proposal. If every NPR affiliate paid a fee—$5,500 for small stations, $8,500 for major markets—the shortfall could be reduced to a manageable level. That idea was greeted by what in the polite world of public broadcasting amounted to derision. Station managers accused NPR of holding *All Things Considered* and *Morning Edition* hostage and denounced Mankiewicz for instigating a tragedy. The NPR chief replied, "We overestimated the response to our programming that would come from the private and foundation sector." The next day, the station managers rejected the rescue plan. That afternoon, the board fired Mankiewicz, although he told the press that he'd resigned. Not only that, he refused to concede that a deficit existed: "There are six months to go in the fiscal year. We'll have a surplus." Then he left. The brochures touting Project Independence were never distributed.

Word of Frank Mankiewicz's dismissal jolted 2025 M Street. There was shock. "It was traumatic," recalled Joe Gwathmey. There was sadness. "We were heartbroken," said Linda Wertheimer. There was also anger—at the individual who had placed NPR in jeopardy. Susan Stamberg was so furious that in a script for an *All Things Considered* story on the Mankiewicz era she pilloried him for his recklessness. But before deadline, Barbara Cohen and Steve Reiner persuaded her to spike the attack, and she did. Some of the hostility toward the deposed president did, however, reach NPR listeners. In a piece by Scott Simon, who flew in from Chicago to report on the meltdown, Jay Kernis said: "I look at Mankiewicz and I think: Why did you let this happen to me?"

In the midst of the turmoil, Mankiewicz returned to M Street to tidy up his affairs. NPR had given him a couple of weeks to work on several underwriting deals and do some lobbying on Capitol Hill. Still, he felt raw. "It was upsetting," he recalled. "I didn't think that's how I should end my career at NPR. I wasn't holding up well." He refused to take responsibility for what had occurred, pinning his demise on plotters—not so much Bill Kling ("I never took him that seriously") but Sharon Rockefeller. "I resigned because it was obvious that she insisted that I resign. The CPB ran the show. If they wanted to shut down public radio, they had the means to do it. Ms. Rockefeller's motivation was political. I wouldn't join her in trying to build CPB." He expressed no remorse for the financial calamity. Assigning blame would be for others, and they would be less reticent. Although most credited

Mankiewicz for elevating NPR—"He connected us to our ambitions for the place," declared Robert Siegel—and everyone agreed that the Reagan budget cuts had put him in a bind and that Kling was a foe, the consensus was negative. Joe Gwathmey went with a metaphor: "He poured fertilizer into the garden until he nearly burned it up." Siegel was blunter: "He fucked up." Later, the postmortems became personal. There was talk of Hollywood and the superciliousness of its princes. There was regret that a Kennedy partisan had been made the head of an objective news organization. There was also mention of Mankiewicz's self-destructiveness. What kind of man bets the farm on an illusion? But as the summer of 1983 began, the larger issue was whether NPR would survive. To make the June payroll, the network borrowed $500,000 from the CPB. While Mankiewicz may have gotten off the best lines, Sharon Rockefeller got the final word: "Only desperate and tough choices at NPR will see all of us through this difficult period."

FOUR

RESURRECTION

A less likely bunch of saviors for America's embattled public radio network would have been hard to imagine. George Miles, who as acting CFO would sift through the financial ruins, was a forty-one-year-old Vietnam veteran who by his own description was "six-three, Black, and loud—a hit man, an enforcer, the bad cop." That Miles held a master's degree in accounting and was on leave from his position as station manager of WBZ television (Boston's NBC affiliate) was something few people at NPR's M Street building ever knew. They couldn't get past his tough-guy demeanor. Although not as physically imposing as Miles, Steve Symonds was for many even more intimidating. Seven years had passed since he'd worked at NPR, but he cast a long shadow. With Al Engelman, Symonds had conducted the 1976 encounter sessions that prompted nasty rumors about staffers' sex lives and resulted in the demise of Lee Frischknecht and Bob Zelnick. He was now interim executive vice president. Then there was Jack Mitchell, one of NPR's original hires, who had named Susan Stamberg host of *All Things Considered* before leaving for member station WHA in Madison, Wisconsin. His new job was acting programming director. He was the "stern uncle," said producer Jeff Rosenberg. "His attitude was, 'You boys and girls have been naughty. Look what you did.'"

Even more unlikely than this trio of radio EMTs was the man to whom they answered. Ronald Bornstein, Frank Mankiewicz's replacement, was unassuming. He stood only five feet, six inches, weighed 150 pounds, and was bald, with enormous ears. A vice chancellor at the University of Wisconsin, former NPR board member who'd championed *Morning Edition*, and erstwhile executive at the Corporation for Public Broadcasting, the forty-nine-year-old Bornstein was a creature of conference rooms and management seminars. "If you saw this guy" on the street, recalled Symonds, who had once worked for him, "you'd walk past him in a New York minute." Bornstein, however, was no pushover. As a former colleague put it, "He was the kind of guy who knew how to say, 'OK—enough with the bullshit.'"

No sooner had the rescuers set up shop at M Street than they realized that National Public Radio was in worse shape than anyone knew. Entering the accounts payable department on their first day, they stumbled on a scene of corporate disarray—six thousand unmailed checks to creditors spilled out of metal file cabinets and onto countertops. The checks, which totaled some $320,000, had been inserted into envelopes but never posted, because the network did not have sufficient funds in its account to cover them. Four months had passed since NPR had paid a bill. Bornstein ordered an emergency audit, and the results revealed the depths of the mess: the network was $9.1 million in debt, a figure far greater than the $5.8 million that Mankiewicz reported. "We were facing no lights, no phone, no building," recalled Bornstein.

It was overwhelming, so much so that a realistic response would have been to shut NPR down. However, the men tapped to clean up the network's finances shared the belief that it had earned a crucial place not only in American journalism but also in the culture. "The team I aggregated just decided that we'd do the right thing," Bornstein said later. "We all knew we were there for the short term. We knew none of us would form lengthy relationships. We'd just fix it the best way we could." Which was why the four, acting like battlefield surgeons, set up a triage operation. Miles ran the numbers to determine how many positions had to be eliminated. Mitchell canvassed department heads to see which employees were expendable. Symonds pounded out pink slips. On May 28, just three weeks after arriving, Bornstein pulled the trigger, firing eighty-four men and women. He dismissed most of the cultural staff, seventeen news reporters and editors, and half the engineers. Combined with the personnel terminated by Mankiewicz, NPR had lost nearly 150 workers in two months, shrinking from a force of 449 to 304.

The resulting pandemonium at M Street offered a sad reverse image of the enthusiasm that had marked Mankiewicz's early days. Terminated journalists came pouring out, followed by many who quit. Barbara Cohen, the news director, jumped to NBC. Sanford Ungar, the former cohost of *All Things Considered*, departed for an academic career, as did Frank Fitzmaurice, the executive producer of *Morning Edition*. Steve Reiner, the producer of *ATC*, left for the *Today* show. It was a stampede. Ira Flatow, on assignment in Detroit, phoned to see if he still had a job.

"Your name is on the list," John McChesney told the science reporter.

"Am I fired?" Flatow pressed.

"I guess you are."

After a second, McChesney, with a chutzpah only an editor could muster, posed the more important question: "Can you file your story for this afternoon?"

Flatow ended up being one of the lucky ones. When he called back a few hours later with his piece, he learned that Robert Krulwich, invoking NPR's financial ties to universities and research institutions, had intervened on his behalf, telling higher-ups, "You can't get rid of this guy. He's bringing in all the grant money for science coverage."

The dismissals were just the start. Bornstein imposed austerity measures on every NPR department. Not only did the corporate AmEx cards disappear, but the newsroom stopped receiving supplies. "I remember coming in and there was no paper," recalled Scott Simon, who continued to cover NPR's crisis for the network (as further proof that NPR was broke, he bunked at the home of one of his sources, Jeff Rosenberg). "I was on" *Morning Edition* "talking to Bob Edwards and said on the air, 'Bob, not to be too dramatic about it, but I came in here today and couldn't type up anything.'" As it happened, someone across the street at CBS News was listening and contributed reams of triplicate typing paper. NPR promptly sent an emissary to CBS to ask for a more intimate staple. An assistant "went over to get toilet paper," Jo Anne Wallace, who'd moved to Washington with McChesney and become a top aide in the news department, said later. "That's how bankrupt we were." The interim managers had no hesitation in justifying the cutbacks. "The survival of the organization was at stake," recalled Mitchell, "and survival required a realistic demonstration that we were going to live within our means." But some staff members, he added, "didn't understand."

No group was more aggrieved than the one that had achieved the greatest status during the Mankiewicz era—the troika. The women had been wary of Bornstein and his team from the start. The night before the interim group began work, Cokie Roberts and Linda Wertheimer buttonholed Jack Mitchell as he was checking into Washington's Renaissance Hotel. At best, the two felt the men charged with saving NPR lacked the political savvy and radio know-how to do the job. More worrying, they feared the men didn't want to save NPR at all. They suspected them of being stalking horses for the network's enemies in the public broadcasting system. "A well-informed guy" had told Roberts, she recalled, that "Bornstein was Robespierre," implying that she expected him, aided by Minnesota Public Radio's Bill Kling, to set up a guillotine at M Street and begin executing Mankiewicz loyalists. "Their attitude," Mitchell said later, "was that Bornstein and I were there to destroy NPR." Worse, he maintained, they dismissed the idea that the network was in extremis. "I realized even before we started that the staff was in deep, deep denial."

Part of the austerity plan was a new rule requiring journalists to submit detailed expense reports for business lunches. "The troika stormed into my office," recalled Steve Symonds, "and said, 'How dare you? We're not going to obey this.'"

"'Then you can get another job.'"

"'This is our First Amendment right.'"

The women believed that revealing news sources they entertained over meals would be tantamount to betraying them.

"Here are the numbers of ABC radio and CBS radio," Symonds replied. "Call up your colleagues. Ask them whether when they file expense reports they have to state the names of the person they took to lunch and the purpose. They'll tell you yes. And by the way, you have no First Amendment rights when it comes to me. I am the goddamn management. You tell me who you take to lunch or pay for it out of your own pocket."

This was just the beginning. A few days later, the troika clashed with

Bornstein over a more highly charged matter—raises. Although Mankie-wicz had approved salary hikes for management, the increases hadn't fil-tered down to the staff. After hearing the women out, the acting president, concluding they didn't know how bad NPR's finances were, responded with a sympathetic no. "It's the wrong time." However, George Miles, who was standing in the office door when the group requested more money, was less understanding.

"Get the hell out of here," Miles exploded.

"I told them," Miles said later, "that we could keep the network running and they could keep their jobs—or we could give them raises and shut the place down. These women were big stars, and they were completely resistant to what we had to do."

From where Wertheimer, Roberts, and Totenberg sat, there was reason for resistance. "We felt the people who came in after Frank didn't have our backs," recalled Roberts. "There was tremendous suspicion on our part that they were either going to do us in or diminish us in such a way that NPR would never again be important in a national scope."

Distrust was rampant in the NPR newsroom. Accordingly, reporters looked for outside help. The help seemed to arrive on June 19 in the form of full-page ads in the *New York Times* and the *Washington Post*. Beneath the headline "Save NPR," an organization calling itself the Friends of Na-tional Public Radio "invited—in fact, urged—listeners to join a group of dis-tinguished citizens in an independent . . . effort designed to save NPR." The citizens were distinguished indeed. They included journalistic heavyweights (Walter Cronkite, Dan Rather, and Ted Koppel), Hollywood figures (Carl Reiner and Jean Firstenberg), wealthy liberals (Max Palevsky and Frances Lear), and some token conservative columnists (James J. Kilpatrick and George Will). US Senator Dick Clark, an Iowa Democrat, chaired the group, but the power behind it was Fred Wertheimer, president of Common Cause and Linda's husband. "Fred got Walter Cronkite and the others to partici-pate," recalled Totenberg, "because he knows how to do that stuff. We knew he was doing it, but we kept our distance." At the time, the reporters bristled at any hint they'd played a part, responding to journalistic inquiries with a terse: "You won't find an answer to your question." Even so, the consensus, as Mitchell put it, was that "the news department, Linda and Cokie," were behind it. That NPR employees were seeking financial support for the network came close to violating what public radio station managers out in the country considered a sacrosanct privilege: the right to conduct pledge drives. "It was way overstepping the bounds," said Susan Stamberg, who nonetheless was pictured in the newspaper ads along with Bob Edwards and Noah Adams, who'd replaced Unger as *ATC* cohost. "They had legal advice, which is why they put it behind the screen 'Friends of.'" Still, local station managers were put off. Perry Echelberger of WUFT in Gainesville, Florida, said that affiliates would "have to find a nice way to tell them we can't do it that way." NPR's interim executives, realizing that for the network to survive it would need the support of its member stations, were appalled. Friends of National Public Radio eventually raised $100,000 for the network, but the skeptical reception and potential pitfalls made it an expensive donation. Besides, NPR needed big money.

To gin up enough working capital to stay on the air, NPR secured a loan from Riggs National Bank, an old-line Washington institution with ties to Westinghouse Broadcasting, the owner of Miles's Boston TV station. (This was the $1 million obtained by Bornstein.) Even with the infusion of cash, NPR sank deeper into the red. When in early June, Oliver Carr, M Street's landlord, called to tell Bornstein that unless he received the back-due rent he would start eviction proceedings, the network chief threatened to report the story on *All Things Considered*. "If you proceed, we'll go on the air and say, 'Oliver Carr is evicting us. There won't be anything you can do.'" It was the sort of stunt you could pull only once, which lent even greater urgency to NPR's dilemma. "We looked at alternative sources of finance," remembered Don Mullally, who'd replaced Myron Jones as NPR's chairman, "and the only one that looked like it had any potential was with the Corporation for Public Broadcasting"—the parent organization that Mankiewicz had done so much to antagonize.

Negotiations began in mid-June in the Corporation for Public Broadcasting boardroom at the corner of Sixteenth and L Street in Washington. The building overlooked the Soviet ambassador's residence, where members of the diplomatic delegation sometimes sunbathed nude on the roof. Sharon Rockefeller and the CPB staff sat around a horseshoe of tables bearing microphones and water pitchers. Bornstein, Mullally, and several lawyers hired as much for their Republican Party connections (a nod to the realities of Reagan-era politics) as for their expertise represented the network. The meeting got off to a bad start. Bornstein believed that Rockefeller "wanted to put me and my team through the ringer for things we had no part in. We were stand-ins for Frank Mankiewicz." The other side was unimpressed with NPR's new leaders. "The characters brought in after Frank were not the best in the world," recalled Linda Dorian, the CPB's general counsel. "Bornstein was a jerk."

By the session's end, the Corporation for Public Broadcasting had agreed to work with NPR—a victory for the network. But it was clear that any financial relief would come at a cost. Recalled Mullally, "CPB would want" something "to bail us out—and what they wanted was more control of NPR."

Over the next several weeks, the Corporation for Public Broadcasting laid out its terms. First came the demand that the network cut its budget by $10 million. Then the demand that the member stations cosign any note. Next the proposal regarding a revolutionary change in the way the CPB distributed funds, which would see the corporation reverse its thirteen-year-old policy of giving money to NPR and instead giving it to the stations. This arrangement, of course, meant that the stations could buy programming from suppliers other than NPR, chief among them Minnesota Public Radio. People at M Street balked. "NPR said that if we gave the money to the stations, the stations could use it to buy shows from Bill Kling," recalled David Brugger, the CPB executive who after working with Mankiewicz grew disenchanted and drafted the no-nonsense rescue plan. He calmed them by replying, "That's possible, but all you have to do to assure that you're competitive is make the stations want your programming instead of Kling's."

NPR executives could agree to CPB's initial demands. Only the last one—control of the Westar satellite and the network distribution system, the transformative technology that had given NPR the ability not just to boost sound quality but also beam its programming from on high—looked like a deal-breaker.

The battle National Public Radio was fighting would involve the United States Congress. The Corporation for Public Broadcasting and NPR answered to the House Energy and Commerce Committee, chaired by John Dingell, a fourteen-term Democrat from Michigan. The son of a former representative and a familiar figure on Capitol Hill since boyhood, Dingell was at once an old-fashioned liberal on social issues and an avid supporter of the National Rifle Association. Gregarious but unflinching, he believed that NPR and Frank Mankiewicz had crossed him. In late June, he charged the network with "financial mismanagement" and declared that those "responsible should be held accountable." In a markup of the bill to authorize the Corporation for Public Broadcasting's 1984 budget, he added language ordering that the agency not release any money to NPR until "the network adopted a system of financial controls." As Steve Symonds said later, "Dingell was super pissed." He was not alone. William Dannemeyer, a Republican representative from Southern California, asserted that the "leftward tilt of biases" at the network justified disbanding it. "The prudent thing to do," he said, "is terminate the life of NPR." Progressives were nearly as angry. David Obey, a Democrat from Wisconsin, remarked, "I have to conclude that the enemies of public broadcasting could not have done as much damage to the system as its friends over the last year or so." Bornstein sent Symonds to the Capitol to mollify the situation.

The troika, journalistic ethics be damned, decided to intercede. Wertheimer, Totenberg, and Roberts—by participating in Fred Wertheimer's Friends of NPR campaign—had signaled a willingness to break rules. The stakes were now higher. They believed that Bornstein and his team lacked the necessary understanding of Washington to succeed in what was a life-and-death battle. The network, they concluded, needed a powerful politician to exert pressure on the Corporation for Public Broadcasting while placating Dingell. Using their knowledge and guile, they chose the lawmaker they felt could turn things NPR's way.

As chairman of the House Subcommittee on Telecommunications, Tim Wirth reported to Dingell's committee. A Harvard-educated, Stanford PhD who sported raffish sideburns, he had capitalized on voters' revulsion at Watergate to sneak into office in 1974 in a traditionally Republican Colorado district. He'd recently presided over the legislation that led to the breakup of the giant Bell Telephone into a collection of "Baby Bells." On top of that, he entertained doubts about Frank Mankiewicz, with whom he'd served on the McGovern campaign. "Dealing with Frank was very unpleasant," he said later. This attitude made him attractive to Dingell—and to Sharon Rockefeller. It also, surprisingly, appealed to the troika. "I was furious at Frank," recalled Wertheimer. "He let us fall into a hole."

Which was why Wirth and David Aylward, his legislative assistant, were parked in the Jeep Cherokee outside the Corporation for Public Broadcasting offices on the night of July 27 and on into the early morning hours of July 28. The agency's negotiations with National Public Radio had come to a final pass. The network's survival was in doubt, and the troika had convinced Wirth to stake out the CPB's meeting and pressure Sharon Rockefeller. "It was hairy," Aylward said later. "We feared they would not reach an agreement."

At two a.m., Wirth's Motorola DynaTAC rang. Rockefeller was calling from upstairs with good news. "It's done," she said. The two sides had resolved the thorniest issue, and they'd done so by making a classic, inside-the-Beltway move. They'd agreed to put NPR's spot on the Westar satellite into a trust supervised by Elliot Richardson, who in 1973 had resigned as US attorney general rather than fire Watergate special prosecutor Archibald Cox, gaining status as one of Washington's wise men. The trust allowed the network to salvage a little dignity (it didn't have to surrender its space on the satellite), while giving the Corporation for Public Broadcasting a victory and a hedge against future financial excesses. "Our board members were persuaded that if NPR went under, we'd have control of the satellite and the interconnection system," recalled Linda Dorian, the corporation lawyer. "We had them by their crown jewels." Even so, she conceded, Bornstein's tough tactics backed up by Wirth's muscle had made a difference. By maintaining an all-night vigil outside the meeting and phoning Rockefeller hourly during the deliberations, the congressman made it clear the Corporation for Public Broadcasting would pay a political price if National Public Radio died. "The board," Dorian said, "didn't want to be seen as doing in NPR."

Soon after Rockefeller called Wirth, Bornstein celebrated his success with a Michelob Lite at his hotel bar. By the terms of the agreement, the Corporation for Public Broadcasting would retire $600,000 of National Public Radio's debt and loan the network $8.5 million, which would be guaranteed by the stations. (Of the network's 281 affiliates, 170 agreed to cosign.) "This was a most creative and fiscally prudent solution," Rockefeller told the

Washington Post. The Corporation for Public Broadcasting was not, however, going to let NPR executives forget who was in charge. The next day, when Bornstein phoned the agency to request that the money be deposited in the network's account via wire transfer, he was told no.

"We'll write you a check."

"That's bush league," Bornstein replied.

But there was no room for discussion. NPR's interim president got up from his desk at 2025 M Street and tromped over to the Corporation for Public Broadcasting. He was at the bank the following morning when it opened.

If Ronald Bornstein believed that just because he rescued National Public Radio, he would be considered a hero at M Street, he was mistaken. Three days after the all-night session at the Corporation for Public Broadcasting, he was on the receiving end of a tirade from NPR's most storied personality.

"I will not go on the air unless you look me in the eye," Susan Stamberg asserted, "and promise that any money we raise this week will not go to pay the debt but will help keep the news department going." The confrontation, which occurred in the sound lock outside the *All Things Considered* studio a couple of minutes before airtime on Monday, August 1, marked the opening day of the "Drive to Survive," an effort on the network's part to take its plight to listeners. The goal, now that NPR had secured the CPB loan, was to restore the organization's editorial budget to something approximating its precrisis level. The Drive to Survive was about journalism, and Stamberg wasn't backing down. Bornstein acquiesced, or she'd scuttle the show.

"Yes, I promise you," he replied—not that he had a choice ("I had him over a barrel," the *ATC* host later admitted). With that Stamberg walked into the studio and joined Noah Adams.

"Welcome to NPR's Drive to Survive, the first day in a three-day effort to raise much-needed money," she began.

"Susan and I are taking time away from our jobs as hosts of *All Things Considered* to ask you to make a contribution right now to National Public Radio," added her cohost.

"Even though we got the loan, even though we can begin paying off our debts, meeting our payroll, National Public Radio is still operating with a

30 percent reduction in our work force and at a budget that is $10 million less than it was," Stamberg explained. "Your help will let us begin to rebuild."

In the manner of a proud family that had stumbled on hard times, NPR proceeded to trot out its best argument for itself—its reporters. Introduced by a series of "Hi yas" from Stamberg, Cokie Roberts discussed covering Congress, White House correspondent Ted Clark weighed in on the Reagan administration, Nina Totenberg talked about the courts, and Daniel Zwerdling, who since joining the network in 1980 had done in-depth pieces on the environment, championed investigative journalism.

Day and night for the better part of a week, NPR begged for money, punctuating the drive with inserts for local stations to solicit donations, which would then be funneled to DC. As a bonus, NPR produced live remotes for the midday hours featuring testimonials from entertainers. At the Sheraton Universal in Los Angeles, Charlie Haid and Michael Warren of *Hill Street Blues* and Ed Asner of *Lou Grant* professed their love for the network, and Steve Allen, the first host of the *Tonight Show*, banged out a song in its praise on an upright piano. At the Saint Regis in New York, the actor Gene Wilder said he listened to NPR religiously, while the musician Bobby Short, responding to a question from Scott Simon about his rumored weakness for fancy pajamas, got off a delightfully un-NPR repost: "Oh, Scott, who wears pajamas?"

The Drive to Survive almost didn't happen. When employees had broached the idea back in June, the NPR board turned them down. Board members regarded the effort as a more invasive version of the Friends of NPR newspaper ads. According to NPR's charter, only the stations could solicit money on the air. But later that month, when Bornstein's crew proposed decreasing the length of *Morning Edition* from two hours to ninety minutes and *All Things Considered* from ninety minutes to an hour, Jo Anne Wallace—who having come up through the public radio system knew most of its local potentates—circumvented the board, going to several major market station managers. Soon enough, she'd signed up WETA in Washington, WBUR in Boston, WNYC in New York City, KCRW in Santa Monica, and most critical, WHYY in Philadelphia, where Bill Siemering, after a long exile in Moorhead, Minnesota, was now manager. Siemering sat on the NPR board.

"I got identified as the salesman," Siemering recalled. "The board had to be sold on this. The station manager in Chapel Hill said I should be impeached." But the creator of *All Things Considered* prevailed. Although less than a third of the member stations would carry the Drive to Survive, the undertaking would give NPR the chance to restore its news operation.

In the end, the Drive to Survive exceeded all expectations. NPR raised $2.1 million. The fundraiser not only preserved the length of NPR's signature shows, but also saved several jobs, among them that of future Pentagon reporter Tom Gjelten. "He was supposed to be cut," recalled Jack Mitchell. The broadcasts also gave the network something else: an opportunity to repay the congressman who'd played a vital part in securing the Corporation for Public Broadcasting loan. At the top of each segment, without mentioning his role in the network's salvation, thus again skirting journalistic standards, NPR gave free chunks of airtime to Tim Wirth, essentially putting him on a loop:

"Seems to me," the Colorado lawmaker told listeners again and again and again, "that National Public Radio provides millions of people in this country a wonderful programming alternative providing extraordinary interesting public affairs programming. The more of that kind of diversity we can have in America the better off this democracy is going to be."

Six months after the crisis started, it was resolved, and Bornstein and his team departed. "The only thanks I got," recalled George Miles, "came from the women in accounts payable. They said, 'We'd been praying for you to get here, and you finally came.'" Theirs had been, Stamberg later agreed, a thankless task. Over time, key figures at both Corporation for Public Broadcasting and NPR concurred that without the work of the interim executives, NPR would have gone under. "Bornstein was an absolute saint for stepping in during NPR's darkest days," said Sharon Rockefeller. Added Stamberg: "He [left] us in a better place than he found us." As to what sort of place that was, Bornstein phrased it succinctly: "Fantasy land was over."

National Public Radio had survived, but as NPR chairman Don Mullally realized, finding someone to run it on a permanent basis would not be easy. "Who in their right mind would become president of an organization that is essentially bankrupt and has no assets?" he asked. Mullally then ticked off a list of NPR's liabilities. It was "run by a group of stations that are fractious." It was controlled by "strong unions." The key staffers all felt "terribly cheated by the fact that this whole thing had come to pass." The downsides, he concluded, were so many that "only someone a little screwy" would be interested in taking over at M Street.

After interviewing a number of candidates, Mullally and his colleagues homed in on the one who seemed least screwy. Douglas J. Bennet, a forty-five-year-old PhD, was in the words of one public radio executive the "consummate bureaucrat." Bennet had begun his career in the early 1960s as an assistant to Chester Bowles, then the United States ambassador to India. Later, he worked in Washington as an aide to Vice President Hubert Humphrey and senators Thomas Eagleton and Abraham Ribicoff. He spent most of the 1970s as director of the Senate Budget Committee. In the 1980s, he became president of the Roosevelt Center for American Policy Studies, a think tank that facing a financial shortfall had recently eased him out. When the NPR opening occurred, he was looking for work.

Bennet's chief qualification for the top position at National Public Radio was that he lacked most of the expected qualifications. "I wasn't interested in finding someone who was really good at public broadcasting," recalled Mullally. "I was interested in finding someone who knew how to put an organization together." Bennet was "the quintessential staff man," Jack Mitchell said later, which, of course, made him the anti-Mankiewicz. True, Bennet was another Democratic operative, but unlike Mankiewicz, he was not an insurgent.

Born in Orange, New Jersey, and reared in Lyme, Connecticut, near the mouth of the Connecticut River, Bennet, in the words of the *Washington Post*, was "a yachtsman, stern and tightly wound." Scott Simon later observed, "He was clinch-lipped and clinch-mouthed. He had to me a kind of clipped, Connecticut 'I only surrender my words with great reluctance' accent." Linda Wertheimer defined the man succinctly: "A Yankee."

Just one thing stood between Bennet and control of National Public Radio: the troika. After embracing then scorning Mankiewicz and then orchestrating the financial bailout from the wings, NPR's three great women reporters were not about to sign off on the network's next leader without weighing in. "The trio interfered in Bennet's hiring, calling to interview him outside the official process," the *Washington Post* reported. "He was quite annoyed." In the end, Totenberg, Roberts, and Wertheimer approved, agreeing with the board that a journalistic neophyte was the right man." As a fellow NPR reporter told the *New York Times*: "He knows how to raise money, deal with Congress, and deal with 280 stations. This building is filled with people with radio experience."

Starting on October 28, 1983—Bennet's first day at M Street—the mantra at National Public Radio became sobriety, propriety, and financial responsibility. After Frank's wild years, NPR would wear the hair shirt. "I hope to show the public that NPR is sound and immaculate financially," Bennet said after arriving. He also wanted to make sure that the staff did not forget how close the enterprise had come to going under. "I don't think we can put the crisis behind us," he said in a late 1983 interview. "I think we've got some lessons that are very important. In terms of my own management mission, part of it is to ensure that nothing like that ever happens again."

Where Mankiewicz entertained great notions and high journalistic ambitions, Bennet was cautious and uninspiring. When asked by a reporter if NPR had any ideas for new shows, he replied, "I'm afraid there isn't time for that now. We must wait until funds are forthcoming." He was there to repair the damage. He spoke about retiring the debt, reaching out to Capitol Hill, and building a foundation for growth. He directed the NPR board to form a committee to study funding arrangements for the future, chief among them the Corporation for Public Broadcasting's plan to start giving money directly to the stations. His principal goal, he said, was to convince Congress and others that NPR was capable of cleaning its own house. Steve Symonds, who stayed on to assist in the transition, remembered: "He was just very determined to get us over this bad patch." There would be no miracles.

The job of making sure that NPR's existing programs didn't lose their way during the lean times fell to Joe Gwathmey and Robert Siegel. Gwathmey had replaced Sam Holt, another Mankiewicz casualty, as programming director. Siegel had returned from London to be news director (Neal Conan, producer of *ATC*, succeeded Siegel abroad). "Robert and I went to lunch just after he got back," Gwathmey said later. "He revealed to me that he wasn't sure that the news department could deliver the way it used to. We'd just gotten started," and due to the fiscal constraints, "we were already behind the eight ball."

As NPR's first foreign correspondent, Siegel had become accustomed to moving in a heady world. With an office at the BBC's Bush House, he'd covered stories ranging from the rise of Margaret Thatcher to the wedding of Prince Charles and Princess Diana. As John Hockenberry put it, "He was every bit a London bureau chief." His attitude had become a tad stuffy and his parlance quite formal. "He returned to Washington an Anglophile," recalled NPR reporter Bill Buzenberg. The straitened new realities at M Street fell short of those that had informed his last six years.

Still, Siegel would do what was required, and to the task of keeping NPR afloat, he would bring a formidable intelligence. As almost everyone at the network never tired of saying, he was exceedingly bright. "He's a very smart guy," recalled Margot Adler. "Smart, really smart," echoed producer Steve Proffitt. He kept *All Things Considered* and *Morning Edition* sounding relevant by showcasing NPR's mainstays, chiefly the troika. We "relied on Nina, Cokie, and Linda," Richard Harris, the new executive producer of *All Things Considered*, said later. For the remainder of the network's content, Siegel fell back on the cheapest form of radio production—extended interviews. "We had to find a way to keep the programs on the air," *Morning Edition* producer Jay Kernis, explained, "and one way of keeping the quality up was doing interviews. They didn't cost anything."

It could have ended up becoming the age of just scraping by, except that NPR's existing programs continued to turn out strong work. At *All Things Considered*, the excellence was due largely to the partnership between Susan Stamberg and her new cohost. Unlike the tortured Mike Waters, the moody Bob Edwards, or the cerebral Sanford Ungar, Noah Adams was even keeled. He was also, in his own surprising way, a daring on-air presence. Stamberg had wanted to team up with him since the two undertook a piece a couple of years before that was hilarious—at Adams's expense. He had visited a New York sound studio that for a fee recorded wannabe rock stars performing versions of hit songs, then pressed them on vinyl. Adams chose "Take It to the Limit" by the Eagles. There was only one problem. "Noah can't sing," recalled Art Silverman, who produced the story. "He is awful. When he finished, I tried to trash the thing. That was the only way I could protect him." But fellow producer Steve Proffitt also listened to the recording and thought it had potential. At his urging Silverman put Adams on *ATC* with Stamberg, cutting back and forth between the one's ear-shattering croaks and the other's uncontrollable cackling. "Susan was laughing so hard she nearly peed in her pants," Silverman said later. Stamberg's lasting reaction was awe. Adams's willingness to expose himself to ridicule was heroic. He was willing to endure public humiliation to make brilliant radio.

The pairing of Stamberg and Adams had a settling effect on *All Things Considered*. They were in many ways opposite. "Susan is this big, brassy New York woman," recalled Silverman, "and Noah is a tiny blond guy from Kentucky." But they had much in common. "They were sweet together. They respected each other. Neither put a real premium on the news of the day," said Harris. "They carved out their own niches."

Stamberg, playing to her greatest strength, provided *All Things Considered* what it needed in an era of diminished budgets—solid interviews, which could be produced at minimal cost.

One evening, Edward Kleban—the lyricist for *A Chorus Line* and, Stamberg informed listeners, her high school classmate—surprised the host by declaring that his favorite song from the show was not the hit "What I Did for Love" but the stinging "At the Ballet," with its account by a sensitive daughter of a devastating put-down by her mother ("Mother always said I'd be attractive / when I grew up ... / 'Different,' she said, 'with a special something / and a very personal flair.' / And though I was eight or nine, ... / I hated her"). Kleban told Stamberg: "I cried when I wrote" the song.

Another night, the novelist Philip Roth, who had not done a broadcast interview since the late 1950s, held forth on the necessity for writers to deal honestly with their lives regardless of the pain it might cause family members. "It's a very unscrupulous profession," he informed Stamberg. "Your material is raw life. Your material is the real thing. And you can't be any more squeamish than a doctor who opens a patient up and sees a big abscess. You have to go in there and take it out."

When Rosa Parks, whose refusal to give up her seat on a Montgomery,

Alabama, bus in 1954 essentially started the civil rights movement, spoke
to Stamberg, the host was initially unsure how to proceed. "I felt reluctant
to ask Mrs. Parks to describe what happened that day," she recalled. "Surely
she'd grown tired of going over it." Ultimately, though, she decided that the
long-ago events remained the story.

"You were arrested," Stamberg began. "Where were you taken?"

"I was taken to jail."

"How long did you stay in jail?"

"Just a short while. A few hours."

"What was the charge, Mrs. Parks?"

"They charged me with violation of their racial segregation law."

"Did you realize how much worse it could have been for you, so much
more than a few hours in jail?"

"At the time of my arrest, I knew that it could have been worse than just
being arrested. I could have been physically injured or possibly killed."

Stamberg's interview with Parks pointed up what had become during her
fourteen years as host of *All Things Considered* her greatest strength: a willingness to pose the obvious question. Many reporters labor to put questions
in a way that will produce unexpected revelations and big news. Not Stamberg. She wanted to know what everyone wanted to know: What happened?
How did it feel?

Adams also possessed a deft touch as an interviewer (his sifting of Dr.
Jack Kevorkian in 1984 introduced America to the assisted suicide doctor's next big idea: harvesting the organs of executed criminals for science).
However, Adams's best work for *All Things Considered* sprang from a continuing desire to produce the sort of radio documentaries he and Deborah
Amos had made under Mankiewicz. In Silverman he found an enthusiastic
collaborator.

On April 29, 1985, Adams fronted a twenty-eight-minute, Silverman-
produced documentary on the tenth anniversary of the fall of Saigon and
the end of the Vietnam War. The two interviewed a cross section of individuals who had been on the ground. Frank Snepp, a CIA officer, described
the chaos at the US embassy. Chung Wan Linh, a young Vietnamese woman
who worked for the South Vietnamese government and had been denied safe
passage from the city, spoke of being among those left behind. Barry Fox, a

TV cameraman, told of the tantalizing appearance of helicopters promising salvation from the sky. Throughout, Silverman cut to static-filled audio from the day's news accounts. All of it was tied together by Adams's calm narration: "A lot of people wanted to get out. Everyone had heard rumors. There would be a bloodbath." The piece had it all, and after weeks of work, Silverman and Adams were ready to put it to bed. Then, just before the air date, they got a call from Richard Sandza. He'd not been in Saigon on April 29, 1975, but his friend, Air Force Second Lieutenant Richard Vande Geer, had been. Vande Geer was one of the helicopter pilots who flew in and out on missions taking people off the embassy roof, and he'd made a contemporaneous tape about the experience. Would they like to hear it? Sandza, who was in New York, went to NPR's bureau there and transmitted the recording to DC. It was incredible. Adams and Silverman reworked the documentary and rewrote its lead. They opened with Vande Geer. The day he made four round-trip flights to and from Saigon had started in a Bangkok hotel. He was on leave after a dangerous mission to Cambodia. "I wanted flowers in the room. I wanted some gin. I wanted the best body massage they had to offer and a woman." What he got instead was a message from the desk. A plane was waiting to take him back into combat. "It was hard to believe that there could be such injustice in the world," he told Sandza, "but be assured, there is." Because of Vande Geer, scores were rescued.

All reporters dream of such a last-second godsend, the interview that transforms a good story into one for the ages. For Silverman and Adams, the Vande Geer tape was that. It concluded with the lieutenant telling Sandza, "Dick, I wish you peace, and I have a great deal of faith that the future has to be ours. Adios my friend."

That's how the Vietnam War ended for most. But for Vande Geer, it was not over, and that gave Adams his kicker:

"Air Force Second Lieutenant Richard Vande Geer had one more helicopter rescue after he made this tape. When the Cambodians seized the SS *Mayaguez* in May of 1975, Vande Geer was called into action. He was airlifting a squadron of marines when a rocket hit his helicopter.

"At the Vietnam Veterans Memorial in Washington, where the names of the dead are listed chronologically, Richard Vande Geer's name is last."

•   •   •

All Things Considered surrounded its interviews and features with commentaries, and in the mid-1980s the show aired more of them than ever. NPR paid $125 per submission, making this the bargain of all journalistic bargains.

The segments were recorded either at M Street or at public radio stations around the country. They were loaded on cassettes kept in a wooden bookcase next to *ATC*'s Road Map, and they were in constant demand. "There was [often] not enough stuff from reporters to fill the show," recalled Silverman. "We filled the holes with commentators. We felt the commentators were good radio." The naturalist Kim Williams remained the mainstay ("I have a pot boiling on my stove, but I don't know if I dare mention what's in it . . . Well . . . earthworms"). Others, however, were on the rise. Silverman would go over to the shelf, he added, and say, "I need three-and a-half minutes of Codrescu."

Andrei Codrescu, a thirty-nine-year-old Romanian poet living in New Orleans, was an emerging force on *All Things Considered* in the Stamberg-Adams era. Ruminative yet fanciful, he spoke with a middle European accent difficult to peg. He could come across as a populist, yet he was also an aristocrat. One evening he might describe his childhood memories of the death of Joseph Stalin, the next his growing love of Louisiana's cultural gumbo. There was a fairy-tale quality to his work ("In a forest far away a bear ate a certain mushroom, and lo and behold he was transformed into a schoolchild," he said mysteriously in his first and many ways defining effort for *ATC*.) "He brought visions from the outside world to play at NPR," said Silverman.

Vertamae Grosvenor, a forty-five-year-old native of South Carolina's Daufuskie Island, was another familiar but distinctive voice. Although raised in New York and Paris, she'd never turned her back on the rich Black heritage of her home state. An actress and activist, she was first and foremost a cook and cookbook writer whose 1970 work, *Vibration Cooking: Or, the Travel Notes of a Geechee Girl*, was one of the first serious efforts to advance the notion that food was a source of not just nourishment but carried with it a story of place and race.

"Vertamae wasn't the sort of person you'd see on the opinion pages of big newspapers," recalled Richard Harris. "Those people are either liberal or conservative. Vertamae contributed an appreciation for a time and a people."

Prompted by reports of impending real estate development on Daufuskie, Grosvenor returned after a four-year absence. In describing her lovely, isolated island, she might well have been describing herself:

> I grew up in the Carolina lowlands, so I understand Gullah speech. Gullah's a patois, a dialect, a way of speaking English with an African rhythm. Sea island people are warm, witty, generous, loyal. But they're very independent, and it takes a while to get to know them and a while for them to get to know you.

After detailing the proposed resort construction and interviewing people on Daufuskie about it, she concluded:

> I don't know what to make of all this. I suppose the people of Daufuskie are just as confused as I am. Progress may save and sacrifice Daufuskie at the same time. But maybe, just maybe, these people are tougher than that, strong enough to hold onto the past as their little island is packaged into somebody else's dream.
>
> Since every good-bye ain't gone, I'll wait and see.

Grosvenor could have become an even bigger presence at *All Things Considered*, but, as Silverman recalled, she was unreliable. "She'd be subject to a deadline and almost violate it. You'd find yourself saying, 'Where are you, Vertamae?'" NPR stuck with her. "We were interested in what she had to say," said Harris.

Morning Edition followed much the same road during the post-Mankiewicz years. Bob Edwards conducted a long interview almost daily. "It allowed him to be a newsman, but it also allowed him to be a person," Jay Kernis said later. "His wry sense of humor came out." Like *ATC*, the a.m. show relied on commentators as well, chief among them Red Barber, a throwback from the golden era of baseball play-by-play announcers.

Ketzel Levine, a twenty-eight-year-old veteran of the defunct arts program *Voices in the Wind*, brought Barber to *Morning Edition*. Best known for producing stories about theater and music, she was also a baseball fan. When the Yankees' star catcher Thurman Munson was killed in a 1979 plane crash, Levine showed up at M Street wearing a black armband. Kernis noticed, and gave her a new job: sports editor. He told her to cover games as if they were performances. Forget about wins and losses. Bring listeners the experience and the culture.

One of Levine's first sports pieces for *Morning Edition* was a profile of Jackie Robinson. While researching the story about the inaugural Black major leaguer and Brooklyn Dodger all-star, Levine stumbled across a name that seemed charged with almost magical resonance for baseball fans in the 1940s and 1950s. Hoping to learn more, she called her father. Arthur Levine was a Long Island CPA, but he grew up in Crown Heights. "My dad grew up in Brooklyn," she said later, "and his youth revolved around the Dodgers. It was classic New York stuff: sitting on a stoop, listening to games on the radio."

"Who is Red Barber?" she asked him.

Starting in 1939, the Mississippi-born, Florida-reared Walter Lanier "Red" Barber was the radio voice of the Dodgers. He'd spent the previous five years doing play-by-play for the Cincinnati Reds, where he'd achieved a bit of immortality by calling the Major League's first night game. But it wasn't until he arrived at Ebbets Field that he came into his own. Although he worked in the heart of the urban North, he peppered his broadcasts with southernisms that became known, over time, as "Barberisms." In Red's parlance, the park on Bedford Avenue, the site of many on-field fracases, was "the rhubarb patch." A sharply hit ground ball was "slicker than oiled okra." Obnoxious players were "suck egg mules." When dem Bums—as the team was affectionately known—held a lead, they were in "the catbird seat."

The son of an English-teacher mother and a distant cousin of the poet Sidney Lanier, Barber informed his on-air patter with all manner of enlightening digressions. He often referred to Keats and Shelley and used multisyllabic words. When an outfielder's error allowed a base runner to advance, he might say the plays were "concomitant."

Barber's at once colloquial yet erudite work at Ebbets Field was inimitable, so much so that James Thurber celebrated the broadcaster in a *New Yorker* short story titled "The Catbird Seat." But there was more to Barber than just a distinctive delivery. Unlike many play-by-play announcers, he considered himself a journalist. He started as a reporter at WRUF in

Gainesville, Florida, and his first boss in the big leagues was Scotty Reston, who prior to joining the *New York Times* was the Cincinnati Reds' traveling secretary. Unlike some of his colleagues in other cities, Barber never pulled for the home team. He was in the news business.

In 1947, when Branch Rickey, the president of the Brooklyn Dodgers, put Jackie Robinson in the club's starting lineup, Barber's journalistic faith was tested. He'd been raised with the racial prejudices of his native region. He told his wife that he intended to quit.

"You don't have to quit tonight," Lylah Barber replied. "You can do that tomorrow. Let's have a martini."

After a night's sleep, Barber decided to stay. His job, as he saw it, was to report, and there could have been no more important story than this one. "Suddenly the scales fell off of my eyes, and I had no problem whatsoever," he recalled. "All I did about Jackie Robinson was report. And I'm happy to say that Mr. Rickey was satisfied, and I know that Jackie Robinson was." As Don Newcombe, another groundbreaking Black Dodger, reflected long afterward: "I remember Jackie saying years ago that Red was a gentleman, and he always was in his corner and he could always depend on Red to give him the necessary backup he needed. Jackie admired Red very, very much."

Barber's role ushering Robinson into the major leagues elevated him in many circles to near sainthood. In 1957, when the Dodgers decamped for Los Angeles, Barber—who'd become a New York character, drinking at Toots Shor's and dining at 21—stayed put. He joined another legend, Mel Allen, as a play-by-play announcer for the Yankees. These were wonderful years in the Bronx—Don Larsen's perfect game, Mickey Mantle, Roger Maris—but by the mid-1960s, the Yankees were in decline, and the tenor in the booth changed. Barber fell out of favor with new owners looking for a rah-rah sound. In 1966, the team's general manager fired him. After thirty-three years as a major league announcer, he was done.

So Red Barber, who'd first stepped behind a microphone during the Great Depression, moved back to the South, settling in Tallahassee, Florida. For the rest of the 1960s and all of the 1970s, he and Lylah traveled while he wrote occasional columns for the *Tallahassee Democrat*. Until the day Ketzel Levine called, he was a forgotten man in his chosen field.

Barber dazzled Levine from the start by inquiring whether the name

Ketzel was Yiddish for kitten. This was a fact not even most of her Jewish friends knew. He then gave her all she needed for her Jackie Robinson story, proving himself as erudite and articulate as her father had promised. "Wow," she said when they finished. On impulse, she asked if he'd consider working at NPR.

Barber said no. He was seventy-one and receiving Social Security. As he understood it, there was a cap on the amount of outside income he could earn. "I decided I would keep track of Red," she said later.

Nearly a year after that first talk, Levine had reason to call Barber again. Elston Howard, a great Yankee from the 1960s, had died, and she hoped the old broadcaster would give her a few insights for her story. Barber obliged, and she again posed the question: "Would you join us?" Answering that he'd recently turned seventy-two, an age at which Social Security permitted higher outside earnings, he surprised her. He said yes.

Red Barber was coming to NPR, but there was a hitch. Bob Edwards didn't want him. The host's resistance to Barber had nothing to do with the broadcaster. Edwards revered the man. It had to do with how the segments would work. Barber wanted to do them like he'd done radio his entire career—live. Edwards hated live radio. Too many things could go wrong.

By the mid-1980s, people at NPR were starting to refer to Edwards's *Morning Edition* work schedule as America's longest recorded experiment in sleep deprivation. The host climbed out of bed each day at one a.m., downed a cup of black coffee, and pulled away from his suburban Virginia home. At that hour the roads were usually empty except for drunks. (One had already hit Edwards, totaling his car.) Once Edwards got to the studio, he wanted no surprises. Jay Kernis did all that was possible to create a controlled environment for his host. Segments were for the most part taped. Interviews were done in advance. "Every word I was to say was written down—even my name," Edwards recalled. "Nothing was left to chance. It was a ridiculous hour. There was no margin for error. I wanted a safe program. And here this broadcast legend wanted to do live radio."

The talk about airing Red Barber live would have been academic except for a startling coincidence: Tallahassee was one of the twelve American cities from which NPR could broadcast remotely. In 1979 when Minnesota Public Radio's Bill Kling convinced the Corporation for Public Broadcasting to establish uplink capacities around the country, WFSU, the Florida State University station, signed on. The station was willing to run a line from its studio to the single-story brick home where Red and Lylah lived. He could do his segments in his study, talking into an Electro Voice 635A mic and using a stopwatch on his desk to track the time. Barber wanted to do it. *Morning Edition*'s wary host acquiesced.

Henceforth at 7:35 a.m. every Friday, *Morning Edition* would convene what Edwards, in a nod to Barber's red hair, dubbed "the Friday meetin' of the church of the ol' Redhead." The segments eventually got around to the commentator's take on the week in sports, but they always started with an account of the weather in Tallahassee. They also usually included a report on Barber's garden (the camellias got all the attention) and a nod to various family pets, particularly an Abyssinian cat and the mockingbirds that dive-bombed it in the yard. Most important, the segments were infused by Barber's faith in what the host called "traditional values: sacrifice and hard work, modesty in ourselves, and charity toward others."

Barber was not only reviving old-fashioned radio, but he was attempting to revive an old-fashioned world. When the great hurdler Edwin Moses was competing for his one hundredth consecutive victory, Barber talked about the inner strength necessary for such a feat.

"Well," he told Edwards, "I think it's wonderful, not only the physical ability, but it's very important to recognize that when someone continues such a continuity of success the price they pay spiritually, for, you know, continuing to want it so badly."

The host pushed Barber about the spirituality part.

"It's so easy when you win a few times, Bob, to then begin to take it easy and to say, 'Well, I just don't have to get up early tomorrow morning.' It's harder to continue at the top."

When Len Bias, the University of Maryland basketball star, died of a cocaine overdose the night after he was selected second in the NBA draft, Barber reached for what he regarded as the only sufficient source of solace, a verse from the Thirty-Ninth Psalm: "For man walketh in a vain shadow, and disquiet himself in vain; he heapeth up riches and cannot tell who shall gather them."

Barber seemed intent on transforming Friday mornings on NPR into a devotional hour. This was no longer the crackling Red Barber who called Dodgers games. For him, sports were now a hook for addressing life and its meaning. "He had no interest for the increasing smarm in sports," Edwards noted later, "the cheating, the greed. He preferred to focus on the positive, the uplifting, and the downright inspirational. He was a lay reader in the Episcopal Church. He was authorized to preach."

Prior to airtime, Edwards never really knew what Barber intended to discuss. The staff—initially Levine and, after she moved to London to return to arts reporting, Mark Schramm—phoned the commentator every Thursday morning to pitch him ideas, but often as not he didn't bite. The conversation would go where it would go.

"You know what I was thinking, Bob," Barber began on a July Friday in 1984, "All the excitement about Geraldine Ferraro, etc., etc. and they've got the British Open going on at Saint Andrews."

"That's right," Edwards agreed. He was baffled. How was Barber going to connect Ferraro, the Democratic nominee for vice president and first woman picked for a national ticket, to a golf tournament?

"Well," Barber continued, "do you know that Mary Queen of Scots was an avid golf player? And when she was a girl, and sent to France to be educated, she took the game of golf with her. And the young men who chased the ball were called, in French c-a-d-e-t-s: *cadets*. But the French pronounced it cadies. And that term came back with Mary to Scotland . . . And when she became queen in 1542, she played golf openly and gave it her blessing. It was in her reign that this famous old course, Saint Andrews, was founded. So you see, we're just a few hundred years behind over here."

"The things you can learn on public radio," Edwards replied, astonished that Barber had used the links to connect the first female ruler of Scotland not just to the British Open but also to the first woman nominated for United States vice president. There was no preparation for it.

Edwards grew increasingly capable of keeping up with his older but more fluent sidekick. Initially, Barber had referred to the host on the air as "young fella," "son," or, in the Mississippi pronunciation of his Christian name, "Robbit." But in time, owing to Edwards's Kentucky roots and to an honorary designation he'd received from his home state, Barber settled on "Colonel Bob." From anyone else, the honorific would have been ironic, but the ol'

Redhead spoke it with respect. Kernis had started the process of building up his host's ego by encouraging him to be more open on the air. Barber took it a step further. "When I talked to Red," Edwards recalled, "he wouldn't allow me to be Bob Edwards, the cool, calm *Morning Edition* host. When I talked with Red, listeners heard the lifting of my journalistic detachment and skepticism. They heard the Colonel. I became a confident, professional host. Red had plenty to do with my maturation—and with the growth of *Morning Edition*'s audience."

Several years into the run, Red Barber was one of NPR's most celebrated personalities. There were other *Morning Edition* commentators. Tom Shales, the TV critic for the *Washington Post*, reviewed films ("Exposure to *Flashdance* makes you think you're getting dumber even as you watch it"). The novelist Ellen Gilchrist contributed accounts of her rural southern childhood that were so evocative they formed the basis of her memoir, *Falling through Space*. Frank Deford, a standout writer for *Sports Illustrated*, weighed in weekly on aspects of sports that Barber ignored. But it was Barber—who on his seventy-fifth birthday received an on-air toast during *Morning Edition* from NPR nemesis and former baseball play-by-play man Ronald Reagan—who helped keep the network fresh as hard times lingered.

Early in 1985, NPR announced the cancellation of *Weekend All Things Considered* after the Corporation for Public Broadcasting rejected a request for $1.2 million to fund the Saturday and Sunday shows and increase overall arts coverage. To lose a program while the network was still recovering from the debt crisis, hurt, especially with Doug Bennet's long-term plans still incubating. Hoping to help, producer Jeff Rosenberg contacted an unusual source—his dad.

Harry Z. Rosenberg was a Fort Lauderdale, Florida, real estate broker who had recently sold a beach place to H. Wayne Huizenga, the millionaire cofounder of the Chicago-based Waste Management Inc., a garbage-hauling company under investigation for accounting misconduct. The elder Rosenberg and Huizenga had become friends, and he told him that his son's employer, NPR, was still financially shaky. Huizenga, who was a fan of public radio, was interested in underwriting a cultural enterprise that, so to speak, would sanitize his business image. Huizinga and Bennet met, and

NPR received a $100,000 check. *Weekend All Things Considered* remained on the air.

Bennet fawned over Huizenga in a *Los Angeles Times* article, praising his "generous gift." Others found the deal distasteful. Many NPR reporters worried that they could not cover environmental issues honestly if the network concluded its broadcasts by thanking Waste Management Inc. for its support. It was no way to run a news outfit. NPR's president assured them this was just a stopgap. By midyear he was ready to introduce what he believed was the real solution—the new relationship with the stations that NPR had agreed to as part of the bailout.

To the station managers who ran public radio, a scheme whereby the Corporation for Public Broadcasting put its funds directly into their hands, allowing them to buy programming from NPR or any other supplier, was an answered prayer. Minnesota Public Radio would become one of the biggest suppliers, competing directly with NPR. But they didn't get all they wanted. Where Kling and others envisioned an à la carte system, Bennet was proposing an integrated service: if stations wanted *All Things Considered* and *Morning Edition*, they also had to take everything NPR broadcast. "They offered no choices," Mitchell said. "It was all or nothing, and since few stations could get by with nothing, nearly all stations had to buy all."

Although Kling and his allies managed to get NPR to amend its plan, allowing stations to negotiate the annual fee they paid the network and giving independents such as Minnesota a better shot in the production game, Bennet prevailed in the bureaucratic battle. The new way of doing business that public radio adopted kept NPR's programming dominance intact while largely removing it from the politicized stigma of federal money. It was part of what Mankiewicz had wanted, just without the downsides.

During his first years as NPR's news director, Robert Siegel, as he later put it, "spent a lot of time preventing things from happening." To keep his department within budget, he reined in expectations, nixing ambitious projects and vetoing prospective hires. He was essentially the executive in charge of saying no. By early in 1985, however, the climate had changed at M Street. The network's business-altering arrangement with the stations meant that it needed to create new programming. If it did not, stations were now free to purchase shows from competitors such as Minnesota's Bill Kling, who offered not only *Prairie Home Companion* but also before decade's end would introduce the daily business program *Marketplace*. To aid NPR, the Corporation for Public Broadcasting, in its most supportive gesture since the crisis, contributed a one-time-only $950,000 development grant. Station managers, motivated by the increasing listenership for *Morning Edition*, wanted a fresh offering that could do for Saturdays what Bob Edwards's program was doing for weekdays. There was just one problem. The system, recalled Siegel, wanted a "best-of" show consisting of repackaged stories that had aired during the week.

For Siegel, the prospect of broadcasting retreads was almost as dismal as the cost-cutting regime he'd supervised since Mankiewicz's departure. "To me, that whole scheme was like death," he said later. "It was like saying, 'NPR used to make these real great radio programs, but that's it.'" A show consisting of recycled stories "would have been a message to everyone at NPR of talent and creativity that the place was finished."

Nonetheless, Siegel appreciated that he'd been given an opening. He decided that if he "framed the Saturday show differently," he might be able to sell a more exciting idea to member stations and to NPR president Doug Bennet. His best argument: An original program would demonstrate that "NPR is expanding and that it's not going to be small time." It would send a message that the network had recovered from its financial nightmare and was ready to grow.

To persuade the stations, Siegel solicited the assistance of Bill Siemering, the founding NPR programming director, who continued to serve on the network board and, more significant, was now chairman of its program committee. The creator of *All Things Considered* was in a perfect spot to champion new productions, and he said yes. Siegel then took on the job of persuading NPR's boss.

After several months of lobbying, Siegel received the go-ahead. NPR was back in the programming business with an order to create its first new show since the Carter presidency. Just what this program might be was far from clear. Siegel hoped it would contain more adventurous stories than those broadcast by *All Things Considered* and *Morning Edition*. He was thinking of longer interviews and features—even documentaries. His chief concern was that the show not reflect conventional public radio wisdom (he opted against using focus groups to assist in its conception) or even traditional ideas of noncommercial broadcast formats. His instinct was that the program would air in the a.m., but as he later noted, "I didn't want the name 'morning' in it, because I thought it might leap into the afternoon." His title was open ended: *Weekend Edition*.

Although Siegel was content to leave the particulars of *Weekend Edition* up in the air, he was not in doubt as to who would create the show. "We took the best producer in the shop—Jay Kernis." After half a decade running *Morning Edition*, Kernis was both burned out and growing in confidence. He was ready to try something new.

As for the host for *Weekend Edition*, Siegel was likewise not in doubt. Station managers almost unanimously wanted Edwards, but NPR's news director wanted Chicago reporter Scott Simon. "I'd worked with Scott when I was an editor, and he is a guy who makes people look great," Siegel said later. "You edit Scott people think you're a great editor. You produce Scott people think you're a great producer." Simon had also excelled as a guest host of *Morning Edition* earlier in the year when Edwards briefly fell ill. His success in the studio was important. NPR was still financially fragile. This thing "had to be great virtually out of the box," Siegel recalled.

For eight years, Scott Simon had been NPR in Chicago. Tall and dark-haired, he dressed well (a weakness for Prince of Wales plaid suits) and was groomed impeccably. His laughter was contagious and he possessed an uncommon ability to project empathy. He knew everyone in America's second city: advice doyenne Ann Landers was a friend as was the *Tribune* columnist Mike Royko. Unlike his famous NPR counterparts in DC, Simon had not attained such status by cultivating influential sources or breaking news. He was something rarer—a literary journalist, more Jimmy Breslin than Cokie Roberts. "He did this very cinematic style of radio," recalled Siegel. "It was not what Linda or Nina were doing. Scott's stories, unlike theirs, weren't ordered by ideas. He didn't do: Here's idea A, which is countered by B with synthesis at C then back again to A. Scott's stories were about place. They said, 'I'm here right now. I'm not in the studio. I'm out of doors. I'm in a field'" or on a factory floor or in a war zone. Simon accomplished this legerdemain two ways. One, he was a wizard at capturing atmospheric sound. He used his microphone much as an artist uses a brush—or as Siegel more pungently put it: "In every story there was a patented Scott Simon bus fart." Just as important, Simon possessed storytelling ability. If Scott did a piece on "the city sanitation department," his colleague Alex Chadwick later said, "it would be glowing."

Simon's ascent as NPR's in-house auteur began on Sunday, July 9, 1978. It was a hot day, and the reporter spent it at Marquette Park in Chicago covering one of the most disturbing and paradoxical incidents of the late 1970s. The National Socialist Party of America, a neo-Nazi group, conducted a major rally that afternoon that attracted thousands of counterprotestors and nearly as many police officers. The American Civil Liberties Union had gone to court to argue *for* the Nazis' right to march. Simon had reported on the legal disputes leading up to the event, and on the big day he taped for seven-and-a-half hours. Considering the buildup, the march was by traditional journalistic standards anticlimactic. No one was killed or badly injured. As a consequence, network TV news shows buried the story, and the *New York Times* printed it inside. Even Simon was relegated to filing just a short piece for Monday's *A Closer Look*, the predecessor to *Morning Edition*, yet he knew that what he'd witnessed—and what he had on tape—merited greater attention. Sunday night he'd phoned Siegel at home. "I said, 'Look, there was so much that went on that was ugly and fascinating and instructive.' I said it was worth doing a postmortem to see exactly what fed into the march, to say: Here's what really occurred." Siegel agreed, and offered to give his reporter time to put together a lengthy piece.

Simon's story led the Wednesday, July 12, edition of *All Things Considered*, and from the moment he started speaking, it was clear that he was taking listeners somewhere broadcast news rarely goes. This was not a report on America's underlying racial and ethnic hostility. This was a portrait of it.

"The neighborhood itself is entirely white, encircled by areas now predominantly black," Simon began. "The residents work mostly in nearby assembly plants, factories, and small stores. Most own their own homes. In a city of apartment dwellers and racially mixed communities, Marquette Park is conspicuously different, and the park itself is considered to be a symbol of that difference."

Simon zoomed in. Against a backdrop of dogs barking and choppers thrumming, he said:

> By mid-morning, police helicopters had come in low over the park, and wind from their blades was spilling leaves from the trees and raising picnic baskets. Lines of police stood along the sidewalks. Women, older men in knee-length shorts, and children in cutoffs filled the face of the small hill along the street leading into the park. Some had brought folding chairs.

As for the crowd's loyalties, Simon caught them in just a couple of sentences:

> Many brought signs reading JEWS GO HOME. Youngsters wore t-shirts embossed with plain black swastikas.

Simon then introduced the protagonists:

> The Nazis arrived almost unnoticed in a white van pulled up to the entrance of the public restroom. Twenty Nazis, several of them only twelve to eighteen years old, entered the restroom in street clothes and came out in brown shirts.

Followed by the antagonists:

> Also in the crowd were organizers from leftist political groups, wading into lines of those who seemed in sympathy with the Nazis.

After which both sides spoke:

> FIRST MAN: I ain't hit a kike in thirty seconds, man. I wanna hit somebody.
> WOMAN: How come you wanna hit one so bad?
> FIRST MAN: 'Cause they got no right to be here.
> SECOND MAN: I'd rather shoot a nigger.
> FIRST MAN: This is white—and we want to keep it white.

WOMAN: Why don't you share?

FIRST MAN: You got Skokie. You don't want us up in Skokie. We don't want
    you here.

Periodically, Simon cut away from such exchanges to feature the chants
of spectators:

Sieg heil! Sieg heil! Sieg heil!

Simon let these words go without comment. He functioned as dispas-
sionate observer until the end of the piece, when he got into a discussion
with a local about why a group had harassed a Black counterprotestor:

SIMON: There was a moment when, back of me and to the right, there was
    one black guy who somehow wandered in. Some people swarmed over
    him and hit him. Why did they do that?

MAN: He was dancing with the Jews.

SIMON: Because a black was dancing with a Jew, they've got to attack him?
    Does it make any sense to you?

"No," the man conceded. "They don't know that particular guy's background or anything. They just know he's black."

SIMON: And in a sense, that seemed the harshest thing of all the diatribes and
    epithets. In the 1970s in the center of the country it was still possible for
    someone to be beaten up simply because he or she was of a certain race.

That's as close as Simon came to expressing his views. This was a dispatch, not a commentary, and he ended it matter-of-factly:

The police removed their riot helmets and began to file into the row of city
buses that had brought them to the park. The Nazis went directly back into
their van and were taken, by escort, to their nearby headquarters. The demonstration at Marquette Park was over. For National Public Radio, this is Scott
Simon in Chicago.

By network TV news standards, nothing happened in the story. But, of course, everything happened. Here was an intimate home movie of an American impasse—the unbridgeable racial gulf that beneath day-to-day accommodations stretched back a hundred years. For one afternoon, it had surfaced, and Simon had captured it.

Following Marquette Park, Scott Simon was on fire. He could be newsy. In the wake of the attempt by John Hinckley Jr. on the life of Ronald Reagan, he retraced a cross-country bus trip the would-be assassin made from Los Angeles to Washington on the eve of the shooting. He could be silly. Working with Jim Nayder, a producer at Chicago's WBEZ, Simon concocted an April Fools' Day spoof of holier-than-thou back-to-the-earth types that would become known in the annals of NPR as the "Pickle Farm" piece. But it was in stories about place that he excelled. When civil wars broke out in Central America, the network sent him there for an extended stay. His work from the battlefront, recalled Smokey Baer—who'd moved to Chicago and mixed many of the reporter's pieces—was exceptional. On one story "I heard a sound I'd never heard before" on tape—the rifling "sound of a bullet. It passed an inch from Scott's microphone." Simon did more than just get close to the action. He continued to get close to the truth.

On the morning of March 19, 1982, Simon, Kim Conroy, a producer, and engineer Leo del Aguila, whose extracurricular activities were behind him, drove to the main hospital in San Salvador, El Salvador's capital. Two days before, four Dutch journalists had been shot to death while trying to get into rebel territory; the government, which was allied with the United States, said the journalists had been caught in a crossfire. Now a dozen or so reporters were gathered at the front of the hospital where the bodies had been taken. They were waiting for another official statement. Simon, however, was looking for more. "We walked around to the back," he recalled. "We figured we'd find something there, and incredibly enough the door we knocked on was for the morgue."

"Where are the bodies?" asked del Aguila in Spanish. He carried a pistol-grip boom microphone and a Sony cassette machine.

"Over here," responded a worker. The doctors in charge had yet to arrive, and the worker pointed the way.

"Can we see them?"

The corpses of Jacob Andries Koster, Jan Kuiper, Johannes Willemsen, and Hans ter Laan lay on embalming tables. One man had been nearly decapitated, two others bore bloody head wounds. They'd been stripped of most of their clothing. As del Aguila taped, Simon walked around describing what he saw—remnants of blue jeans, coagulating blood, and, in his engineer's words, "powder marks on the faces of the guys." In contradiction to the government's account, the journalists appeared to have been shot at close range.

Simon, del Aguila, and Conroy remained in the morgue for twenty minutes. When they emerged, they knew that they had a scoop based on eyewitness reporting. "Fuck," del Aguila remembered thinking. "We've got to get this on the air."

Along with most of the international press corps, the NPR contingent was staying at El Camino Real Hotel. They'd converted a corner of Simon's room into a ministudio: Shure mixer, portable Ampex reel-to-reel recorder, and a couple of broadcast microphones. As del Aguila dubbed from his cassette machine onto the reel-to-reel, Simon wrote his script. The three then assembled a rough cut that contained Simon's descriptions of what he saw at the morgue, the ambient sound, the narration, and tape of an El Salvador official who maintained that the deaths, far from being premeditated, resulted from the fog of war. Next up: transmission. After unscrewing the mouthpiece of the room telephone, del Aguilia used alligator clips to connect a line from the Ampex to the phone's exposed wiring, dialed NPR, and pressed Play, feeding the story to Washington for that night's *All Things Considered.*

"It was a brilliant piece," recalled John McChesney, Simon's editor, who was at M Street when the piece came in. "Scott basically did an on-air autopsy, describing the wounds. The government said they had been accidentally killed. You could make up your own mind. But clearly they were executed."

Although the *Washington Post* and the *New York Times* would eventually quote outside experts casting doubt on the government's account, for twenty-four hours NPR was the lone outlet to challenge the official version. ("The Salvadoran Army said tonight that the newsmen had died when guerrillas accompanying them opened fire on an army patrol," was all the *Times* initially reported.) "We said good night," del Aguila recalled. "I left Scott's room, and I felt very vulnerable."

The NPR contingent in El Salvador was worried that their story could expose them to retaliation. Within days a list attributed to a right-wing group and targeting scores of journalists in the country for death surfaced. Simon's name wasn't on it, but those of many American reporters were. As a result, McChesney flew to San Salvador to propose bringing his people home. The NPR crew decided to stay, but not before agreeing on a code to transmit to M Street if they encountered danger. In words that could only spell trouble coming from a city boy like Simon, it would say: "I'd love to go fishing sometime."

As is often the case with overachieving young reporters, Scott Simon—who frequently spoke of being "existentially present" in his stories—was trying to find himself through his work. Beneath his articulate and extroverted persona lived an uncertain Peter Pan. He was searching for something that always felt just out of reach, and it all went back to his father, who like his son had worked in radio.

Ernie Simon—Big Ern, as he was known in Chicago—was part personality and part tummler. He hosted WJJD's *Curbstone Cutup*, aired live (initially on radio then TV) from a sidewalk on State Street. The show revolved around Big Ern's impromptu interviews with passersby. "What's your favorite food in the summer?" he might ask, or "Is *Bambi* too serious for the kids?" Banter ensued. Occasionally, visiting celebrities—among them Frank Sinatra—joined Simon on the curb to sing a song or promote a concert. He was a Windy City character, so much so that when a local cartoonist and would-be men's magazine publisher, Hugh Hefner, came out with a book of caricatures called *That Toddlin' Town*, he was in it.

Big Ern married a vivacious Irish American girl named Patricia Lyons. An actress and occasional hand model (she appeared in a national campaign for Diet Rite) she was fast with a quip. (When asked what it was like to live with Chicago's funniest man, she replied, "I wouldn't know.") Patricia Simon was also kind, and she and her husband brought up their only child in a supportive household.

For Big Ern, radio and TV were a means to an end, and that end was stand-up comedy. By the late 1950s he believed he'd perfected his act, and he moved the family to California, where he was soon booked into a hot club, San Francisco's The Hungry I. But Simon's routine, long on schmaltz and mother-in-law jokes, did not go over with crowds craving Lenny Bruce. The *San Francisco Chronicle* columnist Herb Caen disliked Big Ern, dubbing him the "big wind from Chicago" and mocking his wardrobe, which ran to polka-dot bow ties.

Big Ern had bombed. The family returned to the Midwest, but Scott, who was just seven, initially didn't perceive a setback. His father's new job was as field announcer for the Cleveland Indians, "the anonymous, unseen basso buffo crackle rasping in stops and starts over the ballpark speakers." What could be better for a boy? During Big Ern's second year in Cleveland, the Simon family imploded. When Scott asked his mother what was wrong, she said, "Daddy's sick." The sickness was alcoholism. Scott went to live with relatives in DC.

By the early 1960s, Big Ern was back in Chicago, but he was no longer a promising young man. As a DJ working WJJD's morning slot, he spun Joey Dee's "Peppermint Twist" and the Kingston Trio's "Where Have all the Flowers Gone?" telling listeners between discs: "The time is exactly 9:30. Have no fear, Big Ern is here." He often was not. With every break, he was in the men's room drinking. There would be a last hurrah—if you could call it that: a nationwide tour playing straight man to Jerry Lewis. A teenage Scott accompanied the duo on their midwestern dates, watching from the wings as his father headed for the exit. At forty-eight, Big Ern died of a cerebral hemorrhage.

Scott Simon's parents had divorced ten years earlier, and his mother was already married to Ralph Newman, the owner of the Abraham Lincoln Book Shop. Her second husband, whom Scott recalled as being "possessed [of] a personal discipline I wish my father had acquired," did his best to be a role model for his stepson, bequeathing a love of history and literature. But it wasn't enough. After graduating from high school, Scott tried college, but he dropped out of both Northwestern and the University of Chicago. He protested the Vietnam War. Then he went to work for WBEZ television. Telling stories enabled him to pick up the pieces. He was doing just that when

Robert Krulwich recruited him to NPR, and it's what he'd continued to do for nearly a decade.

Everything about Simon in his twenties seemed unsettled. Sexually, he was hard to peg. "Scott was always dating women at NPR," recalled John McChesney, but "there was always this rumor that he was confused." Added NPR reporter Margot Adler, he was "someone who never grew up. He was immature. No one knew whether he was straight or gay." Even when Simon, as was his wont, told raunchy jokes featuring women, it felt like a form of overcompensation. Adler said later, "His [jokes] were infantile and puerile."

Simon's obsession with his appearance just enhanced the rumors about his orientation. He took "the longest showers" of any straight man Leo del Aguila ever knew. His wardrobe always had to be exactly so. During reporting trips, del Aguila insisted that Simon schedule his wake-up calls half an hour before other crew members. This would give him enough time to select the right sweater and make certain that his pants were properly creased.

Just as Simon's sexuality seemed mysterious, so, too, did his faith. His father was Jewish, his mother Catholic, and Scott identified as either or both. He was a member of the tribe who carried an image of Saint Francis in his briefcase. Yet he most frequently presented himself as a Quaker. "I happen to be a member of the Society of Friends," he would tell new acquaintances.

People at NPR commonly used the term *arrested development* to describe Simon. His only long-term relationship was with his Mexican cat, Lenore, who had a weakness for enchiladas and salsa and slept under a poster of the Chicago Bulls star Michael Jordan. Simon never learned how to drive. Assignments out of the office required him to beg coworkers for a ride or take subways and buses. Occasionally, there was an upside. During his reporting on the Chicago Nazis, he found himself at party headquarters one day with no way back to the bureau. Nazi president Frank Collin volunteered to give him a lift. Simon whipped along the Dan Ryan Expressway in a van with a swastika on the side. While he got dirty looks from fellow motorists, he won over Collin as a source.

All through the summer of 1985, Scott Simon and Jay Kernis sat across from each other at a table in an isolated office suite at NPR's M Street headquarters.

This section of the building had been depopulated by the 1983 financial crisis. Discarded desks were scattered across the floor, and the doors to empty cubicles swung open. Adding to the general sense of abandonment, the windows looked out on an apartment-complex pool whose algae-green water festered in the sun.

Kernis chose to locate the *Weekend Edition* operation in this dead zone because it was so uninviting. Far from the buzzing hives of *All Things Considered* and *Morning Edition*, it was a perfect spot to create something different. It became a programming laboratory.

Robert Siegel's instructions to Kernis and Simon were tantalizingly vague: "Once you do the news, have a great time with radio. Just play." Over the years, the only prolonged interactions between the two had involved stories Simon pitched to *Morning Edition* from Chicago. "Scott would call and say, 'I need six minutes tomorrow,'" recalled Kernis, "and I'd say, 'I'll give you five and a-half.' He'd say, 'I need six.' And I'd say, 'Tell me what you're reporting on, and I'll consider it.'" However, there was a simpatico, and from the start the relationship clicked. They laughed at each other's jokes. They finished each other's sentences. "It was like we belonged together," Kernis said later.

The basic concept Kernis and Simon came up with for *Weekend Edition* could be boiled down to five words: "Scott's adventures in the news." Where other NPR programs were content-driven, this one would be personality-driven, and it would be so because Kernis realized that Simon possessed a restless nature that needed release. The quirks, the adolescent energy, the inconsistencies, and the seeking sensibility were sources of strength. "Kernis understood that Scott could do it all," recalled John Hockenberry, who kept tabs on the duo. "Caring for Scott Simon was more complicated than caring for Bob Edwards," Hockenberry added. "Bob was happy to stay in the studio in Washington. He didn't need field trips. Scott wanted to go everywhere. Jay's task was to build a show around that."

Selling *Weekend Edition* to the member stations required more than just selling them on Simon as the star. The two needed a hook, and the one they came up with was groundbreaking in the staid universe of public radio. The program would be a celebration of the American weekend. Each episode would ask: What do Americans do with their leisure time? What are they doing for fun? Where are they spending money? "That's how we spoke about the program to the stations," Kernis said later, "and people nodded and we kept talking that way."

The paradox was that the dapper Simon and Kernis knew nothing about the typical American weekend. "Scott and I were the last two people to reflect on this," Kernis recalled. "We didn't do things that Americans did. We didn't golf. We read books." But the two had hit on something. A year into Ronald Reagan's second term, they recognized that the nation was experiencing a happiness explosion. Wealth, sports, and entertainment were in ascendance. The pieties of the 1960s were in eclipse. Siegel may have intentionally resisted using the word *morning* in the title of *Weekend Edition*, but the show would be the first public radio offering to celebrate what the Reagan years were about. It was morning in America at NPR.

Just how determined Simon and Kernis were to make *Weekend Edition* reflect a different, more buoyant America than the one portrayed on *All Things Considered* and *Morning Edition* quickly became clear. "When we were designing the show," Simon recalled, "we thought: What if we produce it in Chicago? We made the case on paper for originating it from the Midwest. We fleshed out what it would sound like." The idea was shot down.

"Not on your life," cracked Robert Siegel. "If there are any two people at NPR who need adult supervision, it's you two."

Simon and Kernis settled for the next-best idea—they would pretend *Weekend Edition* originated from Chicago. They agreed that rather than assign stories in and around DC, they would order them up from Illinois and Indiana. They also agreed that in Simon's on-air patter, he would refer to the Chicago Cubs and da Bears as opposed to eastern teams. They determined that unlike in Washington, where what passed for wit was a steady drumbeat of policy analysis, they would be lighthearted.

Simon selected the small *Weekend Edition* staff, and he made it a point to hire people from Chicago. Smokey Baer relocated to Washington from there to be a producer. Ina Jaffe, an aspiring Chicago actress who'd been contributing freelance pieces to NPR, moved to DC to be the editor. As for the others, while they weren't Chicagoans, they bought into Simon's vision that the show was going to have a midwestern accent.

They also bought into something else: Simon's centrality to *Weekend*

Edition. The show would spotlight what he did best. One of Simon's greatest strengths was his ability to front long features of the sort he'd reported from Chicago. *Weekend Edition* would conclude "each hour with a seventeen-minute segment," Kernis said later. That was a tall order, but the staff took it on. No sooner had Smokey Baer started work than he pitched such a segment based on a poster he'd seen in a New York subway car. Beneath the headline "Subway Criminals," it displayed sixty mug shots. What struck Baer was not how scary the perps looked but how well photographed they were. He "thought Scavullo" took them. Baer contacted the NYPD and was told, "You want to talk to Arthur Weisberger in the Bronx." A few days later Simon was in the Bronx interviewing Weisberger about his technique while capturing the sounds of jail doors slamming, prisoners shuffling into Weisberger's studio, and cameras clicking.

A weekly, two-hour, national radio program, however, could not survive solely on its host's personality. Which was why one late-summer afternoon, Kernis and Simon sat down in an elegant French restaurant for a lunch arranged by Robert Siegel with a broadcasting legend, someone they hoped could do for *Weekend Edition* what Red Barber had done for *Morning Edition.*

Daniel Schorr had reached an age—sixty-nine—and a journalistic plateau—twenty-three years at CBS—at which he might have been content to drift into a respectable dotage as a university lecturer or, if he wanted to cash in, product endorser. Such were the potential rewards for a reporter whose assignments at the Tiffany Network had taken him from postwar Europe to the White House, where as CBS's Watergate correspondent he'd received one of journalism's highest accolades: membership on Richard Nixon's enemies' list.

A shadow, however, had fallen over Schorr's career, and he was seeking redemption. In 1976, while covering a congressional committee investigating the CIA, Schorr had come into possession of what he considered a newsworthy document. After CBS refused to air his piece on the document, he leaked it to the *Village Voice,* the politically rebellious New York weekly. He believed his obligation as a journalist was to get stories to the public, no matter the vehicle. CBS believed he'd betrayed the network and fired him.

Schorr then endured another high-profile setback. Following a personal courtship by Ted Turner, he had signed on at Cable News Network as its first editorial employee. The hire gave the television news buccaneer from Atlanta just what he was seeking: access and clout. At first, Schorr did wonderful stories. In 1981 he stayed on the air for hours from Rhein-Main Air Base in Germany covering the release of the American embassy workers taken hostage in Iran in 1979. Yet again, the job ended badly. During the 1984 Democratic National Convention, Schorr, believing that his journalistic integrity was at stake, refused to serve as a cocommentator with John Connally, Reagan's secretary of the treasury. In his mind, journalists should not appear on the same platform as politicians. CNN did not renew the reporter's contract.

NPR came courting at the right time. To Schorr, a man whose ego needed constant stroking ("I had suffered too much childhood insecurity," he wrote in his memoirs), a new career as host of a morning radio show—the job he believed NPR was offering him—would put him back in the limelight. It would serve as a rebuke to CBS and CNN. When did he start?

Simon and Kernis exchanged nervous glances. The fabled figure sitting across from them had somehow gotten the wrong idea. It fell to Kernis to disabuse Schorr.

"Dan," the *Weekend Edition* producer finally said, "we are operating as if Scott is going to be the anchor of the show." Then he added: "But you're going to have a big part in it."

With that, Simon and Kernis laid out their vision of Schorr's role on *Weekend Edition*. He would handle two major segments in each episode. One would consist of a nine-minute live conversation with Simon about the week's events. The other would be an in-depth essay or feature story. He would not only receive nearly a half hour of airtime each week, but he would be the go-to commentator. The three agreed to a deal that would bring a figure from CBS's glory days to NPR, providing the program its missing piece.

A few seconds before the inaugural episode of *Weekend Edition* began on November 2, 1985, Scott Simon picked up his phone and announced over the M Street intercom: "What a perfect day for a radio show. Let's do two." With that nod to Mr. Chicago, Cubs shortstop Ernie Banks, NPR's first new show in nearly a decade was on the air.

In accordance with Robert Siegel's mandate, *Weekend Edition* led with the news. The South African government had declared a state of emergency to deal with racial unrest, and that morning President P. W. Botha had revoked the media's right to use video or audio tape in covering events, creating an information blackout. Knowing that South Africa was the biggest story of the year and anticipating just such an occurrence, Simon had earlier in the week recorded a phone interview with Bishop Desmond Tutu. "The government is obviously not in control of the situation," the cleric told the host. "We will not have stability or peace until the apartheid system is dismantled." Although Simon pushed back ("White South Africans say, occasionally, 'Bishop Tutu lives in a big house in a rich white neighborhood and is quite beyond the usual considerations of apartheid'"), it was not the time for skepticism. NPR's new offering had a scoop, one that Dan Rather or Ted Koppel would have envied.

Daniel Schorr was up next. In his inaugural Q&A with Simon, NPR's newest special correspondent addressed one of the mid-1980s' other big stories, the Star Wars defense system, explaining as only a Cold War expert could why the Soviet Union objected to this keystone of the Reagan administration's policies. "As far as they are concerned," he said "if Star Wars goes ahead, it is to them . . . an inducement or even an incitement to have more and more offensive missiles." For his other contribution to the first show, Schorr had flown to Berlin and compiled an essay covering twenty-five years of history. "In 1961," he began, "I saw American and Soviet tanks almost muzzle to muzzle at Checkpoint Charlie. In 1982, I was at Checkpoint Charlie with President Reagan. He called the wall an ugly gray gash, a wound that severed a living city." The wall was now gone. No one else at NPR could have spoken with such authority about the topic.

Weekend Edition was not, however, overly concerned with serious issues. It would be what Siegel ordered—a place to play on the radio. John Schulian of the *Philadelphia Daily News* held forth on the Chicago Bears, who were making a Super Bowl run.

The *Los Angeles Herald Examiner* film critic Elvis Mitchell weighed in on the latest from the movie capital: A new Screen Actors Guild contract requiring producers, in light of the AIDS crisis, to inform actors of roles requiring open-mouth kissing.

Along with Robert Krulwich, who would cover business, Schulian and Mitchell would become early cast members. They would function less as reporters than, in the spirit of the program, conversationalists.

The capper was a Simon-reported documentary, and for the debut Kernis chose one on the *Village Voice*, which had recently been purchased by an outsider (Hartz Mountain pet product baron Leonard Stern). The story, which included sounds of the Village—subway trains and taxicabs—focused on the expected points: the racy classifieds, the literary heritage, the navel-gazing. Columnist Nat Hentoff boasted that the paper didn't "want to understand people elsewhere. We're hip and we know better than anybody else." The times, however, had changed at the *Voice*, and Simon's tag, although it was about the paper, could just as well have applied to NPR.

"Inevitably," he asserted, "the charge is heard that the *Voice* is now upscale and uptown, the anger which inspired it through Vietnam, radical feminism, the Attica uprising and the Christopher Street rebellion now baffled by affluence and half-page advertisements for overpriced Italian sweatshirts."

The response to the *Weekend Edition* premiere was positive. "It's the only show we've ever launched," recalled Siegel, "that from day one the whole system said, 'That's fantastic.'" From the first, added Kernis, "it was a hit." Even NPR president Doug Bennet, who was not given to praise, applauded, although he did so with typical restraint. In a staff meeting the next week, he said, "It's a bold new attempt to see if substance can be replaced by youthful charm."

The acclaim both from member stations and at M Street increased the pressure on the *Weekend Edition* staff. The program would have to excel. From the start, recalled Cindy Carpien, the show's director, "there was such a high bar." The most difficult bill to fill would be the documentaries. Nearly every Saturday from here on out, Simon would be on a plane or train just a few hours after the broadcast concluded. Mondays would find him in a seedy precinct of Times Square hanging out with a young crack addict named Hawk or in Louisiana with an alligator hunter or traipsing through the mountains of West Virginia with Bernard Coffindaffer, a businessman who survived heart bypass surgery thanks to what he viewed as divine intervention and had vowed to erect crucifixes on prominent sites in each American state. The host wouldn't get back to Washington until Wednesday. The staff would then "bang the pieces together," remembered Ina Jaffe, "and it wasn't easy."

The dash to get *Weekend Edition* and its big documentaries on the air gave birth to what was known among the show's staffers as "the forty-eight-hour day," a time warp in which Fridays merged into Saturdays in a blur of activity punctuated by moments of dazed incomprehension. "You'd be sleeping on a couch while Scott was writing," recalled Smokey Baer. "Scott is a very good writer, but like every other writer it was very hard work. Sometimes he wouldn't finish until four a.m. Ina would be there to edit him. Then when she finished, we'd mix the piece to have it ready by eight a.m., when we went on the air."

The insane schedule was complicated by Kernis's particular brand of perfectionism. "Jay has a philosophy," Jaffee said later, "which he made clear to all of us: the show sounds good when the host sounds good." For all Simon's skills, his first takes did not always sound good, because inevitably he'd go over the top in several places. "Scott's a cappuccino with too much foam running over the edge," Simon's longtime NPR colleague Frank Browning once observed. The froth had to be edited. Kernis, who listened to everything the host did before broadcast, made most of the tweaks. "Scott had this infectious laugh during interviews," the producer recalled, "and I thought it was overkill. I made it a point to cut the last half of each laugh from each piece. He sat with me as I did it. He trusted me."

The huddles between Kernis and Simon frequently ended with one or the other quoting a famously poignant remark from the Pulitzer Prize–winning play *Tea and Sympathy*. An older woman (Deborah Kerr) tells a young man (John Kerr) whom she introduced to sex: "When you speak of this, and you will, be kind." Such endearing comments were commonplace. "They were like an old gay couple," said Baer. Kernis reflected, "I think most people thought we were lovers. People would ask, 'Are you?' I'd say, 'No, I just produce him.'"

For all their tenderness, however, Simon and Kernis could turn demented. It often "got raunchy," observed Baer. Each had a blistering sense of humor, and either was capable of blurting out inappropriate comments. One evening, in an attempt to goad a Manhattan-based engineer with whom they were feuding, Kernis picked up the phone, dialed a 212 number, and in a twist on an old joke about the location of Carnegie Hall, barked: "Is this the New York bureau, or should I just go fuck myself?"

Weekend Edition, Baer observed, was very much "a boy's club" amidst the matriarchy that was NPR. Even Dan Schorr was a member. The former CBS correspondent adored Simon ("I quickly became very impressed," he wrote in his memoirs), and he felt at home with the relaxed atmosphere, so much so that he soon stopped wearing a suit to work, arriving at M Street for each broadcast in tennis whites. He had a regular Saturday match with Ohio senator Howard Metzenbaum, and this way he could go directly from M Street to the courts. Shortly after Schorr adopted the casual look, he experienced a major wardrobe malfunction. As producer Richard Rarey was adjusting the reporter's microphone prior to the featured back-and-forth with Simon, he looked down and noticed that the great man's penis had escaped the confines of his shorts and was dangling in full view of the staff.

"Little Dan is out," Rarey whispered. Schorr eventually realized what the producer was trying to tell him, and zipped up in time for the broadcast.

Weekend Edition's remote offices were undoubtedly the most uninhibited precinct at NPR. Recalled Carpien, "Jay and Scott were tempestuous children." Kernis agreed. "Did we go too far?" he later asked rhetorically. "Probably. But we were having fun"—and it wasn't just the men. The show's women were on board. "It was a place where people would yell, emote, and express themselves," said Jaffe. "But nobody got angry. We had a great time together." In part, this was because, in Carpien's words, "we were nutty people." But there was something else. With *Weekend Edition*, NPR had reestablished the network's desire to do superlative work. Everyone on the staff was pulling sixty-hour weeks, and they were often trying the impossible. The show had cutaways each hour for the local stations. During that time on other programs, the network typically broadcast filler, but *Weekend Edition* took a different tack. "We decided to make the cutaways remarkable," Kernis said. In essence, they were daring the stations to take a break. "If they cut away, they would miss something wonderful." It was madness of the best kind— exhilarating and inspiring. Life had returned to NPR.

FIVE

CHANGING OF THE GUARD

"Kim Williams," Susan Stamberg began, "What is it that you have heard from the doctor? Please tell us."

"I have terminal cancer. It started out as ovarian cancer, and then I guess it turned into a general cancer of the abdomen."

The July 16, 1986, broadcast of *All Things Considered* was until that instant proceeding like any other during the fourteen years Stamberg had fronted the show. She and Noah Adams cycled through the news of the day. US troops were in Bolivia interdicting drug traffickers. The New York Police Department announced it had halted the investment of pension funds in South African companies. All was on course until the final feature, which was reserved for Williams, the Missoula, Montana, naturalist whose paeans to homespun virtues and foraging for food had made her *ATC*'s most popular commentator.

Stamberg's response to Williams's revelation was a stunned: "Hmm." There was nothing to do but plunge ahead. "Have you been given some kind of time frame, Kim?"

"No, but I would say it's within a month."

"Umm-hmm." Then: "How are you feeling right now, Kim?"

"Well, tired."

"And what are you saying to yourself these days, Kim?"

"I'm saying to myself that it's time to move on."

"I take it that you're turning down any sort of extraordinary means?"

"Yes. I belong to Hospice. I want to die in peace—not in pieces."

"Kim, how would we get in touch with you if we wanted to write?"

"You mean after I've passed to the next dimension?"

"No, ma'am. This minute."

Williams burst into laughter. It was too late for words. But after a pause, she proposed something else. "It's amazing how many letters I've received from people who say they are going to climb a mountain or walk along a river or on a city street, and they will send their thoughts and energies, and they think that they will meet mine."

"I believe that," Stamberg replied.

"I do, too."

"Kim, thank you very much."

"Thank you, Susan."

"Good-bye."

What followed emphasized the starkness of what had just occurred: the click of Williams hanging up the phone. *All Things Considered*'s Neenah Ellis, who produced the conversation, left it on the tape. The sound, Stamberg said later, "tipped me over." For the first time in the host's NPR career, she began to cry on the radio. By clenching her fists, she made it through the sign-off. Once they were out, she could not hold back.

"It's too hard. It's too hard," Stamberg told Noah Adams. Her cohost, she recalled, was "quite alarmed." It was nothing, however, compared with what she felt. The Williams interview would have been difficult under any circumstances, but unbeknownst to colleagues, Stamberg had been diagnosed with breast cancer the week before, and the news of Williams's impending demise struck doubly hard. "The bottom of the world had fallen out. I was sure it was a sentence of death."

At the end of July, Stamberg underwent a lumpectomy and began the prescribed six months of radiation treatment. Early every afternoon she would leave M Street with the seeming nonchalance of someone going out for coffee. At NPR, only Adams and Robert Siegel, both of whom she swore to secrecy, knew that she was headed to George Washington University

Hospital. There, she would lie down on a gurney beneath a device attached to a mechanical arm, and the exorcism would proceed. The machinery was loud—pinging, banging, clanging. To distract herself, Stamberg focused on upcoming interviews and stories. "I've always found work very healing," she said later, "a place to take my mind off other things." Soon enough, however, the diversionary tactics lost their effectiveness, and her thoughts leapt in the opposite direction. The time had come to move on from *All Things Considered*. "I had cancer. I wanted out."

Stamberg's decision was not altogether surprising. From the start, she, more than any other NPR host, had maintained a self-protective distance from the all-consuming nature of life at the network. During her first year fronting *All Things Considered*, she worked only Mondays and Tuesdays, leaving the rest of the week to Mike Waters. She had a young son, and she was determined to be at home for his early childhood. For a while, that was fine with NPR, but soon, the schedule became a problem. Susan "was so good," recalled her original producer, Jack Mitchell. "We wanted her on every day." Here again, Stamberg demanded that the network bend to her will. Starting in 1974, she and Waters (and later Bob Edwards) broadcast together nightly, but the second half hour was always on tape, as were Stamberg's parting words. The accommodation allowed her to work shorter shifts.

In 1983 in a further concession, NPR gave Stamberg Fridays off. Nina Totenberg began cohosting *All Things Considered* in her place. Sanford Ungar, Edwards's replacement, bridled at the arrangement. "I was outraged," he said later. "Why should I have to do it five days a week and the other four?" The answer was obvious. Stamberg was a star, and the job had become a grind. She had been through so many different regimes that she felt she had single-handedly kept the signature program on the air. "I felt like I was hauling that anchor," she recalled. "We had a carousel of producers."

Some at NPR quietly asked whether Stamberg was more trouble than she was worth. "There were conversations in Mankiewicz's office," recalled Ungar, "where Mankiewicz, Barbara Cohen, and I were sitting there talking about who were possible replacements for Susan. I came to understand that Susan would be leaving the program." As it turned out, Ungar was the one who left the program and, along with Mankiewicz and Cohen, ultimately the network. For the next several years Stamberg continued to push hard. "I felt

ike [the show] was my child." But cancer changed everything. "When I had
that diagnosis," she recalled, "I put the other stuff aside." Getting well was all
that mattered. After telling Robert Siegel of her plans, the two went to lunch
at a Marriott hotel near work. To test her certainty, he posed a question that
emphasized what she'd be losing.

"The next time a space shuttle blows up or a great writer dies, are you sure
you don't want to be the person telling the news to two million listeners?"

"Yes."

In September 1986, two months after her interview with Kim Williams and
a month after Williams's death, Susan Stamberg stepped down as host of *All
Things Considered*, the program that had established NPR. The network's
president, Doug Bennet, gave her a going-away party, but otherwise there
was no fanfare and no on-air explanation for her departure. Stamberg's
quiet stoicism impressed Siegel ("She's an emotionally solid person. Today
a host would do a six-part series."), and he felt relief that she would not be
leaving altogether. Emboldened by the success of Scott Simon's *Weekend
Edition*, the network had initiated plans to launch a Sunday version of the
show, and Stamberg had agreed to front it. The new job would allow her to
stay in public radio while diminishing what she felt had been a factor in her
illness—the stress of a daily broadcast. For all that, Siegel was in a bind. NPR
had lost its most identifiable personality, and it was his responsibility to find
a replacement.

The fall of 1986 featured an ever-changing parade of temporary hosts—
Totenberg, Linda Wertheimer, the political reporter Wendy Kaufman—sitting
down opposite the now-indispensable Noah Adams. Meantime, Siegel and
executive producer Ted Clark, formerly NPR's White House correspondent,
contemplated replacements for Stamberg.

The strongest contender was Margot Adler, a reporter in NPR's New York
bureau. Forty years old with long, straight dark hair and a throaty, contralto
voice glinting with mischief, Adler was a graduate of both the University of
California, Berkeley, and the Columbia University School of Journalism. She
was the network's first employee to receive a prestigious Nieman Fellowship at Harvard. Her fund of knowledge ran deep. Along with the physicians
Sigmund Freud and Carl Jung, her grandfather, Alfred Adler, had pioneered

psychoanalysis. From girlhood, Adler lived a life of the mind. Philosophically, she was a free-speech absolutist who'd been in the crowd at Berkeley's Sproul Hall in 1964 when Mario Savio founded the movement. Politically, she was to the left, having visited Cuba in 1969. Spiritually, she was a witch, a Wiccan priestess and the author of *Drawing Down the Moon*, an important history of neopagan beliefs. But her true love was radio. One way or another she had been in the business for twenty years. At NPR, she practiced what she called "anthropological journalism," turning out long, thoughtful stories on everything from the emotional travails of Shanti counselors who worked with AIDS patients in San Francisco to a twenty-minute documentary on the Michigan Womyn's Music Festival, which as she put it was "about eighty-five percent lesbian but felt like it was ninety-nine percent and which I got onto *All Things Considered* even though at the time they were wary of the word 'lesbian.'"

Adler was a natural-born host. Early in her career, she created and anchored *The Hour of the Wolf*, a show of talk and reverie that aired at five a.m. daily on New York's Pacifica outlet, WBAI. "I'd turn the station on some mornings," she recalled. "I'd be sitting essentially in this spaceship, with all the dials flickering. It was like I was the captain. I'd open the phone lines, and at that hour people would say anything. I came to see that radio could be a pure medium of thought, imagination, and revelation." Neal Conan, who met Adler in those days, believed the experience gave her an unparalleled understanding of the demands of fronting a program. "She'd spent so much time on the air as a host that she had utterly absorbed the intricacies of technique that many hosts struggle with."

The greatest raw talent at NPR was John Hockenberry. The forty-year-old broadcaster continued to function in a utility role as the *All Things Considered* newsreader, but he contributed deeply reported and imaginatively produced stories to *ATC* and *Weekend Edition* that one colleague termed "dazzling." It was as if in compensation for his wheelchair-bound existence, he was attempting to walk, sometimes even to fly, on the radio. Part of it was intellectual curiosity. He was open, for instance, to reporting about topics others at the boomer-centric network eschewed—say, hip-hop. "John was the first person I was aware of at NPR to do a piece on rap music," recalled Michael Fields, a Black journalist who started at M Street as a production assistant in 1986. Part of it was style. For a story on Putt-Putt Golf, Hockenberry composed a heroic anthem to celebrate this least heroic of sports and then performed it during the piece, accompanying himself on the ukulele.

Then there was Terry Gross, who although a relative newcomer to NPR was the one person who not only resembled Stamberg in approach to interviewing but also could fairly claim to be the embodiment of the ideas behind *All Things Considered*. A graduate of the SUNY-Buffalo, Gross had started her career as the host of *This Is Radio*, the program launched by Bill Siemering when he was station manager at WBFO and which he regarded as the prototype for *ATC*. In 1975, Gross moved to Philadelphia, where she created a show on WHYY called *Fresh Air* and ended up working for Siemering. With its incisive conversations and its emphasis on reviews and cultural news, *Fresh Air* was what *All Things Considered* might have become had NPR not fired Siemering. After Stamberg left *ATC*, NPR gave Gross a two-week trial.

In the end, none of the homegrown contenders made the cut. With Adler, the basic problem was the witch thing. Although she was a genuine intellect with true sensitivity, she was not above having fun with pointy hats and spells. In 1974, she posed for *Us* magazine in a long, flowing gown while standing in a Central Park pond, and she was frequently identified in the media as a priestess. "It'd been clear for many years that NPR was not comfortable that I was doing this Wicca/pagan stuff," she recalled. As long as she was a reporter, the network tolerated her beliefs, but when the bigger opportunity came along, attitudes changed. "Some station manager sent Doug Bennet a copy of my book and a note saying, 'We can't have that.'" Later, Jude Doherty, who'd recently become director of *All Things Considered*, said, "Bennet was not the kind of guy who knew how to deal with a lusty Jewish witch from New York."

With Hockenberry, the issue was personality. He was "difficult" to work with, recalled Steve Reiner, briefly his producer at *All Things Considered*. "He's a complete asshole," declared the longtime NPR reporter Jacki Lyden. "John is a smart guy," veteran *ATC* editor Smokey Baer said, "but he's not a nice guy."

As for Gross, the Stamberg chair on *All Things Considered* would have disrupted plans already agreed on at NPR. In 1985, the network had begun distributing *Fresh Air* on a limited basis to stations outside Philadelphia. A nationwide rollout was slated for 1987—that, not *ATC*, was Gross's ticket.

There was also something else. At a public radio forum after Stamberg stepped aside, Bennet told the group: "Our programs are not personality driven." The remark wounded Stamberg. "I was hurt. I *was* a personality." The point went to the concept of what NPR would now become. The day of charismatic women and men behind the mic was over. Yes, people like Edwards and Simon remained, but at the top, there was resistance to adding new ones like Adler, Hockenberry, or Gross. "In the future," Bennet told Jack Mitchell, "NPR would de-emphasize distinctive personalities. NPR would attract listeners with its institutional integrity. NPR would have interchangeable and replaceable hosts." The network president envisioned a slate of "competent but colorless hosts. None would stand out. All would embody the NPR style. Listeners would tune in to hear a solid and dependable NPR news product."

Siegel and Ted Clark continued their search. If idiosyncratic NPR talent was part of the receding past, the primary candidate from the world beyond M Street just wasn't interested. In 1983, when NBC television canceled *News Overnight*, its cohost, Linda Ellerbee, who while at NBC *Weekend* coined the signoff "And so it goes," was out of a job. NPR made a run at her, but she wanted to remain in TV and joined ABC's *Good Morning America*. Stymied, NPR turned to its personnel department, which just made matters worse. "It was comical," Siegel said later. They "sent us a woman who did appliance shows—a hostess at industrial shows. That's how they interpreted us."

As 1986 drew to a close, a savior presented herself in the person of a longtime Washington broadcaster who was both an NPR insider and outsider. In 1981, after helping to launch *Morning Edition* and two years of reading the news on the show, Jackie Judd had jumped to CBS radio, where she served as a writer for the commentator Charles Osgood before becoming anchor of the network's hourly five-minute news updates. That was fine for a while, but by 1986, Judd recalled, "I was done at CBS. I'd done everything I could do." When Siegel approached her about the *All Things Considered* job, her heart leapt. The prospect of replacing Stamberg was intoxicating. "I idolized" her." Just as important, she was thrilled at the idea of partnering with Noah Adams. Before joining *Morning Edition*, she and Adams had cohosted

Weekend All Things Considered. "We'd established ourselves as a team, and there was an assumption that this would work again." Siegel shared her view. "I saw Jackie as a straight man to the unconventional Noah." After tense salary negotiations (Judd earned more as a CBS newsreader than NPR could pay her to helm its signature program), the parties came to an agreement.

At which point it all fell apart. "Joe Gwathmey, my boss, had gotten word that Noah was at Minnesota Public Radio being wooed by Bill Kling," recalled Siegel. Although hostility at M Street toward the Darth Vader of public radio had diminished in the years since Mankiewicz departed, wariness remained, and in this instance, it was warranted. Buoyed by the success of his 1985 novel *Lake Wobegon Days* and in love with a woman who lived in Europe, Garrison Keillor was quitting *Prairie Home Companion,* getting married, and moving abroad. Kling hired Adams to replace him. In three months, the broadcaster NPR had counted on to stabilize *All Things Considered* would be gone. "That threw everything off for me with Jackie," Siegel said later, adding that without the quietly imaginative Adams to provide the sparks, she was too matter-of-fact to front a nightly show. Suddenly, the network had no options, but that didn't forgive the way its managers treated Judd. Neither Siegel nor anyone else told her. "We were far down the road," she remembered. Then: "We were nowhere. No pun intended: it was radio silence. It was poorly handled—a terrible thing to do to anyone, but especially terrible to someone with my history at NPR. Someone asked me to the prom, then didn't show up."

Had Jackie Judd been listening to *All Things Considered* on Christmas Eve 1986, she would have heard the debut hosting appearance of the journalist who had improbably become the front-runner to anchor NPR's premier program.

At five foot one, her short, dark hair highlighted by blond streaks, and her wardrobe typically consisting of black blouses, black miniskirts, and lace-up red Capezio boots, thirty-eight-year-old Renee Montagne was even by her own estimation the last person who might have reasonably caught the attention of the people running *All Things Considered.* "I never applied. I never thought about it. *All Things Considered* was way out of my reach."

Montagne, the daughter of a Marine Corps major, grew up in base towns all over the world before attending UC Berkeley. Since 1980, she had worked for NPR's New York bureau. She had a desk and a telephone, but beyond these tools, the network offered her only the barest semblance of support. She was so-called shadow staff, paid $25 per minute for contributions that made the air. If she took a week to knock out a demanding, nine-minute feature, she earned $225. (To survive, she freelanced for the Canadian Broadcasting Corporation.) In a good year she took home $11,700. Thinking back on her deal with NPR, she said, "It was practically illegal."

Montagne lived in a 290-square-foot apartment on Horatio Street in the West Village, but even that was too expensive. Well into her thirties, she received help on the rent from her father. Still, Montagne loved her life. She ran with a crowd of mostly intellectuals and artists, and they stayed out until all hours listening to Henry Threadgill at the Tin Palace, a jazz club down the block from CBGB. Come morning she'd straggle into NPR to do her stories, which were by all accounts excellent. "I knew her as a good reporter," recalled Stamberg. Others had also noticed her work, among them Ted Clark and Noah Adams, who, Siegel observed later, said, "Renee was the best one-day producer at NPR," meaning she was could turn around a news piece quickly.

Montagne's premiere on *All Things Considered* was better than anyone had expected. Adams, who was playing out the string, went to great lengths to make her feel at home. "There was a comfort factor," she recalled. "Noah and I sort of sparkled." Still, Montagne returned to New York expecting to plunge back into anonymity. A few days later, her phone rang.

"After hearing you on Christmas Eve," Ted Clark told her, "we'd like to hear you for two weeks."

Montagne's extended tryout was even more triumphant, in part, she later said, because she was unaware of the position's difficulties. "I didn't get the level of performance needed to carry that job off," she recalled. "I wasn't nervous. It was just really interesting and kind of fun." Siegel and Clark were knocked out.

The last day of Montagne's trial run, Clark asked her to huddle with him in one of the few spots that provided privacy at M Street—an editing booth.

"We want to offer you the job," said Clark.

"That would be hard to turn down," Montagne replied.

Although the two did not discuss terms, Clark, with a penuriousness typical of NPR, said that one point was unnegotiable: the network did not pay moving expenses.

That evening, Montagne ate dinner with Adams at the Tabard Inn. With fading prints on the walls, heavy wood furniture, dim lighting, and a clientele that ran to union organizers and political operatives, the place was to NPR what 21 had once been to New York media titans. Here, the departing veteran advised the heir apparent how to proceed. First, he urged her not to take a cent less than what he was earning: $50,000 a year. For a second, Montagne felt faint. Her salary would quintuple. As she contemplated this, Adams, as a personal favor, asked her to resist a recent management edict aimed at phasing out what from the start had been a tradition on *All Things Considered*—the two words with which the hosts began each broadcast: "Good evening." To Adams, that salutation was a vestige of tradition and radio decorum. ("It really mattered to him," recalled Montagne.) But to Bennet and others, it was an impediment to a moment just beyond the horizon when the program would exist out of time, freed by technology from the clock's constraints.

The next morning, Clark agreed to Montagne's demand for a $50,000 salary and threw in $1,000 to pay for a U-Haul to truck her belongings from New York to Washington. (He would not, however, spring for a hotel during the move; she could room with friends.) As for Adams's hope that Montagne would hold the line on the words "Good evening," she did what she could, but soon enough the greeting went the way of vacuum tubes.

For Robert Siegel and Ted Clark, Renee Montagne was a blessing, but she was only one part of the solution. The two now needed someone to replace Noah Adams. The most visible and vocal possibility was Bob Edwards, the host of *Morning Edition*. After seven years of answering a ghostly one a.m. wakeup call, he believed he'd earned the right to return to the land of the living. "I had paid my dues," he later observed. "Now could I please resume normal sleeping hours?" Siegel, however, was resistant. *Morning Edition* had become just as important to NPR—maybe more so—than *All Things Considered*, and he was not about to tamper with success. Also, he didn't like Edwards. "One of the least pleasant things in my job was dealing with Bob," he recalled. "He was very cranky."

There was a surprise candidate. For the past year, Siegel had wanted out of management. Although he'd taken satisfaction in saving NPR news from the post-Mankiewicz numbers crunchers, he felt his greatest achievement had been undervalued. With *Weekend Edition* "we lobbed an incredibly success-ful show onto the air," he said later. "In commercial broadcasting when you do this, you get rich. In public radio, no one notices that you had anything to do with it. It was at that moment that I pretty well knew that sooner or later I had to get back to being on the radio." Encouraged by Gwathmey, Siegel applied for Adams's job, and Bennet said yes. Around M Street, conspiracy theories sprang up. "There was a vacancy at *ATC*," recalled Alex Chadwick. "Robert Siegel led the search, and lo and behold he discovered Robert Siegel." This was one of the kinder ones. "There were mean things said about Rob-ert," Montagne added. "People said he hired me because he wanted someone he could manipulate after he crowned himself king." (Many believed Siegel had shunned Judd because he already had his own elevation in mind and was threatened by her competence. "It was clear that Robert didn't want to be partnered with me," Judd said later.) Regardless, *All Things Considered* had a new team. Attempting to make sense of it, Montagne floated the view that the match replicated the Stamberg-Adams configuration. "Robert was the new Susan, and I was the new Noah." The show remained in the hands of an Ivy League–educated New York Jew and a gentile from the hinterland. "People at NPR considered things like this," recalled Montagne.

The selection of Renee Montagne and Robert Siegel to host *All Things Con-sidered*, while filling the visible holes opened a new hole that threatened the identity of NPR itself. For more than a decade, NPR news, which pro-duced most of the network's programming, had reflected either Siemering's emphasis on journalism that provided "meaning and joy" (Jim Russell), Mankiewicz's obsession with political power (Barbara Cohen), or a combi-nation of both (Siegel). With Siegel's exit from management, the network's soul was in play.

Neal Conan returned to Washington from London to handle the top news job on an interim basis. During his four years abroad, Conan had followed both his own interests and the vagaries of a changing world. Where Siegel had loved Parliament and being on hand to chronicle the rise of Thatcherism,

Conan got through his tour without filing a single story on British elections. He was drawn to less predictable places. After doing a piece from Austria on the rise to power of Kurt Waldheim, he became obsessed with Europe's inability to shake the allure of fascism. "I kept tripping over Nazis." He was also captivated by the ongoing religious and political strife in Ireland. Renewed tension in the Middle East became a recurring story, as did the Chernobyl nuclear disaster in Ukraine.

American journalistic tradition practically dictated that repatriated London bureau chiefs assumed exulted status, whether it was Peter Jennings after his English posting becoming anchor of ABC's *World News Tonight*, or R. W. Apple following his stint overseas becoming the principal Washington correspondent of the *New York Times*. "Under normal circumstances, Neal would have gotten Siegel's job," Chadwick later noted. "Neal is a very good newsman." Doug Bennet wanted an open selection process, and he engaged a headhunter to put together a list of candidates for the position.

The three finalists for the job included Conan. It seemed an evenly matched group, and each was asked to write a critique of NPR's programming. But from the start there was a clear favorite. According to a substantial *Washington Post Magazine* story by Marc Fisher, the front-runner was Matt Storin, editor of the *Chicago Sun-Times*. A forty-five-year-old Notre Dame graduate, Storin was regarded as a journalist's journalist. He'd risen to prominence at the *Boston Globe*, where he was by turns a writer in the paper's Washington bureau and its Asia editor. The *Sun-Times* gig was a step up, but he tired of the Midwest, and the NPR position offered a return to familiar turf. There was, however, an unstated but mandatory hurdle for employment at M Street—an interview with the troika. Shortly after a session with Wertheimer and Roberts, Storin received a call from a go-between who said "the news staff did not want him at NPR." The *Post* reported that Totenberg was the source of the opposition. "I was told Nina was against me," Storin told Fisher. "I never understood what happened." Around NPR, however, there were no doubts.

The internal resistance to Storin allowed Bennet to pursue his own inclinations. Since his arrival at M Street, the network president had become concerned that while NPR presented itself as an organization that championed equal opportunity, it was, in the words of the Black production assistant

Michael Fields, "a liberal racist institution." The network employed only two Black reporters—Phyllis Crockett on Capitol Hill and Brenda Wilson at the White House. Bennet was committed to making a change. "Bennet felt very strongly about rectifying racial wrongs," recalled Jack Mitchell, who after leaving NPR had not only remained connected to public radio through the University of Wisconsin station but also been elected chairman of the NPR board. During this period, he spoke with Bennet weekly. Bill "Siemering believed in diversity," Mitchell said later, "but Bennet wanted a serious affirmative-action program. With Bennet it was more legalistic."

Which was why, with Storin derailed, the third candidate eclipsed Conan. As Siegel put it, Adam Clayton Powell III "was a dream come true for Doug Bennet."

The name cast a spell. Adam Clayton Powell Jr., Adam III's father, was the twelve-term US congressman from New York, where he was also pastor of the Abyssinian Baptist Church in Harlem. Powell Jr., lifted to power by the likes of poet Langston Hughes, was instrumental in persuading President Dwight Eisenhower to follow through on Harry Truman's desegregation of the American military and helped Lyndon Johnson push through his War on Poverty. He coined the slogan "Black Power." A suave swashbuckler, he was a regular on the Manhattan club scene, usually with a lovely woman, who might or might not be his wife, on his arm. He was a bit of a scoundrel, as willing to attack a liberal ally as go after a hidebound racist. In the late 1960s, following allegations of financial impropriety, the Democratic Caucus stripped him of the chairmanship of the House Educational Committee. As Eisenhower once noted, "Here's a man that's got everything. He's handsome. He's brilliant. But goddammit, he's tricky."

Hazel Scott, the second Mrs. Adam Powell Jr. and Adam III's mother, was an even more dazzling figure than her husband. A native of Trinidad and a child piano prodigy ("I am in the presence of a genius," declared a Julliard professor after hearing a young Scott play Rachmaninoff's Prelude in C-sharp Minor), she made her world premiere at Carnegie Hall at twenty. By that point, she had developed what became a signature style, beginning classical pieces in a conventional manner then, near their conclusion, switching to a syncopated beat that critics termed "witty, daring, modern, but never irreverent." She married Powell Jr. in 1945, and her touring, which featured international dates and regular gigs at Manhattan's High Society nightclub, never slowed. While pregnant with Adam III, she recorded a jazz version of a Chopin waltz.

Adam III, whose parents called him "Skipper" (one day he hoped to become a sailor), grew up a high-end latchkey kid. Although the family maintained an apartment at 138th Street and 7th Avenue, across from the Abyssinian Baptist Church, its main residence was in suburban Mount Vernon. There young Adam would awaken Monday mornings to find carbon copies of his parents' schedules posted in the kitchen: "I'd see that my mother is in Pierre, North Dakota, and my father is in Pensacola, Florida," he recalled. "But they would make it a point of coming home Friday night so that Saturday when I got up, they would be there. Only later did I realize what that involved. I always wondered, 'Why are they sometimes so tired?'"

Weekends were devoted to family life. Mother, father, and son would walk to the nearby Parkland Theater for Abbott and Costello double features or cartoons. In the fall, there were touch football games on the lawn with neighborhood kids. Hazel Scott, who loved sports, always participated. But because she'd insured her hands for $1 million with Lloyd's of London, she kept them tucked under her arms. Evenings were given to opera and talks about racial justice—Adam III sometimes listened in on his father's phone chats with civil rights figures like the Reverend Martin Luther King Jr.

Such interludes did not last. Adam Powell Jr. was an inveterate womanizer, and he made little effort to hide it. In 1957, Scott left her husband and moved to Europe, taking Skipper with her.

Adam Powell III attended high school in Paris, where he grew into a tall young man, became fluent in French, and acquired a sophisticated surrogate family. Notable Black Americans abroad flocked to Hazel Scott's apartment. Skipper talked literature with James Baldwin and music with Max Roach and Dizzy Gillespie. His true interest was science, particularly nautical engineering. After graduation he returned home and enrolled at MIT.

In college, Powell's ambitions changed. He worked at the MIT radio station, and in 1964, thanks to the legendary TV reporter Mike Wallace, a friend of his father's, he landed an internship at CBS News in New York. For the next three summers, Powell hung out at CBS's Black Rock, getting to know Don Hewitt—the producer who invented 60 Minutes—and other network bigwigs. He was then hired by WRVR, the Riverside Church public radio station on Manhattan's Upper West Side, as news director. He met another young broadcaster there—Robert Siegel. Following a stint at WCBS TV, he returned to radio, joining WINS, where he helped introduce the very un-NPR innovation of rapid-fire newscasts promoted by the slogan: "Give us Twenty-Two Minutes and We'll Give you the World." In the late 1970s he was back at CBS television news, where he directed coverage of special events, such as political conventions and NASA launches.

Powell married into an elite, white family. Beryl Slocum of Newport, Rhode Island, was a descendent of the Browns of Brown University and the daughter of Eileen Slocum, known as the most "consummate party giver" in Newport. That she feted Republican politicians—among them Nelson Rockefeller and Gerald Ford—was no surprise, as she was vice chairman of her state's Republican Central Committee and a frequent delegate to Republican national conventions. Eileen Slocum's true stature in society was measured by her work as a clubwoman. She devoted much of her energy to such restricted Newport dives as the Reading Room and the Spouting Rock Beach Association and took great pride that these redoubts had yet to be breached by Hollywood swells or Wall Street barbarians. As she told the *Providence Journal*: "By being rather fastidious about the people in the clubs, we've managed to control the particular atmosphere of the community."

Powell's entrance into this exclusive, inbred world was not smooth. In the words of *Town & Country*, the biracial wedding was "shocking" and some in the Slocum family took it as a "betrayal." Prior to the ceremony, Beryl Slocum's aunt threatened: "If you do this we can never speak to you again." In a textbook act of tribal retribution, the *Social Register* struck the name of Powell's wife from its pages.

By the time NPR sought out Adam Powell III, he had bought and lost control of an Oakland radio station: KFYI. He'd also run a broadcast consultancy and served on the national advisory panel to the Congressional Office of Technology Assessment. He and Beryl, after having two sons, had divorced, and he was living with his oldest boy in the San Francisco Bay community of Sausalito. It was there in the summer of 1987 that he picked up the phone and learned of the opening at M Street.

"Listen to *Morning Edition* and *All Things Considered* for a few days," Doug Bennet said, "and we'll take it from there."

Powell did not at first see this opportunity as serious, believing that at best, NPR might end up being "a nice little consulting gig." Nonetheless, he spent a week listening to the radio and taking notes. He then borrowed his son's Vic-20 computer and typed up his impressions of the network's shows. Unfettered by a strong desire for the job, he wrote what he thought. ("Why did Renee [Montagne] leave out the premise" of her story?) After finishing, he hit Print on "our old fan-fold printer," put the pages in a FedEX envelope, and thought no more of it.

The next morning at five Pacific, Powell was jarred awake by the ringing of his phone.

"Adam."

Powell had not heard from Cokie Roberts since the late 1970s, when she was in Europe stringing for CBS News and he was with the network in New York, but he recognized her voice. The two went back years to when their fathers were both in Congress and they were part of a group of children who roamed the Capitol and referred to themselves as "hill brats."

"Hi, Cokie," he said groggily.

"We love your analysis," Roberts said, adding that Bennet had posted it on the newsroom bulletin board.

Powell's dispatch indeed contained more insight than any of the others. Wrote the *Post's* Fisher: It "was the most impressive" of all the submissions. However, the key thing about the call was the identity of the caller. Many at NPR believed Roberts had been campaigning for her childhood chum all along and that this explained why the troika vetoed Storin.

Later that day, Powell heard from Bennet, who confirmed everything Roberts said, then offered to fly him to Washington.

From the moment Powell walked into Bennet's M Street office, it was clear that he would become the director of NPR News. The two had everything in common, sharing not only a belief in social justice but also a caste: sailing, New England, discretion, breeding, and manners. As Siegel later put it, "Adam Powell III is an extremely intelligent aristocrat."

On Adam Powell's initial day of work at M Street, he took up NPR's racial issues. Although this had always been part of the new executive's agenda, it was not what he intended to do first. But according to Powell, Neal Conan—who as a consolation prize had landed his old job as executive producer of *All Things Considered*—got him thinking. "Neal came in," he recalled, "and said, "'Welcome to NPR, and you've got to get us out from under this court order.'" What followed was a discussion of the ruling that nearly a decade earlier directed the network to hire more Black reporters.

Conan's remarks, Powell said, were ambiguous. Did he mean that the vice president of news (a title never bestowed on Siegel) needed to rectify the genuine problem with minority hiring that led to the consent decree, or that he needed to get the decree rescinded so the network could put the matter behind it? There was a big difference, but for the time being Powell chose to focus on the facts. "When I walked into work in July 1987," he recalled, "NPR had no—zero—minority hosts, correspondents, newscasters, directors, executive producers, or senior editors."

Confident of Bennet's backing, Powell vowed to rectify the situation. "I took that as a mandate," he said later.

In due course, Powell hired a number of Black employees and elevated several already on staff. "When there was finally an opening on the national desk," recalled Michael Fields, a well-informed student of NPR's racial history, "Adam promoted me to that job. That wouldn't have happened without him."

Powell's agenda—which also included a continuation of the Mankiewicz-initiated drive to make NPR a primary news source—was never embraced fully at M Street, even by the many people who agreed with it. The problem was his management style.

As a condition of going to work at NPR, Powell received permission to continue living in Sausalito—he didn't want to take his oldest son out of school there. He flew to Washington on Sunday evenings, kept office hours at M Street the first four days of the week, and flew back to California Thursday nights, spending Fridays at KQED, San Francisco's member station. Bennet justified the arrangement by telling himself that his news director could use the long weekends on the coast to establish personal relationships with a restive community. "What Bennet knew and I didn't was that stations west of the Mississippi were negative about NPR news," Powell said later. "They were not having a good experience with the national desk." The men and women at M Street who decided the domestic stories the network covered had little sensitivity to what happened on the far side of the country.

The issue was serious, although the way Bennet and Midge Ramsey, the vice president of station relations (and Bennet's future wife), put it to Powell accentuated a less urgent angle.

"You're going to go to these regional meetings," Ramsey told Powell, "and dance with the general manager."

"What?"

"Dance with the general manager," she repeated "They always have a social event," and as Powell would discover, NPR's western stations were mostly managed by independent, forceful women. With his grace and charm, he was well equipped to win them over to M Street's side.

So that's what Powell did. To a greater extent than any of his predecessors, he ran the news department by socializing with the female sovereigns on the West Coast who purchased and aired NPR's news shows. During his first six months at the network, he was away from the M Street office 43 percent of the time, and while Bennet always maintained that this was "essential to improving relations with NPR stations," Washington news staffers in need of daily decisions were perplexed. During these absences, their only contact with Powell would be over static-riddled Airfones, the in-seat handsets then in use on commercial flights. "That's how Adam typically participated in meetings. It was not workable," recalled Larry Abramson, an assistant news editor.

Powell's behavior when he was at M Street was also troubling. Even when present there, in a sense he was somewhere else.

During NPR News meetings in his office, Powell often drifted off. At such moments, he would reach into a desk drawer and produce a circular plastic gizmo with adjustable overlays covered by numbers and hash marks. It resembled an old-fashioned proportion wheel of the sort art directors used in the days before computers to size photographs. The device was far more unusual. It was a nuclear bomb effect calculator. After entering a warhead's yield or tonnage, the user, by fiddling with the overlays, could measure the size of its blast, the depth of the resulting crater, and the distance fallout would travel from the point of impact. "It was a conversation starter," Powell said in explaining why he toyed with it in public. But that's not how others saw it. "Adam was fascinated with it far more than whatever NPR issue was under discussion," Smokey Baer remembered.

Cryptic, passive aggressive, oddly strung—these were the analyses that began cropping up at M Street during conversations about Adam Powell III. In-house psychologists, of whom there were many at NPR, devoted hours to fathoming his personality. The consensus was that having grown up the son of fabulous but self-involved parents, then marrying into a wealthy family that due to race and class was on some level impenetrable, Powell—for all his poise and gifts—was a man apart. In fact, he didn't seem comfortable in his own skin. How could he have been, when following his parents' divorce, Adam Jr. remarried and sired another namesake, Adam Diego, who eventually changed his name to Adam Clayton Powell IV? "I came to think of Adam as incredibly well educated and well spoken," Conan recalled, "but he was not grounded. He didn't know who he was. He was a chameleon."

A year into the job, Adam Clayton Powell III was regarded as the most enigmatic executive in the history of NPR news. He seemed, if not indifferent to the network's primary functions—journalism and programming—at the least too distracted to get involved in the particulars. He admitted as much. "When Robert Siegel was head of the news division," Powell said, "he would plunge in every day on how pieces should be edited and so on. I concluded when I got here that there wouldn't be enough time for that." Amplifying on this view, he added, "Before, you had a news director. But now, it was a vice president of news. I'm corporate. I was the first VP. As a corporate officer, that's a different level of responsibility."

Out in the newsroom and in the offices of *All Things Considered* and *Morning Edition*, Powell's insistence on keeping a distance sparked increased grumbling. Some believed that his refusal to get involved in the gritty business of journalism amounted to the risk-avoidance strategy of a slippery careerist. "He managed in a way that when something went wrong, it could never be pinned on him," noted Marcus Rosenbaum, the national editor. As a case in point, Susan Stamberg, who was back at M Street fronting *Weekend Edition Sunday*, recalled that Powell avoided giving straight answers to questions about the contents of her new show. "I'd go in to talk with him about one thing or another, and he'd just sort of bug his eyes at me and push his head in and out like a turtle. And I'd say to him, 'Is that a yes or a no?'" Rosenbaum, whose position determining the stories the Washington staff covered had made him a target of NPR station managers, concluded that the news VP promoted chaos. "He made things difficult. It's easier to keep out of the line of fire when things are crazy. It's easier to say: 'Not my fault.'"

From Powell's perspective, the staffers who chafed at his leadership either lacked the vision he brought to the job or stood in the way of the implementation of the structural changes that the vision demanded. Despite the progress made under Mankiewicz, Powell believed that NPR news still had far to go before its programs were equal to those aired by the major networks. "NPR had a history of being a supplemental news source," he said later. "I thought, along with a number of people, this could become the place you'd come. That would involve a significant shift in the way" the rank and file at M Street "looked at the world."

A major part of that shift would involve reimagining the domestic bureau system that John McChesney had devised and Rosenbaum now managed. Unlike at the commercial networks, NPR did not locate its reporters in metropolitan centers. There were outposts in Chicago and New York, but typically, Rosenbaum recalled, "we put people in slightly off-center" environs. "We wanted them to report about the country," not the big cities. "Our Mountain West person—Howard Berkes—was in Salt Lake City, not Denver; our southern person—Jo Miglino—was in Tallahassee, not Atlanta," and the Southwest correspondent—John Burnett—was in Austin, not Houston. Powell, a product of CBS News, hated the arrangement. "He called me in," added Rosenbaum, "and said, 'I want you to move Miglino to Atlanta.' No discussion. Jo quit." For people on the national desk, Powell's decisions about bureau locations were evidence of what soon became another widely expressed complaint about him: he didn't understand NPR. Quite to the contrary, the VP replied, the old-timers at M Street didn't understand the demands of modern journalism.

Powell's highest priority was the one that he took up his first day of work—rectifying NPR's racial inequities. Although the hiring of Black reporters and producers was part of the solution, it was not all. With Bennet's encouragement, Powell sought to change NPR's content in ways that would increase the number of Black newsmakers to whom reporters spoke. "Somebody got the bright idea that we should be filling out forms to indicate the ethnic identities of the people we were interviewing," recalled Scott Simon. Along with most of his colleagues, the *Weekend Edition* host thought this was ridiculous. "We used to joke with each other, 'Hey, interviewed a Black today—ha, hey, a couple of Scandinavians.'"

Quote quotas were a suspect remedy adopted by many news organizations in the 1980s. Powell was going for something bigger. He wanted his editors to assign more stories on significant Black figures and Black culture. To an extent, he succeeded. Phyllis Crockett did a major interview with the Black director of pediatric neurosurgery at Johns Hopkins University—Dr. Ben Carson. Vertamae Grosvenor, stepping out of her usual role as commentator, contributed a devastating report on a loaded subject—the relationship of promiscuity among Black men to AIDS. ("For black men," a Black AIDS doctor told her, "the way we express our sexuality is by the frequency with which we do it.") Such triumphs notwithstanding, coverage based on skin color did not sit well with many white editors.

"Why don't we fly down to Havana and interview Assata Shakur?" Powell asked the staff one day.

Shakur, a former Black Panther and the step-aunt of the future rap star Tupac Shakur, was living in exile in Cuba after escaping from prison in New Jersey, where she'd been serving a life sentence for the 1973 murder of a state trooper. To the Black community, she was a freedom fighter. To law enforcement officers, she was a killer.

"Adam, are you out of your mind?" snapped John McChesney, who'd recently been named foreign editor. "We're not going to spend a lot of time and money on this."

In the end, Powell folded. McChesney later spoke of the Shakur idea as "an example of the bizarre" lengths the VP would go to impose a racial agenda on NPR's news judgment. To Black reporters, the failure to get the story assigned was evidence that not even their leader could get traction with story ideas. That, they believed, was regrettable but typical. Michael Fields recalled a meeting during the same period when he pitched a story that had nothing to do with skin color. It was about a new weapon in the US military arsenal.

"It would be interesting to get an expert on the air to talk about smart bombs," Fields told a group of editors. They scoffed. Just five minutes later, he said, a white producer walked in and suggested the same story.

"Great idea—let's do it."

As Fields put it, "People were not actively trying to sabotage me, but it was not a supportive or encouraging atmosphere. And it was about race."

The NPR department where most of the racial friction occurred was the national desk. Marcus Rosenbaum was a well-regarded journalist. He'd joined the network in 1978 after working as a copy editor at the *Des Moines Register*. In 1985, following various editorial stints on *All Things Considered*, he moved into management. It was then that Black staffers began to raise questions. "People of color who worked for Rosenbaum might tell you they had a problem with him," said Michael Fields. Brenda Wilson was exhibit A. As the White House reporter, Wilson was on the air almost daily. However, she had trouble hitting deadlines. According to Fields, Rosenbaum not only did little to help her, but a couple of his staffers made matters worse by undermining her.

"Is it going to be on time?" one would ask in a skeptical tone as she pounded away at her typewriter.

"We better have something else ready," another would answer with exaggerated urgency.

Phyllis Crockett, who despite always filing promptly, also occasionally encountered the same sorts of cracks. It got so bad, Fields recalled, that he decided to point out what was happening. Whenever Wilson or Crockett came through, he would jump to feet and proclaim, "I'll be damned. We have fifteen minutes left before deadline. They've done it again."

For Powell, the tension between Rosenbaum and his Black reporters was of a piece with the other issues he had with the national editor. It might not have added up to a dismissible offense, but it was grounds for the sort of second-guessing that sends a strong warning signal. "Powell didn't fire me," Rosenbaum said later, "but I saw the writing on the wall." He resigned to edit the book *Heart of a Wife*, a diary by his grandmother about Jewish life in the South during the early twentieth century.

No sooner had Marcus Rosenbaum left than Adam Powell turned his attention to NPR's foreign desk. In May 1988, Ronald Reagan and Mikhail Gorbachev were meeting in Moscow to discuss nuclear disarmament. As the network's vice president for news saw it, the summit presented an opportunity to showcase NPR's international coverage, putting it on the same level as that of his former employer, CBS. "I said, 'We've got Dan Schorr, who opened the CBS Moscow bureau,'" recalled Powell. "'We have Robert Siegel, who I think knows a lot about the Soviet Union.'"

"Let's send them to Russia a week before," Powell told his assembled editors one early spring day. To make the effort possible would also require dispatching a support team of six producers and engineers. The cost: $70,000, a significant sum for NPR. The network news VP believed that the return on expenses would be enormous.

"They could do pieces and have a major presence on every broadcast—seven days a week, twice a day."

His proposal was met by silence. After an awkward few seconds, someone in the back of the room voiced a sarcastic verdict: "Mr. Commercial Network News!"

The speaker was John McChesney. His views did not go unshared.

Eighteen years into its existence, NPR had established its own version of broadcast journalism, and it rarely included splashy gestures, spot-on story assignments, or extravagant spending. Although the network had over time become more responsive to breaking news, Powell's plans for Moscow struck many at M Street as grandstanding. From the perspective of his foreign editor, who had already clashed with him about the Assata Shakur story, it was a rebuke.

When McChesney took over the foreign desk, it was a bare-bones operation. His number two, Cadi Simon—a tough-minded Sabra who'd been working at *ATC*—handled Middle East coverage. John Dinges, his number three, who'd covered the tropics for the *Washington Post*, concentrated on Central America and Africa. Not that there was a staff in these locations. "We didn't have any foreign correspondents," recalled Dinges. "We had a feed from the BBC—half a dozen forty-five-second spots. Our job was to choose stuff from the feeds to recommend to the shows. We'd run a BBC piece, then do an interview with someone at a Washington think tank to augment the piece." McChesney had changed all that, and he did so by watching his budget and dispatching the few reporters he supervised to spots where they could turn out stories the TV networks missed or oversimplified. Not surprisingly, the approach had required him to nurture—some might have said abuse—underpaid reporters much the same way he had done when constructing the national desk. In return, these men and women became household names.

Sylvia Poggioli was the rising star in the group that McChesney had assembled. The smoky-voiced forty-two-year-old daughter of Renato and Renata Poggioli, Italian intellectuals who because of their anti-Fascist activism had fled to the United States before World War II, Sylvia grew up in Providence, Rhode Island, and Cambridge, Massachusetts. (Her father, an English professor, was an influential figure in the field of comparative literature and a friend of Vladimir Nabokov.) After graduating from Harvard, she moved to Europe with hopes of becoming a Shakespearian actress. Her show business career peaked with the 1971 Burt Lancaster western *Valdez Is Coming*, a production shot in Spain. She played "Segundo's Girl" and had one line: "Come to bed." The film opened her eyes. "It was that experience that convinced me I should never work in the movies," she said. "I couldn't stand it." Poggioli settled in Rome, finding work at the Italian press agency, ANSA. McChesney discovered her there.

The 1985 hijacking of the cruise ship *Achille Lauro* by the Palestine Liberation Front gave Poggioli her break. As the event became an international crisis involving not just the Italian government but also those of Egypt, Syria, Israel, and the United States, most news organizations would have shifted to a more seasoned hand. McChesney, rather than bring Neal Conan in from London, stuck with Poggioli. The complicated negotiations, the execution of the wheelchair-bound American hostage Leon Klinghoffer, the capitulation by Italian authorities that allowed Muhammad Abbas, the Palestinian mastermind, to escape unmolested—Poggioli handled it all. "It was a huge story," she recalled, "and John trusted me. He was my editor. I was extremely grateful."

In the aftermath of the *Achille Lauro* coverage, Poggioli—who'd previously been earning a stringer's wages from NPR—was put on retainer and began reporting on Vatican intrigues and Mafia trials. When she needed interviews translated from Italian then read aloud for broadcast in English, she relied on her bilingual husband. Piero Benetazzo, a special correspondent for Rome's *La Repubblica*, was a key figure in European journalism. Since scoring a scoop in 1968 as the lone Western reporter present in Yugoslavia when Soviet troops rolled in by tank to crush the anti-Communist uprising known as Prague Spring, he had filed major reports from Chile, Iran, and Angola. For his wife, he was not just someone she could use as an on-air voice. He was an endless resource on politics and journalistic craft.

In 1988, Benetazzo started contributing more materially to Poggioli's work, taking her along on his reporting trips. Thanks to him, NPR broadcast her stories from Budapest when the Communist regime lifted restrictions on citizens and from Belgrade, when Slobodan Milosevic, riding an uptick in Serbian nationalism, moved to consolidate power. "Piero's paper paid the bill," she recalled, but they never knew it.

Such spousal assists became the norm as McChesney built his foreign desk. Deborah Amos, who in 1986 had left her producing job at NPR and moved to Amman, Jordan, to become a reporter, piggybacked assignments with her husband, the NBC Middle East correspondent Rick Davis. She used his network's bureau as an office and flew with him on private Arab Wings jets in and out of Damascus for pieces to send back to M Street. Ann Cooper, NPR's Moscow correspondent since 1986, shared work space with her husband, the *New York Times*'s Russian bureau chief Bill Keller. As a result, she was in place to file stories for public radio about the events that led to the breakup of the Soviet Union.

Not every international story McChesney assigned for NPR required financial support from a well-paid journalistic better half. Bill Buzenberg, who replaced Conan in London, contributed pieces not only from Europe but also from Central America and, especially, the Philippines. Reporting for *All Things Considered* in 1986 on a Ferdinand Marcos rally, Buzenberg introduced listeners to the nation's female lead, Imelda Marcos:

> She makes a dramatic entrance to her own fanfare, moving with the regal bearing of a former movie queen. She reaches down into the crowd nearest the stage, much to their delight, not to shake hands but to let people touch hers. At one point, she removes her wristwatch, almost disdainfully dangles it over the edge of the stage for a moment and lets it drop.

Laurie Garrett, after contributing multiple stories from San Francisco on the AIDS crisis, flew to Tanzania to report on the virus in Africa. Appearing on *Morning Edition*, she began her dispatch:

> The waves of Lake Victoria wash up on the shores of Bukoba. Egrets and cranes stand at attention watching children swim. The town is small. . . . Two

years ago, the peace of Bukoba was disturbed by a deadly invisible enemy. Something started killing the young people. . . . The sick came to a government hospital. They seemed to have some kind of strange, venereal disease.

NPR's international coverage was not always this vivid, and there was much the network missed. But when it was good, it was very good. "I was making the foreign desk really competitive," McChesney said.

Now, as McChesney saw it, Adam Powell wanted to ruin his handiwork by spending a fortune to send an armada of employees to Moscow to cover what the foreign editor considered a "largely ceremonial picture story" that had "nothing to do with what NPR is all about." So convinced was he that his boss was committing a sin against the sacred values of public broadcasting that the weekend after Powell's announcement he convened a secret Sunday staff meeting.

"John invited all these people to his house," recalled Alex Chadwick. "John wanted to organize an effort to undermine Adam and figure out how to get NPR to get rid of him." Added Larry Abramson, the session explored ways "to inspire member stations to reject" Powell's leadership. The meeting was the initial stage of a coup.

News of McChesney's plot leaked. For Powell, who was already gunning for the foreign editor because of his irascible attitude, this move was the limit. A day after the meeting, McChesney was out. It was "a tragic mistake," declared Scott Simon, who not only believed the foreign editor was doing a brilliant job but also felt indebted to him for having flown to El Salvador back in 1982 when Simon and his production team were in danger. "I'd do anything for him after that, wouldn't I?" Others at M Street were disinclined to raise a hand. As chief of the national desk, McChesney had not been shy about criticizing the work of Linda Wertheimer and Cokie Roberts, who supported Powell's vision. He gave "Wertheimer a bad evaluation," McChesney said later. "Worse, I told Cokie she sounded bored when she was on the air. She did. But that wasn't something you did." In the end, the best Simon could do for the man who'd always been in his corner was to encourage Doug Bennet to offer him a severance package. With the money, McChesney moved to Northern California to open a bed-and-breakfast.

The departure in rapid succession of Rosenbaum and McChesney, NPR's top news editors, removed Powell's chief enemies. ("Both Marc and John challenged Powell's leadership," recalled Mike Shuster, a New York–based reporter.) But it created a new and different threat. "McChesney," the network board's chairman, Jack Mitchell, recalled, "became an instant martyr and a hero," as did others who opposed the news VP.

Replacing McChesney was easy: Powell elevated the dismissed foreign editor's top deputy, Cadi Simon, who'd already been making many of the assignments anyway. She started the job by assigning John Hockenberry to the Middle East. There, despite his confinement to a wheelchair, the reporter produced a stunning piece when Iranian militants hoisted him onto a helicopter to cover the Ayatollah Khomeini's funeral. "Khomeini's body lay in a box of green glass," he noted. "The glass glinted with each ray of light that broke through the clouds. In the distance, the dust kicked up by the feet of five million mourners walking toward Khomeini's final resting spot was rising on the windless horizon." No other American journalist captured the event so evocatively.

For the position of national editor, Adam Powell went further afield. Isabel Bahamonde, a thirty-five-year-old Cuban American, came to NPR from the Miami-based Univision, America's first Spanish-language TV network. Best known for talk and variety programs (*El Show Cristina* and *Sabado Gigante*), Univision also aired a morning news broadcast. Bahamonde produced segments for the show. She impressed Powell as "vibrant, committed, smart," just the person to shake up his Washington-centric outfit. "When I interviewed her, I thought she had a good grasp of how to interpret the news of the fifty states plus territories. She had a good sense of where the country was moving and how you could measure that with stories."

Bahamonde's appearance at NPR was not warmly greeted. Part of this was cliquishness. "NPR is a place where the cool kids don't like the new kids," John Burnett later observed. Part was genuine dismay. "Isabel was not ready to run a radio news operation," recalled Robert Malesky, who'd been named producer of Stamberg's Sunday show. "She was not a serious news person," added Larry Abramson. As Mike Shuster put it, "Isabel was hired to promote diversity."

Bahamonde did not have broad experience. At first, she tried to win over the staff at NPR with a show of earnest effort. Her charges would arrive each morning to find her with a pair of scissors in hand surrounded by copies of the *New York Times* and the *Washington Post*. She was clipping story ideas. But far from gaining her points, the undertaking was seen as evidence of her cluelessness: she had to cut information out of the newspapers that others already knew. Burnett, a Spanish speaker who liked Bahamonde, said later, she was "a square peg in a round hole." *All Things Considered* producer Art Silverman was harsher. She "was not very good."

M Street's coldness to her stunned Bahamonde, and she retreated into a shell, spending most days in her NPR office glued to Univision telenovelas on a TV. Meantime, the bulk of her work fell to the executive producers at *All Things Considered* and *Morning Edition*. We were "editing her stories," recalled Neal Conan. Three months into the job, Bahamonde was generally referred to at M Street by a cruel, English translation of her surname: "Lower World."

In December, Bahamonde faced a mandatory review. Prior to the session, a group that included most of NPR's editors and producers wrote a brutal critique of her work and presented it to Powell. The charges: lack of judgment, suspect ethics (she allegedly suggested staging a news event), and compromised coverage. The result, as reported in the *Washington Post*: "A crisis in morale and in the productivity of the national desk."

Three weeks later, Powell responded. In a five-and-a-half-page, single-spaced rebuttal, he sided with Bahamonde, accusing those who spoke against the national editor of failing to give her "detailed feedback, orientation, or positive assistance." The reason: "institutional racism."

To a staff largely composed of white liberals who believed they were enlightened on racial issues, the allegation was devastating—so much so that NPR's top producers decided to go over Powell's head. There were "five of us who went to Bennet," recalled Neal Conan. "Bennet lost his cool. He outspokenly accused us of racism. I was furious. My face turned red. Relations were already strained, and they grew more strained from there on out."

Even as the battle over Isabel Bahamonde played out, another, possibly greater threat to NPR was developing. Renee Montagne, Susan Stamberg's successor at *All Things Considered*, was flailing—most would have said failing—at her job. Her promising start had owed more to chutzpah and an ignorance of the position's demands than to skill. She'd enjoyed a phenomenal bit of beginner's luck, but then that luck ran out.

Montagne's difficulties were numerous. First, although she and Robert Siegel were personally close, the warmth did not come through on the air. "I don't think we achieved any chemistry," she recalled. "Robert was a powerful, well-known figure within NPR. I was just a freelancer who'd shown up in the host's chair." Stamberg, who early on did what she could to make her replacement feel confident, concurred. "She was dealing with Robert Siegel, who's brilliant. She got chewed up."

Montagne was also unnerved by the almost nightly need on *All Things Considered* to handle breaking news, which requires sangfroid and the ability to improvise. Cooking up a piece at deadline from scraps of wire-service copy and incoming sound bites is hard even for a veteran. "At *ATC* you had to grasp a story in just a couple minutes," recalled John Dinges, the deputy foreign editor. "You go into a studio and producers are feeding you questions. Renee was unable to do that. She was petrified. She was a wreck."

Then there was Montagne's failure to master a staple of *All Things Considered*—long interviews. Most editions of the show feature two, sometimes three conversations between the hosts and newsmakers. Taped and edited throughout the day, these Q&A's give the program its meatiness. Stamberg, who had a vision of what she wanted and went after it, excelled at them. She was so on point that she typically needed no more than seven minutes with an interviewee to get a broadcast-ready five-minute piece. Montagne, however, required far more time. "I did twenty-minute interviews and told them where to cut the best stuff for a six-minute piece. I'd say, 'Guys, this is a big chunk of marble, but the statue is in there.'" As a consequence, editors had to spend time they didn't have to chisel the host's rambling conversations into airworthy shape.

Finally, Montagne struggled with the most important part of the job—assertiveness. A host, as opposed to a reporter, is master of ceremonies. Montagne, however, was uncomfortable in the spotlight, frequently reverting to the guise of journalistic contributor. She sounded like a guest on her own program.

What it all added up to was someone in deep trouble. "After twenty months," Montagne said later, "I was as miserable as could be." Unfortunately for her, Neal Conan, her direct boss, had also lost patience. "She could not do live interviews on deadline," he recalled. "She didn't apply focus to her work. Every on-air conversation was a fishing expedition."

Although Conan believed that he did what he could to bring Montagne along ("I tried to help Renee," he said later), she saw him as a major part of the problem. She felt that if Ted Clark, the executive producer who'd hired her, had remained in the job instead of returning to reporting, he would have coached her through the rough spots. Conan, she was convinced, was so bitter about not getting the top news post that went to Powell that he'd lost the ability to empathize. "He was aggressive and haughty—something of a bully," she recalled. "In the months I was on the show, he never pulled me aside. He ignored me in editorial meetings. He treated me in a disdainful way in front of the rest of the show."

By the final weeks of 1988, Montagne felt like she was drowning. Shortly after the turn of the year, Conan called her into his office. "I thought, Good," she recalled thinking. "We'll sit down and hash things out." But that's now how it went.

"I'm going to get you out," Conan said with no preliminaries.

"What do you mean?"

"This isn't working."

She was done.

Walking into the M Street newsroom, Montagne felt dazed. "I didn't have a big support base at NPR," she recalled. "People liked me, but I didn't have anyone to go to." The first person she saw was Nina Totenberg. The legal reporter had been, if not kind to the host during her early months, at least considerate. She had counseled her on how to dress in Washington. Lose the punk regalia, she'd advised, and go with pastel blouses and jackets with boxy shoulders—in the capital during the Reagan era, this was feminine yet assertive. Now Totenberg was less understanding. "You know," she told her obviously upset colleague, "when you're gone and they write your obituary, they're not going to say, 'She was a great host.'" There was no reply to that, although Montagne could not fathom the insensitivity. Later, she noted, "There would be talk about the NPR founding mothers—all I can say is that the women weren't motherly to me."

•   •   •

Neal Conan's stated reason for dismissing Renee Montagne, while true, was influenced by several other factors, one of which was the desire of a departed NPR mainstay to return home to M Street.

Things had not gone well for Noah Adams in Minnesota. Rather than try to duplicate *Prairie Home Companion*, the former *All Things Considered* host—assisted by Neenah Ellis, the ex-*ATC* producer he'd brought with him as his top executive and, not incidentally, wife—created an entirely different program. In homage to the old-fashioned on-air salute he loved, he called it *Good Evening*. Gone was the news from Lake Wobegon. Gone were the faux Powdermilk Biscuit ads. Gone was the conceit of a quaint town presided over by a quirky and garrulous monologist. *Good Evening* kicked off on Saturday nights with a jazz arrangement of Dire Straits' "The Walk of Life." Up next were performances by contemporary musical stars (Harry Connick Jr.), sketches by celebrated radio humorists (Stan Freberg), and readings by smart young novelists (Richard Ford). As for Adams's persona, it bore no resemblance to that of his predecessor. Where Garrison Keillor was discursive and imposing, he was direct and modest. Adams's only bow to tradition was that he did the show live from St. Paul's World Theater.

Public radio member stations were less than entranced by *Good Evening*. "It feels like they're struggling to find the right role for Noah," commented the manager of the Ames, Iowa, outlet. Critics were harsher. "Adams," wrote a critic from the Knight Ridder newspapers, "doesn't command center stage the way Keillor did." Alan Bunce of the *Christian Science Monitor* said simply, "The new show feels less idiosyncratic." Adams had his strengths—the guests, for one, were better known than those featured by his predecessor. But the overall result was flat. Listenership fell. On November 1, 1988, barely a year after *Good Evening* debuted, Bill Kling let Adams go.

The Minnesotan's loss was Conan's gain. With the support of Bennet and Powell, the *All Things Considered* executive producer signed Adams to resume his old post atop NPR's longest-running program. The only difference: he would be part of a three-host rotation. This arrangement would allow *ATC* to have one host in the field reporting stories while the other two remained at M Street. For the team's third member, Conan proposed a woman he was convinced would not only complement Adams and Siegel but also, in his words, "was ready to bloom."

For five years, Lynn Neary had been the host of *Weekend All Things Considered*. She was nearly Stamberg's equal when it came to getting interviewees to open up. "She'd already learned the most important part of the job," recalled Conan: "Listening." She was also versed in the arts—that would add balance to the show. Finally, Neary possessed reporting skills. A story of hers for *Weekend All Things Considered* on Washington's troubled Arthur Capper housing project won the 1988 Robert F. Kennedy Award for Journalism.

Conan believed Adams, Siegel, and Neary would constitute the best lineup in broadcast news, and there was one more plus: by moving Neary to *All Things Considered*, he would create a position on weekends for someone who had been passed over two years before: Margot Adler.

By February 1989, Conan had nearly finished his moves. As reported by the *Post*'s Marc Fisher, he offered Neary the top position at *ATC*, and Powell confirmed the hire. "She discussed every detail of her new job—salary, starting date, the whole works." In the halls at NPR and at dinner parties attended by staffers, Neary was accepting congratulations.

Adler had also participated in salary discussions and received a start date. The offer was so firm that in preparation for moving to DC from New York, she did something that once would have been unthinkable—began the process of giving up her apartment. Adler's 333 Central Park West address was one of the best in Manhattan. Her, sprawling, three-bedroom unit had been in her family for two generations, and rent was an unheard-of $970 a month. The building was going co-op, and there was a chance to sell. "Even though I couldn't afford it," she recalled, "I put down one thousand dollars to buy and flip."

Everything was set. Until it wasn't.

Several days before NPR was to introduce the new *All Things Considered* hosts, Linda Wertheimer walked into Adam Powell's office and applied for the position slated for Neary. According to the veteran reporter, the job had not been posted properly, but that was a pretext. Her true reasons for seeking the spot were urgent and personal. After nearly two decades covering politics—a beat that not only required her to be at the Capitol at all hours but also during election years kept her continuously on the campaign trail—Wertheimer was exhausted. The 1988 presidential race between Massachusetts governor Michael Dukakis and Vice President George H. W. Bush had nearly been the end of her. One day she was in California, the next at a debate in Winston-Salem, North Carolina, and the next in Boston. The deadlines for morning and evening shows, the interchangeable hotels, and the ceaseless travel had become too much. To ensure that she could locate her belongings when jet-lagged and groggy, Wertheimer had worked out a color-coordinated luggage set and wardrobe. Everything was red: suitcases, kit bags, even her coat. That way, it would all stand out at one a.m. in any airport, and if she still missed it, the Secret Service agents attached to the candidates would recognize the stuff and grab it. "I was completely dopey," she said later.

Wertheimer's eleventh-hour application for the *All Things Considered* job upended the process. What happened next scuttled it. "Nina and Cokie went to Adam Powell," Adler later asserted, "and said, 'Linda deserves this. She's tired of the campaign trail.'"

Later, Totenberg and Roberts, despite their earlier successes swaying personnel decisions, denied playing a decisive role. Totenberg said that if she spoke to anyone it was "en passant." Roberts said that she had indeed talked with Powell ("I told him frankly what I thought") but contended that her words had no impact.

The evidence suggests that the women were the main actors. "Roberts . . . and Totenberg talked of leaving," reported the *Post*'s Fisher. An unnamed NPR engineer informed him that he overheard Roberts telling colleagues that she'd vowed to quit if Wertheimer didn't get the position. Years afterward, a key NPR figure of the era confirmed that Roberts and Totenberg issued an ultimatum to Powell. "Those two threatened to leave the company if Linda didn't get the job." Then, touching on the incident's relevance to NPR's zeitgeist, the source observed, "It's terrific how much power women had at NPR—then they used it just like men in as vicious and nasty a way as possible."

Confronted by the risk of losing Totenberg and Roberts, Powell seized on a technicality. Bennet had yet to sign the documents memorializing the Neary and Adler promotions. As the news VP later put it, "There is no job offer until it is final."

According to Neal Conan, what followed was duplicitous. "There was an NPR form I filled out offering Lynn the job," he recalled. "Adam rewrote it, putting Linda Wertheimer's name in instead of Lynn's. He erased Lynn's name then put in Linda's then sent it to Bennet—with my signature on it. That's intolerable."

Powell, who'd been wary of Conan since his first-day remarks about the consent decree agreement, did not see it that way. "Is it really the broadcast producer's right," he later asked, "to hire a host?"

Told that Conan thought it was, he shrugged. Then he declared, "Lynn Neary is a terrific person, but not even close to Linda Wertheimer. Linda is an institution."

Told that Conan regarded his actions as deceitful, Powell replied, "Such is life."

Conan responded to the decision by resigning. Neary refused to talk about it on the record then or ever. As for Adler, whose hopes had now been dashed twice in as many years (with Neary stuck in the weekend job, that opening vanished), there was an added insult. While this had been playing out, Powell was in negotiations with a third party to cohost with Neary on Saturdays and Sundays: Emil Guillermo, a thirty-four-year-old journalist at KRON television in San Francisco. The news VP was so eager to hire the Filipino American, thereby bolstering the network's racial diversity, that he acceded to his request not to audition (Guillermo was fearful his station might learn he was in talks with NPR). Under such conditions, the hire was contrary to network procedure, but it was a fait accompli. Adler wasn't even in the running.

Not everyone at NPR was displeased with how things ended. Some agreed with Powell that Conan had overreached. "Neal thought being executive producer gave him much more authority than he actually had," Siegel said later. "Hosts get hired on a presidential level. It's not a small decision." There were also some who like Powell saw Wertheimer as the better choice to front *All Things Considered*. Siegel was in that camp. In a pointed reference to Neary's love of cultural stories, he said, "The lineup was going soft. It was very back of the book. We needed to bring our good journalistic talent to the top. I much preferred Linda Wertheimer."

Nonetheless, the host changes at *All Things Considered* were a disaster. Morale was devastated, reported the *Post's* Fisher. Although Neary and Adler were the most obvious casualties (both filed labor grievances and were subsequently compensated; "They made me a correspondent instead of a reporter," Adler later said), Adam Clayton Powell III was more badly damaged than they. Bennet liked Powell and had looked past previous snafus, but the less-than-candid way his vice president had dealt with these personnel decisions opened a fissure in what had been a solid relationship. "We did not handle that situation well," the NPR president said at the time. "I don't think people should have been misled." So frustrated was Bennet that after a couple of days he summoned Neal Conan to M Street and begged him to stay. "He pleaded with me not to leave." The NPR president asked what he could do to keep him. Realizing that he'd never again have so much leverage, Conan went big: Pentagon reporter. Bennett said yes.

The initial indication that the upheavals at NPR would not soon end came during an early-summer broadcast of what had been one of the few demonstrable successes of the Adam Powell era—*Weekend Edition Sunday*. Even more than *All Things Considered*, the show bore its host's imprint. "It was very personal with me," Susan Stamberg said later. "I wanted it to be like the *New York Times*'s Arts and Leisure section." Every week, the concert pianist Stef Scaggiari—a regular with the National Symphony and a frequent accompanist for the blues vocalist Jimmy Witherspoon—dropped by the studio to play not only the B. J. Leiderman theme music but also the buttons that served as segues between stories. During the first year, each program featured a new chunk of a novel being written in installments by the authors Scott Spencer, Christopher Buckley, and David Leavitt. Adding to the literary power, Jules Feiffer, the cartoonist and screenwriter (*Carnal Knowledge*), served as film critic, and crossword puzzle master Will Shortz as games guru.

Not everything worked. A cooking feature fronted by Alice Waters didn't jell. Over the course of a show, the celebrated founder of Chez Panisse would prepare a meal while talking with Stamberg. "I wanted it recorded in bits and pieces," the host recalled. "'Put this in the oven,'" Waters would say. "Then we'd come back to her." By program's end, Waters would be setting the table. But she couldn't grasp the format. NPR canceled the segment. Such misfires, though, were rare. Early on the show introduced two Massachusetts auto mechanics destined to become public radio stars. Jay Kernis had heard Tom and Ray Magliozzi ("Click and Clack") on Boston's WBUR and brought them to Stamberg's attention. They became regular guests, bantering with the host about piston rods and crankcases. In a year, NPR began syndicating their program: *Car Talk*.

For all this, *Weekend Edition Sunday* had a built-in flaw: It was prerecorded on Fridays, two days prior to broadcast. This irregular arrangement was a concession to Stamberg's post-illness needs. "Cancer changed me as it does everyone it invades," she recalled. "I got scrappier, more impatient." The host, who'd always valued her independence, had become harder to rein in and no longer driven by journalistic gets. Her program carried almost no news. "The show had a reputation for being fluffy," recalled Robert Malesky, adding that Powell, after receiving complaints from the stations, spoke to Stamberg but that nothing changed. A bigger potential problem was that in the event of a breaking story, the host would not be at M Street to handle it. Just in case, the network kept Brenda Wilson and Brian Naylor on standby on Sundays, but they were rarely summoned. News did not happen on Sundays. Then one day it did.

On Sunday, June 4, 1989, the Chinese military marched into Beijing's Tiananmen Square killing several hundred demonstrators revolting against the Maoist government. It all aired live on America's television networks, anchors out front, the confrontation between a lone protestor and Chinese tanks dominating screens. Stamberg, however, was unreachable. "I tried to get Susan in," Malesky remembered, "but that weekend she was out of town—I think Rhode Island. She was not easily available. I went with Brian Naylor." (Stamberg recalled it differently, saying that she was ill.) Regardless, NPR's inability to produce its host during an international crisis sparked repercussions. "There was grumbling among the staff, and the stations were furious," Malesky said later. Board chairman Jack Mitchell at first thought the furor would pass. "I did not regard this failure as fatal." His was the minority view. "Most in public radio were embarrassed, others were outraged."

Powell and Stamberg met to discuss what they could do to avoid the situation repeating itself the next time news occurred on her watch. "We had several conversations," she recalled, "but I was unwilling to do Sundays. I'd given at the office. So that was it with them. I said, 'I'm out of here.'" Although some shook their heads at Stamberg's adamancy, she walked away unscathed. (Her new title at NPR was special correspondent; her first major project was a two-and-a-half-hour documentary titled *Jews of Shanghai* about Jews who fled to Asia to escape the Holocaust.) Powell was not so lucky. In the eyes of many at NPR, the news VP should have nixed the pre-taping setup when stations started complaining.

Powell's position was further weakened a few weeks after Stamberg stepped down by the appearance on the newsroom bulletin board of a plain-tive memo. It read: "Could the person who took the color television please return it as soon as possible?"

In an act of guerilla warfare, an unidentified NPR reporter or producer had absconded with Isabel Bahamonde's sole source of solace—the televi-sion on which she watched telenovelas while the staff labored. The TV was a symbol of Powell's inability or unwillingness to do anything about her. Even as this nasty bit of office politics was eliciting snickers at M Street, the news VP was saying that the issues with Bahamonde were in the past. Later, when pressed regarding her television-viewing habits, he responded, "I knew peo-ple doing a lot worse in NPR offices. As for the telenovelas, they give you an interesting look at what a lot of people in the country are enjoying." Such remarks could not mask Powell's awareness that the national editor had to go. On September 5, the network announced that Bahamonde had resigned. In a statement, the news VP said that she would "return to Miami." He did not acknowledge her failures, although he later allowed, "She didn't work out. She was too much in the commercial mold: Mea culpa."

By the fall of 1989, Adam Clayton Powell III had lost whatever grip he'd once had on NPR's newsroom. He was away from the office too often and when there he seemed away. The anger from the dustups with the national and foreign desks lingered, and many of the minority hires weren't succeeding. Reports also began to reach M Street about his history at other entities.

In 1972, New York's WRVR had dismissed Powell for "rifling" through corporate files. At the time, he denied any wrongdoing, and Robert Siegel, his fellow WRVR alum, was inclined to dismiss the incident. "WRVR was mismanaged, and I think Adam saw himself as a whistleblower." Nonethe-less, the station manager, Arthur Alpert, stood by the allegations, and Powell suffered the indignity of seeing *Jet*, the Black newsweekly, report his demise under the headline: "Adam Powell III Fired from WRVR."

Powell's exit a decade later from KFYI in Oakland was more troubling. In 1984, he raised $3 million to purchase what had been a soul music station, KDIA. With great fanfare, he changed the call letters and instituted an all-news format. But after fewer than four months, twenty-eight of his forty employees walked out. They said they had not been paid in weeks. Days later, the station collapsed. According to the new owner, Powell and other top managers had bled KFYI. "They lived like kings—Cadillac taste on a VW budget." No one at M Street heard about any of this until the *Post*'s Fisher raised the subject while reporting his story. Powell had not disclosed what happened when applying to NPR. All he'd said was that he'd been in the "broadcast ownership and consulting business."

The combination of the current dysfunction at NPR and the looming revelations from Powell's past amounted to a one-two punch. "Adam Powell provoked what you'd have to call a revolution in the news department," recalled Mike Shuster. "Many people concluded Powell didn't know what constituted good journalism and was guilty of bad leadership."

The rebellion began when yet another delegation of NPR employees congregated in Bennet's office. This time, the group included people the network president could not brush off. "We went to Doug about Adam," recalled Susan Stamberg. "We said, 'This isn't working. He isn't qualified. He needs to go.' But Doug resisted. He stood up for him. He was a loyal man." The staff wouldn't back down. "There was so much opposition to him that Doug Bennet was prevailed upon to understand what the problem was," said Shuster. The NPR president proposed a compromise. He would create a new position of managing editor. He did this, Shuster bitingly observed, "so there'd be a journalist between the staff and the news director."

Several candidates vied for the managing editor job, but one vied hardest. In his third year as NPR's London bureau chief, Bill Buzenberg continued to produce big stories, among them an examination of the Thatcher government's decision to treat Sinn Féin, the political branch of the Irish Republican Army, as a terrorist organization and censor news coverage of it. He traveled from England "on my own dime to interview" for the position. "They said they could do it by phone, but I wanted to do it in person."

Buzenberg began work at M Street in September 1989 in a makeshift cubicle just outside Adam Powell's office. The space was inadequate, but the new managing editor later said, "I didn't care. There was a sense we were in trouble. Adam wasn't a real news person. He didn't understand what NPR was—the quality, the tone. He was more interested in entertainment."

Despite the proximity of their workspaces, Powell and Buzenberg steered clear of each other. While Powell retained the more important title, the managing editor exercised full editorial control. "He wasn't involved in any decision making in news," said Buzenberg.

By early 1990, the arrangement had become untenable. According to Buzenberg, "Doug fired Adam after I'd been there six months. Doug said, 'He's not coming back. Will you take this job temporarily?' It became permanent."

There were some sorry to see Powell go—minority staffers, Wertheimer and Roberts, and those who supported his efforts to make NPR's journalism mainstream. (Among Powell's lasting achievements: hourly, on-air news updates.) The staff of *Radio Expeditions*, an ambitious joint undertaking of NPR and the National Geographic Society, also mourned his departure. Reported by Alex Chadwick and produced by his wife, Carolyn Jensen (Siemering's first hire), the production featured dispatches from Peru, Africa, Australia—any place on the map where NPR could cover the natural world in depth and with high-end audio. (As Chadwick later put it, "Carolyn said she wanted the sound to be the equivalent of the photography in *National Geographic*.") *Radio Expeditions* ran for years as a weekly segment of *Morning Edition*, and it wouldn't have existed had not Powell found the funds.

Most cheered Powell's exit. "Bennet made a disastrous decision" in hiring him, Conan said later. "He was just the wrong person for the job." Powell's antagonist then raised a delicate question: "How much did Adam's own failings contribute—and how much did we reject him?"

In Bennet's view, NPR staffers bore a lot of blame. A couple of years afterward, he said, "I think Adam's colleagues didn't give him a respectful hearing." He added, "I hate to say it, but I finally concluded [that] what made Adam Powell's life difficult was a certain amount of racism in the organization." Still, the NPR president was glad to be finished with Powell. "I remember him skipping, jumping up and down about the coming of Buzenberg," Stamberg said later. "I can see him smiling—goofy grin. I said, 'You've done the right thing.'"

For his part, Powell saw his difficulties at NPR as less a function of racism than of the place's clannish nature. "NPR news was not friendly to outsiders," he recalled. "It was as if NPR news was a castle, and the monks had retreated inside and pulled up the drawbridge." Maybe that was just as well. "Three years is long enough anywhere."

Powell's departure coincided not only with the start of a new decade but also with the end of the first two in the life of National Public Radio. The era of the memorable host was over. So, too, was the era of government funding. When Bennet took charge, NPR received 80 percent of its money from the Corporation for Public Broadcasting; by 1990, one-third came from private sources and corporate donations and two-thirds from the member stations. This freed the network from federal meddling but subjected it to a new kind of interference from small-market station managers. ("Bennet stuck us with this crazy governance," Cokie Roberts noted later. "The stations got control.") Although other issues, chiefly the disparity between aspirations for racial equality in hiring and the actual number of minority employees, remained unresolved, the institution had moved forward. It was more conservative, but it was more professional, and in the persons of Conan, Siegel, and Buzenberg (all former London bureau chiefs), worldlier. At a time when international events were starting to dominate the news, NPR's leaders were determined to report them.

SIX

FOREIGN AFFAIRS

The dilemma in which Neal Conan, Chris Hedges of the *New York Times*, and two other reporters found themselves was as confusing as it was terrifying—which made it even more terrifying. They were imprisoned in a Mercedes-Benz wedged between a Russian-made T-72 tank and a group of armored personnel carriers on the banks of the Euphrates River in the biblical city of Ur. A detachment of Saddam Hussein's Republican Guard, which had captured the journalists a few days earlier at the end of the first Gulf War, might execute them at any moment. But a band of Shia militia who'd ambushed the Iraqi convoy of which the Mercedes was a part presented the most pressing danger. They had the vehicles pinned down.

Night had fallen, and a ferocious rain—each drop black and viscous from the oil escaping wells that Saddam had ordered set ablaze as his defeated army retreated into Iraq—pelted the ground. Conan would not have been surprised if one of the rounds the T-72 kept letting go at Shia positions ignited the skies. More likely, a militiaman would roll a grenade beneath a fuel truck parked nearby. That would be the end of them all. "I'd screwed up before in my life," Conan thought, "but this was spectacularly stupid."

The series of circumstances that resulted in Conan's falling into the hands of Iraqi forces had begun several months earlier, 6,400 miles away at National Public Radio's 2025 M Street offices. There, at a meeting in the second-floor conference room, news director Bill Buzenberg announced that the network would cover the looming conflict as thoroughly as anyone in the business. "You'd be able to turn to NPR at any time," recalled Bruce Drake, who'd just joined the organization as Washington editor. "There was going to be wall-to-wall programming. Our correspondents would be everywhere."

To many at NPR, this undertaking initially seemed unrealistic—even questionable. Some in the room worried about the costs. Not only was NPR cash strapped, but its board, haunted by past financial missteps, was disinclined to kick in the necessary funding. Others argued that such coverage would damage the network, transforming it into the audio equivalent of what they regarded as the least substantial outfit in broadcast news: CNN. Finally, there was resistance from dovish old-timers who looked askance at the notion of war reporting. "They thought it was not NPR's role to have this militaristic image," Drake remembered. According to Robert Siegel, these staffers felt the network should serve as the voice of the resistance.

Buzenberg was committed to the idea. If NPR did not exert itself on the international stage during what would be the first major American combat mission since Vietnam, it would decline into irrelevancy. "We needed to grow our coverage to be the kind of serious network that the BBC is," he said later. As for raising the money, Buzenberg had an ingenious plan. Rather than go through channels, he would appeal to NPR's most powerful and independent station managers. Not all were enthusiastic. "I wondered if it mattered whether NPR sent squadrons to cover the actual fighting," recalled Wisconsin Public Radio's Jack Mitchell. But in the end, Mitchell gave into the enthusiastic lobbying of Buzenberg's chief ally, Ruth Seymour of Santa Monica's KCRW. "Ruth was very influential," assistant foreign editor John Dinges later noted. In just weeks, she and her supporters raised $1 million for exclusive use on war reporting. As for those on the inside who accused Buzenberg of hawkishness, he accused them of small-mindedness. In a show of conviction, the news chief arranged for the distribution of thousands of promotional T-shirts emblazoned with a drawing of a military aircraft dropping not bombs but NPR microphones. The slogan: "Air Superiority—NPR News."

The buildup began immediately after the Iraqi army invaded Kuwait—the precipitating incident of the first Gulf War. National Public Radio foreign editor Cadi Simon deployed reporters across the Middle East. "I was in London," Deborah Amos recalled. "I got a call at two a.m. 'Get on a plane.' I went to the United Arab Emirates. I eventually got to Saudi Arabia and checked into the hack hotel"—the Dhahran International. Over the next months as President George H. W. Bush built a coalition named Desert Storm to expel Saddam's troops, other NPR correspondents were on the move. Deborah Wang was assigned to Riyadh, headquarters of General Norman Schwarzkopf, and the US Central Command (CENTCOM). John Burnett flew to the north to cover the Kurds. Jacki Lyden set up in Amman, Jordan. John Hockenberry drew Tel Aviv. Meantime, a revolving group of reporters—among them Scott Simon and Mike Shuster—arrived in Saudi Arabia, where, like Amos, they worked from the Dhahran International. "For NPR, this was pretty good," Dinges said. "We'd never flooded the zone with major reporters."

The quantity of NPR's journalism was overwhelming. The network "provided primary coverage in America," one executive recalled. But the quality wasn't everything that Bill Buzenberg and Cadi Simon wanted—not because of failings by their correspondents but because CENTCOM restricted the movements and access of all correspondents. Only reporters assigned to so-called media pools could work in the field. Officers monitored the chosen reporters and censored their dispatches before forwarding them to the Joint Information Bureau for general distribution to the broader press corps. As a result, the picture of the war presented to the public was cursory, and many journalists spent much of their time lounging at the Dhahran International awaiting handouts and watching CNN. On some occasions, NPR reporters managed to convey the reality of actual events. After hearing a rumor of a friendly-fire incident between coalition troops in a town outside Dhahran, Amos ignored pool protocol, securing an interview with a marine colonel who confirmed the story. But there were repercussions. "When talking to the colonel," she told listeners, a public affairs officer interrupted to inform her, "I can't order you to get out of here, but if you don't I will call the Saudis and have you arrested." Conversely, when the military did offer journalists access, there was often no news. Invited to cover a massive, open-air telecast of the 1991 Super Bowl for homesick US forces, Scott Simon said no. "It felt jingoistic to help the Army use the Super Bowl for crass political purposes. The Super Bowl is supposed to be used for only crass *commercial* purposes."

Neal Conan reached Saudi Arabia in early February 1991, several weeks into what was still largely an aerial campaign. Since being elevated to Pentagon reporter in the aftermath of Adam Powell's tenure, he had briefly returned to the executive suite as managing editor. But soon after Conan took the post, his wife, Liane Hansen, became the host of *Weekend Edition Sunday*, making him her boss. To avoid a conflict of interest, he returned to the Pentagon, a perfect jumping-off point to the Gulf War.

Like Amos and the others before him, Conan worked out of the Dhahran International, where a dedicated phone line to New York provided the primary conduit for transmitting stories to America. "The job was to take in and feed pieces from reporters in the field, write short overview stories, and file spots," he recalled. Such responsibilities, combined with the larger constraints dictated by the pool system, made Conan's life one of drudgery and frustration.

On February 24, after thirty-nine days of aerial warfare, the second stage of Desert Storm began as US-led coalition troops poured into Kuwait. A long, bloody confrontation seemed possible, as Iraqi forces numbered in the hundreds of thousands, but following only one hundred hours of ground combat, Saddam, realizing the futility of his position, surrendered, and his army limped back to Iraq. The war was over. Still, the fighting continued. "There was chaos on the border," recalled Amos. "George Bush was urging the Shia to rise up and turn on Saddam. It was a great story." Just as important, it was an accessible story. With the official end of hostilities, the pool system was no more. Reporters were free to pursue the kind of pieces heretofore off limits, and a gung-ho group was ready to go. As Lyden later put it, "Neal got in with the wild-guy crowd."

The alpha males of the Gulf War I press were driven in part by a desire to cast off the shackles dictated by CENTCOM and in part by testosterone. Several hadn't even waited for Saddam to capitulate before rushing to the front. In the opening hours of the ground war, Michael Kelly, who was freelancing for the *New Republic* and the *Boston Globe*, and Dan Fesperman of the *Baltimore Sun* rented a four-wheel-drive Nissan Safari, used adhesive paper and magic markers to adorn it with the inverted Vs that marked coalition vehicles, donned camouflage, and drove into battle. Unlike the journalists at the Dhahran International, they filed eyewitness accounts of what had become a turkey shoot: scattered Iraqi units, Iraqi equipment destroyed by missile fire. At one point, a group of Iraqi soldiers actually surrendered to the two, who escorted them to the rear for processing.

Another of the alpha males, the *Wall Street Journal*'s Tony Horwitz, also put on fatigues to get around CENTCOM restrictions. "As we pushed deeper," he wrote, "the scene turned much grimmer: blasted bunkers, mangled vehicles, and corpses scattered beside the road. . . . The slaughter was state of the art, the desert plowed with smart bombs. . . . The corpses were scorched and hairless, their faces frozen in expressions of astonishment like Pompeii residents mummified by lava in workaday posture."

Thirty-five-year-old Chris Hedges did not seem the sort Lyden would crown "the king of the wild guys." The son of a New England Presbyterian minister and a graduate of the Harvard Divinity School, he was a thin, balding intellectual who wore thick-lensed glasses. Early in his career he covered revolutions in Central America for the *Dallas Morning News*. For three years, he had been a Middle Eastern correspondent for the *New York Times*.

Hedges's appearance was deceiving. He was "pugnacious, extremely smart, and he did not pay attention to guardrails," recalled Lyden. "Chris took risks," added NPR's Michael Skoler, who came to Kuwait to cover the environmental damage caused by the oil-well fires. More than any American journalist assigned to Desert Storm, Hedges chafed under CENTCOM's dictates. "I wasn't going to sit in a hotel and write up press conferences and pool reports. At that point you might as well take a job with the Pentagon," he said later. "Most of the other reporters there thought I was a bit insane." Hedges's behavior was so provocative that Defense Secretary Dick Cheney contemplated expelling him. Before that could happen, the war ended.

Following Saddam's surrender, Hedges and Conan ran into each other in newly liberated Kuwait City, where the press had reassembled. The two knew each other from Conan's initial stint as executive producer of *All Things Considered*. Part of Conan's job then was to find reporters to cover international news, and he assigned Hedges freelance pieces on the Falklands War. At the time, Conan had thought of Hedges—seven years his junior—as a bright but quiet kid. Hedges now exuded bravado. Like Kelly and Horwitz, he had shed street clothes for combat garb—in his case, a Marine Corps uniform—and he was looking for action. "He said he planned to poke around on the other side of the border," Conan said later, meaning he hoped to find the Shia uprising. The *New York Times* had access to a rented Toyota Land Cruiser. "Chris needed a partner," Amos recalled. "Neal was too fresh to say no." Lyden put it more bluntly: "Anyone in their right mind would have known not to go with Chris Hedges."

On March 5, Hedges and Conan—dressed in a black-and-white check cotton shirt, cargo pants, and a New York Yankees baseball cap—set off for the port city of Basra, one hundred miles to the north, where the Shia rebellion was centered. They were not the only ones on the road. "Sam Donaldson of ABC was in a big camper," recalled Conan. "Tom Brokaw was in a Cortina." But where most of the others traveled only a few miles into the danger zone, Hedges and Conan kept going. "People were trying it," Amos said, "but Neal and Chris went farther than everybody else." Later, Skoler could only shake his head. "They had no way to reel themselves in."

The two drove up the six-lane road known as the Highway of Death. As Michael Kelly, who took the route a day earlier, described it:

> Most of . . . the wreckage . . . remained—roasted, bombed, burned, crashed, blown up, shot to pieces, tangled together in one long, incredible mess. . . . The contents of the wrecked vehicles were spread out in a dirty, smoking, occasionally bloody spume that stretched for miles and miles.

Kelly was content to stop and take inventory of the destruction. Conan and Hedges pressed ahead. They soon reached the last US military outpost. There, a tank driver from the Vermont National Guard gave them several packages of Meals, Ready to Eat (MREs). The reporters drove on.

About halfway to Basra, Conan and Hedges encountered an Iraqi soldier who told them that Saddam had put down the Shia rebellion. Seconds later, a jeep containing three Republican Guardsmen raced up. Hedges, realizing that he could not outrun them, braked to a halt, at which point soldiers appeared at each side of the Land Cruiser, stuck AK-47s into the reporters' faces, jacked them onto the ground, and threw them into the back of the jeep. They asked no questions, which terrified Hedges. In Central America he'd learned that war prisoners' only value was their knowledge. If captors failed to interrogate you, they intended to kill you. At best, he believed he and Conan had just hours to live.

The Iraqis drove the prisoners deeper into the desert, eventually stopping at a Republican Guard camp, where they took their MREs and locked them in a mud-and-wattle command structure. After a brief confinement, the two were marched outside to meet an Iraqi colonel who wore his field jacket draped over his shoulders and his hair and mustache in a crisp cut much like that sported by Saddam Hussein. Hedges, who spoke Arabic, did the talking. Conan was too scared to say anything. Soon a Mercedes arrived with more captured reporters—two Brazilians, a Catalan, and a Uruguayan. It was then that the colonel, who all the while had been stroking the barrel of his Beretta, decided to send everyone north. Conan and Hedges piled back into the jeep. As it pulled away, Conan looked out the rear to see Guardsmen stripping the Land Cruiser.

By this point, news had broken in the United States that Conan, Hedges, and other newsmen had disappeared. "Thirty Journalists Missing after Driving into Iraq," declared the headline atop the front page of the *Washington Post*. At M Street, executives worked the phone to the State Department and the White House trying to get answers. The *New York Times* held bigger cards. "The *Times* got General Schwarzkopf to call the head of the Iraqi Army," Hedges recalled, "and Gorbachev to call Saddam Hussein." Dread fell over the NPR offices. "Everybody was on pins and needles," Drake said later. That was nothing compared with what the network reporters in the Middle East felt. "I knew the Iraqis," Amos recalled. "Of all the Arab regimes, these guys were the most brutal." Reports had now begun to filter out concerning the torture the Iraqis had inflicted on Kuwaitis during the months of occupation. Lit cigarettes and high-voltage electrical wiring were the preferred tools. Rapes had been commonplace, summary executions frequent—and not just of Kuwaitis. Regarding a downed coalition fighter pilot who'd been paraded before the cameras, Amos told a fellow journalist, "He looks like they've buggered him a thousand times."

The truth was that the biggest threat to Conan, Hedges, and the others was not the Republican Guard but the Shia militia the Americans had asked to finish the job of toppling Saddam.

The first stop was Basra, and no matter what that Iraqi soldier had said about regaining control, the Shia rebellion still raged. The prisoners were confined in a science building at Basra University, where following their initial serious interrogation ("One of the officers was taking notes," Conan recalled. "That was good news. If we vanished at least there would be a paper trail") they were kept awake by the roar of Republican Guard howitzers pounding Shia positions and the return fire of Shia mortars. At dawn they were told they were going to Baghdad. After transferring to the Mercedes, they moved out, reaching Ur that afternoon. There, on the banks of the Euphrates in sight of ancient ziggurats and kilns, they were waylaid by the Shia.

"The bullets," Conan observed later, were "buzzing like bumble bees." The only person who stood between the reporters and death was a Republican Guard major spraying fire from his Kalashnikov back at the Shia. During a lull, they all leapt from the Mercedes onto a muddy road, pressing their faces right into the ground. Eventually everyone took cover behind a low wall. Time was elastic, Conan recalled, but after what felt like ten minutes, an Iraqi tank destroyed a tall building that served as the Shia stronghold.

The battle was over. Chris Hedges embraced the Republican Guard major, who doffed his beret. The major then led the prisoners back to the Mercedes, where they spent the long, wet, fearful night by the river. Conan termed it "the worst night of my life." He began to assume an irrational blame for his plight. It was his fault for falling in with Hedges. "If you've been held captive," he said later, "you have the feeling that you've created a terrible situation."

The next morning broke without gunfire. The Shia had disappeared, and the Republican Guard transferred everyone to a different command, which soon transported them to the opposite side of the Euphrates. The following day the Iraqis flew them by helicopter to Baghdad, where they were thrown in with a group of French reporters. The Mukhabarat, the Iraqi intelligence service, was now in charge and locked them all up at the shabby Diana Hotel. Within twenty-four hours, news that they were alive was broadcast over shortwave radio. "We might still be tried for espionage," Conan thought, "but this meant they could no longer just take us out back and shoot us."

On March 10, a week after Conan and Hedges had been apprehended— a week that to the reporters had seemed interminable—the Iraqis turned everyone over to the International Red Cross, which arranged to transport them all to Jordan by convoy. Conan, however, had other plans. Throughout his captivity, he had managed to conceal $5,000 American dollars that he was packing, part of it in a money belt around his waist, the rest tucked into the headband of his Yankees cap. (Coverage in a war zone is a cash business, and Conan was NPR's banker.) Now was time to spend some of it, so he sprang for a $400 cab ride. Once in Amman, he went to Jacki Lyden's hotel room. There he phoned his wife. Then he got to work. "I had a dramatic, first-hand account of a bold, Shia rebellion," he said later. The goal was to finish in time to get it on *Weekend Edition*, where Simon, who'd returned to Washington, would give the story great play. But Conan missed his deadline, settling for a back-and-forth with Lynn Neary on that evening's *Weekend All Things Considered.*

"I have to say, Neal," Neary remarked deep into the conversation "and this is very typical of you, you sound so composed." He was anything but composed.

The next day, the Brazilian embassy in Amman threw a raucous party for the released journalists. "We all did our level best to get drunk," Conan recalled, "but we never managed to overcome the adrenaline still surging through our systems." That was the least of it. "Neal was chastened," Lyden said later. Conan used a stronger word: "Shattered." Emotions welled up in him. "I knew that many others had suffered far more," he later reflected, "but I nursed irrational shame." The root of that shame, he would discover over time, went deeper than just a gnawing sense of personal responsibility. At some point during his captivity he had realized that he would do anything to survive no matter how ignoble. If the Iraqis had ordered him to lie, he would have lied; if they had demanded that he grovel, he would have groveled. In just a week, he had been broken. "The ordeal, it turns out, is the guilt of giving into your fear."

Back at NPR, there was little awareness of Conan's state of mind. "He got out relatively unscathed," Bruce Drake said. "He was OK," added John Dinges. The editors and executives were focused on something else: Arbitron ratings showed that NPR's listenership had jumped 14 percent during the Gulf War, and the gains appeared to be permanent. *Talk of the Nation*, a midday show created just to cover the conflict, was so successful it would become a part of the regular lineup. There was some pushback from the Left. Expanding on the misgivings initially voiced inside M Street, liberal critics accused the network of shilling for the Bush administration. Still in all, Buzenberg's decision to gear up had been vindicated. "The Gulf War was a landmark event for NPR," John Felton, a new deputy foreign editor, later said.

The human cost was undeniable. "It took me a long time to get over it," Conan recalled. "The fears became recurring nightmares—being chased by packs of feral dogs in the desert. Those were my collective fears."

NPR's coverage of the first Gulf War was more than just a tour de force for the network. It was also a validation of its foreign editor. Although Bill Buzenberg had given the go-ahead, Cadi Simon directed the reporters and assigned the stories. "She knew her stuff," the Washington editor Bruce Drake later noted.

Three years into her tenure, Simon had established herself as a tough and effective boss. Short, with curly black hair and a slash of scarlet lipstick worn like war paint, the editor in charge of NPR's international coverage paid little mind to her appearance. Rather, Simon, who had served in the Israeli army, relied on what's known in the military as command presence. "Cadi was an imposing personality," Paul Glickman, her overnight editor, said later.

Stories were legion about Simon's bluntness. Following her dismissal from *All Things Considered*, Renee Montagne ended up freelancing for the foreign desk. In 1991, she was in South Africa. Typically, she focused on the nation's politics, but the biggest news on the continent that year was happening elsewhere. "Zaire had blown up," Montagne remembered. The nation's leader, Mobutu Sese Seko, "was ill on his yacht up the Congo River. The army rioted. The embassy personnel got out. The French and Belgians sent fifteen hundred soldiers. I got a call from Cadi." She asked if Montagne was keeping abreast of developments.

"Yeah," I replied. "Who's there for us?"

Montagne assumed that NPR would have dispatched a warm body, but Simon surprised her. The network had no one in Zaire. What the foreign editor then said was more surprising.

"We're hearing there's gonna be a bloodbath. How soon can you get there?"

The next day Montagne was on a flight to Kinasha.

Simon demanded that NPR's foreign correspondents report from the front lines, of which there were many in 1991. At one thirty one January morning, Ann Cooper, who was covering the last gasps of Soviet communism, stood in front of the transmission tower of Lithuanian National Television in Vilnius observing a battalion of Russian tanks advance on a group of protestors. The USSR was attempting to crush the country's democratically elected government, which had the backing of state TV. The first sound Cooper captured on her Sony recorder was of voices raised in Lithuanian hymns. The next was the roar of a tank barrage. "Several shots have been fired," she said into her mic. "The tanks are shining their spotlights on the tower." By the time it was over, fourteen people in the crowd were dead. On *Weekend Edition Sunday*, Cooper told Liane Hansen, "They were unarmed." She then explained what the confrontation meant. "It's obviously a confused situation, but it's very hard to imagine that this is the Army just going off on its own without Gorbachev's blessing." The Cold War was not over, and NPR had aired tape that proved it.

Cadi Simon, such triumphs notwithstanding, was like many of her colleagues at M Street. She had trouble conceiving of NPR as a primary news source. She wanted her correspondents in the middle of the action, but she preferred for them to file ruminative, second-day accounts that didn't put the network ahead of the major newspapers. For all its progress, NPR remained a cautious institution, and reporters in the field had to fight to get a breaking story on the air. Which was why on August 14, 1992, Sylvia Poggioli, speaking to Simon by phone from her room in the Esplanade Zagreb Hotel in Croatia, started screaming.

"You've got to hold a block for us."

"Don't you want to work on it for later?" the foreign editor replied.

"No," the reporter insisted. "This is news."

Two days earlier Poggioli, her Italian journalist husband, Piero Benetazzo, and several correspondents from Britain's ITV had piled into a white United Nations jeep with the UN high commissioner for refugees, Peter Kessler. "Let's get in," he told the group, and they took off for northern Bosnia, two hundred miles away. Since April, the international press had focused on the ongoing battle between Muslims and Serbs that had followed the partition of Yugoslavia. Most of the attention centered on the mountain city of Sarajevo, which the Serbs had under siege. The bigger news, however, may have been elsewhere. "We were beginning to hear stories about camps of Muslim refugees in Bosnia," Poggioli said later. The reports related that at the least Muslims were being expelled from their homes—at the worst they were being exterminated.

Getting across the border took some doing. "We bribed thuggish guards with cigarettes," Poggioli recalled. They then entered another world, a ruined landscape controlled mostly by Chetnik militias—essentially, roving bands of killers.

Eventually the group reached the town of Sanski Most, where an officer in the Serbian Police, the last vestige of order in the country, agreed to take them to the Muslim quarter. Upon arriving, Poggioli recorded interviews with several women who told her that the Chetniks had forced them to sign over their houses and that the neighborhood men—husbands, brothers, sons—had all disappeared. One slashed a finger across her throat as she spoke.

The Serbian officer then escorted Poggioli and the others to a factory, where 175 men were being held prisoner. Chetnik guards at the place said that the men inside were soldiers, but they did not look like soldiers. Some were old. Some were young. As the contingent made its way out, Poggioli fell behind. "I turned around and started waving like crazy at these men," she said. "The message was, 'We know you're here. We're going to say something. We're not going to let the world forget you.'" As she waved, the realization hit her: this was a death camp.

As Kessler steered the UN jeep away from Sanski Most, the ITV correspondents were grumbling. They were "frustrated," recalled Poggioli. "They said, 'We don't have anything.'" She felt just the opposite. "I said, 'I'm ready to go. I have a great story.'" Unlike the television reporters, for whom images were everything, the NPR reporter could use words—some on tape, the rest her own—to convey what was happening in Bosnia. She could bring a terrorized society to life, painting a portrait of a group of prisoners awaiting execution because of their religion.

Somewhere on the drive back to Zagreb, a band of Chetniks overtook the group. They had "Kalashnikovs and daggers," Poggioli said later. "They were extremely threatening." The men forced Kessler to pull off the road onto a donkey trail that wound down over rough terrain. They were in the middle of nowhere. Everyone feared they would soon be killed, but the NPR reporter nursed another fear. "Shit," she recalled thinking, "If they confiscate my tapes I'm screwed." As the jeep bounced along, Poggioli inserted a blank tape into her Sony and jammed the two tapes that contained her interviews and observations from the day into a crevice behind her seat, where they wouldn't rattle in their plastic cases.

Soon enough captors and captives reached a roadblock separating Bosnia from Croatia manned by Serb police. "It's not a good idea for you to make a group of journalists go away," an officer said to the Chetniks. Meantime, one of the men holding the group stuck his Kalashnikov into Benetazzo's gut and asked, "What do you think of Milosevic?"

Slobodan Milosevic was the architect of Bosnia's anti-Muslim policies and the hero of the Chetniks. A wrong answer and everyone would be dead. But Poggioli's husband responded with a series of vague shrugs and grunts that could have meant anything. They were free to go.

Night had long since fallen, and the group took shelter on the floor of a UN outpost just across the border where they drifted off to the reassuring sound of Elvis on a jukebox. The next day Poggioli, her tapes securely in hand, was back at the Esplanade Hotel and in no mood to get any resistance from Cadi Simon.

After editing her actualities—interviews she conducted in Sanski Most— and writing and voicing her narrative tracks, Poggioli filed her story as NPR reporters in the field always had. She unscrewed the mouthpiece of her room phone, attached a line from her recorder with alligator clips to the exposed wires, dialed the foreign desk, and pressed Play. Then the staff at M Street took over. Julie McCarthy, who'd assisted Simon in directing Gulf War coverage, edited, and Smokey Baer mixed. After several hours of work, the two had shaped Poggioli's account of what she'd witnessed in Bosnia into a ten-minute, thirty-second story. It was twice as long as those that normally aired on *All Things Considered*, but it was so strong that the show led the broadcast with it.

Poggioli's piece was structured as a travelogue. Her guide was the Serb police officer. "Mirko takes a liking to us and agrees to accompany us to the Muslim part of town." There, in Italian, German, and pidgin Slav, the women Poggioli spoke to could be heard telling her their stories. "They have signed documents presented by the Serbs," she explained over the sound of their voices, "saying they voluntarily will leave all their property behind and request to leave the area. A young woman was the most daring. She tells us her mother was taken to a detention camp, and she explains that her brother was killed. She trembles as she speaks."

That was the prelude to the piece's news-breaking moment. "Mirko," Poggioli said, "has agreed to show us a detention camp."

At the camp gates, Mirko and a Chetnik who, as Poggioli phrased it, wanted "to put a stop to this," got into a terrific argument. They reached a compromise that allowed only three members of the group to enter, and the three would be subject to restrictions.

"No," Poggioli said into her mic as guards ordered her to shut off her tape recorder. Then: "OK. OK." The rest of the piece was narration, a testament to the power of acute observation and declarative sentences.

"I go into what was a machine factory," Poggioli related. "It is a large space, 100 yards long and 25 yards wide. About 175 men are evenly divided on each side. They are squatting or sitting cross-legged on wooden, slatted boards only a few inches off the ground. They are in total silence. Nearly all have their eyes averted from us, looking at the floor. Mirko and two guards accompany us. We're told the prisoners were taken in battle. From the looks on their faces, they all seem gripped by terror.

"I try to communicate. They don't respond. I decide to speak with Mirko and the guards to distract them while the others try to speak more freely with the prisoners. One of the reporters is successful. A prisoner tells him he is 42-years-old, a truck driver, and not a soldier. He says he and the others have been detained for 20 days. But he doesn't know why."

Poggioli then described falling back as the group made its way out of the factory. "The men raise their arms and we wave to each other. I think these must be the husbands, brothers and sons of the women we saw in the Muslim quarter, the ones pressured to sign away their homes. This is one of the ways the Serb militiamen carry out what they call *ethnic cleansing*."

Poggioli landed hard on her last two words, for they were new to NPR's listeners. They were new to America. They had first been used in the states

just two weeks earlier by John F. Burns of the *New York Times.* "Serbian nationalists have made war in the name of a myth," he wrote. "Bosnia will not
be safe until the two-thirds of the territory they control has been 'ethnically
cleansed.'" But where Burns introduced the phrase, Poggioli showed what
the practice looked like. "Sylvia Poggioli brought the real meaning of this
repugnant term to life," declared the Peabody Award committee in granting
her that year's prize for best foreign reporting.

Despite the successes under Cadi Simon, there was growing friction surrounding NPR's coverage of the most volatile subject in all of international
news—the Middle East. "Cadi was very much pro-Israel—a Zionist zealot,"
maintained John McChesney, her predecessor in the job and former boss.
John Hockenberry, who reported frequently from the region, took issue
with that assessment. She was, he said later, "meticulously fair." Indeed, during her tenure, the network come under attack from a pro-Israel lobbying
group, the Committee for Accuracy in Middle East Reporting and Analysis
(CAMERA). In July 1992, the organization singled out NPR's Jerusalem correspondent, Linda Gradstein, for her "remorseless hectoring of Israel" in a
story about the difficulties Palestinians faced crossing the Allenby Bridge
from Jordan to the West Bank. Still, to most at the network, Simon's loyalties
and their impact on NPR's reporting were plain. "There's no doubt that Cadi
was more sympathetic to Israel than not," said John Felton.

Hoping to silence critics who saw NPR as too sympathetic to Israel,
Buzenberg decided to bring in a Middle East editor who possessed a different take on the region.

Joyce Davis was thirty-seven when she first walked through the doors at
M Street. She came from the New Orleans *Times-Picayune,* where she'd been,
in her words, the paper's "first legitimate Negro reporter." During her nearly
eighteen years at the *Times-Picayune,* Davis had worked her way up from
the nightside general assignment desk to a spot on the op-ed page, where she
wrote a column that often focused on the Middle East. She'd visited the region
on several fellowships, and in 1989 she'd scored a scoop. She landed an interview with Yasser Arafat. "I went into their compound," she said later. "The
interview came at a time when he was in exile and considered dangerous."

From Davis's perspective, her reception at NPR was not cordial. "Cadi didn't want me there," she recalled. "Cadi was into covering Israeli issues. I was into that, too, but I'd been to Palestine, and I brought another perspective. It wasn't that I was difficult, but there was tension between Cadi and me."

Under the best of circumstances, varying points of view foster open-mindedness. But what ultimately soured the relationship between Simon and Davis is that it surfaced an issue that had vexed NPR since the days of Bob Zelnick through those of Adam Clayton Powell III: race. The conflict revolved around a correspondent hired by Buzenberg at Davis's urging. Sunni Khalid was a thirty-three-year-old Muslim American from Detroit. Standing just over six feet with a broad, expressive face, Khalid carried himself like an athlete. (A welterweight boxer as a young man, he claimed to have sparred with Thomas "Hitman" Hearns.) He arrived at NPR from the *Baltimore Sun*, where he'd been a feature writer, and Davis was thrilled to get him. He had "intimate contacts with and knowledge of the Middle East," she said. "We had few" Muslim and Black "voices at NPR at that time." As Khalid subsequently put it, "I was the only Black male reporter at NPR."

Persuading Cadi Simon to accept Khalid was not easy. "She thought I was a member of the Nation of Islam," he said later. "She had a friend at the FBI do a background check on me." Although Felton later scoffed at Khalid's assertion that Simon ordered an investigation, he agreed that she did not want him at NPR. "Cadi hired Sunni when managers were under pressure to hire minority staff," he said. "The pressure came from Buzenberg. There were pay incentives to hire minority reporters. I'm sure Cadi got an incentive."

Although Khalid was smart and could be charming ("He had a nice personality," recalled Felton), he lacked journalistic skills. "There was a joke that the *Baltimore Sun* staff opened bottles of champagne when NPR took Sunni off their hands," Renee Montagne recalled.

More worrisome, the consensus at NPR was that Khalid was less interested in journalism than in advancing a racial and political viewpoint. "Sunni had an agenda," said Felton. "Black power and the promotion of Islam: not just covering them but promoting them. He was upfront about it. These were his dominant interests."

As Khalid saw it, NPR was so unwittingly racist and unthinkingly in league with Zionist views that a little championing on his part of Blacks and Palestinians was needed to bring the organization into balance. "It's basically state radio," he said later. "If you were not rabidly pro-Israel, you were suspect."

As Simon struggled to deal with Khalid, she was also struggling with a sobering financial truth. The windfall that had enabled NPR to cover Gulf War I and powered the foreign operation through the next months was gone. In 1991, NPR fundraising fell $1 million short of expectations. Fiscal restraint was now the order of the day. There would be no more big pushes as with Desert Storm. Had money been the sole issue, she could have handled it, but it was clear to her that she was not in charge of the foreign desk. "She left because Bill Buzenberg pressured her into hiring Sunni Khalid," Washington editor Bruce Drake said later.

Forty-six-year-old Elizabeth Becker possessed impeccable journalistic credentials. A native of the Midwest, she'd spent most of the 1970s covering Southeast Asia for the *Washington Post* and was among the last journalists to visit Phnom Penh while Pol Pot still reigned. In 1980, she quit the paper to raise a family and write the book *When the War Was Over: Cambodia and the Khmer Rouge Revolution*. She and her husband, the *Post* columnist Jim Hoagland, were plugged into the inner circles of American political power during Bill Clinton's presidency, attending the annual Renaissance Weekend at Hilton Head Island, South Carolina, where they socialized with the likes of Time Inc.'s Walter Isaacson and attorney general nominee Kimba Wood. Buzenberg believed she was just the person to pick up the baton from Simon.

After adjusting to what for a newspaper person is one of the major structural peculiarities of NPR ("You had to go around like a rug salesman and get one of the programs to take your pieces"), Becker zeroed in on staffing issues. As she saw it, the biggest problem on the foreign desk was the inequitable way the network treated its female foreign correspondents. Amos, Cooper, Poggioli, Montagne, Gradstein—none were full-time employees. "They didn't pay for my car," recalled Montagne. "No benefits. I got nothing." Worse, NPR reporters abroad fronted the network money. "Payments from NPR were generally late," Cooper subsequently said. "They'd owe me thousands of dollars. It was a source of tension." Becker's goal was to elevate as many correspondents as possible to salaried jobs. She began with Poggioli, and she hit a wall. Bill Buzenberg "said they were not making Sylvia part of the staff, because she was married to Piero and was living quite well." The answer so infuriated the new editor that defying all good judgment for a just-hired employee she went over her boss's head and appealed to the network board. Which was how, more than ten years after reporting her first story for NPR, Poggioli finally began getting a regular paycheck. With others, Becker was not as lucky. She also "petitioned to get Ann Cooper on staff, but I was not successful, because she was not as famous as Sylvia." Likewise, she failed in her efforts on behalf of Amos, who ended up leaving the network for ABC.

Expanding NPR's foreign presence was another priority during Becker's early months at the network. NPR was trying to cover the world with a patchwork crew. To extend the organization's reach, the new editor took Julie McCarthy off the desk in Washington and assigned her to Tokyo, opening NPR's first Asian bureau. Tom Gjelten, who'd contributed pieces from Latin American during the McChesney era, left his post reporting on labor in DC for Sarajevo, where the siege continued. When the *New York Times* named Bill Keller its Johannesburg bureau chief, Cooper took the same job for the network. (Renee Montagne moved to Los Angeles, where she would cover domestic issues.) Michael Skoler, who'd been reporting on science since returning to M Street following the first Gulf War, set out for Nairobi.

Still, Becker frequently had to improvise. When an earthquake hit Latur, India, in 1993, killing more than ten thousand people, NPR happened to have a technology reporter, Dan Charles, in Bombay working on a science piece. After filing a couple of spot news stories, Charles called Becker and said he did not want to make the twenty-four-hour trip to the scene of the disaster. It would be a waste of time. "This is how we operate," Becker replied. "We get there when we get there, and we ask for help." Chastened, Charles set out for Latur, which he reached in less time than he'd imagined and where he found a couple of ham radio operators who loaned him a satellite phone. *All Things Considered* broadcast a comprehensive account of the earthquake that night.

To be a foreign editor is largely to be a field marshal and an administrator. Neither task interested Becker. What drew her to NPR was the opportunity radio journalism offered to combine facts and audio to produce the kind of powerful work she'd done for the *Post*. The "beauty" of radio reporting is the color of the sounds, she said later. A story told by "the marching of feet or the music of South Africa" appealed to her. There was also something else. Becker, unlike many in Washington, was less interested in policy than in its impact on people.

Thirty-six-year-old Michael Skoler did not have a great voice. It was too nasal and a little wavering. But he possessed more important attributes. He was a graceful writer and a searching journalist who was adept at sound production. Prior to joining the network, Skoler had worked at WGBH in Boston, where he'd apprenticed himself to a group of old-time engineers. Unlike others at NPR, who relied on network-issued Sony recorders, he carried a Marantz PMD430, a high-end but lightweight cassette machine festooned with dials and meters that enabled a user to monitor and adjust sound levels in the field. "I was an audio-driven reporter," he said later. His posting to Africa could not have been better timed for NPR.

In April 1994, just a couple of months after arriving in Nairobi, Skoler heard an incomplete but ominous report over the BBC regarding unrest across Lake Victoria in Rwanda. Airlines had stopped flying into the country, so along with journalists from *Newsweek*, the *New York Times*, and *Time*, Skoler hitched a ride in with a relief convoy from the Red Cross.

Within minutes of crossing the border, Skoler and the rest realized they'd descended into madness. "Bodies were stacked by the side of the road," he said later. "We watched crowds chasing people with machetes. We watched people being killed." The victims were members of Rwanda's Tutsi minority. The murderers were mostly in the Hutu majority. The violence was sparked by a rocket attack, allegedly at the instance of Tutsis, on a plane carrying the nation's Hutu president.

After reaching Kigali, Rwanda's capital, the group checked into the Hôtel des Mille Collines, which would be memorialized in the film *Hotel Rwanda*. There, Skoler phoned NPR for an on-air conversation with Robert Siegel on *All Things Considered*. The next day, he visited a Red Cross hospital to interview the victims. ("I'd see someone—a big chunk of their head would be gone.") By the time he got back to Mille Collines and filed a story about the wounded, the situation in the streets outside had grown dire. Mobs of Hutus were on the prowl. He and the other reporters realized that if they didn't get out they would soon be dead.

"We called our organizations and said we need help," Skoler said later. Back in DC, Elizabeth Becker contacted the State Department. At first, there wasn't much sympathy. They were "scolding us for sending reporters in the first place," recalled Paul Glickman, one of Skoler's editors. Finally, the United Nations dispatched two armored personnel carriers to Mille Collines to extract the group. At the Kigali airport, the UN transport plane chartered to fly everyone to Nairobi came under attack as it rolled down the runway for takeoff. "There were missiles coming," Skoler remembered, adding flatly, "Luckily, they weren't good shots."

It was a narrow escape, but Skoler was not done with Rwanda. "I decided I needed to go back," he said later. "I wanted to tell the story from the ground up—not the geopolitical story but a story that helped people to understand the context and was told by African voices." He returned in May.

This time, Skoler entered Rwanda with a detachment of soldiers from the Rwandan Patriotic Front, the Tutsi militia. Their destination was Gahini, a town about thirty miles outside Kigali. "I saw things before it was cleaned up," recalled the NPR reporter. "It was raw." Using his sophisticated Marantz, Skoler recorded hours of tape. "I interviewed survivors. I interviewed Hutus who'd taken part in the killings. I interviewed officials." Skoler also captured the sounds—sobbing, labored breathing—of a terrorized people. After several days he returned to Nairobi, where he banged out his story and sequenced his audio. "I wrote copious notes on how the producers should cut the tapes and how the story should be mixed." He then put everything into a pouch and sent it to London, where it could be fed from the NPR bureau to M Street. No alligator clips for him. His hope was to get a piece on the air that matched the reportage Poggioli had done in Bosnia while also conveying the atmospherics.

The June 14, 1994 edition of *All Things Considered* featured Skoler's report. The piece clocked in at a hefty twenty-two-and-a-half minutes. In an understated introduction, Robert Siegel said it would reveal "how Rwanda became a country of killers."

Skoler started in a matter-of-fact fashion: "I drove in from the north. The countryside was empty." Then, in the same quiet vein, he showed that death had vanquished life in Rwanda. "Sometimes, the car would fill with the smell of rotting flesh, and we'd notice corpses lying in a field beside of an abandoned house."

One woman in Gahini pulled up her skirt to reveal burn marks. A little boy lifted his shirt to reveal where a spear had punctured his back "right between the shoulders." When the reporter asked a group why their countrymen had wounded and killed so many, one said, "To get rid of the Tutsis."

Ethnic cleansing had come to Africa. "Foreign nations have been hesitant to label the Rwandan massacres genocide because that would force them to act," Skoler explained. "But the evidence that genocide is occurring is hard to ignore."

The story did not require much more explication than that. Skoler took witness-bearing to a high level. At a sanctuary near Gahini, he recorded what he heard—insects, birds—and, in a voice muffled against the stench by a bandana, what he saw.

"Outside the church there are maybe two or three dozen bodies—and the heat here in Rwanda. Many of the bodies are almost fully decomposed. You can see some skulls, some backbones. There seem to be women in brightly colored clothing, as well as children. This is amidst a very beautiful area of Eucalyptus and pine trees."

Skoler went inside.

"There are bodies all over the church." He choked, fighting to retain his composure. "The blood on the floor is so thick it's dried to a muddy, brown crust that may be in some places a quarter inch. Most of the bodies are blackened and decomposing. The stained-glass windows on either side are broken. Above the whole scene, above the altar is a small, wooden statue of Christ with one hand raised."

The descriptions were profound and unsettling. They also begged a critical question. What happened? Skoler let a gravedigger he met outside the sanctuary tell that part. When the genocide began, the man said, Tutsis took shelter in the church. The next day the Hutus attacked. They doused the building with gasoline and tossed grenades through the windows. That killed only some. The Hutus returned with axes, broke down the doors, and murdered the rest with machetes and spears. All told, two thousand people died in this place.

The press had largely dismissed the Rwandan genocide as a tribal clash. The Tutsis were the country's elite, the Hutus its working class. Following the institution of democracy in the early 1960s, Skoler related, the tribes lived side by side for more than thirty years. What led to the hostility? As a former government official told the NPR reporter, political and business factions assassinated the president, armed the Hutus, and stoked buried resentments. Their motivation: financial gain. "They were proud of it. They set up a network of killers, and they did their job." The slaying of some 800,000 Tutsis—the final total—was not a spontaneous eruption of tribalism. It was premediated mass murder.

Michael Skoler's Rwanda story won a duPont-Columbia Silver Baton and a Robert F. Kennedy Award. NPR also won another 1994 duPont-Columbia Silver Baton—for its coverage, directed by Ann Cooper, of South Africa's first all-race elections. The network was securing its stature as a leading outlet for foreign news. Nonetheless, Elizabeth Becker, two years into her tour at NPR, was miserable. Like Cadi Simon, she could not handle Sunni Khalid.

Although Becker included Khalid in the group NPR dispatched to South Africa to cover the elections, she felt that his work was substandard. "He missed deadlines and at times was abrasive under deadline," she said later. She was not alone in this view. "Sunni didn't have the chops," recalled Montagne, who was also part of the South Africa team. Even Joyce Davis agreed that Khalid performed poorly. "There were problems up and down with Sunni, and I was trying to work with him."

For his part, Khalid argued that his competence was not the issue. It was his blackness. He made no effort to disguise it on air, and this made NPR editors uncomfortable. Davis, who saw both sides, concurred. NPR had "an on-air sound," she said later. "It was sophisticated, East Coast. The sound of the Black male was not the NPR sound. Sunni couldn't camouflage his Black male voice. Sunni's cadence and diction were not what they wanted. Did anyone say, 'He sounds like a Black man?' No." But that was the unspoken message.

Through it all, Khalid continued to maintain high hopes for advancement at NPR. "Sunni wanted to be our guy in South Africa," Montagne recalled. But by this time, Cooper was ensconced, and even if she hadn't been, Khalid would not have been considered. "Sunni was not highly regarded," Montagne said.

As bad feelings escalated, Bill Buzenberg took Khalid to lunch and in an effort to repair the damage offered him a new job: Cairo bureau chief. "I thought it would be a good idea to have him in Egypt," the news vice president said later. Khalid was disappointed. "I didn't want to go to Cairo," he recalled. "I wanted South Africa." Montagne later explained, "Sunni saw the Cairo posting as punishment."

But Egypt was where Buzenberg wanted Khalid, and Becker was in charge of making it happen. "I agreed to send him," she recalled. "I told Buzenberg, 'Don't worry. I'll give him Arabic lessons. We'll tutor him about production. We'll have the best reporting out of Cairo that he can give us.'"

Khalid chafed. "Sunni often went to human resources to complain about me," Becker said later. As a consequence, when ironing out the financial details of his Cairo assignment—like most NPR reporters abroad, he would be on contract—the foreign editor took the sort of precautions managers take with potentially litigious employees. She was never alone with him. "I had the contract written and witnessed."

The efforts, Becker said, were fruitless. "He refused the training. He rejected language instruction and the extensive technical training required to record and feed reports more or less on his own." Then, she added, Khalid got to Egypt and claimed he hadn't been properly trained for the job. "He demanded an entirely new contract, more money."

Buzenberg sided with Khalid. "Bill didn't stand up for me," Becker said. Because of the past difficulties with Khalid, NPR's vice president for news, she concluded, was paralyzed by the fear of a racial discrimination lawsuit. "There are ways to handle matters to produce greater diversity," she subsequently said, "and there are ways not to handle them."

Had Becker been in a different place in life, she might have kept at it. But she was going through trying times. She and Jim Hoagland had split. Coworkers often found notes between Becker and her divorce lawyer in the newsroom fax machine. The editor was so distraught that a producer dubbed her "the head achy lady." She was too tired to fight. "Sunni ran roughshod over her," said Bruce Drake.

Becker departed NPR. "If I'd had a stronger stomach, I'd have stayed," she said later. "I didn't handle the Sunni thing well." Shortly after leaving, she landed a position in the Washington bureau of the *New York Times*.

With Becker gone, Sunni Khalid settled into the Cairo job. Reactions to his performance were negative. "His work," Paul Glickman said later, "wasn't strong." Dinges, one of his early advocates, was tougher. "He wasn't productive. In that bureau you had to cover the intifada, but he wouldn't go." That wasn't all. The stories Khalid did get on the air were "vulnerable to the charge that he was pro-Palestinian." Drake was harsher still: "Sunni was a disaster." No one, however, would do anything about it. After a decade of steady progress in coverage abroad, NPR did not have a foreign editor.

In the summer of 1955, sixteen-year-old Loren Jenkins moved to Aspen, Colorado. Slight of build but athletic and confident, he was the son of an American foreign services officer and had spent his early years in Chile. As a young teen, he was deposited at the Lycée Jaccard in Lausanne, Switzerland, on Lake Geneva. There, Jenkins said later, "I learned two very important things. French and skiing."

Aspen in the mid-1950s was a rustic wide spot in the road populated largely by old silver miners, artists, and former members of the army's 10th Mountain Division who'd trained in nearby Camp Hale for high-altitude combat during World War II. For a kid who'd spent most of his life abroad, the town might have seemed insular, yet Jenkins felt at home. It reminded him of the Alps—and the skiing was only part of it. In 1949, Walter Paepcke, the CEO of the Container Corporation of America, enamored of the place's natural beauty and hoping to create a cultural valhalla, founded the Aspen Institute. A transformation was afoot, and in his small way, Jenkins was part of it.

In 1954, E. F. "Army" Armstrong, a former navy attaché, and his wife, Sara, once a violinist with the Boston Symphony, founded Aspen's first international restaurant—the Copper Kettle. Armstrong had served with Jenkins's father in Poland, Moscow, and Iran. While abroad, he and Sara had fallen hard for continental cuisine. They wanted a worldly busboy.

For someone of Jenkins's age and background, the Copper Kettle, located three miles out of Aspen at an abandoned silver mine, was perfect. The downstairs dining room was all exposed bricks and timbers, with big tables adorned by crisply ironed linens. The help slept upstairs in metal sheds that had once housed the pulleys and ropes that lowered equipment into the earth and brought ore to the surface. Each evening featured a new menu. The offerings celebrated the foods of the globe—curries on Wednesday, coq au vin on Thursday. The establishment was a rustic United Nations of food. There was nothing else like it in the Rockies. As Jenkins recalled it, he came to Aspen "and moved into this family of intelligent internationalists."

Although Jenkins worked hard at night, his days were his own. He was a good enough skier that he picked up instructing jobs at the Aspen Ski School. He was also drawn to the town's surrounding peaks. "I started hiking," he said later. "You can mostly walk up the mountains around Aspen." Not every ascent, however, was easy, and Jenkins took lessons, learning how to use pitons and carabiners. He nurtured a vague feeling that in adulthood he would test himself in high places accessible only to those daring and well prepared. He enjoyed the challenge and relished the perspective. "It was danger followed by pleasure, and you shared information with fellow climbers."

To graduate from college in 1961 was not just to have your life ahead of you but to be at the vanguard of John F. Kennedy's New Frontier. With a degree in political science from the University of Colorado, Jenkins joined the recently founded Peace Corps. In 1962 he was part of contingent of volunteers assigned to Sierra Leone, which had just gained independence from the United Kingdom. As one of the group leaders, his main task was to teach French at a secondary school in the capital city of Freetown. "I was also assigned a jeep to go visit the outlying Peace Corpsmen to deliver their mail." At each stop, Jenkins gathered news. He wrote what he learned and printed it in a mimeographed sheet circulated throughout the country.

After the Peace Corps, Jenkins spent time in Algeria, then headed to New York, where he started graduate school at Columbia in philosophy and took part in civil rights protests. Through a family friend, he secured an audience with Ben Bradlee, at the time the Washington bureau chief of *Newsweek*. "We had a good chat, and he asked me to do an article on the campaign of Bill Haddad for the Nineteenth Congressional District of New York—the Lower East Side." Jenkins had an in with the candidate, who'd been a Peace Corps official, although from the start, he knew that Bradlee had no intention of publishing his work. It was an exercise. Still, Jenkins threw himself into the story. It was his first legitimate piece of journalism, and it served as a calling card to get him a job at the *Daily Item* in Westchester County.

Following six months of suburban journalism, Jenkins leaped to the New York desk of UPI. A year later, he transferred to the London bureau and subsequently reported from Madrid and Paris. He soon left to string for *Newsweek* and its sister publication, the *Washington Post*. He ended up in Beirut, where *Newsweek* gave him a full-time job. There was so much news: Black September, the death of Egypt's Gamal Abdel Nasser, the attempted overthrow of Jordan's King Hussein. "I never wanted to cover violence, but it was the story of the moment."

In 1973, *Newsweek* sent Jenkins to Hong Kong. Nixon had opened China, and Katharine Graham, the magazine's publisher, was launching an Asia edition. He learned fast. "I went to Cambodia cold. You land, find people who can be sources and give you a quick fix, write your story, and fly off." *Newsweek* added Vietnam to his area of responsibility. Working from Saigon's Hotel Continental, he covered the last years of American involvement in the war and formed his basic ideas about how a foreign correspondent should operate. One: ignore official sources. Two: stories are everywhere.

The Loren Jenkins who emerged from Vietnam was a foreign correspondent of the old school, and *Newsweek* rewarded him with a posting to Rome. The clean-shaven Peace Corps volunteer had given way to a bearded, stocky bon vivant. Unlike most hacks, who lugged their humble Smith Coronas in dowdy blue cases, Jenkins carried his stylish Olivetti 21 in a custom Gucci tote stenciled with the interlocking logo and set off by the classic, red-and-green striped ribbon. When someone from accounting asked him why he flew first class on an assignment, he retorted, "Because I couldn't find a better way." In part, this was a matter of panache, but it was also provided what Jenkins saw as compensation for enduring the perils of the trade. "To stay civilized when you're covering wars, you had to live well when you could because you knew you were going to be living shittily to do the work you had to do."

No sooner had Jenkins arrived in Rome than the truth of the insight hit home. Before he had found an apartment, his phone rang. Lebanon had descended into civil war. From 1975 until 1979, save for papal trips and the Red Brigade kidnapping of Italy's Aldo Moro, he would write of little else. It was brutal work. In 1980, the *Washington Post* offered Jenkins the chance to make the work more bearable by giving him one of the best jobs in journalism, a six-months-on, six-months-off staff writing position. For half of every year, he would cover not just Beirut but conflict anywhere in the world, racing to El Salvador or Sri Lanka as soon as the shooting began. When the stipulated period ended, he gave way to another *Post* reporter and escaped to a thirty-acre farm he'd bought in Tuscany.

By 1982, the international story was once again Lebanon, which had become the refuge of an increasingly militant Palestinian Liberation Organization (PLO). In June, Israeli president Menachem Begin ordered an invasion. In August, Jenkins flew there.

The large international press corps covering Beirut was headquartered at the Commodore Hotel on the city's Muslim west side. Despite its grand name, the place was eccentric, which made it perfect for reporters. At the check-in counter, the clerk asked arriving guests, "Artillery side or car-bomb side?" The owner, Youssef Nazzal, paid protection money to the PLO, and he'd outfitted the establishment with everything a working reporter required. There were multiple telex machines for transmitting stories and an established system for access to them. You took a number, then waited at the bar for the first availability. For entertainment, a parrot in a nearby cage would periodically mimic the scream of incoming missiles.

The reporters at the Commodore in the summer of 1982 were a stellar lot. They ranged from the talented and young (twenty-nine-year-old Thomas Friedman of the *New York Times*) to the glamorous (ABC's Peter Jennings) and included Tim McNulty of the *Chicago Tribune*. Richard Ben Cramer of the *Philadelphia Inquirer*, winner of the 1979 Pulitzer Prize for his coverage of Israel, was the poet laureate. At night he wandered the halls clad in pajamas downing coffee and composing his stories in his head.

The Lebanon of that summer was careering into insanity. On September 14, it spun out of control with the assassination of president-elect Bashir Gemayel, who was blown up by a remote-control bomb while meeting with members of his Christian Phalangist Party. The outside world had been looking to Gemayel to restore order. The PLO had even withdrawn from Beirut. His death destroyed the hopes for peace.

Jenkins was in his element. Off the bat he pounded out an account of the assassination. The next day, he was back at it. "For the first time fighting in the heart of an Arab capital city, Israeli units fanned through West Beirut's commercial heartland." Then things turned ominous. "Cordons of Israeli tanks surrounded the Shatila, Sabra and Burj el-Barajneh camps," he wrote. A neighborhood that housed thousands of Palestinian refugees was encircled.

On September 18, Jenkins heard that something horrific had happened at the Sabra and Shatila camps. Before dawn the next day, accompanied by his translator, Nora Boustany, and Robert Fisk, a reporter for the *Times* of London, he went there. They were the first reporters to enter. "It was silent except for the flies," Jenkins recalled. "Bodies were everyplace. People at breakfast tables, babies." Slaughter on such a scale could not have occurred without the approval of Ariel Sharon, the commander of the Israeli Army. Jenkins's anger was accompanied by a revulsion that brought him to his knees. In the next morning's *Post*, he wrote: "This correspondent counted 46 bodies lying open in Shatila before being overcome by nausea."

For the next four days, Jenkins broke one story after another about what became known as the Sabra and Shatila massacre. He showed that at the least Israeli forces looked the other way as Phalangists carried out the killing. He named the Phalangist commander. As the *Tribune's* McNulty recalled, "Loren would punch you in the face with the facts." Jenkins did not have the story to himself.

Tom Friedman could not have been more unlike his *Washington Post* counterpart. Where Jenkins was out of a Hemingway novel, the *New York Times* reporter was an Arabic-speaking, golf-playing Oxford grad with a master's degree in Middle Eastern studies. Observed McNulty: "Friedman got the big picture."

On Sabra and Shatila, Friedman started from a disadvantage. After the PLO's withdrawal from Beirut, he'd gone on vacation. The day Gemayel was assassinated he was walking through New York's JFK airport when he heard himself paged. Getting back was hard. The Beirut airport was closed, so Friedman flew to Damascus with the intention of taking a cab to the embattled city, normally a three-hour trip. The roads were blocked. By the time he reached the Commodore Hotel, the killing was over.

Still, Friedman managed to get to Sabra and Shatila only an hour after Jenkins. He then made up for lost time working, as he recalled, "day and night." He also brought his identity as a Jew to his writing. "One part of me wanted to nail Begin and Sharon, to prove beyond a shadow of a doubt that their army had been involved," he later noted. "Another part of me was looking for alibis. . . . Although an 'objective' journalist is not supposed to have such emotions the truth is they made me a better reporter." The result was a ten-thousand-word epic in the September 26 *Times*.

The next spring, the Pulitzer Prize committee anointed both Jenkins and Friedman. The committee felt that their combined work was so unflinching and complete that each merited an award.

Sabra and Shatila shook Jenkins. "I wish I'd never covered the Middle East," he said later, "because it savages you." By the end of 1982, he was gone from Beirut. The CIA had warned him that the Phalangist leader he'd named as the massacre's mastermind had ordered a hit on him. Still, he was a Pulitzer winner, and he capitalized on it. There was a fellowship at the Council on Foreign Relations and stories for *Rolling Stone*. When all that was over, the *Post* asked him to pick back up where he'd left off. This time, the paper planned to base him in Canada, but the location would have little to do with his assignment. "They said, 'With your background, we'll want you to cover whatever conflict there is.'" Jenkins blanched. While reporting in Vietnam, he'd met Keyes Beech of the *Chicago Daily News*. A Pulitzer winner for his coverage of the Korean War, the sixty-two-year-old reporter was still plying his difficult trade. For Jenkins, the sight of the graying Beech busting his gut in a violent country served as a warning. "I thought: I don't ever want to be covering war at his age."

Jenkins left the *Post* and went home to Aspen. He toyed with writing a biography of his former boss, Katharine Graham. Then, he learned that the *Aspen Times* was for sale. The city had grown since his boyhood. Not only were there thousands of wealthy new residents, but they were a lively lot, engaged in issues. "I thought there was a great chance I could take this small-town newspaper and turn it into something—so I taught myself what it takes to run a paper and managed to find five partners who had the cash."

Jenkins filled the *Aspen Times* with tough local stories and pieces from the *Washington Post*'s news service. He also did something that stunned the town—he challenged its powerful real estate industry. "I wrote editorials that were very Bolshoi," he said later. "The only big issue in Aspen is development versus environment. I took on the Aspen Ski Company—the biggest employer in town. We took a pro-environment stance."

Jenkins enjoyed a five-year run at the *Times*, but his critiques won him enemies, among them the co-owners of the paper. "I fell out with my partners. They bought out my share."

At forty-seven, Loren Jenkins was jobless. He was too young to retire but at a loss as to what to do next. That's when he heard that Elizabeth Becker had left National Public Radio and the network was looking for a foreign editor. He made a few calls.

"It was the strangest thing," Jenkins recalled, relating that NPR's management asked him not to come to the network offices but to a neutral site lest anyone on the inside suspect that they were thinking of reaching outside for the hire. The secrecy was warranted. At headquarters, a council of elders was going through the motions of conducting a formal selection process. "They formed a big committee that even included Susan Stamberg," said Bruce Drake, who'd just been elevated to the post of managing editor. "They did extensive interviews."

The leading internal contender for the position was Joyce Davis, and NPR gave her a lengthy hearing. Following Becker's departure, she'd been running the department, and she had her supporters. "She was good," said Ann Cooper. There was, however, a sticky issue. Following the dustups involving Sunni Khalid, Davis formed an all-Black, in-house working group to address racial grievances. She believed the network's largely white leadership was "not living up to" its ideals. Some doubted her motives. "She was a woman who frequently stirred shit in hopes of her own advancement," maintained Drake. Davis countered that her goals were unselfish. She simply wanted the network to hire more Black journalists "NPR was clubby. Positions went to friends of friends."

Considering all this, it's little wonder that NPR's management, as Sylvia Poggioli later put it, saw "Loren Jenkins as manna from heaven." Not only was he a Pulitzer winner who had covered major news stories on nearly every continent but he'd served in the Peace Corps and participated in civil rights demonstrations. "On issues related to race," said Drake, who helped to vet Jenkins, "the higher-ups were impressed. He believed in diversity. That came back very positively." In sum, Poggioli added, Jenkins's credentials were "infinitely better than Joyce Davis's." Bill Buzenberg, the final judge, saw it that way, too. "I hired Loren because he was by far the best candidate."

The possibilities at NPR enthralled Jenkins. Here was a chance to take all he'd learned as a foreign correspondent and use it to build a great international radio news operation. "My strength," he said later, "is that I approach the news not as an American citizen but as a citizen of the world. I had grown up in other cultures. I have a vision of history unfolding that is not limited to the American perspective. Not that American values aren't good, but they're limiting. You have to understand that other people have a different vision."

Before beginning the job, Jenkins summoned NPR's foreign staff to Washington for a daylong retreat. Poggioli, Tom Gjelten, Mike Shuster, Michael Skoler, Cooper, and others flew in. "We're here to educate America about the world we live in," the editor told them. "Good journalism is education." Everyone agreed, but as Jenkins warmed to his topic, some in the group realized that he spoke a language not often heard in the trusting precincts of public radio. He was a skeptic. "Everything that is told to you is questionable," he declared. "Everyone's got spin. Your government's got spin. Generals fighting a war want to let you know it's a great success. The opposition thinks it's a disaster. The CIA tells you something because it fits their vision. The job of the reporter is to listen to all these distortions and pick up a little bit here, a little bit there. The other stuff you discard. The reporter's job is to search for truth in a world of deception and lies." Jacki Lyden, who could not make the session, remembered getting a call from a producer who was there. "We've never had anyone like him," he told her. Paul Glickman, who did attend, felt put off. "He was your classic hard-bitten journalist walking into the NPR newsroom, which was touchy-feely."

None of the misgivings initially mattered. Jenkins had the full support of his superiors, who agreed with his central premise: the foreign desk needed shaking up. "One of the first things he had to deal with was the sense of entitlement at NPR," recalled Drake. Many on the staff, he added, were inclined to go off on tangents while missing the main thrust of the news altogether. The network's international report was soft. Jenkins wasted no time instructing correspondents to fax or email him each morning with a list of the stories they were working on. "I had a rule when I came into the office that everyone had to have left a message of what their days would be like." For a group that in the past had largely followed its own instincts, this was jarring.

It was just the start. The new foreign editor was obsessed with breaking news. Unlike his predecessors, he wanted NPR to beat the *New York Times* on major stories. Jenkins also had little patience for the long, soulful pieces that had previously been the hallmark of the network's international coverage. "Loren felt our job was to tell more and shorter stories," Skoler said later. "He sent out a memo that no story was to be longer than eight minutes, and there should be few of those. I felt that memo was aimed at me."

At the same time Jenkins was giving his reporters their new marching orders, he was informing his editors of a bracing reality: they now answered to him. As a condition of getting the job, he had agreed to keep Joyce Davis as his number two, and she would remain in charge of coverage of the Middle East. He could live with the former but not the latter. "I went to Joyce," he recalled, "and said, 'Joyce, I won a Pulitzer Prize in the Middle East. I know it. You don't. I am going to take over editing of the Middle East.' That pissed her off."

Jenkins's most daunting task would require more than gall. "In offering Loren the job," Montagne said later, it was understood that "he had to become the hatchet man for Sunni Kahlid." Poggioli concurred. "Sunni became Loren's problem." Much as she wanted to protect Khalid, Davis also concurred. "Was Sunni a problem Loren needed to take care of? Probably."

No one knew this better than Jenkins. There was "a racial issue there. Sunni Khalid had bullied his way onto the foreign desk. Then he'd bullied his way to Cairo. His reporting out of Cairo was atrocious. He was approaching the Middle East as if 'I'm here to give the Arab voice.' There was no understanding that it was a two-way conflict. Everyone was afraid of him."

To the extent that he could, Jenkins tried to defer action. Khalid "came back on leave. I was new to the desk—weeks, not a month. Khalid was at the end of the contract he'd signed with Elizabeth Becker, and he wanted an extension." The answer: not so fast. "Look, I just got here," Jenkins recalled saying. "I'm not making any decisions about anything like that until I know the lay of the land." Former assistant foreign editor John Dinges, who'd moved to the national desk to work on election coverage, said that Jenkins in fact tried to give Khalid a second chance. "Loren set some goals." Drake saw it differently: "Sunni was on notice."

While Jenkins figured out how to handle Khalid, he plunged into the day-to-day life of NPR, which for senior staffers revolved around a daily nine thirty meeting. These planning sessions drew the top producers from *All Things Considered* and *Morning Edition*; desk editors (science, national, foreign); the managing editor, Drake; deputies like Davis; and usually Buzenberg. This was where people pitched stories and jockeyed for influence. The tone was light, the mood collegial. That wasn't Jenkins's way. He was loud, opinionated, and challenging. He was also the liveliest raconteur to hit the network since Mankiewicz. He'd been everywhere and knew everyone. Many at NPR (Mankiewicz, Robert Krulwich) had boasted of their association with Hunter S. Thompson, but the gonzo journalist was the best man at Jenkins's wedding. They'd been friends since 1962, when they'd met in Aspen. Before Jenkins became a reporter, he'd asked Thompson whether he should go into the profession. Thompson had replied no, then added that if Jenkins did take the plunge he should remember one thing: "All editors suck." These were the sort of cracks that had kept the correspondents at the Commodore in stitches. However, what played in Beirut did not necessarily play in Washington.

Six months into his tenure, Montagne recalled, "Loren was sitting at the general meeting of all the desks, and he made a remark about ragheads." Derogatory as the crack was, many Middle East hands spoke about Arabs that way, but such talk had rarely been heard around NPR. Minutes after the meeting concluded, the comment was all over the Washington office. Reporters abroad learned soon thereafter. Some staffers were unphased. "I don't think he was bigoted," Drake said later. Montagne concurred but was less forgiving. "Loren is not a racist—just an asshole." Sunni Khalid, however, was livid. "I found out about it in Cairo," he remembered, "Jenkins was a racist. To call Arabs ragheads is deplorable. He has contempt for everybody, but his contempt for Arabs is even greater. I wasn't going to be bullied by him."

From Jenkins's perspective, Khalid's reaction was moot: he'd decided to let the reporter go. Few were surprised. ("I sat kitty-corner from Loren," Jacki Lyden recalled. "He would boast, 'I'm going to fire Sunni.'") The break, however, wasn't clean. NPR brought Khalid back to Washington and put him on the cultural desk. He saw it as a demotion and requested an investigation, claiming "I got run out" for writing stories with a point of view. But it was hard to make the case against Jenkins that he'd made against

Cadi Simon—that the boss was *pro*-Israeli. To many Jewish organizations, Jenkins's coverage of Sabra and Shatila proved him to be *anti*-Israeli. From Buzenberg's perspective, it all evened out. "Jenkins is a force of nature," he said later. More to the point, he was a force of nature driving foreign coverage in the direction Buzenberg wanted. Not surprisingly, the reaction infuriated Khalid. "Sunni was very upset," recalled Davis. That was putting it mildly. "If Loren wanted to get down," Khalid said later, "he picked the wrong guy. I'm from Detroit, man. Give me a motherfucking break." Khalid added that he wished he'd challenged Jenkins to duke it out. Instead, he decided to sue.

Over the years, Lynne Bernabei, a Washington lawyer, had represented many journalists in racial and gender bias cases against news organizations, among them NPR. After listening to Khalid, she concluded that his charges had merit. "Loren said Sunni's pieces were pro-Arab," she said later. "Sunni was supposed to be reporting from the Arab perspective. Loren either pulled him off stories, or his stories didn't run. Loren pulled Sunni back from the Middle East."

On February 12, 1997, in the civil rights division of the United States District Court for the District of Columbia, Judge Royce C. Lamberth presiding, Sunni Khalid sued NPR for $2 million. He took the unusual step of naming Loren Jenkins as a codefendant. Recalled Michael Skoler, who was friendly with Khalid, "it was about Loren." Conceded Buzenberg, the ragheads crack "gave the suit legs."

On February 28, the case was reassigned to a different judge. On March 11, NPR and Jenkins filed a motion to suspend. On March 24, Khalid filed a motion opposing the motion Meetings, memorandums, hearings—much of the spring was taken up with them. While NPR would eventually settle with Khalid, the staff realized that the suit had produced an unintended consequence. The moment he said *ragheads*, recalled Montagne, "Loren's job was protected. They couldn't let him go." Added Skoler, "NPR had to defend Loren."

Which was how, less than a year into his job, Jenkins stood atop a summit from which it would be hard to push him.

SEVEN

BOBAPALOOZA

An outdoor ashtray at the edge of the circular drive that led to the entrance of NPR's new Massachusetts Avenue headquarters marked one of the only spots set aside for employees who smoked. A few minutes before nine a.m. on September 11, 2001, Bob Edwards, the host of *Morning Edition*, stood there taking his first puffs on a Benson & Hedges when a taxi pulled up and Jay Kernis, the show's creator, emerged. During the twenty-two years since the launch of what had become America's highest-rated morning news program, Kernis had gone on not only to start *Weekend Edition* but in 1987 had joined CBS News. There he'd become a producer at *60 Minutes*, supervising many superb pieces, among them a Mike Wallace investigation into the assassination of Malcolm X and a Lesley Stahl probe into the workings of the Betty Ford Center. Earlier in 2001, the prodigal had returned to NPR as senior vice president of programming. Essentially, he now ran the place. As for Edwards, he was basically where Kernis had left him fourteen years before—a celebrated but exhausted front man dragging on a cigarette.

By way of greeting, Edwards told his boss, "A plane just hit the World Trade Center." His tone was mild, suggesting that the seriousness of the crash was unknown. Kernis got the sense it involved a small craft on the order of one that had plowed into the Empire State Building back in 1945. Still, he decided he'd check in at *Morning Edition*'s second-floor offices, the so-called horseshoe. The host remained on the street finishing his smoke.

When Kernis reached the *Morning Edition* area—a cluttered space with computer cables dangling from the ceiling and a whiteboard onto which the contents of the day's show had been scrawled—he realized not only the catastrophic nature of the event but the extent of NPR's failure to respond. The plane had been a commercial airliner. At 8:46, when it crashed into the Trade Center's north tower, *Morning Edition* had been midway into a Susan Stamberg story about Chicago's public school system. Although Edwards broke in ("Sorry to interrupt," he began, then explained the little anyone knew), NPR, unlike its television competitors, had returned to regular programming, which featured the remainder of Stamberg's piece followed by a business commentary from the economist Russell Roberts on the question of whether the George W. Bush administration should tap the Social Security trust fund to pay for other federal programs. As these canned stories aired, Edwards studied some notes for an upcoming interview with Harry Belafonte about the musician's latest project (*The Long Road to Freedom*, a history of the Black American songbook) then dashed downstairs to light up. Kernis felt like his head was exploding. To anyone and everyone, he declared, "You can't tell America the World Trade Center is on fire and go away."

Then Kernis started screaming. "Oh my God, get Bob. Someone, go downstairs and get Bob."

Carl Kasell was delivering the nine a.m. news break when Edwards joined the show's director, Barry Gordemer; producer, Audrey Wynn; editor, Susan Feeney; and a gaggle of others around the television in Studio 2-A watching the north tower burn. At 9:03, they were still standing there as the screen filled with the image of another airliner crashing into the World Trade Center, this one disintegrating into a corner of the south tower.

"Look at that," Edwards said in a voice so flat that the others could tell his brain was having trouble processing what his eyes were seeing.

"Bob was stunned," recalled Wynn—so were they all. "I stood there frozen," she said later. "Everyone started looking at each other," added Gordemer.

No one had moved when a few seconds later Bruce Drake, who'd recently been elevated to the position of vice president of NPR news, burst into the room. "Get on the air," he ordered. "We need to do something."

To which Wynn, a forty-six-year-old Jamaican who after starting as the *Morning Edition* receptionist had risen to the equivalent of daytime show-runner, replied, "What do we do?"

There was no answer. *Morning Edition* was not designed to handle break-ing news. As Ellen McDonnell, the program's executive producer, who was at that moment in her car trying to get to NPR, later put it, "That was not our culture. We told stories. We did interviews. The network was not geared up to go live." Neal Conan, the just-named host of NPR's midday show, *Talk of the Nation*, was blunter. "They hated to break format." *Morning Edition* was locked into an hourly schedule divided into segments—A, B, C, D, and E—for which prerecorded pieces had already been slated. Around the network, these pieces were derided as "nine-minute sausages." The program's produc-ers countered that they were exquisitely crafted gems. "We did not want to sound like CNN," recalled Gordemer. It was no excuse. *Morning Edition* had failed to respond to the biggest story of the new millennium.

Indeed, after Kasell signed off, NPR opened the nine o'clock hour of its 9/11 broadcast day—a day shaping up to be America's most tragic since Pearl Harbor—by doing what it did any other day. On the East Coast, that meant classical music, on the West the same *Morning Edition* feed that had aired at six a.m. on the East. No one uttered a word about two planes slamming into New York's twin towers. This decision was insanity. Most of the staffers wanted to do something. However, the sole person who could have made it happen felt differently.

Drake walked into Edwards's office and said, "Just say what we're seeing on CNN."

"Do you really want me go on the air and fill forty-five minutes with just a few seconds of information?" Edwards replied.

"Yes."

Edwards refused.

Edwards's response was both reasonable and unfathomable. He was with-out resources. Phone lines were down to NPR's New York station, WNYC, so he couldn't get anything from the scene. Reporters were only now straggling into the network's DC headquarters and had nothing to offer. Maybe most crippling, no one was around to function as the host's "buddy," the term used by radio broadcasters for the second party who serves as an in-studio sounding board during live coverage. Even so, the images on CNN were so vivid that merely by describing them Edwards could have fulfilled his journalistic obligations while holding listeners entranced. "A requirement of the job is that you must be able to vamp," Conan later noted. Added Gordemer: "No other host would have required convincing."

As the clock struck nine fifteen, twenty-nine minutes after the first plane hit, NPR remained paralyzed. The paralysis stretched from the *Morning Edition* studio to the network's third-floor conference room, where a dozen executives—department heads, *All Things Considered* producers—were conducting their regular daily planning session. "Every person who was a show producer or editor was in the meeting talking about what to do," recalled John McChesney, the former national and foreign editor who after a lengthy hiatus had just rejoined NPR as a reporter and arrived at work while the session was in progress. "Edwards and Audrey Wynn were left alone."

NPR news's inability to get on the air infuriated its primary constituency—its station managers. "They went batshit," said McChesney. "Many member stations put on" other audio, added Gordemer. Most vocal among the defectors was a champion of the network, Ruth Seymour of KCRW in Santa Monica. "My daughter called from Washington Square in New York. She saw people jumping." Seymour decided to air the audio of NPR's competitor. "I put on CNN."

At 9:20, at Kernis's insistence, NPR began its live special coverage of the 9/11 disaster. "First thing, they hooked me up with Jacki Lyden," Edwards recalled. The veteran NPR reporter was at her home in Brooklyn, but she'd telephoned *Morning Edition* when she realized what was occurring. The windows of her third-floor Vanderbilt Avenue apartment offered a view of the World Trade Center. "Nobody asked me if I was ready to go live," Lyden said later. "They just put me on, and I did the best I could." The result was an impressionistic word portrait in which the reporter captured the contrast between the beautiful day that was 9/11 (she spoke of the "cerulean blue" sky and "crystalline" air) and the deadly spectacle unfolding before her. She described the various shades of smoke pouring from the towers and the flashes of orange flame. "I was winging it," she recalled, but her account was evocative.

Tom Gjelten followed Lyden to the air. The longtime foreign correspondent was now covering the American military in Washington. He had seen both crashes while watching TV at home and driven his wife, the ABC reporter Martha Raddatz, to the State Department ("I'll see you in six months," she said gamely as he dropped her off), then sped to the Pentagon, where a spokesman told him that the two airliners that crashed into the World Trade Center had been hijacked. Edwards got Gjelten on immediately. The host then talked with Larry Abramson. The first of several buddies whom *Morning Edition*'s producers outfitted with headphones and frog-marched into the studio, Abramson had no special insights to offer, but he had once supervised NPR's coverage of the airline industry and could talk about what might occur next in America's skies.

At 9:37, the telephone rang in the *Morning Edition* horseshoe. Franklyn Cater, an *All Things Considered* producer, was calling from his home in Arlington, Virginia, near the Pentagon. He'd just seen a commercial airliner flying barely above ground level outside his window. A second later there was an explosion on the west side of the Pentagon. Cater was certain of what had happened, but rather than put him on live, the show's director instructed Edwards to question Gjelten about the matter. "Absolutely no sign of anything," replied the reporter, who was on the east side of the massive military complex, insulated from what was now the day's third terrorist crash. A few seconds later, when evacuation notices began blaring over the Pentagon's public-address system, Gjelten managed to make a brief correction. "Clearly, something is happening here," he told NPR's listeners. Then he was gone, swept up in the mass exodus from the building. Anything else he might have to say would have to wait. He could not get a cell phone connection.

By ten a.m. eastern, *Morning Edition* had righted itself. "About eighteen minutes apart," Edwards told his audience, "were two crashes. One of the towers has collapsed." The host then shifted among NPR correspondents, who were finally on the ground. Jim Zarroli, a financial reporter, called in from Manhattan. John McChesney had made it to a Pentagon parking lot, where he reported that he'd been drafted to join a stretcher brigade. Peter Overby, a political reporter, was on Capitol Hill, where he quoted a number of evacuating lawmakers, among them Delaware senator Joe Biden. White

House reporter Don Gonyea was on the line from Lafayette Park describing staffers leaving the executive mansion. Lynn Neary was wandering up and down Massachusetts Avenue doing man-on-the-street interviews, while John Burnett was in Texas giving an account of the horror gripping the headquarters of American Airlines in Fort Worth. Two of the downed planes were from its fleet.

Impressive as NPR's reporters were, the aspect of *Morning Edition*'s special coverage that stood out was the result of the anonymous, unglamorous digging by its inside staffers. For more than an hour now, producers and editors had been poring over maps of Lower Manhattan and New York telephone directories, trying to match addresses near the World Trade Center with the numbers of the people who lived there. Meantime they were calling friends and acquaintances to see if anyone knew someone who worked in that part of the city. *Morning Edition* located several eyewitnesses. After the director whispered one or another's names into Edwards's headphones, they were on the air.

"We can't get out the front door," Ginger Miles, who lived just one block from Ground Zero, told the host. "We've wet a bunch of towels and put our cat in a carrier."

"How high up are you?" Edwards asked.

"Eleventh floor."

"Can you see out your window?"

At which point Miles's roommate jumped in. "It seems that the south tower has disappeared," he began, affirming what the host had announced at the top of the hour.

There were other similarly moving exchanges between Edwards and onlookers (one told him that the sight of people running from the Trade Center was like *The Day of the Locust*). Although the host disliked live coverage, he exceled at it. "One of Bob's strengths," recalled Gordemer, "is that he is unflappable." Between interviews, Edwards conversed with an ever-changing circle of buddies, among them Alex Chadwick, and at one point he stated that the wire services were reporting that "Saudi dissident Osama bin Laden" had threatened attacks on American interests several weeks earlier. At 10:20, Lyden was back on the air to confirm the unfathomable: the north tower had also collapsed.

"Can you see that?" Edwards asked.

Lyden said that she could, then added, "That's our Mount Everest. The top is now gone."

Morning Edition finished strong. As even Ruth Seymour admitted, "Edwards recovered." The show would remain on the air live until one p.m. eastern, when Conan would take over, followed by Robert Siegel, Noah Adams, and Linda Wertheimer of *All Things Considered*, then Conan again and, overnight, Scott Simon. For two weeks, this schedule was the new normal.

Once the immediate crisis passed, NPR executives concurred that 9/11 was when the network's relationship with Bob Edwards started to fall apart. True, there was a consensus that *Morning Edition*'s failings that day could not all be pinned on the host. "The screwup was systemic," said Drake. Conan agreed: "The show was not set up to be agile and responsive." Chadwick blamed "the managers of NPR for leaving Bob without anyone to talk to." Nonetheless, Edwards was an impediment. "Bob didn't make it any easier," said Drake. David Folkenflik, who prior to becoming NPR's media reporter covered the network for the *Baltimore Sun*, later observed, "Edwards very much helped define the dysfunction." Despite acknowledging his recovery, Ruth Seymour never forgave his initial missteps. "Bob Edwards should have been fired right then."

The ferocity of such verdicts was a manifestation of a long-simmering conflict. "Things had been building for years," Audrey Wynn said later. "Bob wasn't flexible, engaged, or responsive. Following 9/11, everything bubbled out of whatever can it was in." A new factor had also entered the picture. Jay Kernis had created Bob Edwards and then left NPR. Now he had returned, expecting to find the host functioning just as he had when the two were young and could do no wrong. Instead, Kernis found problems. "The trouble with Jay and Bob began at that point," recalled Gordemer.

For more than two decades, the alarm clock in the master bedroom of the faux Tudor just off Robert E. Lee Highway in Arlington had rung at that ungodly hour of one. Bob Edwards, whose children tucked him in at six each night, often with a bedtime story, had placed the device as far from his pillow as possible, forcing himself to pull back the covers, put his feet on the floor, and stumble through the darkness to shut it off. He was proud of the discipline he exhibited in handling his early call. He was never late to work, and despite occasional crankiness, he was on balance well behaved.

By the mid-1990s, however, Edwards's *Morning Edition* colleagues, who had initially dismissed the host's periodic grumpiness as an annoying but understandable by-product of his schedule, started to detect darker stirrings. The era of office jokes about sleep deprivation was over. At first glance Edwards was still the boyish figure who'd fronted *Morning Edition* since 1979. Same grin. Same mop of blond hair. Same wardrobe—jeans and a flannel shirt. But he had changed. Pale and slumped with nicotine-stained teeth, watery blue eyes, and an attitude that wavered between remote and wary, he looked like someone who was up all night, every night. Although only fifty-three years old, he seemed worn down. The orneriness had soured into prickliness, the nit-picking was compulsive, the silences were edged with sullenness. "He was becoming more and more difficult," recalled his former *All Things Considered* cohost Susan Stamberg. "Bob ossified," maintained Steve Proffitt, his editor during the a.m. show's early years.

Tensions between the *Morning Edition* staff and Edwards increased. What had begun as a relationship marred by periodic spats began to resemble a marriage in crisis. It was the same between NPR executives and the host. Tiny matters could set things off.

One of the earliest bones of contention—and one that would persist—revolved around language, the lifeblood of radio and to Edwards a nonnegotiable matter. The host dubbed the unadorned copy he demanded from *Morning Edition*'s writers "Bobspeak." There were to be no clichés, no wire-service verbiage (*spur, thwart, curb*), few adverbs or adjectives, and nothing cute. It was rigorous but reasonable. Starting in 1991, however, it started to become perverse. That year, while Americans were debating what had or had not happened between US Supreme Court nominee Clarence Thomas and his former clerk, Anita Hill, Edwards was asserting that whatever it was, it was not, as NPR's style manual dictated, Ha-RASS-ment. It was HAIR-ass-ment. The stress belonged on the first syllable. When his editors corrected him, he ignored them. When they pressed the case, he stopped using the word altogether. As Noah Adams recalled, the host found "ways to write around it rather—than in his view—mispronounce it."

Within a couple of years, *Morning Edition* had become a linguistic no-fly zone. Sometimes Edwards had a point. He prohibited squishy phrasing. Why say "two weeks' time" when "two weeks" sufficed? Yet he often went too far. To banish any hint of pretension, he forbade the word *film*. Americans went to the movies. To avoid the possibility of a double entendre, he banned the verb *to come*—it too easily suggested orgasm. When the network launched NPR.org in 1995, giving it a new platform, he balked at using the phrase "Visit our Website." It was *NPR's* website and besides, he did not believe it was his job to shill.

Being a stickler was one thing, but Edwards was becoming a naysayer. He had disdain for the changing culture. His areas of curiosity were narrow and narrowing. "He was interested in very few things," recalled Chadwick: "Sports, primarily baseball, Appalachia, folklore, and Bob Edwards." The host made no apologies for this. "I had a white-collar job and blue-collar sensibilities," he said later. "My parents never read Dr. Spock." He was, in his view, NPR's in-house guardian against the social upheavals and polymorphous predilections besieging the modern world.

Edwards confronted that world in 1992 when Robert Ferrante, who'd just become *Morning Edition's* executive producer after a long career at CBS News producing Diane Sawyer, handed him a tape titled "Santaland Diaries" and asked him to give it a listen. Ferrante wanted to use the eight-and-a-half-minute monologue by David Sedaris as a feature on the show. The piece was a darkly comic account by Sedaris of his misadventures while working as a Christmas elf named Crumpet during the holidays at the Sixth Avenue Macy's. *Morning Edition*, with its need for "nine-minute sausages," was ravenous for this sort of segment. However, there was one big impediment.

"Sedaris was a problem for Edwards," Ferrante said later. The issue: Crumpet and many of his fellow elves were homosexual. "Gays," the producer added, "were not what Bob could handle."

"I disparaged the piece," Edwards conceded later, but not, he insisted, because Crumpet was gay. He'd played the tape for Sharon, his wife, and she took offense. In her view, it mocked the mothers and children who patronize Macy's at Christmas. ("Santaland Diaries" is indeed tough on moms. Near the end Sedaris relates, "Tonight, I saw a woman slap and shake her crying child. She yelled, 'Rachel, get on that man's lap and smile, or I'll give you something to cry about.'") The host believed his wife was right.

"What are we putting this on the air for?" Edwards demanded.

"Because I think it's good radio," Ferrante shot back.

Edwards had taken it as far as he could. Ferrante knew how to deal with talent and had the last word. "Santaland Diaries" debuted on *Morning Edition* December 23, 1992. Sedaris not only became a regular contributor to the show but "Santaland Diaries" became a radio classic, with *Morning Edition* airing it annually during the holidays. The host's intransigence, however, was noted.

Notwithstanding Bob Edwards's decided opinions and don't-tread-on-me defensiveness, he was paradoxically lackadaisical when it came to some aspects of *Morning Edition*. "He was kind of lazy," declared John McChesney. "He was not thought of as working that hard," added Sanford Ungar, who'd replaced him on *All Things Considered*.

Although listeners rarely realized it, Edwards was frequently bored and distracted while on the air. He often just went through the motions, particularly when conducting the host interviews with reporters known as "two-ways" that are a staple of NPR magazine shows. The great utility of two-ways is that they allow the network to air an authoritative conversation with a reporter covering a story without the reporter having to submit an actual story, which costs more money and requires more time. The reporter simply provides a list of questions to the host, and the host asks the questions, making for an informative back-and-forth. For a two-way to work, the host must pay attention to the reporter's answers, reacting with surprise to surprising twists and, if the reporter combines two answers into one, altering the list of questions on the fly. Edwards often failed to take the reporter's cues. He simply plowed ahead.

"Bob didn't listen," recalled Renee Montagne, who as a special correspondent for *Morning Edition* in the mid-1990s was often on the phone with the host. He was doing it by rote. "In a prerecorded interview, you could fix it by editing," editor Susan Feeney said later, but if you were live, look out. He "was just going down the list, reading the questions," recalled Nina Totenberg. "Bob would sound ridiculous," added Feeney. As McChesney put it: "I used to think he could be interviewing the Soviet foreign minister, and the guy could announce they'd just launched a ballistic missile attack on the United States, and Bob would go to the next question."

Nearly every NPR reporter had at least one experience of feeling like they were shouting into the abyss when talking on the air to Edwards. "Bob never changed a question," recalled Sylvia Poggioli. He seemed "brain dead," remembered another foreign correspondent. The *Morning Edition* staff frequently had to perform damage control with reporters. "We just had to apologize to them," remembered Wynn.

Edwards's tendency to slough off certain responsibilities while obsessing over others could often make it seem like he was hardly working at all while simultaneously working harder than anyone. Bouts of sloth would precede bursts of irrational activity, especially when the host was forced to respond to NPR's entry into the 24/7 world of modern media. For years, the network fed *Morning Edition* to the stations starting at six a.m. eastern and finishing at noon. The show rolled across the country following the path of the sun. "When I got there," recalled Drake, "unless something eight on a scale of ten happened, the feeds would stay on touch all the way through." By the end of the 1990s, though, *Morning Edition* was facing competition from online news sources, newspaper websites, and cable outlets. If the show was to stay current, the producers needed to refresh stories throughout its long run, which by 2001 had increased to seven hours. Otherwise, the pieces would go stale. Edwards generally refused to return to the studio to perform these duties.

Instead, Edwards took a tortuous path, instructing *Morning Edition*'s staffers to craft stories that would last for the duration. He insisted that the verbs his staffers wrote at three a.m. had to hold up at eleven a.m. "We'd remove verbs that had a sell-by date," said Gordemer. "We would write in tenses that didn't have a sell-by date." The result was a lot of gerunds—*occurring* instead of *occurred*—and subjunctive mood—*would* or *could* as opposed to *have* or *had*. Added Gordemer, "We would never write, 'So and so will testify in a couple hours.' It was, 'So and so is testifying today.' " For a journalist who professed to be a fan of reporting and precise language, the host was making his show soft and imprecise.

•   •   •

Bob Edwards's beefs with NPR managers, while sometimes involving *Morning Edition*'s content, more typically sprang from his belief that the suits were trying to screw him financially. Although he ultimately earned $200,000 a year, he continued to regard the network much as he had back in the 1970s when he, Totenberg, and a few others took the lead in unionizing it. Edwards, recalled McChesney, "was a hog for overtime." Even so, "he never felt he was rewarded the way he should be," noted Ferrante. The host worked every angle. As he later said, "If there was a short turnaround—less than twelve hours between shifts—I got" a bonus. "There was a nighttime differential—if I worked between twelve and six, I got an extra half hour pay, plus missed meal penalties. I was there every holiday. On Christmas and New Year's Day, I received double time and a half." In 1997, when Edwards flew to London to host NPR's coverage of Princess Diana's funeral (a rare out-of-studio foray), one of his first acts after settling in at the network's bureau was to calculate whether the shift from eastern to Greenwich mean time entitled him to a bump. His zeal not to leave money on the table was so great that it ended up making news. In 1998, a congressional committee opened an investigation into public broadcasting officials who pulled down more than was allowed by a federal salary cap. Most of the alleged offenders were executives. Only one was an on-air personality. The *Washington Post* reported that Edwards had long received an inflated income: "He earns night differential and overtime payments due to starting his work at 1 a.m." The public exposure did not change the host's behavior. Recalled one NPR producer, "We said to him, 'Why do this?'" Edwards was unresponsive, continuing to deluge the accounting department with time sheets.

For staffers and executives alike, dealing with Bob Edwards was not easy. At *Morning Edition*, there were many rules and rituals, yet the host was loath to explain them. "Bob didn't go to the regular meetings," Gordemer said later, and at rare command performances—retreats and the like—he responded to queries in monosyllables. "He didn't want to be interfered with," recalled Frank Fitzmaurice, his original executive producer. Still, woe to the writer or editor who messed up. "He was tough with the staff," McChesney said later. "He'd come out of the studio and chastise people." Added Ferrante, he was a "curmudgeon." Linda Wertheimer, who frequently substitute-hosted for Edwards, recalled, "He was not the sort of person who would say, 'Great job. Wonderful piece.'"

Despite this, Edwards was accorded enormous leeway. With thirteen million daily listeners, *Morning Edition* was a juggernaut, and its host was the main attraction. "They said a lot of things about him," Ferrante said later, "but they didn't say those things to my face, because I defended him. This was the talent. He was the star, bar none. Nobody gave a fiddler's fuck about what was going on with anybody else except that they heard Bob Edwards. He was their image of National Public Radio."

More than that, Edwards's greatest skills remained undiminished. Barbara Rehm, a longtime New York *Daily News* reporter who came to NPR in the late 1990s as an assistant to Bruce Drake, then switched over to foreign editor Loren Jenkins, was dazzled by the host. "I was absolutely stunned by what a lovely writer he is," she recalled. She was not alone. "Bob is a tight, efficient writer," agreed Gordemer. Then there was Edwards's inherent asset. "You couldn't help but love that whiskey and tobacco voice," said Rehm. "It's a calming thing, perfect for the morning." No one else at the network came close. "Bob could talk to people out of their clock radio at an hour when they couldn't bear it," marveled Wertheimer. "The audience could crawl out of bed and stand it."

In 1998, however, *Morning Edition* changed. After eight years atop the program, Ferrante lost out in a bid to become vice president of NPR news and left the network to run Public Radio International's *The World*. Jeffrey Dvorkin, briefly NPR's new news chief, appointed a committee to choose a replacement. Among its members was Chadwick. "We settled on Sean Collins," he said. A longtime *Morning Edition* producer, Collins, like Edwards, was a traditionalist. He was responsible for one of the show's standing features: an annual Fourth of July reading of the Declaration of Independence, which saw the host joined by Cokie Roberts, Stamberg, and others deliver a stirring recitation. It was classic *Morning Edition*, and Collins seemed like a splendid choice. Not everyone saw it that way.

The night before Collins's appointment was to be announced, Nina Totenberg picked up the phone and called NPR's COO. Once again, the not-so-hidden hand behind countless network personnel decisions was exerting its influence.

"Do you know what's happening?" she asked Peter Jablow, a former journalist who'd joined NPR in 1995 to help stabilize its finances. He had a sense of the matter, but he relied on Totenberg to fill in the details. Collins, she said, "was a talented young producer," but there was a greater talent waiting in the wings, "a real manager."

Like Edwards and Kernis, Ellen McDonnell had been a member of *Morning Edition*'s start-up staff. She began as a news writer out of American University, where she'd received a master's degree in journalism, and she'd risen over the years to become Ferrante's assistant. He adored her. She wouldn't put up with "bullshit," he said. Others were puzzled by her ascent. "She was totally without imagination," said John McChesney, adding that she was the sort of mediocrity NPR too often rewards. "If you don't cause trouble, don't raise your voice, just sit still and kind of do your job, promotions will come." Ultimately, the varying views didn't matter. McDonnell had the support of the troika. The three women swore by her. Maybe more important, they, like others at the network, believed Edwards needed closer supervision and that McDonnell could provide it. "He was mentally abusive to everybody on the morning staff," Totenberg said later. "Working for him was a nightmare."

Nearly everything about Edwards rubbed Totenberg, Wertheimer, and Roberts the wrong way. Even some of his strengths stuck in their collective craw. Red Barber was a particular bête noire to Roberts and Wertheimer. Although the *Morning Edition* sports commentator was enlightened about race, he lagged behind on gender equality. He referred to Roberts, who filed weekly pieces for *Morning Edition*, as "little lady." Worse, when Wertheimer guest-hosted, she got the impression that Barber wanted to trip her up on the air. She didn't know a lot about sports, and during one of their live Friday conversations, he devilishly asked her whom she liked in the upcoming Preakness. As it turned out, she followed horse racing, so she replied, "I'm going with the filly." She was proud of the answer, yet she knew that if Barber had inquired about the night's baseball games, she would have frozen. Later, thinking of the moment, she could only mutter, "The bastard."

As with previous putsches by the three women, the Collins reversal was met with some anger. Chadwick said they "bullied" NPR into giving McDonnell the job at *Morning Edition*, but then added, "Ellen was an ally of Cokie." Edwards was resigned, saying, "Ellen McDonnell took care of Nina, Linda, and Cokie, and they took care of her." Nevertheless, the host viewed the decision as a defeat. He now worked for someone he didn't trust.

Ellen McDonnell initially talked up Bob Edwards to NPR staffers, public radio station managers, and the press. "Everyone feels they know Bob," she told the *Los Angeles Times.* "We did research, and the one thing that constantly came through is his warmth. People believe they know Colonel Bob from Kentucky, that he's their friend. It's stunning."

After two years as Edwards's boss, McDonnell had changed her mind. "Bob was burned out. He did not want to do the news. Bob wanted to do the same show he did in 1979."

During the 2000 presidential contest between George W. Bush and Al Gore, Edwards confirmed McDonnell's negative view. After weeks of negotiating, Susan Feeney had secured a major interview for the *Morning Edition* host with the Republican vice-presidential candidate, Dick Cheney. "I went to the wall to set that up," the editor recalled. "It was not easy. The Bush team did not trust NPR." The deal seemed perfect. Cheney would speak to Edwards at two thirty on an early October afternoon. Everyone at the network regarded this interview as a coup—except for the man slated to conduct it.

"No," Edwards replied when McDonnell came to him with the assignment. He said he would have been at work since two a.m. and wasn't staying. He requested that the interview be set for an earlier hour. "He wanted the time changed to accommodate his schedule," recalled Audrey Wynn. "He wanted the candidate to accommodate him."

The *Morning Edition* staff was dismayed, and McDonnell went to Edwards's office to make the case more strongly. "Bob," she said, "this is an important interview. You need to do it." But the host wouldn't budge. "He kept refusing," recalled Wynn. McDonnell summoned the vice president of news.

"Bruce Drake ordered Bob against his will to do it," remembered Feeney.

"I did the interview," Edwards later bragged. Yet as he looked back on his discussion with Cheney, who would become one of America's most powerful vice presidents, he had nothing to say about its substance. He emphasized that because he conducted the interview in midafternoon, he succeeded in "racking up five hours of overtime that day."

·   ·   ·

Because Edwards rarely blew up, what happened in his *Morning Edition* office on September 11, 2002—the first anniversary of the attacks on the World Trade Center and the Pentagon—got the attention of Ellen McDonnell and ultimately Jay Kernis, bringing everything that had happened in the past to a boil.

At least on the surface, NPR—and particularly *Morning Edition*—had been on the uptick since 9/11. Ratings for the a.m. show had increased 31 percent, and the network won the 2001 Peabody for its overall coverage of the disaster and the aftermath. When Bruce Drake stepped onto the stage of the Waldorf Astoria to accept the award from Walter Cronkite, the first name he saw on the accompanying certificate was that of Bob Edwards.

A number of ceremonies were scheduled for the anniversary, and McDonnell hoped that Edwards would not only host the day's regular *Morning Edition* broadcast but also anchor NPR's midday special coverage. When she broached the idea to her superiors, they resisted. "People were not thrilled with Bob's ability to do the news," she recalled. But she lobbied for him. "I said, 'He's the host. I don't want someone else doing it.'" She received a go-ahead, but it was not to be.

"I don't want to do that," Edwards replied when McDonnell proposed the plan, giving his usual rationale: past quitting time. The producer didn't push. This was just Bob. Besides, Neal Conan would do a terrific job. But McDonnell did take note.

The September 11, 2002, installment of *Morning Edition* was a tour de force. It began to the strains of a Scottish march as Edwards intoned: "Bagpipe and drum processions from each of New York's five boroughs are on their way to the site of the former World Trade Center. They've been marching relay style in sets of two for most of the night." This was the prelude to two hours of terrific radio journalism. Among the stories was an interview of Attorney General John Ashcroft, an architect of America's war on terror, and an homage to New York's Trinity Church, just blocks from the downed towers. The program revolved around a flawlessly paced eleven-minute wrap-up of activities from across the country (Hillary Clinton and Colin Powell reading the names of the dead at Ground Zero; President Bush speaking in front of the rebuilt Pentagon.) It all went off flawlessly and offered an example of Edwards at his best. "Bob saw his role to be a steady figure in a chair bringing the world to you," Gordemer later noted. With his seductive baritone, the host embodied certainty. This was the news, but this was also the new millennium. The news now never stopped.

At ten thirty, long after *Morning Edition* had finished its East Coast broadcast and an hour and a half into its West Coast feed, McDonnell walked into Edwards's office carrying a typed script containing a bit of fresh information. On the early version of the program, Edwards had reported that Dick Cheney would join Bush for an event later in the day. The producer had just learned that the vice president had already arrived.

"Bob, I need you to record this update and say, 'The vice president is there,'" she said.

"No," Edwards replied. Then, according to McDonnell, "He took the copy, crumpled it up, and threw it at me."

"I guess that means yes," McDonnell replied, and it did. The host headed to the studio and did his duty. The producer was furious. Enough was enough.

The wadded-up script Edwards fired at McDonnell was the shot heard round the public radio world. Although the host subsequently floated a denial ("I'm not a thrower," he said), he undercut his claim with a taunting question: "Was she sitting next to a waste can?" McDonnell reported the incident to Jay Kernis, saying, "I've taken this show as far as I can."

Kernis told NPR president Kevin Klose. After a career as a reporter at the *Washington Post* (he covered Russia) and director of Voice of America, the sixty-two-year-old Klose had joined NPR in 1998. He had proved himself the best business leader at the network since Don Quayle. "Kevin is the person who demonstrated that you can actually be a successful president of NPR," noted Robert Siegel. He would ultimately have to adjudicate the Edwards affair, but in the short term it was Kernis's problem, and it was a difficult one. "His own staff wanted him off the show," Kernis said later, adding that station managers around the country were also down on the host. "I was attending national meetings, and programmers were saying, 'What are you going to do about Bob? He's disengaged.'" Nonetheless, *Morning Edition* was NPR's biggest hit, and Edwards's was the network's best-known host. Then there was the emotional aspect. Kernis had nurtured Edwards, transforming him from a news reader into a personality. But that was then.

Kernis had come to view Edwards as a willful, surly brother. He decided to do what family members might—stage an intervention.

One afternoon several weeks after the script-tossing incident, Jay Kernis arrived at Bob Edwards's Arlington home. The programming chief had come to tell the host that NPR believed in him and, in the same breath, put him on notice: he had to change his on-the-job behavior.

Edwards and Sharon showed Kernis to a seat on their living room sofa. There, he pulled out a two-page speech he'd been rehearsing incessantly. Voice cracking, eyes welling, he told Edwards that *Morning Edition* wouldn't exist without him and then asked him to recommit himself to the show. He ticked off a list of demands, all involving issues that had been brewing since before 9/11. Edwards needed to treat his coworkers with greater respect. He had to update stories when asked. Most important, he needed to rekindle his enthusiasm.

"You're phoning it in, Bob," Kernis declared.

"Am I?" Edwards asked his wife, who by this point was also in tears.

"Some days."

"I don't think I ever phoned it in," Edwards countered. "I give it my all every day. Getting up at one o'clock in the morning, staying until noon, being responsible for the network from five a.m. until noon."

Looking back on the conversation, Edwards was incredulous. "I was at a loss," he said. "I think Kernis was manufacturing something. I'm puzzled to this day."

Kernis, however, meant what he'd said. The meeting was just the first step. "I'm going to work with him," he told all comers.

Appreciative Inquiry is a consulting technique developed in the late 1980s by two Case Western Reserve University professors dissatisfied with the organizational problem-solving methods then typically used by American businesses. They believed that when dealing with personnel matters, too many human resources facilitators relied on the so-called deficiency model. They asked: What are the problems? What's wrong? AI, as the new theory was dubbed, asked: What is working? What's right? The idea was to identify "the positive core." To do so, counselors would stress "the four d's"—Discover,

Dream, Design, and Deliver. By accentuating employee strengths and work-place triumphs, feuding parties could appreciate one another and, based on past accomplishments and mutual regard, repair frayed relationships. Many companies had embraced the practice, and Kernis thought it would be right not only for NPR, with its communal values, but also for *Morning Edition*, which had brought success to nearly everyone involved.

Once a week starting in the early spring of 2003, Kernis, Edwards, Mc-Donnell, an NPR human resources department coach, and, occasionally, news VP Bruce Drake filed into the network's corporate boardroom on the first floor at Massachusetts Avenue. The goal was to articulate their shared ambitions for *Morning Edition* and reawaken them. Recalled McDonnell, they were "looking for the best" in each other.

From the outset, Edwards, who was wary of expressing feelings and distrusted therapists, resisted. "I never understood any of it," he said later. "There was a facilitator, Jay, Ellen, and me, and we would all contemplate our navels. I don't know what was going on."

Appreciative Inquiry is designed to require only weeks to produce initial results, but in Edwards's case, months dragged by. Despite the protracted process, Kernis believed they were making progress. "I thought he was rein-vesting." Few others saw it that way.

Around NPR, the project was dismissed. As Drake noted, they were "trying to turn Bob Edwards into a human being." The sense was that the task was impossible because the host was too emotionally shut down. "Bob doesn't connect with people," noted Chadwick, who worked with Edwards for thirty years. "There's something deeply absent about the guy."

There was also another factor, one that had less to do with Edwards's personality than with his professional convictions. When it came to *Morn-ing Edition*, the host believed that he was right and that McDonnell and the others were wrong. When they spoke of a changing world and evolving ways of producing the program, he heard trend-driven, data-supported jargon. Just because the cable news networks and online sites were doing something didn't mean NPR should mimic them. As he later wrote, "I'd be sent into the studio for an update of the second feed of *Morning Edition*. This update would replace a real piece of journalism that might have been weeks in the making. Listeners would hear me talking live concerning what the president might say in the Rose Garden. I thought NPR should exercise its own news judgment and not have it determined by a competitive situation." In sum, Edwards felt that his carefully constructed show gave listeners a consistency and reliability unavailable on the error-riddled web or jangly CNN. He provided a foundation for listeners' days; in his mind, McDonnell wanted to chip away at that foundation.

Following a year of Appreciative Inquiry sessions, Kernis and McDonnell concluded that the whole project was a bust. As McDonnell later noted, the AI coach told her, "One option may be that you just discover that people can't work together. What you want to happen isn't going to happen." Edwards had come to the same conclusion.

"I'm not doing it anymore," Kernis recalled Edwards declaring just before they pulled the plug. From the host's perspective, it was a burden off his back, one that would allow him to focus on two occasions he was looking forward to in 2004. First was the publication of his brief biography of a journalistic hero. *Edward R. Murrow and the Birth of Broadcast Journalism* was due out in May. Then, in November, came a far bigger occasion: the twenty-fifth anniversary of *Morning Edition*.

On March 9, 2004, Bob Edwards, responding to an email from NPR's PR department inviting him to a meeting to explore how the network could promote his forthcoming Murrow book, appeared in Jay Kernis's Massachusetts Avenue office. Entering the room, the *Morning Edition* host sensed something amiss. Not only was Andy Danyo, the junior publicist who'd set up the meeting, not present, but those who were there—the programming chief, Bruce Drake, and a representative from AFTRA, the union for NPR's on-air talent—were ill at ease. The gathering had nothing to do with the book. Reading from a prepared text, Kernis got to the point: "We're making a change."

The conversations that led to Edwards's departure from *Morning Edition* had begun almost the minute the Appreciative Inquiry effort broke down. According to Nina Totenberg, "Kevin Klose said, 'I just can't stand this anymore. We need to fire him.'" While NPR's president had pronounced the sentence, the executive who'd discovered Edwards would be the executioner. "Jay, if anybody can pull the trigger, you can," those involved said. Kernis didn't want to do it, but he knew he had to. As he later said, "I was the one."

The news hit Edwards hard. He had no clue how precarious his position had become. This happened "completely outside Bob's ken," recalled Neal Conan. "He was not aware of it. None of us were." As Edwards tried to absorb what felt like a body blow, Kernis tried to ease the pain, offering him a position as a special correspondent starting April 30, the date chosen to be his last as *Morning Edition* host. Edwards barely heard what his former producer was saying.

"What about the twenty-fifth anniversary in November?" he asked.

"The anniversary will be about the future, not the past," Kernis replied, ending any thought of a celebration of Edwards's quarter century atop America's premier morning news show. As Conan later noted, "By the time the decision had been made, all the wheels were in motion. The leading station managers had been informed, and seven other things were happening. It was too late to think about his twenty-five years." The session with Kernis was a formality. "I thought I would die" at NPR, the deposed host said later. "I guess they thought I already had died."

That Edwards was out was soon all anyone could talk about at NPR. Even among those who felt the host had become impossible, the consensus was that the network had treated him shabbily. "Why was Bob Edwards taken off *Morning Edition* six months before the twenty-fifth anniversary?" Chadwick asked. Kernis "handled Edwards so badly," Sylvia Poggioli recalled. Shortly after the programming chief fired the host, he dropped by the office of *Weekend Edition Sunday* producer Robert Malesky, another original member of the *Morning Edition* staff. Kernis wanted his colleague to brief him on how the decision was playing around the building. Malesky accepted some of Kernis's rationale but, he, too, felt Kernis had behaved terribly. He did not hold back. "This tells me," he said, "that you're only as good as yesterday's show and twenty years of incredible creativity means very little" at NPR.

On March 23, NPR issued a press release informing the public that Bob Edwards was finished at *Morning Edition*. The move had been made "to refresh the program and to meet the changing needs of the listeners." It was "part of the natural evolution of the program." Nothing was said about the tensions between the network and the host that had precipitated the decision. "NPR took the high road," McDonnell remembered. "You're not going to talk about personnel matters."

The next morning, papers across America reported the news of Edwards's firing. The intense interest was so predictable that anyone could have predicted it. Anyone, that is, except NPR executives, who professed to being surprised that the dismissal of a national media figure who for twenty-four years had dominated his time slot—only Rush Limbaugh had a bigger a.m. audience—would have drawn attention from the national media. "We were not used to being in the mainstream," contended McDonnell, expressing the network's recurring inability to view itself as something other than a confederacy of college radio stations. The flip side was that the rationale NPR provided to justify the move suggested the arrogance of a conglomerate. Pundits including Ellen Goodman and Linda Ellerbee lambasted the network for its half-baked statements. Harshest of all was the *Washington Post*'s Richard Cohen, whose ex-wife, Barbara, had, of course, run NPR News when *Morning Edition* began. Beneath the headline "Empty Talk at NPR," the columnist asserted:

> The firing of the mellifluous Edwards, my morning companion through all these years, portends bad things. The telling sign was not just that he was axed as the program's host but that no one can tell you why. At NPR, clearly the most erudite of networks, various officials descended into the juvenile babble of TV executives, empty words spilling out of their mouths as if they were determined to fill airtime yet say nothing.

Cohen concluded, "Goodbye, Bob. Get some sleep. You've earned it."

The response by the general public to Edwards's firing was even fiercer. NPR had expected a few hundred letters. Instead, it was swamped by fifty thousand letters and emails. The network had failed to communicate a concrete justification for the move.

"We didn't know what we were doing in the PR part of it," McDonnell later conceded. Kernis was less forgiving. "It was a mess." To counter the bad press, NPR tried to stress the aspect of the story that executives believed indicated that an evolution was indeed coming in *Morning Edition*'s ability to cover the news. The network was replacing Edwards with two hosts. Steve

Inskeep, who after reporting for NPR from Afghanistan had been fronting
Weekend All Things Considered, would hold down a desk in Washington.
Renee Montagne, who had improved her hosting skills while substituting
for Edwards during his vacations, would work out of NPR's new, Culver City,
California, studios, purchased following 9/11 to give the network a base of
operations if Washington again came under attack.

The two-host gambit became NPR's primary, publicly stated grounds for
jettisoning Edwards. In speaking to the press, Kernis, Klose, and McDonnell all said that they'd pitched the idea of a cohost to Edwards and that he'd
declined. Not so, Edwards rejoined. "They never asked me to have a cohost,
and that was in their power." Around the network, such protestations were
regarded as typical Edwards—he was splitting hairs. Maybe the executives
didn't put it to him as a question, but they put it to him. "He fought having
a cohost," recalled Totenberg. The issue was a strong one for NPR, allowing
it to emphasize the advantages of having two people on the job, advantages
that hinted at the actual reasons for the firing.

Having both Inskeep and Montagne fronting *Morning Edition*, Kernis
told the *New York Times*, would allow one host to preside over the broadcast
while the other filed stories from the field—a dig at the typically sedentary
Edwards. Even more pointed, the programming chief declared that with
two hosts always on hand, "updating the show will be easier." The clincher
was 9/11. The *Times* reported that discussions about the host began "when
television morning programs cut immediately to live coverage after the first
airplane crashed into the World Trade Center." The intimation was that
Edwards had been derelict. Kernis wasn't the only one making such statements. Several public radio station managers said it would be nice to have
an "engaged" host.

Nonetheless, NPR's efforts to recover from its mismanagement of Edwards's dismissal were too little, too late. The press viewed the network's
claim that it wanted to "refresh" the show as an unintended revelation. What
it wanted were younger hosts. Senator Richard Durbin, speaking on the
Senate floor about the firing, picked up the theme, accusing NPR of age discrimination. In a rare show of emotion, Edwards also emphasized the point,
telling reporters that he thought Kernis got rid of him because he was "tired
of listening to me." By the vagueness of its statements, the network had left

itself open. (Another theory was that the host, who in early April criticized the Iraq War during a speech in Kentucky, had been pushed out because of his politics.) As Edwards's final *Morning Edition* broadcast approached, the *Los Angeles Times* reported that "doubts and mockery about how NPR had handled the announcement echoed from Hawaii to Washington D.C." To make matters worse, a Georgetown University student launched a website called SaveBobEdwards.com and attracted 26,000 comments, one of which—picked up by the *New York Times*—noted that not since Coca-Cola introduced New Coke had a business entity so mishandled the replacement of a beloved American brand.

As Bob Edwards took his seat in Studio 2-A behind his Neumann U87 mic (he'd been using it since joining NPR) for his farewell broadcast on *Morning Edition*, he was incensed to see Bruce Drake perched on a chair in the adjacent control room. NPR's vice president of news had never sat in on the program live. From the host's perspective, there could be only one reason. "He was expecting me to say something awful," Edwards later maintained. "He had a button and was going to silence me. Like I would say something unprofessional after all these years." Susan Feeney, who was in the control room, witnessed the host's reaction.

"You don't trust me," Edwards roared. "I can't believe you'd insult me like this."

Drake made no apologies. "Some people thought something might happen," he said later. "Bob was so cantankerous, and the job was tied to his identity. Was he going to be unpredictable?"

Drake's concerns were not unfounded. When Edwards announced his dismissal to the *Morning Edition* staff, he told them that there had been three stages to his career at NPR: host, senior correspondent, and "person of interest." This last, he said, was a reference to a recently fired NPR reporter who'd been stalking the Massachusetts Avenue building and had been spotted urinating on company property. To those who knew him, that was just Edwards's black humor, but the network couldn't take a chance.

In the end, Drake's appearance at Studio 2-A was unnecessary. Edwards's tone during the final broadcast, noted the *New York Times*, was "dignified and typically understated." There were moments of joy, among them an interview with CBS's Charles Osgood, who was one of the host's first guests back in 1979. The closest Edwards came to acknowledging that his leave-taking was painful came near the end. Reported the *Times*: "Edwards did not sugarcoat his departure. He told listeners he had been reassigned as a senior correspondent, and noted his 24 years and six months as host of *Morning Edition*," his lone reference to being removed just before his twenty-fifth anniversary.

Edwards's last words could not have been more elegant or generous. He told his listeners, "You're the audience a broadcaster dreams of having."

It was over. Colleagues joined Edwards and his wife and children in the *Morning Edition* horseshoe for a going-away party, but after all the nastiness of recent weeks there was not much merriment and almost no talk about the host's accomplishments. "The cake they gave him had a picture of Edward R. Murrow," remembered Barry Gordemer. "There was nothing about *Morning Edition*."

As the event wound down, Susan Stamberg poked her head in. Considering the history between the two, she might well have avoided this occasion, but as she later said, she had a sense that her ex–*All Things Considered* co-host could use some moral support. The scene, she recalled, was terrible. "No one was talking to him. They were overwhelmed by it all—embarrassed and uncomfortable." Knowing that even the taciturn Edwards had to feel crushed, Stamberg stayed to the end. "I walked out of the building with him. I just thought I needed to do that."

Bob Edwards was gone from *Morning Edition*, but the debate over his firing would not cease. The book tour for his Edward R. Murrow biography, which when he was still fronting the daily show had been slated to run just three weeks, had ballooned into a three-month, multicity extravaganza. Now that Edwards not only reported the news but was making it, managers of every NPR station from the Atlantic to the Pacific wanted him to headline their donor events. He was a draw. The affiliates agreed to put him on local theater stages to discuss both his book and his departure from his hosting gig. He called the whole thing Bobapalooza.

From the perspective of NPR executives in Washington, the prospect of having Edwards at large and unbound all summer was disconcerting, although temperatures seemed to have cooled between the network and the deposed host. His inaugural piece as a special correspondent—a feature about Washington's new World War II memorial for which he interviewed Senators Bob Dole and Fritz Hollings, both combat veterans—aired May 3, and the *New York Times* had reported that once Edwards returned from the road, he was looking forward to taking up his new career in earnest. Still, the idea of a nationwide open-mic night for a high-profile employee with a grudge was not how management would have drawn it up. On the eve of Edwards's departure, he received a summons.

Ken Stern was a thirty-nine-year-old Yale law school graduate who before joining NPR had worked as a litigator in Washington, served as deputy general counsel on the Clinton-Gore 1996 presidential campaign, and, most important to his current career, helped Kevin Klose negotiate a tricky real estate transaction back when the network chief was running Voice of America. Stern was a smart guy, and Klose, who was more interested in journalism than in finances, leaned on him. ("Kevin couldn't have crossed the street without Ken Stern," Drake later cracked.) Stern was also among the first at NPR to embrace the digital future. Not everyone at the network saw things his way. Many believed he disdained the medium of radio, and most were put off by his personality. He not only lacked social graces, but he didn't believe in them. As Ellen McDonnell later put it: "Ken was not good in a crowd."

Stern did not deserve the task now facing him—supervising Edwards's book tour. It was dumped in his lap. ("I didn't decide to fire Bob," he said later. "I regretted backing that. I should have insisted that he be allowed to stay to his twenty-fifth anniversary.") Even so, Stern's solution was maladroit. He'd written up some talking points for NPR's new special correspondent. The list consisted of twenty-four items stipulating what the former host could and could not say on the road. While Stern presented the items as suggestions, Edwards took them as directives.

"With respect to the decision to change hosts and the manner in which it was conducted," read one, "you should indicate that you have moved on and are looking forward to your new role."

"You should always speak positively about your past and future career," read another.

The word *Topic* headed each section of the document. Afterward came specifics spelling out what was "expected" from Edwards should reporters along the way invite him to criticize the network. If they asked him about SaveBobEdwards.com, he was to reply that he appreciated the sentiment but hoped listeners would also support NPR as an organization "because this is worth supporting." If pressed about being denied a chance to finish out twenty-five years as host, he was to say that he was "ready to move on." Should anyone inquire into his feelings about the executives who fired him, he should answer that "the management of NPR has to make tough decisions. At first I was not happy but now I'm ready to move on."

Edwards was appalled. "My reaction alternated between fury at the insult and amusement that [Stern] believed that I'd actually follow his script," he noted later, but he didn't say so at the time, for as soon as he'd finished looking over the list Stern offered him $25,000 to give his assent. It was not so much a nondisclosure agreement as a gag order with benefits. Ordinarily, Edwards later asserted, he would have said no, but he added that since he had "no intention of trashing the organization I helped to build," he said yes. "That was the easiest money I ever made."

With that Edwards was off to see America. Bobapalooza debuted in Norfolk, Virginia, traveled to Edwards's hometown of Louisville, headed to Chapel Hill and Memphis, and then turned west. Normally, NPR would have assigned its head of publicity to accompany the former host and make sure he stayed on message, but he'd been fired for mishandling the press following the host's dismissal. Instead, Andy Danyo, the publicist who'd lured Edwards to his fatal meeting with Kernis and the others, took the assignment—another mistake by the network. "She came to think that Bob was wronged," recalled Drake. She had no interest in functioning as Edwards's minder.

Edwards kicked off every appearance with an homage to the subject of his biography. As he saw it, Edward R. Murrow personified all that was important in broadcast journalism, and he spoke glowingly of him, yet as he did so, a subtext emerged: NPR had dismissed a broadcaster who presented himself as the carrier of Murrow's torch. "Edwards was out there thinking he was Edward R. Murrow," McDonnell said later. It got worse during the Q&A sessions. True to his word, Edwards never disparaged the network, but whenever he was asked why he was sacked, he delivered Stern's platitudes with so much sarcasm that they came across as the empty nothings that they were. "Refresh the show . . . changing needs." The audience would hiss and boo, and someone in the back would bellow, "We love you Bob!" Recalled McDonnell, "He was trashing us from one end to the other" of the country.

As Bobapalooza continued, Edwards sounded less like someone NPR had fired than someone who had fired NPR. This was because he *had* fired NPR—the network just didn't know it yet. Shortly before his last day hosting *Morning Edition*, Edwards received a FedEx package at home from SiriusXM radio. It contained a job offer to host a daily, one-hour interview program called *The Bob Edwards Show*. The details—signing bonus, stock options, a significant increase in salary—were all spelled out. What moved Edwards, however, was a comment Hugh Panero, the satellite network's CEO, made in the cover letter: "Maybe Jay Kernis doesn't want to hear you every day, but I do." Before Edwards hit the road, he had a deal.

SiriusXM planned to break the news regarding *The Bob Edwards Show* at the end of the book tour, but in late July, as Bobaplooza was rolling into Austin, Texas, it leaked. On July 28, Edwards telephoned Kernis and resigned. "Kernis made it difficult." he recalled. "He turned the conversation back to him." Edwards said he replied, this is "about me." They were getting divorced, and neither wanted the other to have the last word. With Bruce Drake, Edwards was nastier and, in a sense, revealed more about himself. "I'm resigning effective tomorrow," he emailed the news VP. "Thanks for the memories."

That it came to such an ugly conclusion said nearly as much about NPR some thirty-five years into its existence as it did about the parties involved. Beneath a professional veneer, the network remained less a business than a dysfunctional family. Everyone acted out, and the damage was personal. In this instance, Kernis, despite having survived professionally, suffered more than the dismissed host—at least his reputation did. As the story was told, the programming chief said later, "I was the vile betrayer, the total idiot." *The Bob Edwards Show* on XM meanwhile won positive reviews. Yet what happened to Edwards at NPR still stung. He professed never to have understood. Seeking an answer, he eventually emailed his old nemesis Drake. "Why was I fired?" he asked. The news vice president was flabbergasted.

Bob "has to be the most pig-headed, self-centered guy in the world—or he has no sense of self-awareness at all." As for *Morning Edition*, it chugged along. In the first year after the upheaval, it added 800,000 listeners as NPR promoted Inskeep and Montagne as the "hosts who leave the studio to investigate the news themselves."

Bill Siemering, creator of
All Things Considered,
at the board of KCCM,
Moorhead, Minnesota,
after being fired by
NPR in 1972.

Siemering at work on
the groundbreaking,
mid-1960s series *To Be
Negro* for WBFO at the
University of Buffalo.

Jeff "El Lobo" Kamen
being beaten while
covering a civil rights rally
in Grenada, Mississippi,
during the late 1960s
for Chicago's WCFL.
Kamen was part of
NPR's start-up staff.

Susan Stamberg, NPR mainstay and longtime host of *All Things Considered*, poses in 1992 in front of a portrait by George Bellows at one of her favorite haunts: Washington's National Gallery of Art.

THE STAFF OF NATIONAL PUBLIC RADIO'S "VOICES IN THE WIND"—Standing from left: Jay Kernis, associate producer; Gigi Yellen, production assistant; Bob Malesky, producer. Seated: Oscar Brand, host.

Left: Fred Calland, NPR's first culture czar, interviewed poet Allen Ginsberg for the inaugural episode of *All Things Considered*.

Right: The mid-1970s staff of *Voices in the Wind*, NPR's first program devoted to the arts. In front: host Oscar Brand. From left to right in rear: Jay Kernis, Gigi Yellen, and Robert Malesky.

Frank Mankiewicz, president of NPR from 1977 to 1983, served as press secretary to Robert F. Kennedy. In 1968, he announced the news of the senator's assassination to reporters at a Los Angeles hospital.

Political reporter and *All Things Considered* cohost Linda Wertheimer outside her home in Washington in 1992.

Legal correspondent Nina Totenberg sits in front of a bust of the late Chief Justice Charles Evans Hughes at the United States Supreme Court in 1992.

Political reporter and *Morning Edition* commentator Cokie Roberts at her Washington home in 1992.

From left: *All Things Considered* assistant producer Gary Covino, national editor John McChesney, and producer Art Silverman at NPR's M Street headquarters on election night, 1980.

Left: Producer Robert Malesky at work in one of M Street's notorious edit booths, where staffers often trysted.

Right: Veteran NPR engineer Leo del Aguila, beloved at the network for both his talent and joie de vivre, outside the Getty Villa in Los Angeles in the early 1990s.

Morning Edition founding staffers. From left: newscaster Carl Kasell, host Bob Edwards, and producer Jay Kernis.

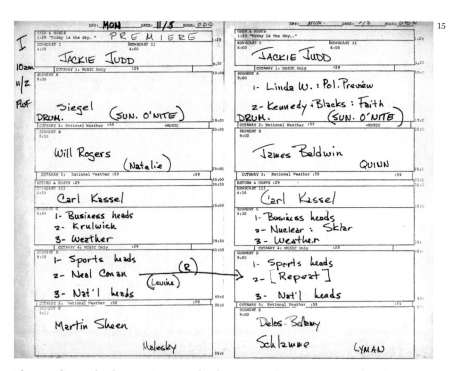

The story lineup for the premiere episode of *Morning Edition*. Most critical is what's missing—any mention of the day's biggest news, the start of the Iranian hostage crisis.

Left: Bob Edwards, who adopted the honorific "Colonel Bob" after he came into his own, relaxes on the lawn of his suburban Virginia home in the early 1990s.

Right: Red Barber, the great play-by-play announcer for the Brooklyn Dodgers during the 1950s, became a commentator on *Morning Edition* in the 1980s, boosting Edwards's confidence. Barber lounges outside his Florida home.

Despite Edwards's resistance, David Sedaris became a *Morning Edition* stalwart during the 1990s, launching his career as an author and performer.

Longtime *All Things Considered* cohost and NPR news director Robert Siegel at his Washington-area home in 1992.

Vertamae Grosvenor, author, actress, and influential *All Things Considered* commentator during the 1980s and 1990s.

Left: Noah Adams, cohost of *All Things Considered* and narrator of the scintillating NPR documentary *Father Cares*, biking in Washington's Dupont Circle in 1992.

Right: Douglas J. Bennet served as president of NPR from 1983 to 1993, stabilizing its finances following Frank Mankiewicz's turbulent reign.

23

WEEKEND EDITION Host Scott Simon, Executive Producer Jay Kernis, and Dr. Ruth Westheimer, who recently spoke with Simon about her role in the new film "One Woman or Two."

Weekend Edition was NPR's first, post-Mankiewicz programming success. From left to right: host Scott Simon, guest Dr. Ruth Westheimer, and producer Jay Kernis during an episode from the show's first year.

25

Left: Daniel Schorr, following a stellar career at CBS News, served as the commentator on *Weekend Edition* for twenty-five years. Schorr reads the *New York Times* at his Washington home.

Right: Scott Simon, relaxing in his Watergate condo. *Weekend Edition* features literate banter and exquisitely produced stories. In 2025, the program will mark its fortieth year on the air.

A year after being taken hostage during the first Gulf War, Neal Conan visits Washington's Air and Space Museum. He ultimately became host of *Talk of the Nation.*

Left: Sylvia Poggioli at work in 1989 in NPR's Rome bureau—a spare room in her home.

Right: Reporter Sunni Khalid at the Islamic Center of Washington, DC, in 1992. Behind him, from left to right, four mentors: Professor Emeritus Samuel Yette of Howard University; Robert J. Cummings, chairman of the Howard University Department of African Studies; Professor Emeritus Ira William Zartman of Johns Hopkins; and former *Washington Post* reporter Leon Dash.

Long-serving *Morning Edition* cohost Renee Montagne at her Los Angeles home during the 1990s.

NPR reporter and Wiccan priestess Margot Adler at her Central Park West apartment in New York.

NPR CEO Kevin Klose announces Joan Kroc's $235 million bequest to NPR in 2003 at the network's Washington headquarters.

Joan Kroc—heiress, philanthropist, activist—in 1984.

33

Foreign Editor Loren Jenkins—in the center in a djellaba and Afghan hat—at a 2011 London party for NPR's international staff. Reporter Deborah Amos (in black jacket) is to Jenkins's left and bottom to top on the right are reporters Ofeibea Quist-Arcton, Sylvia Poggioli, and David Greene.

Left: Foreign correspondent Anne Garrels at her home in Washington during the 1990s in the head garb of her beloved Russia.

Right: Garrels covered some of the bloodiest fighting in the Iraq War while embedded with the Marines in Fallujah in 2004.

NPR reporter and host Jacki Lyden at the network's Washington headquarters. She and Garrels clashed in Iraq.

Controversial commentator Juan Williams after being fired by NPR for his remarks on Fox News in 2010.

38

The launch of *Day to Day*, NPR's first show to originate from California. From left to right: Cyrus Krohn, publisher of *Slate*; network CEO Kevin Klose, and cohost Alex Chadwick.

Ellen Weiss, the talented vice president of NPR News who lost her job in 2011 after she fired both Juan Williams and Alex Chadwick by phone.

Left: NPR CEO Vivian Schiller boosted the network's online presence. She was fired in 2011 after her development team fell victim to a hidden-camera scam staged by conservative provocateurs.

Right: Ira Glass (left) as an NPR intern in 1979 with the innovative producer Keith Talbot.

Glass in 1992 while cohosting *The Wild Room* with Gary Covino for WBEZ in Chicago.

A newly bearded Glass fronting a 2024 episode of *This American Life* in the program's New York studios.

NPR's stylish new headquarters near Capitol Hill in Washington.

EIGHT

BEQUEST

The invitation to lunch at Montagna de la Paloma, the 16,000-square-foot estate of McDonald's heiress Joan Kroc, shimmered with possibilities. "This was not a woman who had people over just for the heck of it," recalled Stephanie Bergsma, the San Diego public broadcasting executive who set up the March 19, 2003, meeting then chauffeured NPR president Kevin Klose and his development director, Barbara Hall, from their downtown San Diego hotel. The drive took the three through increasingly rugged and magnificent countryside and into the hillside community of Rancho Santa Fe, founded in the 1920s by the actor Douglas Fairbanks as a getaway for his showbiz friends. There, on a thirteen-acre promontory, stood Kroc's home.

Few places could have been farther in spirit or distance from NPR's Washington offices. Built in the mid-1980s following the death of Joan's husband, McDonald's CEO Ray Kroc, who parlayed a small hamburger chain founded in 1948 into the world's most successful purveyor of fast food, the Mediterranean-style spread was a sprawling study in its owner's favorite color. The exterior walls were pink stucco. The flower beds overflowed with pink roses. The interior floors were pink marble. Like the dwellings of many wealthy Californians, the house was both ostentatious (two pools, a twelve-car garage) and elegant (Monets and Chagalls in the living room, a Rembrandt sketch in the powder room). But to Joan Kroc, it was where she lived. When Kevin Klose, who seemed a bit overwhelmed by it all, enthused that one of her paintings was beautiful, she smiled and replied that it was nice. She wanted him to feel at ease.

Joining the delegation from public radio were two of Kroc's most trusted friends: Nancy Trestick, the coexecutor of her estate, and Joyce Neu, who after eight years as director of the Conflict Resolution Program at the Carter Center in Atlanta had been appointed executive director of the Kroc Institute for Peace and Justice at the University of San Diego. After introductions, the group sat down at their hostess's round, Lalique crystal dining room table. There was much to discuss. There was also a topic that would not be spoken of directly but would inform everything—the possibility that Kroc, one of America's richest women, might continue down a path she had tentatively started on, a path that could change everything for the financially uncertain NPR.

The events that led to the gathering at Joan Kroc's estate high above the Pacific had started a little less than two years before when in one of life's rare twists, tragedy, charity, and serendipity converged to create an undreamed-of opportunity.

Late on a May night in 2001, Alan Bergsma, a fifty-six-year-old San Diego psychiatrist and Stephanie's husband, picked up a pen and wrote a brief, heartfelt note to Kroc:

> It is 3 a.m. in the San Diego Hospice, and I am personally, eternally grateful to you. This began as one of the worst, miserable, wretched days of my life—nausea, vomiting, severe pain—as sick as I have been in 12 years of cancer. Now I am in my first day of Hospice. It is a delightful, caring place beyond what I ever expected.

Opened in 1991, the twenty-four-bed San Diego Hospice existed because of Kroc. She had given the $18.5 million needed to build it.

Bergsma's note moved Kroc, but when she called the San Diego Hospice to speak to him, he was too ill to come to the phone. She talked instead with his wife. After Alan's death seven days later, Joan asked Stephanie if they could meet. On the surface, they had much in common. Both were widows and, it turned out, both grew up in Minnesota. But there the similarities ended. The seventy-three-year-old Kroc was worth $3 billion, and she looked every cent of it. Her golden hair was perfectly coiffed, her nails buffed to a glossy sheen, and her midwestern accent burnished to a seductive purr by the Virginia Slims she lit up every night over a Scotch. This was the same woman who in the late 1950s had smitten Ray Kroc when he walked into Criterion, Saint Paul's best steak house, where each evening during cocktail hour Joan provided the entertainment. Illuminated by votive candles at her seat behind the restaurant's Hammond organ, she was playing Tony Bennett's "Because of You." The two went on to have a long, tempestuous marriage made spicier because they were politically polar opposites. Ray was a conservative who backed Richard Nixon. Joan was a liberal who hung out with Helen Caldicott, the anti–nuclear weapons advocate. When they weren't fighting, they were buying baseball teams (the San Diego Padres), flying around the globe, and, every Christmas, ringing a bell on lonely street corners for the Salvation Army. They agreed that the rich were obliged to give back.

Joan Kroc was gentle and direct, the kind of person who formed quick, intuitive attachments and never forgot that she'd grown up poor (her father was a telegraph operator). She was also unpretentious. If she noticed that a dinner companion had failed to finish their entrée, she was not shy about stabbing it off their plate with her fork. As for Stephanie Bergsma, while she worked in unglamourous public broadcasting, she did so at its high end. As the development director for KPBS, she spent a fair share of her time with moneyed potential donors. "Stephanie feels at home with people of wealth," observed a colleague. "That makes her rare in the nonprofit world."

No one in San Diego had more money than Joan Kroc, and by the time she and Stephanie became acquainted, the heiress had established herself as the city's most generous philanthropist. Initially, she'd practiced charity in the time-honored fashion of the Rockefellers and the Fords. She'd formed a foundation and adopted the best practices—committees, vetting, waiting. But Kroc was too spontaneous and irrepressible for such as that, and in 1991 she disbanded her foundation. With a $60 million gift to the Ronald McDonald Houses for the care of terminally ill children, she just started giving away cash. In 1996 she donated $3 million to the University of San Diego for interest-free student loans. In 1997 she anonymously handed out $15 million to Grand Forks/East Grand Forks Flood Assistance following a spate of horrible floods in North Dakota. (Her gift only became public because a local reporter jotted down the tail number of her Gulfstream IV when it landed at the Grand Forks airport.) In 1998 she pledged $87 million to build San Diego's Ray and Joan Kroc Community Center for the Salvation Army. As Stephanie and Joan grew close, Stephanie started to suspect that her late husband had written the heiress from hospice in the hopes that just such a friendship might result. Over the years, Kroc had made a few small (for her) donations to KPBS, the largest a $3 million gift to help outfit new studios. Now might be the time for something bigger.

Bergsma's first impulse was to see if she could entice Kroc to give money on a national level to public television. KPBS is a dual license operator, and PBS—with *Masterpiece Theatre, American Experience,* and *Sesame Street*—was by far the sexiest part of the operation. NPR, despite its recent strides, was still just radio. Moreover, Kroc had connections to PBS. She and Fred Rogers, the star of *Mister Rogers' Neighborhood,* were friends (In 1994 she'd given Rogers's Family Communications $400,000). Rogers had accompanied her to the gala KPBS threw to celebrate the gift for its new studios. As a result, Bergsma phoned Pat Mitchell, who'd been appointed CEO of PBS in 2000. There was no response, so Bergsma tried again. "I called Pat Mitchell three times," she said later. "I told them what I was calling about. I felt like I was basically getting blown off." She decided to go another way. "Kevin," she conceded, "was my fallback."

"I've got a donor," Bergsma declared after reaching Klose, who—old newspaper guy that he was—picked up his own phone.

"Who is it?"

When Bergsma told him, the NPR president said he would fly out as soon she set a date.

In October 2002, Klose and his executive vice president, Ken Stern, had a preliminary breakfast meeting with Kroc and Bergsma. They met at Veladora, the restaurant of the Rancho Valencia Resort in Rancho Santa Fe. Bergsma sat Kroc next to Klose, and for the entire morning the two talked almost nonstop. A war was looming in Iraq, and the McDonald's heiress, for whom world peace was an abiding cause (she had endowed not just her institute at the University of San Diego but another at Notre Dame), was, in Joyce Neu's view, "apoplectic" that George W. Bush was about to lead the United States into a ruinous conflict. Klose responded by saying that journalism was the true guardian of peace. He told Kroc that NPR's foreign editor Loren Jenkins had deployed reporters to the Middle East the morning of 9/11 even as the towers of the World Trade Center were still smoldering. Aware that he was speaking to money's emissary, he also emphasized this was good business. NPR's coverage of 9/11, he said, caused the network's audience to grow "by several million. In television, when viewership goes up it goes back down. In public radio it stays up."

Not that Klose believed he reached Kroc. After she departed, the NPR president, Stern, and Bergsma repaired to the Rancho Valencia courtyard. Klose said he'd blown it. "He felt nothing had happened," Bergsma said later. She and Stern disagreed. In their eyes, the tall, white-haired executive had started a potentially fruitful conversation. Bergsma told him he'd been "eloquent."

All through the fall, Klose and Bergsma talked by phone, and he continued to fret, finally asking what more he could do. Bergsma said, "Write her." He said he would if Bergsma edited the letter, which she did. As Klose recalled, he told Kroc about how NPR was formed. "I told her about the core values" articulated by Bill Siemering. "I told her that many of our best reporters were women. They took jobs men wouldn't take because the pay was so low. I told her we did stories nobody else in America cared about."

Klose didn't hold back, but he was still uncertain whether he was getting through. "Have you heard anything?" he asked Bergsma during one of their frequent calls.

"She might drop you a hanky," Bergsma replied, borrowing a phrase used by well-bred Victorian ladies to describe a favored ploy to catch a suitor's eye.

As it turned out, Kroc did more than that. Tucked into the Christmas card she sent Klose at the end of 2002 was a check made out to NPR for $500,000. "That was a big thing for us" recalled Stern. "We thought something significant could be afoot."

No wonder that the March 19 lunch with Kroc at Montagna de La Paloma shimmered with possibilities. But the mood was anxious, even somber. By coincidence, the deadline George Bush had set for Saddam Hussein and his sons to leave Baghdad or face an all-out military assault by the United States and its allies expired that evening. Troops had massed at the Iraqi borders, and destroyers armed with missiles were in the Persian Gulf. For Klose, the imminent conflict was worrying. He'd spent the morning emailing and calling NPR executives back in Washington to assure himself that the network had done everything it could to safeguard Anne Garrels, its correspondent in Baghdad. That the reporter was even there was astonishing. For weeks, Loren Jenkins had lobbied fellow NPR executives on Garrels's behalf. He argued that the correspondent, who'd begun reporting from the city in October, should stay. He maintained that her savvy and abilities, honed over years of working in war zones, would protect her. As Garrels later wrote, Jenkins told higher-ups that his "instincts are that I follow my instincts." Klose had been less certain, and his doubts only increased when other American news outfits began withdrawing their people. On March 12, the Associated Press pulled out its non-Arab staff. ABC and NBC were not far behind. Earlier on the nineteenth, CBS left. So many Western journalists were bailing, Garrels would note that "a steady succession of GMC Suburbans [was] heading for the Jordanian border." Ultimately, the NPR president, in consultation with news VP Bruce Drake, bowed to Jenkins's wisdom. Although John F. Burns of the *New York Times* and Jon Lee Anderson of *The New Yorker* also stayed, Garrels would be the sole American broadcast journalist in Baghdad.

Kroc's worries were more wide-ranging. As she saw it, there was no greater source of human suffering than armed conflict. As the drumbeat preceding the 2003 Iraq War intensified, she had grown convinced that she had to do something to alert America to a looming disaster. During the previous weeks she had flirted with taking out full-page ads in the *New York Times* and the *Los Angeles Times* attacking Bush's plans. The ads would feature an excerpt from one of the most scathing antiwar diatribes ever written, Mark Twain's 1904 short story "The War Prayer." In the passage Kroc wanted to reprint, "an aged stranger . . . his long body clothed in a robe . . . his white hair descending in a frothy cataract," appears before a church group that backed sending young Americans into the Spanish-American War. To them, he delivers his prayer.

Oh Lord, our God, help us to tear their soldiers to bloody shreds with our shells; help us to cover their smiling fields with the pale forms of their patriot dead; help us drown the thunder of the guns with the shrieks of their wounded, writhing in pain; help us lay waste their humble homes with a hurricane of fire; help us to wring the hearts of their unoffending widows. . . . For our sakes who adore thee, Lord, blast their hopes, blight their lives, protract their bitter pilgrimage. We ask it in the spirit . . . of love. Amen.

Kroc believed that if Americans read Twain's bleak prophecy, they might put pressure on Bush to back down. Her friends weren't so sure. "I don't think people will understand," Joyce Neu told her. "It's too solemn. Your reputation might be tarnished." To buttress her position, the former Carter Center official pointed out that in the story Twain's aged stranger is ultimately dismissed by the citizenry as a lunatic. Kroc dropped her plan to take out the ads, but still she agonized.

Over lunch with Klose, Kroc could not stop talking about her fears regarding what might now happen in Iraq. She'd been up at dawn listening to Garrels, who speaking by satellite on *Morning Edition*, set the scene. "I looked out my window at 2 a.m. and saw people packing up stores. I know from Iraqis I've spoken to that they are saying to their wives and children, 'Get out now.'"

Klose could not help but agree with Kroc's grim premonitions. "Whatever happens," he said, "there will be death. People will come back looking whole, but they will have trouble. Some will be maimed for life."

This only made Kroc feel worse. Scrambling, Klose changed course. "We will be there," he promised his hostess. "The great Anne Garrels is there. You should meet her. You will love this woman. She's strong and independent and cares about the things you care about." The NPR chief laid it on, but he believed in what he was saying. That his words constituted the best, off-the-cuff fundraising pitch in public radio history was not lost on the other guests.

"Kevin," Joyce Neu recalled, "was giving a salesman's talk." As for Klose, it was all a blur. "It was extremely intense," he said later. "We were exhausted. We were wrung out. We were strung out."

• • •

Two days after Joan Kroc's lunch with Kevin Klose and the others, Anne Garrels looked out the window of her room at the Palestine Hotel in downtown Baghdad and saw something few people have ever seen—a cruise missile flying at eye level along the banks of the Tigris River. As she told Scott Simon the following morning on *Weekend Edition*, "It hit a target just across the river and exploded into a ball of fire."

The first week of the Iraq War found Garrels filing eight or nine stories every twenty-four hours. Not only was she at the top of nearly each broadcast of *All Things Considered* and *Morning Edition*, but she was also providing spot coverage for the news breaks that punctuate public radio's regular programming. Much of her early work was by necessity terse ("At 5:30 I heard jets overhead then anti-aircraft gunners opened up"). But from the start her pieces included insights that exhibited a deep knowledge of Iraqi politics and society. Regarding Saddam Hussein's initial, postattack news conference, she observed, "He looked puffy. He didn't look himself. To fend off rumors that he had been killed, he specifically mentioned the date, so it would be clear this had not been pre-recorded." Regarding the impact of devastating aerial assaults on the city's residents, she reported, "There are runs on drug stores. There is no valium available. People are giving their kids valium."

Soon enough, Garrels was also filing long, polished dispatches that gave NPR's listeners a view of the human cost of a conflict waged with missiles and bombs that were not always as accurate as American forces advertised. In a three-minute, thirty-six-second story that aired March 26 on *All Things Considered*, she bore witness to the aftermath of an air raid that had gone wrong. Walking through the devastated commercial neighborhood of Al-Sha'ab as sirens blared and survivors wailed, she began with a somber catalog of the dead: "Three in nearby mechanic shops. A 21-year-old in a water heater shop. A family in one of the charred apartments upstairs. At least ten cars which had been lined up to be fixed exploded. Farah Rashid had been working under one. All that is left is a carbonized hulk. A couple that was driving by were caught in the conflagration and were burned to death." The scene set, Garrels shifted tone from hushed to warning. Against a backdrop of increasingly furious voices, she described a crowd of protestors. "A teenager thrust a can he said contained the brains of one of the victims."

She quoted another angry young man. "Is this what you call liberation?" She closed with a dark promise from a student at a Baghdad technological institute. "This war had changed his mind about Americans."

Getting into position to do justice to such a difficult assignment had required more of Garrels than persuading Klose and other NPR executives to allow her to remain in Baghdad. The night before the war began, the reporter had moved into the Palestine after receiving word that the hotel where she'd been staying, the Al-Rashid, was likely on the American target list. To change accommodations meant lugging sufficient provisions to withstand a prolonged attack as well as all her broadcasting equipment from one place to another.

Garrels's quarters at the Palestine—first in a room on the sixth floor, then one on the eleventh—were a cross between a survivalist's hidey-hole and a bare-bones foreign news bureau. Canned tuna fish, peanut butter, coffee, a case of cheap Bordeaux, bags of Kit Kat bars, and, most important, cartons of Marlboro Lights cluttered the floors. In the loo, plastic garbage pails held a week's worth of water—insurance against the likely cutoff of supply. The center of operations was a small desk atop which sat the reporter's Toshiba laptop, a nifty little device that allowed her to convert taped interviews and sound tracks into digital files, and an Iridium sat phone wired to a bulky, three-panel antenna. After positioning the antenna on her room's tiny balcony and syncing it to satellites flying over either the Indian Ocean or the eastern Atlantic, she transmitted her finished work to Washington.

Unlike most network correspondents abroad, Garrels worked alone. No fixer. No staff. No producer. She was not, however, totally on her own. She'd hired an Iraqi driver, a thirty-eight-year-old former military officer she referred to for security reasons as Amer. Resourceful, smart, and fluent in English, he could not only ferry her to assignments and translate quotes but also occasionally even conduct interviews himself. Otherwise, Garrels was a one-woman band, and she was fine with that. "I revel in the freedom of working alone," she subsequently noted. "I like the intimacy this gives me. People, especially here in a police state, are more likely to speak openly."

With or without support, covering an aerial assault from the ground requires the ability to improvise. To ensure that she could get her work back to NPR without official interference, Garrels had decided to defy a regulation

of the Iraqi Information Agency, the government department that monitored foreign journalists, requiring the registration of sat phones. Her gut
told her that should the war start going badly for Saddam, the authorities
would confiscate the devices, making her job impossible. Although she knew
that if security forces, which made periodic sweeps of the Palestine, caught
her with an unregistered phone they would expel her, she had no intention
of getting caught. For one, she believed that John F. Burns of the *New York
Times* was the only reporter Saddam's agents followed. For another, she had
a plan.

Garrels worked a double shift. By day, she covered news conferences
(most of them in the Palestine lobby), conducted interviews, and ventured
with Amer out to parts of the city where the Iraqis allowed access. By night,
she wrote and filed her stories. Because of the nine-hour time difference
between Baghdad and Washington, she transmitted most of what aired on
Morning Edition and *All Things Considered* after dark. The first step was to
switch the lights off in her room. Her movements thus invisible to anyone
watching from outside, she positioned the Iridium phone's ungainly antenna
on her balcony. She then laid a dress out on her bed, stripped off her clothing, and dialed NPR. "This way," she noted in *Naked in Baghdad*, her war
memoirs, "if someone knock[ed] I can pretend they have woken me up, beg
for a few minutes to get dressed, then have time to dismantle the phone and
hide it." All through March and April 2003, Garrels, as she put it, filed her
pieces "in the buff while Robert Siegel remained in blissful ignorance."

Broadcasting in the altogether is not only highly irregular but contradicts
the wisdom of the war reporting fraternity. As Garrels well knew, journalists
in combat typically wear as much clothing as possible. Not only do garments
provide extra protection, but if you have to make a run for it, you can do
so. Nonetheless, NPR's woman in Baghdad had thought things through and
believed that her reasoning was solid. Few foreign correspondents had the
experience in the field she did.

By the time Anne Garrels began transmitting naked from Baghdad, she had
been reporting from dangerous locales for nearly twenty-five years. A Massachusetts native, she grew up in Great Britain but returned to the States
for college. After two years at Middlebury, where she learned Russian, she

transferred to Harvard, graduating with a degree in Russian in 1972. Back in the United Kingdom, Garrels worked as an editorial assistant at the publishing house of Weidenfeld & Nicolson. She spent the mid-1970s as part of a team producing a TV documentary about the Soviet Union. The film never aired, but in 1979 she ended up getting hired by ABC News, which gave her the plum job of Moscow bureau chief almost entirely because of her language skills. She reported on the Soviet Union's involvement in its disastrous proxy war with the United States in Afghanistan, the lives of Muscovites suffering the deprivations of late Soviet communism, and the country's refusenik community. She befriended the Nobel laureate Andrei Sakharov. When the Soviets sentenced the dissident physicist to internal exile in Gorky, Garrels gave his wife a Super 8 film camera with which to interview fellow exiles. ABC aired the footage. Such actions did not play well at the Kremlin. Government goons, the reporter said later, slashed her tires, and "the *Literaturmaya Gazeta*, a major publication, accused me of being a spy." By 1982, just three years into the posting, the reporter sensed that the government was seeking an excuse to silence her. It was at this juncture, she recalled, "that the worst thing that ever happened to me" happened. While driving on a rain-slicked, six-lane highway back to her apartment after covering a dog show for a feature story, she hit two pedestrians. One died. In any other country, this event would have been merely a tragedy. In the Soviet Union, it was a tragedy and a potential international incident. As Garrels later explained, the Soviet government made it clear to ABC and the US embassy that she had to leave. The authorities wanted the network to recall her. "If they expelled me, it allowed the US to expel a reporter from Washington." In hopes of avoiding a diplomatic crisis, ABC sent Pierre Salinger in to clean up the mess. The former press secretary to John F. Kennedy had ascended to the rank of network commentator, but he retained connections from his White House days. The upshot was that the reporter left voluntarily.

What happened in Moscow was a blow, but it did not derail Garrels's TV career. Soon ABC sent her to El Salvador, where she covered that country's civil war and the revolution in neighboring Nicaragua. She jumped to NBC, where she covered the State Department. Smart and attractive ("Her legs went on for days," recalled a former colleague), she was featured on the cover of *TV Guide* with PBS's Judy Woodruff and CBS's Lesley Stahl. Yet as

Garrels's celebrity increased, she grew dissatisfied. Not only did she dislike being, in her phrase, a "TV tart," but she felt that the medium required her to dumb down her work, so she did something radical. "I applied for a job at NPR."

Adam Clayton Powell III, at the time NPR's vice president of news, was intrigued, and invited Garrels to dinner.

"Adam," she said over drinks, "the networks have made me so rich, but I'm so bored."

"Anne," he replied, "we can take care of both of those."

Garrels started at NPR in 1988 at $55,000 a year—$70,000 less than she'd earned at NBC.

Despite her success as a television correspondent, Anne Garrels struggled at NPR. She had "a difficult transition," recalled Bill Buzenberg, who replaced Powell as news VP shortly after Garrels's arrival. "It's about the picture in TV," he added. "In radio it's about the story." Ann Cooper, at the time NPR's Moscow reporter, concurred. "She had to learn how to tell a story without pictures." Furthermore, she needed to learn how to tell a story in depth. Not long after getting to NPR, Garrels said later, *All Things Considered* producer Michael Sullivan approached her before deadline with a story assignment. "Fill four minutes," he ordered. Garrels panicked. "It was nuts—in TV pieces were never longer than a minute and a half." But with the help of staffers like John Dinges, she finished this piece and others that required her to spread out. "She took to it," remembered the former foreign editor.

Garrels turned into one of NPR's top reporters, one of the few who could carry a story on the strength of her prose. Actualities, ambient sound—she'd use them if she got them, but she was fine without them. "She didn't need tape," recalled Renee Montagne. "She was that good." Garrels also boasted another asset. Not since Bob Edwards had anyone at the network had a better voice. That neither Edwards nor Garrels was ever far from a cigarette was part of the explanation. "It was a smoker's voice," recalled Garrels, adding darkly that her engaging rasp was the reward "for my sins." But finally, the reporter's greatest strength was that she threw herself into her work.

Garrels started off covering international affairs for NPR out of Washington, but as Perestroika opened up the Soviet Union, she returned to Moscow, at first sleeping on the sofa in Ann Cooper's apartment. Beginning in 1992, Garrels became the network's full-time correspondent in the country, where her calling was thrust upon her. "The Soviet Union fell apart," she later wrote, "and since then wars have become my metier, as conflicts erupted in places no one had heard of: Georgia, Abkhazia, Nagorno-Karabakh, Chechnya, Tajikistan, Bosnia, and Kosovo. Inadvertently, I became good at covering these kinds of situations."

Garrels might simply have done good work from the world's trouble spots had not Loren Jenkins joined NPR. During the new foreign editor's first week on the job, Michael Sullivan gave the old newspaper guy a crash course in radio journalism. "He would bring me into his office two hours a day," Jenkins recalled. "He played me a good piece of radio journalism, a mediocre piece, and a terrible one." Those by Garrels stood out for their high quality. "The best was a piece she did in Chechnya." The correspondent was trying to get across the border into the country and was "stopped at night by a Russian roadblock. There's this scene of drunken soldiers around a fire with guns drawn. I heard this piece and I can still visualize it. It taught me that good radio journalism makes listeners see through their ears."

In the aftermath of the Chechnyan civil war, Jenkins dispatched Garrels from hot zone to hot zone, expanding the breadth of NPR's international coverage. Along the way, she learned how to survive in the toughest of situations. In Grozny she hid in a basement as outside in the streets a tank battle reduced the city to rubble. In Islamabad the night the *Wall Street Journal* reporter Daniel Pearl was murdered while trying to follow up rumors regarding a radical Islamist group, she declined to join reporters from the *New York Times* and other organizations who for safety reasons moved to a Marriott hotel. What they saw as a circling of the wagons she saw as a heightening of risk. By banding together, they were making themselves an easy target. She instead stayed alone in the house NPR had rented for her where, as she wrote in *Naked in Baghdad*, "I could hunker down in anonymity." That night, she added, was not easy. When the wind picked up and rattled shutters and she answered her ringing phone to hear only silence, she experienced "raw terror."

What made Garrels's life as a journalistic lone wolf bearable was that Jenkins gave her a deal similar to what he'd had at the *Washington Post*: six months of demanding war coverage followed by six months of downtime. In 1986, she'd married Vint Lawrence, a former CIA member and the scion of a wealthy family who'd given up espionage for art. During the 1980s and 1990s, he painted scores of cover illustrations for the *New Republic*. In 1998, the two moved to the vast, verdant Lawrence family compound in Norfolk, Connecticut. After tours of duty, Garrels repaired to this WASP redoubt. There, she and her husband gardened (sixteen raised beds of flowers and produce bordered by dahlias) and played with their chocolate Labs. There, shortly after 9/11, she received her marching orders from Loren Jenkins.

Garrels's first stop was Kazakhstan to cover a long-scheduled visit by Pope John Paul II. She then headed for Afghanistan via Tajikistan. "I hired a car and went across the border at the Hindu Kush with a couple other reporters," she recalled. "One hundred twenty switchbacks on the road. We were at 17,000 feet. We found a safe house. It was a shepherd's hut. We slept with the goats. I waited there for the fall of Kabul." After the US-supported Northern Alliance took the city, she came down from the mountain. In the fall, she went on to Iraq.

Garrels spent her initial tour in Baghdad covering the city much as a general-assignment newspaper reporter might. She made an investment in time and effort getting to know it. She did a piece about the impact of US sanctions on water and sewage treatment and one on the black market in appliances. Following a quick trip home, she returned and continued the process. She profiled the proprietor of the Glast Music Store, which sold bootlegged Britney Spears and Elton John CDs. She covered the rehearsal of the embattled local symphony, whose members played secondhand instruments and received stipends of $12 a month. She was making Baghdad her own, or, as she would later write, creating "a mosaic . . . a picture that approximates reality." This picture would be shattered the next spring.

Through late March and early April 2003, Anne Garrels and NPR owned broadcast coverage of Baghdad. "Anne was front and center in bringing the story home," recalled *The New Yorker's* Jon Lee Anderson, who was trying to make sense of the same events, except for a weekly deadline. "She was unstoppable." As the fighting intensified, the reporter's work just got stronger. She not only covered the news but she channeled the emotional toll of living in a city where the impact of constant bombing registered as both percussive thuds and explosions in the heart. She evaded authorities to interview a thirty-eight-year-old woman in her home, learning that despite US predictions of cooperation, the attacks were stiffening opposition. "Sitting over a cup of dark, sweet tea, Zenab shakes her head at the events of the past week. She didn't anticipate Iraqis would take on the Americans with such fervor. Pride has overtaken paralyzing fatalism."

When Saddam's forces fled the city, Garrels reported, "It started out as a very eerie day. It was quiet, too quiet. And suddenly the blanket of security Iraqis have only known all their lives just disappeared. I mean, I tripped on a cache of surface-to-air missiles that were just left unmanned."

The Americans were caught as much by surprise as the Iraqis. The result was mayhem. From the Iraq Museum, Garrels reported, "Guards stood by helpless as hundreds of looters, many of them armed, broke in. They took sledge hammers to locked, glass display cases. They broke into vaults. In their wake they left a trail of trashed offices, ransacked galleries, and bitterness. . . . Three days of looting destroyed what survived so many invasions and wars of the past."

Garrels's sustained output from the ravaged city was doubly impressive, for as the chaos increased, life at the Palestine deteriorated, forcing her to be even more resourceful. The hotel's power supply was erratic. To assure that she could continue to file her stories, the reporter fell back on a bit of tradecraft she'd learned in Afghanistan. She got hold of cables, an AC/DC converter, and a car battery, toting them all to her room. Ultimately, Garrels hit upon an alternative. The Palestine had a generator that produced just enough electricity to illuminate the single bulb in her quarters. She hotwired the light to a surge strip. "I was able to plug in the computer and the sat phone, and I didn't have to worry about running out of power."

On April 8, the Palestine itself was hit. Although Baghdad was by this point putatively in American control, US forces on the ground believed that snipers loyal to Saddam were firing on them from somewhere in the hotel. A tank from the Third Army fired back, striking a room on the fifteenth floor, killing a Reuters cameraman and fatally wounding one from Spanish TV. "The attack," the *Guardian* reported the next day, "brought pandemonium" to the Palestine.

Garrels was far from deterred. She felt even more committed to what she was doing. On April 9, she scored her biggest scoop from Iraq—not with what she reported but with what she did not. In Baghdad's Firdos Square that day, US Marines took part in pulling down a massive statue of Saddam Hussein. Journalists from American cable networks had begun to filter back into the country, and they presented the event as a celebration. Not so, reported NPR's correspondent, who instead described the reaction of an Iraqi political scientist. "Dr. Saad Jawad," she told listeners of *Morning Edition*, "watched sadly as the Marines helped to topple the statue of Saddam, calling the scene humiliating. No fan of Saddam, he nonetheless warned of wounded pride." Back in DC, Garrels's producers, watching CNN's upbeat account, phoned their reporter to ask if she would edit her story for the network's West Coast feed to reflect what they were seeing on TV. She replied, "No," making NPR the lone American broadcasting entity not to succumb to the unwarranted cheerleading. It would turn out to be the right call.

On April 11, two days after the destruction of the statue of Saddam, Garrels witnessed a deflating scene:

> A convoy of journalists arrived at the Palestine today . . . It's the end of an era in more ways than one. Our intimate war, with no networks and no stars, has turned into the usual gang-bang. When I see Dan Rather and Christiane Amanpour wandering down my floor, I realize it will soon be time for me to leave . . . I call Loren and tell him I've got a week's work left in me.

Come late April, Anne Garrels was back in Connecticut, replaced in Baghdad by NPR's Jackie Northam. To welcome her home, Vint Lawrence planted a huge *A* in purple and yellow crocuses on the lawn. That was just the start of what amounted to a coronation. Susan Stamberg soon arrived to interview her ("She's fine," Stamberg reported. "Needs more sleep, needs to regain some weight but in a forest compound that has been in her husband's family for generations, Anne Garrels can relax"). Stamberg broke the news that her coworker had covered Baghdad in the nude, sending a ripple through the press. Garrels was not only resolute but sexy. Other reporters descended. *Glamour* did a story. *Vogue* published a four-page spread depicting the journalist at ease on the Lawrence estate. "Garrels became our muse," the magazine declared. She was "one of the lone voices who registered the complexities and the sorrows of both the invader and the invaded. . . . People were desperate for details, and Anne gave them what they needed."

Joan Kroc was one of those people. Since her mid-March lunch with Kevin Klose, she had been listening obsessively to Garrels's coverage. Because of that coverage, recalled Stephanie Bergsma of KPBS, the McDonald's heiress "understood the human damage that the war was doing."

Around noon on August 27, 2003, Kevin Klose found himself once again at Montagna de La Paloma. This visit to see Joan Kroc also involved serendipity, charity, and opportunity. But now, there was another element—mystery. During the first weeks of summer, inscrutable signals from "Our Lady of the Golden Arches," as Kroc was sometimes called, had reached NPR headquarters. Something was afoot, but it was beyond the network president's grasp. What is this all about? he kept asking fellow NPR executives. Then he'd received a phone invitation to attend the McDonald's heiress's seventy-fifth birthday party, and he'd flown out the night before. As he was about to depart for the lunchtime event, he learned the truth. Kroc was dying. During a routine examination in June, she'd been diagnosed with rapidly progressing, inoperable brain cancer—glioblastoma. She had the briefest time to live.

As Klose made his way across the pink marble floors through the group of thirty or so who'd gathered for the occasion, he felt stunned. He saw a few familiar faces—chief among them that of Stephanie Bergsma—but most everyone else was a stranger. Maureen O'Connor, the former mayor of San Diego and a friend of Kroc's, was there, as were Linda Bond, the Salvation Army's commander for the West Coast, and Scott Appleby, director of the Kroc Institute for International Peace Studies at Notre Dame. A couple of grandchildren were in attendance, as was the host's neurosurgeon.

Soon enough, the woman they'd all come to celebrate made her entrance, and there was a shock in seeing her. Joan Kroc was in a wheelchair and visibly ill. Although she was stylishly done up and adorned with jewels (she wore Harry Winston and Van Cleef & Arpels), she appeared "like she'd had a stroke," recalled Klose. "Her jaw was weakened and drooping." Added Bergsma, "She looked so fragile."

Kroc had no intention of letting her diagnosis dampen what she intended to be a joyous party. "She wasn't interested in talking about herself," Bergsma said later. Instead, as she wheeled from guest to guest, she made it a point to project good spirits. "How are you, honey?" she invariably inquired. "What's new?" With Bergsma, Kroc homed in on a favorite topic. "She asked if I was dating anybody." With Klose, Kroc's enthusiasm increased even further. She was beaming.

"I'm so happy to see you, Kevin."

The NPR president had brought Kroc a present—a lacquered Russian palekh box. Black with gold filigree, it depicted two swans in flight. He thought it suggested Joan and Ray. She was delighted, but as with her other birthday encounters, she focused her attention on her guest. Taking Klose's hands in hers, Kroc gazed up at him from her wheelchair. For the first time, he noticed that her eyes were a piercing, cornflower blue. He was transfixed. She said, "We're going to do wonderful things together."

It was a promise, maybe a vow. Klose just stood there. He managed a response. "Of course, we are." No sooner had he spoken than he realized how ridiculous he sounded. Not that it mattered. Nothing he said would have mattered. Besides, Kroc had already wheeled away to talk with someone else.

The same thought that was on Klose's mind back in Washington recurred. "I have no idea what this means." He needed to know. Looking around, he spotted a recent acquaintance, a person who in the space of just weeks had improbably become a crucial part of the NPR president's life, the man who earlier in the day had informed him that Kroc was dying.

"Don't worry," Richard Starmann told Klose after learning of the intense but enigmatic exchange with Kroc. "It's been taken care of. When she passes away, I will first call you to say that. Then, several days later, I will call you again to tell you what has been decided."

Richard Starmann, as he would later put it, was not the kind of person NPR generally invited into its boardroom. A raw-boned, six-feet, four-inch conservative, he was, at fifty-eight, still very much the army first lieutenant who as a member of the Special Forces in Vietnam's II Corps took a load of shrapnel in his left side from a rocket grenade. He spoke in a brisk, Chicago accent, softened only slightly by four years at Ole Miss. Direct to the point of bluntness, he'd introduced himself over the phone to Kevin Klose back in

June by telling him no more than that he was with "the Kroc family interests." He left it to the NPR president to find out that he was the just-retired vice president of international communications at McDonald's and Joan Kroc's coexecutor and consigliere.

Starmann had insisted on secrecy for his visit to NPR, and he got it. When he arrived at the network's Massachusetts Avenue offices just a day after that introductory phone conversation, he signed in as John Smith. The only people told his actual name were those who would meet with him—Klose, VP Ken Stern, Barbara Hall, the development director, and John Herrmann, the president of the NPR Foundation, which had been established in the 1990s to provide an independent source of funding for the organization.

Kroc, after learning that she was suffering from terminal cancer, had dispatched Starmann to NPR to conduct due diligence. Not that her emissary revealed many specifics to the assembled executives. Still, there was no doubt that he meant business. "I want to see your books and how you manage yourselves," he began.

Klose gave Starmann NPR's audit reports and its 990s, the forms nonprofit corporations provide to the IRS each year at tax time. Meanwhile, the members of the network contingent did their best to lay out its financial story. Its annual budget was $104 million. During recent years it had made genuine strides, but it was by no means flush. NPR had a cash "reserve of six months," Stern said later. "In an ideal world, you'd want to have one year. We were a distance from where we should be, and we had no idea how to close the gap."

As the conversation progressed, the NPR executives told Starmann as much as they could about the place's history and how it worked. Klose talked about the network's commitment to good journalism. Herrmann explained the function of the foundation, which during the decade since its founding had assembled a board of fifteen trustees and established an endowment of $35 million. Hall outlined the hierarchy NPR had instituted for donors: Silver gave $15,000 a year, gold $20,000, and platinum $25,000.

After an hour of all this earnestness, Starmann was starting to like NPR. ("When I asked them a direct question," he recalled, "they gave me a direct answer.") He was also starting to feel comfortable enough to try a joke. The ability to laugh, he believed, was the greatest asset. Responding to Hall's elucidation of the various levels of corporate giving, he said flatly, "I would hope if Mrs. Kroc made a gift, it would be platinum."

There was initially no reaction. Then the table burst into laughter, Starmann laughing the loudest. Joan Kroc had already given NPR $500,000. Any subsequent gift had to be bigger. They were no longer so formal.

Something else was also happening. Starmann had a weakness for journalists. During his twenty-seven years at McDonald's, he'd interacted daily with reporters (much of his job involved crisis management). At Ole Miss, he'd been managing editor of *The Mississippian*, the student newspaper. He was a bit put off by what he regarded as liberal bias in NPR's news coverage (he was a listener), but that was less important than what he saw as another inherent quality. These people believed in what they were doing just as Ray Kroc and his people had believed in what they were doing. Kroc, while a taskmaster (he hired and promoted vets like Starmann because, in his words, they kept their shoes polished and took orders), had created a culture of excellence. At McDonald's, the saying was, "ketchup runs in our veins." At NPR, journalism ran in the veins.

"If you got to your goals," Starmann asked near the end of his visit, "would you quit?"

"For the weekend," Klose replied.

Following the session, Klose phoned Stephanie Bergsma. After hearing him out, she said, "It's serious." Starmann, meanwhile, hopped in a car and headed to Maryland, to see his son and daughter-in-law. On the way, he phoned Kroc.

"How was your meeting?" she asked.

"Fabulous—really interesting."

"Come out right now."

"I want to stop in Chicago. I don't have fresh clothes."

"I'll send the boys."

The boys were the pilots of Kroc's Gulfstream IV. That night, they flew from San Diego to Washington. Early the next morning, they picked up their lone passenger and flew back west. That afternoon Starmann was in Rancho Santa Fe.

•   •   •

One of Joan Kroc's favorite spots at Montagna de la Paloma was a poolside assemblage of umbrellas and outdoor furniture she'd dubbed "the nook." There, looking out over a stunning landscape of eucalyptus trees and California oaks, she made her decision.

Although Starmann and Kroc were close friends, he always called her "Mrs. Kroc," and he never failed to show deference. On this summer day she was dressed casually, but he wore a sports jacket and tie.

The two talked for three hours. Starmann had taken extensive notes while in Washington. He told his employer about NPR's present finances and its prospects. "The most important thing," he said later, "is that I told her I was impressed" with NPR's people.

Kroc, he recalled, was thrilled. "She had no doubts." At which point he made a humorous stab at slowing her down.

"I think they're further to the left than you do," he said, "but if you want to give your dough to this liberal institution, that's your business."

Kroc smiled. Starmann fulfilled many roles for her, one of which was as a stand-in for her conservative late husband. "I was the right wing of that aircraft," he said later. If he'd entertained genuine worries, he would have spelled them out. She could tell that he was as high on NPR as she was. This conversation wasn't about whether to give the network money. It was about how much.

"What do you think?" she asked.

"I think the big chunk should go to the foundation. They can live off the interest from it. The rest we just give to NPR to do anything they want with it."

"You mean like mad money?"

"Yes, like mad money."

Starmann then proposed a figure. "Even to her," he recalled, "it was a lot of dough. But she didn't flinch."

"Do you think that will knock their socks off?" she asked.

"Yes, I think that will knock their socks off."

"Then that's what I'm going to do."

In the time between this conversation and Kroc's birthday celebration, Starmann worked out the details (most of the bequest would come from charitable remainder trusts). Back at NPR, no one knew anything. The best guess was that Kroc would leave the network between $10 and $20 million. "It would have been huge," recalled Ken Stern, "but it wasn't transformative."

Joan Kroc died on Sunday, October 12, 2003. As he said he would, Richard Starmann phoned Kevin Klose to give him the news, promising to call again on Wednesday to reveal the McDonald's heiress's decision. This plan, it turned out, was overly ambitious. Kroc's consigliere needed one more day to sort matters out—just one, but for Klose, even one prolonged the torture. The six months since the NPR president had first met with Kroc had been overwhelming. The lunch at her home in March when the two discussed the Iraq War and Anne Garrels was intense enough, then the back-and-forth with her at her birthday party brought his emotions to a peak. Klose felt that he and Kroc had touched souls. "I'm not a mystical person," he said later, "but I am a karma person." He sensed that whatever was coming had been predetermined. He was open to anything, but it was out of his hands. When he awoke Thursday at six a.m., he felt he was in the presence of a force bigger than himself. Looking up at his ceiling, he saw a gray cloud. He did not imagine it. He saw it. Emerging from the cloud was a series of numbers. The first was a two. The rest were zeroes. The old question arose: What does it mean? Shaking his head Klose roused himself. The day was here. It was time to dress and leave for work.

Klose was at his desk midmorning when the phone rang.

"Do you have paper?" Starmann asked right off the bat.

"Yes."

"Write down the number two. Now write zero, zero, zero, zero, zero, zero, zero, zero."

He could "barely move," Klose said later. Joan Kroc had left NPR $200 million—the same figure he'd seen on his bedroom ceiling. It had been a sign. It wasn't the kind of thing you could say aloud, but he knew.

The total would reach $235 million by the time the estate settled, what with the interest accruing to various Kroc accounts. "It's divided—$193 million to the NPR endowment, the rest for you do with as you see fit," Starmann explained. "There were no strings attached—no requirement to mention Kroc on the air, no building, no room." Starmann's sole request was that Klose wait several weeks before making an announcement. It would take that long for accountants to finish the paperwork. The only people with whom the NPR president could share the news were those he had been talking to all along—Stern, Barbara Hall, John Herrmann from NPR's foundation, and Stephanie Bergsma.

Kevin Klose announced Joan Kroc's $200 million–plus bequest on November 6 at NPR headquarters. "We are inspired and humbled," he said. The size of the donation attracted front-page headlines. "It is believed to be among the largest ever pledged to an American cultural institution," the *New York Times* reported. (Astonishingly, the NPR gift was not Kroc's biggest. She left $1.5 billion to the Salvation Army to build twenty-five community centers in blighted communities. She also made countless smaller bequests, including one of $500,000 to a San Diego couple who took in laundry from local AIDS patients. In essence, she gave away nearly every cent she had.) At the network's Massachusetts Avenue newsroom, staffers celebrated by ordering in Big Macs and french fries. Susan Stamberg joked that she was changing her name to Susan McStamberg.

Outside NPR, the reaction was more mixed. General managers of public radio stations rejoiced. "Her bequest to NPR is wonderful," enthused Ruth Seymour of KCRW. "Her husband made his fortune creating a populist food. There can't be anything more populist than radio." To many conservative activists, the gift was just more self-dealing by left-of-center elitists. "Mrs. Kroc was a partisan peacenik," declared Tim Graham, the director of analysis at the right-of-center Media Research Group. She "fits right in with NPR's liberal agenda."

In the days after NPR made the news public, the discussion turned to another question: How would the network use the money? Keeping to the terms Kroc laid out, the bulk of it would go into the endowment. "It is to be saved," declared Klose. Still, that left nearly $40 million just waiting to be spent. NPR would dole out $2.4 million of it to its member stations to subsidize the fees they paid for network programming. It would give $700,000 to employees in what the *Los Angeles Times* described as "unusual, company-wide bonuses." (Even the lowliest worker would get $500.) The rest, asserted Jay Kernis, NPR's programming director, would go to the freedom to dream. The network's biggest dream was to increase the quality of its journalism, and the surest way of doing that was to hire new reporters. By mid-November, NPR executives were fantasizing about innovative beats devoted to economics, technology, and media. As for the kind of journalists the network would hire to fill these beats, Kernis couldn't have been clearer. Speaking to a writer from *Current*, the public broadcasting weekly, he asked, "What would our air sound like if we had ten more Anne Garrels?"

NINE

BROKEN IN BAGHDAD

By New Year's Eve 2003, American reporters in Iraq were telling themselves that a period of postwar violence was coming to an end. There had been awful outbreaks since President George W. Bush's "mission accomplished" speech that spring, the worst occurring in August when a suicide bomber struck the Canal Hotel, headquarters of the United Nations in Baghdad. Twenty-two people died, among them Sérgio Vieira de Mello, the UN's special representative. Despite such attacks, hope was ascendant. Tom Bullock, NPR's new senior producer in the city, recalled the last months of 2003 as "a golden era." Nowhere in Baghdad was really off limits. "I found time to swim, safely, across both the Tigris and the Euphrates—though not on the same day," he later noted. Anne Garrels, who returned in high summer following a several-month stay in Connecticut finishing *Naked in Baghdad*, was astonished at the change. "I'm seeing flourishing trade, with new unrestricted imports, especially in satellite phones and satellite dishes, both of which were outlawed under Saddam," she reported in her first piece from the city. "There are money changers lined up under umbrellas on the sidewalks. Traffic clogs the streets in a way I've never seen before. Alcohol is now sold in restaurants and bars."

After Iraq's surrender to coalition forces, NPR relocated its operations from the battle-scarred Palestine Hotel to Al Ebaa's Palace, the downtown Baghdad outpost of a Middle Eastern chain. The atmosphere was relaxed, the freedom to come and go unlimited. "We moved around with insouciance," Garrels said. The network's staff now included translators and a revolving roster of reporters who spelled the chief correspondent during her periodic hiatuses. The best known was Deborah Amos. After a decade at ABC news, she had grown frustrated at the limitations of reporting for television. Upon learning that there would be an opening in Iraq while Garrels wrote her book, she called Loren Jenkins and asked if she could fill it. He said yes, and she went back to NPR. As she later put it, "I didn't even tell ABC."

A relative newcomer, Ivan Watson, was also in the mix. At twenty-seven, he'd covered West Africa and Afghanistan for NPR before reporting from northern Iraq during the invasion. He specialized in breaking news. Rounding out the group were the network veterans Julie McCarthy, who handled general assignments, and Jacki Lyden, who produced features. A piece by Lyden for *All Things Considered* in mid-December headlined "The Booksellers of Mutanabi Street" was NPR's defining effort during this pacific interlude. Named for a tenth-century Arabian poet, the street had been subject to crackdowns during Saddam's rule. Its merchants had been arrested and tortured for selling seditious material. But just months after the regime's fall, the street was flourishing. "We felt secure enough to get out our political books and put them on display," a seller known as Heider the Magazine told Lyden, who concluded her story by proclaiming, "This is the world of knowledge and books. And it is a beautiful world."

Colonel Steven Boylan, the spokesman for the US military in the country, observed that during the waning days of 2003 the press as a whole succumbed to what he termed the "euphoria of liberation." The sense of possibility only increased with the December capture of Saddam Hussein. Armed with a pistol and two AK-47s and in possession of $750,000 in American currency, the deposed dictator was discovered hiding in a ditch near the northern Iraqi town of Tikrit. Watson reported the news for NPR, telling listeners to *Weekend Edition Sunday* that Iraqis were "celebrating in the center of Baghdad, in that famous square where Saddam's statue was pulled down, and that up north the Kurds were rejoicing, while in the South, the Shia are also undoubtedly celebrating." Then came New Year's Eve.

• • •

It was around nine thirty p.m. when cars carrying the Baghdad staff of the *Los Angeles Times* arrived at Nabil, one of the city's most elegant restaurants and a former haunt of Saddam's Baath Party leaders. The place had outdone itself for the big night—tuxedoed waitstaff, live music, belly dancing. Just as the contingent from the newspaper started to enter, a bomb exploded. The blast blew a five-foot-deep hole in front of Nabil, ripped the facade off an adjacent house, and sent flames whooshing fifteen feet into the sky. Five people died, and twenty-one were wounded, among them the *Times* correspondents Tracy Wilkinson, Chris Kraul, and Ann Simmons, as well as one of the news organization's translators, a computer tech, and a driver. The bombing marked the start of a period of ever-worsening atrocities.

As the early 2004 headlines for Anne Garrels's NPR stories indicate, the country soon descended into chaos. "Suicide Bomber Strikes in Central Iraq" (*All Things Considered*, January 14). "Car Bomb Kills Four in Baghdad" (*Morning Edition*, January 28). Garrels conveyed these horrors in her terse but empathic style. "It's now a too-familiar sight, but it continues to shock," she began the January 28 report. "Police cars and ambulances stream toward the sound of the massive blast, the acrid smoke billowing into the dawn leading the way. A smoldering crater with bits of metal in the middle of the street was all that was left of the vehicle carrying the bomb."

The assaults did not stop. Even so, Garrels found ways to keep doing the sorts of pieces she'd been doing all along in Iraq. In a January 16 story for *Morning Edition*, she described the resumption of classes at Baghdad University. "Students entering campus are searched. It's now simply a way of life, as are the bare walls, cold auditoriums, and electricity outages." She lingered on the lack of books. "The central library was burned and other libraries looted while U.S. troops stood by in the early days of the invasion." In a piece that same week for *All Things Considered*, she conveyed the difficulty of attracting health-care workers to facilities in the violence-beset Sunni Triangle. "Here in Baqubah it is getting worse. The hospital director resigned because of threats. The new director found a bomb in his office." In early February she was in Najaf, the center of Iraq's restive Shiite majority, exploring the increasing tension between the moderate ayatollah Ali al-Sistani and the radical young cleric Muqtada al-Sadr. "No one knows whether even the strongest of these leaders has enough power and influence to hold the country's increasingly angry majority together," she reported.

Garrels worked overtime to file nuanced dispatches, but suicide attacks remained her recurring assignment. In a February 11 story for *Morning Edition*, she recounted how earlier that day the driver of a white Cutlass Ciera pulled up to a recruiting station for Baghdad policemen just outside the Green Zone, the headquarters of the coalition government. The ensuing explosion of a five-hundred-pound bomb killed fifty of the recruits. The incident cast doubts on the plans of the American envoy, L. Paul Bremer III, who'd promised to return home rule to Iraq in four months. It also shattered the security of the press corps, whose members, when visiting the Green Zone, parked in a lot adjacent to the blast site. As the army's Steven Boylan noted: "Reporters have no defense."

Although Tom Bullock was titularly NPR's ranking Baghdad employee, Anne Garrels took charge of finding the network's first safe house. Not only did she know the city better than he, but she was NPR's public face. For much of the early winter of 2004, she searched for a spot big enough to accommodate the bureau's growing personnel and secure enough to withstand outside assaults. Other American news organizations were undertaking similar but better-funded searches. The *New York Times* acquired a football field–size block of concrete buildings with forty urinals that had been the home to Saddam's secret police. John F. Burns, the paper's chief Baghdad correspondent, recalled that underbudgeted competitors expressed "bitter opposition." No wonder. Garrels settled on a nondescript home in the Karrada neighborhood. But modest though the place was, she viewed it as "an oasis, with its small patch of lawn and high walls." Here, network staffers could work in anonymity and retire at night with the expectation that they would live until morning.

Precautions were required. NPR's Iraqi translators, fearful of compromising the location of the bureau or incurring reprisals, didn't tell family members where they worked. When leaving the house, reporters adhered to strict protocols. You entered and exited your car only when it was parked behind the compound walls. The streets were too dangerous. Women wore black abayas, in Garrels's words "a necessary if sweltering disguise." While driving to an assignment, you never fastened your seat belt. Buckling up was a telltale sign that you were a foreigner and thus subject to abduction or killing. As often as possible, you changed the routes you traveled.

The forever war had begun, and with it came a difficult question for all reporters in Iraq.

"So, you going back?" That's how *Morning Edition*'s Steve Inskeep put it to Eric Westervelt, a thirty-four-year-old NPR correspondent who after covering the invasion of Iraq became in 2004 another member of the network's Baghdad lineup. From a comfortable hotel in Amman, Jordan, where he'd repaired following his first rotation, Westervelt sighed, then replied, "Yeah, I probably will."

There was no hesitation when interviewers posed the same query to Anne Garrels. Asked by Terence Smith of PBS's *NewsHour*, she answered instantly. "I'm going to keep going back to Baghdad. Having started in this one, I'm going to see this one through." Garrels knew the risks better than anyone, but she maintained that she'd made her peace with them. In a joint appearance with her husband, Vint Lawrence, on *Fresh Air*, she admitted that she was a fatalist. "Yeah, absolutely," she told Terry Gross. Garrels was not in the grips of a death wish. It was about the work. As Lawrence explained, "Look, if you're lucky in life you get to do what you want for 25 years. If you're really lucky in life, you get one time where you can show just how good you are. And this is Anne's time. Far be it from me to ask her to come home."

For Garrels, war-torn Baghdad was an unparalleled story. She had felt somewhat the same about Russia, but where the transformation of the former Soviet Union was a subject of endless interest, it was often too big and amorphous to comprehend, much less convey. In Iraq, the human drama was more accessible. "I was trying to show what Iraqis thought about their own situation and what Iraqis felt about America," she said later. "My window was Baghdad." This city in convulsion presented Garrels with a tableau of life as it is rarely visible. The war, like a series of lightning strikes, illuminated an ordinarily obscured landscape. Love, hate, despair—all were revealed in sharp relief. "I'm not really very interested in the strictly military part," Garrels liked to say. "I'm fascinated by how people survive and how the process affects the attitudes on all sides."

Garrels cranked out ninety-four full-length stories from Baghdad in 2004 and countless shorts for NPR's hourly news breaks. For most of her network colleagues, it was a privilege to watch her go about her business. "She had a great way of getting people to open up to her," recalled Tom Bullock. "She looked them right in the eye." Added Philip Reeves, a former correspondent for the UK *Independent* who joined NPR in 2004 and became part of its Baghdad bureau, "She could comprehend the bigger geopolitical picture and never lose sight of the people on the ground. She moved with absolute ease between the two." John Felton, now an overnight editor at *Morning Edition*, handled Garrels's copy as it flowed into Washington. "Anne is up there," he later said, "with the best three or four reporters I've ever met."

Anne Garrels's NPR peers were not alone in their admiration for her. One year into the war, she had nearly achieved the stature of such network luminaries as Susan Stamberg and Cokie Roberts. She was interviewed on CNN. She spoke on college campuses. *Naked in Baghdad* went into multiple printings. Garrels was a figure of fascination. Not only was she the woman who stayed in Baghdad during the aerial assault, but she was the woman who kept going back. Network executives were ecstatic.

Garrels was one of NPR's greatest assets. The Iraq War overlapped and to some extent sparked an era of empire building by Loren Jenkins. Coverage from abroad had become NPR's most potent generator of growth, increasing listenership, boosting station fundraising, and financing further global expansion.

Even as Garrels and others were braving Baghdad's dangers, Barbara Hall, NPR's director of development, was using their coverage to raise enormous sums of money to finance the network's international ambitions. Having honed her fundraising skills at Washington's Kennedy Center, Hall had a gift for the theatrical (she'd majored in drama at the University of Mary Washington). She could both impress and charm donors. She and Jenkins would travel to New York to pitch the Ford Foundation or to Chicago to woo the MacArthur Foundation. The foreign editor was always the opening act. He'd expound on his philosophy of international coverage. News should "not be limited to the American perspective," he would say. "American values aren't bad, but they're limiting. You have to understand other people."

To achieve that goal, he'd add, you needed reporters on the ground in the world's capitals. Take Anne Garrels. She was there in Baghdad so NPR listeners could understand the complexities of this terrible conflict, one that television, incidentally, didn't bother to explain.

"Ford and MacArthur each gave five-million-dollar chunks at the same time," Hall recalled. The donations were earmarked for "overseas reporting." These injections of money changed NPR's status as a news outlet, transforming it from a network that had traditionally covered the world by interviewing reporters from the *Washington Post* or the *New York Times* to one that hired reporters as good as if not better than reporters from the *Washington Post* or the *New York Times*. "Only a couple of foreign bureaus existed when I got there," recalled Hall, who joined the network in the 1990s. When she left in 2006, there were seventeen.

Launching each new international operation cost NPR roughly $1 million. "We were pretty much able to open a foreign bureau every year," Jenkins said later. As to where they'd be located, NPR largely left those decisions to him. "I'd ask Loren, 'Where should we put them?'" recalled Jeffrey Dvorkin, vice president of NPR News during part of this time. "We ended up in Africa, South America, southeast Asia and all over the Middle East." The result was that new voices—Ofeibea Quist-Arcton, Lourdes Garcia-Navarro, and Eleanor Beardsley, all debuting in 2004—began appearing on *Morning Edition* and *All Things Considered*. Familiar voices—Michael Sullivan, Julie McCarthy, Mike Shuster—began reporting from previously uncovered locales. Through it all there was Garrels.

It would be hard to imagine a foreign correspondent more intrepid than the Anne Garrels of 2004. Reporting from the Green Zone that July, she told *Morning Edition* listeners of surviving a near miss. "Suddenly a 1,000-pound bomb exploded. It knocked people flying. I was only 300 feet away." Ten people died. (Weeks later, enough residue from the blast still adhered to Garrels's skin that she set off a detection device at New York's John F. Kennedy International Airport.) The next test came in the fall, when Garrels was just outside the midsize city of Fallujah, embedded with Bravo Company, First Battalion, Third Regiment of the United States Marines. The unit's 160 men were just two weeks in-country, but they were poised for what by all indications would be the war's biggest battle since the invasion. Their task: to retake Fallujah from Sunni insurgents who after killing and mutilating four Blackwater security contractors there in March had transformed the city into a launching site for terror attacks.

As the assault approached, Garrels was beset by second thoughts. The danger she would now face was unlike any she'd encountered as a war correspondent. Already, eight Marines of the 1-3 had lost their lives in a suicide bomb attack on a seven-ton truck transporting them to the front. (For a piece on the incident, Garrels taped Marines singing "Amazing Grace" during a memorial service at a makeshift chapel outside Fallujah.) Then there were the physical challenges. Bravo was a rifle company that moved by foot. Clad in a blue helmet and Kevlar vest and wearing a fifty-pound backpack into which she'd cram her gear—Sony recorder, mics, sat phone, Panasonic Toughbook, and notebooks—Garrels would be expected to hump right alongside the servicemen. Finally, there was something private. As the reporter later put it, she was an "old woman, and the Marines didn't want me." Although only fifty-four, she was aware that the men she'd been assigned to cover were mostly in their early twenties. "If they had to have someone with them," she added, "they wanted a network babe—or a guy from Fox. They'd never heard of NPR."

Notwithstanding her misgivings, Garrels tried to break through to the Marines the only way she knew how—by asking about their lives. "The night before we went into Fallujah," she recalled, "we sat in the dark, and I recorded everything. They opened up about their families, where they'd come from, and why they'd joined up." They also talked about their feelings for one another. As one told Garrels, "I love my girlfriend. I love my mom and dad. But I can never be as close to them as I am to these guys." The gulf between the reporter and the men closed.

For the next ten days, Garrels stood with the Marines of the 1-3. On *All Things Considered*, she reported that they fought house-to-house "to the heart of the resistance, rarely protected by tanks or troop carriers, working their way through narrow streets. They rarely saw an insurgent—just an outline through their night vision scopes, the scurry of feet on the rooftops above, then the blast of a muzzle."

What the Marines couldn't see, Garrels let NPR listeners hear, using her mic to record gunshots ricocheting around them, rocket-propelled grenades landing nearby, and men crying out when they were hit and talking about their wounds as they awaited evacuation.

"I'll be back tomorrow," a grunt with shattered eardrums told his sergeant. "No, you won't."

Garrels then provided context. "That's Gunny Kelly talking sense to one of his company. He tries to keep it light, though he's got shrapnel in his shoulder." Mostly, however, she let the Marines just speak. "This is not a very nice place to be," said one of the injured. "They don't like us here. We've got to get home."

Garrels remained with the battalion. The experience was intense—and sometimes searing. "One day," she said later, "we were doing house searches, and this young Marine wouldn't let me go in with him. Usually, I went in, He said, 'No, this is too dangerous. There's something weird about this neighborhood.' He went in the house, and he was hijacked. There were people in there on the top. They shot him, and he was killed." Garrels was just outside as all this happened. The Marine had saved her life. His loss was unbearable. Later, she mailed tapes she'd made of him to his mother in Detroit. "That was all I could do."

Garrels ended up spending nearly two weeks with Bravo Company and filed nineteen stories. The Marines, aided by Iraqi troops, took Fallujah. It was the bloodiest battle fought by the corps since Vietnam—forty Marines died, along with two thousand insurgents. However, the terrorist leadership remained intact and would soon reconstitute as an even more lethal force: ISIS. The experience scarred the reporter. At first, she told the *Columbia Journalism, Review*, "You didn't reflect on it." But then: "You just go, 'Jesus!'"

Back in Connecticut for the holidays, Garrels was beset by unexpected demons. "Some kids were celebrating down at the lake just a few hundred yards" from her house. "They set off fireworks, and I found myself curled up, sobbing." Hoping to clear her head, she went skiing in Utah. "I'd been to this place a million times. There are avalanche dangers, and they" dynamite the mountains to diminish the risks. "I've seen this for twenty years. Well, they did it this year, and the next thing I know I'm in the arms of my stepdaughter sobbing my guts out." When the tears passed, anger followed, but it was free floating, without object. It just gnawed at her, waiting to explode.

• • •

Upon returning to Baghdad in early 2005, Anne Garrels seemed to have put Fallujah behind her. Her days in NPR's Karrada bureau started over coffee with Tom Bullock. "Anne and I would joke around," he recalled. Secure in the network's compound, she looked nothing like the Abaya-clad journalist who braved Baghdad's streets or the helmet-topped combat reporter. In the office, she favored what amounted to a cozy but chic uniform: long-sleeved black T-shirts, black Levis, and one of her seemingly infinite pairs of brightly colored French Sole ballet slippers, which she ordered online from the company's shop in New York. "I always wore this instead of sneakers or boots or something appropriate," she said later.

Garrels's bouncy outfits and buoyant workplace patter—reflecting her British girlhood, she called coworkers "loves" and good edits "brilliant"— could not, however, mask that she'd changed. She was more apprehensive, touchier, and Fallujah was only part of it. A new report by the International Federation of Journalists revealed how dangerous working conditions now were. Forty-nine news organization staffers—among them reporters, camera operators, and drivers—had been killed in Iraq in 2004. ABC anchor Peter Jennings, who did a stint in Baghdad in January 2005, told a writer from the *Washington Post* that he'd learned that Sunni militants were offering $2,000 for the abduction of journalists, double the $1,000 bounty for the capture of enemy Shiites. The closest the NPR bureau had come to harm had occurred in the fall during a mortar attack on the Karrada area. No one was hurt, but the staff no longer felt safe there. It was time to move again, and the job of finding a new home once more fell to Garrels. "I knew the lay of the land," she said later. NPR relocated to the periphery of a compound rented by ABC, which employed guards the radio reporters could call on if needed.

It was a fearful time growing more fearful, but it wasn't the fear that got to Garrels—at least not initially. It was her increasing hostility toward others in NPR's Baghdad operation who in her opinion failed to appreciate "what it took to keep a bureau together" in hostile environs. She had started to believe that she alone cared about security, about the Iraqi translators who risked their lives just by showing up, about the intricacies of operating in Iraq's cash-only economy (she frequently served as staff courier, carrying in thousands in US currency each time she returned from the States). "There's no question that a part of me felt ownership," she later reflected. With that feeling came resentment against those who didn't feel the same.

The arrival of a new Baghdad bureau chief crystalized Garrels's issues, giving her a focus for her anger. Not long after NPR moved its operations to the ABC News facility, Jamie Tarabay took command. A former reporter for the Associated Press most recently based in Jerusalem, Tarabay was an Australian of Lebanese descent. Although only thirty, she was well versed in Middle Eastern politics. Just as important, she possessed what Loren Jenkins termed "a very valuable" asset. She was a fluent Arabist. On paper, Tarabay was just the sort of journalist who might complement Garrels. As it turned out, she had no interest in parts of the job that Garrels considered essential. Management tasks like "writing letters to get visas" or dealing with personnel, Tarabay said later, were not her responsibility. "I was the Baghdad correspondent."

Garrels responded negatively to Tarabay's conception of the role of bureau chief. "I'm not sure that Jamie would have given a shit about the broader spectrum of the bureau," she subsequently said. "She didn't get that looking after the fates of the employees was part of the job. She really wasn't engaged, and it was a problem. I had to continue to be, if not in name in reality, the bureau chief."

Some of Garrels's concerns with Tarabay fell under the heading of turf-consciousness. "Anne was territorial," recalled *Morning Edition* cohost Renee Montagne, who was close to a number of reporters in the bureau. "When someone new came in, they wouldn't be met with welcoming arms." For so long, Baghdad had been Garrels's story, and hers alone. Noted Sylvia Poggioli, "This was her beat. She didn't want anyone else from NPR on it."

But Garrels didn't give a hard time to every fresh recruit to Iraq. She was fine with Phil Reeves and Eric Westervelt. Her animus was reserved for journalists of her own sex. "Anne had a thing for any woman whom she saw as a challenge to her in the bureau," Deborah Amos said later. "I took my share of licks" from her.

Recurring nightmares about Fallujah, constant worry about bomb attacks, the failure of newcomers to realize the difficulty of managing a news operation in a war zone, rivalries with female colleagues—Garrels might have been able to navigate them all had she not also started to drink on the job. For a long time, NPR reporters rotating in and out of Baghdad had ignored the star reporter's tippling, which had been largely limited to evenings. But by 2005 when Tarrabay arrived, Garrels had crossed a line. "At eleven a.m. she'd be cracking open a bottle of red wine," the new bureau chief remembered.

Still, beyond an increased irascibility, Garrels displayed few obvious ill effects from her drinking. Throughout her career she'd survived on stimulants. As Vint Lawrence once observed, on the job his wife had only three food groups—"caffeine, nicotine, and adrenaline." Wine during the daytime was just a chemical balancing agent. The drinking "never showed up in her work," conceded Amos. "She was still good on the air."

Garrels's NPR superiors were in the dark about her drinking. As for her Baghdad coworkers, they looked away, regardless of their personal opinions. Life in Iraq was hard, and it wasn't just the threat of violence. "We were all living in the same house," recalled Tarabay. "You often had no electricity or hot water. The food was terrible. We all ended up with Baghdad belly." The result was that the reporters withheld judgment about one another. Despite your doubts about a colleague's coping methods, you said nothing. It was a kind of omertà, and the staff took a version of the hoary oath: What happens in Baghdad stays in Baghdad. Still, Garrels's attitude was deteriorating, and her drinking was disturbing. "You knew it wasn't healthy," Tarabay said later.

For all the unspoken tensions within the bureau, NPR's Baghdad reporters continued to turn out good journalism. Tarabay, her administrative failings notwithstanding, was committed to the mission as Garrels defined it. "We were proud that we did a lot of reporting about the Iraqi civilian experience," the younger reporter said later. "We would do a story on a dance hall or about someone who works in a jewelry store." Garrels appreciated Tarabay's efforts and made periodic attempts to reach out to her. "She had moments where she could be lovely and warm," Tarabay recalled, adding that when she Skyped with her boyfriend, Garrels regularly jumped on the calls to reassure him: "I'm taking care of her. Don't worry."

Further bolstering the Baghdad's staff ability to function at a high level were the daily ministrations of Tom Bullock. The production chief had grown up at NPR (an internship after graduating from American University, a stint at *Morning Edition*, and finally the jump to the foreign desk). Whether arranging an interview with a reluctant source or digging into the first aid kit for a remedy for indigestion, he came up with solutions, functioning as both journalist and fixer.

But ultimately the strains began to show. Beginning in 2006, a new breed of journalists started to appear in NPR's Baghdad bureau, further threatening Garrels's sense of authority and darkening her demeanor. The veteran reporter referred to these mostly fresh faces as "fly-by-nights," believing that they either lacked the experience to cover treacherous territory or unlike even Tarabay weren't in it for the long haul. The reason why such newcomers were now fetching up in Iraq was plain. Three years into the war Baghdad had become so terrifying that most qualified prospects flat-out rejected offers to work there. "Loren was having to scramble to get people," Garrels said later. He was not alone. "The pool willing to go has considerably shrunk," Tim McNulty, the assistant managing editor for foreign news at the *Chicago Tribune* and Jenkins's old running mate in Beirut, noted at the time. As Garrels saw it, this left either careerists hoping that if they survived a season in hell, they'd get promotions, or specialists pursuing niche projects that while important to them were at odds with the Baghdad operation's overall goal of covering the news.

The first fly-by-night to show up in NPR's Baghdad bureau was, it turned out, a familiar face with considerable seniority at the network—Jacki Lyden. Despite her experience in Iraq, Lyden was fixated on a story that struck Garrels as at best a noble indulgence and, at worst, a fishing expedition. The veteran Baghdad reporter was also worried that the new arrival was not answerable to Jenkins. To win the assignment, Lyden had bypassed the foreign desk. While aware of Garrels's skepticism, Lyden wasn't about to back off. She was deeply committed to her idea.

On June 24, 2005, an American sniper, Joe Romero, shot Yasser Salihee dead after the thirty-year-old Iraqi physician appeared to have been preparing to run his car through a checkpoint in the Baghdad neighborhood of Amiriyah. At the time, Salihee no longer practiced medicine, having become a translator for Scripps-Howard newspapers—and for Jacki Lyden, who was on leave from NPR writing a book about the war. Lyden was responsible for the doctor's decision to shift careers. During her 2003 reporting stint in Iraq, she had met him while covering a story, and the two became friends. When Salihee expressed an interest in journalism ("I want to make all the world knowing what's happening inside Iraq," his widow later quoted him saying), Lyden helped him get assignments at the network. News of his death not only devastated her ("Yasser was the sun coming up over the mountain") but spelled the end of her book—she didn't think she could do it without him. But as the weeks passed, Lyden became obsessed with what had happened and what she regarded as the all-too-typical series of events that put the doctor in the gunsight of a thirty-three-year-old Louisiana National Guardsman. In the confrontation she saw everything that was wrong with America's military occupation. Upon returning full-time to NPR, she began planning a major piece.

Ordinarily, Lyden would have pitched her story to Loren Jenkins, but she and the foreign editor could not stand one another. Their relationship was so bad that she almost hadn't gotten to Baghdad in the first place back in 2003. The animus between the two dated to a 1996 complaint made by Lyden to NPR's human resources department involving a foreign desk assistant who'd confided that Jenkins verbally brutalized her at work. According to the reporter, network HR staffers promised not to name her as the source for the allegations, but those promises evaporated in 1997 when the former NPR foreign correspondent Sunni Khalid sued NPR and Jenkins. Khalid's counsel cited other incidents of alleged insensitivity by Jenkins as part of a pattern of behavior, and Lyden's role became public. From that point, she asserted, "Loren was trying to destroy my career." Although she was doing well at NPR (for much of 2002 she cohosted *All Things Considered*), Jenkins rebuffed Lyden's efforts to get the assignment she wanted: Baghdad-based foreign correspondent. He admitted as much, recalling a recurring refrain.

"I want to cover this story," she'd say to him.

"I've got a staff correspondent covering it," he'd reply.

To Jenkins, Lyden was the last person who belonged in a war zone. In his eyes, she was too precious (a self-styled fashionista, she favored vintage clothing, running from appliquéd 1950s blouses to boiled-wool Cossack coats and birdcage earrings) and unreliable, and, not incidentally, she had tried to screw him over. "Jacki," he declared, "was one of those problem children of NPR."

Lyden filed a complaint against Jenkins and the network with the Equal Employment Opportunity Commission, and she won. "The company had to pay my legal fees," she recalled, "and he had to send me to the Middle East." Now, two years later, she needed a way back.

In February 2004, as fantasies swirled around NPR's executive suites about how to spend the Joan Kroc bequest, Jay Kernis read a story in the *New York Times* and then ducked into the office of the network's president, Kevin Klose.

"I think you should talk to this guy," said Kernis.

The guy was fifty-seven-year-old Bill Marimow, and the *Times* article was just one of many about him that winter. "You couldn't pick up a paper without reading about Bill Marimow, the hero," recalled Bruce Drake, NPR's vice president of news. Marimow was editor of the *Baltimore Sun* and a two-time Pulitzer Prize winner (the first came in 1978 for a *Philadelphia Inquirer* series documenting police beatings of suspects and witnesses in homicide cases). Sparking the headlines was Marimow's resistance to orders from the Tribune Company, publisher of the *Sun*, to implement massive staff reductions as part of a cost-cutting measure. Tribune's response was to fire Marimow. To an industry just starting to grapple with the impact of declining revenue, shrinking readership, and changing technology, the editor came across as the rare news executive willing to hold the line against the philistines.

Klose not only called Marimow, but he asked if he could drive to Baltimore to meet him.

"Kevin, I'm the unemployed guy," the ousted editor responded. "Why don't I drive to Washington to see you?"

"No. I'm coming up to Baltimore," Klose insisted.

The two hit it off, each seeing in the other an answered prayer. For Marimow, Klose held the keys to a new career at an organization flush with cash that could give him the chance both to champion strong journalism and also acquire broadcasting skills. For Klose, Marimow was the embodiment of everything the Kroc money could do for NPR. He would elevate the network's reputation and professionalism. Klose "had fallen in love with Marimow," Drake said later.

After a lunch at Washington's Mayflower Hotel attended by Kernis and NPR COO Ken Stern, Klose offered Marimow a job that had never existed at the network—managing editor for enterprise reporting. As the two defined it, the position would give Marimow the responsibility for assigning then editing the sort of time-intensive, investigative stories the network rarely did. Klose promised Marimow free reign.

Marimow wasted no time getting started, quickly dipping into the Kroc money to conduct a raid on his ex-employer. Among the former and current *Sun* reporters he lured to NPR were David Folkenflik, David Greene, and Frank Langfitt. Marimow also identified a number of NPR journalists he believed could turn out the kind of comprehensive stories he'd been hired to promote. He encouraged Snigdha Prakash to pursue a series about Merck pharmaceutical's efforts to pressure med schools to ignore the side effects of its ultimately discontinued painkiller Vioxx, and he persuaded Daniel Zwerdling to look into the excessive use of police dogs in a New Jersey federal prison. (The Prakash stories led to the book *All the Justice Money Can Buy*; Zwerdling's work won a Robert F. Kennedy Award.) No NPR veteran benefited more from Marimow's encouragement than the sixty-five-year-old hippie badass who after having been forced out of his position as foreign editor in the 1990s was now pursuing a second career as a reporter.

Since returning to NPR in 2001, John McChesney had primarily worked from Northern California, covering everything from wine making to Silicon Valley while producing spot features on such local stories as the 2003 reopening of the stylishly renovated San Francisco Ferry Building. Along the way, he got interested in a trial taking place down the coast in San Diego. The United States government was prosecuting two Navy SEALs for the alleged abuse of an Iraqi named Manadel al-Jamadi, who, after being arrested in Baghdad for supplying the explosives for the 2003 bombing of a Red Cross facility, was found dead in a shower room at Abu Ghraib prison. Known as the Ice Man (photographs of his iced-down body with one of his guards grinning at it were published worldwide), al-Jamadi had become a symbol of American military excess. McChesney was just getting started when the government, citing unspecified security concerns, shut the trial down. Prior to Marimow, NPR would not have tried to discover the rationale behind the government's decision, but McChensey wanted to take a shot. "Bill gave me four months to do the story—to go get the classified documents and do half an hour for *All Things Considered*." The piece aired October 27, 2005, and was widely applauded. *The New Yorker*'s Jane Mayer was also investigating al-Jamadi's death, and although McChesney scooped her (Mayer's article, headlined "A Deadly Interrogation," did not see print until November 6), she quoted the NPR reporter in her piece and called Marimow to congratulate him on the network's good work.

McChesney's resurgence under Marimow had a surprise beneficiary—Jacki Lyden. The longtime NPR reporter was a close friend of McChesney, and he introduced her to the new editor. It was her chance to get around Loren Jenkins. "Jacki and John proposed her story to Marimow," recalled Renee Montagne.

As Bill Marimow signed off on it, Jacki Lyden's piece about the death of Yaseer Salihee was a shoot-the-moon proposition. To reconstruct what happened, the editor ordered the reporter to Baghdad to assemble an account of the dead man's life and to probe his death. Simultaneously he sent John McChesney to Louisiana, the home of Joe Romero, to explore the guardsman's past. The piece, Marimow hoped, would put both reporters on the air as they narrated in counterpoint the converging stories of victim and sniper. His sole instruction was that they take all the time required to do the job.

Jacki Lyden's end run around Loren Jenkins would have generated problems even in the best of times. By sending her to Baghdad, Bill Marimow was trespassing on the foreign editor's fiefdom, and he knew it. As Marimow subsequently conceded, "He wanted to have his empire." For Jenkins's part, he regarded Marimow, despite the new NPR editor's sterling reputation, as naive about international news. Most of the foreign staff felt the same. "He is a provincial man," recalled Sylvia Poggioli, adding that he lacked the expertise to direct reporters in a war zone.

Lyden arrived in Iraq to start reporting the Salihee story at the end of February 2006, just as the deadly conflict roiling the country took another terrible turn. On February 22, Sunni insurgents bombed the Golden Shrine, a mosque sacred to the Shia in Samarra, sixty-five miles north of Baghdad. In its aftermath Anne Garrels and Jamie Tarabay were overwhelmed by the task of merely getting out the story.

"Yesterday's bombing has brought Iraq closer than ever to outright civil war," Garrels reported the next day on *Morning Edition*. "Shiites, including grown men, wept, calling on God for help. Followers of Muqtada al Sadr blamed the United States forces. There were calls for retaliation." She ended her dispatch with terrifying news for any reporter. "Today, the bodies of three Iraqi journalists were found near Samarra. They were reportedly killed as they tried to reach the shrine."

Into this moment burst Lyden lugging her outsize project and trailing a tangle of internecine NPR rivalries and resentments. Those rivalries and resentments became apparent immediately. In a move that infuriated Garrels, Lyden refused to reveal the exact nature of her assignment—even though everyone back in Washington seemed to know. "I had been instructed by Marimow not to tell Garrels what the story was about," she recalled, adding that her editor believed that if the established Baghdad reporter got wind of the piece's scope, she might try to scuttle it. In turn, Garrels refused to allow Lyden to work in the network bureau, contending that the newcomer would present a distraction. "I stayed at a room at the Mansour Melia Hotel during the day," Lyden said. In what amounted to an auxiliary bureau, she conducted interviews, pored over evidence, and conferred with members of Salihee's family. The permanent staff made just one concession: Lyden could eat her meals and sleep at their relatively secure digs adjacent to ABC.

From the outset Garrels and Lyden were in a standoff in the world's most dangerous city, and the relationship got only worse. When Garrels learned that Lyden was looking into the death of Yasser Salihee, she was aghast. She was familiar with the incident and felt it was unworthy of exploration. "It was not a story," Garrels said later. Tragic as the shooting was, she believed that the facts were clear. "A translator had run a checkpoint and been killed." The only explanation she could imagine for Lyden's interest was that she had an agenda. "She was trying to go after the military." She had come to Iraq not to investigate but to prosecute, and she had hornswoggled NPR into footing the bill.

According to Garrels, Lyden's Baghdad gambit posed a safety risk to the bureau. Lyden did not know what she was getting into when it came to dealing with Iraqi coworkers. While the longtime Baghdad correspondent valued the efforts of NPR's native staffers, she maintained a healthy wariness. So much about them and their world was impenetrable. Over the years, there had been many culture clashes. Some had been borderline humorous, as when Garrels learned that Iraqi translators were using their NPR computers to download hardcore porn. (One married translator tormented his single colleagues by boasting of "Flying and landing," a euphemism for orgasm.) How to put a stop to the practice? Garrels went to Phil Reeves, who suggested a simple but ingenious fix. The translators sat with their monitors facing inward. "I turned the screens outward," Reeves recalled. No more porn. Still, the chasm between the Americans and the Iraqis was vast, and in some cases volatile. On so vital an issue as religious identification, for instance, native staffers frequently obfuscated. Asked if they were Sunni or Shia, they would reply, "Sushi." In a society sundered by sectarian violence, the response was unnerving. Just one driver with a jihadist friend or one translator hostile to the American press could expose the operation to terrorist attack. The only protection was vigilance, but Garrels said Lyden was oblivious.

Garrels tried to institute some ground rules for Lyden's stay in Baghdad. "I did ask her to tell us who her translators and drivers were and if we could help hire them." The reaction was a curt no. "She blew us off."

Garrels viewed this response as unacceptable. Each morning when Lyden departed for the Mansour Melia and each evening when she returned, unvetted Iraqi drivers accompanied her. "One of the people she hired found out a lot about the bureau," recalled Garrels. "He found out a lot about our staff." The consequence, she said later, was increased exposure. To Lyden, Garrels's concerns were overblown. She seemed like someone stubbornly unwilling to relinquish control.

The tensions erupted on the evening of March 3. Anne Garrels was deep into a bottle of red wine after another day of covering Iraq's madness ("Dozens of Corpses, Hands Bound, Found in Baghdad" would be the headline for her next *All Things Considered* piece). Just before dinner everything came gushing out. "She began insulting me," Lyden recalled. "She said that she was a war correspondent and that I was a war tourist." After a back-and-forth, emotions grew even nastier. "She had a glass of red wine, which she drank from and brandished at me," said Lyden. "Did she throw it at me? I was fixated on the idea that she might or was about to do so. Maybe she just dropped it." Regardless, the wine was now on Lyden.

The entire Baghdad staff, Jamie Tarabay included, witnessed the encounter, which ended with Lyden rushing upstairs to her room without eating dinner. The next morning Garrels left town for an assignment in southern Iraq. Lyden never saw her again, not that she remained silent. She was on the phone with McChesney and others at NPR every chance she got. "It was abhorrent—so embarrassing, so repulsive." For the first time, network executives back in Washington knew there was a problem in the Iraq bureau— not that anyone did anything about it. "Anne was an alcoholic, and Loren Jenkins wouldn't deal with it," Deborah Amos later said. "It was in my view management malfeasance."

The thing about fly-by-nights is that they eventually fly away. Her reporting on the Yasser Salihee story completed, Jacki Lyden returned to the States. As for Anne Garrels and the others in NPR's Baghdad bureau, the parade of deadly news intensified. By the spring of 2006, Garrels was starting each morning not with a call to an American officer or Iraqi politician but by phoning the Baghdad morgue. As she told listeners to *All Things Considered* on March 26, her purpose was to learn "how many unidentified bodies [had] been dumped in the city" the previous day. "With this new wave of sectarian violence, anyone can be a target." Shiites, chiefly members of Muqtada al-Sadr's Mahdi Army, were killing Sunnis. Sunnis, many of them participants in the fighting in Fallujah, were killing Shiites. Americans were killing Sunnis and Shiites. "Thirty bodies were found north of Baghdad," the correspondent ended that late-March story. "Most were beheaded. We don't know why that happened." For security, the time had again come for the network to relocate its Iraq operations.

If safety is found in numbers, NPR found it in its latest Baghdad bureau. Located in what had once been a handsome home not far from the Green Zone on a block entered through a checkpoint, it was surrounded by the Iraq headquarters of various other American news operations. CNN was around the corner, CBS across the street. Down the way was Fox News. Rupert Murdoch's local outpost was a fortress—high walls and a guard tower manned by private security guards toting AK-47s. Whenever Eric Westervelt gave it a look, he shook his head and in a mixture of disgust and awe muttered, "Fox fucking News." Even in a war zone, the network was a bully, but as the NPR staff and others working in what came to be called Media City conceded, it was their bully. As Garrels later said, "We couldn't afford security, so we were piggybacking off them." Not everyone in Washington approved.

"You can't do a deal with Fox," Loren Jenkins cautioned his top correspondent.

"We don't have any choice," she replied, reminding the foreign editor that while public radio now footed the bill for a few rent-a-cops and an armored BMW, it wasn't about to pony up for the big guns.

NPR's latest home was comfortable and spacious. The first floor consisted of a kitchen and dining area and two large, open chambers. One was surrounded by windows and served as the newsroom. The other, decorated with inlaid furniture left behind by the owners, belonged to the translators. Upstairs, several bedrooms clustered around a lone bath. There was also a master suite outfitted with a private bath, an untold luxury in what was otherwise communal living. Outside, a pleasant yard set off by rosebushes provided grounds for staff badminton games and even a weight-lifting station.

The new bailiwick was an improvement, but upon occupying it, NPR's Baghdad staff picked right back up with the bickering. As Renee Montagne later put it, "There was a fight over Anne's room."

Before settling into the Media City compound, the thinking had been that Garrels, by this juncture four years into her Iraq tenure, had dibs on the master suite. Tarabay, the bureau chief, pulled rank.

"I want this room," she told the older reporter.

Garrels was taken aback, but she acquiesced. Her thinking, she said later, was that "it was such a dreadful moment of violence" in Iraq that it wasn't worth fighting about accommodations. So Tarabay moved in, whereupon the matter went from bad to absurd. "Jamie spent the night in the room," the veteran reporter recalled, "and decided she didn't like it—it was noisy. She made me move in. Jamie behaved like an absolute child."

In truth, Tarabay didn't care what room she occupied. The job in Iraq had become too much—she wanted out. "You're on this treadmill for weeks at a time in a stressful environment," she said, thinking back on it all. Prior to accepting the assignment, she'd given her mother power of attorney to make negotiations easier if she were taken hostage. As for the danger and the grind, she'd tried to establish a schedule that would enable her to stand up to it. For a while, she'd spend down time in Cairo. Later she rented an apartment in Paris. But no sooner had she gotten her hair done and enjoyed a few meals at good restaurants than she was due back—to the fear, the claustrophobia, and to Garrels. It was better to transfer to the national desk in Washington, where she was assigned to cover Islam in America, then the mid-Atlantic states.

In the aftermath of Jamie Tarabay's leave-taking, Anne Garrels's position in Baghdad stabilized. Not only was she happy that the young bureau chief was gone, but events at NPR headquarters were breaking in such a way as to secure Loren Jenkins's control over the foreign desk. For better and worse his favorite correspondent could carry on as always.

The piece that had brought Jacki Lyden to Baghdad, while not a disaster, was a disappointment. It did not justify the disruption it had caused in the bureau or the funds involved. "Anatomy of a Shooting"—derisively christened the $120,000 story by NPR wags who'd added up the salaries and expenses that went into producing it—aired June 23, 2006, on *All Things Considered*. Clocking in at twenty-two minutes, thirty-six seconds, it made excellent use of both Lyden's voice and that of John McChesney and featured some powerful moments. Eyewitnesses asserted that the sniper, Joe Romero, gave insufficient warning to Yasser Salihee before firing. An American officer admitted that GIs made everything worse by failing to remove the victim's body from his car, leaving it for his family to find. But ultimately, the piece bogged down in equivocations and quibbles. Beyond a spokesman's concession that the military needed "to recalibrate the rules of engagement" between coalition troops and Iraqi civilians, "Anatomy of a Shooting" offered few revelations and little insight. The best you could say about it was that it was worthy.

Neither Lyden nor McChesney suffered any repercussions for the $120,000 story, but the assigning editor would not get off so easily. Garrels

and Jenkins had not forgotten what they perceived as Bill Marimow's disregard for the foreign desk's chain of command during the reporting of the
piece. By coincidence, both wound up at a dinner with Marimow—who'd
just been elevated to the position of vice president of news—within weeks
of its airdate. The location was Beirut, and the occasion was a Jenkins-
sponsored fly-in for the reporters and producers who staffed NPR's Middle
Eastern bureaus. Over drinks and food, those assembled intended to discuss
how to improve their Iraq coverage while unwinding, but no sooner had the
roughly twenty attendees arrived and the wine begun to flow than Garrels,
in Marimow words, "assailed me about Jacki Lyden." Soon enough the two
were screaming at each other. Before it could get worse, recalled Tom Bullock, "Loren stepped in and quashed it." Yet while the foreign editor played
peacemaker that night, there was no doubt that Garrels was speaking for
him. As John McChesney later noted, Jenkins had "decided that Marimow
should not be a vice president and that he should go."

Had the $120,000 story been Marimow's sole misstep, Jenkins would
have found it difficult to marshal NPR executives to help oust him. But
by 2006, two years into his tenure, Marimow had repeatedly made errors
elsewhere. His biggest was that he failed to adapt to the network culture.
No matter how far NPR had come, it was on some level still college radio,
and executives bought into a collectivist mentality. Although Marimow
understood such thinking, he couldn't bring himself to endorse it. "I gathered pretty quickly that there was a bureaucratic atmosphere at NPR where
things were done by consensus, and committees approved things," he said
later. "My belief is that while consensus is good, great journalism is better."
Marimow's standards were to be lauded, but his disdain for the network's
way of doing business—not to mention social niceties—hurt him. "Bill didn't
play well with others at the management level," recalled Lyden. "He tended
to view the programs as printing presses," McChesney added. "His attitude
was, 'We'll do the pieces. You put 'em on the air.' "

In fairness to Marimow, many of the complaints about him sprang from
NPR's resistance to change. Much of what he was proposing for the network
was in its best interest. He believed that reporters should prize quality over
quantity. He preached that one good story mattered more than several mediocre ones. The organization preached productivity. Recalled Alex Chadwick,

"Bill told a reporter going out to do an interview, 'Don't take your tape recorder. Just have lunch. Develop a source.' This was blasphemy at NPR."

The problem was that Marimow was bullheaded, and over time many at NPR began to suspect that he always had been. The view was reinforced by a character based on Marimow in the HBO drama *The Wire*, which is set in Baltimore. According to the show's producer, David Simon, a former *Baltimore Sun* reporter, his ex-boss was "tone deaf and prize hungry and . . . interested in self-aggrandizement." He gave these same traits to the series' fictional newspaper editor Thomas Klebanow. When she watched *The Wire*," Deborah Amos recalled thinking, "Oh, God, Marimow would say those things in the NPR newsroom."

In August 2006, shortly after Klose, Marimow's initial champion at NPR, was named network chairman (which removed him from day-to-day operations), Jenkins and several others made their move. "They went after him in the most vicious way I've ever seen," recalled McChesney. "I said, 'You know, Bill, they're trying to kill you,'" adding that if he did not fight back he was "'going to go down.'" Marimow disdained office intrigue and refused to get involved. The upshot was that five of his fellow vice presidents signed a letter of no confidence in him. The most powerful of the signatories was NPR's vice president of programming, Jay Kernis, who two years earlier had defenestrated Bob Edwards and was now given the task of shoving aside another protégé.

"Jay gave me a review of my performance, and it was the most abysmal performance review you could imagine," Marimow said later. "Management, leadership, journalism, work ethic—it was F, F, F, F." According to Kernis, the judgment wasn't quite that bad. Most of the failings, as the programming chief saw them, fell under the heading: Doesn't work well with others, and not just those in the NPR brass. "I needed someone who'd pay attention to the stations. I needed someone who'd pay attention to the news directors. He didn't feel he needed to pay attention to them." As a sop, Kernis offered the one-time *Baltimore Sun* editor and two-time Pulitzer winner a position that usually goes to journalists whose futures are behind them: network ombudsman. Marimow did the job for a few weeks. The *Philadelphia Inquirer* then offered him its top spot, and he took it.

For Loren Jenkins, this was a victory. On the surface, it was also one for Anne Garrels. Meddling would now be difficult, but simultaneously she would be ever more isolated, working solely for a man who viewed her through a narrow lens. As the longtime NPR Pentagon reporter Tom Gjelten later put it, Jenkins saw "Anne as a macho woman reporter." He was blind to what others cycling in an out of Baghdad saw. "She needed therapy," Amos recalled, "but she didn't get it. Loren wouldn't hear of it. He was old-fashioned." Said Jacki Lyden, "You had two people who didn't play by the rules and egged each other on."

Life in NPR's Baghdad bureau returned to something approaching normal. In January 2007, George W. Bush used a televised address to introduce "the new way forward," or what would soon be known as "the surge." By June, 20,000 fresh US troops were in Iraq, bringing the total to more than 150,000. This massive deployment, under the command of General David Petraeus, the recently appointed chief of the joint occupying forces, largely succeeded in decreasing the violence in the country. As Eric Westervelt reported on *All Things Considered* in November, the monthly civilian death toll in Baghdad had dropped from 2,000 in January to 317 in October.

As the streets of Iraq's capital quieted (a mother pushing her young son on a park swing told Westervelt, "Before we couldn't even go out our front doors or visit our relatives"), tensions inside NPR's Media City compound subsided as well. Although Tom Bullock returned to America to get married, his replacement was an equally sure hand. At thirty-four, J. J. Sutherland was a ten-year public radio veteran and a legacy hire (his cousin was Neal Conan) who'd handled a number of tough jobs at the network, among them one as founding producer of *Day to Day*. A one-hour NPR newsmagazine fronted by Alex Chadwick and Madeleine Brand and coproduced by *Slate*, the show was launched in 2003 from Culver City, California. Sutherland was "good at keeping a level head when shit goes down," Westervelt said later.

Then there was Garrels. Again, she was filing story after memorable story. For the June 11 edition of *Morning Edition*, she interviewed a pony-tailed, would-be Iraqi suicide bomber who throughout their conversation wore "a homemade suicide vest under his tunic." Abu Abdul Rahman, as he called himself, did not allow the reporter to tape him, but he didn't hold much back, describing his conversion to radical Islam, his affiliation with the newly emergent Al-Qaeda in Iraq, and his ultimate intentions. "Abu Abdul says he will one day blow himself up to kill what he calls infidels. He says he will surrender his soul for the sake of praising God's word. He has already planned how he will do it. He will pose as a woman disguised by a black robe." For the August 6 edition of *All Things Considered,* she reported that despite Petraeus's success in improving security in Baghdad, life remained precarious. "No one trusts anyone."

Garrels produced sixty-four major pieces in 2007. Yet despite having re-emerged as the Baghdad bureau's most prolific reporter, she for the first time began experiencing rough patches. For an October 26 *Morning Edition* story exploring the possibility that Iranian saboteurs were infiltrating Baghdad to sow suspicion between Shia and Sunni factions, Garrels interviewed three prisoners who had been tortured by Muqtada al-Sadr's forces. "There was blood all over their clothes," she reported. "They were in such bad shape that they couldn't walk. They had to be dragged onto chairs, and one of them was just sobbing." By soliciting information from tortured sources, she had entered ethically murky territory, but she pressed ahead, believing that the men might reveal important facts. They did. "They said they went into a con-tested area of Baghdad, pretended they were Sunnis, raped a Shiite girl, and the result was stepped up attacks on Sunnis." This reporting was news, but negative reaction was swift, as critics accused Garrels of being no better than the guards at Abu Ghraib. Even NPR's newly appointed ombudsman, Alicia Shepard, criticized the reporter, accusing her of bad journalistic practice: "Evidence obtained through torture is not credible." In a lengthy follow-up, Garrels defended her actions, asserting that she'd independently verified the information. Then, with the hard-won wisdom of someone who wasn't going to avert her eyes just to satisfy the ACLU crowd, she said that to have shied away from the interviews would have been worse. "If we act like that, then we will ignore the reality of the world."

Garrels's decision to interview tortured captives could be argued either way, but not so some of her other choices during late 2007. The drinking had at last started to take a toll on her work. "I remember a newscast," she said later, where "I had had some wine. Something suddenly happened, and I had to do a spot report. The news editor said, 'I'm not sure you should be doing this.'" The segment required several takes.

On other occasions, Garrels was unable to sober up sufficiently to do broadcast-quality work. "I remember a two-way with Anne where her speech was slurred," recalled Robert Siegel. "She'd clearly been drinking." Although the *All Things Considered* host went ahead and finished the conversation with the Baghdad reporter, the show's producer canned it. "We didn't use it," Siegel said later.

After five years of the most brutal reporting imaginable, Garrels was cracking, and she was alone. "You were stuck in the house," she recalled. "Most of the people there were younger than I. The only thing to do was smoke"—and drink. "I was drinking way too much. I was a wreck."

Despite it all, Garrels never seriously considered putting in for a transfer back to NPR's Washington headquarters—even if some tried to convince her to do so. When he left, Tom Bullock begged her to follow. "I asked Anne to think about doing the same," he said later. "I started seeing what the war was doing" to her. "There was no respite. Burnout was easy." But the veteran reporter demurred. Publicly, she advanced a stock rationale. "We didn't have much of a bench." Then there was Jenkins's hesitancy to intervene. "Drunk or sober, Anne Garrels knew her beat," he said later. "She knew how to function. She was the best. You have to look at a correspondent's totality over a long haul." But even had the foreign editor tried to bring his star reporter home, he would have encountered resistance, and the reasons weren't easily dismissed. Notwithstanding Jamie Tarabay's many disagreements with Garrels, she appreciated her dilemma. "Look at any woman of her generation," Tarabay observed. "It was difficult for females in a newsroom. Anne had to fight for everything she got." Baghdad was where the fight had taken her.

During the early weeks of 2008, the demand for stories out of Iraq did not relent, and Anne Garrels filed constantly. An increase in US bombing strikes on Al-Qaida hideouts, the decision by the government in Baghdad to allow once banned members of Saddam's Baath Party to seek jobs in the bureaucracy, a growing awareness among coalition leaders that Iraqi forces were not yet well-enough trained to take over security duties in the embattled country—Garrels churned out solid pieces on all these topics. She also found time to produce a superb feature about the city of Najaf's massive Valley of Peace cemetery, which she entered rolled up in a Persian rug to avoid detection by Shia militia. Her descriptions of the "towers of sand-colored brick" that marked the graves of the millions interred there and her interviews with body washers and grave diggers brought a mythic place of death to life. Few could maintain such a pace, and following the reassignment of several rotation standbys (Phil Reeves to Pakistan, Ivan Watson to Iran, Deborah Amos to Syria), fulltime reinforcements arrived.

In February, Lourdes Garcia-Navarro assumed the job of NPR's Baghdad bureau chief with Loren Jenkins's enthusiastic endorsement. He had brought her to the network after falling in love with her work. "I had an opening in Mexico City," he recalled. "There were a lot of candidates for the job already there. But I kept hearing from this persistent woman in Cairo. The night before I flew to Mexico City for interviews, I got a CD of a piece this woman had done about going to Cuba to find her ancestors—she's half-Cuban, half-Panamanian, raised in Florida. It was like, 'Wow!'" The piece was that good. "I still had to go to Mexico City, but I decided on the spot I'm going to hire her."

Garcia-Navarro, in her early thirties when she joined NPR, was both a confident on-air presence and an experienced reporter. She had worked at the BBC and also done a turn at the AP, covering Baghdad during the run-up to the American aerial assault. Since joining NPR, she'd covered Mexico (drug cartels, Hurricane Wilma), Latin America, and the Caribbean, reporting on everything from violence-plagued elections in Guatemala to the fading health of Fidel Castro. In 2005, she'd made a temporary return to Iraq when the network experienced one of its recurring personnel shortages.

On the surface, Lulu Garcia-Navarro, as she was generally known, and Anne Garrels should have formed a strong tandem. But Jamie Tarabay, who'd worked with Navarro at the AP and was a friend, had warned her former colleague that there was trouble in NPR's Media City compound and Garrels was its source. The new bureau chief arrived in Baghdad prepared for a confrontation. Meantime her counterpart nursed her own preconceptions. "Lulu was jealous of me," Garrels said later. "I'd stayed during the bombing of Baghdad, and she felt I'd made my name that way. I was the taste of the week. I think that lingered."

Garrels and Garcia-Navarro started off each expecting the worst, and both found what they were seeking. To Garcia-Navarro, Garrels was testy and unwelcoming. "There was a lot of tension between her and me," recalled Garcia-Navarro. "It was a nightmare for her," added Amos. To Garrels, Garcia-Navarro was another fly-by-night. "She didn't care about the bureau or the staff," she said later. What she cared about was career advancement.

While the quality of the work coming out of NPR's Baghdad bureau remained superb, the two principal reporters were at cross-purposes. For one, they possessed conflicting ideas of how to do the job. "Both are strong women but with different approaches," Barbara Rehm, NPR's then assistant foreign editor, recalled. "Anne goes into a story no holds barred. Lulu thinks: 'Is the best entry from this side or that?'" Quite apart from the philosophical disagreements, however, the two just clashed personally. As they sat at their computers writing, Garrels said that Garcia-Navarro often sang softly to herself. "La, la, la, la, la." Added Garrels, "She really knew how to skewer me." Garcia-Navarro denied goading Garrels. Quite to the contrary, she asserted, Garrels goaded her. "I admit," Garrels later conceded, "I was crazy."

Had J. J. Sutherland still been on the job as Baghdad production chief, he could have brokered a truce, but like Tom Bullock before him, he had given way to a replacement. Just twenty-six years old, Jack Zahora was a public radio archetype—an acolyte to its ideals and standards. An international affairs graduate of George Washington University, he'd done a bit of everything since joining the network. He'd assisted Daniel Zwerdling on a series of stories. He'd worked the graveyard shift on *Morning Edition*. He'd schlepped for Scott Simon at *Weekend Edition*. All the while, he never earned a full salary. He was what's known at NPR as a "perma-temp," the kind of faithful striver who'd likely have done the job gratis. He believed that if you kept putting yourself out there, good things happened, and they did when Loren Jenkins brought him onto the foreign desk. Giving such a young journalist control of the Iraq bureau was a risk. It was "not the best thing," Tarabay said later. Added Renee Montagne, "Jack is a nice guy, also smart and caring. However, he might have been out of his element dealing with" someone like Garrels.

Not long after Jack Zahora arrived at NPR's Media City compound, Loren Jenkins hosted another of his periodic correspondents' fly-ins, this one in Istanbul. Anne Garrels, Lulu Garcia-Navarro, and most of the reporters in the network's regular Baghdad rotation attended. Vint Lawrence, Garrels's husband, also came. He and Jenkins were both old southeast Asia hands (Lawrence from his days with the CIA, the foreign editor from his tenure as *Newsweek*'s Saigon bureau chief), and they relished each other's company. But Garrels's husband had not traveled to Turkey just to swap war stories with a friend. He was worried about his wife. "It was clear to him that I shouldn't go back," she recalled. The danger, the anxiety, the drinking, and now the clashes with Garcia-Navarro had shaken her. Although she kept up a cheerful facade during the public parts of the gathering, in private she was distraught. "I basically broke down in front of Vint," she said later. "I cried. I lost it. I was damaged goods." Lawrence was frightened. He'd never seen his wife so rattled, but while he voiced his concerns, he did not presume to tell her what to do. "Vint couldn't get in my face," she said. "We didn't have children." Reporting was Garrels's life, and much as she loved their Connecticut estate with its chocolate Labs and flowers and sunshine days, she could not go home until she had proved some unprovable thing. "I'd tell Vint I was OK," she recalled, "but I wasn't OK."

Back in Baghdad, yet another new correspondent had joined NPR's rotation. By Anne Garrels's definition, Dina Temple-Raston was the quintessential fly-by-night, someone who saw the Iraq posting solely as a vehicle for professional gain. That was only a partial view. Unlike Jacki Lyden or Lulu Garcia-Navarro, Temple-Raston not only knew what she wanted, but she knew what Garrels had to lose. As she would later state: "We were two established journalists, one who was in the sunset of her career—and one who certainly wasn't."

The forty-two-year-old Temple-Raston was new to NPR, having started a mere eleven months earlier following many years in print (Bloomberg, the *New York Sun, USA Today*, and a couple of nonfiction books). Along the way, she had enrolled at the Columbia University School of Journalism, specializing in broadcast news and earning an MA. One of her teachers was the former NPR foreign editor John Dinges.

On April 16, 2007, as Temple-Raston was still getting acclimated at NPR's Washington studios ("They wanted to teach me how to use all the equipment"), a twenty-three-year-old Korean American named Seung-Hui

Cho shot to death thirty-two of his Virginia Tech classmates before turning a semiautomatic pistol on himself. Temple-Raston ditched her orientation sessions to watch the early TV accounts. Before joining the network, she'd written *The Jihad Next Door*, a book about the Lackawanna Six, a group of young Yemeni Americans from the Buffalo, New York, suburbs who'd attended an Al-Qaida training camp in Afghanistan before 9/11. While reporting the project, Temple-Raston, in her words, entered the names of "hundreds and hundreds of FBI agents in my Rolodex." The FBI agent in charge of the mass-shooting investigation was among those she'd met while working on her book. She called him, and he gave her information she hadn't heard on TV. She then emailed David Sweeney, the network's managing editor, telling him, "I know *this* is being reported, but a source *told* me . . . " Following a few exchanges, Sweeney asked her to go live on that afternoon's *Talk of the Nation*. "That's how I hit the scene," she recalled. "Boom. I remember being on every single show for like five days."

Temple-Raston wove a narrative of what was happening at Virginia Tech, most of it told from the point of view of the FBI. Nearly all of her accounts included the phrase: "According to sources I talked to." Unlike typical NPR pieces, which are detached and lack dramatic structure, hers were emotional and suspenseful. "Nobody thought of covering this story that way," she asserted.

In the sedate universe of NPR, Temple-Raston was a sensation, although some at the network expressed reservations. For one, they believed she did not present enough alternatives to the official version. "Dina relied on one or two sources from the FBI," Robert Siegel noted. "It was thin." Others were bothered by her abrasiveness. "She was hard to deal with on a personal basis," Tom Gjelten recalled. (Such observations weren't new. John Dinges, Temple-Raston's Columbia professor, later said. "She's full of herself. It's a lot of all about me.") Temple-Raston made no apologies. "I'm sure you know NPR doesn't break a lot of news," she observed. "I came to NPR to break news."

Temple-Raston became NPR's FBI correspondent, and she continued to dig out scoops, among them one about the bureau's investigation into the Blackwater security agency's involvement in a September 2007 shootout in downtown Baghdad that left seventeen civilians dead. The assignment got her thinking about going to Iraq. Although she was attached to the network's national desk, she knew that Loren Jenkins was having a hard time finding people to send to the conflict zone. Despite the fact that she, like Lyden, would not answer to him, the foreign editor gave Temple-Raston the nod. By March 2008, she was in the Media City bureau.

Temple-Raston had heard that Anne Garrels resented female colleagues and was a drunk. Jamie Tarabay had told her what she'd told Garcia-Navarro. Temple-Raston's response was to express confidence that she and the senior Baghdad reporter would work well together. "I don't think Anne will have a problem with me, because I'm not a young woman," Tarabay recalled Temple-Raston saying. "She might respect me more because I'm her age." Tarabay didn't quite buy it. Not only were the two actually of different generations (Garrels was fourteen years Temple-Raston's senior), but neither was known for being conciliatory.

There was also another matter. Temple-Raston was no fan of Garrels's work. The pieces about the human face of the Iraq war that Garrels prided herself on struck Temple-Raston as beside the point, and she'd said so in print. While at the *New York Sun*, she'd given *Naked in Baghdad* a negative review. Although she conceded that "Ms. Garrels's account works well as a personal memoir," she nailed her for lack of geopolitical sophistication. "For those readers looking for Ms. Garrels to make sense of the war and reflect on the larger messages it provided," she declared, "the book will sadly disappoint."

Unaware of this relevant history, NPR's editors had given Temple-Raston an opportunity to school Garrels. While she was at it, she also had an opportunity to rein in the older reporter. "I was in a unique position to be able to make sure that things that had been going on wouldn't go on any longer," she later said, adding. "I was an adult, I wasn't a twenty-year-old," a reference to Jack Zahora, the bureau's young producer. "I could say, 'This has to stop.'"

The flash point, as it had in part been with Jacki Lyden, was security at the Baghdad bureau, but unlike in that first incident, the question was not who got into the compound but who went out. Since moving to Media City in 2006, the network's correspondents had adhered to a basic rule: they did not accompany Iraqi producers or translators into the field. To travel as a mixed team was too dangerous, as it would expose everyone to kidnapping or worse by any of the parties vying for control of the country. Instead, native staffers, after receiving their orders from Western colleagues, did all the shoe-leather journalism. They could move about the streets, conducting interviews and covering everything from public events to car bombings. They then brought their raw tape back to the bureau, where the correspondents shaped the stories and wrote and recorded narrations. Nobody liked the practice. It was cumbersome. But everyone abided by it. Until one didn't.

Temple-Raston, in what several coworkers concluded was both a bid to make her work stand out and a challenge to Garrels's sway over the operation, launched her Baghdad reporting career by ignoring the protocol.

To anyone listening to *Morning Edition* on March 11, 2008, the story that kicked off the firestorm seemed innocuous. Headlined "Iraq Women Face Risks Behind the Wheel," Temple-Raston's five-minute, seventeen-second piece zeroed in on a school bus operator named Azhar Abbas. "She has long, wild red hair and is partial to tight-fitting, leopard-skin tops," the reporter noted before addressing the dangers females faced on the roads, chiefly arrest by Islamic authorities enforcing laws against showing too much skin. That Temple-Raston was able to gather terrific quotes ("To get gas, I have to wear a headscarf"), and atmosphere (honking horns, laughing children) was because she jeopardized herself and her Iraqi colleagues.

Once the story aired, NPR's Iraqi staffers complained to Garrels. "The staff was worried because they were being exposed," the veteran correspondent recalled. When she presented these objections to Temple-Raston, the two butted heads. Although the merits of the matter seemed obvious, Garrels was now so regularly drunk that it was difficult to take her point seriously. She was also unduly harsh. "I don't suffer fools," she said later. "It enrages me when people take advantage," which she believed had happened. Not surprisingly, Temple-Raston refused to concede anything. Confrontations between the two began. "There were many clashes," Temple-Raston recalled. "She was quite arrogant," Garrels countered.

As during previous dustups, NPR's Baghdad operation avoided collapse into dysfunction by covering the news, and as March drew to an end, there was a lot of it. Conflict between Iraq prime minister Nouri al-Maliki, a Shia, and Muqtada al-Sadr's all-Shia Mahdi Army threatened to undo the gains David Petraeus had achieved during the surge. On the March 27 edition of

Morning Edition, Garcia-Navarro, speaking from the network's Media City compound, reported that nowhere was safe. "We've heard shooting and rocket fire and mortar rounds from the early morning here." On that evening's *All Things Considered*, Garrels related a more foreboding development. "Tens of thousands of young men, many carrying weapons, marched through Baghdad's Sadr City, the stronghold for anti-American cleric Sadr. 'We will fight whoever attacks the Mahdi Army,' they chanted." Even the day's lone feature story, the second part of a Temple-Raston series on efforts to rebuild Iraq's judicial system (told over the shoulder of the FBI agent advising local officials), was dark: "There are about 1,200 judges in all of Iraq. Three dozen of them have been murdered since 2003."

As night fell in Baghdad on the twenty-seventh, the Iraqi government imposed an indefinite curfew, and the US State Department ordered its personnel to shelter in reinforced structures. The NPR bureau was on lockdown, its staff fated to wait it out together for who knew how long.

The infighting started almost immediately and continued for several days. Anne Garrels and Dina Temple-Raston were the principal combatants, but Lulu Garcia-Navarro frequently jumped in. "It was an insane situation," Garcia-Navarro recalled. The recurring issue was Temple-Raston's alleged violation of safety procedures at the Baghdad bureau, but specifics soon vanished and the confrontation became a free-for-all. Due to the curfew, there was no escaping the ugliness, and because now not even Iraqi staffers could venture out, work no longer provided a distraction. There was nothing to do but argue or, more precisely, scream.

Garrels went after Temple-Raston relentlessly. "I was really pissed off at her," Garrels said later. "She felt like she could do whatever she wanted to." Soon Temple-Raston had heard enough, and she dispensed with the bureau's "what happens in Baghdad stays in Baghdad" oath, emailing Loren Jenkins to complain that his pet reporter was tormenting her and disrupting the operation. The foreign editor, rather than call Garcia-Navarro or Zahora to learn for himself what was occurring, forwarded Temple-Raston's email to Garrels with the question: "What the hell is this about?" It was on.

The evening of March 29 had fallen on Baghdad. With Garcia-Navarro, Zahora, and several Iraqi staffers assembled in the bureau newsroom,

Garrels proceeded to suffer what Temple-Raston later termed "a nervous breakdown." It began with Garrels calling Temple-Raston a "cunt." After that there was no holding back. When asked later if Garrels spat at her, Temple-Raston replied, "Talk to Anne." Garrels, however, could not recall. "That night is a blur, but I may have been spitting mad." According to Garcia-Navarro, it happened. "Anne spit at Dina," she said. "Her teeth were black with red wine, her hair disheveled. She was feral."

The exchange stunned those who witnessed it. No one could speak, which Garrels said was typical. "Jack was sweet but useless, and Lulu probably relished it." Eventually, Garrels fled upstairs to her room, where she drank and fumed and formulated a plan so ill advised as to cast doubt on her sanity. She was departing Baghdad immediately, even if she had to walk the nearly fifteen miles to the airport. In light of the renewed hostilities in Iraq, this was a suicide mission. Security experts believed that an unarmed Westerner on the streets would be killed in minutes. But Garrels was desperate. "I felt cornered," she said later.

As Garrels was packing, she experienced a pang of remorse about abandoning NPR's Baghdad operation. She had done much to build it, and there was much still to do. This emotion gave way to one of those ill-conceived ideas that sometimes occur during a bender. The reporter phoned Colonel Steven Boylan, who'd been promoted to chief spokesman for David Petraeus. He was in Washington preparing the general to testify before the Senate Armed Services Committee about the deteriorating conditions in Iraq. But he respected Garrels, and even though it was seven a.m. his time and he was busy, he took her call, hearing her out as she put in a word for, of all people, Garcia-Navarro. "I had issues with Lulu to put it mildly," Garrels said later, "but I was fighting for her. She was doing good work and being stymied" by the military bureaucracy. While that may have been so, Garrels was also trying to exercise her authority one last time. But because she was hammered, she didn't make sense. "She seemed distraught," recalled Boylan. "I could hear the stress in her voice."

During Garrels's conversation with Boylan, several of her colleagues passed by her room on the way to theirs. They could overhear that she was talking to Petraeus's press officer. To them she sounded incoherent. Worried that it was all spinning out of control, Jack Zahora picked up his own phone.

Loren Jenkins was not happy to hear from the Baghdad production chief at such an early hour, and he was even less happy to hear what Zahora had to say. To the news that Garrels was in duress and threatening to walk to the airport, the foreign editor replied, "I don't give a shit."

Jenkins did care—or he at least realized he now had a huge problem. After hanging up with Zahora, he called Eric Westervelt, who'd just become NPR's Jerusalem bureau chief.

"Gunny," Jenkins began, addressing Westervelt as if he were a noncommissioned officer, "I'm sorry to have woken you up, but Anne Garrels has blown a gasket. There's been a big fight, and she's threatening to walk to the airport. I need you to meet her in Amman and take her to dinner."

Westervelt considered Garrels a friend, and he told Jenkins he'd do what was needed, at which point Jenkins, with a characteristic disregard for political correctness, declared, "I'll never send three women into a combat zone again." To him the whole fracas had been a catfight.

Just after dawn Garrels appeared downstairs in the NPR bureau with her luggage. She'd given up her plan to walk to the airport, but her new plan was nearly as unwise—she'd go to a taxi stand and catch a cab. However ineffectual Zahora may have appeared in the past, he took charge, bundling the reporter into the network's armored BMW. Everyone gathered around. "We lined up, begging her not to do it," said Garcia-Navarro, aware that driving to the Baghdad airport was also dangerous. "I was crying: 'Please don't do it.'" Garrels was past reasoning. The Iraqi staffer at the wheel pulled out of Media City onto Damascus Street headed for the Qadisiya Expressway.

Although coalition forces had chopped down aisles of stately date palms that had once provided hiding places for insurgents along the route, attacks were still commonplace on the expressway. The shoulders were littered with the burned-out carcasses of vehicles that had been hit. NPR's car, which while armored was painted baby blue, presented an inviting target. During the thirty-minute trip, Garrels sprawled in the back seat, sobbing then posing the saddest question over and over: "Am I a bad person?"

This grim party soon exited safely onto Airport Road, pulling to a halt at a satellite lot. Garrels emerged from the car and without looking back boarded the shuttle bus that would ferry her to a Royal Jordanian flight. Afterward, she could not remember how she got to the airport or who drove her. Westervelt was waiting for her in Amman and took her to a Marriott, but she remained lost. "She was at her wit's end," he recalled. At least she was alive. A day later, she was back in the States.

Two months after her evacuation from Iraq—months during which she attended weekly therapy sessions—Anne Garrels met Ellen Weiss, Bill Marimow's replacement as vice president of NPR news, at the Connecticut property where she and Vint Lawrence lived. Garrels loved to show off the place, and as she and her visitor strolled the grounds, she held forth on its history. A century earlier, a group of wealthy Yankee capitalists that included Vint's great-grandfather Charles A. Coffin, the first president of General Electric, had bought the land. The Starling Childs mansion, the stately residence of Vint's uncle, stands at the center of several more modest homes, among them Vint and Anne's and those of other relatives. By far the most fascinating structure on the property is the stone, slate-tile-roofed Sports House. It contains not only an indoor basketball court (among the earliest such private courts in New England) but a rare fives court, where players can have a go at a form of handball that has all but petered out except at a few clubs in Great Britain.

After Garrels finished touring Weiss around the property, she invited her in. Although she had asked the news VP to come to Connecticut, Garrels was wary. She knew that she now presented a problem for NPR. Exacerbating Garrels's concern, Weiss had brought another emissary from the network. A former editor of *US News & World Report* who'd recently joined NPR, Brian Duffy had attended Jenkins's March correspondents' fly-in in Istanbul during which Garrels had contemplated not returning to Iraq. She did not know what Duffy knew of her difficulties, but she viewed him as an indication that NPR was building a case against her.

Garrels and Vint had prepared lunch, and once the group sat down, the reporter's worst fears were confirmed. "Ellen said I'd jeopardized people's welfare in Baghdad," Garrels said. "She concocted a story that I made them do something they didn't ordinarily do—take me to the airport." Skipping the fact that a citywide curfew had made the trip in question ill considered, the reporter added that at no point during the conversation did the network news vice president inquire into her emotional well-being.

According to Weiss, the talk preceded differently. "It was my responsibility to try to do what I think was responsible, which is to help someone focus on getting better," she said. During the lunch Weiss handed Garrels a document. Weiss maintained that the document offered the reporter a path to recovery. Garrels saw it as an ultimatum.

Like many major companies, NPR had contracted with a health-care provider to offer psychological counseling to employees. Weiss wanted Garrels to enroll. When the reporter, thinking her boss might not know she was already in therapy, said, "I'm getting help," she said that Weiss replied that if she did not participate in the chosen program, NPR would fire her. "They knew exactly what they were doing," Garrels asserted. ("Dina came back to Washington, and she went to Ellen and said, 'This woman is out of her fucking mind,'" John McChesney later said.) Believing she had no alternative, Garrels signed.

In keeping with what she asserted was a good-faith attempt to abide by NPR's wishes, Garrels made an appointment with a northwest Connecticut office of the network's provider. "They told me I had to stop seeing my own therapist," she recalled. "I could only be part of their program. But the problem was, they had no experience with PTSD—had never even heard of it, practically."

In 2008, few media executives or psychologists realized that war reporters often suffer from posttraumatic stress disorder. As a result, maintained NPR's Phil Reeves, "People played hurt." This was particularly true among members of the Baghdad press corps. "I didn't have a breakdown," said *The New Yorker*'s Jon Lee Anderson, who like Garrels was there from 2002 to 2008. "But the sheer murderousness of it was unlike anything I had experienced." Where his radio colleague numbed herself with alcohol, Anderson, despite his opposition to gun ownership, purchased a 9mm Glock to use if faced with being taken hostage. "The idea was to kill as many of them as possible then kill myself." Thinking back on the dangers he confronted, John F. Burns of the *New York Times*, who was also in Iraq throughout the war, said he returned saddled with a "state of self-reproach." He could not forgive himself for the chances he took.

Garrels caught a break when it came to her mental health. The director of the NPR-contracted facility in her area, realizing that no one at her clinic was qualified to treat someone afflicted with PTSD, allowed the correspondent to continue seeing her own therapist. "I was very lucky," Garrels recalled. "She let me do this without the network's knowledge."

When it came to her career, though, Garrels was in trouble. Loren Jenkins was now fighting for his own job and could no longer help. Weiss had determined that the foreign editor not only knew about his star correspondent's alcoholism and did nothing, but that his ill-advised decision to forward Dina Temple-Raston's email to Garrels was the match that sparked the ultimate conflagration. She suspended him for a week, and she was seeking grounds to fire him. "She called me trying to get me to complain about Loren," Gwen Thompkins, at the time NPR's East Africa correspondent, said later.

Meanwhile, Weiss rewarded Garrels's Baghdad antagonists. Several months after the set-to, she appointed Temple-Raston NPR's New York-based national security correspondent. "Dina got the job because of Anne," said Jacki Lyden. Added Margot Adler, who worked in the network's Manhattan bureau, "They gave it to her as payback." Lulu Garcia-Navarro was also getting ready to move up. She would replace Eric Westervelt in Jerusalem after he was named Berlin bureau chief. In an interview on *All Things Considered* to coincide with her new posting, Garcia-Navarro, in a reference to Garrels, said, "I've seen correspondents who've covered wars for a long time shut down. As long as I can engage and tell people stories the way they deserve to be told, I'll keep doing this."

After Garrels completed a few more months of therapy, she asked NPR to assign her to any of a number of international hot spots. She got nowhere. "It was clear they weren't going to send me anywhere or let me do anything," she recalled. Although Jenkins had held on to his job, he was in no position to assist, and when Garrels went to Kevin Klose, whose triumph with Joan Kroc would not have occurred without her, he refused to lend a hand. "He wouldn't give me the time of day." To which the network chairman responded, "It was difficult and painful, but stuff happens. Life moved on."

As a consolation, NPR made Garrels a roving foreign correspondent working mostly out of Russia, her first love. Because of her journalistic skill and many connections, she couldn't help but stumble across a few meaty stories. Reporting from Kiev in September 2008, she presciently told listeners to *Morning Edition*, "The European Union's failure to support Ukraine could encourage a resurgent Kremlin to believe the country is all alone and ripe for return to the Russian sphere of influence." By and large, she produced light features. The construction of the Olympic Village for the 2014 winter games in Sochi—she was on it. A resurgent Russian Orthodox monastery near Moscow—she had it covered. Her valedictory was a five-part, 2010 series about cruising the length of the Volga River. Describing the trip as "a gilded tour of gilded domes that also raised uncomfortable questions," she noted what had changed along the waterway ("the appearance of new mansions startles passengers") and what had not ("one thing that's untouched is Joseph Stalin's bunker").

With that, Anne Garrels's twenty-two-year career at NPR ended. Jenkins offered to throw a going-away party at the network's Washington headquarters, but the correspondent declined. "I retired by email," she said later. Back in Connecticut, she was soon diagnosed with lung cancer, which she survived, but as she was convalescing, Vint Lawrence contracted leukemia. Within a few months he was dead. Two years later, after seeing *A Private War*, a film about the death of the *Sunday Times* combat reporter Marie Colvin (like the NPR correspondent, an emotional casualty of the profession), Garrels better understood what had happened to her. She took to Facebook to pour out her feelings:

> I was in Iraq too long, but rightly or wrongly I thought I could write the story with knowledge and protect the Iraqi staff as more and more fly-by-nights came in with a desire to make their careers and little concern for the bureau. I was arrogant, but I wasn't wrong. The scars, alas, remain—largely because of Ellen Weiss. She turned up at my house in Connecticut. It was clear I was going to be sidelined in a battle to get rid of Loren Jenkins, with whom Ellen was in a fierce, internal battle. I am getting off my chest (what is left of it after lung surgery) what I have long wanted to tell the community.

Garrels's Facebook posting elicited many sympathetic replies and one judgment from on high. Bill Siemering, the creator of *All Things Considered*, wrote, "The way Anne was treated violated the core values of NPR and of common sense to care for the wellbeing of employees and honor extraordinary talent." For at least some who were involved, the subject of NPR's last dealings with Garrels remained painful. Years later, Eric Westervelt, who went on to run the network's San Francisco bureau, said, "NPR had ridden that talented horse pretty fucking hard without psychological support. Then when the horse fell down, they shot it."

TEN

CAN'T ANYBODY HERE PLAY THIS GAME?

The journalist designated to rescue Rupert Murdoch's biggest television news star walked onto the set of *The O'Reilly Factor* wearing a crisp, navy-blue suit adorned by an American flag lapel pin. Juan Williams was a rarity in the national press: Fox commentator, NPR senior news analyst, successful author (*Eyes on the Prize,* the companion volume to the Emmy-winning PBS documentary series; an acclaimed biography of Supreme Court justice Thurgood Marshall), and Black. On this mid-October evening in 2010, Bill O'Reilly needed him. Appearing on ABC's *The View* a week earlier, the host had ignited a firestorm. During a discussion about the proposed construction of an Islamic center near New York City's Ground Zero, he voiced his opposition by stating, "Muslims killed us on 9/11." Two of the chat fest's panelists—Whoopi Goldberg and Joy Behar—stormed off in protest. (Barbara Walters, the only reporter on the stage, stayed seated.) Afterward, the oft-described "angriest man" on TV took multiple hits. "O'Reilly's claim is unfair, and O'Reilly should understand why," wrote Peter Wehner in *The Atlantic.* "You can't indict an entire faith." The time had come for a figure with standing both inside and, more vital, outside Fox to stop the bleeding.

"Look, Bill, I'm not a bigot," Williams began. "You know the kind of books

I've written about the civil rights movement in this country. But when I get on a plane, I gotta tell you, if I see people in Muslim garb and I think, you know, they're identifying themselves first and foremost as Muslims, I get worried. I get nervous."

Williams had given O'Reilly cover. But he did not absolve him. In what NPR media reporter David Folkenflik later described as an attempt to "bring Bill O'Reilly to a place beyond his own prejudices," Williams added, "There are people who remind us all, as President Bush did after 9/11: 'It's not a war of us against Islam.'" It was too late. By throwing himself atop O'Reilly's reputation, Williams had exposed himself to the cross fire. The first shots came from the Council on American-Islamic Relations (CAIR), which issued a condemnatory statement. The fiercest attack, however, was wielded by Williams's bosses in public radio. As O'Reilly himself noted at the end of the segment, "You live in the liberal precincts. You actually work for NPR."

Executives at NPR were furious at Williams. "This crossed the line for us at NPR," recalled Vivian Schiller, at the time the network's CEO. "Juan's deal was as a news analyst—not an opinion person. A lot of people were angry." No one was angrier than Ellen Weiss, NPR's vice president of news, who just months earlier had dealt harshly with Anne Garrels. By this point, Schiller added, she "was fed up with him."

A former reporter at the *Washington Post*, Juan Williams had joined NPR in 2000 as host of the midday call-in show *Talk of the Nation*. At first, the network was thrilled to have him. Part of the journalist's appeal to NPR was that he'd already been working three years as a commentator for Fox. Public radio executives hoped that his conservative bona fides would bring it new listeners. "He was a Black person who would say unexpected things," said Renee Montagne. "You'd expect a liberal point of view, but Juan would pop out with something different." He did, but he struggled behind the mic. He was only "an adequate host," recalled NPR producer Robert Malesky. "He could be fumble-mouthed." After a year fronting the midday show, Williams became a correspondent, but that was not the right fit, either. "He didn't really know radio," said Montagne. "If he went out on a story, he had to take a producer with him," an unheard-of luxury at a network where nearly everyone worked solo. "You could spend your life at NPR without going out with a producer." Had Williams put in the time to learn broadcasting, his new colleagues might have been more forgiving, but many felt that he was coasting. "When he worked at the *Washington Post*, Juan was wonderful," recalled Nina Totenberg. "But he didn't want to work hard here." Williams believed himself to be bigger than the institution. "Juan saw himself as a star," added Neal Conan, who replaced him on *Talk of the Nation*.

The verdict was not entirely negative. "Williams did some fine work," David Margolick would later write in *Vanity Fair*. And Williams gave NPR access to Republican sources that had typically been unavailable. Few in Washington were better connected to the George W. Bush White House. In 2007 Williams scored a major scoop: NPR's only interview with Bush during his presidency. The get came at a critical time. The Iraq War was going terribly, and the network was thrilled to have Bush on the air addressing it. But in the minds of NPR executives, the scoop ended up underlining a fundamental flaw in the reporter's approach. He was too accommodating.

"People are praying for you," Williams started the interview. "The American people want to be with you, Mr. President. But you know what's going on up on Capitol Hill. The Congress, some in the military, even many Iraqis, according to the polls, don't like the idea of sending more troops into Iraq. I wonder if you could give us something. Say, you know, this is a reason to get behind the president right now."

Ellen Weiss and others at NPR went berserk. "A lot of people in the building thought it was a softball interview," recalled David Greene, at the time NPR's White House reporter. When the Bush administration offered Williams a second interview—this one pegged to the anniversary of the desegregation of Little Rock High School in Arkansas—the network declined. "We're grateful for the opportunity to talk to the president," Weiss informed the *Washington Post*, "but we wanted to determine who did the interview."

Eight years into Williams's tenure, the consensus at NPR was that he was a lackluster performer whose work was marred by a fawning regard for the subjects of his reporting. Weiss renegotiated his terms of employment, taking him off salary and putting him on contract. It was a clear demotion, but to many at the network even this action seemed overly lenient. According to

Robert Siegel, he pulled Weiss into his office in the aftermath of the move to ask a verboten question.

"Was it because he's Black?"

"Yeah," he recalled her answering in a tone he said conveyed "great embarrassment."

Although Weiss's refusal to fire Williams outright disappointed Siegel, he understood her restraint. "She would have been faulted by the board and senior management for parting with a well-known Black employee," he said later. "That was the dogma of the house. They were guided in re-signing Juan because management was always under fire for its lack of Black employees in prominent places." Longtime host Susan Stamberg concurred. "He should have been dismissed," she said, "but we have a problem with people of color. The network, she added is "gun shy. If they're not doing well, we don't fire them." Black network employees did not disagree, but they put a different spin on the matter. "Do I think NPR kept Williams on for years because he is a black man?" asked Farai Chideya, the former host of *News & Notes*, a brief-lived show devoted to Black culture. "Absolutely. Williams's presence on the air was a fig leaf for broader and deeper diversity problems at the network."

While Williams held on to his position at NPR, he was limited to weekly appearances on *Morning Edition* and *Weekend Edition Saturday*, where the hosts liked his work and valued the breadth of opinion he brought to the network. "Juan is smart, funny, and an original thinker," said Scott Simon in explaining why he kept using him. "I thought everything that made him un-NPR-like just made him more interesting."

Soon enough, however, Williams's safe havens at NPR were imperiled, largely due to the provocative opinions he kept uttering on Fox. In 2009, in response to rumors that a video tape existed on which the first lady of the United States used the word "whitey," Williams told viewers of *The O'Reilly Factor*: "Michelle Obama, you know, she's got this Stokely Carmichael in a designer dress thing going. Her instinct is to start with this blame America, you know. I'm the victim. If that stuff starts coming out, people will go bananas, and she'll go from being the new Jackie O to something of an albatross." Ellen Weiss upbraided him for what felt like the umpteenth occasion. "During my time as senior vice president we had increasingly tried to reconcile Juan's relationship with NPR and Juan's other relationships," she said later. "I spent hours talking with Juan." She demanded and received an apology for the Michelle Obama crack. She also demanded that Williams tell Fox to stop identifying him as an NPR analyst. Once a source of pride to the public broadcaster, Williams's high profile in Murdoch world was now a source of chagrin. Weiss was finished with him.

Two days after Juan Williams told O'Reilly that airplane passengers in Muslim garb made him nervous, Ellen Weiss phoned Vivian Schiller on her BlackBerry. Schiller was walking down a street in Atlanta, where she was giving a speech to a gathering of philanthropic donors. Weiss recalled the conversation as being straightforward.

"What do you want to do?" she said the NPR CEO asked.

"I want to end his contract now," she said she replied.

"OK, I agree with that," she said Schiller declared. That was it. The two had consulted and concurred.

According to Schiller, the exchange was far from being so cut and dry. "Ellen said she wanted to 'make a move,'" she recalled Weiss saying. "I don't think I understood what 'make a move' meant. I was distracted. I don't recall if she said, 'Do I have your permission?' It was blurrier than that. I don't want to say that I signed off on it, but I don't want to say that I didn't."

That the leaders of NPR could not agree on the gist of a phone call that would change both of their lives and throw the network into disarray could be taken a number of ways. The first was that one or the other or possibly both were dissembling. The second was that because further communication between the two was mostly via email, neither fully understood what was ultimately decided. A form of management dysfunction in which executives deluged each other with conflicting messages that blurred comprehension plagued NPR during these years. "There were a lot of what I call 'email melees' at the time," recalled Joyce Slocum, the then general counsel at the network. "There would be ten or fifteen people on the distribution list." Slocum, one of those copied during the emails about Williams, said that thoughts about NPR's response were moving so quickly that there was no genuine deliberation about the action under consideration or its potential ramifications. Her suggestion: "Let's get on a call and think things through."

As Slocum saw it, there was a way out of the dilemma. "The interesting thing to me as a lawyer was that Juan was not an employee of NPR. He was an independent contractor, and his contract was due to expire in just a few months. The contract did not give us an obligation to put Juan on the air. My suggestion in the midst of all these emails going back and forth was, 'Let Juan's contract run out. You don't have to terminate him.' But the thing that continues to stand out to me was the urgency to reach a decision. Ellen was adamant that Juan should be terminated immediately. There wasn't going to be a conversation."

The upshot was that late on the afternoon of October 20, Weiss left a voicemail message for Williams and asked him to call, which he did. Weiss dismissed one of her highest profile on-air employees, a ten-year NPR veteran. By phone.

Around eight that night, NPR's David Folkenflik received the first tip about Williams. "I got word that he had been fired. I talked to my senior editor on duty. He was like, 'Yeah, you can do a one-minute spot for the top of the hour.'" The seemingly blasé reaction shocked the network's media reporter.

"This is gonna be a big story," Folkenflik said.

"Nah, I don't think so."

"You don't understand. Juan works for Fox." Which, Folkenflik knew, meant that the most brutally strategic news boss in the electronic media would be orchestrating the Murdoch network's response.

"Roger Ailes will use this as a chance to beat the hell out of NPR for as long as he can."

The Fox barrage began the next evening, and it would continue all night in what amounted to a nonstop attack on NPR. Glenn Beck led off. "America, you're smart enough to know what" Williams's dismissal is "all about," he said. "It's not about setting anything right. It's not about truth. It's about intimidation, bullying, tearing down."

During hour two, Bret Baier aired a story about Long Island Republican congressman Peter King, a vocal critic of American Muslim groups for what he saw as their sympathy for terrorists. He asserted that since NPR appeared to support Al-Qaeda, Congress should defund the network.

The big guns came next. Bill O'Reilly opened the *Factor* by decreeing Vivian Schiller a "pinhead," his favorite term of derision. He then introduced a special guest, the man of the hour. "I don't fit into their box," Juan Williams said in explaining why NPR cast him off. "I'm not a predictable black liberal. They were looking for a reason to get rid of me." O'Reilly responded by offering to do for his guest what his guest had done for him. "We got your back," he promised. Whereupon Karl Rove, George W. Bush's former political adviser, ambled out to emphasize that now was indeed the time for the government to strip NPR of funding. Before the program ended, Laura Ingraham and Megyn Kelly also sounded off.

The assault continued at nine p.m. with Sean Hannity, Fox's emerging mainstay. In speaking of NPR's treatment of Williams, he said, "A good man has been smeared." At which point the pollster Frank Luntz convened a focus group, whose members, he announced, reached a stirring conclusion: "Tell Juan to hang in there, because Republicans and Democrats alike want him to fight for his job."

It was all Juan all night, but Fox struck its harshest blow against NPR off camera. Roger Ailes announced that he was giving Williams a three-year, $2 million contract. For the fiscally cautious, instinctively restrained types who run public radio, it was the ultimate stick in the eye.

NPR was at a loss as how to respond to any of it. In fact, network executives never actually explained why they fired Juan Williams. Ellen Weiss offered the only official rationale. His remarks, she said, "were inconsistent with our editorial standards and practices and undermined his credibility as a news analyst." Vivian Schiller then made matters worse. At a news conference at the Atlanta Press Club, she told reporters that the commentator's decision to sound off about Muslims on *The O'Reilly Factor* led her to conclude that he needed to consult with "his psychiatrist or his publicist." (The remark drew immediate blowback. The National Alliance on Mental Illness accused the CEO of sending "a cruel signal" to Americans grappling with psychological issues.) Dana Davis Rehm, NPR's then senior vice president of marketing and spokeswoman, said later, "We didn't have a sufficient story. We had no defense for ourselves." It soon became apparent that NPR failed to provide a justification for its actions because it saw no need to do so. Neither Weiss nor Schiller "expressed any remorse or felt like they'd done anything wrong," recalled Joyce Slocum. "They felt liked they'd done the right thing. They just had a black-and-white view of Juan's comment and believed that the action they were taking would be lauded."

As had been the case in 2004 when the network refused to give the reasons for dismissing Bob Edwards, its leaders did not appreciate that decisions involving its on-air talent would be of interest to the broader culture. As the *Washington Post* reported, "The real mistake was an assumption shared by Schiller, Weiss, and the rest of NPR's leadership: Releasing Williams would not turn into a public relations disaster." Looking back on it, Renee Montagne was more concise. They were "in a bubble."

Because NPR never articulated its reasons for firing Williams, Fox News continued to fill the void. Speaking to Howard Kurtz of the *Daily Beast*, Roger Ailes ripped Weiss and Schiller, both Jews. "They are, of course, Nazis. They have a kind of Nazi attitude. They are the left wing of Nazism. These guys don't want any other point of view. They don't even feel guilty using tax dollars to spout their propaganda." Jesse Watters, the eventual replacement of Fox titan Tucker Carlson but at the time a gofer for O'Reilly, then staged an ambush interview of Schiller on a Washington street. "As soon as I got out of my car," she said later, "Jesse and his cameraman had a camera in my face. I said over and over, 'Let me put some coins in the meter. Then I will talk to you.' But they wouldn't let me." Watters asked the executive a series of questions regarding an apparent inconsistency in NPR's policies. Why did the network dismiss Williams when it did not dismiss Nina Totenberg for making a nasty comment about Jesse Helms on a television news show in the 1980s? (In response to the refusal of the conservative North Carolina senator to support AIDS research, Totenberg said: If there's "retributive justice, he'll get AIDS from a transfusion or one of his grandchildren will get it.") Schiller had no answer.

Unpleasant as it was to be on the receiving end of Fox's thrashing, NPR faced a more dangerous threat. Conservative politicians intensified the attack against federal funding for the public broadcasting industry. "There's simply no reason to force taxpayers to subsidize liberal programming they disagree with," Republican senator Jim DeMint of South Carolina told *Politico*. Sarah Palin, who'd run for vice president just two years earlier, took to Facebook to ask: "What do we, the taxpayers, get for this [government money]? We get to witness Juan Williams being fired from NPR for merely speaking frankly about the very real threat this country faces from radical

Islam." Arkansas governor Mike Huckabee released a statement saying that he would no longer accept interview requests from NPR.

Inside NPR, the consensus was that Weiss and Schiller had committed a catastrophic unforced error. "We were appalled," foreign correspondent Deborah Amos said later. No matter how much network reporters may have disapproved of Juan Williams, they agreed that his remarks did not warrant dismissal. "It was the last straw, but it was the wrong straw," said Nina Totenberg. "His job was to express his opinion. That's what he did for a living." Robert Siegel added, "He was in a commentary role. That's not a fireable offense." Maybe worse was the graceless manner in which Weiss wielded the ax. "It was really bad form," said Totenberg. Then there was Schiller's jibe about Williams's mental health. "That's not the answer the president of a major news organization gives," said Susan Stamberg. "That's not dignified." Although Weiss and Schiller would subsequently apologize for their behavior ("Calling Juan was one hundred percent wrong," said Weiss. "I made a joke about Juan. That was a mistake," said Schiller), it did not appease network employees. They "totally fucked up," said Siegel.

Fittingly enough at a moment when many Americans were beginning to get their news not from the mainstream press but from social media and cable television, the best assessment of NPR's mishandling of Juan Williams came from Comedy Central's *The Daily Show*. The program began its coverage with a mock exclusive by correspondent Samantha Bee reporting that Williams's firing had nothing to do with his comments about Islam. Weiss canned him, she said, because he was in "direct violation of NPR's never-say-anything-interesting policy." It was the perfect lead in to an analysis by the show's host, Jon Stewart, which for many would serve as the last word:

> Are you kidding me, NPR? You're picking a fight with Fox News? They gave Juan Williams a $2 million contract just for you firing him. NPR, you just brought a tote bag full of David Sedaris books to a knife fight.

The dustup between NPR and Fox over the firing of Juan Williams was arguably the opening battle of the conflict that would define America during the early decades of the twenty-first century—the culture wars. There had been previous skirmishes—notably the one about the nomination of

Clarence Thomas to the US Supreme Court—but this contest was the first to feature the dominant contestants in the fray: the mainstream media and the conservative cable channels. While public radio continued to exhibit some of the institutional insecurity that had marked it from day one, it could now be spoken of in the same breath as the *New York Times* and the *Washington Post*. By 2010, the system boasted 268 broadcast license holders and numbered 784 NPR stations that reached more than 32 million listeners, some 26.4 million of them tuning in specifically for network programming.

Yet despite its dominance, NPR was vulnerable. Although the network by 2010 had all but weaned itself from federal funding, the Corporation for Public Broadcasting continued to provide major sums to member stations, which in turn used the money to buy programming from Washington. Notwithstanding the support from underwriters and windfalls such as the Joan Kroc bequest, the network couldn't afford to alienate the conservative politicians who controlled the CPB. "My sense is that the NPR board panicked at the attention that was going toward us," said David Folkenflik, who covered the story for *Morning Edition* and *All Things Considered*. Increasing the panic was a growing awareness among board members that they couldn't answer a key question: What happened? Did Ellen Weiss act unilaterally, or did Vivian Schiller give her approval? Equally significant, did either of them view the entirety of Williams's appearance on *O'Reilly*? Did they see him qualify his opening remarks about Muslims on airplanes by declaring this was not a war against Islam, or did they proceed based just on his first words? (Many at NPR watched the segment on a progressive website, *ThinkProgress*, which deleted Williams's second thoughts.) The facts were unclear. "The board had the stomach to push back," recalled Joyce Slocum, "but you can't push back when you don't have all the facts. They came to me and said, 'Let's look into it.'"

In early November, several weeks after Williams's dismissal, Slocum advised the NPR board to open an investigation. Typically, she would have led the probe, but because she was angry that Schiller and Weiss had ignored her advice to let the commentator's contract expire, she didn't feel she could be a fair judge. She suggested that the network hire the New York–based law firm Weil, Gotshal & Manges to dig into the management style of the two responsible executives and the back-and-forth between them. "They had done these kinds of reports for other organizations," recalled Dave Edwards, manager of WUWM in Milwaukee and the newly installed chairman of the NPR board. Which meant that a battery of lawyers would scrutinize the network's upper echelons. Since Weiss appeared to be the principal in the firing of Williams, most of the scrutiny would focus on her. Which meant the law firm would be examining the individual many felt was responsible for the successes that had taken the network to the journalistic heights. "Ellen was a big contributor to NPR's progress," declared Robert Siegel. James Fallows, writing in *The Atlantic*, was even more laudatory. "Whatever is admirable about NPR's news ambitions and standards—and to my mind quite a lot is admirable—is to a meaningful degree a reflection of Weiss's own ambitions and standards."

Not since Frank Mankiewicz had there been such a commanding figure at NPR. Ellen Weiss was among the least physically imposing individuals ever to stride the network's hallways. "On a good day," as she put it, she stood at five feet, two inches and weighed between ninety-five and one hundred pounds. Thanks to a rainbow of girlish freckles that spread across her cheeks, the vice president of NPR News was mistaken for a teenager well into her thirties. For all that, Weiss projected so much determination that people reflexively deferred to her. "She would walk around the newsroom, and you knew she was in charge," recalled David Greene.

Weiss's presence owed much to her athleticism. Nearly every day, no matter what was happening in the news, she ran five miles in Rock Creek Park. "She had a runner's energy, a tautness about her," said Robert Malesky. On top of that, unlike many women at NPR, where the preferred dress ran from schoolteacher drab to aging-hippie casual, she was always well turned out in crisp blue skirts and bright blouses. Many people at the network thought she shopped at that bastion of conservative conformity, Talbots. Not true. "The least expensive petites tended to be at Loehmann's," she said later, referring to the discount chain. Even so, Weiss embodied WASPy correctness. "I was mindful that someone of importance might walk into the office and I might need to talk to them," she recalled. "The clothes I wore reflected the idea that I belonged in that position."

Weiss arrived at NPR in 1982. A native of Scarsdale, New York, she'd studied Middle Eastern history at Smith and had admired the network's coverage of the 1981 assassination of Anwar Sadat. Barbara Cohen, the then news boss, hired her as a temp to do advance work for Deborah Amos and Bill Drummond before a reporting trip the two were making to Egypt. "I think I was getting visas," Weiss said later. "Who the heck knows what I was doing? I was doing whatever they needed. In two weeks, I realized I wanted to stay." The feeling was mutual. "Ellen was a very bright, personable young person who showed up like so many of them did," recalled Frank Fitzmaurice, in the early 1980s executive producer of *Morning Edition*. "She made a good first impression."

Weiss's ascent at NPR was better than meteoric. It was inexorable. "I got my foot in the door, and I realized that this was gonna be my journalism school," she said later. While Weiss did such typical temp chores as clipping and filing newspaper stories and answering phones, she soon graduated to the task of editing tape for *Morning Edition* on the four-p.m.-until-midnight shift. "I was surprised by how much I loved the art of cutting tape," she recalled. "I loved the creative aspect of it." Her future, she realized early, would not be behind a mic but behind the scenes.

After a year of temping, Weiss landed a full-time job at *Weekend All Things Considered*. "I was the lowest person on the totem pole, but on a small staff you learn a bit of everything," she said later. The show, as others had found, offered considerable freedom. "Because there aren't that many people there on the weekends, there are fewer people telling you what to do." Weiss regularly got hosts Alex Chadwick and Lynn Neary out of the studios to cover a staple of NPR's weekend programming—the arts. "We did a lot of music interviews at clubs around Washington. We got everything from Mose Allison to Joan Armatrading." Weiss excelled at such stories. "She embraced a fair amount of creativity," recalled her *Morning Edition* counterpart Steve Proffitt.

In 1984 Weiss became an assistant producer on *All Things Considered*. Not only was she now producing pieces for the likes of Noah Adams, but when she got the hosts out of the studio, they were traveling abroad. Following a successful reporting jaunt to Asia with Susan Stamberg, Weiss bumped into Robert Siegel at the M Street Xerox machine. There, in her words, the then-director of NPR news said "the most wonderful thing" anyone had ever said to her.

"You're the future of NPR. You need to run something."

Good to his word, Siegel promoted Weiss to editor of *Weekend All Things Considered*. In 1987 she became the producer. In 1989, Adam Clayton Powell III put Weiss in charge of the daily show. She was only thirty.

Before Weiss could even settle in, she was sending Siegel, who had begun hosting *All Things Considered*, to Germany to cover the fall of the Berlin Wall, Andrei Codrescu to Poland to report on the fall of communism there, and Neal Conan to San Francisco to report on the Loma Prieta earthquake that delayed that year's World Series. "I remember many a long night and day dispatching people and making plane reservations," she said. The next year was even busier, as she was assigning reporters to Saudi Arabia to cover the buildup to the first Gulf War. All the while, she was imposing changes to the way the program sounded. "Ellen understood how to craft the voice of NPR to play to its strengths," recalled John Hockenberry, who at the time was covering the Middle East and South Africa. She stressed "smart radio storytelling. Not a lot of spot news, not a lot of live shots. She wasn't interested in what the cable networks were up to. She wanted to explore the depth and the narrative potential" of broadcast journalism.

In 1994, Weiss supervised the expansion of *ATC* from a ninety-minute to a two-hour show that began at four p.m. "I spent a year doing that," she recalled. "A lot of things had to change. The *All Things Considered* clock was a never-ending pain to the stations, because they had no access to the show." When Weiss was done, she'd created the now-ubiquitous openings for local outlets to break in with updates. Not only that, but by lengthening the broadcast, she added time for the kind of minidocumentaries that hadn't aired on *ATC* in years. While in-house producers contributed strong work, the best came from independents, particularly San Francisco's Kitchen Sisters (Davia Nelson and Nikki Silva). "Lost & Found Sound," a late-1990s Kitchen Sisters series, brought to *All Things Considered* the vanishing aural landscape of the twentieth century. One segment featured Tennessee Williams reading poetry recorded during the 1940s on cardboard discs at a New Orleans penny arcade. Another captured the on-air efforts of Memphis's WHER, the self-proclaimed "First All Girl Radio Station," a 1950s brainchild of Sun Records boss Sam Phillips (the man behind, among others, Elvis, Johnny Cash, and Jerry Lee Lewis) and his wife, Becky. Then

there was the half hour devoted to Vietnamese manicurists, who after fleeing their country during the war set up shop in America and spoke of their
pasts as they buffed wealthy women's nails. These exquisitely produced
pieces won a Peabody.

The Ellen Weiss era at *All Things Considered*—and it was an era, last-
ing just shy of eleven years—saw the program consistently excel. Fronted by
Robert Siegel and Linda Wertheimer, it sometimes seemed so superior to
Morning Edition that its staffers took to referring to it as simply "the show."
Along with the highly produced features were breaking news stories, among
them the first post–Monica Lewinsky interview (conducted by Siegel) with
Bill Clinton, a get so coveted that CNN picked up—some said stole—NPR's
audio and aired it live. "*ATC* was the place to be," recalled Siegel. "When
Ellen left us to become national editor, it was hot."

On September 11, 2001, Ellen Weiss was shopping for Rosh Hashanah at the
Giant Food store off River Road in Bethesda, Maryland. When she reached
the checkout counter, the cashier was sobbing. Two airliners had just plowed
into the World Trade Center. Weiss, who wasn't scheduled to start her job
running NPR's national desk until September 22, dropped her purchases
at home, then raced to the network's Massachusetts Avenue headquarters.
"People were walking out of the city," she said later. "I was basically the only
car going toward the city. I got on an elevator, and I wasn't sure what button to press, because *All Things Considered* was on the second floor, the national desk on the third." Choosing which floor was Weiss's only moment of
indecision that day. Where *Morning Edition*'s host Bob Edwards and many
network editors were paralyzed, she was fixated on doing whatever needed
to be done. "I'll tell you in the most Rahm Emanuel way of saying it," she
recalled, "A crisis is a terrible thing to waste."

Weiss's orders as the incoming national editor had been to go slow and
rethink the job's priorities. "The national desk had needed fixing for a long
time," said Bruce Drake, NPR's news vice president and Weiss's immediate
superior. But as was the case at *ATC* a decade before, events were moving too
rapidly for that. "9/11 fast-tracked the one-year plan into a week," Weiss said
later. "It was an amazing transformational opportunity for a group of people
that just needed a little direction."

Weiss essentially did not leave the NPR offices for the five days that followed the attacks. She viewed her task during that first week as "making sure that people were organized in a way that we were covering the victims, the destruction, and whatever we knew about what happened. It was nonstop trying to understand who did what and who was affected." There was also something else. Because of her encounter with the tearful cashier at Giant Food, Weiss had an insight into how devastating this event was to Americans. She believed NPR needed to present its stories without undue sensation. "We needed information, but we needed not to be made more scared."

Following its shaky start, NPR's performance covering the events stemming from 9/11 was triumphant. As it happened, Siegel was in New York the day of the attacks and was soon filing stories. Meantime Weiss sent reinforcements to the embattled city's bureau while positioning other members of her staff wherever anything relevant was occurring. "When you look at the history of NPR," she later asserted, "the ability to marshal people quickly to do whatever it took was" a watershed moment. "It was like, 'Ah, why can't we do this every day?'"

Hereafter, NPR would be a primary American news source. Weiss was responsible for much of the transformation, but not all. The Kroc bequest played a role. "I was literally one day told, 'Hey, you get six new positions.'" Weiss recalled. "It was when we hired David Folkenflik to cover the media, Frank Langfitt and Adam Davidson as business reporters. Laura Sullivan was hired to cover policing. Elizabeth Shogren was hired to cover the environment. Suddenly, we had expertise on a much larger range of subjects. It was entirely Mrs. Kroc's money."

On a consistent basis, NPR now broke national stories. Daniel Zwerdling exposed jails that were holding prisoners without charge. Carrie Kahn exposed New Orleans hospitals that failed to serve patients in the wake of Hurricane Katrina. Weiss, as she'd done at *All Things Considered*, also continued to stress the aesthetics of radio storytelling. Not long after David Greene joined the network, he stumbled upon a policy backed by the Bush Agriculture Department to produce and distribute broadcast-ready pieces advocating the president's positions to farm-belt radio stations. It was government PR disguised as news. "I was like, 'That's ethically fucked up,'" Greene recalled. "I went to rural Virginia, and captured what it sounded like in a farming community." Greene was pleased with the interviews and atmosphere he got on tape, but when he returned to Washington, he felt he needed insights from an expert on the difference between news and propaganda. He telephoned Marvin Kalb, a former CBS reporter on the faculty of Harvard's Shorenstein Center on Media. What happened next stunned Greene.

"Why is this in the piece?" Weiss demanded.

"It's Marvin Kalb talking about the ethics," Greene responded.

"You just took me out of Virginia," she shot back. "In this script, you're in Virginia. Your listeners are soaking it all in. And suddenly, you're taking me to a phone call?

"You need to think about that," she added. "You're immersing us in a place. Stay there. Don't leave. The bar to leave should be so high."

Weiss was trying to convey to the former newspaper reporter the truth that had animated NPR since the days of Bill Siemering: unlike print journalism, radio journalism relies on sound. To cut away from tape rich in regional accents and the rumble of farm equipment in favor of a disembodied academic was to diminish a story in which the voices of the participants and the ambiance were paramount, allowing listeners to respond emotionally.

"That's the way Ellen's mind works," Greene later observed. "She taught me the magic of audio."

Weiss's ability to expand the scope of NPR's national coverage while championing radio storytelling did not go unnoticed. Bruce Drake later said, "Ellen turned the national desk into just what you wanted in this day and age." Drake, of course, gave way to Bill Marimow, who, of course, was shoved aside, whereupon Ken Stern, who replaced Kevin Klose as CEO, telephoned Weiss. "I met him for drinks," she recalled, "and he told me that Bill was not going to be the vice president anymore. He asked me if I would step in. I said to him, 'Are you asking me, or are you telling me.' He goes, 'Well, when the CEO asks you to do something.'" After ninety percent of the network's on-air correspondents signed a petition supporting her elevation, Weiss said yes. In April 2007, she was named vice president of NPR News.

In twenty-five years, Ellen Weiss had advanced from temp to the head of America's biggest broadcast news organization. It was a phenomenal rise, yet despite the wide admiration for her professional abilities, some of NPR's most talented journalists entertained misgivings about her management style. Mention Weiss's name, and more than a few respond with one word. Robert Siegel: "Divisive." Longtime Africa reporter Gwen Thompkins: "Divisive." Foreign correspondent Deborah Amos: "Divisive." These are some of the kinder judgments. Others call her a "suck up." Still others "vindictive." To square the admiration for Weiss's skills with such harsh assessments of her as a human being, Margot Adler said: "Ellen Weiss had people who loved her and people who hated her. She's a complicated person."

All along, NPR staffers were in accord that Weiss was a careerist. "She was a woman looking first and foremost to career and ambition," recalled the veteran reporter Frank Browning, who worked with her at *All Things Considered*. "That's OK. If you're not like that you're going to be an also-ran." But as time went by, the judgment hardened. Noted a former department head from her heyday with whom she was at odds, "She was transparently ambitious and conniving to move up."

The prevailing view at NPR was that Weiss made major decisions without regard to their impact on others. Runner that she was, she just ran. "Ellen had a million ideas, but she didn't think them through," said Bill Abbott, who worked with her at *Weekend All Things Considered*. Robert Malesky, who as the producer of *Weekend Edition Sunday* was in frequent meetings with her, recalled, "When Ellen decided something, she just went out, did it immediately, and let the chips fall where they may. She often stumbled." When this happened, Weiss typically refused to accept responsibility. "Nothing was ever Ellen's fault," Nina Totenberg said. "She's a political shrewdie," recalled Ruth Seymour, the station manager of Santa Monica's KCRW. Drake, much as he admired Weiss's work as national editor, distrusted her. Summing up her character, he said, "Smart, capable, and dishonest."

Drake was on the receiving end of Weiss's heedlessness. In 1984, when she was executive producer of *All Things Considered*, Weiss hired Mumia Abu-Jamal, the convicted murderer of Daniel Faulkner, a Philadelphia police officer, as a commentator. An ex–Black Panther, a former local radio reporter, and the former president of the Philadelphia chapter of the National Association of Black Journalists, Abu-Jamal was controversial. Liberal celebrities like Ed Asner, the star of *Lou Grant*, argued that Abu-Jamal had been convicted of a crime he did not commit. Law enforcement officials called him a killer. According to Drake, at the time NPR's managing editor and already Weiss's boss, he didn't learn of Abu-Jamal's hiring until he read about it in *Current* a week before his slated debut.

"How come I wasn't told about this?" he said he asked Weiss.

"I thought the ME only oversaw news," she rejoined, suggesting that Drake's purview did not extend to commentators.

On the Sunday before Abu-Jamal's scheduled Monday premiere, Weiss received a furious call from the Philadelphia officer's widow. If the commentaries ran, Maureen Faulkner informed the *All Things Considered* chief, "I'm going to plague you for the rest of your life." Shaken, Weiss phoned Drake.

"I don't want to be left hanging out there on a limb," she told him.

"Ellen," Drake said he replied, "How can you say this to me? I was in the dark about this all the time. You never came to me when you first thought of putting it on to ask what I thought.

"I'll tell you what I'll do," Drake said he added. "I'll go to the office. I'll listen to the tape. And if what I hear is the greatest thing since *The Autobiography of Malcom X*, then I'll say, 'OK. Let's run the thing.'" Drake was not impressed. Abu-Jamal's musings, he said, were pedestrian. "It was neither-here-nor-there stuff—a little commentary on the three-strikes-you're-out law, reflections on prison life. I decided to kill it."

Which was when matters turned ugly. "When I come in Monday morning, I started getting these vitriolic calls," recalled Drake. The most difficult inquiries, however, came from the media. Because of Abu-Jamal's notoriety, this was a big story. As NPR's managing editor, Drake needed to address the criticism publicly (Bill Buzenberg, then the vice president of news, was away), but as he saw it, he couldn't tell the truth, which was that Weiss had blindsided him. "There was no way I could credibly tell the *New York Times*'s reporter that I didn't know anything about this," Drake said. "What would you do as a reporter if you were speaking to somebody called the managing editor, and he told you he was in the dark about this? Plus, I didn't want to air company dirty laundry." There was only one move: Drake took the heat for firing Abu-Jamal and said nothing about the panic that gripped Weiss when things went wrong. While Weiss eventually apologized to him, he felt that she never accepted responsibility.

"It probably showed blind spots all around." Weiss later remarked, seeming to confirm Drake's view. "Because for it to have gotten so far you have NPR . . . promoting it and, umm, maybe not preparing for any kind of blowback or response . . . In retrospect, we probably, as I said, had some blind spots about thinking through the people affected by the death of a loved one . . . But. No. The people in charge did what they thought was best. I think Bruce was the one who decided to pull it . . . I was disappointed. But I think I just moved on—to be honest."

Just as Weiss was regarded harshly around NPR for her unwillingness to own up to her missteps, she was also regarded as someone overly protective of her domain. Her most determined adversary was foreign editor Loren Jenkins, Anne Garrels's champion. The two had been squabbling from the day he started in 1996. "When I got there," Jenkins said later, "the desks of *All Things Considered* and *Morning Edition* were the arbiters of what went on the air. The shows set the agenda for foreign coverage. Having spent my life as a foreign correspondent, I figured I should set the agenda. I said, 'The foreign desk will decide.' That antagonized Ellen Weiss."

The disputes between Weiss and Jenkins went deep. While they fought about everything, they fought most frequently about coverage of the Middle East, a subject about which they held strongly opposing views. Gwen Thompkins was unequivocal in her judgment of Weiss's view: "Ellen was an avowed Zionist." According to John Hockenberry, Jenkins was the polar opposite: "He was a classical T. E. Lawrence Arabist." This led to another charge against Weiss—pro-Israel bias. Robert Malesky felt Weiss stopped short of going over the line. "She has strong feelings" about Israel, he said, but added, "I think she worked not to let them get in the way of her journalistic judgment." While Weiss may have found middle ground regarding what aired on NPR about Israel, many asserted that she showed undue deference to male Jewish colleagues at the network. "Ellen surrounded herself with white Jewish guys," said Renee Montagne. "Ellen loved" Jewish boys, added Margot Adler. They included Adam Davidson, Guy Raz, and David Greene.

The misgivings about Weiss were sufficient that, as was their habit, the troika mounted a last-second, behind-the-scenes attempt to scuttle her appointment as vice president of NPR news. "We tried to tell people she wasn't a good choice," Nina Totenberg said. The three were mad at Weiss for replacing Linda Wertheimer as host of *All Things Considered*, a change that happened in 2002. They also felt, as did others, that Weiss preferred working with men, no matter their faith. "She had trouble with women," said Sylvia Poggioli. The opposition did not prevail. Acknowledging the failure, Totenberg said with a shrug, "The so-called powerful troika."

Once Weiss reached the top, the battles got harder. "Running NPR News is not an easy job," Robert Siegel said later. "There are unexpected bombs along the road." Shortly after Weiss took over as VP, the 2008–2009 financial crisis hit, leaving the network facing a $23 million loss of funding. "We had to cut ten percent of the staff," Weiss recalled, "most of it coming from the news division." Although she said she approached this task with sensitivity, numerous staffers felt she acted callously. In December 2008, NPR slashed sixty-four jobs. Not since the Mankiewicz debacle had the network conducted such mass firings. Among the seasoned reporters let go were John McChesney and Jacki Lyden. Each said that Weiss was excessively brutal. "She lacked an empathic nerve," said McChesney. "Her sense of professional demeanor was that she had to be ruthless." Added Lyden, "If I saw Ellen I would cross the street."

Weiss's firing of the thirty-one-year NPR veteran Alex Chadwick—a celebrated stalwart who'd worked at almost every level at the network and who cohosted *Weekend All Things Considered* when Weiss was an assistant there—became the defining incident. Since 2004, Chadwick and Madeleine Brand had been fronting *Day to Day* from NPR West studios in Culver City. Chadwick was creative ("I think of him in the pantheon with Noah Adams," observed Steve Reiner, the veteran producer of *All Things Considered*), and *Day to Day* reflected his sensibilities. The show was a "fresher, looser NPR news magazine," Chadwick said later. It offered everything from bold coverage of the Iraq War ("I could say things there you couldn't say on the Washington shows," recalled the foreign correspondent Mike Shuster) to commentaries by Brian Unger, a former *Daily Show* cast member, and Michael Kinsley, the editor of *Slate*. On any given program, audiences might hear Chadwick rhapsodizing about wildflowers in the Mojave while standing in a downpour or David Was of the band Was (Not Was) waxing surreal about playing golf while using a Segway as his cart. By 2008, *Day to Day* was airing on two hundred NPR stations—good but in a downturn not good enough. "I was sent to NPR West," Weiss recalled, to cancel two shows (the other was *News & Notes*, also produced in Culver City) and dismiss their staffs.

"The idea," Weiss added, "was we had to tell everybody at the same time." Chadwick was not in the Culver City studio. Rather than inquire where he might be, Weiss picked up the phone. When Chadwick answered, he was at an oncologist's office. His wife, Carolyn Jensen, was dying of cancer. Later, Weiss justified making the call. "I needed him to hear it from me. I didn't want him to read it. I didn't want him to hear it from other people." While her rationale may have had merit, it was also a dodge. Weiss had known Jensen was sick before flying to California. She had been ill for a year. What Weiss did not know was that the disease had progressed. "I did not know that Alex's wife was in chemo," she said. "Perhaps if I had I would have been able to ask my colleagues about how do we handle the situation." But it didn't happen that way. "It wasn't to be cruel. I just needed to let Alex know."

Chadwick was crushed. He learned that his three-decade-plus NPR career was ending at the moment he was preparing to lose his wife. (She died the next year.) Although Chadwick would go on to produce *Burn*, a brief-lived public radio show covering global warming, he was a spent force. Frank Fitzmaurice, a founding producer of *Morning Edition* and an early backer of Weiss, said her actions were unfeeling. Regarding Weiss's treatment of Chadwick, Sylvia Poggioli said flatly, "She's stupid and arrogant."

Part of Weiss's job was, of course, to deliver bad news to employees who for whatever reason needed to be shown the door. There was never an easy way to do it. Even so, she did not possess the intuition to sense the human dimension of this unpleasant responsibility or appreciate that timing was everything. Where others in her position might have stopped to assess, she just acted. Which was why in July 2010, not long after her painful encounters with Chadwick and Anne Garrels, she walked into the office of Daniel Schorr at NPR's Massachusetts Avenue headquarters and got to the point. "Ellen said it was time to make a plan for Dan's retirement," said Scott Simon, the host of *Weekend Edition Saturday*, where Schorr had been a commentator since 1985. No one blamed Weiss for broaching the subject. At ninety-three, the last of Murrow's boys was struggling. "He was drifting, losing his train of thought," said Robert Siegel, who was both a colleague and friend. Schorr had recently started taping his commentaries. After sixty years in the business, he no longer trusted himself to broadcast live. But while Weiss was right to raise the issue, what she said by way of justification was tactless. "We don't want any Helen Thomas incidents."

A few weeks earlier, Thomas, the eighty-nine-year-old former UPI warhorse, had told a well-known rabbi that Israelis should "get the hell out of Palestine and go home." The comment was caught on video, and the Hearst chain, Thomas's new employer, fired her.

"Dan didn't take" the comparison well, recalled Simon, adding that Schorr believed that by prerecording his commentaries, he was protecting NPR from anything untoward. He said that Schorr reassured Weiss about this. "Why should you be worried about me?" he said Schorr asked her.

A couple of days after Weiss spoke to Schorr, Simon's wife and their daughter dropped by Schorr's house to bring a gift to his wife, who'd recently broken her hip. While they were visiting, Schorr stuck his head in to complain about Weiss's remarks to him and to say that his lawyer, Bob Barnett, who serves as an agent for numerous Washington broadcast reporters, was pitching Schorr's commentaries to the producers of PRI's *Marketplace*.

"Dan, that sounds wonderful," Simon's wife enthused. "That'll show NPR."

It was not to be. The next day, Schorr fell ill and checked into a Washington hospital. On July 23 he died. "He died of necrosis of the liver," Simon said. "Now, as powerful as Ellen Weiss may be perceived, she was not responsible for the death of Daniel Schorr. But it's a very bad confluence of events, to say the least." Simon's ultimate conclusion: Weiss "was beginning to operate with an exaggerated sense of her own authority."

Three months after Schorr's death, when Weiss fired Juan Williams, others at NPR were thinking the same.

All through November and early December, current and former NPR employees made their way to the Washington, DC, offices of Weil, Gotshal & Manges. There, they opened themselves to questioning from Yvette Ostolaza, the lead lawyer in the investigation, and her associates. The chief area of inquiry was the series of events leading up to the firing of Juan Williams. But this question was not the Weil team's sole interest. "Standing grievances about Weiss's management style, particularly the way she carried out a series of layoffs and terminations in 2008" were also on the table, reported the *Washington Post*. According to David Folkenflik: "They looked into Ellen's past difficulties with personnel." The sessions were lengthy and exacting.

Equally critical to the Weil lawyers were the countless emails sent between Ellen Weiss and Vivian Schiller during the run-up to Williams's dismissal. "They did a thorough review of those emails," said Joyce Slocum. The electronic communications were revealing, as they included not just the back-and-forth between the two executives but the multiple comments made by the dozen or so other employees on the distribution lists. They offered a virtual portrait of the organization's evolving view of Williams.

The team from Weil sifted through an enormous amount of material, and they were moving fast. The NPR board wanted results promptly to counter the continuing fusillade of criticism from Fox and conservative lawmakers. Under any circumstances, the probe would have been expensive, but the time element made it especially so. Writing in *Vanity Fair*, David Margolick reported that the probe cost "hundreds of thousands of hard-won donor dollars." Inside NPR, many felt that the money could have been better spent on new reporters. Others felt that it should have spent on the current staff.

"Let me get this straight," Scott Simon told Vivian Schiller when she dropped by the *Weekend Edition* office to give an overview of the Weil investigation. "We have just finished contract negotiations where union personnel have been asked to tamp down requests for cost-of-living raises because these are hard economic times. At the same time NPR is paying a blue-chip law firm for a report that will essentially investigate your mistake."

"Well," Schiller replied, "that's one way of putting it."

By Christmas, Weil, Gotshal & Manges was done. "More than a dozen NPR employees, including some of the most well-known hosts" had spoken to Yvette Ostolaza and her associates, reported the *Washington Post*. The only principal in the affair unwilling to cooperate was Juan Williams, who saw no need to help the network understand why it fired him. Even so, the law firm had completed a thorough report laying out the events leading up to his dismissal and exploring the complaints regarding Weiss's previous dealings with other employees.

•   •   •

The NPR board typically holds an informal dinner the night before its regular meetings. The purpose is usually social. But the mood the eve of its January 2011 gathering was different. The Weil, Gotshal & Manges lawyers would present their findings there. Going into the evening, many of the men and women who presided over the network were favorably disposed to their top managers. Dave Edwards, the chairman, believed that Weiss and Schiller had been justified in dismissing Williams. "I've always been concerned when you have journalists appearing on programs, whether that be *Meet the Press* or something on Fox, and they're asked to give their opinions," he said later. "I think Williams's departure was probably warranted." Edwards also held a high opinion of Weiss. "I had known Ellen for a long time in her various capacities at NPR, and I had always respected her."

Yet as Yvette Ostolaza and her associates began to talk—and talk was all they did; fearing that a written report would leak, the firm did not distribute one—Edwards changed his mind. "It became very clear that certain things were not done in the way that you want to manage a news organization," he later said. "The conversations that took place, the things that were said—there were just a lot of things going on that I was not aware of. I was surprised."

The presentation focused on Weiss's firing of Williams. Edwards, who would not reveal the specifics, said the lawyers established that "Ellen was moving too fast." The *Washington Post*, in the only detailed account of all this, reported that the news vice president had indeed fired the commentator without consulting sufficiently with Schiller. "Schiller and Weiss each provided a timeline of the events," wrote the newspaper's Paul Fahri. "What the investigators found was puzzling. Weiss's recollection of the chronology of the episode differed from Schiller's. . . . Weiss had already fired Williams before Schiller signed off." Quoting an unnamed board member, the *Post* reporter added: "'The email traffic supported Vivian's timeline.'"

There was more. As Edwards confirmed subsequently, the Weil report reviewed "other situations that had happened in the newsroom." Again, Fahri was more specific, noting that the lawyers laid out prior incidents in which Weiss had brusquely dismissed employees, including at least one—Alex Chadwick—by phone. "Weiss's decision to fire Williams without benefit of a face-to-face meeting sounded familiar to those who recounted similar episodes." As to whether Weiss considered Williams's ameliorating remarks to O'Reilly about Muslims, the evidence was inconclusive.

Due to the rules of corporate governance, only the NPR CEO had the power to dismiss an employee. The board could, however, express its point of view. "The board made clear what its preference was," Joyce Slocum said later. On January 5, Schiller summoned Weiss to her office and asked for her resignation. The CEO's only explanation was that the news vice president had lost the confidence of the newsroom.

"Vivian," Weiss remembered saying to her boss, "I've been here almost thirty years. Do you think you could tell me why?"

Schiller did not reply.

"She had a script," Weiss said later. "She couldn't veer from the script. That was it."

On January 6, the NPR board announced that Weiss had resigned, although *announce* is far too active a verb for how the network made the news public. The board began its lengthy, evasive memo by stating that Weil, Gotshal & Manges had absolved NPR of wrongdoing in the dismissal of Juan Williams. The board then ticked off several changes the network intended to make to its "internal procedures concerning personnel and on-air talent decisions." NPR would "update" its code of ethics. It would "update" its policies in regard to the role of NPR journalists appearing on other outlets. Not until the twelfth paragraph did the board get to the actual point: "NPR also announced that Ellen Weiss, senior vice president for news, has resigned."

The NPR memo regarding Weiss was not so much a statement of facts as an exercise in avoidance. As had been the case ninety days earlier with the firing of Williams, the network was essentially unforthcoming. For a news organization, the network once more proved incapable of delivering news about itself.

NPR's decision not to reveal the cause of Weiss's departure sparked furious rebukes inside the network. "NPR can hire the most sophisticated investigators in the world," observed Alicia Shepard, the organization's ombudsman, "but how can such a review have credibility if people who care about NPR can't read the full results of it." Shepard demanded that the network make the report public, but that was not going to happen. "For the integrity of the process and to make sure people felt comfortable speaking freely during the review," said Yvette Ostolaza, "the board decided to not have a written report." This position became the party line. As NPR spokeswoman Dana Davis Rehm told journalists, "It would be inappropriate for us to comment on internal conversations."

NPR's stonewalling resulted in another flurry of negative press. Beneath the headline "WEISS WASH," William Saletan, a critic for *Slate*, termed the network board's rationale for firing its news vice president "miserably vague." Declared David Carr in the *New York Times*: "The board took no ownership over the decision. In fact, no one accepted direct responsibility. Ms. Schiller declined to comment to a reporter on how Ms. Weiss's departure came about."

Once again, NPR allowed others to tell its story. The version that gained the most traction held that the network canned Weiss to silence its conservative critics. There would be only scant mention of the difference between the news vice president's explanation of Williams's firing and Schiller's, and little about Weiss's handling of earlier layoffs. An allegorical column by Carr encapsulated the prevailing view:

> A long time ago, in a kingdom beset by tempestuous storms, it was decided that one of the most prized citizens would be fed to the volcano as a sacrifice to appease the punishing gods. After the sacrifice was made and the crowd exulted, a young visitor turned to the man next to him and asked if this ritual always worked. "Nah," said the local. "Does wonders for morale, though."
>
> Confronted by a similar tumult in the wake of the ill-conceived and poorly executed decision to fire the commentator Juan Williams for remarks made on Fox News, NPR recently offered a sacrifice of its own. On the day an outside investigation into the Williams matter concluded, Vivian Schiller, chief executive of NPR, accepted the resignation of Ellen Weiss.

Inside NPR, it wasn't so clear that Weiss's firing was good for morale. "It's outrageous that Ellen Weiss is being pushed aside as some kind of flaming liberal," said Adam Davidson. "She was obsessed with NPR becoming a solid, mature, non-ideological news organization." Not only this, but Davidson believed she was a visionary. "She was trying to shift the voice of NPR to be a more engaging, narrative voice. Ellen got really a raw deal." Others saw it differently. "There was a whole contingent who applauded Ellen's demise," noted Renee Montagne. Among this group was one of Weiss's former supporters. "NPR was obliged to clean house," said Robert Siegel.

Schiller had survived, not that she avoided repercussions. The Weil, Gotshal & Manges report noted that she'd presided over a fiasco. "She was chastised by the NPR board for her handling of the Williams dismissal," reported the *New York Times*. On the same day she fired Weiss, the board rescinded her 2010 performance bonus. But ultimately, the CEO had the board's support.

At fifty, Vivian Schiller embodied NPR's idea of itself as it entered the digital age. Each morning, she awakened in her Georgian home on a wooded lot in Bethesda, flicked on her BlackBerry, and began answering the scores of emails that had arrived overnight. While readying her children for school, she browsed thirty websites. She then climbed into her black Prius, pulled a headset over her short-cropped blond hair, and departed for work, spending the thirty minutes it took to reach Massachusetts Avenue online. "I never actually dial or text except at red lights," she joked at the time, but that didn't mean she failed to feel the urge. She'd still be tethered to her BlackBerry when she got to work, often oblivious to her colleagues as she ascended by elevator to her office.

Digiterati though she was, Schiller was not solely a creature of the internet. A Soviet-studies major at Cornell who also held a master's in Russian from Middlebury, she spent her early work life in the Soviet Union, where she was a translator and guide for touring business groups. One of them, Turner Broadcasting, hired her as a fixer. The job required her to translate during production negotiations and make dinner reservations, but it gave her an entrée to Turner's then-new cable news network. Schiller rose to the position of executive vice president of CNN's documentary unit. She then leapt to the Discovery/Times Channel, a joint venture of Discovery and the *New York Times*. In 2006, the newspaper hired her as senior VP and general manager of NewYorkTimes.com.

Soon after Schiller's arrival at the *Times*, she added blogs and videos to the newspaper's website, which surged past competitors in content and style, winning new subscribers. "During her tenure," the *Times* reported, "the site greatly increased its audience." She became a leading proselytizer for delivering the news online.

Schiller had not been angling to leave the *Times*; NPR came after her. The network, noted *Current*, was "struggling to find a digital content strategy that engaged web audiences and also satisfied its hundreds" of member stations. The tension between NPR and its far-flung outlets had plagued the organization from its earliest years, but the emergence of the web and handheld devices provoked some of the most serious confrontations in its history. Among public broadcasting executives, it was called "the bypass issue." Thanks to digital technology, National Public Radio could now bypass the stations, reaching listeners online. Already, many people downloaded NPR stories onto their computers or tuned in via SiriusXM. Schiller's predecessor, Ken Stern, had encouraged such developments and wanted to go further. Indeed, he advocated for the addition of a button to NPR.org that would enable audiences to donate directly to the network, threatening the funds generated locally by station pledge drives. He also proposed renaming National Public Radio National Public Media, deleting mention of radio from a company whose outlets depended on it. This was nonnegotiable, and the NPR board, which consisted largely of station managers, fired him in 2008.

Schiller took control of NPR in January 2009, at the height of the 2008–2009 financial crisis. "I walked into a buzz saw," she said later. Ellen Weiss had just completed the task of dismissing sixty-four editorial employees, but it wasn't enough. "We were in a nosedive," Schiller recalled. More firings seemed certain. The new CEO believed in the old adage that a business can't cut its way to success. After instituting furloughs and canceling raises across the board, she looked for ways to increase network revenue.

Schiller's first move was to reorganize NPR's underwriting department, where most of the bleeding had occurred. "It was a little sleepy at the time," she said later. "I made a change in the leadership and a change in the metabolism." Schiller then turned her attention to NPR's philanthropic development group. "They were our most promising source of revenue," she said later. Believing that more Joan Krocs were out there, Schiller hired Ron Schiller (no relation) to head the network's fundraising department. Previously the director of development at the University of Chicago, where he raised $2.4 billion in four years, Schiller was a Republican who believed that donations—not federal funding—would provide the answer to NPR's financial needs. He was also attuned to the concerns of member stations, feeling that the network should share donations with them. To close the gap between NPR and its outlets, he launched a "Weekend in Washington" program that brought local managers to the capital to mingle with potential donors and visit the studios. He also expanded the network's fundraising department from twenty-four to thirty-seven employees.

Although righting NPR's finances was Schiller's initial task, her long-term focus was on leading the network into the digital future. By the middle of 2009, she'd redesigned NPR.org, creating what the *New York Times* described as "an easier to navigate site that emphasized written reporting over audio reports." By pushing the text incarnation of NPR pieces online, the CEO extended an olive branch to the stations, ensuring that they'd remain the sole purveyors of the audio incarnation. Schiller also compromised when it came to the rebranding of National Public Radio, retaining at least the salient initial in the new name: NPR.

Many station managers chafed at Schiller's view that in the years ahead NPR would deemphasize terrestrial broadcasting. She also ran afoul of the old guard with the name change. In a widely read self-circulated essay titled "The Three Words You Can't Say on NPR," Bill Siemering, the network's founding programming director, wrote:

> Why did National Public Radio abandon three defining words in favor of letters at this time? The technology has not become obsolete. We have nothing to cover up like British Petroleum. Yet NPR has chosen to remake its identity with a similar bland approach. Words mean more than letters. The words National Public Radio have forty years of meaning something. National is inclusive.

Still, in all, Schiller got off to a terrific start. Even her interactions with NPR employees—once she put her BlackBerry aside and communicated face-to-face—were excellent. "The impression was that she really talked to people," recalled Margot Adler. "When she'd give presentations about where our budget was going, they were always very good. You'd walk out saying, 'I understand what's happening.'"

•   •   •

All of which explains why Vivian Schiller not only kept her job after the Juan Williams scandal but also could have been forgiven for thinking the worst was behind her. It was not. On Saturday, January 8, just two days after Schiller dismissed Ellen Weiss, Arizona congresswoman Gabrielle Giffords was shot in the head at a rally in Tucson, Arizona. NPR received a tip that Giffords was dead from Arizona Public Media's news director, whose wife was in the crowd at the mall where the incident occurred. The network got what seemed like confirmation a few minutes later when reporter Audie Cornish called to say that she'd heard the same on Capitol Hill. Neither source was definitive. No one from law enforcement or a hospital had weighed in. In such cases, staffers were required to contact a senior editor before taking to the air, but with Weiss gone, best practices broke down. At 2:01 p.m., Barbara Klein went live: "Congressman Gabrielle Giffords of Arizona has been shot and killed during a public event in Tucson, Arizona." NPR then tweeted the news, which was soon picked up by other organizations, all of them attributing it to the network. There was only one problem. While Giffords had been badly wounded, she was alive and in surgery. She would survive. It took NPR fifty-nine minutes to correct itself. Not since 1974, when *All Things Considered* erroneously reported that Patricia Hearst had been killed in a shootout in Los Angeles, had the network made such a major error. It both intensified the gloom within NPR and reinforced the outside view that the organization was reeling.

Schiller, with good reason, decided that NPR needed to stop making news and just report it. The CEO informed staffers that from here on out, she alone would make public statements. "Vivian's instruction to the PR team," recalled Joyce Slocum, "was to go dark, go to the mattresses. NPR became very insular."

The dangers confronting NPR were growing, with House Republicans now introducing legislation to end the government's $429 million annual appropriation to the Corporation for Public Broadcasting. During a mid-February episode of *Talk of the Nation* featuring Doug Lamborn, the Colorado representative behind the bill, Neal Conan reported that the likelihood of cuts was better than ever. Lamborn told the host: "I think the future for public broadcasting is bright should it become private broadcasting."

In the face of such increasingly pointed remarks, NPR decided to take the offensive. The National Press Club was the perfect venue. On March 7, with Patricia Harrison, CEO of the Corporation for Public Broadcasting; Paula Kerger, CEO of PBS; and Pat Butler, an industry lobbyist, on the stage in a show of solidarity, Vivian Schiller made the case for NPR's journalism. "We stay on the story when everyone else moves on," she declared, then gave examples. A year after a disaster at the Upper Big Branch coal mine in West Virginia, Howard Berkes was still reporting from there. The same in New Orleans, where Debbie Elliot remained on top of the BP oil spill. Then there were NPR's investments in the sort of coverage no longer guaranteed on the commercial networks. Seventeen foreign bureaus. Check. Reporters assigned to dedicated beats. Check. The CEO was saying that when major news was involved, NPR got things right.

Which brought her to the crux of the matter: how to pay for it all. "We rely on continued government funding," she told her audience, reminding them that this was how the stations stayed afloat. "It's not the largest share of the revenue," she said, "but it is a critical cornerstone." Such money, she added, was particularly vital to rural outlets such as KUYI, the NPR outlet on a Hopi reservation in Arizona, which would have gone off the air during a recent major snowstorm if not for the generators the Corporation for Public Broadcasting had purchased for it.

Schiller's presentation was impressive, linking the reporting NPR did and the services stations provided to continued public support. "It went over really well," she said later. "Pat Harrison came up to me afterwards and said, 'This is perfect, and this is over,'" meaning that the drama that began with Williams had ended.

On the sidewalk in front of the Press Club, a stranger approached Schiller and posed a startling question. "How do you feel about Sharia law? Would you take money from an organization that adheres to Sharia law?" A network staffer shooed the person away, but the CEO knew that something new was amiss. "That," she said later, "was the first inkling."

The eleven-minute, hidden-camera video debuted the next morning on Project Veritas, the site of right-wing mischief-maker James O'Keefe, and the *Daily Caller*, cofounded by future Fox host Tucker Carlson. The setting could not have been better for a sting. Georgetown's Café Milano, with its ceiling mural of Placido Domingo and its reputation as a political gathering spot (Bill Clinton and Newt Gingrich had both hosted events at the restaurant), is one of the capital's most elegant spots. There, over risotto and glasses of expensive wine, Ron Schiller, NPR's top fundraiser, and Betsy Liley, an assistant, were caught on tape lunching with two men who were dangling a $5 million donation to the network if it would help burnish the image of the Muslim Brotherhood, of which Al-Qaeda is an offshoot, and educate Americans to the benefits of Sharia law, whose laudable tenets notwithstanding endorses stoning for such putative crimes as adultery.

The men dining with Schiller and Liley identified themselves as Ibrahim Kasaam, who said he was an oil futures trader, and Amir Malik. They claimed to represent the Muslim Education Action Center. That NPR kept the date was astonishing considering the red flags raised in advance. Following so closely on the dismissal of Juan Williams for anti-Muslim remarks, any overture from a Muslim charity had to be considered suspect, and this one was particularly so. In the days leading up to the lunch, network executives couldn't find any mention of the Muslim Education Action Center in philanthropic databases. "I knew we were dealing with a questionable situation," recalled Joyce Slocum, "but Ron felt NPR could use a major donation." Even at the last second, there were warning signs. Kasaam and Malik chauffeured Schiller and Liley to the restaurant in a stretch limo out of a Vegas fantasy. Still, the NPR contingent was game, and after some informal chitchat Schiller suspended disbelief.

"Now," he said, "I will talk personally, as opposed to wearing my NPR hat."

"I like it when you take off your NPR hat," one of the men replied.

"The current Republican party is not really the Republican party," Schiller said, as the camera and microphone secreted out of sight recorded every word and gesture. "It's not just Islamophobic but really xenophobic. I mean, basically, they believe in sort of a white, middle-America, gun-toting—it's scary. They're seriously racist, racist people."

"It is very clear," Schiller added, that NPR would be "better off in the long run without federal funding."

Then, making it plain that he was receptive to Kasaam and Malik, the NPR fundraising chief said, "I think what we all believe is that if we don't have Muslim voices in our schools and on the air . . . it's the same thing we faced as a nation when we didn't have female voices on the air."

The video, which began circulating before the March 8 workday began, hit NPR like the crack of doom. Joyce Slocum heard of it as she was brushing her teeth. "This is terrible," she recalled thinking. Renee Montagne was at the office. "An executive played the Schiller tape for me, and I said, like you see in the movies, 'Hold on. I've got to sit down.'" Added Slocum: "It was like there was sort of terrible déjà vu. Here we are, back again."

Much as the Juan Williams incident marked the opening battle in the culture wars, the airing of the Ron Schiller video marked the start of a new and slippery era in which ideological pranksters could employ technology to subvert facts (there was, of course, no such organization as Muslim Education Action Center) and undermine the mainstream media. Again, there were antecedents. James O'Keefe had played a similar hidden-camera trick a year earlier by posing as a pimp to lure staffers at ACORN, a quasigovernmental agency that assisted the poor, to support opening a brothel to combat homelessness. Yet by enticing NPR into a similar honeytrap, O'Keefe was aiming higher. He wanted to take down a journalistic institution. Not surprisingly, he had edited the tape to put Ron Schiller in the worst light. As David Folkenflik later reported, the full, two-hour video showed Schiller stating to Kasaam and Malik that they could not buy coverage. Still, even the unexpurgated version was damaging. "The fact is undeniable," noted NPR ombudsman Alicia Shepard, "that Schiller could be heard saying some egregiously offensive things"—among them a cringeworthy paean to the merits of madeira over sherry and port. As Shepard later wrote, "Schiller comes across as an effete, well-educated liberal intellectual—just exactly the stereotype that critics have long used against NPR and other bastions of the . . . media. It is a stereotype that NPR journalists try hard to combat every day."

Before March 8 was over, Ron Schiller, who'd already lined up a job at the Aspen Institute and had given notice, was gone, and Betsy Liley was put on administrative leave. That evening, Dave Edwards convened a teleconference with the NPR board and Vivian Schiller. Recalled Edwards: "The board had a very difficult conversation with Vivian." The group made it clear that in the course of twenty-four hours all the good she did the day before at the National Press Club had been undone. The O'Keefe video—which the board almost certainly did not view in its entirety, just as many at NPR News did not view the Williams video in its entirety—had diminished her standing with station managers, infuriated the Corporation for Public Broadcasting, and provided Republican lawmakers more reason to vote against federal funding. After listening to the complaints, Schiller offered the board members an out.

"If it would be helpful to the organization," she said, "I would be willing to resign." As she recalled it, she then added, "I think that would be a mistake." By capitulating to what she termed "an act of entrapment," NPR would "leave a stain on journalism and legitimate media."

"Why don't you hang up and let us talk about this," the board chairman replied.

Two hours later, Edwards phoned Schiller back to say the board accepted her resignation. As Slocum subsequently put it, "I think the board just felt like enough was enough, and whether she had directly made the decisions or not, they had happened on her watch, and she had to take responsibility." The next day, Edwards named Slocum interim CEO.

The political backlash was immediate. "Our concern is not about any one person at NPR," House Majority Leader Eric Cantor said on March 9. "Rather, it's about millions of taxpayers." Echoing the words of Ron Schiller, Cantor added: "NPR has admitted that they don't need taxpayer subsidies to thrive, and at a time when the government is borrowing 40 cents on every dollar that it spends, we certainly agree with them."

On March 16, the House passed Doug Lamborn's bill to defund the Corporation for Public Broadcasting. The 228–192 vote was mostly along party lines. Although seven Republicans did defect, the majority agreed with Tennessee representative Marsha Blackburn, who asserted, "The time has come for us to claw back this money." Joyce Slocum, in her first act as NPR CEO, countered with a defense of the network: "At a time when other news organizations are cutting back and the voices of pundits are drowning out fact-based reporting and thoughtful analysis, NPR and public radio stations are delivering in-depth news and information respectfully and with civility."

Despite the House vote, public broadcasting executives were confident that the Democratic-controlled Senate would almost certainly not go along. It didn't. Congress funded the Corporation for Public Broadcasting to the tune of $430 million for 2011 (Barack Obama signed the bill on April 15), a slight increase over the previous year. Still, NPR had put itself and its confreres at PBS in danger. As Slocum later noted: "Executives at NPR are better than anyone at shooting themselves in the foot and then immediately reloading and doing it again."

The 2011 White House Correspondents Dinner at the Washington Hilton on April 30 would go down as one of the few that was more than just a self-promotional mosh pit of actors (Sean Penn) and reporters (Jake Tapper). About ten minutes into Barack Obama's headlining remarks, he called out one of the evening's A-list attendees, the real estate developer and *Celebrity Apprentice* host Donald Trump. As it happened, Hawaii had just released a document that Trump had long said did not exist: Obama's birth certificate. (Wide-screen monitors above the podium displayed it for all to see.) While Trump looked on, Obama—with an impressive sangfroid (the American operation that would end with the death of Osama bin Laden in Pakistan on May 2 was already secretly underway as he spoke)—tore into his tormenter.

"No one is prouder to put this birth certificate matter to rest than the Donald," Obama began. Then: "And that's because he can finally get back to focusing on the issues that matter, like, did we fake the moon landing? What really happened in Roswell? And where are Biggie and Tupac?"

The room exploded in laughter. The president doubled down.

"All kidding aside," Obama said speaking directly to Trump, "We know about your credentials and breadth of experience. For example, in an episode of *Celebrity Apprentice* at the steakhouse, the men's cooking team did not impress the judges from Omaha Steaks. There was a lot of blame to go around, but you, Mr. Trump, recognized that the real problem was a lack of leadership, so you didn't fire Lil Jon or Meat Loaf. You fired Gary Busey.

"And these are the kind of situations that would keep me up nights."

As the crowd roared, the object of Obama's japery sat on his hands. The *New Yorker's* Adam Gopnik, who was at a table a few over from Trump, later wrote:

What was really memorable . . . was Trump's response. Trump's humiliation was as absolute and visible as any I have ever seen. His head set in place like a man in a pillory. He barely moved or altered his expression as wave after wave of laughter struck him. There was not a trace . . of the normal politician's or American regular guy's "Hey, good one on me" attitude . . . One can't help but suspect that on that night, Trump's own sense of public humiliation became so overwhelming that he decided, perhaps at first unconsciously, to pursue the presidency.

Obama had eviscerated Trump, but the man who would succeed him in office was not his only or even his first target. The president opened the evening by sticking it to NPR.

"Where's the National Public Radio table?" he asked up top.

A chorus of acknowledgements came back to him.

"You guys are still here? That's good. I couldn't remember where we landed on that."

The same, derisive laughter that would wash over Trump washed over NPR.

"I know you were a little tense when the GOP tried to cut your funding," the president added, "but personally, I was looking forward to new programming like *No Things Considered* or *Wait, Wait, Don't Fund Me*"—this last inspired by the network's weekly news quiz show.

NPR's turn in the barrel was not over. Seth Meyers, then the host of *Saturday Night Live*'s "Weekend Update," was Obama's closer. With the evening winding down, he made sure the audience didn't forget public broadcasting's bad several months, calling attention to a postevent gathering the crowd would be well advised to skip. "NPR is having a party, but I'm sure it will be pretty sedate. How wild can a party get when it's held in accordance with Sharia laws?"

While Barack Obama's jokes were a reminder of NPR's back-to-back-to-back missteps, they were also a validation of the network's place among the journalistic elite. Now that it was an industry leader, it was fair game. Many at the network viewed the whole sequence of events as nothing more than flak. "It was very unpleasant," Nina Totenberg said later, "but it didn't have a lasting impact." Added Dave Edwards, the board chairman, "People picked up the ball and ran with it."

There was, however, a less sanguine judgment. Not only did the errors and comeuppance do NPR substantial harm, but a contingent believed that the outcomes were unjust ("I felt all three of them—Juan, Ellen, and Vivian—got raw deals," said David Folkenflik) and would damage the network in the years ahead.

Juan Williams was one of NPR's few analysts willing to question liberal orthodoxies, and he was Black. "It was stupid to fire the only black Republican at NPR," argued Paul Haaga, who would soon become interim network CEO. Whatever Williams's failings as a radio reporter and despite his sense of himself as being larger than the network, by taking him off the air NPR reinforced Fox's go-to argument that the mainstream media shuns right-of-center views. That's how Williams saw it. "NPR journalism has come to embody elitism, arrogance, and the resentments of its highly-educated, upper-income managers and funders," the deposed analyst wrote in *Muzzled*, his 2011 book about being fired. "Any approach to journalism that is at variance with NPR management's ideas is considered justification for banishment."

The dismissal of Ellen Weiss also drew substantial criticism. She was an innovator. Indeed, even as Weiss was mishandling the departures of Anne Garrels and Alex Chadwick, she'd been cementing a deal between NPR and other public broadcasters to create the network's first podcast, *Planet Money*. It debuted in 2008 with a prescient, hourlong episode that traced the roots of the financial crisis that stuck America that year to the mortgage-backed-securities industry. The program not only won a Peabody, but it also spawned a series of "Planet Money" segments on *Morning Edition* and *All Things Considered* that by 2020 totaled more than one thousand, making it NPR's most successful programming effort in decades.

Adam Davidson, Weiss's pick to cohost *Planet Money*, asserted that many of the NPR veterans who spoke against the news vice president during the Weil, Gotshal & Manges investigation used the probe as cover to go after someone who was challenging institutional precepts. "I think what you saw," he said, "is a kind of high church, abstracted version of objective journalism competing with people like Ellen who followed all the rules of journalism but also advocated a narrative medium. There was a real battle there, and I say when Ellen got fired, the other side won." The result, he contended, was "the kind of lifeless, dull, plodding nature of the NPR sound" during the coming years. "Obviously, none of the people who opposed Ellen would say, 'I think our content should be boring,' but there's a deep editorial risk aversion."

This was something of an overstatement. Although NPR's journalism during the century's second decade may not have been as creatively ground-breaking as it had been under Weiss, it remained formidable. On *Weekend All Things Considered* in October 2012, Guy Raz reported the story of John Lavelle, a four-star air force general who'd been busted down to two-star for ordering unauthorized strikes during the Vietnam War. The riveting, sixteen-minute piece suggested that those strikes were justified by Lavelle's responsibility to protect his pilots. On *All Things Considered* in October 2012, Michelle Kellerman offered a superb summary of the political fallout that resulted from the 2011 attack by Islamic militants on the US diplomatic compound in Benghazi, Libya, that took the life of American ambassador Christopher Stevens. On *All Things Considered* in May 2013, Melissa Block conducted a moving, joint interview with a woman who'd undergone a groundbreaking face transplant and the daughter of the donor, who'd died of a stroke. In an inspiring twist, the two had become friends.

NPR made strides in other realms as well. By 2013, the network's NPR Music website was attracting more than 2.5 million monthly online visitors and nearly 1.5 million to its podcast. Launched as "All Songs Considered" in 1999 by Bob Boilen, a former *All Things Considered* director, as both an homage to the interstitial music segments NPR's shows have always featured and a way to capitalize on the recording industry's increasing embrace of the internet, NPR Music offered album downloads and in-studio performances called "Tiny Desk Concerts." Popular artists—Rufus Wainwright, Robert Cray, Wilco, Lucius—were traveling to the network's Washington headquarters to perform. The median age of the audience: thirty-four, nearly two decades younger than that for *Morning Edition*. Also in 2013, NPR moved into smart new headquarters on Capitol Hill and reinvested in its Culver City, California, operation with a vow to cover the West more thoroughly. Much of *All Things Considered* would soon originate from there. By the fall of 2017, the weekly audience for *Morning Edition* reached 14.9 million, solidifying its place as America's most-listened-to news program.

Still the events of 2011 cast a pall. Vivian Schiller had been building the online delivery system that would ensure NPR's ability to navigate the digital future. "Her firing was an indication of trouble ahead for NPR," declared Jeff Jarvis, a professor at the City University of New York and a proponent of technological innovation in the media. "The network lost a visionary leader who I know, first-hand, was doing great things. . . . While others in the news industry all have the worldview of Eeyore these days. . . . NPR [was] initiating new journalistic endeavors with Vivian's . . . support. . . . There is a strategic cliff ahead, but no one dare speak of it. Watch out."

ELEVEN

THIS AMERICAN IRA

On a Friday morning in the late spring of 2022 in the west side Manhattan studios of *This American Life*, Ira Glass sat at a Shure microphone preparing to record the prologue to "The Parents Step In," episode 771 in his ongoing exploration of living in the United States. The topic of the show: the response by mothers and fathers of gunned-down children to the nation's epidemic of mass shootings. Just three days earlier, in Uvalde, Texas, another attack had left nineteen students and two teachers dead.

With Pro Tools displayed on a ViewSonic computer screen mounted at eye level to highlight vocal tracks and twenty-three-year-old Michelle Navarro, the *This American Life* fellow (the program no longer calls them interns, as entry-level employees now include veteran newspaper and television reporters who've quit steady jobs to apprentice with the master), seated at his side to log the tracks by hand, Glass launched in.

"So, uh, there's a whole infrastructure that springs into action every time a mass shooting occurs. There's the police and SWAT teams, of course, the Red Cross, the Billy Graham prayer truck, therapy dogs—and there's this couple whose daughter died in a mass shooting, and what they do really seems to help."

Following each line, Glass swept his right hand across his body from left to right as if releasing a Frisbee. But when he hit the word *help*, he stopped. Could anything really help? Leaning back from the mic, he pondered the line's wording for a few seconds. Tall, with graying black hair, the sixty-three-year-old host was clad in what he calls his work uniform, a monochromatic ensemble from which he never deviates and which suggests that he leaves little to chance in his professional life. In a tailored black Paul Smith suit (he has a closet full of them at home in the East Village), white Brooks Brothers Milano shirt unbuttoned at the throat (a drawer full of them as well), and chunky black shoes laced up tight, he was at once hip but nerdy. He's worn oversize black glasses most of his career. He now buys them from the high-end eyewear purveyor DITA. It's all thought out—as was the eventual rewording of that troubling line.

"And what they do seems to be *very effective.*"

That was better than *help*—less presumptuous. But it still wasn't right, not the phrasing but the reading. It was weak.

"I don't, uh," Glass muttered to himself. Then, zeroing in on the mic, he went for greater emphasis. "VERY EFFECTIVE." With that, he again swept his hand from left to right.

Nothing is simple about putting together an episode of *This American Life*, but the degree of difficulty has increased in recent years as the program has focused more frequently on breaking news than on the whimsical topics it once featured almost exclusively. "It's just really much more dire times," Glass later noted. "The world is in crisis now in a way it wasn't in the nineties. We live in a country that's completely divided, where no political decision can be made, no cultural thing can happen, without it being reframed into two realities, one that Red America believes and one that Blue believes."

Glass and his staff turned around "The Parents Step In" in the brief period between the Uvalde slayings on a Tuesday and *This American Life*'s Friday deadline because they had two stories devoted to mass shootings in their archives. "Keep Breathing," which first aired in 2018, details the efforts of Sandy and Lonnie Phillips—whose daughter was killed in a 2012 massacre at an Aurora, Colorado, movie theater—to counsel parents who've lost children in subsequent assaults. "Down the Rabbit Hole," which originally aired in 2019, focuses on Lenny Pozner, whose son was murdered in the 2012 bloodbath at Sandy Hook Elementary School in Newtown, Connecticut. He now devotes his life to fighting media propagandists (among them Alex Jones, the host of *Infowars*) and online trolls who deny the event ever happened.

That the stories—each produced by Miki Meek, a *This American Life* veteran—were a bit dated, far from making them stale, made them more relevant. Nothing had changed. The country was reliving this nightmare again and again. That was the headline. As Meek says at the top of her piece on the Phillipses: "Sandy and Lonnie have traveled to eight mass shootings since Aurora: Sandy Hook, then Isla Vista, San Bernardino, Orlando, Las Vegas, Sutherland Springs, Parkland, and then Santa Fe, Texas." They were in Uvalde now.

Both segments of "The Parents Step In" are powerful, but the job of getting audiences to listen fell to Glass. The host's seemingly offhanded but in fact excruciatingly considered opening comments have over the course of *This American Life*'s nearly three-decade run helped make it one of public radio's most popular productions (it attracts a weekly audience of 3.5 million, a small majority now downloading the podcast, the rest tuning in the old-fashioned way), changed how people talk on NPR (imitators of Glass's nasally presence are legion), and resulted in the host's coronation as the suzerain of broadcast journalism storytelling. He is the father of the podcast revolution. Fans of the ur-podcast *Serial* have Glass, whose company produced it, to thank. So, too, have fans of the acclaimed *S Town*, another Glass-related effort. His impact on the narrative form is what makes Glass the most significant figure in contemporary public radio. He ties together the work of such pioneers as Bill Siemering ("If there's anybody who knows the original spoken-word aesthetic of what the real revolutionaries were after, it's Ira," observed John Hockenberry) with that of contemporary practitioners. His influence may be most obvious at the *New York Times*'s successful newscast, *The Daily*, whose stories not only mimic the structure of *This American Life* stories but whose executive producer, Ben Calhoun, was once an editor at both *This American Life* and *Serial*. In an age of declining listenership and fracturing media empires, Glass saw what commercial and other public broadcasters did not—where a big part of the game was headed.

•   •   •

The labor that goes into Ira Glass's spiels is exacting. To construct seven minutes of audio for "The Parents Step In"—two for the prologue and five for the copy between stories—required forty-five minutes. At times, the process seemed unending. Introducing the segment on Lenny Pozner, the host struggled with nearly every line.

"In the second half hour of our show," he began smoothly enough, "we have a dad from Sandy Hook who jumped in and took extraordinary measures—and got results." Again, he just stopped.

"Extraordinary measures," Glass repeated, downplaying the phrase.

"Got results." He downplayed that, too, but he went too far.

"Got *results*." This time he sold harder.

"Got results."

"Got RESULTS."

"Got results."

Following eleven takes, the host was satisfied.

"The performing of the show—actually being on the radio—is the part I dislike most," Glass confessed at the end of the session. "You can go into the studio and just mess up. You want to talk in a way where you're just talking, and you're slowing down to underline things or putting in pauses to underline things—and, not being corny about it, if that makes sense. The whole thing is to achieve a thing where it's just talking, you know. Like if it works, that's what it is."

Fronting *This American Life* is just one of Ira Glass's responsibilities. Producing a weekly news-feature show that tries to respond to major events with alacrity and depth does not leave much downtime. More than ever, Glass's days toggle back and forth between performing and managing, and in the midst of everything he was doing to ready "The Parents Step In," he was managing another big story. As early as the next week, the US Supreme Court would announce its decision in *Dobbs v. Jackson Women's Health Organization*, which would overturn *Roe v. Wade*, the ruling that for nearly fifty years had guaranteed American women the right to an abortion. Glass intended to cover the controversial decision in an hourlong deadline documentary. His goal was to put together a seamless production about a heated moment in history that elsewhere in the media would be told mostly in bits and pieces. Already, he and his staff had scored a coup, securing exclusive permission to record inside the Mississippi clinic at the heart of the case—known because of its color as "the Pink House"—the day the ruling was delivered. But there were other items on the host's wish list for the *Dobbs* episode, and the producer assigned to deliver them was waiting for him in his office down the hall.

Glass's workspace is surprisingly small and modest. The bookshelves hold only a few mementos (among them a mockup of a stage set from a 2014 live performance of *This American Life* at the Brooklyn Academy of Music and a framed photograph of the host, his composer cousin Philip Glass, and the poet Allen Ginsberg). Discarded scripts clutter the floor. At the entrance, a handwritten sign on a piece of copy paper bears a message for colleagues should they arrive and find the door shut: "I Love You Talk Later Go Away."

When Glass entered, Zoe Chace, who was already settled in a seating area, blurted out what they both knew. "Basically, starting Tuesday, it's possible that the decision could come down. That's not ideal."

"Because you and I were both planning on getting our abortions," Glass interjected in an attempt to reduce the producer's anxiety.

"Well, you better get it this weekend," Chace rejoined, her expression relaxing.

The mood lightened, Glass and Chace opened their respective laptops to the same Word document. It was titled "Narrative Version Preferred Structure." This was the blueprint for *This American Life*'s *Dobbs* episode, a show whose main actions had not yet occurred, whose principal interviews had yet to be conducted, and whose contents had mostly not been taped. Which didn't mean that the whole program couldn't be planned then and there and on the air in a week. In consultation with other staffers, the two had conceived a six-act show, and it was outlined in the document:

1. Start with clinic closing
2. Go to patients scrambling
3. Go to catch-in clinic
4. Legislator Mary Elizabeth Coleman
5. What do we do with the babies?
6. Opponents to abortion pills

Item one was self-explanatory. "We can possibly get the last abortion in the state of Mississippi," Chase said.

Everything else, however, was in the works. The story about the catch-in clinics, so called because they were opening to handle referrals from states where abortions would halt after *Dobbs*, would require a *This American Life* reporter to be on the scene when patients began arriving. Several locations seemed likely, but one promised the best access.

"They've already been booking in Illinois," said Chace.

Then there was the piece about Mary Elizabeth Coleman. Chace had been courting antiabortion activists for the episode. ("It's one of the hardest bookings I've ever tried to do," she told Glass. "They only want to speak to religious media.") Coleman, a Missouri assemblywoman who'd written the legislation that would result in the banning of abortions in her state, was among the few interested in what *This American Life* had in mind, which was to spend the day the ruling was announced with her and other pro-lifers and attend a victory party afterward. "She's kind of surprisingly fun to listen to," Chace said. "Young and bubbly and chill." The host was delighted to hear it. While he often asserts "There's no objectivity," he believed it was vital in this episode "to document both sides."

From Glass's perspective, three of the six acts—the closing of the clinic in Mississippi, the catch-in facility in Illinois, and Mary Elizabeth Coleman in Missouri—were coming together. Bringing the meeting to a close, he asked "Anything else?" and got an earful. Chace frequently reports on conservatives (she won a 2018 duPont-Columbia Award for a *This American Life* episode focusing on Republicans opposed to the country's immigration policies) and works to retain them as sources. She was upset that a fellow staff producer named Bim Adewunmi, who was being considered to supervise the catch-in clinic segment, didn't seem to understand that she could not express personal opinions while reporting,

"I'm a little concerned about her politics," she told Glass.

"Cause she's . . . ?"

"So outwardly, publicly angry about *Roe* falling. If she came, I don't want that to be in the tape. I don't want it to be like, 'This is so fucked up.'"

"That's fine," Glass replied. The two left it there. He needed to return to the studio to finish recording a last bit for "The Parents Step In."

"The first feed happens at eight p.m.," Glass said as he settled back in front of the mic. That version, he added, would air on WBEZ in Chicago at seven o'clock central, the show's time slot when it debuted there in 1995. (A final version would be transmitted to *This American Life*'s five hundred other outlets a couple of hours later, followed by the podcast version later still.) While the program has been produced in New York for eighteen years, it maintains a relationship with its old home base, most notably in what has become a signature moment in the closing credits where the host takes a playful bow to Torey Malatia, the former WBEZ station manager who gave him his start. With Michelle Navarro again logging his tracks, Glass delivered an upbeat endorsement of the show's underwriters ("Odoo is a fully integrated business management software solution!") and thanked the staff members who contributed to the episode. Then came his shout-out to Malatia.

"Thanks, as always, to our program's co-founder, Mr. Torey Malatia. He recently tried Axe Body Spray. You know that stuff. He didn't like it."

At which point a voice purportedly belonging to Malatia boomed, "You can't wash that evil off." Except it wasn't Malatia. It was a clip of Alex Jones from the just-finished program. To listeners paying attention, such spin—not too much, not too little—separates *This American Life* from standard public radio fare. The show has a point of view, sometimes absurd, sometimes barbed. It may now cover breaking news, but even as it does so it remains subversive, and nothing could be more subversive than letting Alex Jones hang himself with his own words.

Glass's delivery of the sign-off was enthusiastic and unmarred by any of the stutters or false starts that had plagued him while recording the earlier segments. Which, on brief reflection, struck him as a problem. It was overly glib. He'd raced through the material without considering that it concluded an episode devoted to stories of dead children, sobbing parents, and gun violence. Sighing, the host said to Navarro, "That's really a little too cheerful after all the death in the show. I'm gonna give you another take."

Glass did it again—this time slower, more respectful, but not somber. The Malatia bit guaranteed the program would end with a zinger. He was out.

The weekend had arrived, and Glass would spend it more like a mainstream media big shot than a nonprofit showrunner, which was his privilege.

Unlike anyone else in public radio, Glass is a homegrown multimillionaire. *This American Life* is not only his creation, but he owns it—and a lot else. And what he doesn't own he's sold for serious money. In 2020, the *New York Times* bought Serial Productions, the groundbreaking podcasting company he cofounded with Julie Snyder and Sarah Koenig, for a reported $25 million. "I'm not someone who was trying to make money," he said, standing outside the studio. "But I'm really glad there is money. It feels safe to have it. That's the main thing. And then there are the things I can do with it." The bespoke wardrobe, a techy fold-up Brompton bike whose make he was initially loathe to specify ("It's embarrassingly on brand"), and the freedom to travel.

That night, Glass would catch a flight from JFK to Paris to attend the wedding of friends. He would then fly back to New York Monday and be in the studios early enough to keep shaping not just the Dobbs episode of *This American Life* and every episode to come but to an increasing degree the future of the nation's broadcast news business.

The philosophy that animates *This American Life* can be summed up by a simple come on: "Let me tell you a story." News, almost by definition, rarely conforms to what Aristotle deemed the essential element of storytelling: plot. It consists of dispatches from geographically disparate locales and varying worlds (politics, foreign affairs, finance, sports), and it doesn't adhere to a scenario. Of late, the proliferation of offerings from online outlets has increased choices while fragmenting audiences, creating an age of hot takes and short attention spans. It's hard to get consumers of TV and radio news to stay tuned. "Having a plot is a way to make people stick around and provide something that feels satisfying," Ira Glass noted. "That's the thing about it that's helpful. If you have a plot, the story can be mundane. It can be incredibly everyday. But people just want to find out what's gonna happen, and they'll hang around." Not only this, but plot—or narrative, as its sometimes more grandly called—offers an antidote to the political and cultural polarization changing audience habits. As Glass put it: "The primary problem you have in doing a story about any of the big, emotional issues of our time—was the election stolen, does the vaccine work, what to think of Donald Trump, climate change—is that everybody already knows what they think. If you start any story, everybody's like, 'Yeah, yeah, I know.' There's an enormous hurdle to get over to get people to listen past even the first thirty-five seconds. What do you do? By having characters, scenes, and surprising moments and just letting the thing unfold, you can catch people up in the lives of the people you're documenting. And then they'll keep listening to hear how things work out."

The apotheosis of the *This American Life* approach is its November 15, 2019, episode, "The Out Crowd," winner of the inaugural Pulitzer Prize for audio journalism. When the staff of *TAL* began to put together this show, which focuses on how the Trump administration's Remain in Mexico policy affected asylum seekers trying to cross into the United States, the basic facts of the matter were already familiar. "We knew this had gotten coverage in the *Wall Street Journal*, the *New York Times*, the *Washington Post*, and on the networks," recalled Glass. "It's out there—if you follow this. But all of the stories felt academic." The goal was to capture the human dimensions of a policy that had stranded thousands in desolate shelters deemed unsafe by the US State Department.

"The Out Crowd" opens with a fourteen-minute prologue reported from a tent city in Matamoros, Mexico, just across the Rio Grande from Brownsville, Texas. In it, Glass introduces listeners to an unlikely protagonist—a nine-year-old Honduran refugee named Darwin who along with his mother is hoping to get to America. "I feel like if you said at the beginning that this was a show about immigration, nobody would listen," said Glass. "The fact that the first few minutes of the show can just be a portrait of this completely charming kid, everybody's favorite kid—you wanna hear more. Then you pull the camera back. Then you reveal: OK. Here's what the show is about today."

The show is about the difficulties facing people like Darwin and his family. Some of these difficulties arose from Trump's policies. As outlined by the *Los Angeles Times* reporter Molly O'Toole (*TAL* partnered with the newspaper on this episode), the United States was not just building a physical wall at its southern border but also a bureaucratic one. "We've been asked to do affirmative harm to people," one asylum officer says in explaining rules that send even qualified migrants back to the dangers they are fleeing. Meanwhile refugees faced a more imminent peril: as they awaited a resolution to their cases, cartel members bent on kidnapping them for ransom lurked just beyond their camp gates. To illustrate this part of the tale, Glass introduced Emily Green, a reporter for *Vice*, who'd latched onto some terrifying audiotape—cell phone recordings of negotiations between cartel members and the American sister of a Honduran businessman abducted near his border camp. The hostage was ultimately freed, but the exchanges spoke to why some migrants, among them Darwin's mother, might choose what to most people would be an unthinkable option: sending her son on alone to the United States.

"She doesn't want to let him go," Glass concludes, "but given how things play out, she's not sure what else to do."

In the spring of 2020, when the Pulitzer committee presented its award to *This American Life*, it amounted not just to a recognition of "The Out Crowd" but of Glass's philosophy. The prize saluted what the Pulitzer committee termed the value of "revelatory, intimate journalism." As Glass sees it, work like "The Out Crowd," unlike that of journalists who maintain traditional reportorial distance, does something rare. It encourages audiences to feel. "A lot of so-called conventional sorts of reporting that aren't built around narrative can end up treating people in sort of an anthropological way," he said. "The reporters are just outside anthropologists who are coming in to diagnose questions like, 'Have people been hurt by the economy?' Their reporting doesn't include the possibility of relating to the people. I think the fundamental advantage of narrative is that you can create a context where it's possible to imagine being someone different from yourself."

Over the years, *This American Life* has applied the technique to countless important subjects. In "The Giant Pool of Money," an episode that aired in 2008, reporter Adam Davidson and producer Alex Blumberg make the financial crisis sparked by the collapse of the mortgage bubble comprehensible to just about anyone. In "The Night in Question" in 2015, reporter Dan Ephron and producer Nancy Updike unravel the previously inexplicable motives behind the assassination of Israeli prime minister Itzak Rabin. The method also works for subjects that on the surface seem less profound. In "129 Cars," a 2013 episode produced by Glass and Robyn Semien and reported by, among others, Sarah Koenig and Brian Reed (the mind behind *S Town*), *TAL* explores the lengths to which the staff of Town and Country Jeep Chrysler Ram in Levittown, New York, goes to hit its monthly sales quotas. (To get psyched, one salesman reads Sun Tzu's *The Art of War* at his desk.) In "#1 Party School," *TAL* examines the party-till-you puke ethos of students at Pennsylvania State University while annotating the psychological damage they inflict on themselves and the property damage they do to the town of State College.

Since its debut, Glass's brand of journalistic storytelling has resulted in countless superb installments of *This American Life*. It has also resulted in one devastating misfire. The nadir of the *TAL* approach is its January 6, 2012, episode, "Mr. Daisey and the Apple Factory." When it first aired, this show appeared to be yet another example of Glass's artistry. A reworking of *The Agony and the Ecstasy of Steve Jobs*, a stage production by the monologist Mike Daisey that had been selling out theaters around the country, the program investigates how Americans, in their zeal for iPhones and iPads, have ignored the inconvenient truth that these sleek implements are largely manufactured by workers toiling in brutal conditions at the massive Foxconn complex in Shenzhen, China. Daisey, with the assistance of an interpreter named Cathy who becomes a major character in the story, had recently toured the facility, and he assured Glass of the accuracy of his descriptions of the brutal working environment. After vetting the basic facts about Apple's production process, *TAL* aired his allegations.

"Mr. Daisey and the Apple Factory" opens with the arrival of Daisey and Cathy at Foxconn. It's the kind of simple, arresting scene typical of *This American Life*:

> I get out of the taxi with my translator, and the first thing I see at the gates are the guards. And the guards look pissed. They look really pissed, and they are carrying guns.

More worrying than the guns is what Daisey describes next—the makeup of the labor force:

> In my first two hours of my first day at that gate, I met workers who were fourteen years old, thirteen years old, twelve. Do you really think that Apple doesn't know?

Everywhere Daisey looked, he claimed to have seen evidence of corporate disregard for worker welfare. Some laborers shake from exposure to n-hexane, a toxic chemical used to clean the screens of Apple devices. An elderly ex-worker proffers a hand mangled, Daisey says, during the manufacturing of an iPad case. Because there are few iPads in China, Daisey shows the worker his. The man's eyes light up. According to Daisey, he told Cathy: "It's a kind of magic."

"Mr. Daisey and the Apple Factory" is mesmerizing and flawlessly produced. It became the most-downloaded episode of *This American Life*. There was only one problem. In almost every salient detail, the story was a fabrication.

Glass might never have learned that he'd been bamboozled had not Rob Schmitz, at the time a reporter for *Marketplace* in Shanghai, listened to "Mr. Daisey and the Apple Factory" and realized that key parts of it (Chinese private security guards are prohibited by law from carrying firearms) are untrue. At the suggestion of an executive at American Public Media, the then-distributor of both *Marketplace* and *TAL*, Schmitz called Glass, and Glass engaged him to investigate the entire broadcast.

Glass starts the March 16, 2012, *This American Life*, titled "Retraction," by apologizing for airing "Mr. Daisey and the Apple Factory." The fault, he says, is not so much in Daisey as in himself. He didn't press the monologist regarding a vital piece of intelligence—contact information for Cathy. "He had a cell phone number for her, but it didn't work anymore. He said he had no way to reach her. Because other things Mike told us about Apple and Foxconn seemed to check out, we saw no reason to doubt him, and we dropped this. That was a mistake."

Just how big a mistake becomes plain when Glass cues up act one: Rob Schmitz's probe of Daisey's story. "I decided to track down his translator," the *Marketplace* reporter begins. "I could pretend finding her took amazing detective work. But basically, I just typed 'Cathy and translator and Shenzhen' into Google. I called the first number that came up." Cathy answered. Schmitz met Cathy in Shenzhen, where the bulk of Daisey's story unraveled. Child laborers? The translator says she and the monologist never saw any. Workers suffering from chemical poisoning? "No. Nobody mentioned n-hexane." The man with the gnarled hand. "No, this is not true. Very emotional. But not true."

Schmitz's deconstruction of Daisey's piece (he uncovered at least thirteen lies) remains one of the most unsettling segments ever broadcast on *This American Life*. No sooner did it conclude than Glass introduced an even more harrowing segment—an interview with Mike Daisey, who expresses only one grudging regret: he is sorry he permitted a program dedicated to journalism to air a piece written for the stage.

> Everything I have done making this monologue for the theater has been to make people care. I'm not going to say I didn't take a few shortcuts in my passion to be heard. But I stand behind the work. It's theater. I use the tools of theater to achieve its dramatic arc, and of that arc and that work, I am very proud, because I think I made you care, Ira, and I think I made you want to delve.

As far as Daisey is concerned, the issue was one of inaccurate labeling. Glass didn't buy it.

> I understand you believe this, but I think you're kidding yourself in the way that normal people go to see a person talk. People take it as literal truth. I thought the story was true.

For all that, the host seems less outraged than hurt.

> I have such a weird mix of feelings about this, because I simultaneously feel terrible for you. And also, I feel lied to. And also, I stuck my neck out for you . . . I vouched for you. With our audience, based on your word.

For *This American Life*, Daisey-gate was a mortifying embarrassment. At first, a majority of critics went easy on the program. Seventeen years into its run, it had built a lot of goodwill. David Carr of the *New York Times* saw Ira Glass as the victim: "There is nothing in the journalism playbook to prevent a determined liar from getting one over now and again. It is partly because seekers of the truth expect the same in others." James Fallows of *The Atlantic* praised Glass's retraction, terming it "a superb unraveling of Daisey's inventions" and an "exploration of real journalistic values and the difference between fact and metaphor." Soon enough, the criticism hardened. Some felt that the host's mea culpa was pat. Responding to his comment about having "a weird mix of feelings" concerning Daisey's deceits, David Zurawik of the *Baltimore Sun* wrote, "Despite all the feelings, whoa, whoa, whoa feelings, feeling bad after the crime isn't enough. Talking about your feelings and beating up the lying liar the way Glass did without offering specific actions is more performance and self-absorption than it is genuine contrition." More substantially, a few attacked the central idea of *This American Life*—narrative journalism. In an essay for *The Baffler*, Eugenia Williamson wrote, "Daisey exposed the fact that the aesthetics and conventions of the narrative journey Glass has patented . . . were never designed to accommodate harsh . . . truths . . . Daisey's lies . . . exposed the limitations of *This American Life*'s twee, transporting narratives, the show's habit of massaging painful realities into puddles of personal experience, its preference for pathos over tragedy."

In the end, *This American Life* survived Mike Daisey. "Immediately after that we started working with professional fact-checkers," said Glass. Also, the Daisey scam occurred as *TAL* was phasing out what had long been a staple—monologues by people like Daisey. In its early years the program had often featured works by the comically arch Sarah Vowell and the adventurous Scott Carrier. Later the lineup regularly included the twistedly fatalistic David Rakoff, the twistedly sweet David Sedaris, and the twistedly awkward Mike Birbiglia. But by midway into the millennium's second decade, Glass had decided that the genre was overexposed. "Times changed, and I became less interested in doing memoir, because memoir is sort of everywhere. Basically, the internet happened. People documenting their own lives on social media happened after that. The idea of, 'Let's document people's everyday lives' became less interesting."

As for the larger issue of narrative journalism, not only was Glass not deterred by the harsh assessments of "Mr. Daisey and the Apple Factory," but he upped his bet on the form. "When I talk to journalism students they sometimes freak out when I say, 'You're gonna do a story with a plot.' But all a plot means is: This happened. Then this next thing happened. And that caused this next thing to happen. That will be the thing that's the spine. Then we can digress from there to talk about feelings and make jokes and describe things and have ideas about the world. But the fundamental thing will be: Here's Point A. Here's Point B. Here's Point C. And that's a powerful force. That's part of what gives it such satisfaction at the end."

This is the electronic media movement that Glass started, the one that is attracting not just mainstream journalism outfits like the *New York Times* and giving birth to podcasting pioneers—among them former *TAL* producer Alex Blumberg—but inspiring all those young imitators with iPhones and websites who, in the ultimate tribute to Glass, believe they do a better job than he does.

At the end of his freshman year at Northwestern, Ira Glass faced a choice. The son of an accountant father and psychotherapist mother, he grew up in Willow Glenn, a middle-class neighborhood near Baltimore's elite Jewish enclave of Pikesville. His future seemed predetermined. "My parents really wanted me to be a doctor," he recalled, and he enrolled as a premed student. The model was his uncle Lenny, a surgeon. In fact, Glass already had a part-time job for the summer of 1978 as an orderly at the Maryland Shock Trauma Unit, a facility that specializes in emergency treatment for accident victims. Although Glass wouldn't be allowed to do more than wheel patients around on gurneys, he was intrigued, believing it would be "super interesting to see how it worked."

In his fantasies, however, Glass imagined a different career. During his senior year in high school, he'd started typing up jokes and mailing them to Johnny Walker, a proto–radio shock jock (Robin Quivers, later of Howard Stern fame, was Walker's sidekick) at the Baltimore rock station WFBR. One day the phone rang at the Glass home. The great man was calling. He dispatched his limo to ferry the budding gag writer to a job interview. The upshot was that after graduation, Glass went to work at WFBR for $15 a week. He made coffee runs, but he also wrote more jokes, a few of which got on the air. (Among them was a groaner pegged to the then–hot news that tennis star Richard Raskind had undergone pioneering sex-reassignment surgery, becoming Renée Richards. Glass wrote that "The Renée Richards Ball Toss" at the upcoming Maryland State Fair would pay homage to the transformation: "It used to be three balls for a dollar; now it's no balls.") The time with Walker was a blast, and when Glass got to Northwestern, he signed up at WNUR, the college station, where he produced promos inspired by Dick Orkin, the creator of the radio series *Chickenman*, a spoof on the 1960s TV series *Batman*.

At the end of his first year in Chicago, Glass drove to Washington to meet the executive then heading up NPR's promotional department.

"I want someone to listen to my tapes," Jay Kernis recalled Glass announcing right off the bat. Within minutes, the two were hunched over a reel-to-reel machine in one of M Street's edit booths listening to Glass's efforts for WNUR. "You're really good," Kernis told his gawky visitor.

"Can I stick around and work for free over the summer?" the grateful Glass asked. The answer was yes.

Throughout the summer of 1978, Glass dashed between jobs at Maryland Shock Trauma and NPR, where under Kernis's direction he wrote promos for *All Things Considered* and an innovative new documentary project called *Radio Experience* that was part of the network's *Options* series, which typically aired somnolent seminars from DC think tanks. *Radio Experience* was different. The brainchild of Keith Talbot, the audio autodidact who in NPR's early days was a protégé of Bill Siemering, the show aspired to something unique. In cahoots with another member of the old guard, Mike Waters, the former cohost of *ATC*, Talbot was trying to create broadcast art. Glass's role was to sell the results to listeners. He possessed an uncanny ability to summarize nearly any subject in a few words. "Ira was great" at it, Talbot recalled. He told him, "Come back next summer and be my PA." Glass had landed a full-time position at NPR for the following year.

On one level, Glass's apprenticeship with Talbot was the equivalent of a graduate-level seminar with a brilliant and generous savant. The long-haired, antiauthoritarian producer of *Radio Experience* was the audio version of a New Wave auteur. He conceived of shows based on no more than a philosophical mystery he wanted to explore or a sound he wanted to sample. Although Glass's official job was to churn out promos, he was soon helping mix and edit episodes. One, titled "Attic Ballads," took its cues from the ideas of Carl Jung. "We talked to people about the things they saved, numinous things" recalled Talbot. "A brother and sister holding their father's medicine bag" remembered his work as a doctor. "The concept was mine, but Ira got it right away." Another, titled "Ocean Hour," focused on people who lived near or worked on the seas. The style was spare: No narration, no intrusions from the interviewers (Talbot edited them out). Just sounds of the surf and voices. "The audience has to go to it," Glass recalled, "but it's very beautiful, very thoughtfully designed and paced."

Talbot drove his staff hard. "He was a crazy man," Skip Pizzi, who engineered episodes of *Radio Experience*, said later. "He'd work through the night. He had these high goals and would not quit until he was done." Most evenings Glass lugged stacks of tapes into the edit booths then, using a razor blade and emulsion, cut and spliced sequences. As the hours passed, he pared the cuticles of his thumbs with the razor blade until they bled. "We'd come in the next morning and see a trail, drops of blood leading to the bathroom," Pizzi recalled. "It sounds metaphysical, but in this case, blood was shed on the tape."

Talbot was not the only public radio innovator to exert an influence on Glass during the summer of 1979. Joe Frank, who made his reputation with *In the Dark*, a Saturday-night program of moody monologues and risky improvisations that aired on New York's WBAI, had fetched up in Washington as host of *Weekend All Things Considered*. Frank's style was too out there for *ATC*—and *ATC* was too restrictive for Frank—but he remained at NPR, contributing pieces probing the psychodynamics of his own peculiarities. They aired as standalone episodes of *Options*. In one, Frank invented a character suffering from venereal disease then had him read explicit personal ads aloud. The idea was to examine how illness affects desire. In another, he mocked the sort of panel discussions often broadcast on public radio by impersonating a visitor to New York whose brilliant observations about the city keep getting interrupted by panel discussions. "Joe did some of the weirdest, most off-the-ranch stuff that ever got on NPR," Talbot said later.

The combined impact of Talbot and Frank on Glass was profound. "What I learned," he said later, "is the sheer expansiveness of what radio could be. Before, I hadn't heard anything ambitious on the radio. Johnny Walker was wonderful, but I didn't understand the scale of what radio could be."

In the fall of 1979, Glass transferred to Brown University. He'd never fit in at Northwestern. "It was flat," he said later. "The students weren't engaged." In contrast, Brown was a hive, particularly if you pursued the subject that had become Glass's obsession: semiotics. At the time the school's third-most-popular humanities major, the field stresses the value of signs and symbols as a way of perceiving meanings. At once a bold academic course and a jargon-filled bastion of trendy impracticalities, semiotics lent itself to parody. ("What are you gonna do with semiotics?" asks the skeptic. "Semiosis," answers the believer. "Where?" the skeptic demands. "At the International Center of Semiotics," replies the believer.) For Glass, however, semiotics was not so much an intellectual passion as a laboratory in the topic he'd embraced at NPR: storytelling. While his fellow students were rifling literature for clues to obscure matters, he was searching for techniques he could use to create narratives. In *S/Z*, a book by Roland Barthes central to the discipline, he discovered his bible.

"I got to Brown and read a book that changed everything for me," Glass said later. "What Barthes does in *S/Z* is he takes apart a short story by Balzac ["Sarrasine"], and the thing he's interested in is not what your high school teacher is interested in: 'What are the themes? What is the moral? Who are the characters?' He's not interested in any of that. What he's interested in is 'Why does this get to you?' He's interested in why you keep reading. 'What is the pleasure of the text?' Barthes breaks it down to five things—codes, he calls them—that are operating on you at all times."

As Glass came to see it, two Barthes codes are crucial to narrative. The "proairetic code" holds that if a writer deploys a cunning sequence of details or events in his work, people will follow until the end. Meanwhile the "hermeneutic code" advises that these details or events must engage a deeper meaning. For a story to keep an audience spellbound, it must be more than its parts. There must be a central idea. "Barthes," he said later, "was presenting a tool kit on how to think about what gets to you."

For Glass, *S/Z* amounted to the ultimate storytelling manual. Combined with the skills and inspirations he'd gleaned working for Keith Talbot and observing Joe Frank, it gave him an advantage. How many other twenty-two-year-olds hoping to get into some form of electronic media had this kind of background? There was, however, a problem—and it was big. When it came to putting what he knew into practice, Glass was clueless. He was all theoretical hat and no reportorial cattle. He'd never attended a city council meeting or followed a political campaign. As he said later, "I didn't know anything about journalism."

• • •

The Ira Glass who started as a full-time employee at NPR's M Street head-quarters in 1982 could not have seemed more out of place. This was the era of peak Mankiewicz. The Troika—Wertheimer, Totenberg, and Roberts—was in ascendance. *Morning Edition*, after its rocky start, had become a hit not only with the listening public but also with Washington insiders. The network's free-spirited producers were snorting cocaine and pairing off in the edit booths. In contrast, the recent Brown graduate—who typically wore dorky shirts, patterned sweaters, and aviator shades—came across in the words of several older colleagues as a twelve-year-old. "I used to talk to Mankiewicz in the hall," Glass said later, but to him "I was a kid." As Skip Pizzi later put it: "He was real green."

Glass at twenty-three was amiable and eager to please. He'd done magic tricks (disappearing coins and the like) since his early teens, and on a couple of occasions during his initial months at NPR, he provided the entertainment at events for staffers' children. "He performed as a clown at my daughter's second birthday party," remembered Sanford Ungar, at the time the cohost of *All Things Considered*. For Glass, magic was an icebreaker, a way of making friends.

Even so, Glass, thanks to his apprenticeship with Talbot, possessed an edge. He criticized much of NPR's 1980s programming. "Keith, who seemed to know everything, had contempt for the daily news shows," Glass said later. "He thought they were really square, so I thought they were really square." Glass included in his indictment efforts that at the time network executives held up as groundbreaking. *A Question of Place*, the prestige documentary series produced by Robert Montiegel (creator of *Voices in the Wind*) and dedicated to examining the lives of writers and thinkers struck him as "pious." As for NPR's most ambitious 1980s venture, *Father Cares*, the Noah Adams project about Jonestown, he wrote it off as "an artsy seventies movie driven entirely by emotion." Glass was haughty. For every NPR staffer who adored him ("a great guy" remembered Ungar), others were dubious. "Ira was full of himself," recalled Margot Adler. "An Ivy League college boy."

Conflicting opinions about Glass would never really cease at NPR, but from the start there was accord about two facts: he worked hard, and he was gifted. Because of the demands Talbot had placed on him during those bloody, late-night editing sessions in 1979, he could cut tape with skill, transforming raw interviews into broadcast-ready material on demand. "There weren't many people who could edit audiotape at that level," Glass said later. In the 1980s, "the fastest way to impress people at M Street was to know how to edit reel-to-reel tape."

Glass shuttled from one NPR show to another in his first years, applying his skills to every sort of story. One week he was editing short pieces for *All Things Considered*, the next long pieces for *NPR Dateline*, the brief-lived single-topic series hosted by Ungar as a lead-in to *ATC*. He was a valuable commodity, but he was also expendable. When the Mankiewicz-induced financial crisis hit in 1983, Glass was among the scores of low-level workers shown the door. He used the period to address his weak spot, bolstering his reporting skills by doing freelance stories for Washington's Pacifica station, WPFW.

By 1987, Glass was back at NPR, although just part time. Living in New York, where he'd moved with his first serious girlfriend (a NYU law student), he'd travel to DC to edit stories for *Morning Edition* and *All Things Considered*. At *ATC*, he acquired a new mentor, a network giant whose magnum opus he'd mocked: Noah Adams. "In his interviews, he'd get people to explain what had happened, and then he'd broaden out the story to a thought." Although not a semiotician, Adams practiced what Barthes preached. He infused his work with significance.

When Neal Conan was put in charge of *ATC*, he gave Glass a full-time job to do a specific assignment: Bring out the sense of humor of the show's new cohost. "Neal said to me, 'Robert Siegel is really funny, but he's not funny when hosting. Your job is to go to the morning story meetings, and if Robert says something funny, make him say it on the air that night. I have other producers, but I don't have one who can do that.'" It was an insane task, but Conan was serious, so much so that he extended Glass the kind of offer rarely made at the budget-conscious NPR. The network would fly him from New York to Washington on Sunday evenings, then fly him back on Fridays. He wouldn't have to move.

"There was very little Ira couldn't do," Conan said later. Indeed, Conan soon gave Glass the job of producing Renee Montagne, who after her dazzling start as Siegel's partner had faltered. To address her worst weakness—conducting interviews—Glass dreamed up a feature in which she would always ask subjects the same question: "What music are they listening to now?" The hope was that by repeating one simple query, she would grow more at ease in this part of the job while also eliciting good answers. "We'd talk to guys in a missile silo, and to our surprise they listened to Barbra Streisand," Glass recalled. He also arranged to get Montagne regularly out of the studio. For a Valentine's Day story about first dates, he had her strolling the streets of Washington asking questions and soliciting advice (One interviewee told her not to eat salads because the lettuce gets stuck between your teeth). Montagne was grateful. "God bless him," she said later. "He made it his job to help me find my voice." But it was too little, too late. Conan fired her anyway.

Working with *ATC*'s Alex Chadwick, Glass started generating stories more imaginative than those typically heard on NPR's daily shows. In 1987, the two stumbled upon a brief news item about Jenifer Graham, a fifteen-year-old student at Victor Valley High School near Los Angeles. She had refused to dissect a frog during biology class because she objected to killing a living creature for the sake of science. The matter ended in court, leading to a surprising ruling. The judge said Graham still had to dissect a frog but that her school district had to provide her one that had died of natural causes. Glass booked the wonderfully named naturalist Christy Crawl to hold forth on the relevant biology, and along with Chadwick and an engineer they plunged into northern Virginia's Huntley Meadows Park to see just how hard it is to find a dead amphibian in the wild. "We waded out to where the dark water was knee deep," Chadwick began his report. "Something squawked gently." Interjected Crawl, "That was a frog, a rain frog, making a distress call." Bingo. Except the naturalist added that the body of this frightened creature would most likely never be found. Dead frogs generally ended up in predators' bellies. What had started as a cute story about a kid's resistance to an assignment had become a journey into the mysteries of life and death in the animal kingdom. By this point, Glass said later, he'd learned "the things that divide mediocre radio stories from good ones. In good ones, you break things up: A long stretch of script. Quote. Description. More quote. You vary the rhythms and the sounds and the whole thing laying out." It was the proairetic and hermeneutic codes in action, and there was even a punch line. The only sure way to find a dead frog outdoors is if it's been squashed by a car.

In late 1988, NPR gave Glass, who'd split with his New York girlfriend and was back living in Washington, a trial run as host of *Weekend All Things Considered*. It was a gigantic break, and à la Scott Simon during the early months of *Weekend Edition*, he not only fronted the show but also reported pieces from the field. In many, he put into practice another idea. "I wanted to do stories about everyday people. I just had this feeling that everything around me was not being documented. The way public radio tried to do it was to go for a homespun, country thing. It wasn't capturing the urban life most of us were leading," One of his *WATC* efforts foreshadowed what he had in mind.

Titled "Dead Animal Man," Glass's seven-minute dispatch zeroes in on the life of Clarence Hicks, a worker in the Washington, DC, Department of Sanitation whose job was to drive from one accident scene to the next disposing the remains of all kinds of critters. Glass followed Hicks for a day, mixing snippets of biography and insight with the sound of a shovel scraping concrete and bodies getting tossed. Although sad, the story, told only with sparse narration, never seems morose. This task is necessary, even noble, and Hicks occasionally provides comic relief, such as when he yells at a passerby, "Hey, buddy! You seen a dead cat laying around anywhere?"

Despite Glass's high hopes, his tryout at *Weekend All Things Considered* was a flop. NPR news vice president Adam Clayton Powell III was trying to build a more diverse staff, and he hired the Filipino American Emil Guillermo to front the show. "Being a white candidate for host at that time was not an asset," Glass said later. But skin color was not the main factor. Glass was regarded by a powerful few at the network as someone who valued style over substance. "I was seen as a lightweight," he said. Indeed, a *WATC* producer remarked, "We let him try out, but it was like children's hour on the radio." In a *Washington Post* story summarizing the state of things at NPR in the late 1980s, Glass self-deprecatingly referred to himself as "the Fluff King."

Ira Glass moved to Chicago in 1989 in part because he felt his career at M Street had stalled. In the Midwest, he could freelance for *All Things Considered* while pondering what to do next. More important, he'd fallen in love with a woman whose work required her to be there.

Lynda Barry was well on her way to becoming a star. Syndicated cartoonist (*Ernie Pook's Comeek*), author (*The Fun House*), and regular guest on *Late Night with David Letterman*, she was a redheaded dynamo, funny and brash. "Ira was trying to make it in public radio at that point," recalled Jacki Lyden, then a reporter in NPR's Midwest bureau. "Lynda was already famous." Her first play, *The Good Times Are Killing Me*, was slated to open in Chicago early the next year.

Despite the difference in their levels of success, Barry was the needier of the two. So smitten was she with Glass, she said, "He could have had a six-inch wart growing out of the middle of his forehead . . . and I would have thought he was cute." Of mixed Irish-Filipino heritage, Barry was raised in a polyglot section of Seattle. "We all wanted to be pimps when we grew up," she recalled. "There was a thing in our neighborhood called pimp socks— nylon socks with stripes in them, and they came in bright colors. You kind of had to fold 'em over when you put 'em in your tennis shoes. Then you be pimpin.'" Glass dubbed her "little Ghetto Girl." She did not protest. "I'm sure he meant it in the nicest way," she later wrote.

The Glass who fell for Barry would have been almost unrecognizable to executives at NPR's Washington headquarters—and to his family in Baltimore. He'd grown his hair long, tying it in back into a defiant ponytail, not one of those ratty styles popular with yuppies but a black ball of the sort boasted by samurai warriors. He'd also begun smoking. ("If you lined up everybody in America who started smoking that year," he said later, "it'd be a bunch of twelve- and fourteen-year-olds. I would be the only thirty-year-old.") Here again, there was nothing halfhearted about it. He rolled his own with Drum tobacco and papers. Then there was the booze. "I didn't drink until I got to Chicago," he recalled. "But in Chicago, people drank. I think of myself at the time as being a Chicago drinker." He liked a shot of Jameson followed by a couple of beers—sometimes too many of both. "One night we all went out to a club, Lee's Unleaded Blues, and Ira got completely soused," Lyden said later. "He fell down in my bathroom and got a bloody nose. I put him to bed. The next morning, he said, 'Oh, Jacki, I have learned an important lesson about alcohol.'"

That the Glass-Barry relationship was between a privileged young man trying to figure out his life and a young woman who'd worked her way up from poverty soon led to trouble. Where Barry craved emotional support, Glass sought to prove that he was dominant. "We were reading the *New York Times* one morning a couple weeks in," Barry recalled, "and he looked at me and said, 'You don't know what the IMF is, do you?'" Such petty one-upmanship was typical. During a birthday party in Washington for Glass not long after he and Barry began dating, he was holding forth about profound matters to a table of NPR colleagues. "It was clear she felt left out," Smokey Baer, one of the guests, said later. As the evening wore on, Barry asked Baer if she could borrow a prized possession—a vintage Waterman pen that he happened to have in his pocket. He obliged, and Barry started sketching a cartoon on a placemat. If she couldn't get into the conversation, she could at least amuse herself—and Baer. Ira had "this amazing girlfriend" he recalled, and he wasn't "paying any attention to her."

Glass and Barry stayed together for eighteen fraught months. "They argued a lot," said Lyden. Later, there would be disagreement about who broke up with whom, but it was Barry who took charge of getting the news out, and she did so on national television.

During an early 1991 appearance on *Late Night with David Letterman,* in response to Dave's puzzlement as to why she was so drunk the night before she'd been singing Led Zeppelin songs to a barroom full of strangers, Barry declared, "My boyfriend dumped me."

"I'm sorry to hear that," Letterman replied. "Was it a long-term deal?"

"Yeah, we'd been going out for like a year and a half."

"How did he announce his feelings or lack thereof to you?"

"He gave me a watch. He gave me a watch. I swear to God."

"Like a retirement party," Letterman responded incredulously.

After Barry said that she was finally starting to get over it, Letterman asked, "And where did this guy . . . Is he still in the Chicago area?"

"Yeah. Yeah. He's like a lot of guys. He needed more space. What do you guys do with that space? Why do you need that space?"

"Well, I've got an awful lot of shoes," Letterman offered, putting the matter to rest without Barry ever mentioning Glass by name. Not that anyone outside NPR would have recognized his name. At thirty-one, he was an anonymous toiler in the public radio wilderness. Barry took her final revenge on Glass in *One! Hundred! Demons!*, her next book, by caricaturing him, samurai ponytail and all, sitting in a chair reading a copy of *Lonely Genius Gazette*. Later, Glass said, "I was an idiot. Anything bad she says about me I can confirm."

Glass's initial leap out of obscurity came courtesy of the organization that just a couple of years earlier had shunned him. Although he had continued to contribute stories to NPR since moving to Chicago and occasionally still encouraged humor in Robert Siegel's work for *All Things Considered*, his reputation as a lightweight lingered. One network executive, though, felt different. "I had a little bit of money," recalled Larry Abramson, at the time NPR's national editor, "and I sent Ira to Chicago's Taft High School." The task was to follow a class for a year, reporting on all facets of its academic and social life. "Larry felt that education reporting everywhere was unsatisfying," Glass said later. "He said either the stories are 'Here's how everything is going to hell' or 'Here's how one program is different.' He's like, 'We never get a sense of why it's so hard to fix a school. Why do schools stay mediocre?'" Chicago was in the midst of instituting reforms aimed at decentralizing district control and giving authority back to individual principals. The principal at Taft was "idealistic and wanted to fix the school," Glass recalled. The big-picture project NPR had in mind offered him an opportunity to put into practice everything he'd learned about storytelling.

During the year Glass all but lived at Taft High, he treated its principal, teachers, and students not as if they were journalistic sources but as if they were characters in a play. To capture it all in intimate detail, he purchased at his own expense a Lectrosonics wireless microphone. "It cost as much as my car," he recalled. Because the mic did not restrict his subjects' movements, he could record everyone at will. People were "just talking, forgetting it was there. It was magic." As a result, Glass captured subplots—there was a reform faction and an antireform one—subtext, and gossip. The characters evolved over the course of time. "The leader of the antireform faction was one of the best teachers in the school. He's like, 'It's teaching. You're not gonna change it with reform,'" he recalled. *All Things Considered* aired Glass's effort as a twenty-part series. Abramson was so impressed that he assigned him to do a similar project at Chicago's Washington Irving Elementary School. Together, the series won nearly every education journalism award there is.

The next turning point in Glass's career occurred in the bedraggled studios of Chicago's WBEZ. Situated atop the forty-one-story Bankers Building, a 1927 behemoth in the city's Loop, it required two elevator rides followed by a climb up a steep set of stairs to get there. The views should have been stunning, but there were no exterior windows. As for the decor, it was depressing: stained brown carpet, Rubbermaid garbage can in a corner to collect water leaking from the ceiling. The equipment dated to when the station served as an arm of the Chicago Board of Education. The dials on the ancient green mixing console regularly shorted out. When engineers tried to bring down the volume, the audio sometimes just disappeared. Then there was the mic. It had been lifted from a vintage Dictaphone. As someone who often sat in on recording sessions at WBEZ later wrote, the room oozed "a sickly smell of defeat."

At eight p.m. on Friday, November 30, 1990, Ira Glass, Lynda Barry (the pair had reached a professional rapprochement), and producer Gary Covino crammed into this claustrophobic aerie for the debut broadcast of *The Wild Room*, the precursor to *This American Life*. Not that the parallels were exact. *The Wild Room*, said Covino, would initially consist of "free-form documentary banter." He meant that the program would air standalone radio pieces too ambitious for broadcast elsewhere, works in progress by the hosts and others, and monologues. The three would then dissect and comment on the offerings, each bringing their own perspective to bear. Glass would be shiny and wry, Barry jokey and real, and Covino—who remained the rabble-rouser he'd been back in 1981 when he set in motion the events that led *All Things Considered* to air its infamous interview with a woman ruing that the attempted assassination of Ronald Reagan failed—dark and cynical.

The initial broadcast, which featured several stories about Nelson Mandela, who just months earlier had been released from a South African prison after twenty-seven years, was uneven (the highlight was a conversation with John Matisonn, an ex-NPR correspondent and friend of Mandela). So, too, were the next few episodes. "The shows were a little rough," recalled Covino. Soon enough, though, *The Wild Room* began to deliver, winning a small but devoted audience. "The people were doing brilliant stuff with no spotlight," recalled Shirley Jahad, at the time a reporter for WBEZ. "Friday nights are a forgotten landscape on the radio clock. You had to catch them when you were headed out for your evening. When it sailed, it did so in beautiful ways. It was a source of conversation."

A memorable early installment paid homage to Elvis with a free-associating structure and obsessive level of detail that *Chicago* magazine termed "almost psychedelic." Glass's cohosts presided over the trippy parts. Barry confided that when listening to *Blue Hawaii* as a girl, she would touch Elvis's lips on the album-jacket photo and dream about making out with him. Covino deemed Elvis the American Christ, born not in a manger but "the Mississippi equivalent of it" and said that he performed miracles: "He made white people listen to black music." Glass stuck to the facts, albeit weird ones. On Mercury, the King would have weighed just 99 pounds ("Lean and mean," chortled Barry) but 9,280 pounds on the sun ("Talk about a hunk of burning love," snorted Covino).

The banter among the three could get crazy, but that phase ended, not because anyone matured but because Barry quit. "It had to do with how she felt" about Ira, recalled Covino. Although the two had sufficiently patched things up to work together, she remained wounded. Glass then made things worse when he visited a posh hair salon to get his ponytail cut off and afterward declared on the air that he did so because his ex, who liked it, had dumped him. "Get this," Barry said later. "He dumps me and does this radio piece. That's Ira to a T."

That left just Glass and Covino at *The Wild Room* microphone (they would share the weekly $100 stipend WBEZ had started paying), which in the end was apt, for of the three, they were the true believers. Covino was one of the few people in public radio on par with Glass in skill and ambition. Both wanted to host national programs. In every other way, however, the two could not have been more different.

"If I were to construct a 'Radio Moscow' picket sign for Jesse Helms to tote through Lafayette Park, I'd paste a picture of Gary Covino on it," Sarah Vowell wrote in *Radio On*, her memoir of a year in the 1990s spent binge-listening to everything on America's AM and FM dials, *The Wild Room* included.

Slight (five feet, seven inches), bearded, shaven-headed and given to corduroy jackets, velour pullovers, and jeans, Covino, the son of an Italian American restaurateur, grew up in Brunswick, New Jersey. Like Glass, he was enthralled with radio, but unlike Glass, his taste ran to anarchic stuff. Among his heroes was WBAI's Jean Shepherd, purveyor of one of the medium's great hoaxes. *I, Libertine*, a radio story about a nonexistent book, was so convincing that people swamped New York stores trying to purchase copies. As a student at Antioch College, Covino patterned his work at WYSO, the college station, after Shepherd's. In *The Dark Is Beginning*, he played Frank Despot, "the voice of the people," while on *Popular Radio Front*, he portrayed "Just Plain Joe," a homegrown Stalin.

Covino arrived at NPR in 1979, a year after Glass, and his initial impressions, like Glass's, were mixed, but where Glass's brief was aesthetic, his was political. Covino believed public radio was gutless. "I did not have a great respect for NPR as a news organization," he said later. "It was a conventional wisdom factory. Safe and boring."

Still, Covino, whose first job was as a production assistant on *All Things Considered*, embraced the work. For election eve 1980, he proposed that *ATC* preface each of its stories about the final machinations of the Jimmy Carter–Ronald Reagan campaign with relevant quotes from that great judge of the American polity H. L. Mencken. He further proposed that NPR's in-house expert on such matters, Frank Mankiewicz, voice the bits. Chris Koch, the show's then–executive producer, said yes, and the effort came off brilliantly, so much so that network news chief Barbara Cohen decided to place Covino in charge of a new unit producing half-hour history documentaries for *ATC*. He excelled at it, churning out productions pegged to the twentieth anniversary of the Cuban missile crisis and the tenth anniversary of San Francisco's summer of love.

Covino also excelled in the field. In the mid-1980s, he started producing stories for the foreign desk. In 1986, one—the incendiary election between Ferdinand Marcos and Corazon Aquino—took him and Bill Buzenberg, the future NPR News vice president, to the Philippines. On voting day, Covino was staking out a polling place when it came under attack by Marcos's thugs. As furniture was smashed and people beaten, Covino kept his tape recorder running. He then raced to his hotel, where because of the time difference between Manila and DC, he and Buzenberg could assemble an eight-minute story and transmit it via alligator clips attached to a phone back to M Street in time for that day's *Morning Edition*. NPR was the sole American news outfit to air actual audio of the violence. "Everybody else was saying, 'Today, there's voting in the Philippines. Polls were marred by violence,'" Buzenberg said later.

Yet the verdict at NPR on Covino, just as it was on Glass, was mixed. "Gary could be hard to work with," *Morning Edition* producer Steve Proffitt recalled. He also never abandoned his revolutionary orthodoxy. He had "a left-wing analysis of everything," Smokey Baer said later. "Very suspicious of deviating political values." Covino's doctrinaire leanings led *All Things Considered* to broadcast the disastrous tape about Reagan. As far as Covino was concerned, the interviewee he put on *ATC* expressed the "views of the seventy-percent-Black population of Washington." After Mankiewicz was besieged by station managers and lawmakers furious that the network had aired such an ugly sentiment about the badly wounded president, Covino lost some of his sheen.

The differences between Glass's sensibilities and Covino's gave *The Wild Room* energy. Glass was controlled on the air, his remarks scripted down to the pauses and the laughs. Covino spoke off the cuff. A 1992 episode titled "On the Bus—or Off" illustrates their opposing styles. Glass, who was covering Bill Clinton's presidential campaign for NPR, presented a reasoned account from tape he'd gathered while traveling with the candidate. Covino riffed on a different kind of bus trip—the one taken by Ken Kesey and his Merry Pranksters as they tried to turn America on to LSD. His primary source was recollections by the prankster Neal Cassady included as a flexi disc in a book about the Grateful Dead.

Such disparities were more pronounced when the hosts fronted *The Wild Room* solo, as was often the case, because each had a day job. Glass was contributing more frequently now to NPR, especially to *Morning Edition*, for which he produced the monologues of David Sedaris, whose pieces he'd been airing on *The Wild Room*. Those same pieces, edited down, were perfect for *Morning Edition*. Although the initial one perturbed Bob Edwards, they made Sedaris practically a household name, and they raised Glass's stock in DC. Covino, meanwhile, was producing ambitious segments for *Sound Print*, a public radio documentary series launched in the late 1980s by Bill Siemering.

A typical Glass episode of *The Wild Room* recounted his efforts to retain a relationship with a former girlfriend. "Just friends. Just friends," he begins. "You know you're in trouble when the word 'just' appears in front of the word 'friend.'" He then describes a visit the two made to Saks Fifth Avenue. He accompanies her into a dressing room while she tries on a silk top and mini-skirt. After agonizing over being privy to this moment (Was it appropriate? Was there something still between them?), he comes to a painful realization: the outfit is meant for the eyes of his ex's new love. Her realization: "You're going to talk about this on your radio show."

A typical Covino episode, which aired shortly after the terrorist bombing of the Murrah Federal Building in Oklahoma City, explored the possibility of armed insurrection in America. The host built the hour around a story by Shirley Jahad about the Lake View, Illinois, gun show. Her report was alarming but straightforward. Covino couldn't resist the chance to try to channel the consciousness of a militiaman. "I'm in radio," he cried. "The microphone is my weapon. The microphone is my Uzi." To which Jahad replied, "And you shoot it off a lot, don't you Gary?"

Three years into *The Wild Room*'s run, WBEZ hired a new programming director. Torey Malatia came from commercial radio, and he began making over the station in the mold of his most recent employer, the Chicago powerhouse WLS. The only WBEZ show he didn't touch was *The Wild Room*. "Ira was headed in the right direction, and I started talking with him," he said later.

"Ira would do his show on Friday night then come down from his junky studio to my office." From there the two would repair either to Kon Tiki Ports, where Glass consumed umbrella drinks, or Russian Tea Time, where he ordered lemon Stolichnaya. They struck up a friendship that did not include Covino. "Gary and I didn't hobnob," recalled Malatia.

The conversations between Malatia and Glass grew serious. WBEZ was in the long-overdue process of updating its operations. The station would soon move to state-of-the-art studios at Chicago's glittery Navy Pier on Lake

Michigan. "Torey went to Nick Rabkin at the MacArthur Foundation," Glass said later, "and asked, 'Hey, can you give us money for this project we're doing?'" After studying the station's fundraising efforts, Rabkin concluded that support from MacArthur was unnecessary. WBEZ's new facility already had sufficient financial backing. "'What you need,'" Glass recalled the executive countering, "'are decent programs. I will give you money for a program, but my condition is that you have to have someone with national experience come in and produce.' Torey looked around, and he knew me and Gary, and he turned to me and said, 'Have you got an idea for a show? I can get money for a show.' And I did have an idea."

Malatia excluded Covino from consideration in part because of his friendship with Glass and in part because the kind of program Rabkin wanted would focus more on culture (Glass's interest) than politics (Covino's passion). Malatia also didn't like Covino's on-air persona. It was too unpredictable, too much. "I liked the way Ira did *The Wild Room* when Gary was on vacation," he recalled. "There wasn't much planning with Gary. He was improvisational. Ira sounded improvisational, but it was all written down. So, I talked to Ira."

All of this was fine except no one talked to Covino. "I was deceived," he said later. "Mainly by Ira at this point and by Torey a bit—but also by myself. I sensed what was going on, but I didn't want to face the fact."

In early 1995, Glass and Malatia pitched the MacArthur Foundation a weekly series tentatively titled *Three Things from the Combo Plate*. They asked for a $150,000 grant to produce the pilot and prepare a number of episodes. Rabkin countered with an offer that would cover, but barely, the pilot and a couple of shows: $4,000. Glass and Malatia said yes, and Glass severed his relationship with NPR (he'd been there off and on for seventeen years) and went to work for WBEZ.

Throughout the spring, Glass holed up in his second-floor apartment in Chicago's Irving Park neighborhood. Christmas lights hung over the windows, while the shelves boasted Mexican Day of the Dead skeletons and voodoo bottles. Glued to a wall was the album jacket of Jackie Gleason's *Music for Lovers Only*. Nonetheless, as evidenced by an $1,800 Otari reel-to-reel editing machine in the living room, the place was a production facility. Here, starting daily at seven a.m., Glass—assisted solely by Emily Hanford, a twenty-four-year-old editor he referred to, shades of Lynda Barry, as "little slave girl"—assembled the pilot and first episodes. One featured a screed by Glass against the hit film *Forrest Gump* ("It made me mad. I didn't see why people took it seriously"). Another revolved around a reported story about a hacker who after being sentenced to home confinement figured out how to hack the computer system the court used to monitor him. The third offered a series of interviews with compulsive liars by Margy Rochlin, a Los Angeles writer who'd gotten to know Glass when he produced her pieces for *Morning Edition*.

By late summer, Malatia and Glass had changed the name of their series to *Your Radio Playhouse*, and they'd signed a one-page contract. Several stipulations—WBEZ would provide the show a soundproof studio and up-to-date editing terminals—were meant to guard against the audio glitches common to programs originating from the station's old facility. Most important was a line spelling out the financial relationship between the parties. Glass and WBEZ would co-own the show. Such deals were unheard of in public broadcasting.

Meantime Glass and Covino continued to front *The Wild Room* every Friday night. The evidence that Covino would not be a part of the project his colleague was launching could no longer be denied, although according to Covino, Glass still did not level with him. "Ira kept telling me things that let me hold on to," the illusion, he said later. "He was negative about whether they'd be able to pull it off. I thought maybe they won't be able to do it, and I won't have to face what's going on here." Later, Glass conceded that he'd been less than forthcoming. "I was sort of soft-pedaling it. I'm sorry about that. I'm sorry. I could have handled it by telling him earlier and more assertively. It's a hard thing to tell somebody, frankly."

Your Radio Playhouse became a reality after the MacArthur Foundation, which liked the samples, pledged $150,000. The premiere was slated for Friday, November 17, 1995, at nine p.m. Glass and Covino finally cleared the air. "We had a big dinner before we stopped doing *The Wild Room*," recalled Covino. During the meal, Glass, according to Covino, argued that his forthcoming effort was so unlike *The Wild Room* there were no grounds for Covino to think what he was plainly thinking: Glass was stealing their baby.

"It's a new show," Glass said.

"It's the same show," countered Covino.

"We're gonna do *this*."

"We already do *this*."

"We're gonna do *that*."

"We already do *that*."

Covino said he then demanded, "What's the difference?"

"I'm totally in control," he said Glass replied.

"I felt he'd finally given me an honest answer."

By Glass's lights, Covino not only misremembered the conversation but misapprehended the situation. "He felt like what I was doing was just *The Wild Room* without Gary, which to me seemed wrong on its face. One was a free-form radio show where we would go on with a plan then wing it and end up with something very different. It would go off in wild directions, and that was the premise of the show. Where I wanted this new show to be a completely produced, planned, and edited show."

Later, Covino could only shake his head. "Somewhere in his mind, there was a hierarchy," and live radio "was low in his hierarchy. It takes a lot of talent and skill to do it. It's like being a good jazz musician. But he didn't think that it was as impressive as sitting in front of music and playing the notes. He thought classical music was a higher form."

Following the dinner with Glass, Covino rushed to Torey Malatia's office at WBEZ's new headquarters at the Navy Pier. He had three goals. One, he wanted the station to give him the full, $100-per-episode stipend he and Glass were splitting at *The Wild Room*. Two, he asked WBEZ to cover his parking fee at the new location. Finally, he wanted a reassurance that *The Wild Room* would continue to air at eight p.m., an hour ahead of the slot announced for *Your Radio Playhouse*. Malatia said yes to the $100 but no to the other requests. Not only would *Your Radio Playhouse* not follow *The Wild Room*, it would *precede* it. According to Covino, Malatia basically said, "We're gonna do things to make you feel worse."

Covino spiraled into a depression. "I realized that this thing I'd always wanted, a national show, was never gonna happen. This vision I wanted was being taken away." Self-rebuke became a constant companion. Covino asked himself if he was a willing victim. He felt betrayed. He'd thought of Glass not just as a colleague but as a friend. So stupid. So naive.

Making it all but unbearable was WBEZ's setup at the Navy Pier. *The Wild Room* studio was separated from the *Your Radio Playhouse* studio by nothing but a glass wall. Covino worked alone in his room while Glass was suddenly surrounded by a staff afforded by the MacArthur Foundation. He was "in there with this bevy of servants," Covino said later, "and a big budget. I said servants instead of producers. That was nasty. But that's how he saw these people." Glass was not just succeeding, he was flaunting it. In an attempt to block out the sight, Covino gathered up the debris from the station's move—pieces of cardboard and soundproofing foam—and fashioned a crude curtain between their respective broadcast homes, but while he succeeded in removing his nemesis from sight, he could not remove him from mind.

A week before the premiere of *Your Radio Playhouse*, Gary Covino opened the mic at *The Wild Room* and without uttering Ira Glass's name trashed him. Never in the history of public radio has anyone administered such a nasty, intramural, on-air assault, and the whole monologue was aimed at one listener. To those with no way of knowing the context, Covino's screed seemed merely angry. Only its target would know the reason for the anger.

Covino began with a raw account of his father's years running New Jersey pizza parlors. Carmine Covino was fated to manage but never own the places. Whenever one became available, he was shoved aside. In a nation where everyone wants a piece of the action, he was a day late and a dollar short. For his son, who bussed tables at the joints, the pattern cast doubts on the whole system, and what intensified the doubts was that his father's clientele consisted mostly of Princeton students, smug Ivy Leaguers who seemed to float through their days impervious to the forces that tripped up people like Carmine and Gary. Do you know what it's like to watch your father ground down and realize that the same privileged types who thwarted him will one day thwart you? That's what Covino asked, and he asked it from a barricaded studio where he saw himself as doomed to carry on in anonymity as the Brown graduate next door rocketed into the media firmament. Covino's rant, when it came to uttering truths about the role class plays in who gets ahead in this American life, was as stinging as the novelist John O'Hara at his bitterest. In his tag, he spoke exclusively to his audience of one:

I hate to say it, because I'm feeling at one with my father this week, because it's back to the old realization I had a long time ago. You know, it just seems like in life there are two kinds of people. There's the golden boys, you know, who seem to get what they want. And then there are the other boys. There are the pizza boys. Starting here next week on WBEZ, we'll have two different radio pizza shops—different in name, anyway. One will be run by the golden boy, and the other will be right here at eight o'clock. *The Wild Room*, with me, Gary Covino, your radio pizza boy.

The November 10, 1995, edition of *The Wild Room* was all about those last words. "I did that show for the ending—with the coded meaning," Covino recalled. "Almost nobody got it," he added, except for the intended recipient. Just after the program aired, Glass called "in a half panic," said Covino. "He wanted to come over and we'd listen to it. I said, 'I'll make you a tape and send it to you.'" Years later, Glass was still grappling with what his former cohost had done. "I mean, it really captured his feeling of victimization," he said tentatively. Then: "I don't know. I don't know. I don't know." Finally: "Yeah, I had middle-class Jewish parents, and it was assumed they were preparing me for college. That was my path. And that absolutely gives a person an advantage over one whose parents don't do that." But he could go no further. Again: "I don't know. I don't know. I don't know."

If Gary Covino's harangue was meant to throw his former partner off, it didn't. When seven p.m. the next Friday rolled around, Ira Glass hit the air with the kind of deft bit that would become a staple of *Your Radio Playhouse*, or, as it would soon be renamed, *This American Life*.

"Mr. Franklin?"

"I'm ready."

"It's Ira Glass."

"Oh, you're the emcee of the show, Ira. Hold on a second."

At which point, Glass's inaugural guest, the veteran New York broadcasting personality Joe Franklin, started jabbering with some guy in the background named Tony. All the while, Glass kept his tape recorder on, treating the moment not as a setback but as a gift. Speaking over the chatter, he informed listeners, "One great thing about starting a new show is the utter anonymity. Nobody knows what to expect from you."

The opener felt delightfully offhand, and it introduced what would become another *This American Life* staple—programs devoted to a theme, in this case "New Beginnings." Act one focused on Franklin, whose talk show billed itself as the longest-running series on American television. (Asked the secret to his success, Franklin advised, "Get the plug in fast"). Act two was a monologue by a twenty-seven-year-old who after traveling to Jerusalem and sleeping near the site of Christ's crucifixion was born again into a life of true Christian charity. Up next, Glass tried to interview his parents about his new venture. His father was too busy to come to the phone, while his mother urged Ira to get out of radio and into TV, where he could make real money, adding that she knew he would succeed because he resembled the actor Hugh Grant. To which Glass replied: "Other adults look at me and think: 'Tall Jew.'" Then came another first-person story, this one about an HIV-positive performance artist seeking rebirth during a cross-country road trip with a friend. The premiere episode closed with a reported piece about an ex-con who following release from prison took up the trumpet. Each segment featured innovative use of music (Django Reinhardt during the conversation with Franklin, Billie Holiday's "God Bless the Child" for the finale), and the closing credits listed a group of staffers who would become regulars: Alix Spiegel, Margy Rochlin, and a southern raconteur and magazine writer named Jack Hitt. Liftoff had occurred.

As for Gary Covino, his "pizza boy" monologue proved to be premonitory. A month later in New Jersey, his father died from a heart attack. Before the funeral, Gary attended an open-casket wake. "I'm looking down at my father, and the specifics are different, but I see that he was trapped, and that I'm trapped, too. I wasn't going to let this happen. I decided to end *The Wild Room*, because it was a source of pain. I wasn't going to get what I wanted. So basically, I threw it in Torey Malatia's lap. I wasn't going to stay around while the *This American Life* juggernaut was" beginning. Although Covino would continue to contribute pieces to NPR, he would not front another program. As for his feelings about Glass, he vowed never again to speak his name, and thirty years later, he still would not do so, referring to him as either "the other person" or "the motherfucker."

• • •

For public radio insiders, the split between Ira Glass and Gary Covino was a source of vocal disagreement. "Gary's a great guy," said the longtime NPR editor John Dinges. "Ira shoved him aside." Countered Glass loyalist Margy Rochlin, "Gary Covino is wrong. It's a fantasy on Gary's part that Ira stole the show."

For the start-up staff at *This American Life*, however, the entire thing happened offstage. All they knew, recalled Peter Clowney, one of the show's original producers, was that "Mom and Dad got divorced." The task of cranking out weekly one-hour episodes left no time to look any direction but forward. "We were going around the clock," said Clowney. "The hours were officially mentally ill," added Sarah Vowell, who in the aftermath of the publication of *Radio On* became one of the show's most prolific early contributors.

In the first months of *This American Life*, Glass and his overworked colleagues—among them Nancy Updike (still at *TAL*) and Julie Snyder (now at *Serial*)—turned out a number of engaging, well-produced shows. "Drama Bug" (episode 23) embodies the program's initial preference to address topics with a mixture of monologue (a David Sedaris account of a ninth-grade encounter with a mime who unleashed his inner hambone) and feature journalism (a reported piece by Glass about a suburban Chicago high school production of Neil Simon's *Lost in Yonkers*). "Dawn" (episode 15) offers evidence that from the outset the show was willing to undertake oddball stories. In a mixture of recollection and investigation, Jack Hitt profiles his eccentric boyhood neighbor Gordon Langley Hall, who in the late 1960s set Charleston, South Carolina, on its ear by becoming Dawn Langley Hall Simmons and throwing a coming-out party for her Chihuahua. In "Name Change" (episode 17) the program provides an early example of its transparency (or self-involvement) by exploring the rationale behind the decision to drop *Your Radio Playhouse* ("Public programming directors hate it," conceded the host) in favor of *This American Life*.

Glass, who had adopted an embryonic version of his uniform (black T-shirt, black jeans, black low-top Converse All-Stars, and the trademark black glasses), set the tone for everything. "Listen for the magic of the tape," he would urge reporters struggling to find the best quote in an interview.

"Throw a little banjo music under this and call it a day," he would advise producers obsessing over extraneous details. "He had a vision of what he wanted and he was vocal about it," recalled Julie Snyder. "The netherworld between *Nightline* and *Letterman*" was "what we were going for," said Vowell, adding the whole thing "had a '90s, Northside-of-Chicago aesthetic, which was jokey but lofty, brainy but suspicious of and mystified by up-tight, mainstream America."

On May 6, 1996, just a couple dozen episodes into its run, *This American Life* won a Peabody Award for programming the judges said captured "contemporary culture in fresh and inventive ways." Glass flew to New York for the big ceremony, where following a glowing introduction by Diane Sawyer he thanked his staff and then cheekily chided the well-heeled audience. "Statistics show that only one out of ten of you actually pledges to your local public radio station." He urged anyone who felt guilty about this to sign up at the conclusion of the event.

This American Life was out the chute fast. But no one was listening. After the show aired at seven p.m. in Chicago (while the stories were prerecorded, Glass read the prologue and interstitial copy live in the studio), a staffer would race a tape by car to the northwestern suburbs. WBEZ didn't have a satellite uplink, but WTTW did. From there *TAL* went out to a mere sixty subscriber stations. Across America, the program was not much more than a rumor.

The answer, Glass and Malatia agreed, was to persuade NPR to make *This American Life* part of its lineup. That had basically been the idea all along. Malatia handled the formal pitches. "I was on the phone all the time with the folks in DC," he said later. Glass mailed cassettes of the show to network producers and executives. In a cover letter, he offered to pay each $50 to listen to and critique the episodes. Murray Horwitz, the recently appointed director of NPR's classical music and entertainment programming, was among the recipients. Although he later conceded that some of the program's stories were interesting, he believed the whole enterprise was marred by a fatal flaw, and when he spoke to Glass, he wasn't shy about stating what it was.

"Ira," he asked pointedly, "do you have to be the host?"

"Yes," came back the immediate response in a tone that Horwitz recalled left no room for compromise. To even broach the subject was to have committed a sacrilege.

By 1996, Glass's on-air persona was fully formed. During his early years at NPR, his delivery had been pretty much indistinguishable from that of others at the network. Only after he got to *The Wild Room* did he change it, adopting the pauses, stutters, and occasional laughs he believed increased the intimacy between himself and listeners. A lot of thought went into his approach, but the goal had been to make it seem as if there was no thought at all.

Horwitz couldn't have cared less. He just didn't like the way Glass sounded behind a mic, and he wasn't alone at NPR in feeling that way. Sandra Rattley, the network's vice president for cultural programming, also objected, as did Leslie Peters, the network's director of marketing. "Leslie really had it in for Ira," recalled Horwitz. "She had real animus against him." Where Glass believed that he'd perfected a new way of talking on the radio, these executives and others believed that he was affecting the intonations of a mannered broadcasting mainstay who represented everything that NPR should repudiate.

From the 1940s through the early 2000s, Paul Harvey was the most ubiquitous—and satirized—figure in American electronic media. (He was also one of the most successful. At its peak, *News and Comment*, his daily show, was syndicated by ABC to 1,200 stations.) Harvey's on-air patter, like Glass's, featured stops and starts, italicized phrases, and pauses. "*Hello, Americans*," he began each show. "This . . . is PAUL HARVEY. Stand by for . . . NOOZ!" Once Glass's tapes reached NPR, Horwitz and others could be heard cackling in the halls. "What's with the Paul Harvey delivery?"

The mockery coming out of Washington got back to Glass, prompting him to curtail his efforts to close a deal, leaving Malatia as a sales force of one. "I did most of the pitching to the network because it was upsetting to Ira," the WBEZ boss said later.

NPR executives found other things to dislike about *This American Life*. The program's mix of hard and soft stories was one. "It wasn't quite news, it wasn't quite cultural," recalled Horwitz. Also, the program presented a threat to an in-house project. *Anthem*, which featured performances

(Lucinda Williams, the Reverend Horton Heat) and interviews, was the kind of show the network's cultural executives understood. Horwitz's great success at NPR was *A Piano Jazz Christmas* (Hank Jones and John Lewis came into the studio and played carols). Rattley scored with *Wade in the Water* (a twenty-six-part joint production with the Smithsonian Institution that traced the rise of American gospel music and its relation to soul and R&B). Both loved artistic spectacle, which is what *Anthem* would champion. Glass, with his ideas involving narrative storytelling and plots, left them cold. As for Leslie Peters, she was just a naysayer, infamous at NPR for an edict she issued to reporters and producers on the eve of a network party for station managers: "Don't eat the shrimp." The delicacies, she announced, were intended solely for the honored guests.

Still, NPR did not flatly reject *This American Life*. Negotiations continued, and in May, when *TAL* won the Peabody, Malatia immediately called Horwitz, believing that the honor gave him some much-needed leverage.

"We just won the Peabody," Malatia enthused over the phone to the entertainment czar.

"Oh," Horwitz replied. "We have a whole case of them in our lobby."

It was over. As Malatia said later, "The trophy case line stung."

In June, NPR's six-person programming committee convened in the conference room at the network's Massachusetts Avenue headquarters. Glass did have one supporter in the group. "I said, 'This is great. Let's take it,'" recalled Bill Buzenberg, NPR's vice president of news. The committee rejected *This American Life* by a 5–1 vote.

Glass was crushed. "I always assumed that we would be distributed by NPR," he said later. "I'd grown up there. I knew everybody. But this woman Sandra Rattley and a few others just didn't like the show. They didn't get what about the show was good."

Ultimately, NPR's adverse decision regarding *This American Life* said more about the network than it did about Glass. By the late 1990s, NPR had grown resistant to new approaches and original voices. There was a "lack of regard for brilliant people," proclaimed the veteran KCRW station manager Ruth Seymour, the first broadcaster outside Chicago to air *TAL*. The trend, of course, went back to Mankiewicz and his rejection of *Prairie Home Companion*. The view had been codified by executives like Doug Bennet, who believed the network should stress its overall service as opposed to on-air personalities. To Buzenberg, such thinking defied common sense and NPR's history. "Susan Stamberg: Talent. Scott Simon: Talent. You build shows around talent." The loss of Glass ended up costing the network millions and delayed future innovation. However, as Bruce Drake, who as NPR's managing editor in the early 1990s was Glass's boss, later noted: "It was the best thing that could happen to him."

The same month NPR turned down *This American Life*, Glass and Malatia flew to Minneapolis to meet with Stephen Salyer, the director of Public Radio International (PRI). A fledgling outfit, PRI boasted only one successful program: *Marketplace*. Salyer, who'd come to the company from public television's WNET, was looking to expand the operation, and he loved *TAL*. "Salyer was our champion," said Malatia. "He wanted an exclusive with us, and he gave us an advance, which was great. Nobody else wanted us at all."

Public Radio International promoted *This American Life*. They "doubled our carriage in three months," Glass recalled, meaning that the number of stations carrying the show leapt from 60 to 120. "They were enthusiastic about our business, and very skillful."

Still, *TAL* remained a dicey proposition. "The thing had a fly-by-night feeling," conceded Glass. In the hopes of establishing stability, he and Malatia applied for $100,000 in funding from the Corporation for Public Broadcasting. After pondering the application, Rick Madden, the director of CPB's radio division, made an astonishing counteroffer. "We're gonna give you more money than you're asking for," Glass remembered him saying.

As Madden saw it, *This American Life* would never be more than an also-ran unless Malatia and Glass could persuade station managers nationwide that the program would be around for the long haul. A massive grant, he believed, would convince doubters of the program's viability. After receiving a related reassurance from the board of WBEZ regarding its financial commitment to the show, the CPB gave *TAL* $350,000. "That was big for us," Glass said later.

Its foundation secure, *This American Life* took off. "In year three we started charging stations for carriage and made $100,000," Glass remembered. "By year four we made $300,000. By 2000, we were making almost $1 million."

•   •   •

This American Life's financial ascent was accompanied by a correspond-
ing uptick in the show's journalism. A year after the program's debut, Glass
began reaching outside the world of public radio to hire veteran magazine
editors. One of the first was Paul Tough, a staffer at *Harper's*. As a senior
producer, Tough turned out several strong pieces, among them a smart
profile of Geoffrey Canada, the CEO of the Harlem Children's Zone, which
teaches impoverished parents how to prepare their kids to pursue a higher
education. Tough also increased the professionalism of the operation. "Paul
taught me how to break a story down into its parts," recalled Julie Snyder.
Meantime, *TAL* started engaging well-known authors to turn out pieces.
Michael Lewis (*Liar's Poker*) plumbed the failed presidential campaign of
John McCain. Jonathan Gold, an *LA Weekly* food writer, explored the ethics
of eating chicken after adopting one as a pet. The photographer Joel Mey-
erowitz recounted in loving detail a trip he made with his father after learning that the older man was dying of Alzheimer's.

As always, Glass was central to everything. One evening over dinner
in 1997, when Jack Hitt began regaling the *This American Life* staff with
a tragicomic account of the worst production of *Peter Pan* ever mounted,
Glass shocked everyone by bolting from the table. "I thought he might be
sick—maybe had to pee," recalled Hitt. When Glass returned, he gave his actual rationale. "I didn't want to hear more of that story. We're going into the
studio" to record it. He and Hitt repaired to sound booths, and Hitt started
from the top, allowing Glass, in the role of interviewer and straight man, to
react spontaneously. The result is "Fiasco," one of *TAL's* premier late-1990s
episodes. It starts with an account of a mechanical failure (a device meant
to hoist Tinker Bell and the play's other characters above the stage ends up
pinning them to the rafters), continues with another major prop malfunction (Captain Hook accidentally tosses his appendage into the audience),
and ends with a loud alarm and the arrival of the fire department to rescue
cast and crew.

Five years into the program's run, critics started to take notice. "My favorite piece of new journalism is *This American Life*," wrote Bill McKibben
in *The Nation*. "It takes as its beat, well, life. It's simultaneously 'light,' in
that it doesn't discuss Madeleine Albright . . . budget deficits, the Gephardt

campaign, and 'deep' in that it gets at what matters to most of us most of the time." Writing in the *American Journalism Review*, Marc Fisher declared, "What *This American Life* has brought to the table is the notion that reality can be presented without tabloid hype, that stories can be told in old-fashioned ways in a newfangled format." Although the praise was not universal (Fisher tempered his with what would become a familiar complaint: "The weakest parts of the program sound too self-obsessed, too self-indulgent, too much a product of our tell-all-look-at-me-I'm-a-victim society"), the trend was positive.

As the millennium neared, Ira Glass did what every aesthetic crusader since the founder of futurism has done—he issued a manifesto. *Radio: An Illustrated Guide*, written by Glass and adorned in the style of a graphic novel with sketches by Jessica Abel, starts by laying down a marker. "Radio, when correctly harnessed, can be as emotional, as funny, and as satisfying as the best motion pictures or television show." What follows is an instruction guide. Interviewing: "Doing an interview is like hosting a party. Your guests will follow your lead." Scoring: "Music is the frame around the pictures." Finally, there is the underlying doctrine: "Radio is a didactic medium. There's an anecdote. Then there's a moment of reflection about what that sequence means. It's an ancient storytelling structure—the structure essentially of a sermon."

For the entirety of the twenty-first century, *This American Life* has continued to gain momentum, although as its current focus on news attests, it has changed. Glass never "calcified," observed Adam Davidson, a former NPR and *TAL* staffer and cocreator of *Planet Money*. "It's been a continual reinvention." In this, the show mirrors the transformation of the journalistic institution it most resembles. Just as during and after World War II, *The New Yorker* went from being a magazine of essayists (James Thurber, E. B. White) and wits (Dorothy Parker) to one of witness-bearing correspondents (John Hersey, A. J. Liebling) and sages (Rachel Carson), *This American Life* after 2000 went from being light to if not dark then at least darker. A few old-timers, among them Sarah Vowell, bemoan the loss of the "playful optimism that was possible in those years between the toppling of the Berlin Wall and the Twin Towers," but none question the necessity of the shift.

Aside from airing "Mr. Daisey and the Apple Factory," *This American Life* made one further post-9/11 misstep with its short-lived experiment in television. Like the radio program, Showtime's *This American Life*, which premiered in 2007, features episodes built around a single theme: good ideas turned bad, life at the lowest realms of professional boxing. Also like the radio program, Showtime's *TAL* employs a telltale opening prologue, but with a twist: Glass delivers it from an anchor desk plopped down each week in a different location. The series, however, never caught on, in part because what works on radio does not necessarily work on TV. "Radio listeners can't really fight through Glass's scrim, so they take his word that the story is what he says it is," noted Michael Hirschorn in *The Atlantic*. "In the harsh light of television, however, the affectations of the radio show become glaringly clear." Pictures, in other words, have an integrity that cannot always be finessed by words, especially if those words, as do many of Glass's, tell an audience what to think. Then there was that anchor desk. Showtime thought it was clever, but Virginia Heffernan of the *New York Times* disagreed, dismissing it as "hipster kitsch." Although the television version of *TAL* ultimately won two prime-time Emmys, it left the air following just thirteen episodes.

At some core level, Glass was relieved to be done with television. The host dismissed reports that Showtime canceled *This American Life*, maintaining he "asked to be taken off TV." His reasoning was that the production generated such a heavy workload that the radio program suffered. This did not mean, however, that Glass was done with Hollywood. First through a deal with Warner Bros., then one with DreamWorks, *TAL* has sold dozens of stories to the movies. (Most have not gotten past the development stage, but a few have made it to the screen. The best known is *Come Sunday*, a Netflix production starring Jason Segel and Chiwetel Ejiofor based on the 2016 *TAL* piece "Heretics.") The demand for film ideas from Glass is so great that in 2015 he came to the realization that his partnership with WBEZ restricted his ability to capitalize on it. "There was a story that somebody was adapting, and we wanted a screenwriter to write a draft of the script," he recalled. "That meant I needed to spend $35,000. You can't have a public radio station spend $35,000 without telling the board. It was time-sensitive, and I needed the board to say yes." To cut through the bureaucracy, the host approached Steve Baird, the WBEZ board chairman, in person.

"'It's so weird that you have to ask me this,'" Glass recalled Baird saying.

"'The fact that you guys must go through our nonprofit doesn't make sense. Does it make sense for you to be part of the station anymore, or should we think of some new arrangement?'" The board leader was offering Glass the opportunity to walk away from WBEZ, and he soon did so, acquiring full ownership of *This American Life*. Under the new arrangement, Glass now pays the station an unspecified percentage of earnings from carriage fees, underwriting, and donations.

Independence has been a boon to *This American Life*. The resulting increase in revenues has not only allowed the show to grow (in 2023, *TAL* employed thirty-seven editorial employees) but also to develop its slate of podcasts. "There came a point," Glass recalled, "where Julie Snyder and I had a conversation, and she's like, 'Everyone else is becoming millionaires off podcasts except us. Are we suckers?'" The sale of Serial Productions to the *New York Times* provided a ringing affirmation of *TAL*'s approach. The result is that unlike most media entrepreneurs, Glass enjoys both autonomy and profitability, for which he is grateful—and humble.

In the midst of the same busy spring week that Ira Glass was fronting "The Parents Step In" (the *This American Life* episode pegged to the Uvalde shootings) and assigning stories for "The Pink House at the Center of the World" (the episode pegged to the end of *Roe v. Wade*) he found himself at the stylish East Village home of John McGinn, the chairman of the NPR Foundation and former head of Citigroup's Global Consumer Risk Aggregation Unit. The occasion was a fundraiser for *Radio Diaries*, the Studs Terkel–like interview podcast fronted by Joe Richman and dedicated to documenting extraordinary ordinary lives (Ed Dwight, the first Black astronaut; Fred Harris, the last living member of the Kerner Commission). Glass was there to implore wealthy attendees to donate to his fellow exponent of broadcast storytelling.

Glass might have taken things a bit easier during this frantic week had his new girlfriend not been traveling in Africa. After a 2018 divorce from Anaheed Alani, a writer and editor whom he married shortly before leaving Chicago, he'd spent a few footloose years. But he recently fell for Chris Crawford, a former cook at Berkeley's Chez Panisse who now runs TART, which makes small-batch vinegars at a factory at the Brooklyn Navy Yard. The two were living together, and she's adept at luring him away from the *TAL* office.

But with her out of town, nothing stood between him and his job. He kept grinding.

Almost thirty years into *This American Life*'s run, Glass remains devoted to nearly every aspect of producing and reporting the show. "For a guy named Ira Glass," cracked Sarah Vowell, "he personifies the Protestant work ethic." Julie Snyder concurred. "He'll do edits after six thirty at night," she said, although she conceded that he tires more easily than he once did. Still, she added, "all it takes is a good story to get him excited," and as it happened, he was working on one now. The writer was Michelle Navarro, the *TAL* fellow who'd logged his prologue for "The Parents Step In." Not only did Glass believe that Navarro's piece, titled "Stations of the Double Cross," was excellent, but he wanted to do everything in his power to polish it to a high gloss, as it would mark her *TAL* debut. At the age of twenty-three, she would be on air nationwide for the first time.

While most of the *This American Life* staff was attending a meeting devoted to long-term planning, Glass was in his office making tweaks to "Stations of the Double Cross." As he played and replayed a couple of key sentences, colored bars indicating differing versions of the story (orange for retakes, red for new wording, pink for updated mixes), danced across the screen of his desktop Mac. Following one more listen, Glass noted, "It's totally acceptable, and a lot of radio shows would accept it. But the standard we have is higher."

The process had started two months earlier when Navarro pitched an idea about an issue she'd been grappling with since her teens—her inability to embrace Christianity despite having grown up in a religious home where belief in God had exerted a positive influence on everyone in the family. The aspect of the proposal that spoke to Glass was its specificity. Navarro could pinpoint her crisis to a particular incident. It was the sort of detail that elevated what might have been merely a rumination into a story.

"Stations of the Double Cross" begins with Navarro setting the scene:

I'd been hearing about the retreat for years. It happened every Easter at my local Catholic parish on the southwest side of Chicago. At thirteen, when I was finally old enough, I thought I should go . . . I had been waiting around for a revelation, an epiphany, and thought that this retreat was where I could find it. So, I signed up.

From there, the story digresses into a description of a Good Friday parade that preceded the retreat. The writing is sharp ("Every year, there was a long-haired Jesus, this year performed by a former youth leader whose name was, in fact, Jesus"), but it delayed the pivotal moment. "The plot hasn't kicked in," Glass said as the piece kept playing. "There's no conflict yet. Radio is particularly intolerant of that." To move it all along, he cut a few words. He also sent a Slack message to Stowe Nelson, *TAL*'s production manager, asking him to work some magic. "Hey," he wrote, "I have one other tiny adjustment. Don't hate me. Can you start the music at the end of Jesus? Right now, you start underneath the end of the word." The crisper transition, Glass felt, would give the story more oomph. Now the key passage—Navarro's account of the moment during the retreat that far from awakening her faith destroyed it—arrived a second faster and a bit more emphatically.

Glass kept Navarro—a University of Wisconsin graduate attired in gen Z black T-shirt and jeans—informed on everything that he was doing. "Throughout the whole process," she said, "he's made sure that I sound like myself and that I'm happy. My voice is still there." In this, he was functioning less like Navarro's producer than her instructor—a role he today plays with nearly everyone at *This American Life*.

Now in his midsixties, Glass had become an eminence. "Ira is this singular figure," said Adam Davidson. "In magazines there's all those people at *The New Yorker*—Harold Ross, Mr. Shawn, Bob Gottlieb, Tina Brown, and David Remnick. And you can throw in Harold Hayes at *Esquire*. In documentaries there's the Maysles brothers and Frederick Wiseman. But in audio Ira stands alone. Like Henry Ford, he built an industry and a culture."

For years, teaching was the only profession outside of broadcasting Glass ever imagined pursuing. He first felt its allure during the early 1990s when he reported his multipart *All Things Considered* series about Taft High School, and he held on to the notion. The time, however, had passed. "I've aged out of it," he said.

Yet to see Glass working with Navarro was to see Keith Talbot working with Glass and Bill Siemering working with Talbot. It was also to see Siemering, Navarro's fellow University of Wisconsin alum, standing in a cornfield outside Madison in the 1940s beneath the transmitting tower of WHA listening to *The Farm Program* and *Chapter a Day* as the shows wafted from the small structure that housed the station's equipment operator. *This American Life* is rooted in that most American tradition: storytelling. In Ira Glass, the past was speaking to the future even as he gave no indication that he was done speaking to the here and now.

EPILOGUE: SAME AS IT EVER WAS—BUT DIFFERENT

On April 9, 2024, under the headline "I've Been at NPR for 25 Years. Here's How We Lost America's Trust," Uri Berliner, a senior business editor at the network, leveled an across-the-board broadside at his place of employment. In the essay, which was posted at *The Free Press*, a site on the Substack platform, he accused NPR of abandoning an evenhanded approach to the news. On some of the biggest stories of the day—alleged Russian interference in the 2016 presidential election, the possibility that Covid-19 originated not from an open-air food market in China's Wuhan province but from a lab conducting experiments on bat viruses—Berliner maintained that NPR did not consider all things. Instead, he said the network adopted a rigidly liberal view. The result, he added, was that between 2011, the year after Juan Williams was fired, and 2023, NPR's audience had skewed hard to the left. Where once only 37 percent of the network's listeners identified as progressive, the number had swelled to 67 percent. "An open-minded spirit no longer exists within NPR," he charged. "Predictably, we don't have an audience that reflects America."

Edith Chapin, NPR's new editor in chief, took issue with Berliner's characterizations: "We're proud to stand behind the exceptional work that our shows and desks do to cover a wide range of challenging stories." Katherine Maher, NPR's new CEO, advanced the long view: "The quality of the programming and the integrity of the mission . . . offer a strong basis upon which to build our future."

Central to Berliner's critique of NPR was a set of philosophies and practices known at the network as the "North Star" and instituted by Maher's predecessor, John Lansing. In the wake of the George Floyd murder in 2020, Lansing issued an all-staff memo stating: "When it comes to identifying and ending systemic racism, we can be agents of change." In the future, NPR would not just report on intolerance, but it would call it out in the organization. According the Berliner, the network went too far. "Race and identity became paramount in nearly every aspect of the workplace. Journalists were required to ask everyone we interviewed their race, gender, and ethnicity (among other questions) and had to enter it in a centralized tracking system. We were given unconscious bias training sessions. . . . These initiatives, bolstered by a $1 million grant from the NPR Foundation, came from management, from the top down."

NPR's embrace of what was more broadly known as Diversity, Equity, and Inclusion arrived at a moment when the network found itself struggling financially. During the Covid-19 pandemic, radio-friendly commuters who'd made up a large share of the audience for *Morning Edition* and *All Things Considered* abandoned their daily trips by automobile to and from workplaces for radio-free walks down the hall to home offices. The network's listenership dropped from 60 million a week in 2020 to 47 million in 2023. Simultaneously, corporate sponsorships declined. For 2023, they were off 10 percent—$34 million. In response, NPR dismissed 100 staffers and cancelled four podcasts, among them the much-praised *Invisibilia*, which focused on hidden forces—biological traits, group dynamics—that influence human behavior.

The troubles that surfaced at NPR in the spring of 2024 were not unfamiliar. John Lansing's decision to make racial justice a priority in both the network's work product and at its workplace recalled Lee Frischknecht's efforts during the 1970s to inaugurate a Special Audiences department to broadcast programs focused on ethnicity, gender, and race, while convincing NPR employees to modify their behavior in accord with the directives of Antioch College professor Al Engelman. (Lansing's ideas also suggested those of Adam Clayton Powell III concerning quote quotas.) As for Berliner's jeremiad, it recalled the 5,000-word 1976 attack by then news director Robert Zelnick that accused the network under Frischknecht of shifting its focus from journalism to social issues.

As for the financial difficulties, they were reminders of the even worse crisis that confronted NPR during Frank Mankiewicz's tenure in the 1980s and the hard times following the great recession of 2008 that prompted massive layoffs and the cancellation of such shows as *Day to Day*.

There was, however, a startling and significant difference. Where past discord regarding race was tumultuous and past financial problems convulsive, they occurred during NPR's relative infancy. Despite the network's promise in the 1970s and its achievements during the 1980s, it had yet to become an essential part of the American media. As for the economic turmoil of the early twenty-first century, it happened before print journalism imploded across America during the 2020s and prior to financial losses at the big three commercial television news divisions that led them to cut back.

By 2024, NPR—along with the *New York Times*, the *Washington Post*, the *Wall Street Journal*, and CNN—was one of America's last sources of reliable, comprehensive reporting. More than ever, NPR was a beacon of not just news but, in a divided nation, of fair-mindedness. Whether it remains so will be up to the journalists, executives, and local station managers who write the network's next chapter.

ACKNOWLEDGMENTS

American journalism is better for the existence of NPR. Public radio broadcasts an enormous amount of superb work each day, and throughout its history it's been staffed by some of the smartest people in the news business. While researching *On Air*, I was lucky enough to spend time with many of them. Those to whom I owe the greatest thanks include Jonathan "Smokey" Baer, Bill Buzenberg, Neal Conan, Gary Covino, Leo del Aguila, Bob Edwards, David Folkenflik, Anne Garrels, Ira Glass, Joe Gwathmey, Loren Jenkins, Jay Kernis, Jacki Lyden, Robert Malesky, Frank Mankiewicz, John McChesney, Jack Mitchell, Renee Montagne, Jeff Rosenberg, Jim Russell, Robert Siegel, Bill Siemering, Scott Simon, Susan Stamberg, Keith Talbot, and Nina Totenberg. I am grateful for their countless insights.

In the spirit of full disclosure, my longtime friends Margot Adler and Sylvia Poggioli, both fabled NPR reporters, were also unstinting in their assistance. I tried to treat them as I did everyone else in this book, but my affection for them could not help but influence my prose.

On Air was a massive undertaking—fourteen years in the making. I interviewed scores of people inside and outside NPR, many on multiple occasions. I am thankful to them for their patience and perceptions. They include: Bill Abbott, Larry Abramson, Noah Adams, Deborah Amos, Kurt Andersen, Jim Anderson, Jon Lee Anderson, Jim Angle, David Aylward, George Bauer, Elizabeth Becker, Steve Behrens, Stephanie Bergsma, Howard Berkes, Lynne Bernabei, Ronald Bornstein, Steven Boylan, Bob Boylen, Frank Browning, David Brugger, Christopher Buchanan, Tom Bullock, John Burnett, John F. Burns, Julie Burstein, Cindy Carpien, David Cashdan,

Richard Cassidy, Zoe Chace, Alex Chadwick, Jane Christo, Peter Clowney, Barbara Cohen, Ann Cooper, Adam Davidson, Bill Davis, Joyce Davis, Diane Diamond, John Dinges, Jude Doherty, Linda Dorian, Bruce Drake, William Drummond, Jeffrey Dvorkin, Todd Easton, Dave Edwards, Al Engelman, David Ensor, Karen Everhart, Susan Feeney, John Felton, Michael Fields, Robert Ferrante, Rich Firestone, Frank Fitzmaurice, Ira Flatow, Lourdes Garcia-Navarro, Marilyn Geewax, Rob Gifford, Tom Gjelten, Paul Glickman, Connie Goldman, Sue Goodwin, Barry Gordemer, David Greene, Anya Grundmann, Paul Haaga, Barbara Hall, Richard L. Harris, Jack Hitt, John Hockenberry, Richard Holwill, Sam C. O. Holt, Ina Jaffe, Shirley Jahad, Jackie Judd, Jeff Kamen, John Keator, Michael J. Kennedy, Sunni Khalid, Bill Kling, Kevin Klose, Chris Koch, Howard Kohn, Robert Krulwich, Marc Kuhn, Ron Kramer, Rich Levin, Ketzel Levine, Rick Lewis, Will Lewis, Lawrence Lichty, Steve Lickteig, Pete Lowenstein, Allison MacAdams, Torey Malatia, Kee Malesky, Ben Mankiewicz, John Mankiewicz, Bill Marimow, Kati Marton, Kim Masters, Ellen McDonnell, Tim McNulty, George Miles, Judy Miller, Lisa Napoli, Michelle Navarro, Joyce Neu, Dale Ouzts, Michael Oreskes, Geri Pizzi, Skip Pizzi, Adam Clayton Powell III, Steve Proffitt, Don Quayle, Arun Rath, Phil Reeves, Barbara Rehm, Dana Rehm, Steve Reiner, James Reston Jr., Cokie Roberts, Margy Rochlin, Marcus Rosenbaum, Ernest Sanchez, Vivian Schiller, Ruth Seymour, Jack Shafer, Harry Shearer, Mike Shuster, Art Silverman, Michael Skoler, Joyce Slocum, Julie Snyder, Andi Sporkin, Richard Starmann, Ken Stern, Joel Swerdlow, Steve Symonds, Jamie Tarabay, Dina Temple-Raston, Doug Terry, Mary Tillotson, Gwen Thompkins, Sanford Ungar, Sarah Vowell, Jo Anne Wallace, Tom Warnock, Ellen Weiss, Linda Wertheimer, Eric Westervelt, Minoli Wetherell, Tim Wirth, Bill Wyman, Audrey Wynn, and John Ydstie.

Several people I interviewed for *On Air* spoke to me only on the condition that I would not quote them by name. I respected their requests while profiting from their insights.

I also owe a great debt to the staffs of two archives devoted to American broadcasting: The National Public Broadcasting Archives at the University of Maryland Library and the Walter J. Brown Media Archives and Peabody Awards Collection at the University of Georgia Library. Mike Henry and

James Michael Baxter at Maryland and Mary Miller at Georgia were tireless in locating the documents I needed to read to understand NPR and the recordings I needed to hear to bring its programs to life.

Along the way, I consistently benefited from the wise counsel of Kit Rachlis. For years my editor at *Los Angeles* magazine and now a senior editor at ProPublica, Kit in fact suggested that I write a book about NPR. He said the network was a great story hiding in plain sight, and I agreed. Thanks as well to former *Los Angeles Times* reporter and roving editor extraordinaire Richard E. Meyer, who encouraged me as I was getting started. I also benefited from a Shorenstein Fellowship at Harvard University's Kennedy School of Government, where under the guidance of program director Alex S. Jones I spent a semester researching NPR. Thanks also to the Shorenstein faculty, my fellow fellows, and to William Cole, my able graduate assistant.

In collecting the illustrations for this book, I had the help of several great photographers. They include Murray Bognovitz, who shot portraits of the NPR staff as part of an ambitious project in the 1990s, and Stan Barouh, who shot photos of the staff on election night 1980. Also, Bill Siemering, the creator of *All Things Considered*; Jay Kernis, the original producer of *Morning Edition*; and Robert Malesky, the former producer of *Weekend Edition Sunday*, gave me many vintage photos. Malesky fished some of them from the trash when the network moved from its M Street offices to those on Massachusetts Avenue in the 1990s. Veteran film researcher Brian Tessier helped me track down several other key images. Finally, my erstwhile *Los Angeles* magazine colleague Amy Wallace—daughter of Jo Anne Wallace, longtime station manager at KKGO in San Francisco, and stepdaughter of former NPR editor John McChesney—gave me a stunning photograph of her stepfather and producers Gary Covino and Art Silverman.

On Air would not exist if not for the ministrations of my editor at Avid Reader Press, Ben Loehnen, and his colleagues: publisher Jofie Ferrari-Adler, associate editor Carolyn Kelly, and senior publicity director David Kass. Ben signed this book in 2011 and stuck with it during a long period of gestation. He then edited the manuscript with vigor and style. Thanks also to my former agent, Steve Wasserman, who sold my book proposal, and to agent Katherine Flynn, who saw the project through to completion. I'm grateful as well to Beth Vessel, who believed in me, and to Douglas Johnson, who copyedited *On Air*. I am especially thankful to Tom Colligan, who fact-checked the book.

Most of all, I thank Madeline Stuart, my wife. I couldn't have finished *On Air* without her love and support, or without the company of Mr. Peabody, Phoebe, and dear departed Beatrice, our Parson Russell terriers. They always took me on long walks exactly when I needed them.

NOTES

PROLOGUE: DO OR DIE

1 *With $20,000 in the bank*: "Last-minute salvation for NPR," *Broadcasting*, August 1, 1983.

1 *"I took over a couple"*: Tim Wirth, interview with author, November 13, 2017.

1 *"Sharon met us"*: David Aylward, interview with author, November 17, 2017.

2 *"We don't have much to do"*: Ibid.

2 *"Drinking beer and smoking"*: Ibid.

2 *"It was like a union"*: Ronald Bornstein, interview with author, March 19, 2018.

2 *"You've got to settle"*: Bornstein, interview with author, December 5, 2017.

2 *"Cokie and Linda each called"*: Aylward, interview with author, November 17, 2017.

2 *"I never talked to anybody"*: Nina Totenberg, interview with author, June 4, 2013.

2 *"that the CPB held"*: Aylward, interview with author, November 17, 2017.

2 *"Lots of people had roles"*: Linda Wertheimer, interview with author, August 12, 2015.

3 *"I sensed the urgency"*: Wirth, interview with author, November 13, 2017.

4 *"It deserves to die"*: Jack Mitchell, interview with author, January 30, 2015.

4 *$1 million bank loan*: "Lenders Friendly as Auditors Probe," *Current*, June 7, 1983.

4 *"didn't care about radio"*: Frank Mankiewicz, interview with author, October 21, 2011.

4 *"I thought it already was"*: Mankiewicz, interview with Michael McCauley, August 14, 1995, National Public Broadcasting Archives, University of Maryland.

4 *"there was gross mismanagement"*: "NPR: Resuscitate—But Investigate," *Washington Post*, July 6, 1983.

5 *"wanted control of the satellite"*: Linda Dorian, interview with author, March 20, 2018.

5 *"NPR was the gold standard"*: Bornstein, interview with author, December 5, 2017.

5 *"We hired a law firm"*: Don Mullally, interview with Michael McCauley, July 12, 1995, National Public Broadcasting Archives, University of Maryland.

5 *"Our intent was"*: Aylward, interview with author, November 17, 2017.

6 *"would not only affect"*: "Last-Minute Salvation for NPR," *Broadcasting*, August 1, 1983.

6 *"NPR had become a force"*: Aylward, interview with author, November 17, 2017.

ONE: PHILOSOPHER KING

7   *in an Olds Cutlass*: Bob Greene, "The News from the Street, with a Beat," *Chicago Tribune*, January 6, 1987.

7   *"He would talk back"*: Jeff Rosenberg, interview with author, June 7, 2003.

7   *"niggers and Puerto Ricans"*: Abner J. Mikva, *The Congressional Record*, March 26, 1969, 7837–38.

7   *"Last week a bright"*: Ibid.

8   *"I felt sorry"*: Jeff Kamen, interview with author, March 7, 2012.

8   *"The radio revolution"*: *New York Times*, advertisement, May 3, 1971.

8   *Soon seven thousand people*: "7,000 Arrested in Capital War Protest; 150 Are Hurt as Clashes Disrupt Traffic," *New York Times*, May 4, 1971.

9   *Stephen Banker, an older*: "Stephen Banker," James F. Fallows, *The Atlantic* (Banker's 1955 Harvard class also included David Halberstam and J. Anthony Lukas), May 27, 2010.

9   *"that they filter"*: Jim Russell, interview with author, February 27, 2014.

9   *Frank Sullivan, an official*: Kamen, interview with author, March 22, 2012.

9   *TC-100 cassette tape recorders*: Russell, interview with author, February 27, 2014.

10   *"Let's hold hands"*: Don Quayle, interview with author, October 20, 2011.

10   *We can do this*: Bill Siemering, interview with author, June 9, 2011.

10   *dubbing from cassettes*: Russell, interview with author, February 27, 2014.

10   *Primary sources, multiple perspectives*: Siemering, interview with author, June 9, 2011.

10   *"From National Public Radio"*: National Public Broadcasting Archives, University of Maryland, May 3, 1971.

11   *composed by Don Voegeli*: Siemering, interview with author, June 9, 2011.

11   *"named for Senator Robert F. Kennedy"*: National Public Broadcasting Archives, University of Maryland, May 3, 1971.

11   *"was not horrible"*: Jack Mitchell, interview with author, March 17, 2014.

11   *"Rather than pull in reports"*: National Public Broadcasting Archives, University of Maryland, May 3, 1971.

11   *"Come on and take"*: Ibid.

11   *"Come on, people"*: Ibid.

11   *"Thousands of young people"*: Ibid.

11   *"A line of young people"*: Ibid.

11   *"Sergeant, excuse me"*: Cokie Roberts et al., *This Is NPR* (San Francisco: Chronicle Books, 2010), 26–27.

12   *"We're gonna shut"*: National Public Broadcasting Archives, University of Maryland, May 3, 1971.

12   *"The Weathermen organization"*: Ibid.

12   *"It is true"*: Ibid.

12   *"Today in the nation's capital"*: Ibid.

12   *"In this age of unshorn"*: Ibid.

13   *"Drugs are a source of peace"*: Ibid.

13   *"He was off in dreamland"*: Mitchell, interview with author, March 17, 2014.

13   *"We'd at least"*: Ibid.

13 *"I winced when I heard"*: Russell interview with author, September 30, 2011.

13 *"It was a happy day"*: Siemering, interview with author, March 10, 2014.

14 *learned that Edward P. Morgan*: "Edward P. Morgan, 82, Anchor and Reporter for TV and Radio," *New York Times*, January 29, 1993.

14 *The programming chief didn't want*: Siemering, interview with author, June 9, 2011.

14 *"plastic, faceless men"*: Joseph Brady Kirkish, "A Descriptive History of America's First National Public Radio Network" (PhD dissertation, University of Michigan, 1980), 68.

15 *"share the human experience"*: Ibid., 69.

15 *"rip and read"*: Ibid., 68.

15 *"bring the people"*: Ibid.

15 *"Siemering had this vision"*: Russell, interview with the author, September 30, 2011.

15 *"One of the most critical"*: Kirkish, "Descriptive History," 70.

15 *"I tried to offer"*: Siemering, interview with McCauley, August 8, 1995, National Public Broadcasting Archives, University of Maryland.

15 *"Bill didn't hire people"*: Mitchell, interview with author, March 17, 2014.

16 *"What did your father do?"*: Linda Wertheimer, interview with author, March 22, 2012.

16 *"He decided that I wasn't"*: Ibid.

17 *"He hired me as a safety"*: Russell, interview with author, February 27, 2014.

17 *lightweight Sony cassette recorders*: Ibid.

17 *"How about All Things Considered?"*: Quayle, interview with author, October 20, 2011.

17 *Nagra, the state of the art*: Mitchell, interview with author, March 17, 2014.

17 *"round robin"*: George Cassidy, interview with author, March 30, 2014.

18 *Cassette machines record*: Ibid.

18 *Sprawled across the floor*: Rosenberg, interview with author, July 26, 2014.

18 *"This is exactly"*: Stamberg, interview with author, October 21, 2011.

18 *"It had never occurred"*: Stamberg, interview with McCauley, August 16, 1995, National Public Broadcasting Archives, University of Maryland.

18 *"Granted, there are different situations"*: Siemering, interview with author, June 9, 2011.

19 *That's what she dubbed him*: Stamberg, interview with author, October 21, 2011.

19 *"We'd hired all these people"*: Quayle, interview with author, October 20, 2011.

19 *"We have a blank canvas"*: Michael P. McCauley, *NPR: The Trials and Triumphs of National Public Radio* (New York: Columbia University Press, 1995), 28.

19 *The twin transmitting towers*: Siemering, interview with author, June 9, 2011.

19 *"The teacher would turn on"*: Ibid.

19 *"From first grade"*: Ibid.

20 *"typical of America"*: "Roosevelt Lauds Chautauqua," *The Chautauquan Daily*, July 25, 2015.

20 *"It was hard work"*: Siemering, interview with author, June 9, 2011.

20 *WHA was located*: Ibid.

21 *"broadcast specialist"*: Ibid.

21 *"The Heart of the Nation Station"*: Ibid.

22 *"unconditional positive regard"*: Carl R. Rogers, *On Becoming a Person* (New York: Mariner Books, 1995), 62.

22 *To Be Negro*: Siemering, interview with author, June 9, 2011.

22 *The Nation within a Nation*: Ibid.

22 *"I remember one woman"*: Ibid.

23 *"The Chicago activist Saul Alinsky"*: Ibid.

23 *"It wasn't quite what they have"*: Ibid.

23 *"I wanted to use radio"*: Ibid.

23 *Foss had founded the Creative Associates*: Ibid.

23 *"It's said there's music"*: Ibid.

23 *"We broadcast a kind of"*: Ibid.

24 *show called* This Is Radio: Ibid.

24 "This Is Radio *was Bill's experiment"*: Ira Flatow, interview with author, November 25, 2013.

24 *"This Is Radio—damn it!"*: Siemering, interview with author, June 9, 2011.

25 *"the utilization of a great technology"*: Jack Mitchell, *Listener Supported: The Culture and History of Public Radio* (Westport, CT: Praeger, 2005), 31.

25 *"wonder and variety"*: Ibid., 33.

25 *When Sandler learned*: McCauley, *NPR*, 21–22.

25 *the words* and radio: Drew Lindsay, "Has Success Spoiled NPR?," *The Washingtonian*, March 2007.

25 *But following a campaign*: Mitchell, 33–42.

25 *the Public* Broadcasting *Act*: Ibid., 35.

25 *CPB's Al Hulsen*: Ibid., 46.

26 *From an office in Harvard Square*: Sam Holt, interview with author, March 19, 2012.

26 *"It was pitiful"*: Ibid.

26 *"tightly formatted, in-depth"*: Mitchell, 45.

26 *saw things Holt's way*: Ibid., 46.

26 *NPR would broadcast* and *produce*: Ibid., 46–47.

26 *During the winter meetings*: McCauley, *NPR*, 23.

26 *"National Public Radio," Siemering began*: Kirkish, "Descriptive History," 21–22.

27 *"Do you think that if"*: Quayle, interview with author, October 20, 2011.

27 *"I did it on the spot"*: Ibid.

27 *Ten days after* All Things Considered *debuted*: Kirkish, "Descriptive History," 93–95.

27 *"Our child has been born"*: McCauley, *NPR*, 29.

27 *Jim Russell contributed*: National Public Broadcasting Archives, University of Maryland, May 4, 1971.

28 *Jeff Kamen, covering yet another*: Ibid., May 5, 1971.

28 *Mike Waters, in a montage*: Todd Easton, interview with author, February 27, 2014.

28 *"fabulous"*: Stamberg, interview by author, October 21, 2011.

28 *"He just grabbed me"*: Kati Marton, interview with author, April 11, 2014.

28 *"At the start"*: Rosenberg, interview with author, June 7, 2013.

28 *Siemering played Crosby, Stills*: National Public Broadcasting Archives, University of Maryland, May, 4, 1971.

29 *"We were castigated"*: Mitchell, interview with author, March 17, 2014.

29 *"I think we have a good program"*: Kirkish, "Descriptive History," 93–95.

29 *"the shifting sands of policy"*: Rich Firestone, interview with author, March 23, 2014.

29 *"Mercury, most of us know"*: National Public Broadcasting Archives, University of Maryland, May 6, 1971.

29   *Alice B. Toklas hash brownies*: Doug Terry, interview with author, March 20, 2012.

29   *"The guy on paper"*: Russell, interview with author, February 27, 2014.

30   *"His idea was"*: Wertheimer, interview with author, March 22, 2012.

30   *"Oh, you mean the place"*: Terry interview with author, March 20, 2012.

30   *"wonderful and glib"*: Mitchell, interview with author, March 20, 2014.

30   *"I'd hear comments about him"*: Easton, interview with author, February 27, 2014.

30   *"His grasp of reality"*: Mitchell, interview with author, March 17, 2014.

30   *"The kids who cut tape"*: Firestone, interview with author, March 13, 2014.

30   *"He was pompous"*: Marton, interview with author, April 11, 2014.

30   *"I think he felt above"*: Rosenberg, interview with author, June 7, 2013.

30   *"Conley leaned back in his chair"*: Wertheimer, interview with author, March 22, 2022.

30   *"shape, form, style and personality"*: McCauley, *NPR*, 30.

31   *"Bill didn't like confrontation"*: Rosenberg, interview with author, June 7, 2013.

31   *"could be brilliant"*: Siemering, interview with author, June 9, 2011.

31   *"producer/on-air voice/director"*: Kirkish, "Descriptive History," 37.

31   *applied to be a* Playboy *bunny*: Russell, interview with author, September 30, 2011.

31   *"He had reporting chops"*: Stamberg, interview with author, October 21, 2011.

31   *"He had the entire package"*: Easton, interview with author, February 27, 2014.

31   *"Lace curtain Irish"*: Rosenberg, interview with author, June 7, 2013.

31   *"He had this impish quality"*: Siemering, interview with author, June 9, 2011.

31   *"I got a call from Siemering"*: Russell, author interview, September 30, 2011.

32   *"This is* The Big Old Fat Old Jimbo Show*"*: Flatow, interview with author, November 25, 2013.

32   *"We sent out two versions"*: Russell, interview with author, February 27, 2014.

32   *"Oh, shit. Take two"*: Ibid.

32   *"I had messages from stations"*: Ibid.

32   *"He was under a lot of self-imposed pressure"*: Mitchell, interview with author, March 17, 2014.

32   *"That's a bridge over trouble waters"*: Terry, interview with author, March 20, 2012.

32   *"having a cathedral in his head"*: Susan Stamberg, *Every Night at Five* (New York, Pantheon Books, 1982), 8.

32   *"George insisted on it"*: Cassidy, interview with author, March 30, 2014.

33   *"Non-Professional Radio"*: Joe Gwathmey, interview with author, February 26, 2014.

33   *"Not until I heard Kamen's work"*: Mitchell, interview with author, March 17, 2014.

33   *"In TV," said Kamen*: Kamen, interview with author, March 22, 2012.

33   *"you just couldn't manage him"*: Stamberg, interview with author, October 21, 2011.

33   *"He was not fitting in"*: Rosenberg, interview with author, June 7, 2013.

33   *"People would make jokes"* Easton, interview with author, February 27, 2014.

33   *"I'm impulsive, self-absorbed"*: Kamen, interview with author, March 22, 2012.

33   *"Hey, Kamen, we don't"*: Kamen, interview with author, March 7, 2012.

34   *"It's just batteries"*: Ibid.

34   *"It never occurred to him"*: Quayle, interview with author, October 20, 2011.

34   *"stubby fingers"*: Mitchell, interview with author, March 20, 2014.

34   *"To Quayle's buddies"*: Mitchell, interview with author, March 17, 2014.

34   *"panic buttons"*: "The ATC Time Line," 30th Anniversary Celebration of *All Things Considered*, NPR.org, 2001, https://news.npr.org/programs/atc/atc30/timeline/index.html.

35   *"What I found"*: Gwathmey, interview with author, February 20, 2014.

35   *"sloppy"*: Ibid.

35   *"George might have genuinely disliked"*: Ibid.

35   *"I wasn't intimidated"*: Ibid.

35   *"Turn on your TV"*: Quayle, interview with author, October 20, 2011.

35   *"He was passionate"*: Stamberg, interview with author, October 21, 2011.

36   *"He had a nice way"*: Wertheimer, interview with author, March 22, 2012.

36   *"And now they tell us"*: Stamberg, *Every Night at Five*, 62.

36   *"All around me people are screaming"*: Terry, interview with author, March 20, 2012.

36   *"I was schooled"*: Ibid.

37   *"Another demonstrator arrested"*: "Police Halt March on White House," *Washington Star*, October 27, 1971.

37   *"I was opposed to the war"*: Terry, interview with author, March 20, 2012.

38   *"She's too New York"*: Mitchell, interview with author, March 20, 2014.

38   *"conservative, male, midwestern"*: Ibid.

38   *"I wasn't nearly as radical"*: Stamberg, interview with author, October 21, 2011.

38   *"She was the perfect diplomat's wife"*: Mitchell, interview with author, March 17, 2014.

38   *"She had enthusiasm"*: Siemering, interview with author, June 9, 2011.

38   *"working the numbers"*: Susan Stamberg, *Talk: NPR's Susan Stamberg Considers All Things* (New York: Perigee Books, 1993), 13–16.

38   *"What came across"*: Jim Anderson, interview with author, June 5, 2012.

39   *"I learned the art"*: Flatow, interview with author, November 25, 2013.

39   *"The program needs to be"*: Kirkish, "Descriptive History," 100.

39   *"We had a staff full of egos"*: Mitchell, interview with author, March 17, 2014.

39   *"It was," said Mitchell*: Ibid.

40   *"I thought the telephone"*: Ibid.

40   *"They did not build the studio"*: Ibid.

40   *"Susan took charge"*: Ibid.

40   *"On the phone, I'm not distracted"*: Stamberg, *Every Night at Five*, 41.

40   *"What surprised me"*: Mitchell, interview with author, March 17, 2014.

41   *"The Quayle people"*: Mitchell, interview with McCauley, April 28, 1995.

41   *"he became more psychedelic"*: Mitchell, interview with author, March 17, 2014.

41   *"kind of a flower child"*: Marton, interview with author, April 11, 2014.

41   *"Carol was not engaged"*: Siemering, interview with author, March 10, 2014.

41   *"Siemering had an aura"*: Easton, interview with author, February 27, 2014.

41   *"He lived as a free man"*: Mitchell, interview with author, March 17, 2014.

41   *"I think there were women"*: Russell, interview with author, April 2, 2014.

41   the *"Dream Attic"*: Keith Talbot, interview with author, March 21, 2014.

41   *"I drove all over the country"*: Ibid.

42   *"I don't think Bill"*: Ibid.

42   asked to write a job title: Siemering, interview with McCauley, August 8, 1995, National Public Broadcasting Archives, University of Maryland.

42   *"We have a problem"*: Flatow, interview with author, November 25, 2013.

42 *"A light bulb went off"*: Russell, interview with author, April 27, 2014.

43 *"I think it's time"*: Siemering, interview with author, June 9, 2011.

43 *"He comes in"*: Jonathan "Smokey" Baer, interview with author, October 21, 2011.

43 *"I was shocked"*: Flatow, interview with author, November 25, 2013.

43 *"I couldn't believe it"*: Stamberg, interview with author, October 21, 2011.

43 *"I'd known for six months"*: Quayle, interview with author, October 20, 2011.

44 *"I went down to the* Washington Post*"*: Siemering, interview with author, June 9, 2011.

TWO: ENCOUNTER SESSION

45 *"An expectant standing-room-only"*: Josh Darsa, May 17, 1973, quoted in David Welna, "Russia Investigation Has Echoes of Watergate Probe," *Weekend Edition Sunday*, May 17, 1973, and April 1, 2017, https://www.npr.org/2017/04/01/522284658/russia-investigation-has-echoes-of-watergate-probe.

45 *Jermyn Street suits*: John Keator, interview with author, October 26, 2017.

46 *"Reporter Josh Darsa talked to the Beatles"*: CBS News, November 21, 1963; https://www.recmusicbeatles.com/public/files/saki/1963.html.

46 *Nagra tape machine*: Keator, interview with author, October 26, 2017.

46 *"was dramatic and pretentious"*: Mitchell, interview with author, March 20, 2014.

46 *"Live . . . from the nation's capital"*: Flatow, interview with author, November 25, 2013.

47 *"He was like a cross"*: Russell, email to author, September 12, 2016.

47 *"If it wasn't vivid before"*: Linda Wertheimer, ed., *Listening to America: Twenty-Five Years in the Life of a Nation, as Heard on National Public Radio* (Boston: Houghton Mifflin, 1995), 41.

47 *"I remember very, very long days"*: Easton, email to author, September 14, 2016.

48 *"He slept at the office"*: Stamberg, interview with author, January 14, 2017.

48 *NPR's live coverage*: Walter J. Brown Media Archives and Peabody Awards Collection, University of Georgia Special Collections Library, May 17, 1973.

48 *"Only on public radio"*: "Music," *Richmond Times-Dispatch*, August 26, 1973.

48 *"The National Public Radio Network"*: "Senate Hearings Add Big Boost to Public Radio," *Cincinnati Enquirer*, August 12, 1973.

48 *"Since many of the pieces"*: Firestone, interview with author, March 13, 2014.

49 *"She was our investigative reporter"*: George Bauer, interview with author, September 30, 2016.

49 *"She fancied herself"*: Easton, interview with author, September 13, 2016.

49 *"What's advocacy and what's not?"*: Kirkish, "Descriptive History," 144.

49 *"I smelled a rat"*: Ibid.

49 *"I thought that was the single most boring"*: Russell, interview with author, September 30, 2011.

50 *"I'm buying a can of peas"*: Ibid.

50 *"God damn it, that's the last time"*: Ibid.

50 *"The Village Well"*: Kirkish, "Descriptive History," 103.

50 *"Commercials for Nicer Living Contest"*: Walter J. Brown Media Archives and Peabody Awards Collection, University of Georgia Special Collections Library. October 13, 1973.

50 *"We'll create an ad"*: Stamberg, interview with author, August 21, 2014.

50 *"Cherry pie, apple pie"*: Flatow, interview with author, November 25, 2013.

50 *"Life got you down?"*: Walter J. Brown Media Archives and Peabody Awards Collection, University of Georgia Special Collections Library, October 13, 1973.

51 *"After two hundred years"*: Wertheimer, *Listening to America*, 70.

51 *"The young, sexy, smoldering-voiced"*: Ibid., 69.

51 *"Fill!"*: Stamberg, interview with author, January 14, 2017.

51 *"Would you like to dance?"*: Deborah Amos, interview with author, May 13, 2011.

51 *"It was like we'd just met"*: Stamberg, interview with author, January 14, 2017.

51 the Peabody Award: Walter J. Brown Media Archives and Peabody Awards Collection, University of Georgia Special Collections Library, October 13, 1973.

52 *"We haven't ever got a shot"*: Ibid.

52 *"The young people"*: Ibid.

52 *"There are many who say"*: Ibid.

53 *"He kept this screwy organization"*: Mitchell, interview with McCauley, April 28, 1995, National Public Broadcasting Archives, University of Maryland.

53 *"He knew how to schmooze"*: Flatow, interview with author, November 25, 2013.

53 *"the Mormon industrial complex"*: Totenberg, interview with author, June 4, 2013.

53 *"Quayle was not a good Mormon"*: Mitchell, interview with McCauley, April 28, 1995.

53 *"the worst professional decision"*: Quayle, interview with author, October 20, 2011.

53 *"Quayle went off to CPB"*: Rosenberg, interview with author, March 27, 2015.

54 *"Unfailingly polite"*: "Lee Conrad Frischknecht," *Deseret News*, January 3, 2005.

54 *"He was not by any stretch"*: Gwathmey, interview with McCauley, August 3, 1995, National Public Broadcasting Archives, University of Maryland.

54 *"them versus us"*: *Dick Cavett Show*, March 22, 1973, as quoted in James Day, *The Vanishing Vision—The Inside Story of Public Television* (Berkeley: University of California Press, 1995), 236.

54 *"to get the left-wing commentators"*: Richard Nixon Papers, October 15, 1971, quoted ibid.

54 *"The long-predicted emasculation"*: "Nixon Reaching for 'Off' Switch," *Los Angeles Times*, January 15, 1973.

55 *"I'm so glad we're not"*: Russell, interview with author, September 30, 2011.

55 *"I looked at all my colleagues"*: Ibid.

55 *"It is possible"*: Walter J. Brown Media Archives and Peabody Awards Collection, University of Georgia, May 7, 1973.

55 *"I remember him dancing"*: Baer, interview with author, August 18, 2014.

55 *I wonder how many*: Wertheimer, *Listening to America*, 36–38.

56 *"I went down there"*: Stamberg, interview with author, January 14, 2017. NPR producer Robert Malesky also retrieved some of the transcript. Malesky, email to author, September 3, 2016.

56 *"I was assigned to be someone"*: Stamberg, interview with author, January 14, 2017.

56 *You're listening to*: Walter J. Brown Media Archives and Peabody Awards Collection, University of Georgia, May 4, 1974.

56 *Nixon: Hi, John*: Ibid.

57 *"It was not great"*: Malesky, interview with author, February 16, 2018.

57 *"You had a sense of"*: Anderson, interview with author, June 5, 2012.

57 *"There was something about us"*: Stamberg, interview with author, January 14, 2017.

57 *"I felt as if we had reached out"*: Wertheimer, *Listening to America*, 50.

57 *"I'd rush into the studio"*: Easton, interview with author, September 27, 2016.

57 *"Our broadcast the day Nixon"*: Wertheimer, *Listening to America*, 50.

57 *"That was great"*: Malesky, interview with author, February 16, 2018.

58 *"Josh was in his zone"*: Easton, email to author, September 14, 2016.

58 *"What happened next"*: Ibid.

58 *"There has been a report"*: Easton, interview with author, February 27, 2014.

58 *"And so the saga"*: Baer, interview with author, October 21, 2011.

58 *"No heads rolled"*: Ibid.

59 *"Josh had been drinking"*: Anderson, interview with author, June 5, 2013.

59 *"It's what he wanted"*: Ibid.

59 *"The editorial process"*: Malesky, interview with author, June 6, 2013.

59 *"I recall making calls"*: Russell, interview with author, December 26, 2013.

60 *"fed up"*: Mitchell, interview with McCauley, September 19, 1995, National Public Broadcasting Archives, University of Maryland.

60 *"Lee was interested"*: Ernest Sanchez, interview with author, March 6, 2017.

60 *"He was the only one"*: Jack Mitchell to McCauley, April 28, 1995, National Public Broadcasting Archives, University of Maryland.

61 *"The head of the* Observer*"*: Nina Totenberg, interview with author, June 4, 2013.

61 *"I asked for a full account"*: Robert Zelnick, interview with author, January 31, 2015.

61 *"It was a rat's nest"*: Anderson, interview with author, June 5, 2012.

61 *"She was officious"*: Ibid.

61 *"Nina was full of herself"*: Easton, interview with author, September 13, 2016.

61 *"real liberals and crazy"*: Richard Holwill, interview with author, January 16, 2017.

61 *"He was our White House correspondent"*: Zelnick, interview with author, January 31, 2015.

62 *"She was like a dog"*: Stamberg, interview with author, January 14, 2017.

62 *"44 to 66 pounds"*: "Kerr McGee Challenges Missing Plutonium Story," *Wall Street Journal*, December 31, 1974.

62 *"She went out and came back"*: Russell, interview with author, December 26, 2013.

62 *"She tried too hard"*: Firestone, interview with author, March 13, 2014.

62 *"Barbara ransacked Silkwood's"*: Stamberg, interview with author, January 14, 2017.

62 Plutonium: A Question: Walter J. Brown Media Archives and Peabody Awards Collection, University of Georgia, March 23, 1975.

62 *"Karen Silkwood was right"*: Ibid.

62 *"Barbara rubbed a lot of people"*: Howard Kohn, interview with author, September 10, 2016.

63 *"When Zelnick took over"*: Judy Miller, interview with author, October 30, 2014.

63 *"He thought I was very funny"*: Ibid.

63 *"There were some important people"*: Holwill, interview with author, January 16, 2017.

63 *"Lend me your ears"*: Oscar Brand, Walter J. Brown Media Archives and Peabody Awards Collection, University of Georgia, October 13, 1974.

63 *"a report on the creative experience"*: Robert Malesky, "The Great NPR Program You Never Heard," Reporter's Notebook, NPR.org, February 22, 2004, https://www.npr.org/2004/02/22/1690692/the-great-npr-program-you-never-heard.

64 *"If you flower"*: "Oscar Brand, More than a Radio Personality," NPR press release, September 4, 1975, National Public Broadcasting Archives, University of Maryland.

64 *"I'll try anything"*: "Bringing the Arts to Public Radio," NPR press release, September 4, 1975, National Public Broadcasting Archives, University of Maryland.

64 *"He was one of those people"*: Malesky, interview with author, October 16, 2011.

64 *"Voices wasn't designed"*: Malesky, "Great NPR Program You Never Heard."

65 *"maimed monument"*: "The Round Museum Building Impresses a Critic as a 'Maimed Monument on a Maimed Mall,'" *New York Times*, October 10, 1974.

65 *"We must tell our eager listeners"*: Gore Vidal on *Voices in the Wind*, November 17, 1974, Walter J. Brown Media Archives and Peabody Awards Collection, University of Georgia.

65 *"The show"*: Jay Kernis, interview with author, November 30, 2011.

65 *"probably only 100"*: Ibid.

66 *"He fell apart"*: Easton, interview with author, September 13, 2016.

66 *"One night"*: Bob Edwards, interview with author, October 26. 2015.

67 *"The lipstick is"*: Stamberg, *Every Night at Five*, 9.

67 *"I'll buy if you'll fly"*: Skip Pizzi, interview with author, August 21, 2014.

67 *"A tall boy"*: Bob Edwards, interview with author, October 26, 2015.

67 *"I really learned"*: Ibid.

67 *"He was tall"*: Stamberg, interview with author, August 21, 2014.

67 *"We had a Black engineer"*: Edwards, interview with author, October 26, 2015.

67 *The water ran brown*: Pizzi, interview with author, August 21, 2014.

68 *"All the years, it seemed"*: Wertheimer, *Listening to America*, May 27, 1975, 79–81.

68 *ship named the* Glomar Explorer: Jack Mitchell, memo to NPR Information Programming Staff, March 19, 1975, Frischknecht papers, National Public Broadcasting Archives, University of Maryland Library.

68 *"At the meeting Colby"*: Ibid.

68 *"We had the information"*: Ibid.

69 *"Anderson is a Mormon"*: Mitchell, interview with author, February 5, 2015.

69 *"The question then became"*: Ibid.

69 *"This earned Jack"*: Russell, interview with author, September 30, 2011.

69 *"Richard Cohen"*: Mitchell, interview with author, February 5, 2015.

69 *"He wanted NPR"*: Russell, interview with McCauley, August 3, 1995, National Public Broadcasting Archives, University of Maryland.

70 *"NPR made a bigger effort"*: Mitchell, interview with author, September 6, 2017.

70 *"They sat on one side"*: Mitchell, interview with McCauley, September 19, 1995, National Public Broadcasting Archives, University of Maryland.

70 *"When I took over"*: Zelnick, interview with author, January 31, 2015.

70 *"covered a press conference"*: Ibid.

70 *"to protect the congressmen's reputation"*: Ibid.

70 *"Zelnick wanted to fire"*: Mitchell, interview with author, September 6, 2017.

71 *"She needed a lot"*: Zelnick, interview with author, January 31, 2015.

71 *"You can now let Green"*: Mitchell, interview with author, September 6, 2017.

71 *"was without merit"*: Russell, email to author, September 6, 2017.

71 *"identity politics that championed"*: Mitchell, *Listener Supported: The Culture and History of Public Radio*, 79.

71 *"NPR was embarrassed"*: David Cashdan, interview with author, June 11, 2021.

72 *"Zelnick claimed any decisions"*: Ibid.

72 *"Jim Russell put the material"*: Sanchez, interview with author, June 15, 2021.

72 *"The lawyers told me"*: Cashdan interview with author, June 11, 2021.

72 *"Marti tried to commit"*: Mitchell, interview with author, September 6, 2017.

72 *"resolve the case"*: Cashdan, interview with author, June 11, 2021.

72 *"financial settlement"*: Mitchell, interview with author, September 6, 2017.

72 *"civil rights lawyers"*: Cashdan, interview with author, June 11, 2021.

72 *"NPR agreed that"*: Sanchez, interview with author, June 15, 2021.

73 *"At NPR, everyone"*: Totenberg, interview with author, June 4, 2013.

73 *"adamant"*: Mitchell, interview with author, September 6, 2017.

73 *"I invited the Teamsters"*: Totenberg, interview with author, June 4, 2013.

73 *"Nina was loud"*: Gwathmey, interview with author, September 7, 2017.

73 *"People were asking"*: Russell, interview with author, December 26, 2013.

73 *"I was trying to keep"*: Gwathmey, interview with McCauley, August 3, 1995, National Public Broadcasting Archives, University of Maryland.

74 *The "minnow" . . . hoped "to swallow"*: Mitchell, interview with author, February 5, 2015.

74 *"NPR had been born"*: Sanchez, interview with author, March 6, 2018.

74 *"water sign"*: Mitchell, interview with author, March 20, 2014.

75 *"institutional assessment"*: Al Engelman, interview with author, July 17, 2015.

75 *"big body, big personality"*: Mitchell, interview with author, January 21, 2015.

75 *"They were concerned"*: Engelman, interview with author, August 10, 2015.

75 *"There were enclaves"*: Ibid.

76 *"relate to the long-range"*: Ibid.

76 *"When goals don't define"*: Ibid.

76 *"Engelman was trying to take apart"*: Russell, interview with McCauley, August 3, 1995, National Public Broadcasting Archives, University of Maryland.

76 *"Engelman's philosophy was"*: Mitchell, interview with author, January 21, 2015.

76 *"They'd go on for hours"*: Rosenberg, interview with author, March 27, 2015.

76 *"It was about making trouble"*: Ibid.

77 *"There was an incredible amount"*: Anderson, interview with author, March 8, 2016,

77 *You've been* role-ified": Engelman, interview with author, August 10, 2015.

77 *"I was in a meeting"*: Anderson, interview with author, March 8, 2016.

77 *"Masturbation is good"*: Talbot, interview with author, September 19, 2014.

77 *"Engelman and Symonds were sleeping"*: Rosenberg, interview with author, March 27, 2015.

77 *"was a cold fish"*: Steve Symonds, interview with author, February 19, 2016.

77 *"a sex-starved JAP"*: Ibid.

77 *"was Captain Kangaroo"*: Ibid.

77 *"There was a fury"*: Wertheimer, interview with McCauley, August 18, 1995, National Public Broadcasting Archives, University of Maryland.

77 *"My job was to do an assessment"*: Engelman, interview with author, August 10, 2015.

77 *"There was a lot of pent-up"*: Symonds, interview with McCauley, September 25, 1995, National Public Broadcasting Archives, University of Maryland.

78 *"I don't recall Engelman"*: Rosenberg, interview with author, March 27, 2015.

78 *"We saw ourselves"*: Symonds, interview with author, February 19, 2016.

78 *"Where are they from?"*: Engelman, interview with author, August 10, 2015.

78 *"People not familiar"*: Wertheimer, interview with McCauley, August 18, 1995, National Public Broadcasting Archives, University of Maryland.

78 *"The Department of Program Content"*: "Reorganizing Public Radio," *Washington Post*, April 24, 1976.

78 *"Special Audiences"*: Ibid.

79 *"a lack of familiarity"*: Mitchell, Stamberg, and Zelnick to Frischknecht, n.d., Frischknecht papers, National Public Broadcasting Archives, University of Maryland.

79 *"Our first thought"*: Ibid.

79 *"an outstanding job"*: Ibid.

79 *"No one," they wrote*: Ibid.

79 *"We cannot say too strongly"*: Ibid.

79 *"Because of the predictable withdrawal"*: Stamberg, handwritten addendum to Mitchell, Stamberg, and Zelnick, Ibid.

80 *"began to physically eject him"*: Jack Mitchell to Presley Holmes, April 28, 1976, Ibid.

80 *"artsy-fartsy"*: Holwill, interview with author, January 16, 2017.

80 *"breaking" his confidence*: Frischknecht to NPR staff, April 16, 1976, Frischknecht papers, National Public Broadcasting Archives, University of Maryland.

80 *"We must stop the brutalizing"*: Frischknecht, n.d., Ibid.

80 *"This shit must stop"*: Ibid.

81 *"News will include"*: Frischknecht reorganization plan, April 20, 1976, Ibid.

81 *"Socializing the basic philosophy"*: Ibid.

81 *"Widespread acceptance of our goals"*: Ibid.

81 *"a regurgitation of raw data"*: Robert Zelnick to Jack Mitchell, April 19, 1976, Ibid.

81 *"The memorandum takes refuge"*: Ibid.

82 *"Mouthing Off"*: *Washington Star*, May 6, 1976.

82 *"Ear just hates it"*: Ibid.

82 *"National Public Radio Network Downplays News"*: *New York Times*, May 10, 1976.

82 *"to alert those concerned"*: Zelnick to Mitchell, May 3, 1976, Frischknecht papers, National Public Broadcasting Archives, University of Maryland.

82 *"Perhaps the survival of NPR"*: Zelnick memo to NPR staff and station managers, May 5, 1976, Ibid.

83 *"Distribution of it"*: Frischknecht to Zelnick, May 7, 1976, Ibid.

83 *"discontinuing his public opposition"*: Zelnick resignation letter, May 9, 1976, Ibid. After leaving NPR, Zelnick assisted David Frost on a four-part TV interview series with Richard Nixon. Zelnick then became a reporter for ABC.

83 *"For reasons that have not"*: Harrison Salisbury, CBS News, May 24, 1976, Ibid.

83 *"I was very distressed"*: Stephen Goldfarb to Frischknecht, May 18, 1976, Ibid.

84 *"represented a distortion"*: Frischknecht to Paul Darling, May 25, 1976, Ibid.

84 *"She was devastated"*: Mitchell, interview with author, January 21, 2015.

84 *"We thought they were"*: Stamberg, interview with author, January 14, 2017.

84   *"We'd go to these meetings"*: Ibid.

84   *"I had panic attacks"*: Ibid.

84   *"Terrible. I was just popping"*: Ibid.

84   *"She had a psychological breakdown"*: Mitchell, interview with author, January 21, 2015.

84   *"I am neither in the habit"*: Zelnick resignation letter, May 9, 1976, Frischknecht papers, National Public Broadcasting Archives, University of Maryland.

84   *"Our job," recalled Symonds*: Symonds, interview with author, February 19, 2016.

85   *"My job was to get Hunter"*: Robert Krulwich, interview with author, December 4, 2012.

85   *"Well, Zelnick's just been offed"*: Ibid.

85   *"Russell made up some title"*: Ibid.

85   *"I don't think so"*: Stamberg, interview with author, January 14, 2017.

85   *"New York depressive"*: Robert Siegel, interview with author, August 20, 2014.

86   *"I was at the microphone"*: Ibid.

86   *"Tim found this plausible"*: Krulwich, interview with author, December 4, 2012.

86   *"I have a stepson"*: Ibid.

86   *"I took the cassette"*: Ibid.

87   *"He looked like he'd swallowed"*: John McChesney, interview with author, April 30, 2011.

87   *"He's the college professor"*: Stamberg, interview with author, August 21, 2014.

87   *"Let's play on the radio"*: Krulwich, interview with author, December 4, 2012.

87   *"I inadvertently adopted a Texas accent"*: Ibid.

87   *"You can't do that"*: Ibid.

87   *"Where are you from?"*: Ibid.

87   *"This is not in any way good"*: Ibid.

88   *NPR suspended him*: "Has Success Spoiled NPR," *The Washingtonian*, March 2007.

88   *"His gift for voices"*: Totenberg, interview with author, June 4, 2013.

88   *"Susan and I would put on"*: Krulwich, interview with author, January 18, 2017.

88   *"Paging Al Engelman"*: Engelman, interview with author, August 10, 2015.

88   *"We love you too Barbara"*: *New York Times*, October 4, 1976.

THREE: CITIZEN MANKIEWICZ

90   *"I have a short"*: Gladwin Hill, "Kennedy Is Dead, Victim of Assassin," *New York Times*, June 6, 1968, 1.

90   *"McGovern's alter ego"*: Hunter S. Thompson, *Fear and Loathing on the Campaign Trail '72* (San Francisco: Straight Arrow Press, 1973), 120.

91   *"His reputation preceded him"*: Quayle, interview with author, October 20, 2011.

91   *"Mankiewicz could be abrasive"*: Shirley MacLaine, *You Can Get There from Here* (New York: Norton, 1975), 67.

91   *"we'd wanted to hear from Lee"*: Wertheimer, interview with McCauley, August 18, 1995, National Public Broadcasting Archives, University of Maryland.

91   *"We'll take care of this"*: Kernis, interview with author, January 30, 2011.

92   *"After he got the laugh"*: Ibid.

92   *"It was a shithole"*: Russell, interview with author, September 30, 2011.

92   *"Frank, I'm really feeling paranoid"*: Flatow, interview with author, November 25, 2013.

92   *"Morale was terrible"*: Frank Mankiewicz, interview with McCauley, August 14, 1995, National Public Broadcasting Archives, University of Maryland.

93   *"Mankiewicz came in"*: Totenberg, interview with author, June 4, 2013.

93   *"$15,000—suddenly it was $25,000"*: Ibid.

93   *cost NPR $474,000*: Ernie Sanchez to NPR Executive Committee, August 26, 1977, Frank Mankiewicz papers, National Public Broadcasting Archives, University of Maryland.

93   *"Frank agreed to everything"*: Gwathmey, interview with author, February 26, 2014.

93   *"There's a certain attitude"*: Mankiewicz, interview with McCauley, August 14, 1995, National Public Broadcasting Archives, University of Maryland.

93   *"I don't know of any decision"*: Siegel, interview with McCauley, August 21, 1995, National Public Broadcasting Archives, University of Maryland.

93   *"Whatever is necessary"*: "National Public Radio's Voice at the Top," *Washington Post*, February 25, 1979.

94   *"Frank's interest"*: Siegel, interview with McCauley, August 21, 1995, National Public Broadcasting Archives, University of Maryland.

94   *"Mankiewicz was not a corporate leader"*: Russell, interview with author, December 26, 2013.

94   *"Mankiewicz wanted those women"*: Rosenberg, interview with author, March 27, 2015.

94   *"Frank made you feel great"*: Stamberg, interview with author, August 21, 2014.

94   *"wanted to be big shots"*: Russell, interview with author, December 26, 2013.

95   *"Do you want brains"*: Amos, interview with author, May 11, 2013.

95   *"Nina figured out"*: Siegel, interview with author, August 20, 2014.

95   *"The New York Post suggested"*: Totenberg, interview with author, June 4, 2013.

95   *termed Totenberg's piece stunning*: William Safire, "Equal Justice under Leak," *New York Times*, April 28, 1977.

96   *"We can't do it"*: Russell, interview with author, September 30, 2011.

96   *"Tell you what, gentlemen"*: Ibid.

96   *"Mankiewicz had the big picture"*: Ibid.

96   *"If NPR ever had any listeners"*: "Radio Is Pro Tem in the Senate for Canal Debates," *Broadcasting*, February 13, 1978.

97   *"It went on and on"*: Gwathmey, interview with author, February 26, 2014.

97   *"turning point"*: Noah Adams, interview with author, March 31, 2013.

97   *"Steve came to NPR"*: Totenberg, interview with author, June 4, 2013.

97   *"I know her from Wellesley"*: Ibid.

97   *"I sneaked her in"*: Mankiewicz, interview with McCauley, August 14, 1995.

97   *"A whole chain"*: McCauley, *NPR: The Trials and Triumphs of National Public Radio*, 48.

98   *"The news division"*: Chris Koch, interview with author, November 30, 2012.

98   *"She was so disliked"*: Russell, interview with author, September 30, 2011.

98   *"She was a nut bag"*: Easton, interview with author, February 27, 2014.

98   *"She was egoistic"*: Rick Lewis, interview with author, April 13, 2015.

98   *"She was brassy and Brooklyn"*: Frank Fitzmaurice, interview with author, June 5, 2013.

98   *"got together on something"*: Russell, interview with author, September 30, 2011.

99   *"This is a lady"*: Russell, interview with author, December 26, 2013.

99   *"You can if the entire staff"*: Ibid.

99   *"She was always asking"*: Rosenberg, interview with author, March 27, 2015.

99   *"made Newman uncomfortable"*: Russell, interview with author, December 26, 2013.

99   *"We gave her a negative"*: Siegel, interview with author, August 20, 2014.

99   *"He clearly undermined"*: Russell, interview with author, December 26, 2013.

99   *"out of his depth"*: Neal Conan, email to author, April 27, 2015.

100   *"It was a legitimate piece"*: Mankiewicz, interview with McCauley, August 14, 1995.

100   *"There was an awful lot"*: Holt, interview with author, March 19, 2012.

100   *"The tree's willing"*: Stamberg, *Every Night at Five*, 54.

100   *"It's like you breathe"*: Ibid.

101   *"You heard that story"*: Wertheimer, ed., *Listening to America*, 116.

101   *"I think the high-water mark"*: Gwathmey, interview with McCauley, August 3, 1995.

101   *"In Japanese"*: Stamberg, *Talk: NPR's Susan Stamberg Considers All Things*, 100–102.

101   *"In childhood boys are trained"*: Ibid., 115–17.

101   *"Was it Buddy De Sylva"*: Ibid., 103–9.

102   *"a blinkered, parochial"*: Conan, email to author, April, 27, 2015.

102   *"Life is what you heard"*: Conan, interview with author, June 6, 2011.

102   *"No, you stay"*: Conan, email to author, April 28, 2015.

103   *"Rick was in charge"*: Conan, email to author, March 13, 2015.

103   *"We blew up the show"*: Conan, interview with author, June 6, 2013.

103   *"tired, dull hole-fillers"*: Conan, email to author, April 27, 2015.

103   *"We decided to make it"*: Conan, interview with author, June 6, 2013.

103   *"Susan was the star"*: Lewis, interview with author, April 13, 2015.

103   *"I love your work"*: Ibid.

103   *"Frank used to say"*: Russell, interview with author, September 30, 2011.

104   *" 'Frank, I don't think' "*: Russell, interview with author, October 26, 2013.

104   *"I wanted to make this"*: Mankiewicz, interview with author, October 17, 2011.

104   *"He was marginalized"*: Lewis, interview with author, April 13, 2015.

104   *"Frank . . . wanted somebody"*: Conan, email to author, April 25, 2015.

104   *"I see the* Star*"*: Barbara Cohen, interview with author, March 19, 2012.

104   *"Do you think it's now"*: Ibid.

105   *"I was one of the few"*: Ibid.

105   *"Sam Holt was always saying"*: Mankiewicz, interview with author, October 17, 2011.

105   *"It was clear"*: Lawrence Lichty, interview with author, April 17, 2015.

106   *"Start a morning radio"*: Mankiewicz, interview with author, October 17, 2011.

106   *"I'd been at the* Star*"*: Cohen, interview with author, March 19, 2012.

107   *"sorority rushes"*: Ibid.

107   *"We voted not to let"*: Lewis, interview with author, April 13, 2015.

107   *"This is an opening"*: Fitzmaurice, interview with author, June 5, 2013.

108   *"All of a sudden, I realized"*: Cohen, interview with author, March 19, 2012.

108   *"Susan Stamberg thought"*: Kernis, interview with author, June 11, 2011.

108   *"The person who was most hostile"*: Lichty, interview with author, April 17, 2015.

108   *"I stood my ground"*: Stamberg, interview with author, October 21, 2011.

108   *"They thought they would"*: Mankiewicz, interview with author, October 17, 2011.

108   *"not anxious to do"*: Cohen, interview with author, March 19, 2012.

108   *foot-dragging to hostility*: Ibid.

108   *"I remember Nina"*: Steve Reiner, interview with author, June 12, 2013.

108   *"She was ruthless"*: Stamberg, interview with author, August 21, 2014.

109   *"My notion about"*: Krulwich, interview with author, December 4, 2012.

109   *"I met with everybody"*: Harry Shearer, interview with author, September 22, 2011.

109   *"I was championing difference"*: Krulwich, interview with author, December 4, 2012.

109   *"I called a lot of psychologists"*: Mankiewicz, interview with author, October 17, 2011.

109   *"move All Things Considered"*: Chris Koch, interview with author, November 30, 2012.

110   *"How do you create a show"*: Reiner, interview with author, June 12, 2013.

110   *"Here's my title"*: Bob Edwards, *A Voice in the Box: My Life in Radio* (Lexington: University Press of Kentucky, 2011), 68.

110   *"Public radio was never good"*: Kernis, interview with author, July 24, 2015.

111   *"The motivation for hiring"*: Ibid.

111   *"informed on nothing"*: "Harden and Weaver for President?" *New York Times*, February 25, 1985.

111   *"It was a lot about nothing"*: Marc Kuhn, interview with author, July 29, 2015.

111   *she was "thrilled"*: Mary Tillotson, interview with author, June 16, 2015.

111   *"We didn't have time"*: Kuhn, interview with author, July 29, 2015.

112   *"Outsiders were not welcome"*: Tillotson, interview with author, July 16, 2015.

112   *"They made us feel"*: Kuhn, interview with author, July 29, 2015.

112   *"To me they just wanted"*: Kernis, interview with author, July 24, 2015.

112   *"Kernis was a snooty"*: Kuhn, interview with author, July 29, 2015.

112   *"It sounded more like WMAL"*: Fitzmaurice, interview with author, June 5, 2013.

112   *"It was a bomb"*: Edwards, *Voice in the Box*, 68.

112   *"They hated it"*: Mankiewicz, interview with author, October 17, 2011.

113   *"They had Landphair call us"*: Tillotson, interview with author, June 16, 2015.

113   *"Do you think"*: Kernis, interview with author, June 11, 2011.

113   *"Bob, can we see you"*: Stamberg, interview with author, August 21, 2014.

113   *"He thought he was gonna"*: Ibid.

113   *"He never felt"*: Ibid.

113   *"If it had been Hurricane Susan"*: Koch, interview with author, November 30, 2012.

114   *"pointed"*: Ibid.

114   *"Barbara and Sam were tense"*: Fitzmaurice, interview with author, June 5, 2013.

114   *"It was an emergency"*: Bill Drummond, interview with author, July 22, 2013.

114   *"We tried to hash"*: Jackie Judd, interview with author, September 9, 2015.

114   *"By the end"*: Fitzmaurice, interview with author, June 5, 2013.

115   *"You designed the format"*: Kernis, interview with author, July 24, 2015.

115   *"frantic"*: Judd, interview with author, September 9, 2015.

115   *"It wasn't all hands"*: Ibid.

115   *"We'd watch the rats"*: Lichty, interview with author, April 17, 2015.

115   *"Bob was not only"*: Kernis, interview with author, July 24, 2015.

115   *"He was striking looking"*: Cohen, interview with author, March 29, 2012.

116   *"He looked like"*: Drummond, interview with author, July 22, 2013.

116   *"You know there are people"*: Margot Adler, interview with author, June 8, 2011.

116   *"diva-ish about Jay"*: Drummond, interview with author, July 22, 2013.

116   *"Part of the reason"*: Kernis, interview with author, June 11, 2011.

116   *"People had their doubts"*: Lewis, interview with author, April 13, 2015.

116   *"Jay was a good"*: Judd, interview with author, September 9, 2015.

116   *"was not impossible"*: Edwards, *Voice in the Box*, 70.

117 *"The NPR reporters"*: Kernis, interview with author, July 24, 2015.

117 *"We all went"*: Lichty, interview with author, April 17, 2015.

117 *"What are you listening to?"*: Mankiewicz, interview with author, October 17, 2011.

117 *"It was the first day"*: Ibid.

118 *"Edited and read by"*: "Robert J. Lurtsema, Region's *'Pro Musica'* Host, Dies at 68," *Boston Globe*, June 14, 2000.

118 *"There was a lot of opposition"*: Fitzmaurice, interview with author, June 5, 2013.

118 *"the same impact"*: Jeff McLaughlin, "The Birds Will Be Back," *Boston Globe*, February 9, 1980.

118 *"the Junior League nasalities"*: David B. Wilson, "Unwelcome Intruder of the Airwaves," *Boston Globe*, March 3, 1980.

119 *"ad-libbing the important"*: McLaughlin, "Birds Will Be Back."

119 *95 percent of the mail*: William A. Henry, "Lurtsema's Way Wins at WGBH," *Boston Globe*, March 4, 1980.

119 *"We said, 'Screw WGBH'"*: Lichty, interview with author, April 17, 2015.

119 *"Every radio station"*: Siegel, interview with author, August 20, 2014.

119 *"NPR was the first national service"*: Pete Lowenstein, interview with author, March 23, 2012.

119 *"Someone wanted to know"*: Holt, interview with author, March 19, 2012.

120 *They thought the host*: Mankiewicz, interview with author, October 21, 2011.

120 *"I asked them to put some static"*: Ibid.

121 *"NPR's view was"*: Lewis, interview with author, April 13, 2015.

121 *"He had a graphic"*: Ibid.

121 *"We need 12 uplinks"*: Bill Kling, email to author, June 18, 2015.

121 *"He was more used"*: Ibid.

122 *"Let me tell you"*: Mankiewicz, interview with author, October 21, 2011.

122 *"When you've met one"*: Siegel, interview with author, August 20, 2014.

122 "Frank was always saying," Dale Ouzts, interview with author, May 16, 2016.

122 *"With the satellite"*: Wertheimer, interview with McCauley, August 18, 1995, National Public Broadcasting Archives, University of Maryland.

123 *"That was the only way"*: Drummond, interview with author, July 22, 2013.

123 *"a six-foot shit-kicker"*: Frank Browning, interview with author, July 8, 2011.

124 *"I wanted us to have roots"*: John McChesney, interview with author, January 2, 2016.

124 *"I came out of the community radio movement"*: Ibid.

124 *bring in 1,400 stories*: "Caught in the Act of Thinking," *Current*, April 27, 1981.

125 *"Hey, you're working"*: Howard Berkes, interview with author, September 28, 2013.

125 *"He could find good reporters"*: Conan, interview with author, June 6, 2013.

125 *"He was bluff"*: Ibid.

125 *"John wore his balls"*: Reiner, interview with author, June 12, 2013.

126 *"You walked through this lobby"*: Steve Proffitt, interview with author, May 7, 2011.

126 *"We were on some sort of crusade"*: Amos, interview with author, November 1, 2014.

126 *"We just worked"*: Drummond, interview with author, July 22, 2013.

126 *"the Fallopian Jungle"*: Ibid.

127 *"Notch me, sync me"*: Proffitt, interview with author, September 7, 2012.

127 *"edit faster than anybody"*: Baer, interview with author, October 21, 2011.

127 *"There wasn't a day"*: Reiner, interview with author, June 12, 2013.

127 *"It was hard to have a conversation"*: Drummond, interview with author, July 22, 2013.

127 *"It was insular"*: Proffitt, interview with author, May 7, 2011.

128 *"We were all in bed"*: Amos, interview with author, November 1, 2014.

128 *"Everybody . . . was fucking"*: Drummond, interview with author, July 22, 2013.

128 *"It was the only place"*: Malesky, interview with author, October 16, 2011.

129 *"Those two are doing"*: Proffitt, interview with author, May 7, 2011.

129 *"Boy A and Girl A"*: Proffitt, interview with author, September 7, 2012.

129 *"To be on NPR"*: David Ensor, interview with author, December 7, 2015.

130 *"It's Carl"*: Geri Pizzi, interview with author, September 18, 2015.

130 *"What the media had brought"*: *People*, January 14, 1980.

130 *"a fairly tall person"*: Nora Ephron, *Heartburn* (New York: Alfred A. Knopf, 1983), 8.

130 *"Damn near everybody"*: McChesney, interview with author, April 30, 2011.

130 *"There was an epidemic"*: Koch, Facebook post, October 24, 2014.

131 *"Leo del Aguila, call 6492"*: Drummond, interview with author, July 22, 2013; Alex Chadwick, interview with author, October 22, 2013.

131 *"The voice of . . . Communism"*: "Birth of a Salesman," *New York Times Magazine*, October 26, 1975.

132 *"Abalone"*: Guy Raz, "Radio Free Georgetown," *Washington City Paper*, January 29, 1999.

132 *"He was so charismatic"*: Skip Pizzi, interview with author, August 21, 2014.

132 *"I've got a party"*: Raz, "Radio Free Georgetown."

132 *"At first"*: del Aguila, interview with author, May 28, 2013.

132 *"In those days"*: del Aguila, interview with author, May 24, 2013.

132 *"great quality coke"*: Ibid.

133 *"That's where I would go"*: Edwards, interview with author, October 26, 2015.

133 *"There was coke at every party"*: del Aguila, interview with author, May 24, 2013.

133 *25 percent indulged*: Amos, interview with author, November 1, 2014.

133 *put it at 30 percent*: del Aguila, interview with author, May 24, 2013.

134 *"Of the group that was my peers"*: Ibid.

134 *"Word had gotten out"*: Ibid.

134 *"I had nothing there"*: Ibid.

134 *"Many of the people"*: Ibid.

134 *"We saw some people"*: McChesney, interview with author, January 26, 2016.

134 *"Chris Koch and I"*: McChesney, interview with author, April 30, 2011.

134 *"We were all sitting around"*: Koch, interview with author, November 30, 2012.

135 *"that Leo was selling drugs"*: Fitzmaurice, interview with author, June 5, 2013.

135 *"It was the FBI"*: McChesney, interview with author, April 30, 2011.

135 *"Mankiewicz started a rumor"*: Koch, interview with author, November 30, 2011; Koch, Facebook post, October 24, 2014.

135 *"It ended, and"*: McChesney, interview with author, April 30, 2011.

136 *"It was a fad"*: Edwards, interview with author, October 26, 2015.

136 *"We moved on"*: Ibid.

136 *"Drugs were not"*: McChesney, email to author, February 1, 2016.

136 *"Cokie, Linda, and Nina"*: Drummond, interview with author, July 22, 2013.

136   *"What pieces didn't"*: Kernis, interview with author, June 11, 2011.

137   *"Bob had walls up"*: Fitzmaurice, interview with author, June 5, 2013.

137   *"a very good instrument"*: Stamberg, interview with author, October 21, 2011.

137   *"Jay helped Bob loosen up"*: Cohen, interview with author, March 19, 2012.

137   *"negotiating stuff with them"*: Fitzmaurice, interview with author, June 5, 2013.

138   *"I think hiring me"*: Sanford Ungar, interview with McCauley, August 16, 1995.

138   *"He was bright"*: Stamberg, interview with author, August 21, 2014.

138   *"She thought he was stiff"*: Cohen, interview with author, March 22, 2012.

138   *"I think she wanted"*: Ungar, interview with author, October 27, 2015.

138   *"I think at our best"*: Ungar, interview with McCauley, August 16, 1995.

138   *"We were actually"*: Koch, interview with author, November 30, 2012.

138   *"Chris was an interesting"*: Ungar, interview with author, October 27, 2015.

139   *"He always wanted to keep"*: Bill Abbott, interview with author, January 13, 2014.

139   *"I liked going to work"*: Mankiewicz, interview with author, October 17, 2011.

140   *wiped out*: "Public Broadcasters State Their Budget Case before House," *Broadcasting*, March 30, 1981.

140   *"When an agency is threatened"*: "Caught in the Act of Thinking," *Current*, April 27, 1981.

140   *"can of worms"*: "A Public Broadcasting Dilemma," *Chicago Tribune*, March 1, 1981.

141   *"People don't realize"*: "National Public Radio at 10: Excellent but in Danger," *New York Times*, April 16, 1981.

141   *"How do you feel"*: Rob Rosenthal, "Father Cares, The Last of Jonestown," *Transom*, September 22, 2015, https://transom.org/2015/father-cares-the-last-of-jonestown-with -deb-amos-and-noah-adams/.

142   *He declassified the material*: James Reston Jr., interview with author, March 11, 2016.

142   *"Jones was brutally crushing"*: Ibid.

142   *"This was an auditory"*: Ibid.

142   *"I walked over to NPR"*: Ibid.

142   *"The executives left them alone"*: Proffitt, interview with author, September 7, 2012.

143   *"They gave us"*: Amos, interview with author, November 1, 2014.

144   *"Jonestown's greatest hits"*: Reston, interview with author, March 11, 2016.

144   *"The sounds were bleeding"*: Ibid.

144   *"My job was to structure"*: Amos, interview with author, November 1, 2014.

144   *"We decided to break"*: Ibid.

144   *"There was a lot of guff"*: Reston, interview with author, March 11, 2016.

144   *"The character is flat"*: Adams, interview with Rob Rosenthal, in Rosenthal, "Father Cares."

145   *"A guy walked in"*: Ibid.

145   *"Dad climbed up into"*: Ibid.

146   Father Cares *cannot conceivably*: Anthony Lewis, "Nightmare Brought to Life," *New York Times*, April 23, 1981.

146   *"We interviewed Maureen Reagan"*: Koch, interview with author, November 30, 2012.

146   *"I just had this habit,"* Gary Covino, interview with author, May 20, 2021.

147   *"Hi, thanks for calling"*: Representative Al Swift to Frank Mankiewicz, June 13, 1981 (excerpt from broadcast attached), Mankiewicz papers, National Public Broadcasting Archives, University of Maryland.

147   *"They saw it as a threat"*: Koch, interview with author, November 30, 2012.

147   *"went bonkers"*: Ibid.

147   *"I got on and said"*: Ibid.

147   *"The taped comment"*: Richard R. Storms to Representative Jerry Huckaby, May 4, 1981, Mankiewicz papers, National Public Broadcasting Archives, University of Maryland.

147   *"The folks at National Public Radio"*: Reed Irvine and Cliff Kincaid, "Media Monitor," distributed by Accuracy in Media, reprinted by *Broadcasting*, May 25, 1981.

148   *"NPR is a private"*: Mankiewicz to Representative Jerry Huckaby, June 16, 1981, Mankiewicz papers, National Public Broadcasting Archives, University of Maryland.

148   *"break the back"*: Cokie Roberts, email to author, June 7, 2016; Mankiewicz, interview with author, October 12, 2011.

148   *"every profession except"*: "Every Profession but the Oldest; NPR Is Going Private for Public Radio," *Broadcasting*, November 16, 1981.

149   *"Public Radio Means Business"*: "We Mean to Survive," *Current*, April 30, 1982.

149   *"Off the Fix"*: Gwathmey, interview with author, February 2, 2014.

149   *"like a jackrabbit"*: *Current*, April 30, 1982.

149   *"You better watch out"*: Ibid.

149   *"schizophrenic"*: Ibid.

150   *"will be a total"*: "FM Public Radio Stations to Broadcast Software; Service to Offer Game of the Week and Data Hotel," *InfoWorld*, July 12, 1982.

150   *"data hotels"*: Ibid.

150   *"NPR Goes on Line"*: Ibid.

151   *"Frank stated to me"*: Tom Warnock, interview with author, March 23, 2012.

151   *"McKinsey koshered the nuts"*: Siegel, interview with author, August 21, 2014.

151   *"The campaign is coming along"*: Margie Bonnett, "Frank Mankiewicz, a Rebel with Causes, Rides to the Rescue of America's Endangered Public Radio Network," *People*, May 24, 1982.

151   *"A Rebel with Causes"*: Ibid.

151   *"The bottom line"*: Warnock, interview with author, March 23, 2012.

152   *"It looks like a Diane Arbus photograph"*: Amos, interview with author, November 1, 2014.

152   *"They were very high"*: David Brugger, interview with author, October 19, 2011.

152   *"was very pretty"*: Warnock, interview with author, March 23, 2012.

153   *"The device"*: Brugger, interview with author, October 19, 2011.

153   *"It didn't sound believable"*: Ibid.

153   *"When I heard about it"*: Siegel, interview with author, August 20, 2014.

153   *You wanted to believe*: Brugger, interview with author, October 19, 2011.

153   *"Frank was known"*: Siegel, interview with McCauley, August 21, 1995.

153   *"Mama don't allow"*: "Emergency at NPR: This Is Not A Test," *In These Times*, May 4–10, 1983.

153   *"On Monday, Tom"*: "No Villains, Just Miscast Characters in Budget Saga," *Current*, August 9, 1993.

154   *"such a quick devolution"*: Gwathmey, interview with McCauley, August 3, 1995.

154   *"a stringent cash flow"*: "No Villains, Just Miscast Characters."

154   *"People found him in bars"*: Warnock, interview with author, March 23, 2012.

155   *"Art-to-Tom-to-Frank"*: "No Villains, Just Miscast Characters."

155   *"I didn't have to"*: Ibid.
155   *"the agencies of the government"*: Mankiewicz, interview with author, October 25, 2011.
155   *"I don't want my epitaph"*: "No Villains, Just Miscast Characters."
155   *"Nobody knew where we were"*: Gwathmey, interview with author, February 26, 2014.
156   *"This is a show we think"*: Bill Kling, interview with author, June 17, 2015.
156   *"Frank's answer was not"*: Ibid.
156   *"I didn't like" the program*: McCauley, *NPR: The Trials and Triumphs of National Public Radio*, 53.
156   *"We're permitting you suburban people"*: Mankiewicz, interview with author, October 21, 2011.
156   *"It was the first yuppie"*: Mankiewicz, interview with McCauley, August 14, 1995, National Broadcasting Archives, University of Maryland.
156   *"Any money I give to you"*: Kling, interview with author, June 17, 2015.
156   *"He wanted half"*: Ouzts, interview with author, May 16, 2016,
156   *"all outside production"*: Kling, interview with author, July 21, 2016.
156   *"We sat on chairs"*: Kling, interview with author, June 17, 2015.
157   *"If Garrison Keillor gets laryngitis"*: Mankiewicz, interview with author, October 21, 2011.
157   *"Kling was obviously"*: Ibid.
157   *"They made Kling"*: Hockenberry, interview with author, June 5, 2012.
157   *"People at NPR thought"*: Ungar, interview with author, October 27, 2015.
157   *"I don't think Bill"*: Lewis, interview with author, April 13, 2015.
158   *"We had arguments"*: Mankiewicz, interview with author, October 17, 2011.
158   *"We had this argument"*: Ibid.
158   *"It works today"*: Brugger, interview with author, October 19, 2011.
158   *"The problem was"*: Warnock, interview with author, March 23, 2012.
159   *"We thought* Star Wars*"*: Holt, interview with author, March 19, 2012.
159   *"David, we need"*: Brugger, interview with author, October 19, 2011.
159   *"He so clearly didn't want"*: Warnock, interview with author, March 23, 2012.
159   *"These vice presidents"*: Siegel, interview with author, October 20, 2014.
159   *"We had been in a period"*: Warnock, interview with author, March 23, 2012.
159   *"Coming up in public radio"*: Stamberg, interview with author, August 21, 2011.
160   *"I didn't have to itemize"*: Siegel, interview with author, August 20, 2014.
160   *"It's in my nature"*: "The Sunday Show," *Washington Post*, April 4, 1982.
160   *"I remember people saying"*: Ungar, interview with McCauley, August 16, 1995.
161   *"I wanted to see"*: Quayle, interview with author, October 20, 2011.
161   *"The problems were bad"*: Brugger, interview with author, October 19, 2011.
161   *"It could have been solved"*: Mankiewicz, interview with author, October 17, 2011.
161   *"I'm not sure I wanted"*: Mankiewicz, interview with McCauley, August 14, 1995.
161   *"bored"*: Conan, interview with author, December 15, 2013.
161   *"never seriously considered"*: Rich Levin (retired spokesman for Major League Baseball), email to author, August 5, 2016.
161   *"took me out"*: Warnock, interview with author, March 23, 2012.
161   *"Warnock wasn't giving"*: Fitzmaurice, interview with author, June 5, 2013.
162   *"the fall guy"*: Ungar, interview with McCauley, August 16, 1995.
162   *"Billy said we"*: Cohen, interview with author, March 22, 2012.

162   *"there had been rumors"*: Kling, email to author, August 5, 2016.

162   *"the sacrificial lamb"*: Kling, email to author, August 7, 2016.

162   *"giving us the full picture"*: Kling, email to author, August 5, 2016.

162   *"Darth Vader approaches"*: Ron Kramer, interview with author, July 20, 2017.

162   *"Who has the bottom-line"*: Kling, email to author, August 5, 2016.

162   *"$5.8 million"*: "NPR Gets Interim Chief," *Washington Post*, April 22, 1983.

163   *"We overestimated the response"*: Mankiewicz, April 18, 1983, Minnesota Public Radio 30th Anniversary CD, January 22, 1987, courtesy Bill Kling.

163   *"There are six months"*: Laurence Zuckerman, "Has Success Spoiled NPR?," *Mother Jones*, June/July 1987.

163   *"It was traumatic"*: Gwathmey, interview with McCauley, August 3, 1995.

163   *"We were heartbroken"*: Wertheimer, interview with McCauley, August 18, 1995.

163   *"I look at Mankiewicz"*: "NPR Turns Microphone on Itself," *Current*, May 24, 1983.

163   *"It was upsetting"*: Mankiewicz, interview with author, October 17, 2011.

163   *"I never took him"*: Mankiewicz, interview with author, October 21, 2011.

163   *"I resigned because"*: Ibid.

163   *"He connected us"*: Siegel, interview with author, August 20, 2014.

164   *"He poured fertilizer"*: Gwathmey, interview with author, February 26, 2014.

164   *"He fucked up"*: Siegel, interview with author, August 20, 2014.

164   *"Only desperate and tough"*: "What Went Wrong at National Public Radio?," *The New York Times*, June 12, 1983.

FOUR: RESURRECTION

165   *"six-three, Black, and loud"*: George Miles, interview with author, March 29, 2018.

165   He was the *"stern uncle"*: Rosenberg, interview with author, October 24, 2017.

166   *"If you saw this guy"*: Symonds, interview with McCauley, September 25, 1995.

166   *six thousand unmailed checks*: Bornstein, interview with author, December 5, 2017.

166   *"We were facing no lights"*: Ibid.

166   *"The team I aggregated"*: Bornstein, interview with McCauley, July 3, 1995.

167   *"Your name is on the list"*: Flatow, interview with author, November 25, 2013.

167   *"I remember coming in"*: Simon, interview with McCauley, August 23, 1995.

167   *"went over to get"*: Jo Anne Wallace, interview with author, October 26, 2017.

168   *"The survival of the organization"*: Mitchell, *Listener Supported: The Culture and History of Public Radio*, 109.

168   *"Bornstein was Robespierre"*: Cokie Roberts, interview with author, June 27, 2016.

168   *"Their attitude"*: Mitchell, interview with author, November 28, 2017.

168   *"The troika stormed"*: Symonds, interview with McCauley, September 2, 1995.

169   *"It's the wrong time"*: Bornstein, interview with author, December 5, 2017.

169   *"Get the hell out"*: Miles, interview with author, March 29, 2018.

169   *"We felt the people"*: Roberts, interview with author, June 27, 2016.

169   *"Save NPR"*: *The New York Times*, June 19, 1983.

169   *"invited—in fact, urged"*: Ibid.

169   *"Fred got Walter Cronkite"*: Totenberg, interview with author, June 4, 2013.

169   *"You won't find an answer"*: "NPR Dilemma: How Can You Slap Uncle Walter in the Face?" *Current*, June 21, 1983.

170 *"the news department"*: Mitchell, interview with author, November 11, 2017.

170 *"It was way overstepping"*: Stamberg, interview with author, February 22, 2018.

170 *"have to find a nice way"*: "NPR Dilemma: How Can You Slap Uncle Walter in the Face?" *Current*, June 21, 1983.

170 *"If you proceed"*: Bornstein, interview with author, December 5, 2017.

170 *"We looked at alternative sources"*: Mullally, interview with McCauley, July 12, 1995.

171 *"wanted to put me and my team"*: Bornstein, interview with author, March 19, 2018.

171 *"The characters brought in after Frank"*: Dorian, interview with author, March 20, 2018.

171 *"CPB would want"*: Mullally, interview with McCauley, July 12

171 *"NPR said that if"*: Brugger, interview with author, October 19, 2011.

172 *"financial mismanagement"*: "NPR Gets the Bad News," *Broadcasting*, June 20, 1983.

172 *"the network adopted"*: "FCC Authorization Clears Dingell et al. with Focus on Public Broadcasting Rider," *Broadcasting*, July 4, 1983.

172 *"Dingell was super pissed"*: Symonds, interview with author, March 4, 2018.

172 *"leftward tilt of biases"*: "FCC Authorization Clears Dingell."

172 *"I have to conclude"*: "GAO Probes as Lawmakers Lean on CPB," *Current*, July 12, 1983.

173 *"Dealing with Frank"*: Wirth, interview with author, November 13, 2017.

173 *"I was furious at Frank"*: Wertheimer, interview with author, August 12, 2015.

173 *"It was hairy"*: Aylward, interview with author, November 17, 2017.

173 *"It's done"*: Ibid.

173 *"Our board members"*: Dorian, interview with author, March 20, 2018.

174 *"This was a most creative"*: "Accord Reached to Bail Out Troubled NPR," *Washington Post*, July 29, 1983.

174 *"We'll write you a check"*: Bornstein, interview with author, December 5, 2017.

174 *"I will not go on the air"*: Stamberg, interview with author, October 21, 2011.

174 *"Yes, I promise you"*: Ibid.

174 *"Welcome to NPR's Drive to Survive"*: *Drive to Survive*, August 1, 1983, National Public Broadcasting Archives, University of Maryland.

174 *"Susan and I"*: Ibid.

175 *"Even though we got the loan"*: Ibid.

175 *"Oh, Scott, who wears"*: Rosenberg, interview with author, October 24, 2017.

176 *"I got identified"*: Siemering, interview with author, November 30, 2017.

176 *"He was supposed to be cut"*: Mitchell, interview with author, November 29, 2017.

176 *"Seems to me"*: *Drive to Survive*.

176 *"The only thanks I got"*: Miles, interview with author, March 29, 2018.

176 *a thankless task*: Stamberg, interview with author, February 22, 2018.

176 *"Bornstein was an absolute saint"*: "Public Radio's Reorganizer Signs Off," *New York Times*, October 22, 1983.

176 *"He [left] us in a better place"*: Ibid.

176 *"Fantasy land was over"*: Bornstein, interview with McCauley, July 3, 1995.

177 *"Who in their right mind"*: Mullally, interview with McCauley, July 12, 1995.

177 *"consummate bureaucrat"*: Bornstein, interview with McCauley, July 3, 1995,

177 *"I wasn't interested in finding"*: Mullally, interview with McCauley, July 12, 1995.

177 *"the quintessential staff man"*: Mitchell, *Listener Supported*, 112.

177   *"a yachtsman, stern"*: "The Soul of a News Machine," Marc Fisher, *Washington Post Magazine*, October 22, 1989,

177   *"He was clinch-lipped"*: Simon, interview with author, November 27, 2012.

177   *"A Yankee"*: Wertheimer, ed., *Listening to America*, 217.

178   *"The trio interfered"*: Fisher, "The Soul of a News Machine."

178   *"He knows how to raise money"*: "Ex-Aid Director Heads Public Radio," *New York Times*, October 29, 1983.

178   *"I don't think we can put the crisis"*: Wertheimer, *Listening to America*, 218.

178   *"I'm afraid there isn't"*: "Douglas Bennet Tries to Get the Money Ball Rolling Again at NPR," *Christian Science Monitor*, March 14, 1984.

178   *"He was just very determined"*: Symonds, interview with author, March 4, 2018.

178   *"Robert and I went to lunch"*: Gwathmey, interview with author, February 28, 2014.

179   *"He was every bit a London"*: Hockenberry, interview with author, June 5, 2012.

179   *"He returned to Washington"*: Buzenberg, interview with author, August 18, 2014.

179   *"He's a very smart guy"*: Adler, interview with author, June 8, 2011.

179   *"Smart, really smart"*: Proffitt, interview with author, May 7, 2011.

179   *"relied on Nina, Cokie"*: Richard Harris, interview with author, September 7, 2018.

179   *"We had to find a way"*: Kernis, interview with author, April 9, 2018.

180   *"Noah can't sing"*: Art Silverman, interview with author, August 20, 2018.

180   *"Susan was laughing so hard"*: Ibid.

180   *"Susan is this big, brassy"*: Ibid.

180   *"They carved out"*: Harris, interview with author, September 7, 2018.

180   *"Mother always said"*: Stamberg, *Talk: NPR's Susan Stamberg Considers All Things*, 196.

180   *"I cried when"*: Ibid.

180   *"It's a very unscrupulous"*: Ibid., 209.

181   *"I felt reluctant"*: Ibid., 212.

181   *"You were arrested"*: Ibid., 213.

182   *"A lot of people wanted to get out"*: Wertheimer, *Listening to America*, 71.

182   *"I wanted flowers"*: Ibid.

182   *"It was hard to"*: Ibid.

182   *"Air Force Second Lieutenant Richard Vande Geer"*: Ibid., 79.

183   *"There was [often]"*: Silverman, interview with author, August 20, 2018.

183   *"I have a pot boiling"*: Stamberg, *Talk*, 272.

183   *"I need three-and-a-half"*: Silverman, interview with author, August 20, 2018.

183   *"In a forest far away"*: Wertheimer, *Listening to America*, 207.

183   *"He brought visions"*: Silverman, interview with author, August 20, 2018.

183   *"Vertamae wasn't the sort"*: Harris, interview with author, September 7, 2018.

184   *"I grew up in the Carolina lowlands"*: Wertheimer, *Listening to America*, 201.

184   *"She'd be subject to a deadline"*: Silverman, interview with author, August 20, 2018.

184   *"We were interested"*: Harris, interview with author, September 7, 2018.

184   *"It allowed him to be"*: Kernis, interview with author, April 9, 2018.

185   *"My dad grew up in Brooklyn"*: Ketzel Levine, interview with author, August 23, 2018.

185   *"Who is Red Barber?"*: Bob Edwards, *Fridays with Red: A Radio Friendship* (New York: Simon & Schuster, 1993), 18.

185 *"Barberisms"*: Ibid., 43.

185 *"The Catbird Seat"*: *The New Yorker*, November 6, 1942.

186 *"You don't have to quit"*: Edwards, *Fridays with Red*, 91.

186 *"Suddenly, the scales fell"*: Ibid., 92.

186 *"I remember Jackie saying"*: Ibid., 184.

186 *Barber dazzled Levine*: Ibid., 18.

187 *"I decided I would"*: Levine, interview with author, August 23, 2018.

187 *"Would you join us?"*: Ibid.

187 *"Every word I was to say"*: Edwards, *Fridays with Red*, 27.

188 *"the Friday meetin'"*: Ibid., 146.

188 *"traditional values: sacrifice"*: Ibid.

188 *"Well," he told Edwards*: Ibid., 204.

188 *"For man walketh"*: Ibid., 143.

189 *"He had no interest"*: Ibid., 138.

189 *"You know what I was thinking"*: Ibid., 205.

189 *"That's right"*: Ibid.

189 *"The things you can learn"*: Ibid., 206.

189 *"young fella"*: Ibid., 20.

189 *"Colonel Bob"*: Ibid.

190 *"When I talked to Red"*: Ibid., 57.

190 *"Exposure to* Flashdance*"*: Wertheimer, *Listening to America*, 208.

191 *"generous gift"*: "New Weekend Life for 'All Things Considered,'" *Los Angeles Times*, July 22, 1985.

191 *"They offered no choices"*: Mitchell, *Listener Supported*, 113.

191 *"spent a lot of time preventing"*: Siegel, interview with author, August 20, 2014.

192 *a "best-of" show*: Ibid.

192 *"To me, that whole scheme"*: Ibid.

192 *"would have been a message"*: Siegel, interview with McCauley, August 21, 1995.

192 *"framed the Saturday show"*: Siegel, interview with author, August 20, 2014.

192 *"NPR is expanding"*: Siegel, interview with McCauley, August 21, 1995.

193 *"I didn't want the name"*: Siegel, interview with author, August 20, 2014.

193 *"We took the best producer"*: Siegel, interview with McCauley, August 21, 1995.

193 *"I'd worked with Scott"*: Siegel, interview with author, August 20, 2014.

193 *"had to be great"*: Siegel, interview with McCauley, August 21, 1995.

193 *"He did this very cinematic"*: Siegel, interview with author, August 20, 2014.

194 *"In every story,"* Ibid.

194 *"the city sanitation department"*: Chadwick, interview with author, April 21, 2011.

194 *"I said, 'Look'"*: Simon, interview with author, March 30, 2012.

194 *"The neighborhood itself"*: Stamberg, *Every Night at Five*, 33.

197 *"I heard a sound"*: Baer, interview with author, January 25, 2017.

197 *"We walked around"*: Simon, interview with author, November 27, 2011.

197 *"Where are the bodies?"*: del Aguila, interview with author, May 24, 2013.

198 *"powder marks on the faces"*: Ibid.

198 *"Fuck"*: Ibid.

198 *"It was a brilliant"*: McChesney, interview with author, April 13, 2011.

198   *"The Salvadoran Army said"*: "4 Dutch Newsmen Slain on a Trip to Film Guerrillas in El Salvador," *New York Times*, March 19, 1982.

199   *"I'd love to go fishing"*: Scott Simon, email to author, June 27, 2018.

199   *"existentially present"*: Browning, interview with author, July 2, 2011.

199   *"What's your favorite"*: Simon, email to author, June 28, 2018.

199   *"I wouldn't know"*: Simon, interview with author, November 27, 2012.

200   *"big wind from Chicago"*: Scott Simon, *Home and Away* (New York: Hyperion, 2000), 4.

200   *"the anonymous, unseen basso buffo"*: Ibid., 41.

200   *"Daddy's sick"*: Ibid., 51.

200   *"The time is exactly"*: Scott Simon, "A Saturday Morning with Ernie Simon," NPR, July 14, 2008, https://www.npr.org/2008/06/14/91514684/a-saturday-morning-with-ernie-simon.

200   *"possessed [of] a personal discipline"*: Simon, *Home and Away*, 200.

201   *"Scott was always dating women"*: McChesney, April 30, 2011.

201   *"someone who never grew up"*: Adler, interview with author, June 8, 2011,

201   *"the longest showers"*: del Aguila, interview with author, May 24, 2013.

201   *"I happen to be a member"*: Simon, interview with McCauley, August 23, 1995.

201   *Frank Collin volunteered*: Simon, interview with author, March 30, 2012.

202   *"Once you do the news"*: Kernis, interview with author, December 11, 2017.

202   *"Scott would call"*: Ibid.

202   *"It was like we belonged"*: Ibid.

202   *"Scott's adventures in"*: Ibid.

202   *"Kernis understood that"*: Hockenberry, interview with author, June 5, 2012.

202   *"That's how we spoke"*: Kernis, interview with author, December 11, 2017.

203   *"Scott and I were"*: Ibid.

203   *"When we were designing"*: Ibid.

203   *"Not on your life"*: Ibid.

204   *"each hour with"*: Ibid.

204   *"thought Scavullo"*: Baer, interview with author, January 25, 2017.

205   *"I had suffered"*: Daniel Schorr, *Staying Tuned: A Life in Journalism* (New York: Pocket Books, 2001), 261.

205   *"Dan . . . we are"*: Kernis, interview with author, December 11, 2017.

205   *"What a perfect day"*: Ibid.

206   *"The government is"*: *Weekend Edition*, November 2, 1985, NPR.org.

206   *"White South Africans say"*: Ibid.

206   *"As far as they are concerned"*: Ibid; https://www.npr.org/2010/10/31/130954134/25-years-of-weekend-edition-from-our-first-show.

206   *"In 1961"*: Ibid.

207   *"want to understand"*: Ibid.

207   *"Inevitably . . . the charge"*: Ibid.

207   *"It's the only show"*: Siegel, interview with author, August 20, 2014.

207   *"it was a hit"*: Kernis, interview with author, December 11, 2017.

207   *"It's a bold"*: Simon, interview with author, November 27, 2012.

207   *"there was such a high bar"*: Cindy Carpien, interview with author, February 2, 2018

208   *"bang the pieces together"*: Ina Jaffe, interview with author, January 18, 2018.

208 *"the forty-eight-hour day"*: Baer, interview with author, June 14, 2013.

208 *"You'd be sleeping"*: Ibid.

208 *"Jay has a philosophy"*: Jaffe, interview with author, January 18, 2018.

208 *"Scott's a cappuccino"*: Browning, interview with author, July 1, 2011.

208 *"Scott had this infectious"*: Kernis, interview with author, December 11, 2017.

208 *"When you speak of this"*: Simon, interview with author, November 27, 2012.

208 *"They were like an old"*: Baer, interview with author, January 25, 2017.

208 *"I think most people"*: Kernis, interview with author, December 11, 2017.

208 *"got raunchy"*: Baer, interview with author, January 25, 2017.

209 *"Is this the New York bureau"*: Simon, interview with author, November 27, 2012.

209 *"a boy's club"*: Baer, interview with author, January 25, 2017.

209 *"I quickly became"*: Schorr, *Staying Tuned*, 322.

209 *"Little Dan is out"*: Carpien, interview with author, February 2, 2018.

209 *"Jay and Scott were tempestuous"*: Ibid.

209 *"Did we go"*: Kernis, interview with author, December 11, 2017.

209 *"It was a place"*: Jaffe, interview with author, January 18, 2018.

209 *"we were nutty"*: Carpien, interview with author, February 2, 2018.

209 *"We decided to make"*: Kernis, interview with author, December 11, 2017.

FIVE: CHANGING OF THE GUARD

210 *"Kim Williams"*: Stamberg, *Talk: NPR's Susan Stamberg Considers All Things*, 273.

211 *"tipped me over"*: Stamberg, interview with author, November 5, 2018.

211 *"It's too hard"*: Stamberg, *Talk*, 276.

211 *"The bottom of the world"*: Stamberg, interview with author, November 5, 2018.

212 *"I've always found work"*: Ibid.

212 *"I had cancer"*: Stamberg, interview with author, February 22, 2018.

212 *"was so good"*: Mitchell, interview with author, January 28, 2019.

212 *"I was outraged"*: Ungar, interview with McCauley, August 16, 1995.

212 *"I felt like I was hauling"*: Stamberg, interview with author, February 22, 2018.

212 *"There were conversations"*: Ungar, interview with McCauley, August 16, 1995.

212 *"I felt like [the show]"*: Stamberg, interview with author, February 22, 2018.

213 *"The next time a space shuttle"*: Siegel, interview with author, November 9, 2018.

213 *"She's an emotionally solid"*: Ibid.

214 *"anthropological journalism"*: Fisher, "The Soul of a News Machine," *Washington Post Magazine*, October 22, 1989.

214 *"about eighty-five percent lesbian"*: Adler, interview with author, June 8, 2011.

214 *"I'd turn the station on"*: Ibid.

214 *"She'd spent so much time"*: Conan, interview with author, January 22, 2019.

214 *"dazzling"*: Montagne, interview with author, May 5, 2011.

214 *"John was the first person"*: Michael Fields, interview with author, February 18, 2019.

215 *"It'd been clear"*: Adler, interview with author, June 8, 2011.

215 *"Some station manager"*: Adler, interview with author, December 1, 2012.

215 *"Bennet was not"*: Jude Doherty, interview with author, February 25, 2019.

215 *"difficult"*: Reiner, interview with author, June 12, 2013.

215 *"He's a complete asshole"*: Lyden, interview with author, June 11, 2013.

215 *"John is a smart guy"*: Baer, interview with author, January 25, 2018.

216 *"Our programs are not"*: Stamberg, interview with author, November 5, 2018.

216 *"I was hurt"*: Ibid.

216 *"In the future"*: Mitchell, *Listener Supported: The Culture and History of Public Radio*, 116.

216 *"It was comical"*: Siegel, interview with author, November 9, 2018.

216 *"I was done at CBS"*: Judd, interview with author, December 12, 2018.

216 *"I idolized"*: Ibid.

217 *"We'd established ourselves"*: Ibid.

217 *"I saw Jackie"*: Siegel, interview with author, November 9, 2018.

217 *"Joe Gwathmey, my boss"*: Ibid.

217 *"That threw everything off"*: Ibid.

217 *"We were far"*: Judd, interview with author, December 12, 2018.

217 *"I never applied"*: Montagne, interview with author, November 14, 2018.

218 *so-called shadow staff*: Ibid.

218 *"It was practically illegal"*: Ibid.

218 *"I knew her"*: Stamberg, interview with author, November 5, 2018.

218 *"Renee as the best"*: Siegel, interview with author, November 9, 2018.

218 *"There was a comfort factor"*: Montagne, interview with author, November 14, 2018.

218 *"After hearing you"*: Ibid.

218 *"I didn't get the level"*: Ibid.

218 *"We want to offer you"*: Ibid.

219 *"Good evening"*: Ibid.

219 *"It really mattered"*: Ibid.

219 *"I had paid my dues"*: Edwards, *Voice in the Box*, 87.

219 *"One of the least pleasant"*: Siegel, interview with author, November 9, 2018.

220 *"we lobbed an incredibly"*: Siegel, interview with McCauley, October 21, 1995.

220 *"There was a vacancy"*: Chadwick, interview with author, April 5, 2011.

220 *"There were mean things"*: Montagne, interview with author, May 5, 2011.

220 *"It was clear that Robert"*: Judd, interview with author, December 12, 2018.

220 *"Robert was the new Susan"*: Montagne, interview with author, November 14, 2018.

220 *"People at NPR"*: Ibid.

221 *"I kept tripping"*: Conan, interview with author, December 14, 2018.

221 *"Under normal circumstances"*: Chadwick, interview with author, December 3, 2018.

221 *"the news staff did not want him"*: Fisher, "The Soul of a News Machine."

221 *"I was told Nina"*: Ibid.

222 *"a liberal racist"*: Fields, interview with author, October 18, 2019.

222 *"Bennet felt very strongly"*: Mitchell, interview with author, January 28, 2019.

222 *Bill "Siemering"*: Ibid.

222 *"was a dream come true"*: Siegel, interview with author, November 9, 2018.

222 *"Black Power"*: Wil Haygood, *King of the Cats* (Boston: Houghton Mifflin, 1993), 322.

222 *"Here's a man"*: Ibid., 239.

222 *"I am in the presence"*: "Hazel Scott, 61, Jazz Pianist, Acted in Films, on Broadway," *New York Times*, October 3, 1981.

222 *"witty, daring, modern"*: Ibid.

223   *"I'd see that my mother"*: Adam Clayton Powell III, interview with author, February 20, 2018.

223   *"consummate party giver"*: "Eileen G. Slocum, 92, Dies; Society Doyenne and Republican Stalwart," *New York Times*, August 1, 2008.

224   *"By being rather fastidious"*: Ibid.

224   *"shocking"*: "Inside the Auction of Eileen Slocum's Astounding Newport Mansion," *Town & Country*, September 28, 2018.

224   *"If you do this"*: Ibid.

224   *"Listen to Morning Edition"*: Powell, interview with author, February 20, 2018.

225   *"a nice little consulting"*: Ibid.

225   *"Why did Renee"*: Ibid.

225   *"Adam"*: Ibid.

225   *"hill brats"*: Ibid.

225   *"Hi, Cokie"*: Ibid.

225   *"was the most impressive"*: Fisher, "The Soul of a News Machine."

225   *"Adam Powell III is an extremely"*: Siegel, interview with author, November 9, 2018.

226   *"Neal came in"*: Powell, interview with author, February 20, 2018.

226   *"When I walked into work"*: Fisher, "The Soul of a News Machine."

226   *"I took that as"*: Powell, interview with author, February 20, 2018.

226   *"When there finally was an opening"*: Fields, interview with author, February 18, 2019.

226   *"What Bennet knew"*: Powell, interview with author, February 20, 2018.

227   *"You're going to go"*: Ibid.

227   *"Dance with the general managers"*: Ibid.

227   *43 percent of the time*: Fisher, "The Soul of a News Machine."

227   *"essential to improving"*: Ibid.

227   *"That's how Adam"*: Larry Abramson, interview with author, January 30, 2019.

227   *"It was a conversation"* Powell, interview with author, February 20, 2018.

227   *"Adam was fascinated with it"*: Baer, email to author, February 1, 2018.

228   *"I came to think"*: Conan, interview with author, December 14, 2018.

228   *"When Robert Siegel was the head"*: Fisher, "The Soul of a News Machine."

228   *"Before, you had a news director"*: Powell, interview, with author, February 20, 2018.

228   *"He managed in a way"*: Marcus Rosenbaum, interview with author, October 29, 2018.

228   *"I'd go in to talk with him"*: Stamberg, interview with author, February 22, 2018.

229   *"He made things difficult"*: Rosenbaum, interview with author, October 29, 2018.

229   *"NPR had a history of being"*: Powell, interview with author, February 20, 2018.

229   *"we put people in slightly off-center"*: Rosenbaum, interview with author, October 29, 2018.

229   *"Somebody got the bright idea"*: Simon, interview with McCauley, August 23, 1995

230   *"We used to joke"*: Ibid.

230   *"For black men"*: Wertheimer, ed., *Listening to America*, 306.

230   *"Why don't we fly down"*: McChesney, interview with author, April 30, 2011.

230   *"Adam, are you out"*: Ibid.

230   *"an example of the bizarre"*: Ibid.

230   *"It would be interesting"*: Fields, interview with author, February 18, 2019.

230 *"People were not actively trying"*: Ibid.

231 *"People of color"*: Ibid.

231 *"Is it going to be"*: Ibid.

231 *"I'll be damned"*: Ibid.

231 *"Powell didn't fire me"*: Rosenbaum, interview with author, October 29, 2018.

231 *"I said, 'We've got Dan Schorr'"*: Powell, interview with author, February 20, 2018.

232 *"Let's send them to Russia"*: Ibid.

232 *"They could do pieces"*: Ibid.

232 *"Mr. Commercial Network News!"*: Ibid.

232 *"We didn't have any"*: John Dinges, interview with author, August 9, 2019.

233 *"Come to bed"*: Sylvia Poggioli, interview with author, July 6, 2011.

233 *"It was that experience"*: Ibid.

233 *"It was a huge story"*: Ibid.

234 *"Piero's paper paid"*: Poggioli, interview with author, March 26, 2010.

234 *"She makes a dramatic"*: Wertheimer, *Listening to America*, 258.

234 *"The waves of Lake Victoria"*: Ibid., 263.

235 *"I was making the foreign desk"*: McChesney, interview with author, April 30, 2011.

235 *"largely ceremonial"*: Fisher, "The Soul of a News Machine."

235 *"John invited all these people"*: Chadwick, interview with author, December 4, 2018.

235 *"to inspire member stations"*: Abramson, interview with author, January 30, 2019.

235 *"a tragic mistake"*: Fisher, "The Soul of a News Machine."

235 *""Wertheimer a bad evaluation"*: McChesney, interview with author, April 30, 2011.

235 *"Both Marc and John"*: Mike Shuster, interview with author, March 8, 2018.

236 *"McChesney . . . became an instant"*: Mitchell, *Listener Supported*, 137.

236 *"Khomeini's body lay"*: John Hockenberry, *Moving Violations: War Zones, Wheelchairs, and Declarations of Independence* (New York: Hyperion Books, 1995), 288.

236 *"vibrant, committed"*: Powell, interview with author, February 20, 2018.

236 *"When I interviewed her"*: Ibid.

236 *"NPR is a place"*: John Burnett, interview with author, March 29, 2019.

236 *"Isabel was not ready"*: Malesky, interview with author, February 16, 2018.

236 *"She was not a serious"*: Abramson, interview with author, January 30, 2019.

236 *"Isabel was hired"*: Shuster, interview with author, March 8, 2018.

237 *"a square peg"*: Burnett, interview with author, March 29, 2019.

237 *"was not very good"*: Silverman, interview with author, August 20, 2018.

237 *"editing her stories"*: Conan, interview with author, February 12, 2018.

237 *"Lower World"*: McChesney, interview with author, April 30, 2011.

237 *"A crisis in morale"*: Fisher, "The Soul of a News Machine."

237 *"detailed feedback"*: Ibid.

237 *"Institutional racism"*: Ibid.

237 *"five of us who went"*: Conan, interview with author, February 12, 2018.

238 *"I don't think we achieved"*: Montagne, interview with author, November 14, 2018.

238 *"She was dealing"*: Stamberg, interview with author, November 5, 2018.

238 *"At ATC you had to grasp"*: Dinges, interview with author, January 8, 2019.

238 *"I did twenty-minute"*: Montagne, interview with author, November 19, 2018.

238 *"After twenty months"*: Montagne, interview with author, May 5, 2011.

239 *"She could not do"*: Conan, interview with author, December 14, 2018.

239 *"I tried to help"*: Ibid.

239 *"He was aggressive and haughty"*: Montagne, interview with author, November 14, 2018.

239 *"I thought, Good"*: Ibid.

239 *"I'm going to get you out"*: Ibid.

239 *"I didn't have a big support base"*: Ibid.

239 *"You know"*: Ibid.

239 *"There would be talk"*: Ibid.

240 *"It feels like"*: "Fresh Voices Hope to be Far from Wobegone," *New York Times*, December 13, 1987.

240 *"Adams . . . doesn't command"*: "The Ghost of Garrison Keillor Lives . . . But in the Footpath Left Behind," *Star Press* (Muncie, IN), January 16, 1988.

240 *"The new show feels less"*: "Noah Adams Show Bows in Old Keillor Time Slot. For 'Prairie Home' Fans, the New 'Good Evening' Has a Semi-Familiar Sound," *Christian Science Monitor*, January 13, 1988.

240 *"was ready to bloom"*: Conan, email to author, January 22, 2019.

241 *"She'd already learned"*: Ibid.

241 *"She discussed every detail"*: Fisher, "The Soul of a News Machine."

241 *"Even though I couldn't"*: Adler, interview with author, December 1, 2011.

242 *"I was completely"*: Wertheimer, interview with author, August 12, 2015.

242 *"Nina and Cokie went"*: Adler, interview with author, December 1, 2011.

242 *"en passant"*: Fisher, "The Soul of a News Machine."

242 *"I told him frankly"*: Ibid.

242 *"Roberts . . . and Totenberg"*: Ibid.

242 *"Those two threatened"*: Name withheld at request of source, interview with author.

242 *"There is no job offer"*: Fisher, "The Soul of a News Machine."

242 *"There was an NPR form"*: Conan, interview with author, December 14, 2018.

243 *"Is it really"*: Powell, interview with author, February 20, 2018.

243 *"Lynn Neary is"*: Ibid.

243 *"Such is life"*: Ibid.

243 *"Neal thought being"*: Siegel, interview with author, November 9, 2018.

243 *"The lineup was going soft"*: Ibid.

243 *Morale was devastated*: Fisher, "The Soul of a News Machine."

244 *"They made me a correspondent"*: Adler, interview with author, December 2, 2011.

244 *"We did not handle"*: Fisher, "The Soul of a News Machine."

244 *"He pleaded with me"*: Conan, interview with author, December 14, 2018.

244 *"It was very personal"*: Stamberg, interview with author, February 22, 2018.

244 *"I wanted it recorded"*: Ibid.

245 *"Cancer changed me"*: Stamberg, *Talk*, 276.

245 *"The show had a reputation"*: Malesky, interview with author, February 16, 2018.

245 *"I tried to get Susan"*: Ibid.

245 *"There was grumbling"*: Ibid.

245 *"I did not regard"*: Mitchell, *Listener Supported*, 117.

245 *"We had several"*: Stamberg, interview with author, February 22, 2018.

246 *"Could the person"*: Fisher, "The Soul of a News Machine."

246 *"I knew people doing"*: Powell, interview with author, February 20, 2018.

246 *"return to Miami"*: Fisher, "The Soul of a News Machine."

246 *"She didn't work out"*: Powell, interview with author, February 20, 2018.

246 *"rifling"*: Siegel, interview with author, November 9, 2018.

246 *"WRVR was mismanaged"*: Siegel, email to author, November 16, 2018.

246 *"Adam Powell III Fired"*: "Adam Powell III Fired," *Jet*, August 23, 1972.

247 *"They lived like kings"*: Fisher, "The Soul of a News Machine."

247 *"broadcast ownership"*: Ibid.

247 *"Adam Powell provoked"*: Shuster, interview with author, March 8, 2018.

247 *"We went to Doug"*: Stamberg, interview with author, February 22, 2018.

247 *"There was so much opposition"*: Shuster, interview with author, March 8, 2018.

247 *"on my own dime"*: Buzenberg, interview with author, November 28, 2018.

248 *"I didn't care"*: Ibid.

248 *"He wasn't involved"*: Ibid.

248 *"Doug fired Adam"*: Ibid.

248 *"Carolyn said she wanted"*: Chadwick, interview with author, December 4, 2018.

248 *"Bennet made a disastrous"*: Conan, interview with author, February 12, 2018.

248 *"I think Adam's colleagues"*: Bennet, interview with McCauley, July 31, 1995.

248 *"I remember him skipping"*: Stamberg, interview with author, February 22, 2018.

249 *"NPR news was not friendly"*: Powell, interview with author, December 20, 2018.

249 *"Bennet stuck us"*: Roberts, interview with author, June 27, 2016.

SIX: FOREIGN AFFAIRS

250 *"I'd screwed up before"*: Neal Conan, *Play by Play* (New York: Crown, 2002), 109.

251 *"You'd be able to turn to NPR"*: Drake, interview with author, August 10, 2019.

251 *"They thought it was not NPR's"*: Ibid.

251 *According to Robert Siegel*: Mitchell, *Listener Supported: The Culture and History of Public Radio*, 142.

251 *"We needed to grow"*: Cokie Roberts et al., *This Is NPR* (San Francisco: Chronicle Books, 2010), 148.

251 *"I wondered if"*: Mitchell, *Listener Supported*, 141.

251 *"Ruth was very influential"*: Dinges, interview with author, August 9, 2019.

252 *"I was in London"*: Amos, interview with author, September 6, 2019.

252 *"For NPR, this was"*: Dinges, interview with author, August 9, 2019.

252 *"provided primary coverage"*: Mitchell, *Listener Supported*, 142.

252 *"When talking to the colonel"*: Wertheimer, ed. *Listening to America*, 349.

252 *"It felt jingoistic"*: Simon, *Home and Away*, 210.

253 *"The job was to take in"*: Conan, email to author, June 30, 2019.

253 *"There was chaos"*: Amos, interview with author, September 6, 2019.

253 *"Neal got in with"*: Lyden, interview with author, September 13, 2019.

254 *"As we pushed deeper"*: Tony Horwitz, *Baghdad Without a Map* (New York: Plume, 2002), 282-283.

254 *"the king of the wild guys"*: Lyden, interview with author, September 13, 2019.

254 *"pugnacious, extremely smart"*: Ibid.

254 *"Chris took risks"*: Michael Skoler, interview with author, January 19, 2020.

254 *"I wasn't going to sit"*: "Chris Hedges Unmasks American Empire," *TruthDig*, November 10, 2016.

255 *"He said he planned to poke around"*: "Gulf War Flashback, NPR's Neal Conan Reflects," NPR.org, March 27, 2003.

255 *"Chris needed a partner"*: Amos, interview with author, September 6, 2019.

255 *"Anyone in their right mind"*: Lyden, interview with author, September 13, 2019.

255 *"Sam Donaldson"*: Conan, interview with author, June 27, 2019.

255 *"People were trying it"*: Amos, interview with author, September 6, 2019.

255 *"They had no way"*: Skoler, interview with author, January 19, 2020.

255 *"Most of . . . the wreckage"*: Michael Kelly, *Martyrs' Day* (New York: Random House, 1993), 230.

256 *"Thirty Journalists Missing"*: "Thirty Journalists Missing," *Washington Post*, March 6, 1991.

256 *"The* Times *got General Schwarzkopf"*: "Chris Hedges Unmasks."

256 *"Everybody was on pins"*: Drake, interview with author, August 10, 2019.

256 *"I knew the Iraqis"*: Amos, interview with author, September 6, 2019.

256 *"He looks like"*: Conan, *Play by Play*, 104.

257 *"One of the officers"*: Ibid., 109.

257 *"The bullets"*: Ibid., 113.

257 *Time was elastic*: Ibid.

257 *"the worst night"*: Ibid., 109.

257 *"If you've been held"*: Conan, interview with author, December 15, 2013.

257 *"We might still be tried"*: "Gulf War Flashback."

258 *"I had a dramatic"*: Conan, *Play by Play*, 116.

258 *"I have to say, Neal"*: Wertheimer, *Listening to America*, 353.

258 *"We all did our level best"*: Conan, *Play by Play*, 115.

258 *"Neal was chastened"*: Lyden, interview with author, September 13, 2019.

258 *"Shattered"*: Conan, interview with author, December 15, 2013.

258 *"I knew that many others"*: Conan, *Play by Play*, 116.

258 *"The ordeal, it turns out"*: Ibid.

258 *"He got out relatively"*: Drake, interview with author, August 10, 2019.

258 *"He was OK"*: Dinges, interview with author, August 9, 2019.

258 *listenership had jumped*: Mitchell, *Listener Supported*, 142.

259 *"The Gulf War was a landmark"*: John Felton, interview with author, March 10, 2020.

259 *"It took me a long time"*: Conan, interview with author, December 15, 2013.

259 *"She knew her stuff"*: Drake, interview with author, August 10, 2019.

259 *"Cadi was an imposing"*: Paul Glickman, interview with author, January 6, 2020.

259 *"Zaire had blown up"*: Montagne, interview with author, September 12. 2019.

260 *"Several shots have"*: Wertheimer, *Listening to America*, 344.

260 *"They were unarmed"*: Ibid., 345.

260 *"You've got to hold a block"*: Poggioli, interview with author, June 5, 2018.

260 *"Let's get in"*: Ibid.

261 *"We were beginning to hear stories"*: Ibid.

261 *"We bribed thuggish guards"*: Ibid.

261 *"I turned around"*: Ibid.

261 *"frustrated"*: Ibid.

261 *"Kalashnikovs and daggers"*: Ibid.

262 *"Shit"*: Ibid."

262 *"Mirko takes a liking"*: Transcript, *All Things Considered*, August 14, 1992, Walter J. Brown Media Archives and Peabody Awards Collection, University of Georgia.

263 *"The men raise their arms"*: Ibid.

264 *"Serbian nationalists have made"*: John F. Burns, "The Dying City of Sarajevo," *New York Times Magazine*, July 26, 1992.

264 *"Sylvia Poggioli brought"*: "Peabody Award Acceptance Speech," May 17, 1993, YouTube video, https://www.youtube.com/watch?v=Zrc8smjxmxY.

264 *"Cadi was very much"*: McChesney, interview with author, April 30, 2011.

264 *"meticulously fair"*: Hockenberry, interview with author, June 5, 2012.

264 *"remorseless hectoring"*: "Thumbs Down to Linda Gradstein," *Camera*, July 30, 1992.

264 *"There's no doubt"*: Felton, interview with author, March 10, 2020.

264 *"first legitimate Negro"*: Joyce Davis, interview with author, November 26, 2019.

264 *"I went into their compound"*: Ibid.

265 *"Cadi didn't want me"*: Ibid.

265 *"intimate contacts with"*: Ibid.

265 *"I was the only Black"*: Sunni Khalid, interview with author, March 8, 2019.

265 *"She thought I was a member"*: Ibid.

265 *"Cadi hired Sunni"*: Felton, interview with author, March 10, 2020.

265 *"He had a nice personality"*: Ibid.

265 *"There was a joke"*: Montagne, interview with author, November 19, 2018.

265 *"Sunni had an agenda"*: Felton, interview with author, March 10, 2020.

266 *"It's basically state radio"*: Khalid, interview with author, March 8, 2019.

266 *"She left because"*: Drake, interview with author, August 10, 2019.

266 *"You had to go around"*: Elizabeth Becker, interview with author, December 18, 2019.

266 *"They didn't pay for my car"*: Montagne, interview with author, November 11, 2017.

266 *"Payments from NPR"*: Cooper, interview with author, January 13, 2020.

266 *"said they were not"*: Becker, interview with author, December 18, 2019.

267 *"petitioned to get Ann Cooper"*: Ibid.

267 *"This is how we operate"*: "The Earthquake," *Inprint*, February, 1994.

267 *"beauty"*: Becker, interview with author, December 18, 2019.

267 *"the marching of feet"*: Ibid.

268 *"I was an audio-driven"*: Skoler, interview with author, January 25, 2020.

268 *"Bodies were stacked"*: Ibid.

268 *"I'd see someone"*: Ibid.

268 *"We called our"*: Ibid.

269 *"scolding us for sending"*: Glickman, interview with author, January 6, 2020.

269 *"There were missiles"*: Skoler, interview with author, January 25, 2020.

269 *"I decided I needed"*: Ibid.

269 *"I saw things"*: Ibid.

269 *"I wrote copious notes"*: Ibid.

269　*"how Rwanda became"*: "Rwanda," *All Things Considered*, June 13, 1994, remix, courtesy Michael Skoler.

269　*"I drove in from the north"*: Ibid.

271　*"He missed deadlines"*: Becker, email to author, May 20, 2020.

271　*"Sunni didn't have the chops"*: Montagne, interview with author, September 13, 2019.

271　*"There were problems"*: Davis, interview with author, November 27, 2019.

271　*"an on-air sound"*: Davis, interview with author, November 26, 2019.

271　*"Sunni wanted to be our guy"*: Montagne, interview with author, September 13, 2019.

271　*"Sunni was not highly"*: Montagne, interview with author, November 19, 2018.

271　*"I thought it would be a good idea"*: Buzenberg, interview with author, November 28, 2018.

272　*"I didn't want to go to Cairo"*: Khalid, interview with author, March 8, 2019.

272　*"Sunni saw the Cairo posting"*: Montagne, interview with author, September 13, 2019.

272　*"I agreed to send him"*: Becker, interview with author, December 18, 2019.

272　*"Sunni often went to human resources"*: Ibid.

272　*"I had the contract"*: Ibid.

272　*"He refused the training"*: Ibid.

272　*"He demanded an entirely"*: Becker, email to author, May 20, 2020.

272　*"Bill didn't stand up"*: Becker, interview with author, December 18, 2019.

272　*"There are ways to handle"*: Ibid.

272　*"the head achy lady"*: Rosenberg, interview with author, August 8, 2019.

272　*"Sunni ran roughshod"*: Drake, interview with author, August 10, 2019.

272　*"If I'd had a stronger stomach"*: Becker, interview with author, December 18, 2019.

272　*"His work"*: Glickman, interview with author, January 6, 2020.

273　*"He wasn't productive"*: Dinges, interview with author, August 20, 2014.

273　*"vulnerable to the charge"*: Dinges, interview with author, August 8, 2019.

273　*"Sunni was a disaster"*: Drake, interview with author, August 10, 2019.

273　*"I learned two"*: Loren Jenkins, interview with author, March 20, 2019.

274　*"and moved into this family"*: Jenkins, interview with author, May 29, 2020.

274　*"I started hiking"*: Ibid.

274　*"It was danger"*: Ibid.

274　*"I was also assigned"*: Jenkins, interview with author, March 20, 2019.

274　*"We had a good chat"*: Ibid.

275　*"I never wanted to cover violence"*: Ibid.

275　*"I went to Cambodia"*: Ibid.

275　*"Because I couldn't find"*: Poggioli, interview with author, June 5, 2018.

275　*"To stay civilized"*: Jenkins, interview with author, March 20, 2019.

276　*"Artillery side"*: "Hotel's Fall Mourned in World's Press Club," *Chicago Tribune*, March 1, 1987.

276　*"For the first time"*: "Israelis Complete Occupation of West Beirut," *Washington Post*, September 17, 1982.

276　*"Cordons of Israeli tanks"*: "Israelis Hunt Palestinian Sympathizers in Beirut," *Washington Post*, September 18, 1982.

277　*"It was silent"*: Jenkins, interview with author, March 20. 2019.

277　*"Bodies were everyplace"*: Jenkins, interview with author, May 29, 2020.

277   *"This correspondent counted"*: "Scores of Palestinians Killed in Beirut," *Washington Post*, September 19, 1982.

277   *"Loren would punch"*: Tim McNulty, interview with author, June 14, 2020.

277   *"Friedman got the big picture"*: Ibid.

277   *"day and night"*: Thomas Friedman, *From Beirut to Jerusalem* (New York: Farrar, Straus and Giroux, 1989), 165.

277   *"One part of me"*: Ibid.

278   *"I wish I'd never covered"*: Jenkins, interview with author, March 21, 2019.

278   *"They said, 'With your'"*: Jenkins, interview with author, March 20, 2019.

278   *"I thought: I don't"*: Ibid.

278   *"I thought there was a great"*: Ibid.

278   *"I wrote editorials"*: Ibid.

279   *"I fell out"*: Ibid.

279   *"It was the strangest thing"*: Ibid.

279   *"They formed a big committee"*: Drake, interview with author, August 10, 2019.

279   *"She was good"*: Cooper, interview with author, January 13, 2020.

279   *"not living up"*: Davis, interview with author, November 26, 2019.

279   *"She was a woman who"*: Drake, interview with author, August 10, 2019.

279   *"NPR was clubby"*: Davis, interview with author, November 27, 2019.

279   *"Loren Jenkins as manna"*: Poggioli, interview with author, June 5, 2018.

279   *"On issues related"*: Drake, interview with author, August 10, 2019.

279   *"infinitely better than Joyce"*: Poggioli, interview with author, June 7, 2019.

279   *"I hired Loren"*: Buzenberg, interview with author, August 8, 2014.

280   *"My strength"*: Jenkins, interview with author, March 21, 2019.

280   *"We're here to educate"*: Jenkins, interview with author, March 20, 2019.

280   *"Everything that is told to you"*: Ibid.

280   *"We're never had anyone"*: Lyden, interview with author, September 19, 2019.

280   *"He was your classic hard-bitten"*: Glickman, interview with author, January 6, 2020.

280   *"One of the first things"*: Drake, interview with author, August 10, 2019.

280   *"I had a rule"*: Jenkins, interview with author, March 21, 2019.

281   *"Loren felt our job"*: Skoler, interview with author, January 19, 2020.

281   *"I went to Joyce"*: Jenkins, interview with author, March 20, 2019.

281   *"In offering Loren"*: Montagne, interview with author, November 19, 2018.

281   *"Sunni became Loren's problem"*: Poggioli, interview with author, June 7, 2019.

281   *"Was Sunni a problem"*: Davis, interview with author, November 27, 2019.

281   *"a racial issue"*: Jenkins, interview with author, March 20, 2019.

281   *"came back on leave"*: Ibid.

281   *"Loren set some goals"*: Dinges, interview with author, August 9, 2019.

281   *"Sunni was on notice"*: Drake, interview with author, August 10, 2019.

282   *"All editors suck"*: Jenkins, interview with author, March 20, 2019.

282   *"Loren was sitting"*: Montagne, interview with author, November 19, 2018.

282   *"I don't think he was bigoted"*: Drake, interview with author, August 10, 2019.

282   *"Loren is not a racist"*: Montagne, interview with author, November 19, 2018.

282   *"I found out about it"*: Khalid, interview with author, March 8, 2019.

282 *"I sat kitty-corner"*: Lyden, interview with author, September 19, 2019.

282 *"I got run out"*: Khalid, interview with author, March 8, 2019.

283 *"Jenkins is a force"*: Buzenberg, interview with author, August 20, 2014.

283 *"Sunni was very upset"*: Davis, interview with author, November 26, 2019.

283 *"If Loren wanted"*: Khalid, interview with author, March 8, 2019.

283 *"Loren said Sunni's pieces"*: Lynne Bernabei, interview with author, August 8, 2019.

283 *"it was about Loren"*: Skoler, interview with author, January 25, 2020.

283 *"gave the suit legs"*: Buzenberg, interview with author, August 20, 2014.

283 *NPR would eventually settle*: *Khalid v. Natl. Public Radio, et al.*, U.S. District Court, District of Columbia, Civil Docket, Case #: 1:97-cv-00291-RCL.

283 *"Loren's job was protected"*: Montagne, interview with author, November 19, 2018.

283 *"NPR had to defend Loren"*: Skoler, interview with author, January 25, 2020.

SEVEN: BOBAPALOOZA

284 *"A plane just hit"*: Kernis, interview with author, June 10, 2011.

285 *"Sorry to interrupt"*: Barry Gordemer, interview with author, October 7, 2020.

285 *"You can't tell America"*: Ibid.

285 *"Oh my God"*: Kernis, interview with author, June 10, 2011.

285 *"Look at that"*: Edwards, interview with author, October 6, 2020.

285 *"Bob was stunned"*: Audrey Wynn, interview with author, October 5, 2020.

285 *"Everyone started looking"*: Gordemer, interview with author, October 7, 2020.

286 *"Get on the air"*: Wynn, interview with author, October 5, 2020.

286 *"What do we do?"*: Ibid.

286 *"That was not our culture"*: Ellen McDonnell, interview with author, March 23, 2012.

286 *"They hated to break"*: Conan, interview with author, June 27, 2019.

286 *"nine-minute sausages"*: Ibid.

286 *"We did not want to sound"*: Gordemer, interview with author, October 7, 2020.

286 *"Just say what we're seeing"*: Wynn, interview with author, October 5, 2020.

286 *"Do you really want"*: Gordemer, interview with author, October 7, 2020.

287 *"A requirement of the job"*: Conan, interview with author, undated.

287 *"No other host"*: Gordemer, interview with author, October 7, 2020.

287 *"Every person who was"*: McChesney, interview with author, April 30, 2011.

287 *"They went batshit"*: Ibid.

287 *"Many member stations put on"*: Gordemer, interview with author, October 7, 2020.

287 *"My daughter called"*: Ruth Seymour, interview with author, March 26, 2010.

287 *"First thing, they hooked"*: Edwards, interview with author, October 6, 2020.

287 *"Nobody asked me"*: Lyden, email to author, October 26, 2020.

287 *"I was winging it"*: Ibid.

288 *"I'll see you in six months"*: Tom Gjelten, interview with author, October 22, 2020.

288 *"Absolutely no sign"*: Tom Gjelten, "My Peaceful City Had Been Transformed Into a War Zone," NPR Extra, September 11, 2011, NPR.org.

288 *"About eighteen minutes"*: "World Trade Center Attack # 1," September 11, 2001, NPR .org, https://www.npr.org/2001/09/11/1128838/world-trade-center-attack-1.

289 *"We can't get out"*: Ibid.

289 "The Day of the Locust": Ibid.

289 *"One of Bob's strengths"*: Gordemer, interview with author, October 7, 2020.

289 *"Saudi dissident Osama bin Laden"*: "World Trade Center Attack, #1."

290 *"Can you see that"*: Ibid.

290 *"That's our Mount Everest"*: Ibid.

290 *"Edwards recovered"*: Seymour, interview with author, March 26, 2010.

290 *"The screwup"*: Drake, interview with author, August 10, 2019.

290 *"The show was not set up"*: Conan, interview with author, September 24, 2020.

290 *"the managers of NPR"*: Chadwick, interview with author, April 4, 2011.

290 *"Bob didn't make it"*: Drake, interview with author, August 10, 2019.

290 *"Edwards very much helped"*: David Folkenflik, interview with author, December 4, 2012.

290 *"Bob Edwards should have been fired"*: Seymour, interview with author, March 26, 2010.

290 *"Things had been building"*: Wynn, interview with author, October 5, 2020.

290 *"The trouble with Jay and Bob"*: Gordemer, interview with author, October 7, 2020.

291 *"He was becoming more"*: Stamberg, interview with author, August 21, 2014.

291 *"Bob ossified"*: Proffitt, interview with author, September 7, 2012.

291 *"Bobspeak"*: Edwards, *Voice in the Box*, 103.

291 *"ways to write around it"*: Noah Adams, *On All Things Considered: A Radio Journal* (New York: W. W. Norton, 1992), 245.

292 *"two weeks' time"*: Gordemer, interview with author, October 7, 2020.

292 *"He was interested in very few"*: Chadwick, interview with author, October 22, 2013.

292 *"I had a white-collar"*: Edwards, interview with author, October 29, 2015.

292 *"Sedaris was a problem"*: Robert Ferrante, interview with author, September 30, 2013.

292 *"I disparaged the piece"*: Edwards, interview with author, October 29, 2015.

292 *"Tonight, I saw a woman"*: David Sedaris, "Santaland Diaries," NPR, December 23, 1992, https://www.npr.org/2021/12/23/1065187420/david-sedaris-santaland-diaries.

293 *"What are we putting"*: Ferrante, interview with author, September 30, 2013.

293 *"He was kind of lazy"*: McChesney, interview with author, April 30, 2011.

293 *"He was not thought of"*: Ungar, interview with author, October 27, 2015.

293 *"Bob didn't listen"*: Montagne, interview with author, March 22, 2012.

293 *"In a prerecorded interview"*: Susan Feeney, interview with author, November 30, 2020.

293 *"was just going down the list"*: Totenberg, interview with author, June 4, 2013.

293 *"Bob would sound ridiculous"*: Feeney, interview with author, November 6, 2020.

294 *"I used to think he could be"*: McChesney, interview with author, April 30, 2011.

294 *"Bob never changed"*: Poggioli, interview with author, July 5, 2011.

294 *"brain dead"*: Anne Garrels, interview with author, August 5, 2019.

294 *"We just had to apologize"*: Wynn, interview with author, October 5, 2020.

294 *"When I got there . . . unless"*: Drake, interview with author, August 10, 2019.

294 *"We'd remove verbs"*: Gordemer, interview with author, October 7, 2020.

294 *"We would never write"*: Ibid.

295 *"was a hog for overtime"*: McChesney, interview with author, April 30, 2011.

295 *"he never felt he was rewarded"*: Ferrante, interview with author, September 30, 2013.

295 *"If there was a short turnaround"*: Edwards, interview with author, October 29, 2015.

295 *"He earns night differential"*: "House Panel Probing Salaries at NPR, PBS," *Washington Post*, March 2, 1998.

295 *"We said to him"*: McDonnell, interview with author, March 23, 2012.

295 *"Bob didn't go"*: Gordemer, interview with author, October 7, 2020.

295 *"He didn't want to be interfered"*: Fitzmaurice, interview with author, June 5, 2014.

295 *"He was tough with the staff"*: McChesney, interview with author, April 30, 2011,

295 *"curmudgeon"*: Ferrante, interview with author, September 30, 2013.

295 *"He was not the sort of person"*: Wertheimer, interview with author, August 12, 2015.

296 *"They said a lot of things about him"*: Ferrante, interview with author, September 30, 2013.

296 *"I was absolutely stunned"*: Barbara Rehm, interview with author, August 9, 2019.

296 *"Bob is a tight"*: Gordemer, interview with author, October 7, 2020.

296 *"You couldn't help but love"*: Rehm, interview with author, August 9, 2019.

296 *"Bob could talk to people"*: Wertheimer, interview with author, March 22, 2012.

296 *"We settled on Sean Collins"*: Chadwick, interview with author, April 5, 2011.

297 *"Do you know what's happening?"* Totenberg, interview with author, June 4, 2013.

297 *"a real manager"*: Ibid.

297 *"bullshit"*: Ferrante, interview with author, September 30, 2013.

297 *"She was totally without"*: McChesney, interview with author, April 30, 2011.

297 *"He was mentally abusive"*: Totenberg, interview with author, June 4, 2013.

297 *"little lady"*: McDonnell, interview with author, September 30, 2020.

297 *"I'm going with the filly"*: Wertheimer, interview with author, March 22, 2012.

297 *"The bastard"*: Ibid.

297 *"bullied"*: Chadwick, interview with author, April 5, 2011.

297 *"Ellen McDonnell took care"*: Edwards, interview with author, October 29, 2015.

298 *"Everyone feels they know"*: "A Decade as NPR's Amiable Morning Man," *Los Angeles Times*, November 2, 1989.

298 *"Bob was burned out"*: McDonnell, interviews with author, March 23, 2012, September 30, 2020.

298 *"I went to the wall"*: Feeney, interview with author, October 6, 2020.

298 *"No"*: Wynn, interview with author, October 5, 2020.

298 *"He wanted the time changed"*: Ibid.

298 *"Bob," she said*: McDonnell, interview with author, March 23, 2012.

298 *"Bruce Drake ordered Bob"*: Feeney, interview with author, October 6, 2020.

298 *"I did the interview"*: Edwards, *Voice in the Box*, 147.

298 *"racking up five hours"*: Ibid.

299 *"People were not thrilled"*: McDonnell, interview with author, March 23, 2012.

299 *"I don't want to do that"*: Ibid.

299 *"Bagpipe and drum processions"*: *Morning Edition*, NPR.org, September 11, 2002, https://www.npr.org/programs/morning-edition/2002/09/11/13053475/.

299 *"Bob saw his role"*: Gordemer, interview with author, October 7, 2020.

300 *"Bob, I need you to record"*: McDonnell, interview with author, March 23, 2012,

300 *"He took the copy"*: Ibid.

300 *"I guess that means yes"*: McDonnell, interview with author, September 30, 2020.

300 *"I'm not a thrower"*: Edwards, interview with author, October 26, 2015.

300 *"Was she sitting next to"*: Ibid.

300 *"I've taken this show"*: McDonnell, interview with author, March 23, 2012.

300 *"Kevin is the person"*: Siegel, interview with author, August 20, 2014.

300 *"His own staff wanted him"*: Kernis, interview with author, June 11, 2011.

300 *"I was attending national meetings"*: Ibid.

301 *"You're phoning it in"*: Kernis, interview with author, November 30, 2011;

301 *"Am I"*: Ibid.

301 *"I don't think I ever"*: Edwards, interview with author, October 26, 2015.

301 *"I was at a loss"*: Edwards, interview with author, October 6, 2020.

301 *"I'm going to work with him"*: Kernis, interview with author, June 11, 2011.

301 *"the four d's"*: Suza Trajkovski, Virginia Schmied, Margaret Vickers, and Debra Jackson, "Implementing the 4D Cycle of Appreciative Inquiry in Health Care," *Journal of Advanced Nursing* 69, no. 6 (June 2013): 1224–34, https://doi.org/10.1111/jan.12086.

302 *"looking for the best"*: McDonnell, interview with author, March 23, 2012.

302 *"I never understood any of it"*: Edwards, interview with author, October 26, 2015.

302 *"I thought he was reinvesting"*: Kernis, interview with author, November 30, 2011.

302 *"trying to turn Bob Edwards"*: Drake, interview with author, August 10, 2019.

302 *"Bob doesn't connect"*: Chadwick, interview with author, October 22, 2013.

302 *"I'd be sent into the studio"*: Edwards, *Voice in the Box*, 139.

303 *"One option may be"*: McDonnell, interview with author, March 23, 2012.

303 *"I'm not doing it"*: Kernis, interview with author, November 30, 2011.

303 *"We're making a change"*: Edwards, *Voice in the Box*, 130.

303 *"Kevin Klose said"*: Totenberg, interview with author, June 4, 2013.

303 *"Jay, if anybody can"*: Kernis, interview with author, November 30, 2011.

303 *"I was the one"*: Kernis, interview with author, June 11, 2011.

304 *"completely outside Bob's ken"*: Conan, interview with author, December 15, 2013.

304 *"What about the 25th"*: Edwards, *Voice in the Box*, 130.

304 *"The anniversary will be about"*: Ibid.

304 *"By the time the decision"*: Conan, interview with author, December 15, 2013.

304 *"I thought I would die"*: Edwards, interview with author, October 26, 2015.

304 *"Why was Bob Edwards taken off"*: Chadwick, interview with author, April 5, 2011.

304 *"handled Edwards so badly"*: Poggioli, interview with author, July 6, 2011.

304 *"This tells me"*: Malesky, interview with author, October 16, 2011.

304 *"to refresh the program"*: Edwards, *Voice in the Box*, 133.

304 *"part of the natural evolution"*: Ibid.

304 *"NPR took the high road"*: McDonnell, interview with author, March 23, 2012.

305 *"We were not used to being"*: Ibid.

305 *"Empty Talk at NPR"*: "Empty Talk at NPR," *Washington Post*, March 25, 2004.

305 *"We didn't know what we were doing"*: McDonnell, interview with author, March 23, 2012.

305 *"It was a mess"*: Kernis, interview with author, November 30, 2011.

306 *"They never asked me"*: Edwards, interview with author, October 26, 2015.

306 *"He fought having a cohost"*: Totenberg, interview with author, June 4, 2013.

306 *"updating the show will be easier"*: "Morning Minus Bob," *Current*, April 12, 2004

306 *"when television morning programs"*: "NPR Stations Had Pushed for Change," *New York Times*, March 30, 2004.

306   *"engaged"*: Ibid.

306   *"tired of listening to me"*: "Morning Minus Bob."

307   *"doubts and mockery"*: "Stormy Days for NPR," *Los Angeles Times*, March 29, 2004.

307   *not since Coca-Cola*: "NPR Stations Had Pushed for Change."

307   *"He was expecting me to say"*: Edwards, interview with author, October 26, 2015,

307   *"You don't trust me"*: Feeney, interview with author, November 30, 2020.

307   *"Some people thought something"*: Drake, interview with author, August 8, 2019.

307   *"person of interest"*: Edwards, *Voice in the Box*, 131.

307   *"dignified and typically understated"*: "Bob Edwards Signs Off as He Signed On in '79," *New York Times*, May 1, 2004.

308   *"Edwards did not sugarcoat"*: Ibid.

308   *"You're the audience"*: Ibid.

308   *"The cake they gave him"*: Gordemer, interview with author, October 7, 2020.

308   *"No one was talking to him"*: Stamberg, interview with author, August 21, 2014.

309   *"Kevin couldn't have crossed"*: Drake, interview with author, August 10, 2019.

309   *"Ken was not good in a crowd"*: McDonnell, interview with author, March 23, 2012.

309   *"I didn't decide to fire"*: Ken Stern, interview with author, February 25, 2021.

309   *"With respect to the decision"*: Edwards, *Voice in the Box*, 144.

309   *"You should always speak positively"*: Ibid.

310   *The word* Topic: Ibid., 145.

310   *"because this is worth supporting"*: Ibid.

310   *"ready to move on"*: Ibid., 144.

310   *"the management of NPR"*: Ibid., 146.

310   *"My reaction alternated"*: Ibid.

310   *"no intention of trashing"*: Ibid.

310   *"That was the easiest money"*: Ibid.

310   *"She came to think"*: Drake, interview with author, August 10, 2019.

310   *"Edwards was out there"*: McDonnell, interview with author, March 23, 2012.

311   *"Refresh the show"*: Edwards, *Voice in the Box*, 157.

311   *"He was trashing us"*: McDonnell, interview with author, March 23, 2012.

311   *"Maybe Jay Kernis doesn't want"*: Edwards, interview with author, October 26, 2015.

311   *"Kernis made it difficult"*: Edwards, *Voice in the Box*, 159.

311   *"about me"*: Ibid.

311   *"I'm resigning effective tomorrow"*: Edwards, email to Bruce Drake, July 29, 2004.

311   *"I was the vile betrayer"*: Kernis, interview with author, November 30, 2011.

311   *"Why was I fired?"*: Drake, interview with author, August 10, 2019.

312   *"has to be the most pig-headed"*: Ibid.

312   *"hosts who leave the studio"*: "Some Closure on Bob Edwards's Departure," NPR.org, April 20, 2005.

EIGHT: BEQUEST

313   *"This was not a woman"*: Stephanie Bergsma, interview with author, June 1, 2011.

314   *"It is 3 a.m."*: "Billions Served," *Washington Post*, March 14, 2004.

315   *"Stephanie feels at home"*: Kevin Klose, interview with author, April 28, 2011.

316   *"I called Pat Mitchell"*: Bergsma, interview with author, June 1, 2011.

316   *"Kevin . . . was my fallback"*: Ibid.
316   *"I've got a donor"*: Klose, interview with author, April 28, 2011.
317   *"apoplectic"*: Joyce Neu, interview with author, February 22, 2021.
317   *"by several million"*: Klose, interview with author, April 28, 2011.
317   *"He felt nothing had happened"*: Bergsma, interview with author, June 1, 2011.
317   *"eloquent"*: Ibid.
317   *"Write her"*: Klose, interview with author, April 28, 2011.
317   *"I told her about"*: Ibid.
317   *"Have you heard anything?"*: Ibid.
317   *"She might drop"*: Ibid.
317   *"That was a big thing"*: Stern, interview with author, February 25, 2021.
318   *"instincts are that I"*: Anne Garrels, *Naked in Baghdad* (New York: Farrar, Straus and Giroux, 2003), 92.
318   *"a steady succession"*: Ibid., 105.
318   *"The War Prayer"*: Joyce Neu, email to author, February 22, 2021.
319   *"Oh Lord, our God"*: Mark Twain, *The War Prayer* (New York: Harper Colophon, 1971).
319   *"I don't think people"*: Neu, interview with author, February 22, 2021.
319   *"I looked out my window"*: Garrels, *Morning Edition*, March 19, 2003, https://www.npr.org/programs/morning-edition/2003/03/19/13036947.
319   *"Whatever happens"*: Klose, interview with author, April 28, 2011.
319   *"We will be there"*: Ibid.
319   *"Kevin . . . was giving"*: Neu, interview with author, February 22, 2021.
319   *"It was extremely intense"*: Klose, interview with author, April 28, 2011.
320   *"It hit a target"*: "Targets Associated with Saddam and Sons Bombed," *Weekend Edition Saturday*, March 22, 2003, Walter J. Brown Media Archives and Peabody Awards Collection, University of Georgia Special Collections Library.
320   *"At 5:30 I heard jets"*: "Baghdad Reaction," *Morning Edition*, March 20, 2003, https://www.npr.org/programs/morning-edition/2003/03/20/13062500/.
320   *"He looked puffy"*: Ibid.
320   *"There are runs"*: "More Than 350 Killed," *Morning Edition*, March 27, 2003, https://www.npr.org/programs/morning-edition/2003/03/27/13059455/.
320   *"Three in nearby mechanic shops"*: "War Update Baghdad," *All Things Considered*, March 26, 2003, Walter J. Brown Media Archives and Peabody Awards Collection, University of Georgia Special Collections Library.
321   *"I revel in the freedom"*: Garrels, *Naked in Baghdad*, 18.
322   *"This way"*: Ibid., 99.
322   *"in the buff"*: Ibid., 100.
323   *"the Literaturmava Gazeta"*: Garrels, interview with author, August 4, 2019.
323   *"the worst thing that ever happened"*: Ibid.
323   *"If they expelled me"*: Ibid.
323   *"Her legs went on"*: Jamie Tarabay, interview with author, November 25, 2013.
323   cover of TV Guide: "Why There Are Still No Female Dan Rathers," August 6–12, 1983.
324   *"TV tart"*: Garrels, interview with author, August 4, 2019.
324   *"I applied for a job at NPR"*: Garrels, email to author, March 22, 2021.
324   *"Adam . . . the networks"*: Powell, interview with author, February 20, 2018.

324 *"a difficult transition"*: Buzenberg, interview with author, August 20, 2014.

324 *"She had to learn how to tell a story"*: Cooper, interview with author, January 13, 2020.

324 *"Fill four minutes"*: Garrels, interview with author, August 6, 2019.

324 *"It was nuts"*: Garrels, interview with author, August 4, 2019.

324 *"She took to it"*: Dinges, interview with author, August 20, 2014.

324 *"She didn't need tape"*: Montagne, interview with author, September 13, 2019.

324 *"It was a smoker's voice"*: Garrels, interview with author, August 5, 2019.

325 *"The Soviet Union fell apart"*: Garrels, *Naked in Baghdad*, 51.

325 *"He would bring me"*: Jenkins, interview with author, March 20, 2019.

325 *"The best was a piece"*: Ibid.

325 *"I could hunker down"*: Garrels, *Naked in Baghdad*, 182.

325 *"raw terror"*: Ibid.

326 *"I hired a car"*: Garrels, interview with author, August 5, 2019.

326 *"a mosaic"*: Garrels, *Naked in Baghdad*, 18.

326 *"Anne was front and center"*: Jon Lee Anderson, interview with author, April 19, 2021.

327 *"Sitting over a cup"*: "One Iraqi Family," *Weekend Edition Sunday*, March 30, 2003, Walter J. Brown Media Archives and Peabody Awards Collection, University of Georgia Special Collections Library.

327 *"It started out as a very eerie day"*: "Fall of Baghdad," NPR Special Coverage, April 9, 2003, ibid.

327 *"Guards stood by helpless"*: "Looting Decimates Iraq Museum Collection," *All Things Considered*, April 14, 2003, ibid.

327 *"I was able to plug in"*: "Anne Garrels: Back in the U.S.A.," *Morning Edition*, April 23, 2004, https://www.npr.org/2003/04/23/1240401/anne-garrels-back-in-the-u-s-a.

327 *"The attack"*: "Pandemonium at the Hotel Reporters Called Home," *The Guardian*, April 9, 2003.

328 *"Dr. Saad Jawad"*: "Reporting from the War Zone; Garrels Reflects," *Talk of the Nation*, April 5, 2010, https://www.npr.org/programs/talk-of-the-nation/2010/04/05/125588122/.

328 *"No"*: Ibid.

328 *"A convoy of journalists"*: Garrels, *Naked in Baghdad*, 200.

328 *"She's fine"*: "Anne Garrels: Back in the U.S.A."

328 *"Garrels became our muse"*: "Louder than Bombs," *Vogue*, July, 2003.

329 *"understood the human damage"*: "Magnanimity & McMuffins," *Washington Post*, November 7, 2003.

329 *"like she'd had a stroke"*: Klose, interview with author, April 28, 2011.

329 *"she looked so fragile"*: "Philanthropy that Was Deeply Personal," *Los Angeles Times*, January 31, 2004.

330 *"She wasn't interested in talking"*: Ibid.

330 *"How are you, honey?"*: Ibid.

330 *"She asked if I was dating"*: Bergsma, interview with author, June 1, 2011.

330 *"I'm so happy to see you"*: Klose, interview with author, April 28, 2011.

330 *"We're going to do wonderful things"*: Ibid.

330 *"Of course, we are"*: Ibid.

330 *"I have no idea what"*: Ibid.

330 *"Don't worry"*: Ibid.

331 *"the Kroc family interests"*: Ibid.

331 *"I want to see your books"*: Ibid.

331 *"reserve of six months"*: Stern, interview with author, February 25, 2021.

331 *"When I asked them a direct question"*: Richard Starmann, interview with author, June 13, 2011.

332 *"I would hope if Mrs. Kroc"*: Ibid.

332 *"If you got to your goals"*: Klose, interview with author, April 28, 2011.

332 *"It's serious"*: Ibid.

332 *"How was your meeting?"*: Starmann, interview with author, June 13, 2011.

332 *"I'll send the boys"*: Ibid.

333 *"The most important thing"*: Ibid.

333 *"I think they're further to the left"*: Ibid.

333 *"I was the right wing of that aircraft"*: Ibid.

333 *"What do you think?"*: Ibid.

333 *"I think the big chunk"*: Ibid.

333 *"Even to her"*: Ibid.

333 *"Do you think that will knock their socks off?"*: Ibid.

334 *"It would have been huge"*: Stern, interview with author, February 25, 2021

334 *"I'm not a mystical person"*: Klose, interview with author, April 28, 2011.

334 *"Do you have paper?"*: Ibid.

334 *"Write down the number"*: Ibid.

334 *"barely move"*: Ibid.

334 *"It's divided"*: Ibid.

334 *"There were no strings attached"*: Starmann, interview with author, June 13, 2011.

335 *"We are inspired"*: "Kroc Leaves $200 Million Gift to NPR," *San Diego Union-Tribune*, November 7, 2003.

335 *"It is believed"*: "Billions and Billions Served, Hundreds of Millions Donated," *New York Times*, November 7, 2003.

335 *"Her bequest to NPR"*: "Kroc Bequest Goes to NPR," *Los Angeles Times*, November 7, 2003.

335 *"Mrs. Kroc was a partisan peacenik"*: "Kroc Widow Wills $200 Million to NPR," *Washington Times*, November 6, 2003.

335 *"It is to be saved"*: "Kroc Bequest Goes to NPR."

335 *"unusual, company-wide"*: "Dishing Out the Hamburger Money," *Los Angeles Times*, May 16, 2004.

335 *the freedom to dream*: "Billions and Billions Served."

336 *"What would our air sound like"*: "Kroc's $200 Million Gift Frees Pub Radio's Dreams," *Current*, November 17, 2003.

NINE: BROKEN IN BAGHDAD

337 *"a golden era"*: Tom Bullock, "Life in War: Journalist's Assignment in Iraq Ends," *Morning Edition*, October 22, 2007. In *Fiasco*, his definitive account of the Iraq War, Thomas E. Ricks posits that this quiet period was used by insurgent Iraqis to plan the bloody attacks that followed.

337 *"I found time to swim"*: Ibid.

337 *"I'm seeing a flourishing"*: "U.S. Soldier Killed in Iraq," *Weekend Edition Sunday,* August 3, 2003, https://www.npr.org/2003/08/03/1383963/u-s-soldier-killed-near-baghdad.

338 *"We moved around"*: Garrels, *Naked in Baghdad,* 233.

338 *"I didn't even tell"*: Amos, interview with author, September 6, 2019.

338 *"The Booksellers of Mutanabi Street"*: "The Booksellers of Mutanabi Street," *All Things Considered,* December 21, 2003, https://www.npr.org/2003/12/21/1554766/the-book sellers-of-mutanabi-street.

338 *"euphoria of liberation"*: Steven Boylan, interview with author, August 24, 2021.

338 *"celebrating in the center"*: "Iraqis Rejoice at Saddam's Capture," NPR, December 14, 2003.

339 *Five people died*: "Baghdad Bomb Kills at Least 5 at a Restaurant," *New York Times,* January 1, 2004.

339 *"Suicide Bomber Strikes"*: "Suicide Bomber Strikes in Central Iraq," *All Things Considered,* January 14, 2004, https://www.npr.org/2004/01/14/1597547/suicide-bomber -strikes-in-central-iraq.

339 *"Car Bomb Kills"*: "Car Bomb Kills Four in Baghdad," *Morning Edition,* January 28, 2004, https://www.npr.org/2004/01/28/1622086/car-bomb-kills-four-in-baghdad.

339 *"Students entering campus"*: "Baghdad University," *Morning Edition,* January 16, 2004, https://www.npr.org/2004/01/16/1600699/baghdad-university.

339 *"Here in Baqubah"*: "Suicide Bomber Strikes in Central Iraq," *All Things Considered,* January 14, 2004, https://www.npr.org/2004/01/14/1597547/suicide-bomber-strikes -in-central-iraq.

339 *"No one knows"*: "Analysts Ponder Sistani's Leadership of Shiite Iraqis," *All Things Considered,* February 3, 2004, https://www.npr.org/2004/02/03/1640151/analysts-ponder -sistanis-leadership-of-shiite-iraqis.

340 *"Reporters have no defense"*: Boylan, interview with author, August 24, 2021.

340 *"bitter opposition"*: John F. Burns, interview with author, May 10, 2021.

340 *"an oasis"*: Garrels, *Naked in Baghdad,* 235.

340 *"a necessary if sweltering"*: Ibid.

341 *"So, you going back?"*: "The Dangers of Reporting in Iraq," *Morning Edition,* June 7, 2004, https://www.npr.org/2004/06/07/1941072/the-dangers-of-reporting-in-iraq.

341 *"I'm going to keep going"*: Garrels to Terrence Smith, *The NewsHour with Jim Lehrer,* October 7, 2003.

341 *"Yeah, absolutely"*: "Naked in Baghdad," *Fresh Air,* September 11, 2003, https://www .npr.org/2003/09/11/1427922/naked-in-baghdad.

341 *"Look, if you're lucky"*: Ibid.

341 *"I was trying to show"*: Garrels, interview with author, August, 2019.

341 *"I'm not really very interested"*: Garrels, *Naked in Baghdad,* 182.

342 *"She had a great way"*: Tom Bullock, interview with author, June 14, 2013.

342 *"She could comprehend"*: Philip Reeves, interview with author, October 7, 2019.

342 *"Anne is up there"*: Felton, interview with author, March 10, 2020.

342 *"not be limited to the American"*: Jenkins, interview with author, March 20, 2019.

343 *"Ford and MacArthur each gave"*: Barbara Hall, interview with author, August 7, 2019.

343 *"Only a couple of foreign bureaus"*: Ibid.

343 *"We were pretty much able"*: Jenkins, interview with author, March 20, 2019.

343 *"I'd ask Loren"*: Jeffrey Dvorkin, interview with author, October 24, 2019.

343 *"Suddenly, a 1,000-pound bomb"*: "Deadly Car Bomb Rocks Iraq," *Morning Edition*, July 14, 2004, https://www.npr.org/2004/07/14/3384003/deadly-car-bomb-rocks -baghdads-green-zone.

343 *enough residue from the blast*: Garrels, interview with author, August 5, 2019.

344 *"Amazing Grace"*: "Fallujah Braces for Assault," *Morning Edition*, November 3, 2004, https://www.npr.org/2004/11/03/4141471/fallujah-braces-for-u-s-assault. The fall 2004 offensive is known as the second battle of Fallujah to distinguish it from fighting in that city earlier in the year.

344 *"old woman"*: "The Embeds: What Is Gained and What Is Lost," *Columbia Journalism Review*, November/December 2006.

344 *"If they had to have"*: Garrels, interview with author, August 5, 2019

344 *"The night before"*: Ibid.

344 *"I love my girlfriend"*: "A Marine Unit's Experience in Fallujah," *All Things Considered*, November 2, 2004, https://www.npr.org/2004/11/22/4182427/a-marine-units-experi ence-in-fallujah.

344 *"to the heart of the resistance"*: Ibid.

345 *"I'll be back tomorrow"*: Ibid.

345 *"This is not a very nice place"*: Ibid.

345 *"One day"*: Garrels, interview with author, August 5, 2019.

345 *"That was all I could do"*: Ibid.

345 *"You didn't reflect on it"*: "The Embeds."

345 *"Some kids were celebrating"*: Ibid.

345 *"I'd been to this place"*: Ibid.

346 *"Anne and I would joke"*: Bullock, interview with author, June 14, 2013,

346 *"I always wore this"*: Garrels, interview with author, August 4, 2019.

346 *$2,000 for the abduction*: "Anchors Try to Get Close to the Story in Baghdad," *Washington Post*, January 27, 2005.

346 *"I knew the lay of the land"*: Garrels, interview with author, August 5, 2019.

346 *"what it took"*: Ibid.

347 *"There's no question"*: Ibid.

347 *"a very valuable"*: Jenkins, interview with author, March 20, 2019.

347 *"writing letters to get visas"*: Tarabay, interview with author, November 25, 2013.

347 *"I was the Baghdad correspondent"*: Ibid.

347 *"I'm not sure that Jamie"*: Garrels, interview with author, August 5, 2019.

347 *"Anne was territorial"*: Montagne, interview with author, September 13, 2019,

347 *"This was her beat"*: Poggioli, interview with author, October 5, 2019.

347 *"Anne had a thing"*: Amos, interview with author, September 6, 2019.

348 *"At eleven a.m."*: Tarabay, interview with author, November 25, 2013.

348 *"caffeine, nicotine, and adrenaline"*: Garrels, *Naked in Baghdad*, 71.

348 *"never showed up"*: Amos, interview with author, September 6, 2019.

348 *"We were all living"*: Tarabay, interview with author, November 25, 2013.

348 *"You knew it wasn't healthy"*: Ibid.

348 *"We were proud"*: Ibid.

348 *"She had moments"*: Ibid.

349 *"fly-by-nights"*: Garrels, interview with author, August 5, 2019.

349 *"Loren was having to scramble"*: Ibid.

349 *"The pool willing to go"*: "Anchors Try to Get Close."

350 *"I want to make all the world"*: "Anatomy of a Shooting," *All Things Considered*, June 23, 2006, https://www.npr.org/2006/06/23/5506353/anatomy-of-a-shooting-a-civilians-death-in-iraq.

350 *"Yasser was the sun"*: Lyden, interview with author, September 13, 2019.

350 *"Loren was trying to destroy"*: Lyden, interview with author, September 19, 2019.

350 *"I want to cover this story"*: Jenkins, interview with author, March 20, 2019.

351 *"Jacki . . . was one"*: Ibid.

351 *"The company had to pay"*: Lyden, interview with author, September 19, 2019.

351 *"I think you should talk"*: Kernis, interview with author, April 9. 2018.

351 *"You couldn't pick up a paper"*: Drake, interview with author, August 10, 2019.

351 *"Kevin, I'm the unemployed guy"*: Bill Marimow, interview with author, June 13, 2013.

352 *"had fallen in love"*: Drake, interview with author, August 10, 2019.

353 *"Bill gave me four months"*: McChesney, interview with author, April 30, 2011.

353 *"A Deadly Interrogation"*: Jane Mayer, "A Deadly Interrogation," *The New Yorker*, November 6, 2005.

353 *"Jacki and John proposed"*: Montagne, interview with author, November 27, 2018.

353 *"He wanted to have"*: Marimow, interview with author, June 13, 2013.

353 *"He is a provincial man"*: Poggioli, interview with author, June 7, 2019.

354 *"Yesterday's bombing has brought"*: "Protests and Violence Follow Bombing of Samarra Shrine," *Morning Edition*, February 23, 2006, https://www.npr.org/2006/02/23/5229437/protests-and-violence-follow-bombing-of-samarra-shrine.

354 *"I had been instructed"*: Lyden, interview with author, September 13, 2019.

354 *"I stayed at a room"*: Lyden, email to author, September 18, 2019.

354 *"It was not a story"*: Garrels, interview with author, August 5, 2019.

354 *"A translator had run"*: Ibid.

354 *"She was trying to go after"*: Ibid.

355 *"Flying and landing"*: Ibid.

355 *"I turned the screens"*: Reeves, interview with author, October 7, 2019.

355 *"Sushi"*: Name withheld at request of source, interview with author.

355 *"I did ask her"*: Garrels, interview with author, August 5, 2019.

355 *"One of the people she hired"*: Ibid.

355 *"Dozens of Corpses"*: "Dozens of Corpses, Hands Bound, Found in Baghdad," *Morning Edition*, March 8, 2006, https://www.npr.org/2006/03/08/5252283/dozens-of-corpses-hands-bound-found-in-baghdad.

355 *"She began insulting"*: Lyden, email to author, September 16, 2019.

356 *"She had a glass"*: Ibid.

356 *"Did she throw it"*: Ibid.

356 *"It was abhorrent"*: Ibid.

356 *"Anne was an alcoholic"*: Amos, interview with author, September 6, 2019.

356 *"how many unidentified bodies"*: "Growing Sectarian Strife Roils Baghdad," *All Things Considered*, March 26, 2006, https://www.npr.org/2006/03/26/5302561/growing-sectarian-strife-roils-baghdad.

356 *"Thirty bodies were found"*: Ibid.

357 *"Fox fucking News"*: Eric Westervelt, interview with author, December 20, 2021.

357 *"We couldn't afford security"*: Garrels, interview with author, August 5, 2019.

357 *"You can't do a deal"*: Ibid.

357 *"There was a fight"*: Montagne, interview with author, September 13, 2019.

357 *"I want this room"*: Garrels, interview with author, August 5, 2019.

357 *"it was such a dreadful"*: Ibid.

357 *"Jamie spent the night"*: Ibid.

358 *"You're on this treadmill"*: Tarabay, interview with author, November 25, 2013.

358 *"Anatomy of a Shooting"*: "Anatomy of a Shooting."

358 *the $120,000 story*: Montagne, interview with author, November 19, 2018.

358 *"to recalibrate the rules"*: "Anatomy of a Shooting."

359 *"assailed me about Jacki"*: Marimow, interview with author, June 13, 2013.

359 *"Loren stepped in"*: Bullock, interview with author, June 14, 2013.

359 *"decided that Marimow"*: McChesney, interview with author, April 30, 2011.

359 *"I gathered pretty quickly"*: Marimow, interview with author, June 13, 2013.

359 *"Bill didn't play well"*: Lyden, interview with author, June 11, 2013.

359 *"He tended to view the programs"*: McChesney, interview with author, April 30, 2011.

360 *"Bill told a reporter"*: Chadwick, interview with author, April 5, 2011.

360 *"tone deaf and prize hungry"*: Margaret Talbot, "Stealing Life: The Crusader behind 'The Wire,'" *The New Yorker*, October 14, 2007.

360 *"Oh, God, Marimow"*: Amos, interview with author, November 1, 2014.

360 *"They went after him"*: McChesney, interview with author, April 30, 2011.

360 *"Jay gave me a review"*: Marimow, interview with author, June 13, 2013.

360 *"I needed someone"*: Kernis, interview with author, April 9, 2018.

361 *"Anne as a macho woman"*: Gjelten, interview with author, May 13, 2021.

361 *"She needed therapy"*: Amos, interview with author, September 6, 2019.

361 *"You had two people"*: Lyden, interview with author, June 11, 2013.

361 *"Before we couldn't even go"*: "Iraqis Skeptical New Sense of Security Can Last," *All Things Considered*, November 1, 2007, https://www.npr.org/2007/11/01/15812025/iraqis-skeptical-new-sense-of-security-can-last.

361 *"good at keeping a level head"*: Westervelt, interview with author, December 20, 2021.

361 *"a homemade suicide vest"*: "Portrait of a Suicide Bomber," *Morning Edition*, June 11, 2007, https://www.npr.org/2007/06/11/10931837/portrait-of-a-suicide-bomber.

362 *"Abu Abdul says"*: Ibid.

362 *"No one trusts anyone"*: "Two Neighborhood's Illustrate Baghdad's Divide," All Things Considered, August 6, 2007, https://www.npr.org/2007/08/06/12542846/two-neighborhoods-illustrate-baghdads-divide.

362 *"There was blood"*: Iraqi Group Accuses Iran of Fueling Violence," Morning Edition, October 26, 2007, https://www.npr.org/2007/10/26/15655331/iraqi-group-accuses-iran-of-fueling-violence.

362 *"They said they went"*: Ibid.

362   *"Evidence obtained through torture"*: "NPR Defends Torture-Based Reporting: Network Ombud Agrees with Critics," Fair.org, November 5, 2007.

362   *"If we act like that"*: "Letters: Shiite Militia," *Morning Edition*, November 1, 2007, https://www.npr.org/2007/11/01/15835066/letters-shiite-militia.

362   *"I remember a newscast"*: Garrels, interview with author, August 5, 2019.

363   *"I remember a two-way"*: Siegel, interview with author, October 5, 2021.

363   *"We didn't use it"*: Ibid.

363   *"You were stuck"*: Garrels, interview with author, August 5, 2019.

363   *"I was a wreck"*: Ibid.

363   *"I asked Anne"*: Bullock, interview with author, June 14, 2013.

363   *"We didn't have much of a bench"*: Garrels, interview with author, August 4, 2019.

363   *"Drunk or sober"*: Jenkins, interview with author, March 20, 2019.

363   *"Look at any woman"*: Tarabay, interview with author, November 25, 2013.

364   *"towers of sand-colored brick"*: "Millions of Muslims Rest in Najaf's Valley of Peace," *All Things Considered*, February 1, 2008, https://www.npr.org/2008/02/01/18615547/millions-of-muslims-rest-in-najafs-valley-of-peace.

364   *"I had an opening"*: Jenkins, interview with author, March 20, 2019.

364   *"Lulu was jealous"*: Garrels, interview with author, August 5, 2019.

365   *"There was a lot of tension"*: Lourdes Garcia-Navarro, interview with author, April 11, 2024.

365   *"It was a nightmare"*: Amos, interview with author, September 6, 2019.

365   *"She didn't care"*: Garrels, interview with author, August 5, 2019.

365   *"Both are strong women"*: Barbara Rehm, interview with author, August 9, 2019.

365   *"She really knew how"*: Garrels, interview with author, August 5, 2019.

365   *"I admit"*: Ibid.

365   *"not the best thing"*: Tarabay, interview with author, November 25, 2013.

365   *"Jack is a nice guy"*: Montagne, interview with author, September 13, 2019.

366   *"It was clear to him"*: Garrels, interview with author, August 5, 2019.

366   *"I basically broke down"*: Ibid.

366   *"Vint couldn't get in my face"*: Garrels, interview with author, August 4, 2019.

366   *"I'd tell Vint"*: Ibid.

366   *"We were two established"*: Dina Temple-Raston, interview with author, October 1, 2013.

366   *"They wanted to teach me"*: Ibid.

367   *"hundreds and hundreds"*: Ibid.

367   *"I know this"*: Ibid.

367   *"That's how I hit the scene"*: Ibid.

367   *"Nobody thought of covering"*: Ibid.

367   *"Dina relied on one or two"*: Siegel, interview with author, October 5, 2021.

367   *"She was hard to deal with"*: Gjelten, interview with author, May 13, 2021.

367   *"She's full of herself"*: Dinges, interview with author, August 20, 2014.

367   *"I'm sure you know"*: Temple-Raston, interview with author, October 1, 2013.

368   *"I don't think Anne"*: Tarrabay, interview with author, November 25, 2013.

368   *"Ms. Garrels's account works"*: "In Brief," *New York Sun*, October 22, 2003.

368   *"For those readers looking"*: Ibid.

368   *"I was in a unique position"*: Temple-Raston, interview with author, October 1, 2013.

369   *"Iraq Women Face Risks"*: "Iraq Women Face Risks behind the Wheel," *Morning Edition*, March 11, 2008, https://www.npr.org/2008/03/11/88091798/iraqi-women-face-risks-behind-the-wheel.

369   *"She has long, wild red hair"*: Ibid.

369   *"The staff was worried"*: Garrels, interview with author, August 5, 2019.

369   *"I don't suffer fools"*: Ibid.

369   *"There were many clashes"*: Temple-Raston, interview with author, October 1, 2013.

369   *"She was quite arrogant"*: Garrels, interview with author, August 5, 2019.

370   *"We've heard shooting"*: "Militant Fighting Spreads across Southern Iraq," *Morning Edition*, March 27, 2008, https://www.npr.org/2008/03/27/89140765/militant-fighting-spreads-across-southern-iraq.

370   *"Tens of thousands"*: "Fighting between Iraqi Forces, Militias Continues," *All Things Considered*, March 27, 2008, https://www.npr.org/2008/03/27/89163652/fighting-between-iraqi-forces-militias-continues.

370   *"There are about 1,200 judges"*: "Iraqis on Slow Road to Building Judicial System," All Things Considered, March 27, 200, https://www.npr.org/2008/03/27/89162530/iraqis-on-slow-road-to-building-judicial-system.

370   *"It was an insane situation"*: Garcia-Navarro, interview with author, April 11, 2024.

370   *"I was really pissed off"*: Garrels, interview with author, August 5, 2019.

370   *"What the hell is this about?"*: Name withheld at request of source, interview with author.

371   *"a nervous breakdown"*: Temple-Raston, interview with author, October 1, 2013.

371   *"cunt"*: Gjelten, interview with author, May 13, 2021.

371   *"Talk to Anne"*: Temple-Raston, interview with author, October 1, 2013.

371   *"That night is a blur"*: Garrels, interview with author, August 5, 2019.

371   *"Anne spit at Dina"*: Garcia-Navarro, interview with author, April 11, 2024.

371   *"Jack was sweet"*: Garrels, interview with author, August 5, 2019.

371   *"I felt cornered"*: Ibid.

371   *"I had issues"*: Garrels, interview with author, October 24, 2019.

371   *"She seemed distraught"*: Boylan, interview with author, August 24, 2021.

372   *"I don't give a shit"*: Name withheld at request of source, interview with author.

372   *"Gunny . . . I'm sorry"*: Westervelt, interview with author, December 20, 2021.

372   *"I'll never send three women"*: Ibid.

372   *"We lined up, begging"*: Garcia-Navarro, interview with author, April 11, 2024.

372   *"Am I a bad person?"*: Name withheld at request of source, interview with author.

373   *"She was at her wit's end"*: Westervelt, interview with author, December 20, 2021.

373   *"Ellen said I'd jeopardized"*: Garrels, interview with author, August 5, 2019,

374   *"It was my responsibility"*: Ellen Weiss, interview with author, July 14, 2023.

374   *"I'm getting help"*: Garrels, interview with author, August 5, 2019.

374   *"They knew exactly"*: Garrels, interview with author, September 5, 2019.

374   *"Dina came back to Washington"*: McChesney, interview with author, April 30, 2011.

374   *"They told me I had to stop seeing"*: Garrels, interview with author, September 5, 2019.

374   *"People played hurt"*: Reeves, interview with author, October, 7, 2019.

374   *"I didn't have a breakdown"*: Jon Lee Anderson, interview with author, April 19. 2021.

374   *"state of self-reproach"*: Burns, interview with author, May 10, 2021.

375 *"I was very lucky"*: Garrels, interview with author, September 5, 2019.

375 *"She called me trying"*: Gwen Thompkins, interview with author, September 28, 2013.

375 *"Dina got the job"*: Lyden, interview with author, September 19, 2019.

375 *"They gave it to her as payback"*: Adler, interview with author, June 8. 2011.

375 *"I've seen correspondents"*: "NPR Reporter Looks Back on a Year in Iraq," *All Things Considered*, April 25, 2009, https://www.npr.org/2009/04/25/103495152/npr-reporter -looks-back-on-a-year-in-iraq.

375 *"It was clear they weren't"*: Garrels, interview with author, August 5, 2019.

375 *"He wouldn't give me the time"*: Ibid.

375 *"It was difficult and painful"*: Klose, interview with author, July 19, 2019.

375 *"The European Union's failure"*: "In Ukraine, A Conflict Over Russian Relations," *Morning Edition*, September 5, 2008, https://www.npr.org/2008/09/05/94297069/in -ukraine-a-conflict-over-russian-relations.

376 *"a gilded tour of gilded domes"*: "Russia's Troubled Waters Flow with the Mighty Volga," *All Things Considered*, November 1, 2010, https://www.npr.org/2010/11/01/130837658 /russias-troubled-waters-flow-with-the-mighty-volga.

376 *"I retired by email"*: Garrels, interview with author, August 5, 2019.

376 *"I was in Iraq too long"*: Garrels, "Former Nippers," Facebook, November 19, 2008.

376 *"The way Anne was treated violated"*: Ibid.

377 *"NPR had ridden that talented horse"*: Westervelt, interview with author, December 20, 2021.

TEN: CAN'T ANYBODY HERE PLAY THIS GAME?

378 *"Muslims killed us on 9/11"*: "Bill O'Reilly on 'The View': "Muslims Killed Us on 9/11," CBS News, October 14, 2010.

378 *"O'Reilly's claim"*: "Because Muslims Killed us on 9/11!," *The Atlantic*, October 15, 2010.

378 *"Look, Bill, I'm"*: The O'Reilly Factor, YouTube, October 18, 2010.

379 *"bring O'Reilly to a place"*: Folkenflik, interview with author, May 18, 2023.

379 *"There are people who remind us"*: The O'Reilly Factor, YouTube, October 18, 2010.

379 *"You live in the liberal precincts"*: Ibid.

379 *"This crossed the line"*: Vivian Schiller, interview with author, May 12, 2013.

379 *"He was a Black person"*: Montagne, interview with author, March 31, 2011.

379 *"an adequate host"*: Malesky, interview with author, October 16, 2011.

379 *"He didn't really know"*: Montagne, interview with author, March 31, 2011.

380 *"When he worked"*: Totenberg, interview with author, July 24, 2023.

380 *"Juan saw himself"*: Conan, interview with author, December 15, 2013.

380 *"Williams did some fine work"*: "National Public Rodeo," *Vanity Fair*, January 17, 2012.

380 *"People are praying"*: David Folkenflik, *Murdoch's World: The Last of the Old Media Empires* (New York: Public Affairs, 2013), 105.

380 *"A lot of people"*: David Greene, interview with author, May 19, 2023.

380 *"We're grateful for"*: Folkenflik, *Murdoch's World*, 106.

381 *"Was it because he's Black"*: Siegel, interview with author, October 5, 2021.

381 *"great embarrassment"*: Ibid.

381 *"That was the dogma"*: Siegel, interview with author, July 21, 2023.

381 *"He should have been"*: Stamberg, interview with author, August 21, 2014.

381 *"Do I think NPR"*: "National Public Rodeo."

381 *"Juan is smart"*: Ibid.

381 *"whitey"*: Folkenflik, *Murdoch's World*, 107.

381 *"Michelle Obama, you know"*: Ibid.

381 *"During my time"*: Weiss, interview with author, July 14, 2023.

382 *"What do you want"*: Weiss, interview with author, June 20, 2023.

382 *"Ellen said she wanted"*: Schiller, interview with author, May 12, 2023.

382 *"There were a lot of"*: Joyce Slocum, interview with author, April 18, 2023.

382 *"Let's get on a call"*: Ibid.

382 *"The interesting thing"*: Ibid.

383 *"I got word"*: Folkenflik, interview with author, May 18, 2023.

383 *"Roger Ailes will use this"*: Ibid.

383 *"America, you're smart enough"*: Folkenflik, *Murdoch's World*, 111.

383 *"pinhead"*: Ibid.

383 *"I don't fit into"*: Ibid.

384 *"We got your back"*: "National Public Rodeo."

384 *"A good man"*: Folkenflik, *Murdoch's World*, 112.

384 *"Tell Juan to hang in"*: Ibid.

384 *"were inconsistent with"*: "NPR Ends Williams' Contract after Muslim Remarks," NPR .org, October 21, 2010.

384 *"his psychiatrist or"*: "The Revenge of Juan Williams," *American Journalism Review*, March 9, 2011.

384 *"We didn't have a sufficient"*: Dana Davis Rehm, interview with author, March 20, 2012.

384 *"expressed any remorse"*: Slocum, interview with author, April 18, 2023.

385 *"The real mistake"*: "NPR Firing Prompts Review of Leadership," *Washington Post*, January 28, 2011.

385 *"in a bubble"*: Montagne, interview with author, March 31, 2011.

385 *"They are, of course, Nazis"*: "Fox News Chief Roger Ailes Blasts National Public Radio Brass as 'Nazis,'" *Daily Beast*, November 17, 2010.

385 *"As soon as I got out"*: Schiller, interview with author, August 11, 2023.

385 *"retributive justice"*: "Ambush-Journalist Confronts NPR CEO about Firing of Juan Williams," *Hollywood Reporter*, October 25, 2010.

385 *"There's simply no reason"*: "Defunding NPR? It's Not That Easy," *Politico*, October 23, 2010.

385 *"What do we, the taxpayers"*: "Juan Williams Firing Leads Palin, Huckabee to Call for Defunding NPR," CBS News, October 21, 2010.

386 *"We were appalled"*: Amos, interview with author, May 13, 2011.

386 *"It was the last straw"*: "National Public Rodeo."

386 *"He was in a commentary"*: Siegel, interview with author, July 21, 2023.

386 *"It was really bad form"*: Totenberg, interview with author, June 4, 2013.

386 *"That's not the answer"*: Stamberg, interview with author, October 21, 2011.

386 *"Calling Juan was 100 percent"*: Weiss, interview with author, June 20, 2023.

386 *"I made a joke"*: Schiller, interview with author, May 12, 2023.

386 *"totally fucked up"*: Siegel, interview with author, July 21, 2023.

386   *"direct violation of"*: "Night Watch: Stewart on Williams," *New York Times*, October 26, 2010.

386   *"Are you kidding me"*: "A Tote Bag to a Knife Fight," *Politico*, October 26, 2010.

387   *"My sense is"*: Folkenflik, interview with author, May 18, 2023,

387   *Many at NPR watched*: "NPR's Juan Williams Fired for One Too Many Opinionated Comments," *Current*, November 11, 2010.

387   *"The board had the stomach"*: Slocum, interview with author, July 29, 2023.

387   *"They had done these kinds"*: Dave Edwards, interview with author, July 26, 2023.

388   *"Ellen was a big contributor"*: Siegel, interview with author, October 5, 2021.

388   *"Whatever is admirable"*: "Ellen Weiss Out at NPR," *The Atlantic*, January 6, 2011.

388   *"On a good day"*: Weiss, interview with author, July 11, 2023.

388   *"She would walk around"*: Greene, interview with author, April 19, 2023.

388   *"She had a runner's energy"*: Malesky, interview with author, October 16, 2011.

388   *"The least expensive petites"*: Weiss, interview with author, July 11, 2023.

388   *"I was mindful"*: Weiss, interview with author, July 14, 2023.

389   *"I think I was getting"*: Weiss, interview with author, July 11, 2023.

389   *"Ellen was a very bright"*: Fitsmaurice, interview with author, June 5, 2013.

389   *"I got my foot"*: Weiss, interview with author, July 11, 2023.

389   *"I was surprised by how much"*: Ibid.

389   *"I was the lowest person"*: Ibid.

389   *"We did a lot of music interviews"*: Ibid.

389   *"She embraced"*: Proffitt, interview with author, May 7, 2011.

389   *"the most wonderful thing"*: Weiss, interview with author, July 11, 2023.

389   *"You're the future"*: Ibid.

390   *"I remember many"*: Ibid.

390   *"Ellen understood how to craft"*: Hockenberry, interview with author, June 5, 2012.

390   *"I spent a year"*: Weiss, interview with author, July 11, 2023.

390   *"Lost & Found Sound"*: *All Things Considered*, 1999, https://exchange.prx.org/series /2269-lost-found-sound.

391   *"the show"*: Malesky, interview with author, October 16, 2011.

391   "ATC *was the place"*: Siegel, interview with author, October 5, 2021.

391   *"People were walking out"*: Weiss, interview with author, July 11, 2023.

391   *"I'll tell you"*: Ibid.

391   *"The national desk had needed"*: Drake, interview with author, August 10, 2019.

391   *"9/11 fast-tracked"*: Weiss, interview with author, July 11, 2023.

391   *"making sure that people"*: Ibid.

392   *"We needed information"*: Ibid.

392   *"When you look"*: Ibid.

392   *"I was literally one day"*: Weiss, interview with author, July 14, 2023.

392   *"I was like"*: Greene, interview with author, April 19, 2023.

393   *"Why is this in the piece?"*: Ibid.

393   *"That's the way Ellen's mind"*: Ibid.

393   *"Ellen turned the national desk"*: Drake, interview with author, August 10, 2019.

393   *"I met him for drinks"*: Weiss, interview with author, July 14, 2023.

394 *"Divisive"*: Siegel, interview with author, July 21, 2023.

394 *"Divisive"*: Thompkins, interview with author, September 28, 2013.

394 *"Divisive"*: Amos, interview with author, May 13, 2011.

394 *"suck up"*: Totenberg, interview with author, June 4, 2013.

394 *"vindictive"*: McChesney, interview with author, April 30, 2011.

394 *"Ellen Weiss had people who loved her"*: Adler, interview with author, June 8, 2011.

394 *"She was a woman looking"*: Browning, interview with author, July 8, 2011.

394 *"She was transparently"*: Jenkins, interview with author, March 20, 2019.

394 *"Ellen had a million"*: Abbott, interview with author, January 16, 2014.

394 *"When Ellen decided"*: Malesky, interview with author, October 16, 2011.

394 *"Nothing was ever Ellen's fault"*: Totenberg, interview with author, June 4, 2013.

394 *"She's a political shrewdie"*: Seymour, interview with author, October 16, 2010.

394 *"Smart, capable, and dishonest"*: Drake, interview with author, August 10, 2019.

395 *"How come I wasn't told"*: Ibid.

395 *"I'm going to plague you"*: Ibid.

395 *"I don't want to be left hanging"*: Ibid.

395 *"I'll tell you what"*: Ibid.

395 *"When I come in Monday"*: Ibid.

395 *"There was no way"*: Ibid.

396 *"It probably showed"*: Weiss, interview with author, July 11, 2023.

396 *"When I got there . . . the desks"*: Jenkins, interview with author, March 20, 2023.

396 *"Ellen was an avowed Zionist"*: Thompkins, interview with author, September 28, 2013.

396 *"He was a classical"*: Hockenberry, interview with author, June 5, 2012.

396 *"She has strong feelings"*: Malesky, interview with author, October 16, 2011.

396 *"Ellen surrounded herself"*: Montagne, interview with author, April 22, 2011.

396 *"Ellen loved"*: Adler, interview with author, June 8, 2012.

396 *"We tried to tell people"*: Totenberg, interview with author, June 4, 2013.

397 *"She had trouble with women"*: Poggioli, interview with author, July 6, 2011.

397 *"The so-called powerful"*: Totenberg, interview with author, June 4, 2013.

397 *"Running NPR news is not"*: Siegel, interview with author, October 5, 2021.

397 *"We had to cut ten percent"*: Weiss, interview with author, July 14, 2023.

397 *"She lacked an empathic"*: McChesney, interview with author, April 30, 2011.

397 *"If I saw Ellen"*: Lyden, interview with author, June 11, 2013.

397 *"I think of him in the pantheon"*: Reiner, interview with author, June 12, 2013.

397 a *"fresher, looser"*: "The Second Coming of NPR West," *Los Angeles*, April 2014.

397 *"I could say things there"*: Ibid.

398 *"I was sent to NPR West"*: Weiss, interview with author, July 14, 2023.

398 *"The idea"*: Ibid.

398 *"I needed him to hear it"*: Ibid.

398 *"I did not know"*: Ibid.

398 *"It wasn't to be cruel"*: Ibid.

398 *ruined Chadwick's life*: Fitzmaurice, interview with author, August 4, 2014.

398 *"She's stupid and arrogant"*: Poggioli, interview with author, June 4, 2014.

398 *"Ellen said it was time"*: Simon, interview with author, November 27, 2012.

399   *"He was drifting"*: Siegel, interview with author, July 21, 2023.

399   *"We don't want"*: Ibid.

399   *"get the hell out of Palestine"*: "Helen Thomas Comes under Fire for Remarks on Jews, Israel," CBS News, June 7, 2010.

399   *"Dan didn't take"*: Simon, interview with author, November 27, 2012.

399   *"Why should you be worried"*: Ibid.

399   *"Dan, that sounds wonderful"*: Ibid.

399   *"He died of necrosis"*: Ibid.

399   *"was beginning to operate"*: Ibid.

400   *"Standing grievances about"*: Paul Fahri, "NPR Firing Prompts Review of Leadership," *Washington Post*, January 28, 2011.

400   *"They looked into Ellen's past"*: Folkenflik, interview with author, May 18, 2023.

400   *"They did a thorough review"*: Slocum interview with author, April 18, 2023.

400   *"hundreds of thousands"*: "National Public Rodeo."

400   *"Let me get this straight"*: Simon, interview with author, November 27, 2012.

400   *"More than a dozen NPR employees"*: "NPR Firing Prompts Review."

401   *"I've always been concerned"*: Dave Edwards, interview with author, July 26, 2023.

401   *"I had known Ellen"*: Ibid.

401   *"It became very clear"*: Ibid.

401   *"Ellen was moving"*: Ibid.

401   *"Schiller and Weiss"*: "NPR Firing Prompts Review."

401   *"other situations"*: Dave Edwards, interview with author, August 7, 2023.

401   *"Weiss's decision to fire Williams"*: "NPR Firing Prompts Review."

402   *"The board made clear"*: Slocum, interview with author, April 18, 2023.

402   *"Vivian . . . I've been here"*: Weiss, interview with author, July 14, 2023.

402   *"She had a script"*: Ibid.

402   *"internal procedures"*: "NPR's Costly Mistake," NPR.org, January 7, 2011.

402   *"NPR also announced"*: "A Sacrifice to Appease NPR's Gods," *New York Times*, January 8, 2011.

402   *"NPR can hire"*: "NPR's Costly Mistake."

402   *"For the integrity of the process"*: Ibid.

403   *"It would be inappropriate"*: "NPR Firing Prompts Review."

403   *"WEISS WASH"*: "WEISS WASH," *Slate*, January 7, 2011.

403   *"The board took"*: "A Sacrifice to Appease NPR's Gods."

403   *"A long time ago"*: Ibid.

403   *"It's outrageous"*: Ibid.

403   *"She was trying to shift"*: Adam Davidson, interview with author, March 29, 2003.

404   *"There was a whole contingent"*: Montagne, interview with author, March 31, 2011.

404   *"NPR was obliged"*: Siegel, interview with author, July 23, 2023.

404   *"She was chastised"*: "Vivian Schiller, NPR Chief Executive, Resigns," *New York Times*, March 9, 2011.

404   *"I never actually dial"*: "NPR Amps Up," *Columbia Journalism Review*, March-April 2010.

404   *"During her tenure"*: "Times Executive Resigns to Lead NPR," *New York Times*, November 11, 2008.

405 *"struggling to find"*: "Schiller Hit 'Every Point' on NPR's CEO Wish List," *Current*, November 24, 2008.

405 *"I walked into a buzz saw"*: Schiller, interview with author, May 12, 2023.

405 *"We were in a nosedive"*: Ibid.

405 *"It was a little sleepy"*: Ibid.

405 *"They were our most promising"*: Ibid.

406 *"Weekend in Washington"*: "The Right Jabs Public Radio with Video Sting Using NPR Fundraiser's Words," *Current*, March 21, 2011.

406 *"an easier to navigate site"*: "NPR Moves to Rewire Its Approach to the Web," *New York Times*, July 26, 2009.

406 *"The Three Words"*: Manuscript in author's possession.

406 *"The impression was"*: Adler, interview with author, June 8, 2011.

407 *congresswoman Gabrielle Giffords was shot*: "NPR's Giffords Mistake: Re-Learning the Lesson of Checking Sources," NPR.org, January 11, 2011.

407 *"Vivian's instruction"*: Slocum, interview with author, April 18, 2023.

407 *the likelihood of cuts*: "Public Broadcasting Funds Caught in Budget Battle, *Talk of the Nation*, February 17, 2011, https://www.npr.org/2011/02/17/133842355/Public-Broadcasting-Funds-Caught-In-Budget-Battle.

408 *"We stay on the story"*: "NPR President and CEO Delivers Keynote Speech at National Press Club Today," NPR.org, March 7, 2011.

408 *"We rely on"*: Ibid.

408 *"It went over really well"*: Schiller, interview with author, August 11, 2023.

408 *"How do you feel about Sharia law?"*: Ibid.

409 *"I knew we were dealing"*: Slocum, interview with author, April 18, 2023.

409 *"Now," he said*: "Right Jabs Public Radio."

409 *"The current Republican party"*: "NPR General Counsel Serving as Interim CEO," *Salon*, March 10, 2011.

409 *"It is very clear"*: "The Revenge of Juan Williams," *American Journalism Review*, March 9, 2011.

409 *"I think what we all believe"*: "NPR Executive Caught Calling Tea Partiers 'Racist,'" *New York Times*, March 8, 2011.

410 *"This is terrible"*: Slocum, interview with author, April 18, 2023.

410 *"An executive played the Schiller tape"*: Montagne, interview with author, March 31, 2011.

410 *"It was like"*: Slocum, interview with author, April 18, 2023

410 *"The fact is undeniable"*: "Never Take Your Hat Off in Public," NPR.org, March 17, 2011.

410 *"Schiller comes across"*: "No One Seems to Be Taking Care of NPR," NPR.org, March 9, 2011.

410 *"The board had a very difficult"*: Dave Edwards, interview with author, July 26, 2023.

411 *"If it would be helpful"*: Schiller, interview with author, August 11, 2023.

411 *"Why don't you hang up"*: Dave Edwards, interview with author, July 26, 2023.

411 *"I think the board just felt"*: Slocum, interview with author, April 18, 2023.

411 *"Our concern is not about"*: "Vivian Schiller, NPR Chief Executive, Resigns."

411 *"The time has come"*: "House Votes to End Money for NPR, and Senate Passes Spending Bill," *New York Times*, March 17, 2011.

411 *"At a time when other news organizations"*: Ibid.

412 *"Executives at NPR"*: Slocum, interview with author, April 18, 2023.

412 *"No one is prouder"*: "Inside the Night President Obama Took on Donald Trump," *Frontline*, September 22, 2016, https://www.pbs.org/wgbh/frontline/article/watch-inside -the-night-president-obama-took-on-donald-trump/.

412 *"All kidding aside"*: Ibid.

412 *"What was really memorable"*: Adam Gopnik, "Trump and Obama: A Night to Remember," *The New Yorker*, April 12, 2015.

413 *"Where's the National Public Radio table?"*: " 'The President's Speech' at the White House Correspondents' Dinner," May 1, 2011, National Archives, https://obamawhitehouse .archives.gov/blog/2011/05/01/president-s-speech-white-house-correspondents-dinner.

413 *"You guys are still here?"*: Ibid.

413 *"I know you were a little"*: Ibid.

413 *"NPR is having a party"*: "Seth Meyers at the 2011 White House Correspondents Dinner—Full Transcript," *Scraps from the Loft*, April 9, 2017.

413 *"It was very unpleasant"*: Totenberg, interview with author, July 24, 2023.

413 *"People picked up the ball"*: Dave Edwards, interview with author, July 26, 2023.

414 *"I felt all three of them"*: Folkenflik, interview with author, May 18, 2023.

414 *"It was stupid"*: Paul Haaga, interview with author, June 29, 2022.

414 *"NPR journalism has come to embody"*: Juan Williams, *Muzzled: The Assault on Honest Debate*, (New York, Crown, 2011), 277.

415 *"I think what you saw"*: Davidson, interview with author, March 29, 2023.

415 *Guy Raz reported the story*: "Family Fights for Honor of 'Rogue' Vietnam General," *Weekend All Things Considered*, October 12, 2012, https://www.npr.org/2012/10/13 /162789031/family-fights-for-honor-of-rogue-vietnam-general.

415 *Michelle Kellerman*: "Hillary Clinton Offers Mea Culpa in Libya Attack," *All Things Considered*, October 16, 2012, https://www.npr.org/2012/10/16/163037215/hillary-clinton -offers-mea-culpa-in-libya-attack.

415 *Melissa Block*: "Falling in Love Again," *All Things Considered*, May 3, 2013, https:// www.npr.org/sections/thetwo-way/2013/05/03/180892483/falling-in-love-again-face -transplant-donors-daughter-meets-recipient.

415 *more than 2.5 million*: "The Improbable Rise of NPR Music," *Wall Street Journal*, March 15, 2013.

415 *Also in 2013*: "The Second Coming of NPR West," *Los Angeles*, April 2014.

415 *14.9 million*: "NPR Retains Highest Ratings Ever," NPR press release, March 28, 2018.

416 *"Her firing was an indication"*: Jeff Jarvis, "NPR's Inevitable Conflict," *Buzz Machine* (blog), March 9, 2011, https://buzzmachine.com/2011/03/09/nprs-inevitable-conflict/.

ELEVEN: THIS AMERICAN IRA

417 *"So, uh, there's a whole"*: Ira Glass, interview with author, May 27, 2022.

418 *"And what they do"*: Ibid.

418 *"I don't, uh"*: Ibid.

418 *"It's just really much more dire times"*: Glass, interview with author, July 14, 2022.

418 *"The Parents Step In"*: "The Parents Step In," *This American Life*, May 27, 2022, https:// www.thisamericanlife.org/771/the-parents-step-in.

419 *"If there's anybody"*: Hockenberry, interview with author, June 5, 2012.

420   *"In the second half"*: Glass, interview with author, May 27, 2022.

420   *"Got results"*: Ibid.

420   *"The performing of the show"*: Ibid.

421   *"Basically, starting Tuesday"*: Zoe Chace, interview with author, May 27, 2022.

421   *"Because you and I"*: Glass, interview with author, May 27, 2022.

422   *"We can possibly get the last"*: Chace, interview with author, May 27, 2022.

422   *"They've already been booking"*: Ibid.

422   *"It's one of the hardest"*: Ibid.

422   *"She's kind of surprisingly"*: Ibid.

422   *"There's no objectivity"*: Glass, interview with author, May 24, 2022.

422   *"I'm a little concerned"*: Chace, interview with author, May 27, 2022.

423   *"The first feed"*: Glass, interview with author, May 27, 2022.

423   *"Odoo is a fully integrated"*: Ibid.

423   *"Thanks, as always"*: Ibid.

423   *"You can't wash that evil"*: "The Parents Step In."

423   *"That's really a little too cheerful"*: Glass, interview with author, May 27, 2022.

424   a reported $25 million: "New York Times to Buy Production Company Behind Serial Podcast," *New York Times*, July 22, 2020, https://www.nytimes.com/2020/07/22/business/media/new-york-times-serial.html.

424   *"I'm not someone"*: Glass, interview with author, May 27, 2022.

424   *"It's embarrassingly"*: Ibid.

424   *"Having a plot"*: Glass, interview with author, December 27, 2022.

424   *"The primary problem"*: Ibid.

425   *"The Out Crowd"*: "The Out Crowd," *This American Life*, November 15, 2019, https://www.thisamericanlife.org/688/the-out-crowd.

425   *"We knew this had gotten coverage"*: Glass, interview with author, December 27, 2022.

425   *"I feel like if you said"*: Ibid.

426   *"revelatory, intimate journalism"*: "The Pulitzer Prizes 2020," https://www.pulitzer.org/prize-winners-by-year/2020.

426   *"A lot of so-called conventional"*: Glass, interview with author, December 27, 2022.

426   *"The Giant Pool of Money"*: "The Giant Pool of Money," *This American Life*, May 9, 2008, https://www.thisamericanlife.org/355/the-giant-pool-of-money. With the assistance of NPR's Ellen Weiss, this episode of *TAL* became the pilot for the podcast *Planet Money*.

426   *"The Night in Question"*: "The Night in Question," *This American Life*, October 16, 2015, https://www.thisamericanlife.org/570/the-night-in-question.

426   *"129 Cars"*: "129 Cars," *This American Life*, December 13, 2013, https://www.thisamericanlife.org/513/129-cars.

427   *"#1 Party School"*: "#1 Party School," *This American Life*, December 18, 2009, https://www.thisamericanlife.org/396/1-party-school.

427   *"Mr. Daisey and the Apple Factory"*: "Mr. Daisey and the Apple Factory," *This American Life*, January 6, 2012, https://www.thisamericanlife.org/454/mr-daisey-and-the-apple-factory.

428   *"Retraction"*: "Retraction," *This American Life*, March 16, 2012, https://www.thisamericanlife.org/460/retraction.

429 *"There is nothing in the journalism"*: "Theater, Disguised as Real Journalism," *New York Times*, March 18, 2012, https://www.nytimes.com/2012/03/19/business/media/theater-disguised-up-as-real-journalism.html.

429 *"a superb unraveling"*: James Fallows, "The Sad and Infuriating Mike Daisey Case," *The Atlantic*, March 17, 2012.

430 *"Despite all the feelings"*: "Is Ira Glass Getting a Pass on His Mike Daisey Gatekeeping Failures?," *Baltimore Sun*, March 20, 2012.

430 *"Daisey exposed the fact"*: "Oh, the Pathos: Presenting This American Life," *The Baffler*, July 2012.

430 *"Immediately after that"*: Glass, interview with author, December 27, 2022.

430 *"Times changed"*: Ibid.

430 *"When I talk to journalism students"*: Ibid.

431 *"My parents really wanted"*: Glass, interview with author, May 26, 2022.

431 *"super interesting"*: Ibid.

431 *"The Renee Richards Ball Toss"*: Glass, interview with author, May 24, 2022.

432 *"I want someone to listen"*: Kernis, interview with author, June 11, 2011.

432 *"You're really good"*: Ibid.

432 *"Can I stick around"*: "To Get Things More Real: An Interview with Ira Glass," *New York Review of Books*, August 8, 2019.

432 *"Ira was great"*: Talbot, interview with author, March 21, 2014.

432 *"We talked to people"*: Ibid.

432 *"Ocean Hour"*: https://www.thirdcoastfestival.org/feature/ocean-hour.

433 *"The audience has to go"*: Glass, interview with author, May 26, 2022.

433 *"He was a crazy man"*: Pizzi, interview with author, August 21, 2014.

433 *"Joe did some of the weirdest"*: Talbot, interview with author, September 19, 2014.

433 *"What I learned"*: Glass, interview with author, May 26, 2022.

433 *"It was flat"*: Ibid.

434 *"What are you gonna do with semiotics"*: "Jokes Concerning Semiotics," Live Journal, October 24, 2013.

434 *"I got to Brown"*: Glass, interview with author, May 26, 2022.

434 *"Barthes . . . was presenting"*: Ibid.

434 *"I didn't know"*: Ibid.

435 *"I used to talk to Mankiewicz"*: Glass, interview with author, December 19, 2012.

435 *"He was real green"*: Pizzi, interview with author, August 21, 2014.

435 *"He performed as a clown"*: Ungar, interview with author, October 27, 2015.

435 *"Keith, who seemed to know"*: Glass, interview with author, May 26, 2022.

435 *"pious"*: Glass, interview with author, December 19, 2012.

435 *"an artsy seventies movie"*: Ibid.

435 *"a great guy"*: Ungar, interview with author, October 27, 2015.

435 *"Ira was full of himself"*: Adler, interview with author, June 8. 2011.

436 *"There weren't many people"*: Glass, interview with author, May 26, 2022.

436 *"In his interviews"*: "To Get More Real."

436 *"Neal said to me"*: Glass, interview with author, May 26, 2022.

436 *"There was very little"*: Conan, interview with author, September 24, 2020.

437   *"What music are they"*: Glass, interview with author, May 26, 2022.

437   *"We'd talk to guys"*: Ibid.

437   *"God bless him"*: Montagne, interview with author, November 14, 2018.

437   *"We waded out"*: *All Things Considered*, undated.

437   *"the things that divide"*: Glass, interview with author, May 26, 2022.

438   *"I wanted to do stories"*: Glass, interview with author, December 27, 2022.

438   *"Dead Animal Man"*: "A Touch of Glass," *Chicago*, March 1995.

438   *"Hey, buddy!"*: Ibid.

438   *"Being a white candidate"*: Glass, interview with author, May 26, 2022. As noted in chapter 5, Margot Adler also sought this position.

438   *"I was seen as"*: Ibid.

438   *"We let him try out"*: Lyden, interview with author, June 11, 2013.

438   *"the Fluff King"*: Fisher, "The Soul of a News Machine."

438   *"Ira was trying"*: Lyden, interview with author, June 11, 2013.

439   *"He could have had"*: "What Becomes of the Brokenhearted," *Chicago Reader*, November 19, 1998.

439   *"We all wanted to be pimps"*: Lynda Barry, *Late Night with David Letterman*, 1988, YouTube video, posted by "Cliporama," https://www.youtube.com/watch?v=sL_uvZU_-jI.

439   *"little Ghetto Girl"*: Linda Barry, *One! Hundred! Demons!* (Montreal: Drawn and Quarterly, 2017), 21.

439   *"If you lined up everybody"*: Glass, interview with author, May 26, 2022.

439   *"I didn't drink"*: Ibid.

439   *"One night we all went out"*: Lyden, interview with author, June 11, 2013.

440   *"We were reading"*: "What Becomes of the Brokenhearted."

440   *"It was clear she felt"*: Baer, interview with author, August 18, 2014.

440   *"this amazing girlfriend"*: Ibid.

440   *"They argued a lot"*: Lyden, interview with author, June 11, 2013.

440   *"My boyfriend dumped me"*: Lynda Barry, *Late Night with David Letterman*, 1991.

441   *Lonely Genius Gazette*: Barry, *One! Hundred! Demons!*, 21.

441   *"I was an idiot"*: "What Becomes of the Brokenhearted."

441   *"I had a little money"*: Abramson, interview with author, October 13, 2020.

441   *"Larry felt that education"*: Glass, interview with author, May 26, 2022.

441   *"idealistic and wanted to fix"*: Ibid.

441   *"It cost as much"*: Ibid.

441   *"The leader of the antireform"*: Ibid.

442   *"a sickly smell"*: Sarah Vowell, *Radio On: A Listener's Diary* (New York: St. Martin's Press, 1996), 104.

442   *"free-form documentary banter"*: "What Becomes of the Brokenhearted."

442   *"The shows were a little"*: Covino, interview with author, June 23, 2021.

443   *"The people were doing brilliant"*: Shirley Jahad, interview with author, September 18, 2020.

443   *"almost psychedelic"*: "A Touch of Glass."

443   *"the Mississippi equivalent"*: Vowell, *Radio On*, 141.

443   *"Lean and mean"*: Ibid., 142.

443 *"Talk about a hunk"*: Ibid.

443 *"It had to do with"*: Covino, interview with author, May 19, 2021.

443 *"Get this"*: "What Becomes of the Brokenhearted."

443 *"If I were to construct"*: Vowell, *Radio On*, 75.

444 *"the voice of the people"*: Covino, interview with author, June 25, 2021.

444 *"Just Plain Joe"*: Ibid.

444 *"I did not have a great respect"*: Ibid.

445 *"Everybody else was saying"*: Buzenberg, interview with author, August 20, 2014.

445 *"Gary could be hard"*: Proffitt, interview with author, September 7, 2012.

445 *"a left-wing analysis"*: Baer, interview with author, August 18, 2014.

445 *"views of the seventy-percent-Black"*: Covino, interview with author, May 20. 2021.

445 *"On the Bus—or Off"*: Covino, interview with author, June 3, 2021.

446 *"Just friends"*: "Just Friends," *This American Life*, November 15, 1996, https://www .thisamericanlife.org/42/get-over-it. This story originally aired on *The Wild Room. This American Life* rebroadcast it.

446 *"I'm in radio"*: Vowell, *Radio On*, 79.

446 *"Ira was headed"*: Torey Malatia, interview with author, August 21, 2020.

446 *"Ira would do his show"*: Ibid.

446 *"Gary and I didn't hobnob"*: Ibid.

447 *"Torey went to Nick"*: Glass, interview with author, July 13, 2022.

447 *"'What you need'"*: Ibid.

447 *"I liked the way Ira"*: Malatia, interview with author, August 21, 2020.

447 *"I was deceived"*: "What Becomes of the Brokenhearted."

448 *"little slave girl"*: "A Touch of Glass."

448 *"It made me mad"*: Glass, interview with author, July 13, 2022.

448 *"Ira kept telling me things"*: "What Becomes of the Brokenhearted."

448 *"I was sort of soft-pedaling"*: Ibid.

448 *"We had a big dinner"*: Covino, interview with author, June 23, 2021.

448 *"It's a new show"*: Covino, interview with author, June 25, 2021.

449 *"I'm totally in control"*: "What Becomes of the Brokenhearted."

449 *"I felt he'd finally"*: Ibid.

449 *"He felt like"*: Glass, interview with author, July 13, 2022.

449 *"Somewhere in his mind"*: Covino, interview with author, June 23, 2021.

449 *"We're gonna do things"*: Covino, interview with author, June 3, 2021.

449 *"I realized that this thing"*: Ibid.

450 *"in there with this bevy"*: Covino, interview with author, June 25, 2021.

451 *"I hate to say it"*: "What Becomes of the Brokenhearted."

451 *"I did that show"*: Covino, interview with author, June 23, 2021.

451 *"in a half panic"*: Ibid.

451 *"I mean, it really captured"*: Glass, interview with author, June 13, 2022.

451 *"Yeah, I had middle-class Jewish"*: Ibid.

451 *"I don't know"*: Ibid.

451 *"Mr. Franklin"*: "New Beginnings," *This American Life*, November 17, 1995, https:// www.thisamericanlife.org/1/new-beginnings.

452 *"One great thing"*: Ibid.

452 *"Get the plug in"*: Ibid.

452 *"I'm looking down"*: Covino, interview with author, June 3, 2021.

452 *"the other person"*: Covino, interview with author, June 23, 2021.

452 *"the motherfucker"*: Covino, interview with author, June 25, 2021.

453 *"Gary's a great guy"*: Dinges, interview with author, August 20, 2014.

453 *"Gary Covino is wrong"*: Margy Rochlin, interview with author, August 15, 2022.

453 *"Mom and Dad got divorced"*: Peter Clowney, interview with author, June 4, 2021.

453 *"The hours were officially"*: Sarah Vowell, email to author, July 18, 2022.

453 *"Drama Bug"*: "Drama Bug," *This American Life*, May 10, 1996, https://www.thisameri canlife.org/23/drama-bug.

453 *"Dawn"*: "Dawn," *This American Life*, February 28, 1996, https://www.thisamericanlife .org/15/dawn.

453 *"Name Change"*: "Name Change," *This American Life*, March 21, 1996, https://www .thisamericanlife.org/17/name-change-no-theme.

453 *"Listen for the magic"*: Clowney, interview with author, June 4, 2021.

454 *"Throw a little banjo music"*: Julie Snyder, interview with author, August 1, 2022.

454 *"He had a vision"*: Ibid.

454 *"The netherworld between"*: Vowell, email to author, July 18, 2022.

454 *"contemporary culture in fresh"*: https://peabodyawards.com/award-profile/this-ameri can-life/, May 6, 1996.

454 *"Statistics show that"*: Ibid.

454 *"I was on the phone"*: Malatia, interview with author, August 21, 2020.

454 *"Ira . . . do you have"*: Murray Horwitz, interview with author, September 4, 2020.

455 *"Leslie really had it in"*: Ibid.

455 *"What's with the Paul Harvey"*: Ibid.

455 *"I did most of"*: Malatia, interview with author, August 27, 2020.

455 *"It wasn't quite news"*: Horwitz, interview with author, September 4, 2020.

456 *"Don't eat"*: Art Silverman, interview with author, September 21, 2020.

456 *"We just won"*: Malatia, interview with author, August 21, 2020.

456 *"The trophy case line"*: Malatia, interview with author, August 27, 2020.

456 *"I said"*: Buzenberg, interview with author, August 18, 2014.

456 *"I always assumed"*: Glass, interview with author, July 13, 2022.

456 *"lack of regard for brilliant"*: Seymour, interview with author, August 26, 2010.

457 *"Susan Stamberg: Talent"*: Buzenberg, interview with author, August 20, 2014.

457 *"It was the best thing"*: Drake, interview with author, August 10, 2019.

457 *"Salyer was our"*: Malatia, interview with author, August 21, 2020.

457 *"doubled our carriage"*: Glass, interview with author, July 13. 2022.

457 *"The thing had a"*: Ibid.

457 *"We're gonna give you more"*: Ibid.

457 *"That was big"*: Ibid.

457 *"In year three"*: Ibid.

458 *"Paul taught me"*: Snyder, interview with author, August 1, 2022.

458 *"I thought he might be"*: Jack Hitt, interview with author, August 20, 2020.

458 *"Fiasco"*: "Fiasco," *This American Life*, April 25, 1997, https://www.thisamericanlife.org /61/fiasco-1997.

458 *"My favorite piece"*: "Media Matters: This American Life," *The Nation*, November 24, 1997.

459 *"What* This American Life*"*: "It's a Wonderful Life," *American Journalism Review*, July/ August 1999.

459 *"The weakest parts"*: Ibid.

459 *"Radio, when correctly"*: Jessica Abel and Ira Glass, *Radio: An Illustrated Guide* (Chicago: WBEZ Alliance, 1999), introduction.

459 *"Doing an interview"*: Ibid., 10.

459 *"Music is the frame"*: Ibid., 22.

459 *"Radio is a didactic"*: Ibid., 6.

459 *"calcified"*: Davidson, interview with author, March 29, 2023.

459 *"playful optimism"*: Vowell, email to author, July 18, 2022.

460 *"Radio listeners can't"*: "Quirked Around," *The Atlantic*, September 2007.

460 *"hipster kitsch"*: "The Myth of the Omniscient Narrator, and Other Stories," *New York Times*, March 22, 2007.

460 *"asked to be taken"*: "About Our TV Show," This American Life, n.d., https://www .thisamericanlife.org/about/tv.

460 *"Heretics"*: "Heretics," *This American Life*, March 21, 2018, https://www.thisamerican life.org/about/announcements/trailer-for-our-new-film.

460 *"There was a story"*: Glass, interview with author, May 24, 2022.

460 *"It's so weird"*: Ibid.

461 *"There came a point"*: Glass, interview with author, May 26, 2022.

461 *"The Pink House"*: "The Pink House at the Center of the World," *This American Life*, July 1, 2022, https://www.thisamericanlife.org/774/the-pink-house-at-the-center-of -the-world.

462 *"For a guy named Ira"*: Vowell, email to author, July 18, 2022.

462 *"He'll do edits"*: Snyder, interview with author, August 1, 2022.

462 *"Stations of the Double Cross"*: "Stations of the Double Cross," *This American Life*, June 3, 2022, https://www.thisamericanlife.org/772/the-kids-table/act-three-7.

462 *"It's totally acceptable"*: Glass, interview with author, May 25, 2022.

462 *"I'd been hearing"*: "Stations of the Double Cross."

463 *"Every year, there was"*: Ibid.

463 *"The plot hasn't kicked in"*: Glass, interview with author, May 25, 2022.

463 *"Hey . . . I have one"*: Glass, Slack message, May 25, 2022.

463 *"Throughout the whole"*: Michelle Navarro, interview with author, May 26, 2022.

463 *"Ira is this singular figure"*: Davidson, interview with author, March 29, 2023.

463 *"I've aged out"*: Glass, interview with author, July 14, 2022.

EPILOGUE: SAME AS IT EVER WAS—BUT DIFFERENT

465 *"I've Been at NPR for 25 Years"*: Uri Berliner, "I've Been at NPR for 25 Years. Here's How We Lost America's Trust," *The Free Press*, April 9, 2024.

465 *"An open-minded spirit"*: Ibid.

465 *"We're proud to stand behind"*: "NPR Roiled by Editor Claiming Liberal Bias," *New York Times*, April 12, 2024.

466 *"The quality of the programming"*: "Inside the Crisis at NPR," *New York Times*, April 28, 2024.

466 "When it comes to identifying": Berliner, *The Free Press*, April 9, 2024.

466 "Race and identity": Ibid.

BIBLIOGRAPHY

ARCHIVES AND LIBRARIES

National Public Broadcasting Archives, University of Maryland Libraries, College Park, Maryland.

Walter J. Brown Media Archives and Peabody Awards Collection, University of Georgia Special Collections Library, Athens, Georgia.

UNPUBLISHED AND MISCELLANEOUS MATERIAL

Khalid v. Natl. Public Radio, et al., U.S. District Court, District of Columbia, Civil Docket, Case #: 1:97-cv-00291-RCL.

Kirkish, Joseph Brady, "A Descriptive History of America's First National Public Radio Network," (PhD dissertation the University of Michigan, 1980).

Minnesota Public Radio 30th Anniversary CD, January 22, 1987, courtesy Bill Kling.

Siemering, Bill, "The Three Words You Can't Say on NPR," n.d., manuscript courtesy of the author.

NEWSPAPERS

Baltimore Sun

Boston Globe

Chicago Tribune

Christian Science Monitor

Cincinnati Enquirer

Current

Daily Beast

Deseret News

Guardian

Inprint (in-house publication of National Public Radio News)

Los Angeles Times

Star Press (Muncie, IN)

New York Press

New York Times

Politico
Richmond Times-Dispatch
Wall Street Journal
Washington Post
Washington Star

ARTICLES

"Adam Powell III Fired," *Jet*, August 23, 1972.

Adams, Michael Henry. "Inside the Auction of Eileen Slocum's Astounding Newport Mansion," *Town & Country*, September 28, 2018.

Burns, John F. "The Dying City of Sarajevo," *New York Times Magazine*, July 26, 1992.

Coburn, Marcia Froelke. "A Touch of Glass," *Chicago*, March 1995.

Cox, Ana Marie and Joanna Dionis. "Ira Glass: Radio Turn-On," *Mother Jones*, August 11, 1998.

Dreifus, Claudia. "To Get Things More Real: An Interview with Ira Glass," *New York Review of Books*, August 8, 2019.

Drew, Jill. "NPR Amps Up," *Columbia Journalism Review*, March/April 2010.

"The Embeds: What Is Gained and What Is Lost," *Columbia Journalism Review*, November/ December 2006.

"FCC Authorization Clears Dingell et al with Focus on Public Broadcasting Rider," *Broadcasting*, July 4, 1983.

Fallows, James. "Ellen Weiss Out at NPR," *The Atlantic*, January 6, 2011.

———. "The Sad and Infuriating Mike Daisey Case," *The Atlantic*, March 17, 2012.

Fisher, Marc. "The Soul of a News Machine," *Washington Post Magazine*, October 22, 1989.

———. "It's a Wonderful Life," *American Journalism Review*, July/August 1999.

Gopnik, Adam. "A Night to Remember," *The New Yorker*, April 12, 2015.

Hirschorn, Michael. "Quirked Around," *The Atlantic*, September 1, 2007.

Johnson, Rebecca. "Louder than Bombs," *Vogue*, July, 2003.

Lindsay, Drew. "Has Success Spoiled NPR," *The Washingtonian*, March, 2007.

McKibben, Bill. "Media Matters: This American Life," *The Nation*, November 24, 1997.

Margolick, David. "National Public Rodeo," *Vanity Fair*, January 12, 2012.

Mayer, Jane. "A Deadly Interrogation," *The New Yorker*, November 6, 2005.

Miner, Michael. "What Becomes of the Brokenhearted," *Chicago Reader*, November 19, 1998.

Oney, Steve. "The Second Coming of NPR West," *Los Angeles*, April, 2014.

Piantadosi, Roger. "Stamberg Considered," *New York*, October 22, 1979.

"Public Radio Stations to Broadcast Software; Some to Offer Game of the Week and Data Hotel," *Infoworld*, July 12, 1982.

"Radio Is Pro Tem in the Senate for Canal Debates," *Broadcasting*, February 13, 1978.

Raz, Guy. "Radio Free Georgetown," *Washington City Paper*, January 27, 1999.

Rieder, Rem. "The Revenge of Juan Williams," *American Journalism Review*, March/April, 2011.

Salaten, William. "WEISS WASH," *Slate*, January 7, 2011.

Sherman, Scott. "Good, Gray NPR," *The Nation*, May 23, 2005.

Talbot, Margaret. "Stealing Life: The Crusader behind 'The Wire,'" *The New Yorker*, October 14, 2007.

Wehner, Peter. "Because Muslims Killed us on 9/11!," *The Atlantic*, October 15, 2010.

Williamson, Eugenia. "Oh, the Pathos: Presenting This American Life," *The Baffler*, July, 2012.

Zuckerman, Laurence. "Has Success Spoiled NPR," *Mother Jones*, June/July 1987.

BOOKS

Abel, Jessica and Ira Glass. *Radio: An Illustrated Guide*. Chicago: WBEZ Alliance, 1999.

Adams, Noah. *All Things Considered: A Radio Journal*. New York: W. W. Norton, 1992.

Adler, Margot: *Heretic's Heart*. Boston: Beacon Press, 1997.

Amos, Deborah. *Lines in the Sand: Desert Storm and the Remaking of the Arab World*. New York: Simon & Schuster, 1992.

Barry, Lynda. *One! Hundred! Demons!* Montreal: Drawn and Quarterly, 2017.

Barthes, Roland. *S/Z*. New York: Hill & Wang, 1975.

Breslow, Peter. *Outtakes: Stumbling Around the World for NPR*. Mojo Hand Publishing, 2023.

Collins, Mary. *National Public Radio: The Cast of Characters*. Washington, DC: Seven Locks Press, 1993.

Conan, Neal. *Play by Play*. New York: Three Rivers Press, 2002.

Day, James. *The Vanishing Vision—The Inside Story of Public Television*. Berkeley: University of California Press, 1995.

Edwards, Bob, *A Voice in the Box: My Life in Radio*, Lexington, Kentucky, the University of Kentucky Press, 2011.

———. *Fridays with Red: A Radio Friendship*. New York: Simon & Schuster, 1993.

Ephron, Nora. *Heartburn*. New York: Alfred A. Knopf, 1983.

Filkins, Dexter. *The Forever War*. New York: Alfred A. Knopf, 2008.

Folkenflik, David. *Murdoch's World: The Last of the Old Media Empires*. New York: Public Affairs, 2013.

Friedman, Thomas. *From Beirut to Jerusalem*. New York: Farrar, Straus and Giroux, 1989.

Garrels, Anne. *Naked in Baghdad*. New York: Farrar, Straus and Giroux, 2003.

Haygood, Wil. *King of the Cats: The Life and Times of Adam Clayton Powell, Jr.* New York: Houghton Mifflin, 1993.

Hillen, Andreas. *1973 Nervous Breakdown: Watergate, Warhol, and the Birth of Post-Sixties America*. New York: Bloomsbury, 2006.

Hockenberry, John. *Moving Violations: War Zones, Wheelchairs, and Declarations of Independence*. New York: Hyperion, 1995.

Horwitz, Tony. *Baghdad without a Map*. New York: Plume, 1992.

Kelly, Michael. *Martyr's Day: Chronicle of a Small War*. New York: Random House, 1993.

Kern, Jonathan. *Sound Reporting: The NPR Guide to Audio Journalism and Production*. Chicago: University of Chicago Press, 2008.

MacLaine, Shirley. *You Can't Get There from Here*. New York: W.W. Norton, 1975.

Marton, Kati. *Enemies of the People*. New York: Simon & Schuster, 2009.

McCauley, Michael P. *NPR: The Trials and Triumphs of National Public Radio*. New York: Columbia University Press, 2005.

Mitchell, Jack. *Listener Supported: The Culture and History of Public Radio*. Westport, CT: Praeger, 2005.

Napoli, Lisa. *Ray and Joan*. New York: Dutton, 2016.

———. *Susan, Linda, Nina & Cokie*. New York: Abrams Press, 2021.

Packer, George. *The Assassins' Gate: America in Iraq*. New York: Farrar, Straus and Giroux, 2005.

Phillips, Lisa A. *Public Radio: Behind the Voices*. New York: CDS Books, 2006.

Raske, Richard. *The Killing of Karen Silkwood: The Story Behind the Kerr-McGee Plutonium Case*. New York: Houghton Mifflin, 1981.

Ricks, Thomas E. *Fiasco: The American Military Adventure in Iraq, 2003 to 2005*. New York: The Penguin Press, 2006.

Roberts, Stamberg, et al. *This Is NPR: The First Forty Years*. San Francisco: Chronicle Books, 2010.

Schorr, Daniel. *Staying Tuned: A Life in Journalism*. New York: Pocket Books, 2001.

Simon, Scott. *Home and Away*. New York: Hyperion, 2000.

Stamberg, Susan. *Every Night at Five*. New York: Pantheon, 1982.

———. *Talk: NPR's Susan Stamberg Considers All Things*. New York: Perigee Books, 1994.

Thompson, Hunter S. *Fear and Loathing on the Campaign Trail '72*. San Francisco: Straight Arrow Press, 1973.

Twain, Mark. *The War Prayer*. New York: Harper Colophon, 1971.

Vowell, Sarah. *Radio On: A Listener's Diary*. New York: St. Martin's Press, 1996.

Wertheimer, Linda, ed. *Listening to America: Twenty-Five Years in the Life of a Nation, as Heard on National Public Radio*. Boston: Houghton Mifflin, 1995.

Williams, Juan. *Muzzled: The Assault on Honest Debate*. New York: Crown, 2011.

Witherspoon, John, et al. *A History of Public Broadcasting*. Washington, DC: Current Publishing Committee, 2000.

INDEX

PHOTO CREDITS

ABOUT THE AUTHOR

STEVE ONEY is a longtime journalist who worked for many years as a staff writer for the *Atlanta Journal-Constitution Magazine* and *Los Angeles* magazine. He has also contributed articles to many national publications, including *Esquire*, the *Wall Street Journal, New York* magazine, *GQ*, and the *New York Times Magazine*. His history of the lynching of Leo Frank, *And the Dead Shall Rise*, won the American Bar Association's Silver Gavel Award and the National Jewish Book Award. Oney was educated at the University of Georgia and at Harvard, where he was a Nieman Fellow. He lives in Los Angeles with his wife, Madeline Stuart.